Thinking About
AMERICA

The United States
in the 1990s

Annelise Anderson
Dennis L. Bark

• ——— editors ——— •

HOOVER INSTITUTION PRESS
Stanford University, Stanford, California

Hoover Press Publication 375

Copyright 1988 by the Board of Trustees of the
  Leland Stanford Junior University

Distributed by arrangement with
  National Book Network
  4720 Boston Way
  Lanham, Maryland 20706

First printing, 1988

Manufactured in the United States of America

Jacket and book design by P. Kelley Baker

94 93 92 91 90 89   9 8 7 6 5 4 3 2

Library of Congress Cataloging-in-Publication Data

Thinking about America: the United States in the 1990s / Annelise
    Anderson, Dennis L. Bark, editors.
        p.   cm.—(Hoover Press publication)
    Includes index.
    ISBN 0-8179-8751-7.   ISBN 0-8179-8752-5 (pbk.)
    1. United States—Foreign relations—1981– 2. United States—
Politics and government—1981– I. Anderson, Annelise Graebner.
II. Bark, Dennis L.
E876.T47 1988   88-12273
327.73—dc19   CIP

Contents

◆ II. International Economics Issues ◆

◆ III. Domestic Policy and National Purpose ◆

◆ IV. Philosophical Perspectives: Peace, Prosperity, Liberty ◆

Foreword

♦ In 1980 the Hoover Institution Press published *The United States in the 1980s,* a book of 29 essays on domestic and foreign policy issues facing the United States at the time. The purpose of the book was to provide readers—from the candidates in the 1980 election who might come to hold the office of the presidency to citizens and voters thinking about issues— with the analysis and judgment of the best thinkers on the various issues we were able to find.

The book was successful. It was published in four editions, and more than 25,000 copies are in print. It was translated into several foreign languages, including Chinese, Japanese, and Korean, and was reviewed in newspapers and magazines throughout the United States and abroad.

Partly as an accident of history and partly owing to a convergence of historical trends, the book became unusually newsworthy. Ronald Reagan was elected president during the year it was published, and of the 37 people who contributed to the volume as writers, editors, or senior advisers, 8 served the Reagan administration full-time for some period following the Reagan inauguration in 1981 and another 9 held part-time appointments on various boards or commissions, most of them at the highest level of government.

What made the book newsworthy, however, was not this normal contribution of scholars to the practice of government but Mikhail Gorbachev's comment, following his ascendancy to the leadership of the Soviet Union, that the book was the blueprint for the policies of the Reagan administration and that the Hoover Institution was a sort of intellectual Politburo for the administration. "We know what you think," he said to the secretary of state and the president's national security adviser. "We have read this book and watched all its programs become adopted by the Reagan administration." A great deal of what the book recommended had indeed come to pass.

What Gorbachev failed to understand, of course, is the extraordinary diversity of the policy process in the United States, the independence of individuals at universities and other research organizations from the institutions where they happen to be located, and also the independence of any administration from any group of scholars. After all, an administration appoints over 5,000 people to run the government. Finally, Mikhail Gorbachev no doubt failed to understand the nonpartisan nature of both research organizations and the individuals who do their work in these organizations, for they are first of all thinkers and advisers and only by the requirements of the particular jobs they take—and sometimes not even then—representatives who take the part of a particular candidate or administration.

This volume—*Thinking About America: The United States in the 1990s*—proposes to serve the political process in the United States in the same way the 1980s volume served it almost a decade ago: by providing the best we have to offer in defining, analyzing, and recommending courses of action to address the policy problems that confront us today. The authors of the many articles in this book are well-known and often world-renowned scholars, and many of them are experienced in government and have participated actively in the political process over many years. They are thoughtful people who care deeply about the future of the United States, diverse in background and interests but always worthy of the reader's attention.

The United States will elect its 41st president this year. He will take office in January 1989, following the administration of the first president since Dwight Eisenhower to serve, barring the unexpected, two full terms in office. The Hoover Institution wishes him well, whoever he may be, and hopes that this book will make a contribution to his success and that of the United States in the 1990s.

W. Glenn Campbell
Director, Hoover Institution
Stanford University

Acknowledgments

♦ As the editors of this volume, our first debt is to the authors of the essays in this book. They took precious time and care from other professional commitments as scholars and statesmen to write essays giving the essence—the best—of their long years of learning and experience. It is not just that they contributed to the book; they are the book.

Our second debt is to the four advisers to this project, who read and commented on the initial drafts of the essays: George J. Stigler, Nobel laureate and Charles R. Walgreen Distinguished Service Professor Emeritus and director, Center for the Study of the Economy and the State, University of Chicago; Robert A. Scalapino, Robson Research Professor of Government and director, Institute of East Asian Studies, University of California, Berkeley; James Q. Wilson, Collins Professor of Management, University of California, Los Angeles; and Donald W. Treadgold, chairman, Russian and East European Studies, University of Washington. They made many suggestions that we in turn made available to the authors. The authors were, of course, the sole decision makers on what they wanted to say and how they wanted to say it and were free to accept or reject the suggestions.

We also want to thank another group of individuals whose measure of time and support has been enormous and unsung. Sharon Greene has been the project administrator. She has not only carried on her shoulders a wide variety of different responsibilities but has done so with efficiency, attention to detail, and the common sense that humor and wit make possible. Elizabeth Preston was the careful and attentive typist of the manuscript, creating the electronic record used for typesetting.

The designer, Pat Baker, and the marketing coordinator, Lenore Mc-Cracken, have consistently met deadlines of "yesterday" and have done so with unerring attention to both the importance of the production schedule and the value of the volume itself; that is to say, ensuring publication of this book at a critical time when Republicans and Democrats in our nation are exchanging ideas in the American arena of public debate preceding the 1988 national elections.

Other people have also helped to bring this volume to the attention of the public: Jed Lyons, of the University Press of America, who has worked with us on marketing and distribution; and Ronald Getz, the head of Public Affairs at the Hoover Institution, and his staff, headed by Gloria Walker. We want to give a special, and important, word of appreciation—and it is more than just a word—to Virginia Gurrola and to Janet Dutra, in the offices of Annelise Anderson and Dennis L. Bark, respectively.

Our final debt is to W. Glenn Campbell, the director of the Hoover Institution, who conceived, guided, and supported this project. His leadership over the last decades built the Hoover Institution, and this book is in essential respects a product of the institution he built and continues to lead. Many of the authors are resident scholars at Hoover; others are associated with the institution as advisers, nonresident fellows, and friends. His leadership has made possible this unique collection by experts, Nobel laureates, presidents, and other statesmen—including Hoover's four honorary fellows.

ANNELISE ANDERSON
DENNIS L. BARK

Contributors

RICHARD V. ALLEN, senior fellow at the Hoover Institution, was assistant to the president for national security affairs from 1981 to 1982. He is also a member of the Presidential Commission for the German-American Tricentennial and chairs the Asian Studies Center Advisory Council of the Heritage Foundation.

ANNELISE ANDERSON, senior research fellow at the Hoover Institution and former associate director of the Office of Management and Budget, is a member of the President's Commission on Privatization, the National Science Board, and the Board of Overseers for the Rand/UCLA Center for the Study of Soviet International Behavior.

MARTIN ANDERSON, senior fellow at the Hoover Institution, was assistant to the president for policy development, 1981–1982, and is currently a member of the President's Economic Policy Advisory Board and the General Advisory Committee of the Arms Control and Disarmament Agency. He is author of the recently published book *Revolution*.

DENNIS L. BARK, senior fellow at the Hoover Institution and director of its national security affairs program, serves as a director of the United States Institute of Peace and is coauthor with David Gress-Wright of the forthcoming book *In the Balance: An Interpretive History of the Federal Republic of Germany, 1945–1987*.

Contributors

LAWRENCE J. BRAINARD, senior vice president and head of international economic and political analysis at Bankers Trust Company New York, has served as an adviser to the Atlantic Council, the Dartmouth Conference, the Office of Technology Assessment of the U.S. Congress, and the National Security Council.

JAMES M. BUCHANAN, winner of the Nobel prize for economics in 1986, is currently general director for the Center for Study of Public Choice and Harris University Professor at George Mason University.

JIMMY CARTER is the 39th president of the United States.

JOHN F. COGAN, senior fellow at the Hoover Institution, has held positions at both the Department of Labor and the Office of Management and Budget, where he was an associate director. He is a White House adviser and vice chairman of the Seminar on the Family and American Welfare Policy.

GERALD A. DORFMAN, senior fellow and curator of the Paul and Jean Hanna Archival Collection on the Role of Education at the Hoover Institution, is a member of the Public Policy Foundations Committee of the U.S. Information Agency and the Educational Planning Panel of the Atlantic Council of the United States.

PETER DUIGNAN, senior fellow, Stella and Ira Lillick Curator, director of the African and Middle East program, and director of Western European studies at the Hoover Institution, has written and edited 32 books on sub-Saharan Africa, including the five-volume *Colonialism in Africa*.

JOHN B. DUNLOP, senior fellow at the Hoover Institution and an expert on the contemporary Soviet Union, has written *The New Russian Nationalism* and coedited *Solzhenitsyn in Exile*.

GERALD FORD is the 38th president of the United States.

MILTON FRIEDMAN and ROSE D. FRIEDMAN, both economists, are the authors of *Capitalism and Freedom* and *Free to Choose*. Milton Friedman, recipient of the Nobel prize for economics in 1976, is senior research fellow at the Hoover Institution and Paul Snowden Russell Distinguished Service Professor of Economics, Emeritus, at the University of Chicago.

L. H. GANN, senior fellow at the Hoover Institution and a leading historian on colonial Africa, has written and edited more than twenty books and articles on African history.

PHILIP C. HABIB, senior research fellow at the Hoover Institution, has served as special presidential envoy to the Philippines, Central America, and the Middle East. From 1974 to 1976 he was U.S. ambassador to Korea. He received the Presidential Medal of Freedom in 1982.

ROBERT E. HALL, senior fellow at the Hoover Institution and professor of economics at Stanford University, is the coauthor (with Alvin Rabushka) of *The Flat Tax*.

The late PAUL R. HANNA was a senior research fellow at the Hoover Institution and Lee L. Jacks Professor of Education, Emeritus, at Stanford University.

AVIGDOR HASELKORN, an expert on Middle Eastern and Soviet affairs, is president of Haselkorn & Associates, Inc., a California-based consulting firm on defense and foreign affairs.

F. A. HAYEK, one of the twentieth century's strongest defenders of the free market and the liberal social and economic order, received the Nobel prize for economics in 1974 and is an honorary fellow at the Hoover Institution.

SIDNEY HOOK, senior research fellow at the Hoover Institution, is professor emeritus of philosophy, New York University. His most recent book is his autobiography, *Out of Step: An Unquiet Life in the 20th Century*.

ADMIRAL B. R. INMAN, USN (Retired), is chairman, president, and chief executive officer of Westmark Systems, Inc., and former deputy director of the Central Intelligence Agency.

D. GALE JOHNSON is the Eliakim Hastings Moore Distinguished Service Professor of Economics at the University of Chicago.

MELVYN KRAUSS, senior fellow at the Hoover Institution, is an expert on international trade and development issues and on the European Common Market. His most recent book is *How NATO Weakens the West*.

EDWARD P. LAZEAR, senior fellow and director of the domestic studies program at the Hoover Institution, is the Isadore Brown and Gladys J. Brown Professor of Urban and Labor Economics at the University of Chicago.

SEYMOUR MARTIN LIPSET, senior fellow at the Hoover Institution and Caroline S. G. Munro Professor of Political Science and professor of sociology at Stanford University, received the Gunnar Myrdal Prize for his work *The Politics of Unreason* and coedits the journal *Public Opinion*.

CHARLES E. McLURE, Jr., senior fellow at the Hoover Institution and former deputy assistant secretary of the Treasury for tax analysis from 1983 to 1985, has been vice president of the National Bureau of Economic Research and a senior economist on the President's Council of Economic Advisers.

EDWIN MEESE III, attorney general of the United States, served as counsellor to the president, 1981–1985, and was professor of law and director of the Center for Criminal Justice Policy and Management at the University of California at San Diego, 1977–1981.

THOMAS GALE MOORE, senior fellow at the Hoover Institution, is currently on leave as a member of the President's Council of Economic Advisers.

RAMON H. MYERS, senior fellow at the Hoover Institution, has written widely on Chinese and Japanese economic and political developments in the nineteenth and twentieth centuries.

RICHARD NIXON is the 37th president of the United States.

JUNE O'NEILL, director of the Center for the Study of Business and Government and professor of economics at Baruch College, City University of New York, has served as assistant staff director for programs, policy, and research at the U.S. Commission on Civil Rights and research associate at the Brookings Institution.

ALVIN RABUSHKA, senior fellow at the Hoover Institution, is a political scientist and coauthor (with Robert E. Hall) of *The Flat Tax*.

RONALD REAGAN is the 40th president of the United States.

RITA RICARDO-CAMPBELL, senior fellow at the Hoover Institution, is an expert on the health care sector, the economic and political problems of the Social Security system, and the pharmaceutical industry. She is a member of the President's Economic Policy Advisory Board and the National Endowment for the Humanities and author of *The Economics and Politics of Health*.

ROGER W. ROBINSON, JR., president of the international consulting firm RWR Inc., was senior director for international economic affairs at the National Security Council from 1982 to 1985.

NATHAN ROSENBERG, professor of economics at Stanford University, is a leading expert on the history of technology and coauthor of *How the West Grew Rich*.

HENRY S. ROWEN, senior fellow at the Hoover Institution and the Edward B. Ruse Professor of Public Policy and Management in the Graduate School of Business at Stanford University, is a former president of the Rand Corporation and has held a number of national security posts in the federal government. He and Charles Wolf are the authors of *The Future of the Soviet Empire*.

THOMAS J. SARGENT joined the Hoover Institution as a senior fellow in 1987. From 1971 to 1987 he taught at the University of Minnesota and has held visiting positions at the University of Chicago, Harvard University, and Stanford University. He is the author of *Dynamic Macroeconomic Theory*.

GEORGE SHULTZ is the U.S. secretary of state and has served as secretary of labor, director of the Office of Management and Budget, and secretary of the Treasury. He is an honorary fellow at the Hoover Institution and a member of the faculty (on leave) of Stanford University's Graduate School of Business.

ALEKSANDR SOLZHENITSYN, recipient of the Nobel prize for literature in 1970, is an honorary fellow at the Hoover Institution. He was exiled from the USSR in 1974 after serving terms in prison and Siberian exile and now lives and writes in the United States.

THOMAS SOWELL, senior fellow at the Hoover Institution, specializes in social theory and the history and economics of racial and ethnic groups. His most recent book is *A Conflict of Visions*.

RICHARD F. STAAR, senior fellow at the Hoover Institution and director of its international studies program, was U.S. ambassador to the mutual and balanced force reduction negotiations in Vienna from 1981 to 1983 and has been a professor of foreign affairs at Emory University and the National War College. He is the author of *USSR Foreign Policies After Détente* and *Communist Regimes in Eastern Europe*.

VICE ADMIRAL JAMES BOND STOCKDALE, USN (Retired), is senior research fellow at the Hoover Institution and recipient of the Congressional Medal of Honor. He served on active duty in the navy for nearly 37 years. Shot down during his second combat tour in Vietnam, he was a prisoner of war for seven and one-half years. He is the author of *North Vietnam Experience: Ten Years of Reflection* and *In Love and War*, coauthored with his wife, Sybil.

EDWARD TELLER, senior research fellow at the Hoover Institution, was a member of the Manhattan Project, University Professor of Physics at the University of California, and director of the Lawrence Livermore National Laboratory. His most recent book is *Better a Shield Than a Sword*.

WILLIAM R. VAN CLEAVE, senior research fellow at the Hoover Institution, is university professor and director of the Center for Defense and Strategic Studies at Southwest Missouri State University, Springfield, Missouri. He has served in various governmental positions involving arms control negotiations, defense, and intelligence and has written widely on strategy, arms control, and national defense issues.

CASPAR W. WEINBERGER served as secretary of defense from January 1981 through November 1987 and has held many other key positions in government and business, including secretary of health, education, and welfare, and director of the Office of Management and Budget.

ROBERT WESSON, senior research fellow at the Hoover Institution, specializes in Soviet and Latin American issues and served for several years in the U.S. foreign service. He is coeditor of *Latin American Views of U.S. Policy* and author of *Democracy in Latin America*.

AARON WILDAVSKY is professor of political science and public policy at the University of California at Berkeley. He has written *The New Politics of the Budgetary Process* and *Searching for Safety*.

JAMES Q. WILSON is the James Collins Professor of Management, UCLA. The author of many books on government and crime, he is a member of the U.S. Attorney General's Task Force on Violent Crime.

CHARLES WOLF, JR., senior research fellow at the Hoover Institution and dean of the Rand Graduate School, has written *Markets or Governments: Choosing Between Imperfect Alternatives* and edited (with Katherine Webb) *Developing Cooperative Forces in the Third World*.

ANDREW YOUNG, mayor of Atlanta, Georgia, was U.S. ambassador to the United Nations in the Carter administration.

An Introductory Overview

♦ This book offers 47 essays on the major public policy issues facing the United States in the next decade. The authors are distinguished scholars and statesmen who bring to their subjects a wide range of experience and expertise. They were asked to address issues of critical importance and to offer their conclusions and recommendations. Although they wrote independently of each other, several powerful themes recur in many essays.

The book has four parts. Part I, "Foreign Policy and National Security," and Part III, "Domestic Policy and National Purpose," are the usual breakdowns one expects to find in such a book. Part II, "International Economic Issues," deals with matters that might in another time have seemed limited to either the foreign or the domestic arena but today have worldwide implications. Part IV, "Philosophical Perspectives: Peace, Prosperity, Liberty," offers essays of unusual scope often bearing on foreign policy, international economic developments, or domestic issues—or all three. This introduction identifies some of the major themes and summarizes the individual essays but does not always follow the order in which the essays appear in the book.

In general the authors share the view that what the United States does in the 1990s matters because we remain the most powerful nation in the free world, with enormous resources and influence. In the next decade our country faces more responsibilities and more challenges than some Americans would like to accept. What the United States does—or more correctly, what the people of the United States encourage and permit their government to do—will affect not only our future in the twenty-first century but democracy and freedom in countries around the world.

A trend underlying the analysis and recommendations in a number of the essays is the continuing worldwide revolution in communications, information, and transportation. This revolution has made the competitive marketplace increasingly international in ideas, products, and finance. Countries are less and less able to isolate themselves from developments in the rest of the world. At the same time, industrial development and economic growth in other nations of the free world have produced economic competitors for the United States—as well as powerful allies. Several contributors to this volume urge policies to increase the competitiveness of the U.S. economy by relying on market mechanisms; others also consider trade and access to U.S. markets a major strength and opportunity in relations with the Third World and counsel against protectionism.

Democracy in the Third World, the U.S. role in encouraging freedom, and the Western cultural heritage that is the basis for our understanding of liberty and democracy are the concern of several writers. So too are the quality of education, especially public education, and personal character and public virtue. A related domestic theme is the internal problems created by the welfare state. Some of these essays concern fundamental internal challenges to our strength as a nation, reflected in our philosophical values, our educational system, and our inability to unite behind our leaders and reach consensus even on matters affecting our national interest.

Meanwhile, economic and political competition with the Soviet Union continues, and Western military power remains challenged by the Soviets and the East Bloc. What is new in the last decade, and what will affect policies worldwide in the 1990s, is the growing recognition of the failure of socialist, centrally controlled economies and the global trend toward market incentives and decentralization—a trend presenting challenges, opportunities, and risks.

As Richard Nixon writes:

> For the balance of this century and the beginning of the next, the dominant players on the world stage will be the United States and the Soviet Union . . . One of the most promising developments has been Gorbachev's recognition of the need to deal with the desperate internal problems of the Soviet Union. He is admitting that in important respects the Soviet system has failed . . . He needs a generation of peace—or to put it more precisely, a generation without war. Our task is to formulate an agenda to exploit those twenty years for the cause of freedom and real peace . . . If we have only twenty years before a reinvigorated Soviet Union turns its sights to renewed expansion, we have no time to lose.

Charles Wolf, Jr., outlines how various governments have responded to the failure of central planning. "The cardinal economic choice," he writes, "concerns the degree to which markets or governments—with their respective flaws—should determine the allocation, use, and distribution of resources." He views the expanded attention to market forces in Western countries as a mid-course correction; in the communist and developing countries it is a genuine innovation.

Wolf finds Gorbachev's *perestroika* "a surprising recognition by a communist state of the need to rely more on market forces," but he notes the contradictions inherent in efforts to reconcile centrally planned socialism and central political control with an expanded role for the market. In their study of the Soviet Union, Henry S. Rowen and John B. Dunlop emphasize the economic problems of the Soviet Union and the political challenge and internal conflict involved in *glasnost'* and *perestroika*. They see a struggle for power between the Gorbachev forces and opponents of change and conclude that both the economic and political outcomes are in doubt.

Ramon H. Myers provides an equally sober assessment of the potential for reform in China. Its new leaders "have no intention of abandoning socialism, nor are they true friends of the West. They are contemptuous of capitalism and liberalism and only concerned with acquiring Western capital, technology, and managerial expertise as quickly as possible to make China strong and prosperous." The "violent zigzag pattern" resulting from attempted reform will continue as long as the Chinese Communist Party remains dominant and credible. But "the gradual, steady chipping away of that credibility might also lead to the erosion of ideological control . . . Should that happen, we could observe the first successful destruction of a Marxist-Leninist regime through peaceful means." The challenge to U.S. foreign policy, Myers concludes, is to foster more trade with the West to encourage ideological pluralism without providing technology that accelerates China's military modernization.

Nathan Rosenberg explores the failure of socialist economies to innovate. He argues that capitalism has been especially effective in accommodating the innovative process, whereas Soviet socialism has failed not only to develop new technologies but even to use effectively those developed elsewhere. In the West the marketplace came to determine the success or failure of innovations, a process that requires "freedom from arbitrary and unpredictable interventions by government authorities." Rosenberg links the success of capitalism to the Western political and economic institutions and policies that make experimentation and innovation possible. "It is extremely difficult," he concludes, "to make socialist societies more amenable to technological change without at the same time making them more capitalist."

The first systematic analysis of the economic and political problems of central planning was F. A. Hayek's 1944 book, *The Road to Serfdom*. In his contribution to this volume, the Nobel laureate and longtime honorary fellow of the Hoover Institution writes:

> Before the obvious economic failure of East European socialism, it was widely thought . . . that a centrally planned economy would deliver not only social justice but also a more efficient use of economic resources. [But] the totality of resources one could employ in such a plan *is simply not knowable to anybody* and therefore can hardly be centrally controlled.

Understanding the communication of information through market prices lets us understand the extended order of human cooperation on which our civilization depends, "an order more commonly, if somewhat misleadingly, known as capitalism." Hayek concludes that greater knowledge and wealth are generated with decentralized control over resources and the competitive market order than are possible in a centrally directed economy.

In looking at the changes of the last twenty years, Martin Anderson sees a revolution in the recognition of the intellectual bankruptcy of statism (whether communism, socialism, or dictatorship) and the acknowledgment of capitalism, characterized by individual freedom and private property, as the system leading to prosperity. He emphasizes the radical departure from basic elements of communist economic theory in China's adoption in the early 1980s of three new principles: "Seek truth from facts," "Practice is the sole criterion of truth," and "Emancipate the mind from dogma." He finds Gorbachev's statements on *perestroika* also extraordinary and concludes that in the competition between the two major ideologies of the twentieth century for the loyalties of people all over the world, capitalism is winning, having shown itself a powerful vehicle for "enhancing individual liberty, generating economic prosperity, and making possible a strong national defense."

In an essay we will return to later, Sidney Hook also remarks on the failure of socialism as an economic system in the semisocialized countries of Western Europe as well as in communist countries and the Third World, but cautions that Leninism remains a powerful political ideology. Several of our authors, then, see major change in the intellectual outlook influencing policies worldwide. Milton Friedman and Rose D. Friedman present their hypothesis of how such changes occur: "major change in social and economic policy is preceded by a shift in the climate of intellectual *opinion*." This intellectual tide spreads to the public at large and, through public pressure on government, affects the course of events—economic, social, and political policy. As the tide in events reaches its flood, the intellectual tide starts to ebb, offset by reactions to the practical consequences attributed to the earlier intellectual tide.

The first tide the Friedmans present is the Adam Smith tide—the rise of laissez-faire beginning in the eighteenth century with the publication of Adam Smith's *The Wealth of Nations* and the Declaration of Independence in the United States. The resulting ideas came to influence public policy over the course of the following century. The Friedmans date the beginning of the Fabian tide, leading to Britain's welfare state and an extensive expansion of U.S. government regulation and federal spending, to the founding of the Fabian Society in 1883. The third tide they describe—the Hayek tide, marking the resurgence of free markets—is still incomplete. Intellectual argument persuaded people that government failure was as real as market failure, the Friedmans argue, but they give experience the greater weight in changing the climate. "Experience," say the Friedmans, "turned the great hopes that the collectivists and socialists had placed in Russia and China to ashes. Indeed, the only hope in those countries comes from recent moves toward the free market." Experience also dampened the hopes placed in Fabian socialism and the welfare state in Britain and the United States, an experience reinforced by the stagnation of less-developed countries engaged in central planning in comparison to the rapid progress of those adopting free-market policies. The Friedmans warn that the tide can still be reversed, given the powers of vested interests. But "once a tide in opinion or in affairs is strongly set, it tends to overwhelm counter-currents and to keep going for a long time in the same direction . . . Yet it is also worth recalling that their very success tends to create conditions that may ultimately reverse them."

Secretary of State George Shultz, an honorary fellow at the Hoover Institution, finds democracy and the demand for political openness and participation one of the most important political forces of our time. "Confronted by daunting internal and external challenges, new democracies will look to us for ideas, assistance, and understanding. In response, we cannot shut our eyes or close our doors." Like Rosenberg, Hayek, Anderson, and Ronald Reagan, Shultz sees a link between the political and economic arenas:

> Others have come to recognize what we have known all along—that democracy and free markets go together . . . Free markets cannot function in an environment of stifling political regulation or interference . . . All nations share a common responsibility, and must work together, to promote market forces and to ensure the maintenance of an open international

economic system ... Markets, not governments, determine economic results, and there is no way to overrule the market more than momentarily.

Shultz also addresses the realities of today's world:

The Soviet Union will remain our central security concern for the foreseeable future ... Whatever *perestroika* may finally come to mean, the terms in which it has been defined thus far suggest that Mr. Gorbachev and his colleagues understand that a closed society is a dead end for advanced development. And implicit in the parallel concept of *glasnost'* may be a recognition that the free flow of ideas and information that will fuel growth in the future requires greater intellectual and political freedom ... [But] the continuing reality before us means that U.S. political resolve must remain constant, our defense posture robust.

Aleksandr Solzhenitsyn, in words first spoken as an honorary fellow at the Hoover Institution in 1976 but even more important today, stresses the importance to Western scholars of understanding Russian history. A major error is the assumption that the transition from prerevolutionary Russia to the USSR was a continuation rather than "a fatal fracture of the spine."

The distortion of the Russian historical past ... has persistently taken on the form of a tendentious generalization about ingrained "perennial Russian slavery" and "Asiatic tradition" ... [which] dangerously misleads contemporary scholars ... and disregards numerous forms of remarkable social independence among our people ... For the United States, Russian and Soviet history is not merely the history of one among 120 foreign countries, and the fate of your great and beautiful country will depend in the very near future on whether the American continent has understood—adequately and soon enough—that history.

Roger W. Robinson, Jr., writes about Western financing of the East Bloc. He notes that the USSR has consistently put economic and financial ties with the West on a separate track from other issues, hoping to expand them even while the Soviet military buildup, Third World adventurism, and violations of the Helsinki accords continue. The Soviets intend, he believes, to use their economic relations with the West to address their economic problems, especially by tapping Western capital markets for untied general-purpose loans. He recommends a multilateral, voluntary Western initiative to strengthen the discipline and transparency of Western lending practices toward potential adversaries, improvements in Western statistical reporting so that analysts can estimate more precisely the funds available to Warsaw Pact states and their clients, and consultations among Western finance ministers on the security aspects of the January 1988 Soviet entry into international securities markets.

Lawrence J. Brainard addresses management of the trade deficit and the foreign debt of the United States in a way that will not lead to instability, recession, or threats to our national security. "Stability requires," he says, "that debt created within a financial system be tied to production or underlying asset values." Brainard describes the increasing importance of capital flows rather than trade flows in the last twenty years and the globalization of financial markets, leading to capital flows that are not tied to underlying trade balances. He advises that foreign investment in the United States will reduce the debt overhang, is beneficial to the U.S. economy, and should be encouraged. At the same time the United States needs to follow policies encouraging economic growth, investment, and exports, including reducing the budget deficit in ways that encourage rather than discourage growth. Security measures need to accompany this approach: sharing the military burden with our allies, especially Germany and Japan; preventing the transfer of untied general-purpose loans from the West to the East; and continuing to manage the debt crisis in the less-developed countries not by forgiveness but by encouraging economic reforms that will restore the confidence of lenders.

Nixon, Shultz, and Solzhenitsyn would all place the Soviet Union at the center of U.S. concern in the last decade of this century. Richard F. Staar provides a detailed analysis of Soviet expansionism. Staar argues that "if most of Central Europe can be called the contiguous empire of the USSR, then certain Third World states comprise the extended empire." He cites massive Soviet support for national liberation movements not only in Africa but also in Afghanistan and Latin America, where "the enormous quantities of weapons shipped to Nicaragua suggest that the USSR is using the country for stockpiling military equipment in anticipation of a protracted struggle throughout Central America and the Caribbean." Given the scope of Soviet activities abroad and the consistent effort to support the "world revolutionary process," Staar too concludes that the Soviet Union poses the greatest threat to U.S. national interests.

The pattern of Soviet activity abroad is also a challenge for the Third World. In an essay on Latin America and the Caribbean, Robert Wesson notes that Latin America is

> a testing ground of democracy and the ideals of freedom, where they at the same time have great promise and are threatened by economic and social problems and political tensions. It is the area above all others where the outcome is in doubt and may be influenced by American policies. If the United States can wisely fulfill its responsibility, its neighbors should be friends and partners.

Like Melvyn Krauss, Wesson argues that "American policy should be directed toward helping needy neighbors help themselves through production and exports" and that we should "tear down barriers to exchanges with our Latin American–Caribbean neighbors." His proposed free-trade area would not only contribute to political stability and national security but create confidence, encourage investment and production, and stabilize the economies of the region.

Although "success in Africa has been outweighed by failure," Peter Duignan and L. H. Gann find reason for optimism. But the continent must overcome serious constraints identified by the World Bank: "undeveloped human and material resources, difficult climate and geography, rapid population growth, alien unassimilated political institutions and insecure political legitimacy." Like Wesson, Duignan and Gann argue that "the West, including the United States, can best contribute to . . . development by lowering trade barriers against . . . exports. Such barriers restrict markets, impede foreign contacts, inhibit productive investment, exacerbate unemployment, and restrict the spread of skills." The authors recognize that widespread political problems are often exacerbated by Soviet-sponsored insurgency movements. But they argue that the United States can provide "counsel, aid, and expert advice" as well as technical assistance and "a restrained diplomacy that emphasizes mutual interests."

Melvyn Krauss also argues for the importance of trade rather than aid in relations with the Third World. "The United States has probably spent too much time and too many resources containing communism, and too little time and too few resources spreading capitalism. The marketplace is this country's strongest institution, and the United States must learn to use it to help poorer countries develop a vested interest in the capitalist system." He argues that food aid often fails to reach the hungry and is often used by recipient governments to subsidize elites and keep themselves in power, and it may encourage them to undertake economic policies that fail to address their countries' real problems. But to encourage capitalism abroad, Krauss concludes, protectionism must be discouraged at home.

Closely connected to the concerns of foreign aid is the ability of the world to feed its population. D. Gale Johnson points out that "world food production per capita is at its highest level in human history"; yet hunger persists despite this "global cornucopia." Johnson concludes that barriers to trade and protectionist policies impede measures to increase agricultural productivity in both industrial and developing countries. Although industrial countries should "help developing countries improve their national agricultural research systems," food aid is not the answer because it neither eradicates the conditions nor corrects the policies that lead to low agricultural production.

One of the most volatile and strategically important areas of the world is the Middle East. Two essays address the conflicts and the prospects for their resolution. The first of these, by diplomat Philip C. Habib, finds that "the interests of the United States . . . are linked directly to political, economic, and strategic developments in the area." He acknowledges that conditions of instability, national rivalry, and uncertainty in the Middle East will complicate the search for peace, but he is nevertheless convinced that the peace process must continue. Habib concludes:

> If the United States is not willing to devote itself fully to the search for peace, it will disappoint those who exercise moderating influence in a turbulent region. The voices in Israel and among many Arabs supporting the peace process will give way under the pressure of those who are satisfied with the status quo or who dream and plan for dominance through force.

In a related essay, Avigdor Haselkorn presents the Middle East as a place of interwoven interests and conflicting views on political, economic, and military issues. Haselkorn shares Habib's view that the United States has a responsibility to revitalize the role of diplomacy in the region. Two circumstances make this increasingly possible: Israel's opportunities for greater diplomatic flexibility given its advantageous position in the regional conflict system and the Arab leaders' need to contain the consequences of their strategic decline.

Looking at the Pacific Basin, Richard V. Allen sees enormous opportunity as well as challenge for the United States following the significant progress of the 1980s. "The security and well-being of the inhabitants of the region have been enhanced beyond even the most optimistic forecast," he writes. "The engine of growth has gathered momentum in every vital sector, and change has come in a dynamic acceleration of modernization, economic growth, social change, and political evolution." These developments are seen in South Korea, Taiwan, Japan, Australia, and China. The Pacific also offers great rewards for both Asians and Americans if both avoid "narrow and counterproductive nationalist goals."

The challenge for American policy will be to enhance our economic ties and not constrict them: "The United States will be the loser in any sustained trade conflict with our Pacific Basin trading partners . . . Managing the trade policy of a new administration may become the new president's most challenging task." In addition, the United States will continue to have major security commitments in the area, Allen notes, and must encourage the nations of the region, especially Japan, to assume greater responsibility for their own defense. "The future of U.S. interests in the Pacific Basin is linked directly to the new president's ability to lead, constructively and pragmatically, the nation and Congress to support a clearly articulated policy to defend those interests," Allen concludes.

Although the United States is concerned with developments throughout the world, its heritage is that of Western civilization—based on a belief and commitment to "the enduring values of the civilized world of Europe contained in its thought and literature, its art and music, and its economic and political legacy." As Dennis L. Bark writes, "the responsibility for preserving these traditions is ours, as the primary spokesman and defender of the spirit of liberty and the value of freedom in the twentieth century." The purpose of NATO "rests on the premise that we and our European allies share the values of freedom and liberty and the desire to live in a peaceful world . . . It would be impossible to exaggerate the importance of this common bond when committing all our political, economic, and military resources to preserving our way of life." Bark concludes that "the defense of Western civilization is the defense of the joint heritage of our societies in Europe and in North America. The day this heritage is forgotten and we fail to lend material and moral support to the maintenance of freedom . . . we place our future in jeopardy."

In his essay on defense policy, former Secretary of Defense Caspar W. Weinberger asks: "What are the threats to our freedom and our peace, and what must we do to preserve our peace and freedom in a world inhabited also by the Soviet Union, with its strong military capability and its unchanging goal of world domination?" He points out that although we can easily afford the national defense we need, there is a risk that we will fail to do enough: "It is the fate, the paradox, and possibly the ultimate destruction of free, open democratic societies that they are frequently unwilling to spend the amounts necessary to keep themselves free."

Weinberger considers it important for the United States to be prepared in the 1990s to use the many elements of power at its disposal—diplomatic, economic, and moral—to support and complement the application of military force. The successful development of the Strategic Defense Initiative is essential, he says, if the United States is to move "the world away from the threat of mutual assured destruction and toward a greater reliance on defensive systems."

How the United States may meet the challenges of defense and arms control is addressed by Edward Teller and William R. Van Cleave. Teller analyzes the opportunities and challenges open to the United States as a consequence of its superior economic and technological development. He argues that test ban treaties and arms limitation agreements have not prevented the Soviet Union from developing a missile defense capability far exceeding that of the United States and that to be vulnerable to attack does not make us safe. He considers it mandatory that the United States develop a strategic defense in the 1990s: "Today the United States cannot prevent a single . . . missile from wreaking havoc. Yet such limited defense has been possible for two decades."

Van Cleave writes on strategic deterrence, defense, and arms control. Although the U.S. government through successive administrations has been committed to all three aspects of this military equation, "the strategic balance increasingly favors the Soviet Union." Van Cleave argues that today arms control considerations seem to limit the "options available to the United States to improve the strategic balance, including progress in the Strategic Defense Initiative (SDI)." Indeed, "there are no more critical security problems for the United States than the state of the U.S.-Soviet strategic balance, the future of SDI, and the influence over these of arms control."

To evaluate the threats and challenges to our national security in the 1990s—and thereby to maintain peace and preserve freedom—the quality of information and intelligence available to our nation's leaders is of paramount importance. As Admiral B. R. Inman emphasizes, "it is fundamental to the success of intelligence operations within a democracy that they be conducted effectively within the laws of the country." Inman observes: "It is impossible to predict when religious fundamentalists or crosscurrents of cultural decay in other countries will spur activities inimical to the long-term interests of the United States." Therefore, "to avoid long-term damage to the effectiveness of U.S. intelligence activities in a troubled world, we must find more effective mechanisms for reaching a bipartisan consensus between the executive branch and Congress on the proper scope, oversight, and execution of intelligence activities." Indeed, Inman reminds us that "a great nation will remain great only if it accurately assesses conditions in the outside world and deals with them intelligently."

Among the essays addressing major domestic economic and social issues, Nobel laureate James M. Buchanan considers the most fundamental question: the nature of the constitutional order for an economically viable and free society. "Where is the wisdom that understands the Constitution as a set of constraints on executive, legislative, and judicial intrusions into the lives of citizens?" he asks. "It is critically important," he asserts, "that we recapture the eighteenth-century wisdom of the need for checks and balances and that we shed once and for all the romantically idiotic notion that as long as processes are democratic all is fair game."

Buchanan finds our economic constitution in disarray. He notes that there are no constitutional limits on absolute levels of taxation or spending. Nor does our economic constitution protect the value of our money, place any limits on transfer payments, or limit the regulation of value-enhancing market activity. Buchanan makes a number of specific recommendations, including formal restoration of fiscal rules of responsibility by means of a constitutional amendment.

Several essays on domestic policy deal with the areas of economic concern on which Buchanan touches. Aaron Wildavsky looks at the problems the U.S. Congress has had in producing a federal budget and deciding how much revenue should be raised, who should pay, and how much should be spent on what.

Wildavsky identifies two opposing views, that of the dominant liberal faction of the Democratic party, "whose main purpose in achieving power is to do good deeds with public money," and that of the major faction of the Republican party, which favors limited government. Republicans seek equality before the law and equal opportunity; Democrats seek more equal results. Liberals want higher, more progressive taxes, lower defense spending, and more welfare programs; conservatives want the opposite. These fundamental differences are the source of conflicts over budgeting, and thus there is a fundamental "dissensus": public officials cannot agree on the budget because they are fundamentally at odds over policy.

Wildavsky, like Buchanan, supports a constitutional amendment to balance the budget and limit federal spending. Support for the amendment reflects a preference for limiting the public sector—a choice of fundamental importance for the nation's future. The choice will be made, he thinks, in a battle over whether to increase taxes by such means as a value-added tax (a giant revenue raiser) and will determine whether we remain capitalist or become semisocialist.

John F. Cogan sees the federal budget deficit as the single most important domestic challenge confronting the next president and other political leaders in the 1990s. Economic growth alone will not produce enough revenue to finance federal programs at their current levels. He analyzes federal spending as two separate budgets: one for trust fund programs and the other for general fund programs.

Trust funds enable Congress to dedicate revenues from particular sources to finance specific expenditures. By contrast, general fund revenues—mostly from income taxes—are pooled. The trust funds (which now take in 40 percent of revenues) are in surplus; taxes are greater than expenditures. The general fund, however, is in increasing deficit, and these recent trends, unprecedented in U.S. fiscal history, will continue well into the 1990s. Cogan suggests that the taxing committees are biased in favor of trust fund taxes because they also control the expenditures made possible by these revenues, whereas the expenditure control over general revenue is divided among multiple committees. To ensure comparisons of different programs on their merits and to create political accountability, he recommends combining all spending authority for general fund programs into a single committee, and he would strip the tax-writing committees of authority over expenditures.

Two essays analyze tax policy: one by Robert E. Hall and Alvin Rabushka, who first proposed a simple flat tax in 1981, and another by Charles E. McLure, Jr., who participated as deputy assistant secretary of the Treasury in creating the tax proposals leading to the Tax Reform Act of 1986. Both deal primarily with how revenue ought to be raised.

Hall and Rabushka emphasize the dramatic accomplishments of the 1981 and 1986 tax reforms, which lowered marginal rates from a high of 70 percent on individuals and 46 percent on corporations to 28 and 34 percent respectively. They support further rate reductions as both desirable and possible, urging a simple flat tax at 19 percent for individuals and corporations applying to a comprehensive measure of income.

According to Hall and Rabushka, the greatest problem with the current tax system is its severe penalty for risk taking, or entrepreneurship, owing to the remaining double taxation of dividends and taxes on capital gains. This bias penalizes the corporate form of organization and favors debt over equity. They argue that the elimination of penalty taxes on entrepreneurial success is the most critical tax issue of the 1990s, one only partially addressed by reducing capital gains taxes. Instead, a coherent reform taxing all income at uniformly low rates would be simple and would save billions of dollars in the preparation of tax returns. "As the full benefits of the lower rates enacted in 1986 take hold in 1988," they conclude, "we hope that Congress and the executive can work together to make a low, simple flat tax a reality."

McLure finds the current federal tax system—despite the 1986 reforms—seriously flawed when evaluated by the standards of fairness, economic neutrality, and simplicity (standards implicit in Hall and Rabushka as well). These standards are met by taxing all real economic income consistently, regardless of its source or its use. The 1986 Tax Reform Act broadened the tax base, lowered marginal rates, and reduced opportunities for tax shelters, thus improving the equity and neutrality of the system. McLure would like to broaden the base further by eliminating the deduction for mortgage interest, disallowing employer deductions for fringe benefits (including health insurance), and eliminating the deduction for state and local income and property taxes.

But in preference to adjustments to the current system or a value-added tax, he would substitute a system of direct taxation based on consumption, a tax system that would not discourage saving, would eliminate many complicated timing issues for business, and would be substantially simpler—an approach similar to Hall and Rabushka's.

In a related essay, Thomas J. Sargent argues that despite our institutional separation of responsibility for fiscal and monetary policies, the independence of monetary policy from fiscal decisions is a fiction. Monetary policy makers are constrained by fiscal (taxing and spending) decisions because fiscal policy determines the size of the government debt the Federal Reserve Board must manage. The Fed's job is to choose, through open-market operations, how much will be held in interest-bearing debt and how much will be held as currency and bank reserves.

Great powers for producing good or bad economic effects are attributed to those who administer monetary policy; but "in truth," Sargent says, "monetary policy is much less powerful than is often depicted." Sargent explains that monetary policy cannot be used to influence the rate of unemployment, real interest rates, or the timing of inflation, and thus it cannot permanently prevent inflation if the budget is in deficit. Nor can monetary policy makers stabilize the price level and at the same time control the value of the dollar with respect to foreign currencies (or act as a lender of last resort) unless supported by appropriate fiscal policy. In concluding, Sargent cites the old maxim of central banking circles: "With a tight fiscal policy that hands the monetary authority a small portfolio of government debt to manage, it is easy to run a noninflationary monetary policy; but under a deficit-spending policy, it is *impossible* to run a noninflationary monetary policy." Sargent's analysis and warning are especially appropriate given the fiscal policy of recent years. In short, we may be expecting too much of monetary policy.

Thomas Gale Moore argues that deregulation has brought substantial benefits to U.S. industry and consumers. This success is the result of two policies: the reduction of marginal tax rates to their lowest levels since the 1920s, and a low and decreasing level of government control over markets in specific industries and in antitrust activity. Little has been done, however, to make safety, environmental, and social regulations less burdensome.

Moore reviews the bipartisan program to reduce economic regulation in transportation, communications, financial services, and energy from the mid-1970s to the mid-1980s, noting that the agenda is far from complete. "In the long run," Moore says, "the only way to maintain a vibrant, strong economy that can compete in the world is to preserve its flexible markets ... The 1990s will be the critical decade for maintaining these gains and accomplishing what remains to be done ... Continuing the trend toward deregulation is critical to U.S. jobs and to the U.S. position in world markets."

In her essay on Social Security and Medicare, Rita Ricardo-Campbell presents a demographic overview of the United States as an aging society and analyzes programs for the aged, offering an extensive set of recommendations. Like other countries, the United States has programs to protect the aged from the risks of lower incomes and the higher expenses of ill health—programs funded by the working population. These generous benefits, indexed to the cost of living, favor the elderly over younger people and one-worker families over two-worker families: Social Security taxes on an individual basis but pays out on a family basis. In the next century there will be fewer workers whose earnings can be taxed to fund retirement for the baby boomers as they reach their mid-sixties. Can we continue to afford this generous system, she asks, when the financial status of the aged is in fact better than that of the rest of the population and their poverty rate lower?

Meanwhile Social Security trust fund balances are growing, as taxes exceed the amounts needed to pay current benefits. This surplus is likely to create pressure for benefit increases; but other programs need funding, and workers need lower taxes on earnings to pay day-to-day bills. Ricardo-Campbell recommends rolling back the existing payroll tax rate, establishing a national commission to review the actuarial status of the funds, reducing the annual cost-of-living adjustment for high-income recipients, and gradually increasing the early retirement age.

Health care costs are still rising rapidly, owing to increased utilization as well as price increases. "Government subsidies of medical care seem to be self-defeating because they foster overutilization and inflation," she notes. The best hope to contain the costs of medical care is the provision of information to consumers, which can be primarily a private effort. Finally, Ricardo-Campbell calls for more public awareness about Social Security and Medicare and more frankness on the part of the Social Security Administration.

In an essay on labor markets and international competitiveness, Edward P. Lazear makes the point that the government should be reluctant to take actions that diminish the economy's ability to adapt rapidly to change and should limit its role to enforcing private contracts and providing information. Lazear reviews for both Europe and the United States the increase in government control of labor markets and thus the erosion of the doctrine of employment at will—the principle that the worker serves at the pleasure of the employer.

In analyzing the decline of labor unions in the United States, Lazear considers the possibility that U.S. business unionism, with its emphasis on wages, makes U.S. industries less competitive than their foreign counterparts, especially when an economy must respond rapidly to changing conditions. As a consequence, foreign-produced durables are substituted for U.S. ones. But government can mimic the operations of a union with legislation that dictates wages, working conditions, and layoff penalties. "Care should be taken," he warns, "to avoid doing by fiat what the market is in the process of undoing. Much proposed labor legislation attempts to establish by national decree what labor unions have tried unsuccessfully to win through the bargaining process." Public policy should promote rather than hinder the efficient functioning of labor markets to ensure a mobile and responsive labor force and to encourage rapid growth in labor productivity in a changing economy.

Annelise Anderson assesses immigration policy, especially the Immigration Reform and Control Act of 1986. The most significant immigration legislation enacted since 1965, it sought to limit illegal immigration by establishing penalties—fines and ultimately prison sentences—for employers who hire anyone not eligible, according to the government, to work in the United States. A general amnesty for those here illegally was also made part of the law, as was a requirement for worker identification and a review of these provisions leading to the establishment, if necessary, of a more secure system of identification—a provision that could lead to a national identity card.

Anderson outlines standards by which immigration policy might be judged—peace, prosperity, and liberty—and provides some basic facts that should be considered. She concludes there may be no set of immigration policies that meets all the objectives or embodies all the values we would like to achieve, but that in the pursuit of peace, our immigration policy should favor the economic integration of the North American continent; in the pursuit of economic growth and competitiveness, more immigrants than we are now admitting may be desirable; and in the pursuit and protection of liberty, employer sanctions should be repealed.

June O'Neill addresses the basic dilemma of poverty policy: "the provision of income to those who meet the poverty standard is bound to weaken the incentive to be self-supporting" and "may in time lead to a permanent underclass of individuals dependent on the state." O'Neill explains how we define and measure poverty in the United States, noting that although two-thirds of benefits to the poor are now delivered as in-kind income (such as food stamps, Medicaid, and subsidized housing), the official measure of poverty considers only cash income. Adjustment of poverty statistics for in-kind income reduces poverty rates; nevertheless, the greatest real declines in poverty come with robust economic growth.

O'Neill also analyzes the Aid to Families with Dependent Children (AFDC) program and its relation to out-of-wedlock childbearing, the disintegration of the family, and the seeming persistence of a dependent underclass. O'Neill counsels that policy proposals should consider the complexity of human behavior in response to simple plans: "It is difficult if not impossible for the government to demand responsible behavior from recipients of welfare grants." But, for example, greater vigilance in requiring fathers to contribute to the support of their children (including those born out of wedlock) may help, as would placing a time limit on AFDC benefits to convey the message that the program is intended to be temporary help for emergencies. Because circumstances around the country vary widely and a large number of policy changes are possible, O'Neill considers it desirable to permit states to experiment with policy changes. She notes that measures building skills, such as basic education, may also contribute to a reduction in welfare dependency.

Seymour Martin Lipset analyzes the unanticipated consequences of recent events in U.S. politics. He concludes that unanticipated consequences are inherent in democracies and should not, in fact, lead us to "vote for the other guy." He demonstrates his premise with a variety of examples. "Apart from the American one," he says, "most revolutions rarely establish the kind of government or society their ideological program calls for." Unanticipated consequences also result from "moderate efforts to reform stable democratic societies, such as those designed to aid the poor, to balance national budgets, or to create a more democratic polity." In analyzing changes in U.S. politics since the 1960s, Lipset concludes that efforts to reduce the influence of established groups and increase participation have greatly weakened the power of political parties but have also increased the power of the ideologically motivated in choosing candidates. He finds no solution, given the many complex processes involved in social actions.

Gerald A. Dorfman and the late Paul R. Hanna address the question of educational reform. They review the problems with our schools today and summarize the proposals for reform of the major commissions and groups that have addressed the issue in the last five years. But their concern is with the obstacles to implementing educational reforms. Education policy is always politically charged, and social upheavals and the resulting demands on schools have left in their wake cynicism and distrust. Nevertheless, Dorfman and Hanna do not believe the situation is hopeless, and they consider education important (as do Sidney Hook and James Q. Wilson). The public schools alone can provide common concepts, values, and skills essential for the survival and progress of our democratic society; this fundamental purpose would be sacrificed in confusion, rivalry, and variety of curriculum in a voucher system, which they therefore oppose. "The next president can make a great difference in the progress toward educational excellence," they write. "But he is going to need to rebuild confidence . . . so that the new path will be carefully and effectively developed over a long period of time—and so that the participants in the process will have a stake in its success rather than in its destruction."

Cities, says Andrew Young, are "the most challenging political entity because they are where the action is . . . they are the free market of politics." Young emphasizes that political geography is too narrow a base for the city; a more extensive entity with more flexible boundaries is an economic necessity. This flexibility makes possible regional planning for transportation, water resources, and utilities but can leave schools and police locally controlled. "The most successful cities are able to find ways to help their region function as a cooperative economic unit beyond the limitations of political categories."

Young sees privatization as an opportunity cities are seriously considering because of the decline in federal and state resources for infrastructure and other assistance. Citizens want local government action but oppose increased taxes, and so the city goes to the bond markets and the private sector. Young finds privatization applicable to programs subsidized by the general public that serve the interests of only a few people, such as specialized recreation facilities. He notes that services such as waste management can be provided by private contracts and cities can guarantee development ventures in their high-risk phase and then sell them at a profit.

Finally, Young sees the city as a place of culture and values, of spiritual resources "that have brought us together in one place and will enable us to live together in unity despite our tremendous diversity and our boundless desire for freedom." Crime and drugs threaten the security and stability of cities; ultimately a national and international approach will be needed to solve this problem, but meanwhile cooperation between community leaders and the police is critical.

Crime, Edwin Meese III points out, affects the quality of life and our daily decisions and experience—where to live, educational excellence, the choice of transportation. Meese reviews the major changes that have taken place in criminal justice in the last 25 years: the increase in crime rates, court decisions expanding the rights of defendants and limiting police and prosecutorial powers, efforts to improve the treatment of victims, an emphasis on nonprison alternatives to sentencing (leading to a decline in the probability of incarceration for convicted felons), and an increase in the use of narcotics.

Meese considers the historical roles in criminal law enforcement of different levels of government and suggests several priority areas where the federal government can support state and local efforts: technological research; narcotics prevention and control (he suggests an international effort through the United Nations Fund for Drug Abuse Control); improvements in information used by courts in sentencing and in dealing with rearrested probationers; increased use of "team policing" approaches to patrolling;

federal support of higher education for those in or entering police service; and the establishment, in collaboration with an institution of higher learning, of a federally funded residential educational institution and research center for senior police officers.

Several contributors to this book address not specific issues but fundamental concerns about the United States and the world. Sidney Hook writes that "the most important problem confronting mankind . . . is whether the free and open society of the West . . . will survive or whether it will be overwhelmed by some form of secular or religious totalitarianism." We have already had occasion to mention Hook's assessment of socialism as an economic system. But his critical point is that we need to "recognize the importance of strengthening intelligent allegiance to the democratic faith of the West and its institutions," for we live in a time when ideology—"the set of ideas and ideals that constitute the legitimizing rationale of a society one is prepared to defend"—is decisive. He finds that the historical legacy of American liberalism has been transformed into doctrines and practices of illiberalism. One important manifestation is judicial activism and a view that the courts rather than the legislative process are the chief defenders of our basic freedoms. To accept this activism, says Hook, "is to abandon the principles of democracy and both the letter and the spirit of the Constitution."

A second manifestation is the systematic perversion by government agencies and the courts of the language of the Civil Rights Act of 1964 and Executive Order 11246, both of which forbid discrimination against any individual on grounds of race, religion, sex, or national origin. Instead, the principles of affirmative action have become instruments of policies of reverse discrimination and preferential hiring—in practice, quota systems. Most worrisome is the impact of such an approach on the prospects for a liberal education and "the abandonment of the quest for excellence on the ground that it leads to an invidious emphasis on the achievement of the elite." Hook concludes:

> As long as we are committed as a nation to the defense of free societies, we can live without a consensus on the shifting pressures and conflicts of domestic policy. All the more necessary therefore is a consensus on a foreign policy that puts freedom first . . . A genuinely democratic consensus cannot be established by manipulation but only by discussion, debate, and rational persuasion. The capacity to engage in this process and the quality of thought displayed in the decisions that emerge from it will reflect the character of the education—especially the public education—Americans receive. That is why wherever we are and whatever else we do, we must begin by improving our public education.

Thomas Sowell notes that "preferential policies are not unique to the United States or to our times . . . Seeing the rationales and consequences of preferential policies in other societies may also help us to understand the logic of American efforts in this area, and how the outcomes here look against the background of international patterns." Sowell defines preferential policies as all government-imposed group preferences, distinguishing them from purely individual preferences lacking the force of law and from policies mandating equal treatment of individuals, although both mandated preferential policies and mandated equal treatment are lumped together in the United States as "civil rights." Preferential policies commonly favor the majority; minority preferences are more recent.

Sowell points out that we are well aware of the rationales for preferential policies but know little about the actual consequences. He reviews preferential policies in a wide range of societies, finding that in many instances they "have benefited, primarily or exclusively, the most fortunate segment of the groups designated as beneficiaries," whereas those harmed most are usually the least fortunate members of nonpreferred groups.

Sowell questions the assumption made by supporters of preferential policies that "an even distribution of groups would occur in the absence of discrimination": "uneven distributions are commonplace in countries around the world, in the most trivial and the most serious activities, in activities in which others might discriminate" and in those solely at the discretion of the individual.

The most serious consequences of preferential policies have been polarization, hostility, and violence. Sowell attributes three civil wars of this generation to official group preferences pitting one group against another. "Given the great heterogeneity of the groups receiving preferential treatment around the world, and the vast differences between the societies in which they live, the emergence of some common patterns is especially striking—and ominous."

In an essay on public policy and personal character, James Q. Wilson observes that "controls on will and appetite in the United States have been insufficient to maintain the minimum levels of order, amenity, and decency essential to maintaining a free society." He finds the United States unique not in the rise of crime and drug abuse, but in having an underclass that is not only poor but has few chances of escaping poverty. The problem, he says, is not just poverty—it is behavior.

Wilson considers two ways to achieve a more civilized society: internal controls and external controls. Both the conservative inclination toward tougher and more certain penalties and the liberal inclination toward attractive job opportunities emphasize external controls. Wilson supports maintaining and enhancing both, but his primary concern is with internal controls: building character. "U.S. leaders must now support efforts to improve the internal controls on which human character, and ultimately human behavior, depend." Character formation is widely misunderstood; it is neither a matter of choice, as those suspicious of conventional mores would have it, nor a matter of proper indoctrination, as those committed to conventional standards hold, but rather a product of habituation. A good character comes about through the regular repetition of right actions, not through instruction or personal discovery. "Behavior is controlled by its consequences," Wilson asserts, citing evidence that early efforts to mold character can succeed.

But it may not be possible to make the changes necessary to improve educational attainment and youthful behavior, so great are the political constraints on public schools. Wilson, unlike Dorfman and Hanna, therefore supports the revival, expansion, and evaluation of tuition grants, educational vouchers, and the like, so that parents can choose the school their child attends. On the federal government level he also recommends tests of alternative preschool education programs, the design and testing of parent training programs and drug education programs, requiring work as a condition of aid for recipients, and long-term studies of how high-risk children grow up. Finally, public leaders must set a moral tone emphasizing the importance of character to a free society.

Character is also the concern of Vice Admiral James Bond Stockdale. In an eloquent essay Stockdale reveals the demoralizing effects of public apathy, "paralyzing self-interest," and the lack of leadership in the U.S. Congress. The ability to defend our freedom and our democracy depends on our commitment "to civic virtue, public virtue, . . . personal responsibility, and the placing of the overall good of the body politic above personal ambition and gain."

In the conduct of the Vietnam War, Stockdale argues, political expediency and divisive congressional sentiment eschewed consensus and made a virtue of protest for self-serving purposes at a time when American soldiers were being asked to make a commitment to defend U.S. interests abroad but were not given the unequivocal support they required. His conclusion is as sobering as it is critical: men and women defending the United States in the future will "march off to their deaths only so long as they don't feel they have to die alone for what will be abandoned causes."

We conclude with three essays written especially for this volume by Presidents Gerald Ford, Jimmy Carter, and Ronald Reagan.

President Ford presents three changes he believes necessary in this country: a return to fiscal responsibility, a restoration of balance of power, and "a resurgence of the innate confidence and sense of community that . . . makes us all Americans." The cause of the annual escalation of expenditures is, he says, "the huge federal entitlement programs whose growth is preordained by law and perpetuated by powerful political blocs of voters, whose wrath both parties fear." He urges us to face fiscal reality and accept responsibility for our economic health, for "without economic strength, military strength is essentially meaningless, and neither peace nor prosperity can be indefinitely sustained. Freedoms we cherish for ourselves and defend for others depend on a sound and growing economy at home."

What, he asks, should we demand of those who win (and lose) the 1988 elections? "*We must expect and demand balance*" between the legislative and executive branches. "Our Founding Fathers knew what they were doing when they gave the congressional body closest to the people the power to declare war and the commander in chief the power to wage and win it . . . when military force is used or contemplated, a president's hands should not be tied arbitrarily and automatically by the Congress." Ford cites specifically the War Powers Resolution of 1973. He remains convinced that it is unconstitutional, impractical, and needlessly constraining, recounting six examples of his own experience with it as president. "What we need is more balance, comity, give and take, reasonable compromise, and readiness to cooperate on the vital issues that affect the general welfare—indeed the survival—of our nation and the future of freedom in the world." He calls in this election year on the distinctively American spirit of unity in diversity and individuality in community.

President Carter writes that finding ourselves in the center of world politics and meeting the challenge of world leadership will continue to be difficult for the United States. He notes we have never sought world domination, as did former leading powers, but have used our influence to encourage self-government and free enterprise. He considers one of our most important problems the increasing disharmony and lack of understanding between rich and poor countries, lamenting the lack of "commitment to comprehend what is happening within the less-developed countries, to communicate with them, and to help alleviate their most critical problems." He describes the activities of the Carter Center in a variety of projects, noting that "each partnership arrangement is designed to strengthen the ability of recipients to be more self-sufficient . . . There is no reason why our foreign aid programs cannot be guided by similar principles."

Carter addresses international issues ranging from Central America to the Middle East. But how to deal with the Soviet Union and the new leader is the challenge he finds most provocative. "Some of Gorbachev's actions and proposals have been symbolic, some substantive, and others perhaps superficial or false . . . Predictably, all these moves have been carefully designed to benefit the Soviet Union." He recalls his support for the INF treaty, but notes that this INF agreement helps bring about a long-standing goal of Soviet leaders: to reduce the nuclear-deterrent capability of NATO and leave the Warsaw Pact nations with a clear preponderance of conventional forces. How to follow on with further reductions in weaponry that will bring a stable balance in nuclear *and* conventional forces is one of the most serious challenges that our nation must face.

He too is concerned about budget deficits, citing a need for an increase in revenues and a substantial reduction in expenditures. "Entitlement programs cannot be exempt," he writes, in agreement with President Ford. Carter also points to the issues of energy and AIDS; on the latter, he is critical of the United States for imposing restrictions on family planning efforts and defaulting on treaty obligations to finance our share of World Health Organization programs. Finally, he emphasizes the protection of human rights around the world as a goal worth pursuing despite the difficulty of maintaining a consistent position and at the same time taking into account other factors affecting policy.

The last essay in this volume is a statement by President Reagan, since 1975 a Hoover honorary fellow, of the objectives he has sought as president and the opportunities for the future. He notes that he faced in 1981 (and has accomplished) three urgent foreign policy tasks: to restore our nation's economic strength and help reinvigorate the world economic system, to restore our military strength after a decade when defense investment was neglected, and to restore the nation's dynamism and self-confidence as a world leader. Thus the stage is set for further achievements in foreign policy in the 1990s.

Like other contributors to this volume, Reagan notes the worldwide trend toward giving greater scope to market forces to liberate the natural productive forces in every society. He recalls the consensus reached at the Bonn Economic Summit in 1985 that reducing "structural rigidities and excessive state control" was critical to growth in their economies; a similar conclusion was reached by African governments in 1986. Communist governments are tentatively recognizing the same realities. Reagan sees us entering the Information Age, a consequence of innovation that occurred for good reason in the free nations and is a major challenge to communism:

This new industrial revolution poses a stark dilemma to a system that is terrified of the free flow of people, information, and ideas across national boundaries, a system that keeps photocopiers under lock and key as a threat to its monopoly of information. The communist system faces a clear choice: if it permits the conditions to develop that allow it to exploit information technology for economic growth, it risks a challenge to the party's monopoly of power; yet if it resists this new phase of modernization out of fear for its political control, it will fall further and further behind. Probably it has no choice . . . these regimes will find they *cannot* resist the forces of change and the power of the human spirit.

Reagan reiterates a commitment to free trade as essential to rapid economic growth worldwide, noting historical agreements establishing free-trade areas with Israel and Canada. "It would be a worthy goal for the next administration," he says, "to reduce further the barriers to global economic interaction and global prosperity."

With respect to democracy, Reagan writes that we need "an active, vigorous, and *sustained* American policy with the flexibility and resources to assist democratic friends around the world." A closely related issue is support for anticommunist insurgencies resisting totalitarian oppression in the developing world—in Afghanistan, Nicaragua, Cambodia, Angola, and elsewhere—with the goal of resolution through negotiation rather than military means. "We have made some progress," he notes, "and there is a lesson here for American policy in the 1990s. Where we have received bipartisan support in the Congress, our policies have been effective. Where we Americans have been at odds among ourselves, we have courted failure."

On arms control, Reagan writes that his philosophy has been to work for agreements that would truly enhance our national security and to seek deep reductions in nuclear arsenals rather than ceilings permitting a continuing buildup. Most important, he concludes, is the program of research, development, and testing that constitutes the Strategic Defense Initiative, offering the hope of making the security of the free world less reliant on the threat of offensive destruction and more reliant on deterrence. "Perhaps among the most important legacies I will leave to my successors are these advances we have made in enhancing strategic security," he says. But "just as significant progress has been made, so future decisions can undo it."

Like Ford, Reagan is concerned with the powers of the presidency. "I believe future historians will look back with favor at the advances made during this period in the cause of political and economic freedom around the world. So too will they judge our efforts to establish a less-dangerous strategic equilibrium to ensure the peace that must accompany our freedom." But, he continues, he is "well aware that, in other circumstances, we could have done much more. My own achievements and disappointments have convinced me that a successful foreign policy requires a strong executive branch with the freedom to act decisively, as well as a cooperative relationship between the Congress and the executive." He recalls the gridlock in executive-congressional relations in the 1970s, leading to a paralysis of American power that provided opportunities for Soviet gains throughout the world. "No legacy would make me more proud," he says, "than a bipartisan consensus that this nation will never again permit such a situation to come to pass." But he concludes, as do we for the many reasons presented in this volume: "The future is bright for the cause of freedom."

ANNELISE ANDERSON
DENNIS L. BARK
Stanford, California
May 1988

Thinking About
AMERICA

• PART I •

Foreign Policy and National Security

RICHARD NIXON

◆ ———————————————— ◆

A New America

◆ Like most great historical figures, Charles de Gaulle had the gift of pre-science. Long before others, he saw the danger posed by the rise of Hitler, the awesome potential of motorized armed forces, and the possibility that France, defeated and humiliated in 1940, could recover and emerge from the war on the side of the victors. During his state visit to Washington in 1959, he turned his powers of insight to American politics. With the 1960 campaign only months away he told me, "I do not want to interfere in American politics, but my advice to a candidate for President would be to campaign for 'a new America.'" He was right. As Vice President, I could not take advantage of that advice, for it would appear I was repudi-ating President Eisenhower. But John Kennedy did run on that theme, and he won.

I would give that same advice to a candidate for President in 1988. Like Eisenhower, Ronald Reagan has been a very popular President. The Ameri-can people have supported his leadership. They are glad America now stands tall abroad and has experienced a long period of growth and pros-perity at home. They admire the way he has restored respect for America and the respectability of patriotism in America. But Americans are never satisfied with success. A candidate who tries to be a carbon copy of President Reagan and promises only to continue his policies will be left at the starting gate.

A call for a new America strikes a deep chord in the American temperament. Complacency is not an American characteristic. American history alternates between periods of quiet and periods of energetic change. But the quiet is always more apparent than real. A restless energy seethes beneath the surface. The status quo is at best a temporary rest stop on the road to greater endeavors—a pause to recharge our batteries before taking on new challenges. It is only a question of time before the other side of the cycle of American history bursts forth. For a great nation as well as a great man, true fulfillment comes not from savoring past achievements but only from embarking on new adventures.

With the beginning of the twenty-first century only twelve years away, there will be added appeal to call for a new America. A growing sense will develop that we need to gear up for new times, to prepare America for leadership in the next century. What we choose to do will profoundly affect what will become of the world. How we choose to lead and who is chosen to lead us are vitally important questions. What is at stake is nothing less than the future of civilization. Our actions will determine in large part whether the next century will be the best or the last one for mankind.

We have to ask ourselves what role the United States should play in the twenty-first century. Will the baton of world leadership pass to another nation after 1999? Is the United States—the oldest democracy in history—over the hill after two hundred years? To paraphrase Churchill, are we witnessing the beginning of the end or the end of the beginning of the great American experiment? All individuals go through the same experiences—birth, life, and death. Most individuals die when they no longer have a reason to live. Nations also experience birth and life. But for a nation, death is inevitable only when it ceases to have a reason to live. America has powerful reasons to live—for the sake of our posterity and for the sake of others.

To understand what is special about America, we should study our history. Without a shared vision of our past, we will find ourselves without a true vision of our future. As we celebrated the two-hundredth anniversary of our Constitution, some superficial observers propagated the myth that the American concept of government sprang almost by magic out of the minds of the remarkable men who assembled at Philadelphia. Even some of the Founders spoke of creating a "new order for the ages." But while the Constitution initiated a new order for the future, it was firmly grounded on old principles from the past. The ideas of English philosopher John Locke are reflected in both the Declaration of Independence and the Constitution.

But as Paul Edward Gottfried has observed, "While Locke's teachings influenced both the American and French revolutions, other principles, Judeo-Christian, classical, even medieval, also contributed to the American government's founding and growth."

The Founders had the advantage of painting on a new canvas. But while they were not inhibited by the dead hand of the past, they borrowed liberally from the great thinkers of the past. Putting together those great old ideas, they produced a new idea, superior to any one or to the sum of the parts.

They were idealists, but they were very practical men. They had no illusions about building a new utopia, where human beings would cease acting like human beings. They knew that while people should strive for perfectibility, they could never hope to achieve it—that they lived in an imperfect world, inhabited by imperfect people. They knew that idealism without pragmatism is impotent, and that pragmatism without idealism is meaningless. They wanted to build a solid structure that would survive after they were gone. Never in history have any men built so well.

While they had been revolutionaries, they knew that a violent revolution would destroy what they had built. They therefore provided a process whereby the goals of revolution could be accomplished by peaceful change.

One principle motivated them above all others. They might not have read the works of Baruch Spinoza, but their handiwork represented the practical application of his words: "The last end of the state is not to dominate men, nor to restrain them by fear; rather it is to set free each man from fear, that he may live and act with full security and without injury to himself or his neighbor. . . . The end of the state is really liberty." While praising the concept of equality, they rejected any system that would impose equality at the cost of stifling individual liberty, which is essential for the flowering of human creativity.

After experiencing the chaotic years under the Articles of Confederation, during which government was too weak, they wanted a strong government—one strong enough to protect the rights of people but not so strong as to threaten those rights. They had the genius to set up a system in which each of three strong branches of government, the executive, the legislative, and the judicial, would be a check on the strength of the others. In their wildest dreams they could not have imagined the megapower today of giant corporations, big labor unions, and media monopolies. But they would have been wary of any concentration of power that might threaten the rights of people because they believed that a free, strong people is indispensable to progress.

These practical men were motivated by what can only be described as a mystical faith in what they had created. It cannot be found in the words of the document, but they believed they were building not just for themselves but for others, not just for their nation but for other nations, not just for their time but for all time. They were not so presumptuous as to think of America as a world power, but they believed they were participating in a cause far greater than themselves.

They were not soft-headed do-gooders, but they believed in moral and spiritual values. They would have been appalled by the philosophy that seems so dominant in the capitalist world today—when so many seem motivated only by selfish, secular, materialist values and for whom the only god is money. They were conservatives, but their conservatism was leavened with compassion.

They wanted America to be not just a great country, but a good country. They were passionately patriotic, but they knew that patriotism, literally interpreted, means love of country. They wanted their country to be worthy of love.

To understand America's role in the future, we must first understand what America has meant to the world in the past. We have not been just another country on the world scene. We have been at the center of the revolutionary progress in man's material condition and have often been a decisive influence in the great political and military struggles of recent times. But we have been more than that. We have also been an ideological beacon—the physical embodiment of a unique philosophy of the relationship between the individual, society, and the state.

At the beginning of the twentieth century, America was not a world power. Economically, we were behind Britain and Germany in relative terms. Militarily, we were not even in the picture. While the great fleets of the imperial powers ruled the seas, we had only recently succeeded in sending a small flotilla around the world—and our land forces were even weaker than our navy. Politically, we were following a policy of deliberately avoiding involvement in the snits and quarrels of the Old World.

At the same time, the ideals that animated the American system carried a profound effect. They gave us boundless optimism about the promise we held out to the world. From the time of our national independence, Americans have believed that we represent ideals that are bigger than ourselves. Thomas Jefferson said, "We act not just for ourselves but for all mankind." Abraham Lincoln spoke of America as the "last, best hope of earth." Albert Beveridge spoke lyrically of America's "manifest destiny." Woodrow Wilson said, "A patriotic American is never so proud of his flag as when it comes to mean to others as to himself a symbol of liberty."

All these statements were made *before* the United States became an authentic world power. We believed deeply in the principles for which we stood. Our influence stemmed not from our military or economic power but from the enormous appeal that our ideals and their success had in the rest of the world. We were the only great power in history to make its entrance on the world stage not by the force of arms but by the force of its ideas.

In the course of this century, we have stayed true to our ideals. We have been a force for good in the world. We sought to temper the vindictive peace of the Treaty of Versailles. We were a decisive factor in preventing Hitler from making good on his promise of a thousand-year Reich. We have tried to hold the line on Soviet expansionism in Europe and Asia. We have certainly made mistakes in trying to uphold our ideals. But American idealism—sometimes naive, sometimes misguided, sometimes overzealous—has always been at the center of our foreign policy. One of our greatest strengths and greatest weaknesses as a world power has been the fact that we have never learned to act with the cold cynicism of Old World *Realpolitik*.

After his Kitchen Debate with me in Moscow in 1959, Khrushchev tried to demonstrate his flexibility as compared with his doctrinaire colleagues. Pointing to his Vice Premier, he said contemptuously, "Comrade Koslov is a hopeless communist." Khrushchev was ribbing Koslov for his dedicated idealism. In a sense, Americans have always been Koslovs. They have been dedicated idealists in their approach to the world but, unlike Koslov, not dedicated to foisting their ideals on the world. This had been to our credit. For Americans, a foreign policy must not be justified only on the ground that it serves our interests. It must also be consistent with our ideals. In a deeper sense, our interests are served only when we believe that what we do is right.

We stayed our course despite the sweeping changes that transformed the world in this century. In 1899 no one could have predicted this century's unprecedented material progress which has improved living conditions everywhere, with even the poor now enjoying better food, better housing, better health care, and a longer life span. No one could have predicted that man would smash the atom, explore space, and invent the computer. No one could have predicted that over one hundred million people would lose their lives in two world wars and more than a hundred smaller wars. No one could have predicted that the United States and the Soviet Union would replace Britain, France, and Germany as the principal world powers, that the European empires would collapse, or that totalitarian communism would rule 35 percent of the world's population.

As great as these changes have been, they will seem insignificant by comparison to those coming in the twenty-first century. It is therefore imperative that we decide today what role America should play in the future.

Our potential seems unlimited. We are the strongest and the richest country in the world. We can project our military power around the world, and we can influence all the great political issues of our time. Our culture, our ideas, and our economic and political systems have greater international appeal than ever before. It is no exaggeration to state that if allowed, hundreds of millions of people from around the world would emigrate to the United States.

But ironically, a new negativism afflicts America today. A growing chorus of pundits, professors, and politicians speak of the decline of American economic power and political leadership. They say that we have seen the end of the American century. They argue that American civilization has peaked and now faces an irreversible decline. They point out all around us the symptoms of decline—the problem of drug addiction among our young people, the crisis in education, the call for protectionism, and the appeal of isolationism. Brazil even beat us in basketball!

Are the new negativists correct? Does all this prove America's greatest days are behind us? Those who propound the new negativism will prove correct only if we permit their pessimism to become a self-fulfilling prophecy. Unlike the Marxists, we do not subscribe to a determinist view of history. We know we have a choice to make. We have the resources, the power, and the capacity to continue to act as a world leader. We can be a force for good in the twenty-first century. But there is still one unanswered question: Do we have the national will to play that role?

The new negativists argue that American national will power has collapsed. After his famous seance with his advisers at Camp David, President Carter declared that the United States was suffering from a deep-seated malaise. He was right in identifying a problem. But he was wrong in arguing that the malaise afflicted the American people. In fact it was a deadly virus which had infected the American leadership class. The same is true of the new negativism. The American people are not defeatist. They will respond to strong, responsible leadership. The problem has been that our leader class has failed to provide it.

If Moscow ever wins the U.S.-Soviet rivalry, the reason will be the failure of the American leadership class. As Robert Nisbet wrote, "We appear to be living in yet another age in which 'failure of nerve' is conspicuous; not in the minds of America's majority but in the minds of those who are gatekeepers for ideas and intellectuals." In the last forty years, the upper crust of America in terms of education, money, and power has lost its sense of direction in the world. It has become enamored of every intellectual fad that has caught its attention. Disarmament and pacifism are today's rage, and that could have a disastrous impact on the fate of the West. If our society's decision-makers and those who influence them lose the will to lead, there is a great danger that America's majority might not be able to reverse the slide to defeat.

President Reagan has proved how potent strong leadership can be. Despite the almost universal opposition of those who call themselves the brightest and the best, he won overwhelming victories in 1980 and 1984. He did so because he called on Americans to turn away from the negativism and isolationism of the 1970s and to move forward into a new era of opportunity at home and leadership abroad. The merits of the Reagan administration's domestic and foreign policies are fair subjects for debate. But no one can deny that President Reagan's buoyant and confident style has restored Americans' can-do spirit. While the Iran-contra affair tarnished the Reagan presidency, one of his major legacies will be that the spirit of the American people will be far better when he leaves office than it was when he entered it.

Yet there are those both on the right and on the left who ask why the United States should play a role on the world stage when we have so many urgent problems at home. Many were disillusioned by our failure in Vietnam. Others have despaired at the sight of corrupt leaders in developing countries wasting billions of dollars in American aid on graft and government boondoggles. And they have been outraged to hear those same leaders berate us at the United Nations. Critics on the right think the United States is too good to sully itself with the grimy politics of the world; critics on the left think the United States is not good enough to be able to contribute anything to the world. These old and new isolationists seek to shift to the Europeans and the Japanese, whose economies have long since recovered from the devastation of World War II, the primary burden of world leadership.

In addressing the future world role of the United States, we need historical perspective. At the beginning of this century, it did not matter whether America played a world role or not. Others who shared our values could do so. As we approach the beginning of the next century, that is no longer true. It is absolutely vital for America to play a major role. If the United States withdraws into a new isolationism, there is no other power that shares our values and possesses the resources and the will to take our place. At the same time, we can be sure that another power hostile to our values and interests, the Soviet Union, will do so.

If we pull back, we will turn over to Moscow the role of undisputed leadership; we will have made the world safe for Soviet domination and expansionism; we will see the rapid demise of peace and freedom, and the dawn of the twenty-first century will open a new age of barbarism on a global scale. If we pull back, we will eventually find that we have become an island in a red sea. We will have peace. But it will be the peace of retreat and defeat.

We must therefore reject the new isolationist agenda of withdrawing from Europe, curtailing our nuclear guarantee to our allies, erecting a wall of protectionist tariffs, cutting off support to freedom fighters, and retreating from the battle of ideas. In the superpower rivalry, to the extent that the United States prevails, the world will be safe for free nations. To the extent that the Soviet Union prevails, the world will be unsafe for free nations. Soviet-style tyranny survives by expanding. Liberty will expand by surviving. But to expand, it must first survive.

We must continue to assume the burden of leadership not just for the sake of others but also for our own sake. De Gaulle wrote, "France is never her true self except when she is engaged in a great enterprise." This is true for all nations. It is true for individuals. But it is particularly true for America. Only if we commit ourselves to be an active force for good in the world can America keep faith with its founding principles. Only if we commit ourselves to take part in the great enterprise of shaping the future of human civilization can we be true to ourselves.

In the twenty-first century, man will remake the world. We must play a central role in this great enterprise. We will remake the world materially through an explosion of technological innovation. We must try to remake the world politically through a strategy to achieve real peace. At the same time, we must not fail to address ourselves to the spiritual dimension of man.

Advances in science will transform the material world in the twenty-first century. It is estimated that 90 percent of all scientific knowledge has been developed in the last three decades. That knowledge will double by the turn of the century. In the years beyond, science will advance at an exponential rate. We are on the verge of an explosion of knowledge so tremendous that in its wake literally nothing in the world will remain the same.

In the years beyond 1999, we will see whole new industries develop and revolutionize our lives. Chemical fuel cells will enable us to build electric cars that can travel over a thousand miles without recharging. Superconductors will transform the transmission and production of electricity. Synthetic-fuel technology will create a permanent oil glut. We will conquer the problems of the fusion nuclear reactor and thereby develop an inexhaustible form of clean energy. Our descendants in the twenty-first century will look back and wonder what the energy crisis was all about.

We will see great advances in medical technology. In biotechnology, we will develop reliable artificial human organs for transplants. We will invent ways to regenerate damaged brain and nerve tissue. We will devise substances to lubricate arthritic joints. We will build machines that can scan inside the human body to diagnose problems and illnesses. Through DNA research, we will eradicate scores of diseases, perhaps even cancer and AIDS. For our descendants, life spans of 100 years will no longer be unusual.

We will be able finally to solve the problems of world hunger and poverty. We will see DNA researchers create new strains of crops that produce greater yields, that make more efficient use of sunlight, that resist disease and insects, and that thrive in poor soil. Famine will exist only in the history books. Futurist Herman Kahn predicted that the per-capita income of the world, which was $200 when our country was founded and which is about $2,000 today, will grow to $20,000 in the twenty-first century.

We will see a continuing revolution in computers. We will perfect the voice-operated word processor. We will increase the speed of computers by whole orders of magnitude at a time. We will create artificial intelligence—computers that can not only execute complex calculations but also think creatively. We will see robot technology take over traditional manufacturing industries. In just twenty years, a computer as small as a cigar box will be able to store the equivalent of ten Libraries of Congress. And that will be child's play compared with the technology that we will develop later in the century.

These are just a few of the changes we can anticipate—and they will be dwarfed by those that cannot yet be foreseen. America needs to stay at the cutting edge of the technological revolution. To do so, we must enhance our competitiveness in the global economic system. Our business leaders must start to think about the next century rather than being obsessed only with the profit figures of the next quarter. Our educators must become serious about creating a first-rate school system at every level. Our political leaders must resist the protectionist impulse, for building tariff walls is the refuge of weak and declining powers.

We must also overcome the antitechnology syndrome of the 1960s. This is particularly true in the area of nuclear power. Antinuclear lobbyists have made building a nuclear power plant impossible. They claim to be concerned for the danger to the environment. But the fact is that nuclear power is the cleanest form of energy. Moreover, unlike the Soviet power plant at Chernobyl, Western nuclear plants have multiple safety systems. In addition, we will see advances in technology create nuclear power plants that are inherently safe, that will shut down the nuclear chain reaction automatically if the reactor temperature becomes too hot. In nuclear power, we have seen the future—and it works.

If America is to capitalize on the tremendous promise of the next century, we must reject the call of the antitechnologists. If we accept the advice of these modern-day Luddites, with their mindless opposition to scientific progress, we will condemn America to the status of a technological backwater.

We must also rededicate ourselves to the exploration of space. We will exploit space for practical purposes, such as communications satellites and space stations with laboratories for creating medical vaccines and flawless industrial crystals in perfect weightlessness. But we must do more than that. We must renew our spirit of exploration. Shortly after the Russians launched Sputnik in 1957, one of America's premier scientists was briefing the National Security Council on what we could gain from the exploration of space. He pointed to a chart which listed ten possibilities, including such items as weather, communications, and medical research. Then he turned to President Eisenhower and said, "Mr. President, probably the most important discovery we will make is not on this chart." No better case could be made for space exploration. After all, those who discovered America thought they were going to find the East Indies.

In the twentieth century, man landed on the moon; in the twenty-first, he will walk on Mars and then reach beyond our solar system, to the stars. We must be involved if only to take part in the thrill of the adventure and the challenge of the enterprise. In these great endeavors, we can ennoble the American spirit, we can unite ourselves in the pursuit of a common goal, and we can take pride in achieving together what none of us could have achieved alone.

As we transform the material world, we must try to remake the world politically. In the twentieth century, our technological progress outstripped our political progress. We must not let this happen in the next century, because our material progress has reached the point where failure to match it with political progress can lead to our total destruction. In the twenty-first century, if we are to maximize material progress not only for ourselves but for all mankind, we must find ways to match our scientific advances with greater political progress in reducing the chances of war and sharing the benefits of peace.

Compared with creating new and better inventions, our political tasks will be infinitely more difficult. We can expect massive changes in the political and economic balance of power in the twenty-first century. While the United States and the Soviet Union will remain the dominant powers at the turn of the century, all bets are off thereafter. At present growth rates, Japan will surpass the United States in GNP, and it will be as strong militarily as it chooses to be politically. China will become an economic and military superpower. If Western Europe matches its economic prowess with political unity, it too will join the ranks of the superpowers. We will no longer be able to lead by virtue of our superior economic and military power. Instead, we will have to lead by virtue of superior political vision.

For the balance of this century and the beginning of the next, the dominant players on the world stage will be the United States and the Soviet Union. We will see this great rivalry—so insightfully foreseen by Tocqueville—reach its climax. We will face two key questions: Can we avoid nuclear war? Can we avoid defeat without war? We must work to find ways to avoid seeing the scientific capacities that can produce unlimited progress used to produce unlimited destruction. We must at the same time defend our system and our values, not only for ourselves, but also for our posterity.

One of the most promising developments has been Gorbachev's recognition of the need to deal with the desperate internal problems of the Soviet Union. He is admitting that in important respects the Soviet system has failed. He knows that his superior military power—which was created at tremendous expense—cannot be used against his main adversaries without courting catastrophe. He knows that his internal economic problems constrain his capacity to compete for influence around the world. He knows that Moscow's steady expansionism into contiguous territories has now run up against formidable opponents on all fronts. He knows that the problems he faces will require at least a generation to solve. He needs a generation of peace—or to put it more precisely, a generation without war.

Our task is to formulate an agenda to exploit those twenty years for the cause of freedom and real peace. We must first of all reject the counsel of the new negativists in our great universities, in the news media, in big business, and in politics. One of the most disturbing aspects of their approach is the new isolationism. Unlike the old isolationists, those afflicted with the new strain of this deadly virus oppose not only American involvement abroad but also defense programs at home. They are obsessed with the twin fears of another Vietnam and of nuclear war and are incapable of facing up to the threat posed by the Soviet Union. Whenever Western interests are at risk, they can only tell you how not to do it. Their knee-jerk response to a crisis is to turn it over to the United Nations—which means, in effect, to do nothing.

If we have only twenty years before a reinvigorated Soviet Union turns its sights to renewed expansion, we have no time to lose. We must think boldly and act boldly. We must seek to shape the world; but we should not seek to remake the world in our image. We must recognize that a system which works for us may not work for others with different backgrounds. We must reject the fashionable but intellectually sterile doctrine of moral relativism. We deeply believe in our values. But one of the fundamental tenets of those values is that we will not try to impose them on others. Only by example and never by force will our values be extended to others.

We must restore the credibility of the U.S. strategic deterrent by reducing its vulnerability to a Soviet first strike. We must bolster our conventional forces for key theaters—like Europe, Korea, and the Persian Gulf—so that Soviet leaders will never believe they could win a war with conventional forces alone.

We must take advantage of Moscow's flagging economic strength to improve our competitive position around the world, fortifying our friends and improving ties with those we wish to be our friends. We must continue to build our cooperative relations with the other major power centers in the world: Western Europe, Japan, and China. We should help those who are fighting to prevent a communist victory and those who are trying to overturn a communist victory. We should also work to improve living conditions in other countries in order to undercut the political appeal of communist slogans. We should make it clear that even if there were no communist threat we would devote our efforts to reducing the poverty, misery, disease, and injustice that plague most of the people in the world. By investing in progress abroad, we are ensuring progress at home.

We should use our negotiations with Moscow to demonstrate our resolve in areas of irreconcilable conflict, to work toward mutually beneficial accords in areas of possible agreement, to increase contact between Soviet society and the West, and to structure as constructive a relationship with the Soviets as their international behavior permits.

Most of all, we must not fall into the trap of thinking that a reduction in U.S.-Soviet tensions means the end of the conflict. If Gorbachev stresses the need to solve his internal problems, we should not be conned into thinking that the system has changed or that the threat to the West has ended. Those in the West who believe he has abandoned the Soviet goal of a communist world should note the conclusion of his speech on the seventieth anniversary of the Bolshevik revolution: "In October 1917, we parted with the old world, rejecting it once and for all. We are moving toward a new world, the world of communism. We shall never turn off that road." Even as he pushes forward with reforms, Gorbachev will still press for Soviet interests and challenge ours—and he will be back in full force in twenty years. If we take the needed actions in the years before 1999, we will be ready for him.

We must avoid the danger of complacency. As Paul Johnson wrote, "One of the lessons of history is that no civilization can be taken for granted. Its permanency can never be assured; there is always a dark age waiting for you around the corner, if you play your cards badly and you make sufficient mistakes." We cannot allow Western civilization to meet with that fate. We have the needed physical and moral reserves, but we still have to demonstrate that we have the skill and the will to prevail.

As we attend to material needs and political problems, we must not ignore the need to address the spiritual dimension of mankind.

America stands for certain philosophical ideas. When the new negativists carp about America's demise, they are arguing not only that the United States has lost the will to lead but also that it has lost its faith in itself. They are right to point out the problem. Great civilizations in the past have declined not only because they have tired of the sacrifices necessary for leadership but also because they lost their sense of purpose and direction. A nation that has lost faith in its ideals cannot expect its ideals to have appeal to others.

To restore our faith we must look to our roots. Two centuries ago, the United States was weak militarily and poor economically. But the country created in the American Revolution caught the imagination of the world. Our appeal stemmed not from our wealth or our power but from our ideas. Too often today we emphasize only our military and economic power. While we pay homage to our founding principles on special days, our day-to-day dialogue is dominated by the message of materialism.

But there is more to this world than per-capita GNP statistics. When historians write about our times several hundred years from now, they will tell the story of a titanic struggle between two clashing conceptions of man and his place in the world. The American-Soviet contest is a struggle between the opposite poles of human experience—between those represented by the sword and by the spirit, by fear and by hope. The Soviets' system is ruled by the sword; ours is ruled by the spirit. Their influence is spread through conquest; ours is spread by example. We know freedom, liberty, hope, and self-fulfillment; they know tyranny, butchery, starvation, war, and repression. Those qualities that make the prospect of Soviet victory so frightful are the same ones that make it possible.

We believe in the primacy of the individual; the Soviets believe in the primacy of the state. We believe in a government with limited powers; they believe in a totalitarian system with all power in the hands of the party and the state. Our system was designed to give the individual the greatest scope for action consistent with public order and the rights of others. We have unlocked the creative energies of individuals, while the Soviets have locked up their most creative individuals. We have created a dynamic system—which is most admired not for its products but for its freedom—while the Soviets have built a stagnant society suffocated by bureaucracy.

The power of Moscow's sword cannot defeat the power of the West's spirit. In deriding the ability of the Church to affect world events, Stalin once wryly asked how many divisions the Pope commanded. That comment bespoke a failure to understand what moves the world. Ideas, not arms, ultimately determine history. That is especially true when statesmen who understand the way the world works are armed with powerful ideas.

Pope John Paul II is a perfect example. He is the most influential religious leader of the twentieth century. What is the secret of his enormous appeal to men and women of all faiths, all nations, all races? It is not just his exalted office with its magnificent pageantry and vestments. It is not that he is one of the world's most gifted linguists, has a warm personality, and knows how to use television. People listen to the Pope because they want to hear what he has to say—not just about religion but about the mysteries of life and the intricacies of statecraft. He lifts people out of the drudgery, drabness, and boredom that plague life for both rich and poor. He gives them a vision of what man can be if he will listen to what Lincoln called the better angels of his nature. Against such a faith as this, communism, the antifaith, cannot prevail.

When the new Soviet leader eventually travels to other parts of the United States, far more important than having him see our swimming pools, our shopping centers, our millions of automobiles is for him to see and to sense the spirit and the ideas that made these things possible. If we compete with the Soviets materially, we will win because our system works and theirs does not. But our greatest strength—from the time of our national independence—has been our ideas. Moscow cannot even compete on that level. Marxism-Leninism has nothing left to say to the world. Our freedoms enable us to search for new meaning in changing times.

America was founded by individuals who sought religious freedom, who wanted the right to worship God in their own way and to look for meaning in life on their own terms. We must not lose sight of this animating principle of our country. We should not allow our competition with Moscow to degenerate into a contest over which side can create the most bombs, the tallest buildings, and the highest per-capita GNP. If material wealth is our only goal, we are no different from the communists. We should heed Max Weber's warning against the destructive, selfish materialism—the bureaucratization of the human spirit, an "iron cage" for the West. We should channel the U.S.-Soviet competition into a debate over whose ideas will result in not only the strongest or the richest economy but also the most just society.

The communists deny there is a God, but no one can deny that communism is a faith. We believe it is a false faith, but the answer to a false faith can never be no faith. When America was weak and poor two hundred years ago we were sustained by our faith. As we enter our third century and the next millennium, we must rediscover and reinvigorate our faith.

Our greatest challenge in this respect is to enable all our citizens to share fully America's success. In creating a system based on equality and liberty, our Founding Fathers threw down a challenge to those who would follow. They knew that their society did not measure up to their ideals, particularly because of slavery. But they hoped that over time our system would evolve and someday match their vision. We must continue that pursuit. We must solve the problems of the urban underclass, the homeless, the poor, the disadvantaged. We must rectify the inequalities from which blacks and other minorities suffer. The fact that much of the black community in America is no better off today than it was twenty-four years ago when the Civil Rights Act was passed is a blot on our past and a challenge for our future. We must recapture the sense of compassion that was so eloquently demonstrated by millions in America and others throughout the world a few months ago when the plight of an eighteen-month-old baby girl trapped in an abandoned well touched our hearts.

We should not return to the failed government programs of the past. But we must not use those failures as an excuse to quit trying. We need new approaches to these problems. There will have to be profound changes in the attitudes of the poor and in society's attitudes toward the poor. We have learned that solving poverty is more complicated than simply giving poor people money. Before we can have constructive action against poverty, we need creative thought about the problem.

We will make no progress if the creativity of our young people is consumed in the purely selfish pursuit of financial gain and social status. Nietzsche wrote that he foresaw the day when such secular, rationalistic values would triumph and in doing so bring about the demise of civilization. He warned against what he called the "last man," a creature totally obsessed with security and comfort and incapable of throwing himself into a higher cause. Nietzsche rightly saw the last man as a repellent creature. We do not have to accept Nietzsche's nihilism to agree with his assessment. The West will become impotent as a moral force if its guiding philosophy degenerates into what Russell Kirk has called a kind of cosmic selfishness.

In the 1960s, we accepted the mistaken belief that we could create a great society simply by ensuring that its people were well fed, well housed, well clothed, well educated, and well cared for. All these are important, but a life limited to the realm of material possessions is an achingly empty one. We should remember the biblical admonition, "Man does not live by bread alone."

The search for meaning in life has gone on since the beginning of civilization. It will never end, because the final answer will always elude us. But it is vitally important that we engage in the search, because we will thereby develop a fuller, better life for ourselves. Some believe the answer will be found in the classics; others seek it in religion. Of this we can be sure: Meaning cannot be found in sheer materialism, whether communist or capitalist. The Supreme Court has ruled that our Constitution requires that we not teach religion in our schools. But removing religion from our schools should not mean rejection of religion in life. It is because they addressed spiritual values and fulfillment that the world's great religions—Judaism, Christianity, Islam, and Buddhism—have inspired people for centuries.

We need to restore faith in our ideals, in our destiny, in ourselves. We are here for more than hedonistic self-satisfaction. We are here to make history—not to ignore the past, not to destroy the past, not to turn back to the past, but to move onward and upward in a way that opens up new vistas for the future.

In addition to the great foreign-policy issues before us, we need to direct ourselves to a very basic question: How do we want America to be remembered? Do we want to be remembered as a people who built the biggest houses, drove the fastest cars, wore the finest clothes, produced the best athletes? Do we want to be remembered as a society in which rock stars were more admired than great teachers? In which beautiful people were more admired than interesting people? In which telegenic quality was more important than brains, bad manners more than decency, sensationalism more than truth, scandal more than good deeds? Or do we wish to be remembered as a people who created great music, art, literature, and philosophy, who acted as a force for good in the world, and who devoted themselves to the search for meaning and a larger purpose?

We need to realign our philosophical bearings—to return to the animating principles of our country and rededicate ourselves to perfecting our society according to those ideas. It is a tragic fact that war traditionally calls forth our greatest talents. War produces unity in a common purpose and stretches man to his ultimate. That is more difficult to achieve in peacetime—but we should make it our goal to do so. The total effort required to fight a war must be mobilized to build a better peace. Our best answer to Gorbachev's "new thinking" is a new America.

Saint Thomas Aquinas observed, "If the highest aim of a captain were to preserve his ship he would keep it in port forever." The sea may be stormy, but conflict is the mother of creativity. Without risks, there will be no failures. But without risks there will be no successes. We must never be satisfied with success, and we should never be discouraged by failure. In the end, the key is the call, the commitment, the power of a great cause, a driving dream bigger than ourselves, as big as the whole world itself.

In war, the Medal of Honor is awarded for conduct beyond the call of duty. In peacetime we must not be satisfied with doing only what duty requires—doing what is right only in the sense of avoiding what is wrong. A morality of duty is not an adequate standard for a great people. We should set a higher standard, what Lon Fuller described as the morality of aspiration—dedicating ourselves to the fullest realization of our potential, in a manner worthy of a people functioning at their best.

Let us be remembered not just as a good people who took care of themselves without doing harm to others. Let us be remembered as a great people whose conduct went beyond the call of duty as we met the supreme challenge of this century—winning victory for freedom without war.

Are we witnessing the twilight of the American revolution? Are we seeing the first stages of the retreat of Western civilization into a new dark age of Soviet totalitarianism? Or will a new America lead the way to a new dawn for all those who cherish freedom in the world?

In his Iron Curtain speech at Westminster College in 1946, Winston Churchill said, "The United States stands at this time at the pinnacle of world power. It is a solemn moment for the American democracy. For with primacy in power is also joined an awe-inspiring accountability for the future." Those words are as true today as when he spoke them forty-two years ago. We hold the future in our hands.

EDWARD TELLER

◆ ───────────── ◆

Deterrence? Defense? Disarmament?

The Many Roads Toward Stability

◆ Almost exactly 50 years before this book was published, an editorial in a British scientific journal discussed the beginning of a "new era in the history of the world," which would have "peaceful methods of settling disputes between nations." But the optimistic editorial ended abruptly on a different note:

> We hope and believe that the resolution now made between the German Führer and Chancellor and the British Prime Minister will have more lasting influence than that reached by Disraeli, of whose treaty it was said soon afterwards:
>
>> "Once 'peace with honour' home was brought;
>> And there the glory ceases.
>> For peace a dozen wars has fought,
>> And honour's all in pieces."[1]

Five months later, in March 1939, Hitler took the portions of Czechoslovakia that the Munich agreement had not given him. The Allies began rearming. By May 10, 1940, when Hitler began his invasion of the Low Countries, the combined Allied armies outnumbered the Germans. But by June 24 all the allied democracies but Britain had capitulated.

The men who went to Munich were eminent politicians devoted to the cause of peace and freedom. The problem was not that the democracies failed to negotiate or had too few military forces, but that in a time of economic depression they ignored changes in military technology. Modern Nazi tanks and aircraft proved completely overwhelming.

The price of that error was five horrible years of war and 50 million lives, but it might easily have been higher. Today the oceans are no longer barriers; a world war could be fought and irrevocably lost far faster than Hitler's conquest of continental Europe. Historical parallels are incomplete and untrustworthy. But they should not be disregarded.

Two Approaches

The contemporary controversy about military affairs concerns defense. The most fruitful discussion I have ever had on that topic was with a dozen leaders of the AFL-CIO. Organized labor thinks that we have both an enemy of exceptional military strength and values worth preserving. It does not oppose the current strategic defense program. Defense is opposed by many academics, by the majority party in politics, and by many members of the media. In 1980 those opponents were attacking the nightmare of mutual assured destruction through the nuclear freeze movement. Three years later the same people were claiming that mitigating the destructiveness of a nuclear attack by using defense technology is wrong.

As the century ends, the call for peace is as strong as ever. No one disagrees about the goal, only about how best to attain it. One approach to peace is traditional: problems with the Soviet Union need only a political solution. Another approach looks to the future: ever-changing technology must be considered and used appropriately. The traditional proposal has remained uniform: peace must be based on negotiated agreement between the two superpowers, and it must concentrate on disarmament, particularly on eliminating nuclear weapons. Contemporary negotiations have addressed three areas, limiting testing, attack weapons, and defense. They should be viewed separately.

Test Bans

When negotiations with the Soviet Union became feasible after Stalin's death, the United States had a big lead in nuclear technology and weapons. No agreement could be reached on reducing the latter, but further development of nuclear weapons could be impeded by a test ban.

An informal nuclear test moratorium was established in 1958. The United States assumed that Soviet plans to resume testing would be identified in time to prepare its own tests. But on September 1, 1961, with one day's notice from the Soviets and no notice from the Central Intelligence Agency (CIA), the Soviet Union began the world's largest test series. The United States conducted a hastily assembled test series; the Soviets, a second extensive test series; and then a ban on atmospheric testing went into effect.

Although theory can predict what should occur, only testing can provide confidence. The Soviet 1961–1962 tests studied the effects of nuclear explosions on incoming ballistic missiles. The United States, lacking interest in defense, did not do so before the ban was implemented. A defensive nuclear explosion of less than a 1,000 tons' yield, detonated as low as five miles above the surface of the earth, can destroy a nuclear warhead of megaton yield (equivalent to a million tons of TNT) without harmful effects at ground level.

That type of defense was the first developed; many still consider it the most reliable. But observations of nuclear explosions in the atmosphere ceased with the Soviets in a superior position, which they have retained since that time.

The absence of atmospheric tests had another consequence. Soviet progress in weapons development could be observed by collecting and analyzing the radioactive material produced by the tests. That valuable source of information was cut off in 1963. The United States set out to limit knowledge and succeeded in limiting its own. The Soviet Union believed in progress and reaped the advantage.

The limited test ban treaty did not impede the development of nuclear attack weapons, since they could be tested underground.[2] Limiting the indiscriminate damage done by weapons had high priority in U.S. weapons research and has led to smaller weapons that could fulfill military purposes. Indeed, the U.S. stockpile in 1980 had only one-third the blast and radioactivity of the 1960 stockpile. Few people are aware of the two-thirds reduction that research and testing have already accomplished.[3] The Soviet stockpile in the late 1980s, higher in explosive power than the U.S. stockpile ever was, seems to be declining, possibly because the Soviets are introducing similar weapons.

Following an extensive underground Soviet test series in 1985, General Secretary Mikhail Gorbachev announced (on the anniversary of the Hiroshima bombing) a unilateral cessation of testing and began a major effort in propaganda and diplomacy for a comprehensive test ban. The Soviet Union resumed testing in early 1987, but the pressure for a nuclear test ban continues.

Arms Limitation

A test ban treaty does not restrict the number or the power of weapons; it has no effect on an arms race. Rather, it is a restriction on research, on the acquisition of new knowledge. Arms limitation was not attempted until the early 1970s. The first treaty, the strategic arms limitation treaty (SALT I), concluded in 1972, limited the systems that deliver nuclear weapons—missile silos, airplanes, and submarines—not the number of nuclear weapons, which cannot be checked in the Soviet Union. The United States wanted verification and accepted what was feasible: counting the carriers. National means of verification (more plainly, refined satellite photography) provide some assurance that fixed silos, airplanes, and submarines can be counted and that estimates of mobile launchers may be reasonable.

The treaty disclosed the superiority of the Soviet nuclear forces. The course leading to that surprising situation is clearer in retrospect. After the 1957 Sputnik launch, many people concluded that Soviet nuclear-armed rockets were already aimed at the United States. That was an imagined missile gap. Years of complacency followed the early apprehensions. But according to the CIA, by 1969 the missile gap was real.

That fact was kept secret. I became aware of it before 1970, but U.S. senators were told only when they were confronted with the treaty in 1972. The Soviets had a threefold advantage in weight that could be lifted by rockets, which corresponds roughly to a threefold advantage in nuclear explosive power. The Senate demanded that future treaties be based on parity, a demand that may never be met.

SALT I dispelled the illusion of overwhelming U.S. superiority. But the balance of forces cannot be measured simply by rocket throw weight or by explosive power. During the early deployment of nuclear missiles, U.S. rockets had more accurate guidance systems. By the early 1980s both sides had the same effective level. In the late 1960s the United States developed multiple independent reentry vehicles (MIRVs), which could direct several nuclear explosives on one rocket to different targets. Within five years, much sooner than the CIA expected, the Soviets had also installed MIRVs.

The United States has fallen far behind the Soviet Union in quantity of every type of weaponry. Many claim that the disadvantage is offset by the qualitative superiority of our weapons. At the same time work on weapons is denigrated as part of an arms race. We cannot count on a technical advantage if we are divided about its necessity and its value.

Under Presidents Ford and Carter a further arms limitation treaty was drawn up. Although SALT II was signed in 1979, Senate ratification was interrupted by the invasion of Afghanistan. Nevertheless, the United States observes both SALT agreements.

U.S.-Soviet treaties lack parity in more than the quality and quantity of weaponry: they are both enforced more comprehensively and interpreted more strictly in the United States than in the Soviet Union. The enforcement disparity stems from the difference between an open society and a closed one. The effective Soviet intelligence service would quickly identify any U.S. treaty violation. Our free press automatically and rightfully provides further safeguards for the Soviets. For those simple reasons treaty enforcement in East and West will differ for the foreseeable future.

The disparity in interpretation is more essential. The SALT I treaty was intended to limit the number of missiles by limiting the number of delivery systems; each U.S. silo can deliver only a single missile. But the treaty did not specify nonreloading silos. No one is sure whether all or only some of the Soviet silos can be reloaded. The SALT agreements do specify the kind of new rockets that can be introduced. The details of the new Soviet SS-20 through SS-25 missiles are not clear, but there is no question that only the broadest interpretation of the treaties would permit their introduction.

The political impact of the SS-20 series was great. More than a thousand intermediate-range nuclear explosives were aimed at Europe. The United States countered by planning and later deploying missiles in Western Europe aimed at the Soviet Union. In 1981 President Reagan proposed the zero-zero option: the elimination of all medium-range rockets. The intermediate-range nuclear forces (INF) treaty, signed in 1987, is the first treaty to reduce the number of nuclear weapons. Such a reduction, if it happens, could be highly significant. Because it makes the difficult task of rocket defense a little easier, deterrence by defense may become more effective.

Planning for treaties that would reduce the number of rocket launchers, and possibly the number of nuclear arms, continues. Such plans should be assessed on how well reductions can be verified and on whether the reductions will be significant enough to make defense more feasible. For example, the Soviet SS-20 series missiles are launched from mobile carriers. Therefore a reduction in numbers (as opposed to elimination) is almost impossible to verify.

Restrictions on Defense

The Soviet Union has won the race in weapons of attack, but at least the United States ran the race. That has not been the case with defensive weapons. From the earliest beginnings of the rocket age the Soviet Union has planned not only for missile attack but for defense against missiles as well. The rationale for this decision was given by Aleksei Kosygin, premier of the Soviet Union, in 1967: "A defensive system that prevents attack is not a cause of the arms race . . . Perhaps an anti-missile system is more expensive than an offensive system, but its purpose is not to kill people, but to save human lives."[4]

Nevertheless, in 1972 the United States and the Soviet Union signed the antiballistic missile (ABM) agreement: each side could defend two sites (later reduced to one) by rockets from 100 silos. The Soviets began deploying defenses around Moscow in 1972 and have continued through 1987 to upgrade those defenses. They have thus had the opportunity not only to work out difficulties in the system but also to train personnel. The United States decided to defend its North Dakota missile site. Development stopped without deployment, since the defense was thought ineffective against the number of missiles that might be sent against it.

In 1972 Henry Kissinger convinced me that ratifying the treaty was reasonable. He noted the treaty would not have an actual effect on U.S. deployment of defenses—Congress would not vote the money with or without a treaty. The ABM treaty languished as an unimportant footnote to history until 1983, when President Reagan announced the Strategic Defense Initiative (SDI). Then the treaty suddenly became the main obstacle to U.S. defense in space. The ABM treaty is a clear demonstration of the difficulties of writing meaningful agreements about future possibilities.

The Soviet circumventions and violations of the ABM treaty are much more significant than those connected with offensive weapons. Research on directed-energy weapons is permissible under the ABM treaty; deployment of such weapons is defined as a violation. The U.S. Department of Defense has stated that the Soviets have deployed a laser at the Sary Shagan weapons testing center.[5] Installations at other sites have not been discussed because the CIA wants to document a violation fully before mentioning it. Such caution has some worth. But if made doubly obscure by an added cloak of secrecy, the virtue becomes vice.

In addition to laser weapons, the Soviets have deployed an advanced surface-to-air missile, the SA-12. It provides defense against airplanes as claimed; it almost certainly can also be used against incoming rockets. The same holds even more clearly for inland radars (like the Krasnoiarsk radar station).[6] Together with tracking devices on the SA-12s (which are launched from mobile carriers), the radars can support a defensive system for the entire Soviet Union.

The Strategic Defense Initiative

In the late 1950s Air Force General E. E. Partridge invited me to the observation and communication facilities at Cheyenne Mountain. He also gave me reasons to think positively about the efficacy of defense. More than twenty years later, presidential candidate Ronald Reagan visited the same facility. After viewing the elaborate means of observing a missile approach its U.S. target, he asked: "Then what can we do about it?" He was told. Nothing.

Most Americans still do not understand that simple fact. In looking for defense against a catastrophic attack, the United States has neglected to establish any defense—even against one missile. Vulnerability is a fact of life in our modern technological world, but we need not make a virtue of it. President Reagan does not like total vulnerability. He collected advice, considered, and eventually announced that scientists should try to enlist technology to defend against nuclear weapons.

That decision unleashed a debate and a development. The debate has been violent, unwieldy, and unproductive. The opponents correctly argue that defense will never be complete and that devastation, even by a few atomic bombs, would be terrible. Their second, more controversial, objection is that defense will lead to overconfidence and the temptation to strike first. The second objection is in obvious conflict with the first. Defense can never be perfect. Overconfidence may be claimed in the heat of debate but not in the real world. By making the success of an attack doubtful, defense strengthens deterrence of war.

Deployment of defenses would also ease tensions; today the United States cannot prevent a single accidentally fired missile from wreaking havoc. Yet such limited defense has been possible for two decades. What is served by having to trust Soviet technology and operational skills as well as Soviet intentions—or the intentions of anyone else?[7]

On the positive side, SDI, though limited in scope, has been remarkably effective. It has been accepted as an international undertaking in treaties between the United States and Great Britain, West Germany, Italy, Israel, and Japan. The Israeli SDI effort, carried by a right-left coalition government, is concentrating on defense against SS-21 missiles (with a range of 100 miles) that might be used against its mobilization centers. That shortest-range defense project, operating in the shortest time span and requiring the least money, is at one extreme of the SDI spectrum. At the opposite extreme are the lasers and other beam weapons. High-intensity lasers, engineered as defensive weapons, are in an advanced research stage in the United States, but unlike their counterparts in the Soviet Union, they are not ready for deployment.

The examples above should make it clear that SDI is looking for a whole array of defensive instruments. The system likely to be available for deployment first may involve a few thousand remarkably small, simple devices that can seek out and collide with Soviet rocket boosters.[8] Deployed in space, the devices could home in on rockets as they take off. The use of miniaturization, electronic observation, and improved computers all suggest that modern technology gives small defensive objects a good chance of being cost-effective. The technical questions connected with the development of defense will in the end be decisive. I predict that defense will be deployed if we can demonstrate that it is effective.

The Technological Advantage

When President Reagan took office, he made the shocking statement that the Soviet Union had become the world's greatest military power. The statement was overdue. Still the general belief is that Soviet leadership is only quantitative, not qualitative: the advantage in technology lies with the United States. In a rapidly changing technological situation, elusive questions about leadership must be approached with care. Part of our technical preeminence was established in seven years, the time between the discovery of fission and the test of the first atomic bomb. The speed was possible because the whole scientific and engineering community worked to achieve that goal. In the interim our leadership in nuclear energy has been lost, and the unity and dedication that produced it are no more.

When discussing military strength in the 1990s, at least three technical developments must be considered: electronics, space, and lasers. The United States has been and still is preeminent in the first area: computers, sensors, and communications. The United States is also best at miniaturization. Electronic devices the size of a pinhead are a great achievement, but a radically smaller jet engine is also significant. Both electronics and miniaturization can be important for defense, provided we work on it.

The U.S. position in the second area, space, is different. The Soviets gave high priority to rocket development long before we did. Sputnik made the first space flight. Subsequently the United States put a man on the moon. Despite the enthusiasm generated by that success, the U.S. space effort was not sustained, and since the tragic Challenger accident in 1986 it has almost come to a standstill. In 1985 the Soviets launched at least ten times as many rockets (and thereby put ten times as much weight in space) as we. The military importance of space cannot be overestimated. Official Soviet military doctrine calls not only for a presence in space but for domination of space. When England was our adversary, the United States insisted on freedom of the oceans; now that we are contending with the Soviets, we must insist on freedom of space.

The third great area of modern defense technology is the development of beam weapons. The highly localized effects of such weapons are the opposite of the indiscriminate destructiveness of large nuclear explosives. Beam weapons, particularly lasers, can be directed with such accuracy that after a thousand miles of travel, the beam need be no more than five feet wide. For many years the Soviets have spent more than a billion dollars annually on lasers alone. It should not be surprising that the best technical publications on beam weapons are of Soviet origin.

In the broad field of strategic defense, the Soviets seem to have the technological lead in directional weapons as well as in the use of space. The United States is ahead in electronics and in miniaturization. If the United States does not develop and deploy defenses using its own technical advantages, it will have lost all hope of maintaining a military balance.

By the year 2000 the technological picture may be greatly changed. The first high-temperature superconductor was discovered in 1986. Any or all of the technologies connected with electromagnetism—from electronics to energy transmission—may be affected by that discovery. Research on superconductivity began and continues to blossom in the international arena. Even the Soviets have begun to publish openly on the topic. The technology is important for defense, but its impact on economics and on collaboration may be fully as important. There is change; there is danger; there is also promise.

The Choice

The possibility of introducing realistic defenses following five years of modest effort on SDI (at a level of 1 percent of the Pentagon budget) looks promising. SDI has shown that excellent defense against a single missile, even against a dozen missiles, is feasible. It has also shown that the effectiveness both of retaliation and of a devastating first blow may be challenged in the next few years, certainly well before the end of the century. There is no possibility of an impenetrable shield, but there is a real possibility of protecting the most vital targets.

The year 1987 ended with the positive prospects of arms reduction and of defense. Will those two reinforce or cancel each other? In the 1970s the ABM treaty stopped our defensive efforts. Those on the right believe that treaty and defense will once again prove incompatible. Those on the left assert that SDI is provocative. Which of those two absurdities is more absurd?

A recent joint U.S.-Soviet summit statement declared:

> Taking into account the preparation of the Treaty on Strategic Offensive Arms, the leaders of the two countries also instructed their delegations in Geneva to work out an agreement that would commit the sides to observe the ABM Treaty, as signed in 1972, while conducting their research, development, and testing as required, which are permitted by the ABM Treaty, and not to withdraw from the ABM Treaty, for a specified period of time. Intensive discussions of strategic stability shall begin not later than three years before the end of the specified period.[9]

If those arguing for the treaty and those favoring strategic defense are not to clash head-on, those sentences must be clarified. President Reagan has consistently argued for both disarmament and defense. He may be the only prominent man in the world whose approach is on middle ground. That road is not a compromise but an innovative, promising new direction to securing peace.

As the United States enters the last decade of the twentieth century, we face an unprecedented discomfort: a deep influence on U.S. party politics by a foreign power. Increased disunity is visible not only between Republicans and Democrats but also within the parties themselves. A coherent, unified, and reliable vision of our nation's relation to the rest of the world is critical.

SDI has been accepted as an international undertaking. The next question is whether a bridge can be built between negotiations and defense so that their combined effectiveness can make peace and freedom more secure. A treaty cannot provide a 100 percent guarantee of peace; a defense system cannot be 100 percent effective against missiles. But the combined effect of fewer missiles of attack and the best of imperfect defenses could constitute a sturdy insurance of peace.

The Third Millennium

As we approach the last decade of the twentieth century, talk about the end of mankind is commonplace. Religious fears of an apocalypse had wide currency in the years just before A.D. 1000. Today's nightmares are similar except that they are based on science rather than on religion. That does not mean that they are more closely connected with reality.

Changes in technology will make the third millennium very different from the past. The incredible story of the twentieth century can lead to no other conclusion. Developments in communication (radio and television), transportation (automobiles and airplanes), nuclear energy, electronics, computers, and space travel have shrunk the world and opened the universe.

Much of that accomplishment is a result of theory, that is, of our understanding of the world. Old rigid conceptions of space, time, and even causality have been replaced. The universe has expanded a thousand times over what was envisaged in the nineteenth century. Nebulous concepts about atoms have been replaced by precise mathematical models. The practical applications of those new insights reach from semiconductors and high-temperature superconductors to new polymers that are replacing metals and to genetic engineering. The most consistent characteristic of all that change is its increasing rapidity.

In human dimensions the population of the planet has grown from little more than two billion to more than six billion. Malthus's pessimistic predictions have proved false: ingenuity has outpaced fertility. The biggest catastrophes of our century were its two horrible wars, but even those were not unprecedented. The Mongol invasion and the Thirty Years' War left proportionally far fewer survivors.

In human values achieved and human values violated, the twentieth century may be no better and no worse than those that went before it. But the rapidity of change we face as the century ends is a new experience. Technology makes interaction among all parts of the globe both possible and necessary. The decisions we make in the 1990s will not only influence the United States and the Soviet Union but determine the nature of the third millennium for the entire globe.

As the interdependence of the world increases, the need for organization becomes more pronounced. Before many more decades pass, the nations of the world will decide whether that order will be imposed on them or cooperatively created by them. In the past, order has always been introduced by conquest. There is reason to hope that conquest has gone out of fashion. The only country that captured other nations during the twentieth century and still holds them is the Soviet Union.

As the 1990s begin, the Soviets still have a monopoly on defense technology. If they succeed in maintaining it, a second Munich may be in the making, and the year 2000 may mark the founding of a Soviet world empire. The United States is the only existing power that may be able to hold its own against the Soviet Union. But the United States has no coherent plan for the future.

The United States does have some remarkable accomplishments. One is its unprecedented move to restore the vitality of its former enemies. Following World War II the United States provided rehabilitation funds to Germany and assistance to Japan that sped their economic recovery. Because of

that support, the Western world is functioning with unprecedented harmony. The United States also accelerated decolonization. The process may
have been too radical and rapid, but certainly it established new and important responsibilities in the Third World. And most recently the United States
has led the way in a cooperative international venture to lift the threat of
nuclear missiles. For better or for worse, the United States has taken initiatives in harmony with the moral principles to which we subscribe.

There is an even deeper side to the character of the United States. We
are a mixture of cultures. More than half of our annual population increase
comes from immigration. By modifying immigration procedures to legalize
formerly illegal immigrants, we have recognized immigration as helpful.
One can look at the United States as a model of a wider international society. Like the United States, that society is flexible, has vague goals rather
than plans, and has doubts rather than absolute truths. Such uncertainty is
both its peril and its hope. The survivability of such a fragile organization,
however, is inexorably linked to its appreciation of technology.

Technology has been called dehumanizing. Human values will not be
created by technology, but they will not be realized without it. Technical
progress has helped create material abundance; it also points to deficiencies
in human relations. By accepting technology as an ever-active component
of human existence, the United States in the 1990s can create the conditions
that will lead to a better approach to coexistence on our planet.

Notes

1. "The Promotion of Peace," *Nature* 142, no. 3597 (October 8, 1938): 629.

2. A further test ban limiting underground tests to a yield of 150 kilotons, signed
in 1974 but unratified, has been observed. There is little interest in multimegaton
explosives because at such high yields an increasing fraction of the energy released
is directed upward (militarily useless) rather than laterally along the earth's surface.

3. By comparison, the reduction promised by the INF treaty is a low percentage
of the stockpiles.

4. *Pravda* (TASS report from London), February 11, 1967, p. 1.

5. Department of Defense, *Soviet Military Power* (Washington, D.C.: Government Printing Office, 1984), p. 33.

6. Department of Defense, *Soviet Military Power* (Washington, D.C.: Government Printing Office, 1985), p. 44.

7. The destruction of the Korean airliner in 1983 and the 1987 Chernobyl accident suggest the Soviets have room for improvement.

8. In the boost phase, rockets, heavily laden with fuel, are slow and vulnerable.

9. President Ronald Reagan and General Secretary Mikhail Gorbachev, *Joint
U.S.-Soviet Summit Statement*, U.S. Department of State, December 10, 1987.

WILLIAM R. VAN CLEAVE

♦ ———————————————————— ♦

Strategic Deterrence, Defense, and Arms Control

♦ "How can we fight our enemies if we kill our own people?" the great military leader Xenophon asked his army.[1] The same question might be asked today, rephrased in the modern language of deterrence: How can we credibly threaten to fight our enemies, and thus be able to deter their attacks, if we do not defend our own people? By not defending them, they are supposed to be hostages to deterrence, but their vulnerability works against the effectiveness of our own deterrent. How can we respond credibly to attacks if this means we kill our own people?

This is the paradox of mutual assured destruction, a so-called strategy that no longer exists in official policy but is prolonged in practice by the lack of effective means for limiting damage to ourselves in the event that deterrence fails. Ironically U.S. policy has long linked the effectiveness of deterrence to the ability to control destructiveness. Successive U.S. administrations have agreed that the ability to use nuclear weapons carefully and rationally to control escalation and to limit damage constitutes both the best deterrent and the best capability should deterrence fail.

A combination of Soviet actions and relative U.S. inaction, however, has placed in grave jeopardy the ability of the United States to carry out this policy. For nearly twenty years, including the eight years of the Reagan administration, Soviet strategic nuclear programs have far outstripped U.S. efforts to maintain the capabilities that U.S. governments have deemed essential. As a consequence, the strategic balance increasingly favors the Soviet Union.

It is not as provocative as it once was to observe that arms control has contributed to this unfavorable situation. It has asymmetrically constrained U.S. strategic modernization while masking the momentum and obscuring the objectives of the Soviet buildup. Today arms control considerations seem to limit the best options available to the United States to improve the strategic balance, including progress in the Strategic Defense Initiative (SDI).

This essay will briefly explore these problems and suggest a few ways the next administration might deal with them more effectively. I would argue that there are no more critical security problems for the United States than the state of the U.S.-Soviet strategic balance, the future of SDI, and the influence over these of arms control.

The Reagan administration came to office with the avowed intention of establishing a comprehensive military strategy and a policy to ensure that both arms and arms control decisions were consistent with that strategy. It leaves office with a mixed record, which on balance falls short of what has been required even when requirements are based solely on officially established strategic doctrine and objectives. By those standards, the gap between the requirements and the capabilities to meet them has grown as surely as the gap between Soviet and U.S. strategic nuclear force (SNF) capabilities.

The Strategic Balance

The importance of this strategic imbalance may be appreciated by a review of the roles that SNFs play in U.S. policy. Their importance is based not only on the grave consequences of a failure of nuclear deterrence but also on the impact of SNFs on deterrence at lower levels. The strategic nuclear balance is the high ground that casts a shadow over all other military balances. The success of U.S. extended deterrence, on which other nations depend, rests ultimately on the SNF balance. An imbalance at that level magnifies deficiencies at the theater nuclear and general purpose force levels and erodes the effectiveness of these forces.

The official document *National Security Strategy of the United States* points this out: "While deterrence requires capabilities across the entire spectrum of conflict, its essential foundation is provided by our strategic deterrent forces and the doctrine which supports them."[2] The doctrine for these forces, which establishes standards for evaluating their adequacy, has remained remarkably constant through successive administrations.[3] It is not based on a policy of minimum deterrence or on the theoretical ability to inflict damage to cities and populations in response to attacks. As the Carter administration put it, U.S. SNFs must have the capability and plans for "attacks which pose a more credible threat than an all-out attack on Soviet industry and cities . . . while retaining an assured destruction capacity in reserve."[4]

Whether enunciated by Secretary of Defense Schlesinger, Rumsfeld, Brown, or Weinberger, U.S. strategic doctrine has called for forces capable of surviving any Soviet attack with a variety of selective attack options against a wide range of Soviet targets. These options are selected for (1) their contribution to deterrence and (2) their contribution to U.S. political-military objectives should deterrence fail. The most important of the latter are denying enemy objectives, controlling escalation, and limiting damage. It is U.S. doctrine that these objectives not only have intrinsic value but are also essential to deterrence. As the Carter administration said: "Our surest deterrent is our capability to deny gain from aggression . . . There is no contradiction between this attention to militarily effective targeting . . . and our primary and overriding policy of deterrence."[5]

For deterrence, then, not only must U.S. forces be able to retaliate effectively, but the retaliatory threats must be credible both to the enemy and to ourselves. Credibility requires the ability to use weapons rationally and carefully. The Reagan administration has not changed this approach: "If we are forced to retaliate and can only respond by destroying population centers, we invite the destruction of our own population. Such a deterrent strategy is hardly likely to carry conviction as a deterrent."[6] Additionally, in both peacetime and after any failure of deterrence, U.S. SNF capabilities should be essentially equivalent to those of the Soviet Union.

These requirements clearly call for more robust, diversified, and flexible forces than those necessary only for counter-city responses. They also call for highly survivable forces. The basic standards of strategic stability (freedom from the risk of surprise attack) and crisis stability (denying the Soviets any incentive to strike first in a crisis) require the absence of major force vulnerabilities. This fundamental consideration gave rise to the concerns that President Reagan voiced during the 1980 presidential campaign about the window of vulnerability. Unfortunately the window of vulnerability has not been closed; instead, U.S. SNFs have become even more vulnerable to the types of attacks the Soviets can now launch.[7]

An analysis of the strategic balance by the prestigious Committee on the Present Danger concluded that "the U.S. strategic force posture vis-à-vis the Soviet Union has deteriorated sharply, and is considerably worse than official estimates."[8] In his annual report to Congress for fiscal year 1985, Secretary of Defense Caspar Weinberger declared that Soviet capabilities had "undermined the retaliatory effectiveness that was at the heart of our policy of deterrence."[9] And his annual report for fiscal year 1988 concluded that U.S. SNFs "are not equivalent in their actual capabilities" to Soviet SNFs.[10] Two strategic analysts have recently concluded:

> The overall pattern of Soviet activities in recent years—the ICBM buildup and the burgeoning ABM capability—suggest that the USSR is intent on positioning itself for a first strike. As a consequence of the resultant threat to the effectiveness of our retaliatory forces, the theory of deterrence by Mutual Assured Destruction is collapsing like a house of cards ... they will not be deterred by the fear of retaliation, because we will not be able to retaliate.[11]

The above conclusions reflect Soviet success in developing counterforce capabilities against the principal nuclear deterrent forces of the West. These counterforce capabilities are supported by a large strategic nuclear reserve force intended in the event of war to dissuade the United States from retaliating with degraded forces. That reserve is backed up by impressive and still-developing active and passive defenses to safeguard against Western retaliation. Defenses that may not look strong against the hypothetical contingency of an unfettered U.S. first strike may be very effective indeed against a force that has already suffered Soviet attacks. The Soviets have been working with steady determination on those capabilities for years, and they continue to do so today despite their public emphasis on arms control and *glasnost'*.

In contrast, U.S. SNF programs have vacillated between what is required by the threat and what is deemed compatible with arms control. At times the latter consideration has unduly influenced the administration's decisions; at other times, arms control constraints have been imposed on U.S. programs by Congress. As a result, U.S. forces today do not confidently possess the capabilities required by U.S. doctrine. Forces likely to survive Soviet attacks lack flexibility and damage-limiting capabilities. Strategic defenses to strengthen deterrence by enhancing the survivability of U.S. retaliatory forces and to limit damage from enemy attacks do not exist. Ironically U.S. policy makers place more emphasis on limiting damage to the USSR *from U.S. strikes* than on limiting damage to the United States *from Soviet attacks*.

The United States has proceeded in an appropriate direction in strategic nuclear doctrine, concepts, and objectives, but its capabilities have not kept pace. This lag raises a serious question as to what is U.S. policy. It also raises an important question for the 1990s: Should standards and goals be reduced to fit existing capabilities, or should capabilities be expanded to conform with existing standards? It is perfectly appropriate to have military objectives that cannot be met by existing capabilities if (1) those objectives are used as guidelines for force planning and modernization and (2) active programs are designed to erase the gap between capabilities and objectives. In neither case, however, is the Reagan administration's record good. Dealing with this problem should be at the top of the agenda of the new administration.

The Strategic Defense Initiative (SDI)

Will a defense of the United States against ballistic missile attack be deployed? As this volume goes to press, some five and one-half years have passed since President Reagan's visionary announcement of a program to develop a ballistic missile defense (BMD) for the nation. Although the technical progress fostered by the program has placed a variety of BMD systems and technologies at our command, deployment of a defense has not drawn correspondingly nearer. As Wyoming Senator Malcolm Wallop pointed out in a June 1987 address:

> More time has passed since March 23, 1983, than elapsed between Pearl Harbor and VJ Day. During that time, this country built and armed most of the world, and developed a huge technical infrastructure necessary to construct the atom bomb from scratch. Yet four years after the President's 1983 announcement, we appear no closer to a strategic defense.[12]

Moving deterrence away from a reliance on offensive retaliatory threats alone and toward a greater emphasis on the ability to defend—saving lives rather than avenging them—cannot proceed without a decision to begin deploying a BMD. Yet U.S. government policy still limits SDI to research and selective development and links the question of eventual deployment to arms control.

U.S. strategic doctrine, as described above, logically requires strategic defenses to augment and provide survivability for offensive capabilities and to limit damage from attacks. These are now feasible objectives when stated reasonably. Yet official descriptions of SDI remain oriented toward the most ambitious long-term goals for defense. This approach establishes standards that work against the early deployment of feasible limited defenses. It also lends support to the exceedingly high cost estimates generated by SDI opponents. Ironically even though the more ambitious goals dominate, the SDI program is being deliberately restrained by a decision to conform to the most narrow interpretation of the antiballistic missile (ABM) treaty.

The Soviets, however, are proceeding to deploy a BMD, and a strategic nuclear balance based on defense as well as offense is shaping up solely through Soviet actions. A February 1988 *Wall Street Journal* editorial cited new intelligence that the Soviet Union is breaking out of the ABM treaty and proceeding to deploy a nationwide BMD. The *Journal* correctly called this "an official stamp on what has been apparent all along."[13]

The choice for the United States is whether to continue to defer deployment, standing by and watching the Soviets add a BMD to their offensive superiority, or whether to acquire the benefits of defense against threats of ballistic missile attack. Technologically the United States could counter and diminish Soviet strategic advantages through a BMD—which is precisely why the Soviets so ardently seek to limit U.S. BMD development.

For twenty years the United States has expended considerable energy seeking means to provide its deterrent forces with adequate survivability against Soviet threats to those forces. In 1969 the United States planned to provide this survivability by a BMD. In 1972 it agreed not to do so. That agreement, based on the unfulfilled condition that the Soviets refrain from developing a threat to U.S. deterrent forces, should now be reversed. Defending threatened U.S. deterrent forces is an appropriate beginning for U.S. BMD deployment. It would also have an attractive advantage over such alternative survivability measures as intercontinental ballistic missile (ICBM) mobility: it would do more. ICBM mobility addresses only the threat to ICBMs; a BMD of ICBMs would also address a range of threats to populations and other civil or military assets under the protective umbrella of the defense. Consequently defending ICBMs and defending the population are not alternatives; they are complementary. Despite a tentative phase-one plan for a deployment that would do both (based on the 1987 Marshall Institute recommendations), no decision has been made to proceed, and none is planned until about 1993.[14]

Two other purposes for a limited BMD have recently been suggested, one highlighted by Democratic Senator Sam Nunn of Georgia and the other by the Pentagon commission on long-range strategy. The first is defense against what Senator Nunn called the "frightening possibility of an accidental or unauthorized missile launch." Senator Nunn suggested using the one site of BMD allowed by the ABM treaty for an accidental launch protection system, or ALPS. This is intrinsically a good idea. Coupled with an ICBM defense at the one site, it would provide a valuable operational system test center for further BMD development and deployment.[15] Beginning BMD deployment with Senator Nunn's suggestion might also promote stronger bipartisan support for BMD. A second purpose could be protection against future third-country threats. The Pentagon commission warned that newly industrialized and even less-developed countries could acquire nuclear weapons and ballistic missile systems by the twenty-first century. These capabilities would not only add new dimensions of threat directly to the United States but would also limit the ability of the United States to support its security interests around the world.[16]

Any of these options could form the basis for beginning the deployment of a BMD that could strengthen deterrence and move progressively toward greater effectiveness. What is needed is a deployment policy to proceed with feasible objectives now. Without beginning deployment, however limited, the political-psychological barrier to BMD will continue, and without deployment SDI will fade into a poorly funded research program.

Arms Control

Unless U.S. policy changes, the future of SDI will depend more on arms control politics than on technical progress and strategic considerations. U.S. policies, tying BMD to arms control, are retarding SDI progress and diminishing the prospects of deployment.

To promote an agreement on offensive arms, the United States has formally offered not to withdraw from the ABM treaty through 1996. The Reagan administration argues that this is *not* a nondeployment commitment, and published U.S. statements of the proposal usually use the careful wording "not to withdraw from the Anti-Ballistic Missile (ABM) Treaty for the purpose of deploying strategic defenses not permitted by the ABM Treaty."[17] But it is difficult to avoid the conclusion that such a commitment would really be a nondeployment pledge. The wording of the Joint U.S.-Soviet Summit Statement—"not to withdraw from the ABM Treaty, for a specified period of time"[18]—departed from the usual formulation.

At the end of 1987 Soviet and U.S. officials, including President Reagan, made conflicting statements about whether an understanding limiting SDI testing had been reached.[19] Inevitably speculation arose about secret agreements or implicit understandings with the Soviets.[20] At the same time, the administration accepted, in fact if not in principle, congressional constraints on testing that conformed to the narrow treaty interpretation the Soviets have sought to impose on the United States. In February 1988 Secretary of Defense Frank Carlucci told Congress that no SDI tests are scheduled through fiscal year 1989 that would be beyond the narrow interpretation of the ABM treaty.[21] While constraining the United States, the treaty has not prevented the Soviet Union from deploying the base for a nationwide BMD.

The administration, however, has suggested a "negotiated transition" toward defense, "sharing the benefits of strategic defense" technology with the Soviets.[22] It is one thing to set forth conceptually, and publicly, the advantages of a more defensively based strategic relationship with the USSR in which both deemphasize offensive forces. But to expect to plan such a relationship jointly, or to base it on arms control agreements with the USSR, is a fundamental mistake that would defy the lessons of experience. An equally great mistake would be to share U.S. BMD technology with the Soviets. Sharing this technology would greatly reduce our ability to offset Soviet strategic advantages with a U.S. defensive advantage.

What the Soviet Union really seeks are constraints on SDI that would delay deployment and limit development—in effect, constraints fatal to the program—in return for the Soviet *promise* of reductions. In 1972 the United States agreed to forgo deploying a BMD to secure future reductions of the Soviet threat. Instead, once effective constraints were established on the U.S. BMD program, the Soviets proceeded to expand their forces beyond any official prediction at the time. They also gained the time to catch up with the United States in BMD technology.

What would the United States gain in the arms control bargain? Presumably a strategic arms reduction (START) agreement with an emphasis on reductions, not on improving stability. The U.S. START proposal does not derive from U.S. strategic force and targeting requirements or from existing force posture planning; it was formulated largely apart from such considerations. If there is to be a START agreement reducing force levels, it could be made safer and more tolerable if there were a simultaneous and corresponding U.S. deployment of a BMD. The problem is that BMD deployment and the future of SDI are being bargained away to achieve a reduction agreement.

With a BMD the *threat* of ballistic missiles will be reduced. Negotiated reductions of ballistic missiles may follow, but ballistic missiles will have been devalued, with or without an agreement. Without BMD even deep reductions will not devalue ballistic missiles or their threat, especially if—as in the currently formulated START agreement—targets for ballistic missile warheads are reduced proportionately more than ballistic missile warheads. The value of ballistic missiles could then increase. The threat of Soviet cheating, the strategic significance of covertly produced ballistic missiles, would be far greater without a U.S. BMD. Consequently BMD deployment should be a necessary concomitant of reductions. It would decrease the vulnerability of the reducing forces, compensate for Soviet defenses, and safeguard the United States against Soviet cheating and breakout from the agreement.

In its emphasis on reductions, or eliminations, of nuclear weapons, the Reagan administration has transformed arms control back into disarmament. Disarmament, in contrast to arms control, seeks the reduction of armaments as a goal in itself, proceeding from the assumption that armaments per se, rather than aggressive policies, cause war. Arms control in concept subordinates reductions to the goal of enhancing stability—that is, improving the survivability of our deterrent forces through agreements that reduce the threat more than they reduce our ability to cope with the threat. What is now occurring is what two arms control experts call the "return of radical arms control . . . [and] older notions of disarmament." [23]

The need for a realistic reexamination of the course and effects of arms control, its indirect and asymmetrical consequences in democratic societies, and its impact on the future of defenses is urgent. In attributing sincerity and common arms control goals to the Soviet Union, the Reagan administration seems to ignore a rich learning experience to the contrary. It also seems to ignore the asymmetrical constraints the arms control process has always imposed on the West.

In a recent *Foreign Affairs* article, Professor Samuel Huntington concluded that the Reagan administration had made a "breathtaking" reversal of its position on the central issues of nuclear arms control and the Soviet Union: "By 1986 and 1987 it was alarming realistic moderates (and many allies) by its apparent willingness to weaken nuclear deterrence, its eagerness to reach agreements with the Soviets, and its new found faith that the Soviets had abandoned their expansionist goals. The naiveté concerning the Soviets that President Carter abandoned in 1979 President Reagan appeared to embrace in 1987." [24]

Conclusions about arms control, articulated forcefully in the early days of the Reagan administration, have been set aside. [25] These conclusions were that the Soviet Union has used arms control as an instrument to gain strategic advantage. Through arms control it has sought to restrict U.S. defense programs and to inhibit U.S. technologies that might deny strategic superiority to the Soviets. The Soviets have also used arms control for propaganda and the pursuit of political goals in Europe. If these conclusions are correct, and experience certainly validates them, it is necessary to ask whether Soviet policies or strategic objectives have changed fundamentally. Ongoing Soviet strategic programs do not suggest such a change, in which case the Soviets are again exploiting Western hopes for arms control.

Despite optimism in some quarters about arms control, we must remember that the United States has engaged in intensive arms control efforts for twenty years while the military balance has shifted away from U.S. security and toward Soviet superiority, from survivable deterrent forces to vulnerable ones, from strategic stability to a situation where Soviet capabilities for surprise attack have increased. In sum, the period saw a shift in the strategic balance more adverse than any in the history of the United States.

Many years ago Walter Lippmann summarized the historical lesson of arms control: "The disarmament movement was . . . tragically successful in disarming the nations that believed in disarmament" [26]—leaving the aggressors free to arm without a determined opposition.

Notes

1. Xenophon, *The Persian Expedition*, trans. Rex Warner (Baltimore: Penguin Books, 1965), p. 206.

2. The White House, *National Security Strategy of the United States*, January 1987, p. 21; ibid., January 1988, p. 14. The same statement is in both documents.

3. This continuity was emphasized in the FY 1984 defense report to Congress, which contained an appendix showing the similarity of doctrinal statements by former secretaries of defense; see Secretary of Defense Caspar Weinberger, *Annual Report to the Congress, FY 1984* (Washington, D.C.; Government Printing Office, 1983), app. A.

4. Secretary of Defense Harold Brown, *Annual Report to the Congress, FY 1981* (Washington, D.C.: Government Printing Office, 1980), p. 66.

5. Ibid., p. 67.

6. Secretary of Defense Caspar Weinberger, *Annual Report to the Congress, FY 1984* (Washington, D.C.: Government Printing Office, 1983), p. 55.

7. For a discussion and summary analysis, see William R. Van Cleave, "Surprise Nuclear Attack," in Brian D. Dailey and Patrick J. Parker, eds., *Soviet Strategic Deception* (Lexington: D. C. Heath, Lexington Books, 1987), pp. 449–66.

8. Committee on the Present Danger, *Can America Catch Up? The U.S.-Soviet Military Balance* (Washington, D.C.: Committee on the Present Danger, 1984), p. iii.

9. Secretary of Defense Caspar Weinberger, *Annual Report to the Congress, FY 1985* (Washington, D.C.: Government Printing Office, 1984), p. 56.

10. Secretary of Defense Caspar Weinberger, *Annual Report to the Congress, FY 1988* (Washington, D.C.: Government Printing Office, 1987), p. 26.

11. Robert Jastrow and James Frelk, "Emasculating America's Deterrent," *Policy Review* 41 (Summer 1987): 34.

12. Senator Malcolm Wallop, *The Case for a Strategic Defense Force*, Heritage Lectures, no. 125 (Washington, D.C.: Heritage Foundation, 1987), p. 3.

13. "Breakout," *Wall Street Journal*, February 25, 1988, p. 20.

14. George C. Marshall Institute, *Missile Defense in the 1990s* (Washington, D.C.: George C. Marshall Institute, 1987).

15. Senator Sam Nunn, "Arms Control in the Last Year of the Reagan Administration" (Speech before the Arms Control Association, January 19, 1988), pp. 10–11.

16. Commission on Integrated Long-Term Strategy, *Discriminate Deterrence* (Washington, D.C.: Government Printing Office, 1988), pp. 9–10.

17. See "Nuclear and Space Talks: U.S. and Soviet Proposals," *Issues Brief* (U.S. Arms Control & Disarmament Agency), June 16 and September 9, 1987.

18. "Joint Statement by Reagan, Gorbachev," *Washington Post*, December 11, 1987, p. A-34.

19. See *New York Times* and *Washington Post*, November–December 1987.

20. See, e.g., "Is There a Secret Deal?" *National Security Record* 107 (November 1987).

21. "Star Wars Defense Plan Loses Steam," *Washington Post*, February 20, 1988, p. A-3.

22. See "Nuclear and Space Talks."

23. Charles H. Fairbanks, Jr., and Abram N. Shulsky, "From Arms Control to Arms Reductions," *Washington Quarterly* (Summer 1987): 59–73.

24. Samuel P. Huntington, "Coping with the Lippmann Gap," *Foreign Affairs* 66, no. 3 (1988): 463.

25. For early Reagan administration statements, see William R. Van Cleave, "The Arms Control Record: Successes and Failures," chap. 1 in Richard F. Staar, ed., *Arms Control: Myth Versus Reality* (Stanford: Hoover Institution Press, 1984).

26. Walter Lippmann, *U.S. Foreign Policy: Shield of the Republic* (Boston: Little, Brown & Co., 1943), p. 55.

HENRY S. ROWEN
JOHN B. DUNLOP

$\blacklozenge$ ───────────────── $\blacklozenge$

The Soviet Union
The Crisis of the System and Prospects for Change

$\blacklozenge$ By the mid-1980s it was becoming increasingly apparent to the rest of the world that the Soviet Union was having serious difficulties. The economy, the health of the population, the condition of the environment, the state of the party—all were in trouble. The situation as perceived by many people inside the country was much worse than appeared to most Western observers. Then in 1985 a radical reformer, Mikhail Gorbachev, became general secretary. Since then much has happened: decisions have been announced to decentralize decision-making power in the economy, a major effort has been underway to revive détente, there have been moves to make the operation of the party and of the workplace more "democratic," and the cultural scene is much more open. It has become abundantly clear that these actions, fostered by Gorbachev, have stimulated a strong resistance in terms of both policies and personalities.

The Contest Over Policy and Power

One objection within the ruling group concerns revelations about the past, especially revelations about the Stalin era that it fears will undermine the legitimacy of the system. Too much *glasnost'* could bring into the open too many skeletons from too many closets—not all of them ancient. On the economy there is also disagreement, at least about the pace and apparently also about the extent of the reforms. The opposition holds that *perestroika*,

if pushed too fast and too far, would weaken discipline, unleash open inflation, disrupt output, and perhaps produce conditions similar to those from
which Solidarity emerged in Poland. And the military objects to decisions
they believe result in diminished status and perhaps smaller budgets and
lower priority.

A personal element is central to these differences. The logic of Soviet
politics "inclines the leader to seek absolute power over the leading group,
but the same logic also impels them to strive to inhibit or prevent the prime
leader from acquiring it." [1] The struggle for power, however, varies in intensity. A cautious, consensus-seeking leader like Leonid Brezhnev who does
not seek radical change can achieve relative harmony among the top leadership, though the struggle always continues. A reform leader like Nikita
Khrushchev or Mikhail Gorbachev necessarily maximizes stress among the
leadership. There is an inevitable tension between those who promote innovation, more material rewards for performance, less centralization, and
more resources to consumers and those who emphasize ideology, limits on
de-Stalinization, central control, heavy-industry orientation, and control
over the intelligentsia.

Peter Reddaway has pointed out the extraordinary similarity of Khrushchev's and Gorbachev's programs: "Khrushchev's goal, after the stifling *im-
mobilisme* of [Joseph] Stalin's later years, was to 'get the country moving
again.' He wanted to reinvigorate the economy and society, put less emphasis on world revolution . . . [and] gave high importance to firing a number
of Stalinist officials . . . One of his major instruments for doing this—and
boosting his program as a whole—was *glasnost'*." [2] As a result Khrushchev
was nearly thrown out in 1957, only a year after his epoch-making secret
speech, and was jettisoned in 1964.

Gorbachev enjoys the fervent support of a few highly intelligent and
remarkably energetic men, but his support is paper-thin in numbers. One of
his principal supporters, Boris Eltsin, has already been purged. [3] On the basis
of history, we should predict a victory by the conservatives. This would
probably take the form of an accession by Egor Ligachev. Gorbachev and
his supporters know their history, however, and, being intelligent and re-
sourceful men, they might be able to defeat the odds.

The basic division within the system is between the "Gorbachevites,"
who favor a more open, Lenin-like strategy, reminiscent of the 1921 New
Economic Policy, which entails more use of market forces, and the "neo-
Andropovites," who favor more discipline in the system. Of course, it would
be an oversimplification to regard policy views as polar; they are not opposed on all important matters. There seems to be agreement on the need
to cut down on alcohol use, on anticorruption measures, on some moves
toward decentralization, and on the need to revive détente with the West.

The differences center on the limits of *glasnost'*, on the revision of party history, on the turnover and privileges of party cadres, on the degree and pace of economic reform, and on how much democracy to introduce into the party.

The arena of Gorbachev's greatest accomplishments so far has been in foreign policy. There appear to be few disagreements on this front, especially in contrast with domestic affairs. Here are some salient facts:

1. Heavy Soviet borrowing from the West, including a $10 billion increase in foreign debt in the past two years

2. Soviet industry's evident need for Western technology

3. The challenge from Western military technology, symbolized by the U.S. Strategic Defense Initiative (SDI)—a challenge the Soviet economy is in no position to respond to

4. The long-term implications for Soviet security of an economically powerful China and Japan in the East, a rich if politically fragmented Europe in the West, and a United States that promises to remain the world's largest economic and military power for the indefinite future

Even if General Secretary Gorbachev had an unchallenged position, which he might attain in the next several years, it would be impossible to forecast accurately the future course of events. For instance, would Gorbachev (or any likely Soviet leader) cut back the massive investment in military power or forego extensions of the Soviet empire to sustain the benefits of increased Western investment and freer access to Western technology? He might, but that would run counter to deeply embedded traits. Following precedent, the Soviets will do something in the next five or ten years to disrupt or destroy the new era of good feelings. Put differently, if whichever faction wins the struggle doesn't sustain the military buildup or doesn't engage in expansionist foreign behavior or in repressive behavior internally or in Eastern Europe, something important will have changed in the Soviet system.

The Decay of the System

After the long dreary Brezhnev years with their growing economic stagnation, corruption, and erosion of the limited freedoms permitted under Khrushchev, the longing for more liberties and more consumer goods must have become enormous. We are in an age of improved communications, and the contrast between developments outside the country and inside must have become increasingly evident even to the ruling establishment. Despite increasing news coverage and scholarly analysis of Soviet developments in the West, there is still inadequate appreciation of the depth of the economic and social backwardness and deterioration of that system. Evidence has been emerging, much of it recently in Soviet publications, on the near stagnation of the economy since the early 1970s.[4] There have been assertions—disputed by official Soviet statisticians—that Soviet national income has been grossly exaggerated since the late 1920s. A recent claim is that unreported inflation in consumer goods since the late 1950s has averaged 3–4 percent a year.[5] If true, not only has there been little or no economic growth in the past decade, but growth over the past 30 years averaged only 3.0–3.5 percent annually, with most growth occurring early in this period. Such a rate is not only far below Soviet official claims but also below the assessments of almost all Western scholars. Of course the latter have been aware of the bias of Soviet statistics and have deflated them, though perhaps not by enough. Still, these internal critics may not be correct; performance may not have declined as much as they say. But even if overall growth since the mid-1970s was better than widely estimated by Western experts, the Soviet economy did not gain on the West. Without improvement, it will be condemned to permanent inferiority.

In the 1970s a few keen Western observers noticed signs of social pathology. They included an increase in infant mortality after 1970; a decrease in the life expectancy of adults; a high and perhaps growing incidence of various diseases, most long ago brought under control in advanced nations; a high incidence of alcoholism; and an unparalleled degree of poisoning from bad alcohol. The causes of this decay seem multiple: the shortcomings of an impoverished system of health care, poor work and home conditions for mothers, a polluted environment, dangerous workplaces, and neglect (especially of the aged).

What caused this stagnation and retrogression? The neo-Andropovites would point to the loss of discipline and growing corruption during the Brezhnev era. Western economists—and the Gorbachevites—would emphasize growing difficulties of controlling an economy once it got beyond providing the minimums of shelter, clothing, and food, the increased distortion of prices from high money supply growth combined with price controls, the slowdown in investment, and the exhaustion of the process of "extensive" investment.

The investment process has created an industrial sector that produces huge quantities of steel and other metals. The energy sector produces more than half as much electric power as the United States, the world's largest amounts of oil and gas, and large quantities of coal and hydropower. The Soviet stock of machine tools is enormous. How could a society so underdeveloped in many ways have such a large industrial base, including such an advanced military-industrial sector? The answer is that the highest goal of this society (and of communist systems in general) is state power, including military power; this goal has the same supreme status as consumer welfare in the United States. Heavy industry is seen as the basis for military power and also almost as an end in itself. So steel plants, machinery plants, and power stations have been multiplied with little regard to efficiency in production or in the use of their outputs. Consequently the Soviet Union consumes, per unit of total output, more than three times as much steel as the United States and nearly twice as much energy. Many of these resources might as well have been heaped into pyramids to commemorate the work of Marx, Lenin, and Stalin. Weapons aside, only a modest flow of goods emerges from this vast industrial establishment. The heavy-industry sector should be considered a nearly closed system that absorbs large quantities of inputs and reproduces itself but emits only a small stream of products usable outside that system.

The command system contains another important source of inefficiency. In a market system resources for public purposes are allotted through budget allocations and through laws regulating behavior. When cost overruns occur, legislators sometimes adopt a tolerant attitude; soft budget constraints are not unknown in market systems. But they are the rule in command economies. Because of systemic excess demand, continuing bureaucratic interventions are needed to assure that resources go to the military and other high-priority sectors. Such a system forces low-priority sectors, like the health care system, to absorb most of the shortfalls that an overstressed economic system is bound to experience.[6] For example, when the railroads become congested, the defense sector gets its shipments and low-priority sectors get the shortages. Consequently enterprise managers try to hoard materials and labor. One result is a healthy military-industrial establishment and a sick population.

The operation of this priority system is made more consequential by the large share of output taken by the military, which absorbs nearly 20 percent of GNP. In addition are various levies by the military on the civilian economy and the costs of supporting the Soviet empire in Eastern Europe and abroad. Altogether these security-related activities absorb over 20 percent of GNP, perhaps around 25 percent.[7] Moreover, this share grew during the 1970s and early 1980s; probably a third to a half of incremental output over these years went to the security sector.

Many in the elite perceived the economic and social decline. But the military sector and the empire abroad did very well and individual welfare has low standing. Therefore, one disposed to do so could maintain that things were going fairly well. But the early 1980s brought a widespread sense that things were seriously amiss. Most observers now recognize that the country will continue to lag far behind the West—perhaps increasingly—unless it improves performance. Continued economic stagnation implies a relative decline in Soviet military power over time. Moreover, the rise to economic superpower status of Japan and the rapid growth of China must have impressed the Soviet leadership. Chinese GNP has doubled in the past decade; if China stays on its market-oriented course, GNP could double again by 2000. In twenty years China might approximate the Soviet Union as the world's third largest economy after the United States and Japan.

The General Secretary's Strategy

Gorbachev has realized that a program of discipline and slow reform could neither guarantee his continuance in power nor get the country moving again. Considerations of power and policy required him to act rapidly and sweepingly. His first priority has been rapid turnover of cadres—removing opponents and fence-sitters at all levels of the party and state machinery. The takeover of the Union of Filmmakers in May 1986 was a model of how to gain dominance over an organization. Gorbachev also attempted to have his supporters seize control of as much of the mass media as possible. He and his followers have been using the press as a sword and a club.

In addition to his cadres policy, Gorbachev's two most risky steps have been his attempt to revise the history of the party and his campaign to involve the Soviet masses in the political process in order to use them as a battering ram against his opponents. It was such high-risk endeavors that brought about Eltsin's fall and might bring about Gorbachev's.

If Gorbachev wishes to maximize his chances of survival, he should cease advocating policies that hurt him politically: *demokratizatsiia* and the turnover of cadres, cutting back the perks of the *nomenklatura*, the radical revision of party history, and the attempt to unleash "the living creativity of the masses." If he plays a more cautious waiting game, his chance of prevailing goes up. Certain issues work on his behalf: the state of the economy, arms control, and Afghanistan. If he can protect his clients and strong allies and continue to use the media effectively, he could slowly build support.

It is difficult to remove a sitting general secretary. Gorbachev knows this, and it is a major advantage. If he is cautious and wily, he could survive.

The Leading Opponent's Strategy

Ligachev, the leader of the conservatives, has opposed Gorbachev on both power and policy levels. He has chosen to speak out as an opponent of the excesses of *perestroika, glasnost'*, and *demokratizatsiia* and has been using the press to boost his authority. To strengthen his position, Ligachev has formed a close alliance with Viktor Chebrikov, the head of the KGB, and with elements in the Soviet military (including Defense Minister Dmitrii Yazov and Marshal Sergei Akhromeev, according to some reports). He has given firm support to anti-Gorbachev elements in the Union of Soviet Writers and Union of Writers of the Russian Socialist Federated Soviet Republic, has forcefully pushed the campaign against "groupism," and has adopted some of the issues of centrist and right-wing Russian nationalists (such as their hatred of Western mass culture and their concern for the preservation of monuments).

Ligachev has a realistic chance to effect Gorbachev's demotion or removal from the Politburo, although it is far from certain. The purge of Eltsin was an important step in this direction. Ligachev might attempt to demote or oust Gorbachev in 1988, perhaps at the June party conference. Ligachev's chances to become general secretary are at least as strong as Gorbachev's chances to hold on to the post.

Will Economic Performance Improve?

The June 1987 Party Plenum announced far-reaching changes in the economic system.[8] These have already begun to be implemented and are to be completed by 1991. They include overhauling the wage and salary system, restructuring the foreign trade system, increasing private and cooperative economic activities, and decentralizing power to regional authorities. But the central command system will be retained. Most investment will be controlled centrally, and much of production will still be centrally directed.

Enterprises are supposed to develop their own plans, based on nonbinding control figures, state orders, and contracts with other firms. Routine investment is supposed to be self-financed. Wholesale trade will be determined by direct contract among enterprises or with state wholesale organizations. Managers will be elected by workers—but with the approval of higher authorities. Authority over foreign trade has been decentralized and incentives to encourage foreign investment offered.

Gosplan will henceforth focus on long-range planning and the development of indirect, especially financial, levers of control and will coordinate all economic activities and decide on state orders. Banks will control credits more tightly. The ministries will shrink in function and size but will still be responsible for seeing that demands are met. All prices will be reset, some centrally and some independently by enterprises, but all will be determined by central rules.

Wages will be altered with the aim of increasing differentials related to skills, tying bonuses more closely to performance, tightening work norms, and encouraging work effort. Changes in retail prices are not to reduce workers' living standards.

Individual and collective activities are encouraged, taxes on private income are being reduced, and penalties for corruption have increased. In agriculture, farms can sell more output at market prices and are allowed to operate somewhat more independently.

For this program to turn the economy around, it will have to overcome major obstacles: Ministries are still responsible for seeing that goals are met. State orders will preempt other outputs of enterprises. Prices will not be market driven but will be set by the center or must follow the center's guidelines and must be stable. The monopoly power of enterprises will remain.

If prices are made more flexible, a much-needed reform, there will be high inflation. Cuts in the huge subsidies on food and housing (which amount to around seventy billion rubles, about 10 percent of GNP) would make prices more rational, but prices of consumer goods would skyrocket. Although wages could be raised in compensation, there are bound to be losers as well as winners in such a process. Popular disturbances could result. All of these considerations suggest that implementation is likely to be slow.

Despite these obstacles, there is scope for improved performance, especially in the encouraging of individual and collective private activities and the increased differential in wages. But there is also a potential for disruptions in the supply system as a result of these changes. In the end the Politburo might not implement this plan or might delay it or might pull back as problems emerge. It will take a strong and sustained push from the top to make *perestroika* take place as advertised, and there is good reason to doubt that this will happen.

Future Possibilities

Looking ahead, we can identify several main outcomes. We also need to recognize the possibility of surprises.[9] A middle outcome is arguably most likely: The struggle between the Gorbachevite and neo-Andropovite factions continues. *Glasnost'* is partially rolled back from the level of openness attained in 1986–1987. Slow implementation of *perestroika* brings little improvement in the economy in the next five years. Private service activities expand. Some foreign firms make investments, but there is no rush to invest. Changes in foreign behavior are few—with the possible exception of a major agreement on strategic nuclear weapons. Gorbachev remains general secretary, but his bold aims are not fully met.

A second outcome entails victory by the conservatives. Gorbachev is demoted and probably ousted and is replaced by Ligachev or another conservative. The party line shifts to emphasize discipline and the extraction of the hidden reserves in the system. This path is compatible with a greater degree of openness than in the Brezhnev era and some decentralization of economic decision making, but the system would remain unchanged in all essentials. The foreign policy line associated with this path is not obvious; presumably defense would continue to have highest priority, but economic realities could force some trimming. The détente line now being pursued might well be continued. It is also possible, however, that a new chill in East-West relations might set in.

A third path is the consolidation of power by Gorbachev. This implies the preservation of *glasnost'* and full implementation of *perestroika*. Although more promising for economic progress, this outcome by no means assures that the Soviet economy will thrive. Retarding forces, which in time might be overcome, could include preemption of resources for the security sector, a still-modest role for money in the system, the continuation of centrally set prices, and a failure to promote competition. Major improvement would require bolder steps toward the market. If Gorbachev is well and truly in control, this could happen.

This path also suggests bolder foreign policy initiatives: perhaps significant steps toward a settlement with Japan on the northern islands dispute, much better relations with China, and a conventional arms agreement with the North Atlantic Treaty Organization (NATO) that would reduce forces in Europe. A key question is whether a Gorbachev-dominated Soviet Union would continue to press the expansion of the empire in the Third World. Such expansion was instrumental in bringing about the collapse of détente in the 1970s and could do so again in the 1990s. If the Politburo restrains its behavior on this front, a signal change in strategy will have occurred.

Possible Reversals and Discontinuities

The outcomes outlined above assume several alternative, more or less steady, future courses. But steadiness might not occur and does not even seem likely. For example, it is plausible to expect that if *perestroika* and détente result in economic gains and reduced pressure from the West, the regime would then revert to its normal condition. This reversal would parallel events after Khrushchev's liberalization.

Moreover, events might not even remain entirely under the leadership's control. Possible events include civil disturbances resulting from dissatisfaction over high inflation together with continued poverty, politically motivated disturbances by minority peoples (similar to the one in Alma Ata in late 1986—perhaps on a larger scale), and disturbances in Eastern Europe. Another possibility that has attracted some Western speculation is that of a military coup, although party control over the military seems firmly established.

A question worth noting—but one on which only conjecture is possible—is whether such disruption is more likely if Gorbachev fails or if he succeeds. If he fails, continued stagnation would be increasingly seen as a systemic failure, one that eventually prompts strong action by some parties. For example, Russian nationalists (including those in the military) might decide to move against a system that has been destructive of the Russian people and their values and that is demonstrably unable to deal with the country's problems. If Gorbachev succeeds, he might prove Alexis de Tocqueville's theory that expectations that run ahead of reality produce a revolutionary situation. In any case, serious disruption of some kind is likely inside the Soviet empire, and perhaps within the Soviet Union, within the next decade or two.

Western Influence

It would be a mistake to assume that the West has much influence over developments within the Soviet Union: the central issues appear to be domestic, our knowledge of the forces at work inside the system has important limitations, and Western governments are divided in their aims. Still, in some circumstances and on some matters Western actions might make a difference.

1. The most important thing for Western political leaders to understand is that Soviet leaders don't want to change their system or the types of behavior that threaten the West. They will change only if they must. Making things easier for them enables them not to change.

2. We should not seek to prop up the Gorbachev faction on the theory that he is a benign influence or that making communists fat will make them peaceful. This is too tenuous a basis on which to act.

3. Western leaders need to understand that the Soviet Union is in a weak strategic position. For example, there was widespread surprise when the Soviet leadership abandoned its insistence that SDI be constrained as a condition for the intermediate-range nuclear forces (INF) treaty. A quid pro quo or linkage approach should be adopted for any

economic interactions between Western nations and the Soviet Union that go beyond normal unsubsidized trade. For instance, Western countries should condition economic benefits on Soviet military cuts in Eastern Europe.

Excessive expectations in the U.S. and the West about the Soviets have often been dashed, from Uncle Joe Stalin through Khrushchev to the early 1970s' détente. Following precedent, this will happen again—but we need to keep an open mind.[10] Gorbachev may have the potential to move the Soviet Union, as Michel Tatu puts it, from a totalitarian to an authoritarian state. That would be a considerable change—one that might, but wouldn't necessarily, make the Soviet Union easier to deal with.

Notes

1. Carl Linden, *Khrushchev and the Soviet Leadership, 1957–1964* (Baltimore: Johns Hopkins Press, 1966), p. 14.

2. Peter Reddaway, "Gorbachev the Bold," *New York Review*, May 28, 1987, p. 22.

3. Western analysts are uncertain what precisely happened at the critical October 21, 1987, Central Committee meeting that led to Eltsin's downfall. The available evidence suggests that Michel Tatu's dispatch in *Le Monde*, November 13, 1987, had it right. Gorbachev's version, which appeared in the November 13 *Pravda*, represents an unconvincing attempt at political damage control. On this episode, see also Michel Tatu, *Gorbatchev* (Paris: Centurion, 1987), pp. 165–66, 243–49.

4. V. Selyunin and G. Khanin, "Cunning Figures," *Novy Mir*, no. 2 (February 1987): 181–201.

5. Oleg T. Bogomolov, *Moscow News*, as reported by Agence France Presse, September 16, 1987.

6. Christopher M. Davis, "Priority and the Shortage Model: The Medical System in the Socialist Economy," in *Models of Disequilibrium and Shortage in Centrally Planned Economies* (London: Chapman & Hall, forthcoming).

7. Andrew W. Marshall, in "Gorbachev's Economic Plans," *Joint Economic Committee, Congress of the United States*, vol. 1, November 23, 1987. See also Henry S. Rowen and Charles Wolf, Jr., eds., *The Future of the Soviet Empire* (New York: St. Martin's Press, 1988).

8. The following discussion draws on an excellent article by Gertrude E. Schroeder, "Anatomy of Gorbachev's Economic Reforms," *Soviet Economy* 3, no. 3 (July–September 1987): 219–41.

9. Rowen and Wolf, *Soviet Empire*, pp. 259–324.

10. Vladimir Bukovsky, "Gorbachev's Reforms: Where's the Beef?" *Wall Street Journal*, December 22, 1987.

ALEKSANDR SOLZHENITSYN

Difficulties in the West with the Study of Russian History

A Speech at the Hoover Institution in 1976

◆ The tragic circumstances of Soviet history have in general created rather extraordinary conditions for the study of Russian history. One cannot help fearing that the abnormality of the conditions which underlie the study of Russian history, similar to a general displacement of geological strata, creates, through no fault of the scholars themselves, a common *systematic* error, as mathematicians would say. This error displaces and distorts all the results of research.

The abnormality I speak of lies, first of all, in a paradox: the fact that the country being studied is your contemporary—it leads a real and stormy existence—and yet, at the same time, it behaves like the archeologists' prehistory: the spine of its history has been fractured, its memory has failed, it has lost the power of speech. It has been denied the possibility of writing the truth about itself, to tell honestly how things are, to discover itself.

Consequently, foreign scholars who study this living country find themselves, as it were, in the position of archeologists: they are lacking links, materials, connections, and most of all they lack access to the spirit either of vanished old Russia or of the contemporary USSR, which has been so skillfully sealed off—the country's atmosphere, without which it is impossible to recreate its history, even when the objective materials appear to have

Translated by Terence Emmons, professor of history at Stanford University. Published with Mr. Solzhenitsyn's permission.

been collected. Of course, it is foreign scholars who are most affected by the lack of this root connection with the soil.

Yet this is not calm, indifferent antiquity, nor even merely one among 120 contemporary countries to whose academic study one of 120 institutes is devoted. No. This country decisively determines the course of current world history and powerfully influences the course of American history, so that the work of every American scholar on the Soviet Union becomes superheated: your own, American, history may vitally depend on whether it is truthful or erroneous, profound in its understanding or superficial.

There is a third, even more complex aspect of the problem: to judge by appearances, this country we speak of is far from silent. It constantly, actively, and quite aggressively serves up great quantities of what is supposedly information about itself, but what is in fact programmed lies.

And fourthly: the situation is complicated by the fact that committed socialist circles in the West passionately grab up this false Soviet information, and as a result the historian is subjected, as it were, to a wrenching sidewise hurricane that hurls sand in his eyes, twists his whole body, and turns his head toward a calmer and more comfortable, but false, tack. He must turn his gaze away from the shards of truth, in the direction the wind of the epoch compels him.

How can the conscientious Western scholar imagine, how can he conceive that, for example, in the principal Great Encyclopedia of that country *not a single line* can be accepted *a priori* as the truth, but by the prudent must be suspected of containing either a lie, a concealment, or a cunningly distorted formulation?

Not to mention such tragicomic cases as the individual whose work on the 1920–21 peasant rebellion in Tambov province against the Bolsheviks I saw in the Hoover Institution. Being well acquainted with that subject, I could appreciate how painstakingly and persistently that American scholar had sought out, during a visit to the Soviet Union, all accessible materials, and even virtually inaccessible ones.

But beside the most important of them in his bibliography I found the following comment: "Unfortunately, all my notes from this source were stolen from my hotel in Moscow, so I was unable to use them in my work." That, I must say, did not surprise me: the simpletons at the library slipped up and gave the foreigner unauthorized material, but the KGB tracked down the error and corrected it!

(In order just to have the opportunity of such visits—just to get closer to the material—other scholars pay with cautious and discreet formulations, so as not to anger their hosts. Like any compromise with the truth, however, the price is not worth paying.)

The prerevolutionary Russian administration never thought to inform world public opinion about life in Russia. Given the slow movement of history at the time and the lack of communication among countries, it could not even conceive that the future of its own people, and of others, would soon depend on just such informed opinion.

By contrast, the revolutionary and other opposition-minded emigres from Russia sensed its importance here in the West, and spared no effort to influence it; they invested in it all their emotional bitterness, the intolerance and lack of objectivity of men temporarily frustrated in their aims of subversion and revolution.

They drew for the West a distorted and biased picture of several centuries of Russian history—partly owing to their fanaticism, and partly because many of the emigres were young people with an artificial and one-sided upbringing. They were quite unable to know and understand the depths of the millennial life of the people; indeed, they did not even wish to.

And so, at the very moment of her most reassuring economic and social development on the eve of the First World War, Russia's image in the West was fashioned by men who rejected and hated Russia, her way of life and spiritual values, and by force of inertia this image has persisted to this day.

Here we confront the fifth serious complication, that primary displacement of an entire stratum which has shifted all the basic points of reckoning for Western scholars, and with them any possibility for a correct comparison between bygone Russia and the contemporary Soviet Union.

A whole series of myths and legends has been strung out and even dressed up with meaningless statistics concerning the economy or social stability, the character of the revolutionary movement or the magnitude of repressions (I have dealt with several distortions in various parts of the *Gulag Archipelago*). And so the distortion of the Russian historical past, the lack of understanding of Russia in the West, has persistently taken on the form of a tendentious generalization about ingrained "perennial Russian slavery" and "Asiatic tradition."

This generalization dangerously misleads contemporary scholars and hinders them from understanding the essential socialistic nature of what has happened in the USSR. It deliberately neglects centuries-long periods, overlooks vast territorial expanses, and disregards numerous forms of remarkable social independence among our people: Kievan Rus, Suzdalian Orthodoxy, the intense religious life in the limitless ocean of forest, the centuries of exuberant democracy in Novgorod and Pskov, the spontaneous popular initiative and resistance at the beginning of the seventeenth century, the judicious Assemblies of the Land, the free peasantry of the vast North, the free cossacks on a dozen rivers of the South and Siberia, and strikingly independent Old Believers, and, finally, the peasant commune, whose workings even in the nineteenth century were compared to English parliamentary practices by the astute English observer Mackenzie Wallace.

All this has misleadingly been pushed into limbo by two centuries of serfdom in the central region by the Petersburg bureaucracy. The great Russian folklore, the people's brilliant and truest testimony about itself, was scorned in the construction of such a false notion. It was overshadowed by the pamphlets of not very gifted critics whose command of the Russian language left much to be desired.

Even events dear to American memory, such as Russia's support for the North in your Civil War, the warm Russian-American friendship during the reign of Alexander II, whose great reforms were cut short by foolhardy terrorists—all this was forgotten and crossed off, as if it had never been.

Is it surprising in these circumstances that a prominent American scholar has published a pseudoacademic book about old Russia that is full of mistakes, exaggerations, and perhaps premeditated distortions (considering that *caricatures* have been deliberately selected as illustrations for this *scholarly* book)? Is it surprising that in such circumstances every young American historian, writer, or journalist when undertaking a Russian theme automatically succumbs to the postulate that the USSR is the natural continuation of old Russia?

In reality, the transition from prerevolutionary Russia to the USSR was not a continuation, but a *fatal fracture of the spine*, which nearly ended in complete national destruction. Soviet development is not an extension of Russian development, but its diversion in a completely new and unnatural direction which is inimical to her people (as well as to her neighbors and to all other peoples on earth).

Not only are the terms "Russian" and "Soviet," "Russia" and "USSR," not interchangeable, not equivalent, and not unilinear—they are irreconcilably contradictory and completely exclude each other. It is a gross mistake and scholarly slovenliness to confuse them or use them inappropriately, yet how carelessly this substitution has spread in contemporary Western usage. And how disastrously for Western understanding of historical perspective!

It is the persistent, penetrating wind of the epoch, the wind of socialism, that throws sand in the eyes of the scholar and prevents him from looking steadily at the truth—that takes courage! The entire Western world is presently being swept toward socialism, and how alluring it was for several decades to find one's ideal realized on earth!

But when it became apparent that the Soviet system differed drastically from even the most approximate ideal, then the identification of the terms "Soviet" and "Russian" came in handy: all the crimes, defects, and failings of *Soviet* socialism were falsely written off to the *Russian* "servile tradition," so as to snatch the paper angel of socialism from the fire. Of course it could not have succeeded with the *Russians*, but *here*, in the West, it will be altogether different, pure as the driven snow.

So I recommend to you the works of two Russians—not historians, for professional historians in the USSR have either been liquidated or compelled to lie, but scholars from the exact sciences: the internationally known mathematician Igor Shafarevich and the outstanding physicist Iurii Orlov, who has been ruthlessly persecuted for 20 years now—since 1956, the year of the "thaw" following the Twentieth Congress, when he dared in the Academy of Sciences to draw the natural conclusion from Khrushchev's speech that *this* Party and *this* government should retire.

In his extensive study of socialism, based on a vast number of historical facts, Shafarevich shows that socialist systems are by no means modern inventions, that in history they have always and without exception assumed a ruthless totalitarian character, and that even all Western—yes, *Western*—theoreticians and prophets of socialism have proudly proclaimed just these brutal principles.

With the methods and language of physics, Iurii Orlov has convincingly shown us (his samizdat work has just arrived in the West) that even in theoretical terms consistent socialism can take *no other form than the totalitarian*, just as two gears must mesh or an accelerated wheel cannot fail to turn.

Orlov shows that even the mildest methods of introducing socialism, so long as they are consistent and steadfast, can only lead to totalitarianism; that is, to the total suppression of individuality and the human spirit.

I think I have mentioned the main dangers and obstacles that have so far prevented Western scholars from laying bare—to the benefit of their own country, of my country, and of the entire course of history—the strata of the last century of Russian history that have been buried and hidden from us.

For the United States, Russian and Soviet history is not merely the history of one among 120 foreign countries, and the fate of your great and beautiful country will depend in the very near future on whether the American continent has understood—adequately and soon enough—that history.

RAMON H. MYERS

◆ ———————————————————— ◆

Mainland China's March Toward a New Socialism

◆ The new leaders of the People's Republic of China (PRC) have no intention of abandoning socialism, nor are they true friends of the West. They
are contemptuous of capitalism and liberalism and only concerned with acquiring Western capital, technology, and managerial expertise as quickly as
possible to make China strong and prosperous. They also understand how
to use their organs of control and surveillance to rebuff demands for more
liberty and democratization. Yet by the turn of the century the PRC will
pose no threat to its neighbors except the Republic of China on Taiwan
(ROC) because the country will still be poor and the economy afflicted with
inefficiency; and the population of over 1.1 billion people will demand the
state's full attention to matters of control and stability.

The new leaders, who in late 1987 replaced the old leadership that had
ruled China since 1949, will continue to modify the socialist system but will
not replace that system with something else. These adaptations have been
taking place for the past decade and can be expected to continue until the
year 2000 and beyond. They were undertaken because of the former leadership's ill-conceived policies, which had split the Chinese Communist
Party (CCP), weakened popular support for socialism, and damaged the
country's economic and educational system.

These policies had produced famine in the late 1950s and early 1960s,
virtual civil war in the late 1960s, and constant turmoil throughout most of
the 1970s. Consequently the economy had remained backward and poor,
and the people had become disillusioned with the CCP and socialism. These

developments forced the aging leadership under Deng Xiaoping to chart a new course of action in 1978. In that year the party leadership hammered out a new line, which was upheld in October 1987 at the Thirteenth Party Congress, when a new generation of leaders replaced Deng and his colleagues.

This new party line called for modernizing China by relying on reform and more contact with the West to acquire advanced technology. To legitimize this new line, the party pledged to uphold the four cardinal principles: adhering to the socialist road, upholding the dictatorship of the proletariat, maintaining the dictatorship of the CCP, and adhering to Marxism-Leninism and Mao Zedong thought. This doctrine permits only the CCP to rule society and interpret how society will evolve. The new party line also downplays fomenting revolution abroad and waging class warfare at home. It enabled Deng and his supporters to justify making numerous adaptations, which Deng's successors will continue: changing the leadership, reorganizing the socialist economy, separating the party and the state, and managing foreign affairs.

Changing the Leadership

During the 1980s Deng and his key supporters, Hu Yaobang and Zhao Ziyang, reshuffled personnel and prepared officials for new party jobs in order to select the right people with the "correct thinking" and "proper behavior." They worked especially hard to rid the party of Maoists and of those who wanted speedy liberalization of the party. By steering a course of gradualism, Deng and his supporters concentrated on rebuilding the CCP and consolidating their networks of support. By the time the Thirteenth Party Congress convened, Deng could complete the leadership changeover, as the following results confirm.

The CCP's Central Committee shrank from 210 to 175 members, with one-third being elected for the first time. The average age declined by several years. The old guard no longer actually ruled: Chen Yun left to head the Central Advisory Commission; Li Xiannian (82) was gone and Deng (83) an elder statesman. But Hu Yaobang, who stepped down as party general secretary in early 1987 under heavy criticism, remained. His protégés from the Communist Youth League, which Hu chaired for many years, make up a client network probably more extensive than that of any other party leader. Gone was conservative ideologue Deng Liqun (72), former minister of propaganda. Li Peng (59), Soviet-trained and raised by Zhou Enlai, is now acting premier; Zhao Ziyang (68) is the party's new general secretary; Qiao Shi (63) heads the Discipline Inspection Commission; Hu Qili (58) manages ideology and education; and Yao Yilin (70) presides over economic matters. These five dominate the party's Politburo, which is the nerve center for the Central Committee.

Equally important was the shake-up of top military leaders. The army chief of staff, Yang Dezhi (77), was replaced by Ji Haotian (59), a political commissar and former deputy chief of staff. General Yu Qiuli (73), who directed the General Political Department, was replaced by Yang Baiping (66), another political commissar of the Beijing military area. General Hong Xuezhi (74), director of the General Logistics Department, was replaced by Zhao Nanqi (early 50s), his deputy. These new leaders have approved the party's decision to cut back the size of the military and reduce the number of leaders with military experience in the party's Politburo.

Reorganizing the Socialist System

Zhao Ziyang and his colleagues realize the extent of China's backwardness and its limited technological capabilities. They realize that China cannot leapfrog into socialism. They tell the Chinese people that the road to socialism will be tortuous, requiring even a century or more to realize. They admit that China will "inevitably remain a country with a backward economy and culture for quite a long time after taking the socialist path." They claim that China is only in the "initial stage of socialism" and therefore needs to make various reforms to develop beyond this early stage.

To complete this initial stage of socialism, the country must modernize by implementing comprehensive reforms and obtaining much-needed modern technology from the West. The country also must have a new economic structure, but public ownership will continue to play a dominant role. There also must be a new political system in which party control and guidance can be separated from the operation of the state bureaucracy. Such a system would also provide more decentralized decision making and consultation with people at the grass roots. A new "spiritual civilization" must be built with socialist ideology and ethics. These tasks now preoccupy the leadership and will dominate the policy agenda for the coming decades.

Although China's leaders admit that socialism in the initial stage means underdeveloped socialism, they want to build a new China with enough wealth for the people to enjoy a decent living standard comparable to that of the Four Tigers, the newly industrialized countries of the Pacific Basin. They want enough wealth for China to project regional power, attain equivalence with the developed countries, and eventually even match the superpowers. They perceive that China has fallen far behind the Four Tigers, and they realize their economic system is inefficient and backward.

They will not abandon their socialist dream, which means retaining the party's monopoly power, depending on public ownership of resources, and relying on the basic doctrines of communism as developed in the writings of Marx, Lenin, Stalin, and Mao. These new leaders say the party will build a new Chinese-style socialism, which will have less direct control over society but will still guide the economy to become more efficient and modern.

China's leaders are confident they can always control through policy guidance and ideological leadership. The party now plans to establish a public service examination system based on new rules. All state officials who now serve or intend to serve would take these exams. The officials who pass would be expected to uphold communist doctrine and the virtues of socialism and to have general expertise in the rules of governance. The leadership wants to separate party control from the state bureaucracy so that bureaucratic decisions are made by experts who merely carry out the instructions of the party. The party, naturally, will not tolerate any competing political party or alternative political views. It will guide but will not try to control and monitor every state bureaucrat. It will even permit elections at the county (*xian*) level, so that local people can select the leaders they believe are able and trustworthy. But the party will orchestrate the candidates to be selected for popular voting.

Rather than try to dominate every nook and cranny of China's huge landmass, the CCP wants more local talent to be elected by the people. But the party also wants its policy decision making to be based on "democratic centralism" and not democracy as practiced in the West. In other words, after the party center debates an issue and a policy is agreed on by the majority, all party members must abide by that decision and faithfully support and implement the new policy. Past party experience shows that a minority can skillfully have the majority do its bidding even in the face of considerable opposition. But party intellectuals can be expected to challenge this procedure and demand greater Western-style democratization. Even so, the party should be able to deflect these challenges for the next decade or so.

Just as the bureaucracy will be guided by the party, so the new economic system will be regulated rather than directly controlled. Since the early 1950s central planning determined what goods and services would be produced, how much investment would be made, and which resources would be allocated. That system has failed. The CCP now proposes to reduce the scope of mandatory planning to an undisclosed number of essential goods and services. Then the state will "regulate the market," and the "market will guide the state and collective-owned enterprises" as well as some privately owned and managed enterprises. That means that state and collective enterprises will be allowed to contract with other firms in regulated, rather than free, markets. Various organs will monitor prices and regulate movement. Other organs will rely on taxes, interest rates, and the money supply to direct market forces according to the dictates of the state. Although a small private sector of households hiring scores of workers is also expanding in services and manufacturing, their activities will be controlled through licensing, monitoring, and taxing. Finally, foreign firms now cooperate with Chinese enterprises or hire Chinese labor and buy materials primarily for export, although eventually limited sales might be allowed in the domestic market.

The scope of free and regulated markets in China expanded in the 1980s and will continue to expand in the 1990s and beyond, until the party believes an appropriate balance with the mandatory planned sector has been reached. Some areas, like Guangdong province in southeast China, have become an experimental region for political and economic reform. More than 60 percent of all foreign investment now goes to Guangdong; Hong Kong businessmen operate several thousand factories there, and they subcontract to another ten thousand enterprises. A few areas like Guangdong, Shanghai, and the special economic zones created in the 1980s outpace the rest of the country, but the party now affirms that some people can become richer than others. As more enterprises transact outside their provinces, trade and specialization flourish, and households contract and hire free labor. As some areas prosper, with new houses and factories being constructed and more consumer goods circulating, the competition for scarce resources between the state planned sector and the less-regulated sector becomes more intense, driving prices upward.

Finally, the party also expects the people to cultivate "idealistic, moral, cultured, and disciplined new socialist ethics." Young and old alike must adhere to the rules of a collective society, and individual behavior will be restrained. Collective rights and duties, as well as organizational discipline, take precedence. The party will continue to purify its ranks through educational campaigns and testing. The leadership recognizes that the party must wage an unceasing war against foreign ideas that threaten to undermine communist doctrine, which upholds the superiority of socialism, the party's right to rule and interpret the correct thought, and the veracity of Marxism-Leninism and Mao Zedong thought. In 1978 Deng said that "to undermine any of the four cardinal principles is to undermine the whole cause of socialism in China, the whole cause of modernization."[1] In mid-1987 Zhao told a meeting of propaganda officials that "the overwhelming majority of our society must understand that the four cardinal principles are like food and clothing to us and that we cannot be deprived of them even for a moment."[2] To make certain that the people do not forget, the party will use state security bureaus, the judiciary, and its huge network of labor camps to elicit compliance with party rule.

The Reforms and the Difficulties of Implementation

From the cautious, deliberate reforms launched so far, a definite pattern of difficulties has emerged that will continue as long as the CCP strives to maintain its dominance over society. At first the rural reforms were easy. When the state ordered the rural areas in 1982 to adopt the new contract-responsibility system, the country obeyed with alacrity and produced favorable results. Households acquired the right to farm plots of land rather than have their members work under team management, and the rate of farm production doubled. But reforming the huge bureaucratic hierarchy to manage the new farming system was another matter. In every county the state organs that formerly managed capital investment, finance, planning, resource allocation, and labor management remained in power, along with new agencies regulating the contract-responsibility system of local officials and village production teams, even though many planning organs had become obsolete. Above each county are the prefectural and provincial organs, and between the provinces and the political center are 41 ministries and commissions with crisscrossing branches that link all provinces and subprovincial organs to the political center. These bureaucratic layers have not been restructured; each reform creates more regulatory organs, so that enormous inertia has afflicted the state apparatus controlling the economy.

Local officials now allow households to use their land freely (contracts can extend to fifteen years), and an unprecedented boom in new factories and services has occurred in many rural areas. But the country must still employ over a hundred million young people in the coming decade. Moreover, every step to liberalize releases enormous spending and an upsurge in the velocity of money, so that inflation and shortages have become severe. Because households now manage capital investment, public works formerly under brigade or team supervision are deteriorating. Acute shortages of building materials, spare parts, and transport vehicles afflict many areas. In other words, the countryside is a mixed picture, with some areas becoming extremely rich while other areas are plagued with problems. Furthermore, as households shift from one production line to another in response to relative price changes, the supply of some products has become scarce, as reflected in the rationing of pork, sugar, and cooking oil in many cities by late 1987 and the resumption of importing fourteen million tons of grain at the cost of a billion U.S. dollars in 1987.

Similarly the urban reforms announced in late 1984 have yet to produce an enterprise bankruptcy law or any statute permitting enterprises to contract with other firms in free markets. Only limited experiments in enterprise bankruptcy, joint stock companies, urban stock exchanges, and enterprise transaction have been allowed in Shenyang (Manchuria), Beijing (the capital), Chongqing (Sichuan), and elsewhere. Inefficiency, waste, and poor-quality goods are still common. Refrigerator doors fall off, bicycle frames crack as they are wheeled from stores, and the hands of doughnut-size watches fail to keep time. The problem of quality control remains especially serious for enterprises that depend on machine tools, lifting and transport vehicles, and other machinery for their assembly lines. Enterprises have great difficulty in securing official approval to contract with other firms, particularly foreign enterprises, to increase their sales in order to purchase new equipment to upgrade productivity. High transaction costs afflict every enterprise in the country, since enterprises must obtain bureaucratic approval for nearly every transaction outside the mandatory plan.

As for economic contacts with foreign countries, the PRC accepted $20.5 billion in foreign loans between 1979 and 1986. Direct foreign business investment only came to $8.2 billion, and between 1984 and 1986 even that spending declined, with smaller amounts invested in fewer projects. Foreigners increasingly prefer to lend rather than invest, because investment returns are uncertain and signing a deal is costly. Therefore loans amount to 70 percent of all outside funding to the PRC. About 50 percent of foreign investment is concentrated in the hotel business, with only 10 percent going to energy and industry; transport and communication receive even less. PRC authorities insist that investors make available their advanced technology, a stumbling block for expanding future investment. The PRC unit of account, the *renminbi*, has been steadily depreciating since 1982, so that importing materials becomes more costly for foreign firms doing business there. Unless the above trends are reversed, foreign investment will not provide the PRC with the new technology and capital its leaders expect.

The PRC's overall trade increased dramatically after the late 1970s. But the country ran trade deficits on current account of some $14.9 billion and $11.9 billion for 1985 and 1986 respectively, although in 1987 a $4.0 billion surplus enabled the authorities to keep foreign exchange reserves at around $10–11 billion. The regime should be able to regulate foreign trade to maintain sufficient reserves, but tight control over foreign trade will not permit that trade to become the powerful engine of growth it has been for many Pacific Basin countries. But unlike other Pacific Basin states, the PRC has extensively diversified its exports and imports so that neither export nor import with any single country exceeds 15 percent of its total foreign trade. Japan, the PRC's largest bilateral trading partner, exports more than twice its imports from the PRC, and Japan's generous loans for machinery and vehicles allow this trade gap to persist. Because foreign trade is so controlled, foreigners have not been able to penetrate this market of more than a billion consumers. Only Guangdong province and Hong Kong enjoy a special relationship of investment, trade, and smuggling. The trade potential for southeast China is conceivably great, but only if provincial authorities can resist controls from Beijing.

To reform science and technology, the leadership mainly rejuvenated the old Chinese Academy of Science, the leading research organ of the 1950s. A few new institutes were established in some universities and factories, but there has been no significant attempt to decentralize research (except to some universities) to enterprises and the private sector. The PRC's capacity to increase research and development (R and D) spending will remain weak in the coming decades unless the authorities make better use of the students they have sent overseas for advanced study and truly reform the present R and D system.

Whenever the CCP relaxes its control over what people can say and write, the new freedoms immediately spawn tremendous debate and eventually an outburst of criticism, which forces the party to clamp down on public criticisms of its policies. In 1977–1978 private pamphlets and journals began circulating in the large cities, but the party stamped out such activity in 1979–1980. Debate and criticism of party policies mushroomed in 1983, only to be suppressed late that year by the Anti–Spiritual Pollution Campaign. In December 1986 and January 1987 demonstrations broke out in nine universities, involving some ten thousand or more students, but they were quickly suppressed, to be followed immediately by the party's Anti–Bourgeois Liberalization Campaign throughout 1987. Rather than subject all of society to the massive campaigns of the past, the party now targets key critics, discredits them, and purges them from the party or brings them before the courts on charges of counterrevolutionary activity. This happened to Yang Wei, a U.S.-trained researcher in Shanghai, who was arrested in late January 1987 and not seen again until he was tried, convicted, and sentenced to two years in prison in December 1987.

Perhaps the most significant adjustment has been to trim the four million–strong People's Liberation Army (PLA) by at least one million (and perhaps more) and to move troops back to the barracks for disciplining, reeducation, and training. Because of drastic cuts in the PLA's budget and a clampdown on the purchase of exotic weaponry from abroad, commanders have had to develop home-produced items like the Chinese Silkworm ground-to-ground missile sold to Iran in 1986–1987 and used so effectively in the Persian Gulf war. Despite the difficulties of retiring officers and noncommissioned officers and shunting them into civilian occupations, the government has upgraded the PLA's weaponry and slowly expanded a small blue-water fleet of frigates and destroyers. The leadership intends to develop and operate a small but highly effective fighting force based on some 1,250 nuclear warheads deployed in a rudimentary triad of strategic nuclear forces (land-based and sea-based missiles as well as manned bombers). The leadership counts on having enough nuclear power to deter a first strike from any aggressor, but should an aggressor strike first, it would resort to nuclear retaliation and use the surviving PLA ground forces to withstand any invasion while reverting to guerrilla war.

Reforms so far have been limited, chiefly because of the party's obsession with personnel appointments and the reeducation of party members. But adaptations will continue, with the party and state slowly experimenting, then encouraging discussion, and finally allowing more experimentation before adopting a reform. Yet every reform brings unexpected outcomes. Allowing enterprises to engage in more transactions increases their spending, which then increases the velocity of money in circulation and produces inflation. As free marketing expands, enterprises demand more materials, and the inflationary pressures intensify. When farmers shift production, various products become scarce, and the regime must reimpose rationing. Giving more people the freedom to speak and write only leads to criticisms of the party, thus forcing party leaders to impose harsh sanctions. Therefore the unintended trade-offs of the reforms form a violent zigzag pattern that will certainly continue into the 1990s and beyond.

Over the next decade or so the party will be able to brake the momentum from the new market forces and ideas that might otherwise change the political center's control over society. But whether the leadership after 2000 can continue to control the new forces of ideas and the marketplace is doubtful. The new complexities associated with China in the decades after 2000 will have to be managed through greater decentralization and less control from the political center. At that time the party's monopoly controls over ideology and society will very likely weaken.

PRC Foreign Policy and Asian-Pacific Security

The PRC will not closely ally with either of the superpowers but will continue to tilt slightly toward the United States, Japan, and Western Europe. In the late 1970s the PRC deliberately tilted toward the United States by normalizing relations, but it never induced Washington to break with the Republic of China on Taiwan (ROC). Then in the mid-1980s the PRC began to improve relations slightly with the Soviet Union but continued to be linked more closely with the West through trade, investment, and cultural exchange. Yet the PRC only strongly supports the United States when its immediate interests in countervailing the Soviet Union become paramount. In the majority of cases the PRC voted against the resolutions sponsored or backed by the United States in the United Nations. The CCP continually denounces the evils of U.S. capitalism at home but acknowledges U.S. technological superiority and the necessity of having good relations to acquire that technology.

Beijing's leaders will continue to cultivate trade and technical cooperation with the developed countries of Europe and Japan. They will continue to criticize Japan's gradual military buildup and to remind its leaders and people of the past crimes Japan committed in China. But they will welcome Japanese trade and investment, especially the latter. The PRC also supports friendly developing countries and tries to elevate its status among them by portraying itself as a developing country trying to counter superpower imperialism.

South Korea will try to negotiate with the PRC to expand trade and informal communications in order eventually to normalize relations, especially to isolate North Korea and force it to negotiate with South Korea on more favorable terms. The PRC wants peace to prevail on the Korean peninsula, and its leaders would like to see improved relations between the North and South Korean regimes. Beijing's new leaders would like to have formal relations with South Korea, since they wish to further isolate the ROC. But until there is a substantive leadership and/or policy change in North Korea, the PRC will be permitted only to expand informal ties with South Korea instead of normalizing formal relations.

The battle of wills with Vietnam will continue. Vietnam promises to withdraw its troops from Cambodia in 1990, but until all guerrilla resistance against its client government ends, it may defer that promise. Likewise, the PRC will continue to supply the Khmer forces to keep the pressure on Vietnam-backed Cambodia. Crucial in this conflict is Soviet military and economic aid to Vietnam, worth several billion dollars each year, in exchange for Soviet use of Cam Ranh Bay and the Danang airfields. This struggle could go on for years.

The PRC will take formal control of Hong Kong in 1997, partially realizing its dream of unifying China under its rule. According to the "one country, two systems" formula, Beijing says that communist officials can replace British civil affairs officers and nothing will change; in fact everything will probably change. First, a crisis of confidence will most likely hit in the early 1990s as financial capital and businessmen and their families leave the colony. Second, by 1997 the CCP will have links with every civil organization through the several hundred cadres sent into Hong Kong every month. By penetrating the local organizations, the party can orchestrate the selection of Hong Kong leaders who will be totally subservient to Beijing. Once these leaders are in power, they can pass new laws that gradually eliminate the many freedoms Hong Kong society has enjoyed in order to create conditions propitious to molding the new citizen, *Homo socialisticus*.

The ROC is another matter. Its successful economic modernization is often mocked by some PRC experts as one-sided because of the island's huge foreign trade dependency, although others state that much can be learned from the ROC's experience. PRC experts also allude to the oppression of Taiwan's working people "by foreign capitalists and compradores concealed behind an economic prosperity." But the economic miracle of the ROC and even the recent political reforms to end martial law in July 1987 and allow new political parties to mushroom are increasingly recognized as significant developments worthy of the attention of party members and intellectuals. Although party pundits explain these events as "new trends that forced the KMT leadership to change," the party obviously worries that its citizenry will demand more Western-style democracy at home.

Whereas the PRC asks that the ROC negotiate unification according to the "one country, two systems" principle, mainland people are not to listen secretly to Taiwan radio or television broadcasts. But the PRC consistently appeals to nationalistic sentiments for unification by arguing that "the two sides of the Straits are linked by common mountains and water . . . so the mainland cannot do without Taiwan and Taiwan also cannot be separated from the mainland."

The ROC leadership has refused to negotiate on Beijing's terms. Its leaders believe that their economic successes and recent democratization will challenge the Beijing leadership to accelerate its reform of the economy and polity. If such reforms do come, especially by the year 2000, each one will produce the unintended consequences outlined above. Gradually, in the decades beyond the year 2000, those changes might facilitate more pluralism of ideas to challenge the credibility of communist doctrine. The gradual, steady chipping away of that credibility might also lead to the erosion of ideological control on the mainland within at least another generation (roughly 25 years). Should that happen, we could observe the first successful destruction of a Marxist-Leninist regime through peaceful means. Therefore the presence of the ROC and the United States' continued support of that state through the Taiwan Relations Act could help bring about such a peaceful transformation.

China by the Year 2000

The above dynamics suggest that after Deng's death the PRC should experience neither a major power struggle nor any momentous policy changes. Although Hu Yaobang might gain greater prominence, the current leaders should be able to rule the Chinese mainland without major disagreements. Those leaders will continue to emphasize personnel changes and party indoctrination while pursuing their cautious reform. The party will gradually withdraw from directly controlling the state; a new economic structure will slowly evolve; security and judicial organs will still maintain order and harshly punish dissidents. But these reforms will be afflicted by all the difficulties cited above. Even so, the party should be able to maintain order and stability. The party will continue to be challenged by party intellectuals, students, and perhaps even workers, but its organs of control should effectively rebuff those challenges.

By the year 2000 the PRC will still be a poor developing country with a per capita income of less than $1,000. But some of its industries will produce a gross output larger than those of some advanced countries. Most important of all, because mainland China should not have experienced any serious threat to its national security, its leaders' energies can focus on solving domestic problems, maintaining party control, and building socialism. To use the concept developed by Thomas A. Metzger, mainland China by the end of the 1990s will probably still be a society with an "uninhibited political center" in which the party and its leaders are still not constrained in their use of power and society lacks sufficient power to force the political center to make the changes it desires. Mainland China will still be too weak to threaten its regional neighbors, but it will have acquired Hong Kong. Meanwhile, the ROC should still be independent, and its successful development experience might influence China's younger leaders to speed up the liberalization of the political and economic system. The West can breathe a sigh of relief that the PRC will still not have enough wealth or power to become a threat in the region, except to the ROC. But what will happen after the year 2000? Much will depend on the ability of China's future leaders to maintain their monopoly control over ideology. If that control weakens, the Chinese polity and economy will become more decentralized. China will still desperately need Western technology to deal with its problems of energy, food supply, and so on, and for reasons of self-interest PRC leaders will remain more friendly toward the West than toward the Soviet Union.

U.S. Policy Toward the PRC

The U.S. position toward mainland China should be one of toughness tempered by realism. The United States should insist that the PRC (as well as the Soviet Union) improve its human rights record. It should permit PRC citizens (as it now allows Soviets and East Europeans) to have political asylum in the United States. It should refrain from any transfer of technology or weaponry that greatly accelerates the modernization of the PRC's military system. It should insist that PRC (as well as Japanese) markets be opened to U.S. businessmen. And it should put some real teeth into the Taiwan Relations Act to prevent the PRC from using its growing military power to threaten and blackmail the ROC into negotiations that would endanger that state's security. In other words, U.S. foreign policy should foster more trade and technology dependency on the West and should facilitate those domestic forces that can challenge the CCP to initiate ideological pluralism.

Finally, the United States need not fear the resumption of the 1950s alliance between the Soviet Union and the PRC in the next decade or so. PRC and Soviet leaders will remain suspicious of each others' intentions. In particular, Beijing still demands that the Soviet policy of encircling and threatening China must end and that the Soviets must remove all troops from Afghanistan, greatly reduce troop strength along China's northern border, and cease supporting Vietnam's occupation of Cambodia. Until Moscow's military buildup in Asia and the Pacific stops, relations between the PRC and the Soviet Union will remain cool.

Notes

1. Committee for Compiling Original Communist Chinese Materials, *San-chung ch'üan-hui i–lai: chung-yao wen-hsien hsüan-pien* (First compilation of basic documents since the Third Plenum) (Taipei, Taiwan: Chung-kung Yen-chiu Tsa-chih-she, 1983), p. 97.

2. *People's Daily*, July 10, 1987, p. 4.

PHILIP C. HABIB

◆ ─────────────────── ◆

Looking at the Middle East

◆ The United States has had important and long-standing interests in the Middle East since the end of World War II, and these will not change in the future. There is wide bipartisan and public support for continuing a strong commitment to the existence and security of the state of Israel. In addition, the United States has a vital interest in maintaining free access to the extensive oil resources of the region for itself and for its allies and friends. The Middle East is also significant in the global competition with the Soviet Union for presence and influence in the world. Further, the United States has a direct interest in nurturing cooperative relations with friendly moderate Arab states, in particular Egypt, Jordan, and Saudi Arabia. In the widest sense the interests of the United States in the Middle East are linked directly to political, economic, and strategic developments in the area and the nurturing of peace and harmonious relations with and among the nations involved.

The 1980s began with some hope that during the decade there could be some progress in the long-term search for peace and stability in the Middle East. The 1970s had produced successful disengagement agreements between Israel and neighboring states and then the Camp David Accords, which led to peace between Israel and Egypt. But the revolution in Iran and the taking of American hostages in 1979 were the opening act in the drama surrounding the Persian Gulf. With the release of the hostages in January 1981, however, it seemed that interested parties could begin to consider more comprehensive solutions to the region's frequent conflicts and widespread instability. Instead, the 1980s turned out to be a time of more war, no progress in the search for peace, and greater uncertainty over the future.

Will the 1990s correct the errors of the past? Will a revitalized peace process deal justly with the Arab-Israeli conflict? Will the Persian Gulf have peace and stability? Will terrorism supported from within the region continue to be active, and to what extent will it be directed toward the United States? Will religious fundamentalism reach such a scale that reason will become the victim of emotion and hatred? Will this crisis-ridden region see the sudden appearance of new conflicts or the revival of those lying dormant? Will the last decade of the twentieth century be the turning point away from the violence of the past toward a period of sufficient harmony among people and nations to allow for greater economic and social progress?

The Arab-Israeli dispute has been a dominant feature in the Middle East and is likely to remain so. Unfortunately the danger of escalation and wider war in the Persian Gulf has diverted attention from the longer-term search for peace between Israel and its neighbors. Thus assessing the outlook in the 1990s requires considering prospects for peace or war in the troubled Gulf as well as attending to the basic confrontation between Israel, the Palestinians, and the neighboring Arab states.

There is no sign that the bloody war between Iran and Iraq will end before 1990. Although it began with Iraq's move to gain territory from bordering areas in Iran, it has grown into a struggle in which Iran's demands include a change in Iraqi leadership and the establishment of an Islamic state in Iraq. The conflict has also affected the Arab Gulf states that have been supporting Iraq and that feel threatened by Iran's power and ambitions.

Although the United Nations (U.N.) pursues its resolutions and the war drains the antagonists, an early end to hostilities is unlikely. There will be periods of greater or lesser action, but neither side seems capable of a sudden victory. Even a change in circumstances, such as the death of Ayatollah Ruhollah Khomeini or economic or military sanctions, cannot readily resolve the dispute. Iranian demands are unacceptable to Iraq, and Iraqi military capabilities remain formidable and sustainable.

The effort set in motion in 1987 with the passage of U.N. Security Council Resolution 598 provides the best hope for ending the war. Its call for a cease-fire and for the Secretary-General to participate in the search for a negotiated settlement opens the way for further U.N. efforts. A negotiated settlement will require both parties to move from their present positions. There is some hope that both Iraq and Iran may be seeking a way out of the costly affair, but each side insists on its own terms. There are fundamental differences between the adversaries on how the war can be ended. Thus it may be some time before an end to the conflict is achieved. Despite the implicit threat of retaliation against a party that defies the Security Council, sanctions, if imposed, will probably not in themselves do the job.

Thus the 1990s may begin with the conflict still unsettled. It is difficult to gauge how much time will pass before a valid peace process can be brought to bear. Given his advanced age, we can expect Khomeini to pass from the scene during the decade, if not before. Although no substantial change in Iran's policies are likely as long as Khomeini is the ultimate power, predicting change thereafter is highly speculative. Khomeini's designated successors reflect his purposes. Nevertheless, his death would be a possible point of departure for the U.N. and others to encourage a more reasonable approach to a solution through the new leadership.

The importance of Middle East oil resources, particularly in the Persian Gulf states, will grow in the 1990s and on into the twenty-first century. In proven reserves available for export, no other region in the world can meet expected international needs. Following the oil embargo of the 1970s many oil-importing nations diversified their sources. Conservation measures and alternative sources of energy in the face of high prices reduced demand. Production capacity in the Gulf has not been fully exploited since then, and vast resources remain available for at least several decades. Meanwhile, demand has risen again and, barring a drastic global economic collapse, is likely to continue to rise.

Thus free access to the resources of the area, friendly relations with the oil-producing nations, and stability within the region will continue to be important to the rest of the world, especially to importing nations. It will also become increasingly important to the United States. In recent years U.S. dependence on Persian Gulf oil has been slight, but this situation will change. Reserves in the United States are down and are expected to decrease further. With the de facto ban on new nuclear-based power in the near future, the need for oil will grow beyond the ability of substitution and conservation to compensate. The U.S. economy will be more dependent on imported oil and thus more vulnerable to any threat to the flow from the Gulf.

Even if the Iran-Iraq war were to end, Iran would probably remain a source of instability in the Persian Gulf. Inspired by the fervor of narrow Islamic fundamentalism and governed by an expansionist mentality, Iran may well continue to pose a threat to the regimes in the region.

Islamic fundamentalism as an expression of religious fervor has become the tool of nationalist ambitions. Although most evident in Iran, it plays an important role in Libya and other Islamic nations. It has now become an exportable item from one Islamic nation to another and a major factor contributing to intraregional disputes. Fundamentalism has pitted the two major branches of Islam, Shia and Sunni, against each other, with all the excesses that can stem from religious confrontation. This conflict was evident in the clashes in 1987 between Iranian Shia pilgrims and the Sunni-led Saudi regime. Sustained by passion, wealth, and a martyr complex, Iran's role as the base for Islamic revolution can be expected to continue into the 1990s unless there is some unforeseen and unpredictable change in the nature of the Iranian regime.

Although Shia fundamentalism has attracted particular attention, there has also been a smaller, if not as apparent, movement among the Sunni Muslims. The activities of Sunni Muslim Brotherhoods in Egypt and Syria have survived despite government suppression. Directed toward fundamentalist aims internally (for example, restrictions on the freedom of women and the applicability of the *shari'a*, or Koranic law, as the source of law and justice), these movements have been revolutionary. They are also anti-Western and to a certain extent antimodern.

In the circumstances envisaged, free passage in the Gulf and the security of the small bordering states will remain problematic. Even if the crisis mood that began in 1987 will have worked itself out by 1990, the United States and its allies will still need to continue their strong support of open seas and nonaggression. The moderate, internationally oriented nations of the region will also need Western support. Iranian-style radical fundamentalism needs to be answered in the Islamic context. If it is not altered by a less radical version of Islam, at least those Islamic nations that tend toward moderation (such as Jordan, Saudi Arabia, and some of the small Gulf states) must be able to resist an onslaught directed against them. Nowhere is this more apparent than in the Middle East, the heartland of Islam. It is equally relevant whether the problem derives from Shia or Sunni extremists.

Soviet ambitions are another important factor in considering the role the region plays on the world scene. Traditionally the Soviets have viewed the Gulf as an opening to warm waters. Iran in particular has been the target of past Soviet efforts to gain influence in the region at the expense of Western Europe and the United States. As the largest Gulf nation, Iran has been a prize objective. At the end of World War II the Soviets attempted to seize Azerbaijan in northern Iran but were rebuffed by British and U.S. determination to keep a united Iran oriented to the West. Political penetration through the Tudeh party also failed to bring Iran into the communist orbit, and the Tudeh cadres have been weakened and dispersed by the Islamic government that replaced the shah.

The other nations in the Gulf have not succumbed to Soviet blandishments or given way to communist subversion. The rulers are anticommunist and the environment for Soviet political subversion has been unfavorable in the period of high incomes and dependence on Western markets for oil. Nevertheless, we should expect the Gulf to remain an attractive region for

Soviet expansionist efforts and a major arena for U.S.-Soviet confrontation. Thus, whereas the United States must protect its interests by preventing an unfriendly Iran from dominating the Gulf, it must also be constantly alert to the threat of Soviet efforts to take advantage of the situation.

The likely continuation of instability, national rivalry, and uncertainty in the Persian Gulf will have a negative effect on the search for peace in the Arab-Israeli conflict. But it should not prohibit the peace process.

The tragic situation in Lebanon shows no sign of improvement either at this time. The differences between sects, the need for political reform, the presence of external forces within the country, and the breakdown of central authority have brought about a political, economic, and social disaster. By now there is widespread concern that the state may not survive. This pessimism may be unwarranted, but at this time no process is dealing with the problem in a comprehensive manner. In fact, Lebanon's future may be linked directly to the process that will deal with the wider conflict between Israel and the Arabs. Certainly any international effort to resolve that conflict in a comprehensive framework should not neglect Lebanon and the restoration of its sovereign rights. That restoration may in turn ease the task of achieving sufficient national harmony to deal with the internal issues of religion, political power, local authority, and external links that divide Lebanon. Lebanon's neighbors and the international community may agree on its sovereignty, but until the Lebanese agree on how to govern their country, Lebanon will remain the sick man in the region.

The Arab-Israeli conflict will continue to demand the close attention of the United States. Since 1948 the region has faced a recurrent problem—namely, how to bring about a solution in which Israel and its neighbors can live together under mutually satisfactory conditions without the constant threat of conflict. Most likely this problem will still be with us in 1990, although some steps in the right direction may be possible in 1989. By then a new administration will be in office in the United States, and a new government will have succeeded the immobile government of national unity in Israel. It is even conceivable that in the last year of the Reagan administration the underbrush of procedural differences could be sufficiently cleared to give the successor administrations in both countries a head start, beginning the 1990s with a vigorous move toward peace through negotiation. The new decade would thus open with renewed emphasis on a peace process that has proceeded in fits and starts since Camp David.

The search for peace between Israel and the Arab nations must go on with the understanding that it will be a long road. The problem is complex and the issues difficult to treat. Deep animosities have developed between the adversaries. Among the Arab parties and within Israel are major differences on matters of substance, so that neither side approaches negotiations with a completely unified position. We cannot expect the confrontation to give way directly to the ultimate goal of a just, durable, and comprehensive peace. Intermediate steps and transitional arrangements will be needed so that peoples and nations can adjust to living together.

The history of past efforts warns of possible pitfalls as well as useful precedents. To list them may give the impression of failure or incomplete achievement, but together they help define the problem, identify the issues, and suggest a solution. These significant milestones are U.N. Security Council Resolutions 242 and 338, the Camp David Accords and the associated Israeli-Egyptian Peace Treaty, the Arab Summit Declaration at Fez in 1982, the peace initiative proclaimed by President Ronald Reagan on September 1, 1982, the efforts in 1985 led by King Hussein of Jordan and involving the Palestine Liberation Organization (PLO), and the attempt in 1987 to convene an international conference under the aegis of the permanent members of the Security Council.

Whatever course the peace process takes in the 1990s, attention will be directed toward both form (which includes procedure) and substance. The two are linked. Whether negotiations are bilateral or multilateral, under whose auspices they may be held, with what representation, and where—these are questions involving different attitudes toward the issues. To resolve these differences of form will require agreement before negotiations can occur. They will need to be resolved without preconditions on issues that more correctly belong on a comprehensive agenda.

The issues that will be the subject of negotiations are well known and have not changed substantially over the past twenty years or so. Whenever negotiations occur they will need definition, compromise, and agreement. Without compromise there is no negotiation, and without negotiation there will be no agreement.

The major issues concern recognition, security, land, and the fate of the Arab Palestinians. The Arabs must accept the right of Israel to exist within secure and recognized borders. The concept of land for peace will be present as suggested in Resolution 242, applied at Camp David, and reiterated in the 1982 Reagan initiative. The legitimate rights of the Palestinians will need definition and agreement in a manner that will support a durable peace. Solving differences over the status of Jerusalem will require imagination and flexibility. How a transition period can bridge the problems of administration, security, and autonomy in the occupied territories will challenge mediators and adversaries alike. Concepts of sovereignty and national rights will call for equal attention.

Dealing with form and procedure is likely to be the first hurdle as the interested parties reemphasize the peace process. The proposal to convene an international conference as a vehicle for negotiations has received substantial support in the Arab world, in the West, and within the Soviet bloc. The precise nature of such a conference remains to be delineated. It is a subject of great political debate in Israel, with significant differences between the major parties (the Likud bloc and the Labor alignment) that will undoubtedly be a subject of debate in the elections scheduled to be held no later than October 1988. The United States has given a measure of support for the concept but has been waiting for a more definitive position by the Israeli government before taking any action. Meanwhile, the proposal will remain on the table to be taken up with more or less vigor depending on the chances of success. Other options will include modifications of the present proposal and attempts to return to strict bilateralism, depending on the immediate circumstances, including the degree to which further instability threatens.

Diplomacy in the 1990s must seek to bring the parties to the table with some prior understanding of what will be on the agenda. If the agenda is incomplete—that is, if one side or the other attempts to ignore an important issue—there will be less likelihood of a meeting, let alone a meeting of minds. All of the well-known issues cited above will need to be on the table.

In the past the impasse created by differences over the nature of Palestinian Arab representation have frustrated the peace process in its early stages. The PLO's insistence that it be recognized as the sole legitimate representative of the Palestinians and that it play a direct role in the negotiations has plagued the process. Whatever argument is put forth on the legitimacy of the position, it is evident from the past record that for the foreseeable future no Israeli government would survive if it were to deal directly with the PLO. The situation calls for the utmost skill and a strong measure of constructive ambiguity. The PLO need not give up its claim to sole legitimacy. Thus it can choose not to make an issue of its formal representation and satisfy itself that the Palestinian representatives at the table are valid proponents of the Palestinian point of view. Just as Israel cannot accept the PLO, no Arab nation can ignore it; but PLO acquiescence or blessing in one form or another of Palestinian representation is feasible. Finding Palestinians from the West Bank and Gaza who are not blatantly identified with the PLO has been widely viewed, in and outside Israel, as the way out of the impasse. This was foreseen in the Camp David Accords, and it should not be difficult for either side to make the necessary adjustment in its position.

If the parties can find their way to the table through the maze of procedural problems, they will then face the much more difficult task of compromising on differences of substance. Looming large among these issues is the question of Palestinian Arab rights. Palestinian spokesmen, supported in large measure by the Arab nations, have insisted that any agreement must include the right of Palestinians to self-determination. Philosophically the right to self-determination cannot be denied. It is deeply imbued in the U.S. political tradition and is an integral element in democratic revolution. In the context of the Middle East peace process, however, the words have come to mean the establishment of an independent Palestinian state in the West Bank and Gaza. The Israelis will not contemplate conceding to the establishment of such a state. This attitude is unlikely to change in the early stages of negotiations, if ever.

Instead, attention has been directed toward the possibility of the West Bank and Gaza becoming associated with Jordan. With substantial local autonomy, such a Palestinian homeland would not require immediate definition of sovereignty or nationhood. Elections and a referendum of the sort outlined in the Camp David Accords could then be viewed as an exercise of self-determination. The concept outline was endorsed in the 1982 Reagan initiative and has been one of the more potentially useful proposals discussed in the intervening period. It will undoubtedly receive continued attention in the next round of the peace process.

If the West Bank and Gaza were no longer occupied, it is readily conceivable that acceptable conditions and arrangements could be agreed upon to assure the security of Israel. Various suggestions for demilitarization, peacekeeping forces, arms limitation, special border arrangements, and other means of limiting threats to the peace have been proposed. Any association of the West Bank and Gaza with Jordan would need to satisfy legitimate Israeli security concerns. Israel would need safeguards during and after the projected transition period, and the future of existing Israeli settlements would have to be resolved.

There is no assurance that the above issues will be resolved as indicated. There may be other options, and there are other related issues. But it is clear that there is enough chance of success if Arabs and Israelis are sufficiently willing to negotiate. Pursuing this goal calls for an active diplomacy on the part of those who seek a just and durable peace.

In Israel and the Arab world there is some hope for greater understanding of the desirability of peace over continued conflict. Modern warfare has become so devastating in its cost and losses that finding a better alternative to the settlement of disputes becomes imperative. In the case of Israel there is greater recognition of the futility of war as an answer. Israeli political leaders and the public are sensitive to casualties, in part because of the closeness of the society. They also recognize that limited success in warfare does not resolve the strategic problems the nation faces. The Arabs, meanwhile, increasingly recognize that social and economic progress will not accelerate without peace, particularly in the confrontation states on the borders of Israel—Syria, Jordan, and Lebanon. This factor contributed greatly to the bold actions of Anwar Sadat in the late 1970s and helps sustain the peace between Israel and Egypt.

The disunity among Israel's Arab adversaries complicates the peace process. An Arab consensus has become increasingly important if for no reason other than the difficulty for one Arab party to pursue negotiations on its own. What Sadat was able to do is not as easy for the leaders of Jordan or Lebanon. Clearly in 1983 and again in 1985 Syrian and Palestinian objections stopped what otherwise appeared to be forward movements in the search for peace. Syria in particular plays a crucial role. It is a confrontation state with a large Soviet-supplied military force, close relations with radical Palestinian factions, and a firm vision of its basic demands. Syrian leadership has been willing to sustain the confrontation despite the cost. Syrian opposition to bilateral negotiations between Israel and its neighbors is not likely to change. But Syria is in principle committed to participating in an international conference involving the permanent members of the U.N. Security Council. How it will approach such a comprehensive process is uncertain. We can anticipate that Syria will demand Israel's return to 1967 borders. This raises the question of what happens on the Golan Heights—a prime example of the difficulties inherent in any Israeli-Syrian negotiation.

No people, no nation, and no problems between nations remain static. Although the basic issues remain, changes in circumstances occur and new problems emerge, especially in a conflict as long-lasting as that between Israel and its Arab neighbors. Thus 20, 30, or 40 years ago when various attempts at peace were being pursued, circumstances that are important now were not yet evident. Islamic fundamentalism has become an increasingly important factor. Similarly demographic factors now weigh more heavily in the search for solutions. For example, the high rate of growth of the Palestinian population in Israel and the occupied territories of the West Bank and Gaza has been called a demographic time bomb. It will have a direct bearing on proposals designed to deal with the Palestinian question in all its aspects.

Similarly the population explosion that has produced a heavy preponderance of young people born and growing to maturity under conditions of continuing conflict, with little opportunity and no sense of belonging, also adds to the complexities of this central issue in the search for a peaceful settlement. Combined with Palestinian frustration at the prospect of endless Israeli control, these factors were at the origin of the anti-Israeli riots that broke out on the West Bank and Gaza in early 1988.

The prospect of peace and the willingness to seek mutually acceptable solutions to seemingly insoluble differences must be rejuvenated in the 1990s. The process should be viewed comprehensively, excluding none of the confrontation states, even if progress in the end may involve bilateral rather than multilateral efforts. In the long run peace in the Arab-Israeli context is not divisible. A multilateral framework is attractive because it can bring in all of the interested parties. Its difficulties stem in part from the differing views and ambitions of the Arab participants. Moreover, differences within Israel over the desirability of a multilateral approach remain. Here again, however, proposals based on bilateral negotiations under a multilateral umbrella can break the impasse. They would also help deal with the competition between the United States and the Soviet Union that would arise in a more rigid multilateral formula.

For one reason or another, the peace process in the Arab-Israeli conflict has depended historically on the active involvement of outside powers. Efforts to generate movement through direct contact between the adversaries bog down without that added support and make progress when it is most evident. The success of the Camp David process would not have occurred without the dedication of the Carter administration. The stalemate that ended King Hussein's efforts in 1985 was probably hastened by the relatively meager participation of the United States, although in the end Palestinian inflexibility and Syrian opposition frustrated the Jordanians.

If the 1990s are to see progress toward peace between the Arabs and Israelis, with or without a multilateral forum, the U.S. role is likely to be crucial. That role is not as evident in the Iran-Iraq war, where the emphasis should be more universal and should include the neutral representatives of multinational organizations. The United States will be supportive but not solely capable—a participant, not a catalyst.

In the Arab-Israeli dispute the United States has traditionally played a unique role in the peace process, in part because both sides accept it. The Israelis know the strength of the U.S. commitment to them, the moderate Arabs look to the United States for support, and all Arabs recognize the United States as the nation with the most influence on Israeli views.

Internal political factors in the United States will continue to influence U.S. policy, just as political divisions in Israel produce strong and differing points of view and political pressures within the Arab world hamper those ready to end the confrontation with Israel. Each of the parties needs to find in the benefits of peace a reason to resist inflexibility.

The opportunity to revitalize the peace process in the Arab-Israeli conflict is likely to arise on the threshold of the last decade of this century. It should be seized. If there is no active peace process, the relatively favorable circumstances may change for the worse. Any local crisis will threaten the search for peace. Incidents involving violence and threatening escalation into wider hostilities will weaken efforts to resolve differences by peaceful dialogue. If reasonable proposals are not forthcoming or are abandoned, less useful ideas will come from those with opposing interests and objectives. In this sense the suggestions for dealing with the issues set forth in the 1982 Reagan initiative remain valid and worthy of continued attention. They were based principally on the concept of land for peace, security and recognition for Israel, association with Jordan for a Palestinian West Bank and Gaza, a transition period of five years, and an undivided Jerusalem within a negotiated framework.

If the United States is not willing to devote itself fully to the search for peace, it will disappoint those who exercise moderating influence in a turbulent region. The voices in Israel and among many Arabs supporting the peace process will give way under the pressure of those who are satisfied with the status quo or who dream and plan for dominance through force.

The United States should act as a catalyst to overcome diplomatic inertia. At one time or another the U.S. role as participant, mediator, intermediary, and innovator will be needed. The role of the go-between is traditionally understood in all the cultures of the Middle East. Arrangements requiring subtlety, ambiguity, compromise, and resolution of differences through negotiation are a way of life in both Israel and the Arab world.

As this book goes to press, the Reagan administration is exploring the possibility of a major effort to revitalize the Middle East peace process in the last year of the administration. The approach is based upon an interlocking series of negotiations, including an international mechanism to bring the parties together, bilateral negotiations between Israel and its neighbors, Palestinian autonomy in the West Bank and Gaza during a transitional period, and final status talks to begin on a certain date. The concept maintains the role of U.N. Security Council Resolution 242 in all its aspects (territorial, security, recognition). It also provides for a full partnership role for the United States at the request of the parties and presumes agreement on a limited role for the international conference.

To the extent that this approach succeeds, the resulting process will undoubtedly carry over into the first year of the new presidency and into the 1990s in regard to certain elements. If it fails or relapses into a moribund state, then the new administration will face the task of revitalization. The precedent of past efforts will be available to it, and the issues will not be much different. The United States will again be called upon to play a vital role in the search for a just and durable peace between Israel and its Arab neighbors. In such circumstances the 1990s will determine how soon a settlement can be reached, on what terms, and on what schedule of implementation.

AVIGDOR HASELKORN

◆ ──────────────────────── ◆

Strategic Currents and Patterns of Conflict in the Middle East

◆ Conflict systems—constellations of opposing forces acting perpetually to neutralize each other—may be the subject of significant transformations even if their basic character endures. Historically the pattern of rivalry may change abruptly and demonstratively or gradually and subtly. For example, the development of atomic weapons in the late 1940s and early 1950s had long-lasting effects on the U.S.-Soviet conflict system within a relatively short time. Conversely a major shift in the structure of the Middle East conflict system has been under way for almost two decades now, although it has only recently begun to attract attention.

Bipolarization of the Middle East Conflict System

As many Arab leaders have recently observed, the Arab strategic position in the Middle East has progressively worsened because of the rise into regional dominance of Israel and Iran.[1] Moreover, although the Middle East conflict system is currently being polarized between the two emerging forces, Arab leaders cannot ignore the inherent anti-Arab orientations of both power poles.

Israel's strategic supremacy became apparent in the wake of the 1967 war. In six days "a small state had displayed [the Arab] historical inadequacy," leading to disillusionment with pan-Arab doctrines, on the one hand, and to disenchantment with secularism in favor of Islamic fundamentalism, on the other.[2] Even more important, Israel is believed to have developed in the early 1970s a bomb-in-the-basement posture, with nuclear weapons providing a last resort in case the country's survival was in jeopardy.[3] As a result, Arab prospects of "eliminating the Zionist entity" were sealed (barring a commitment of national suicide), and their countries were locked into a position of strategic inferiority.

Even the most serious Arab military challenge to Israel—the 1973 Yom Kippur War—was conceived by Egyptian President Anwar al-Sadat as a *limited* campaign and fought beyond Israel's Green Line to minimize the risk of an Israeli resort to the nuclear option.[4] Moreover, as the attack on Iraq's nuclear reactor demonstrated in June 1981, Israel had signaled a readiness to exercise its improved conventional option to maintain its nuclear monopoly and thus strategic supremacy in the region.

Arguably the 1979 Egyptian-Israeli peace agreement has also contributed to Israel's position in the Middle East conflict system. The accord aggravated Syria's isolation while making it easier for Israel to concentrate on its northern and eastern fronts.[5] More important, it dealt a severe psychological blow to the notion of Arab unity in the face of the Israeli "menace."

Iran's rise to a position of regional dominance could be explained by a combination of four factors:

1. *Combat performance.* Iran was able to roll back the invading Iraqis, even though the objective situation in September 1980 suggested a quick Arab victory. Consequently the standing of Arab countries in the Middle East has waned, to Tehran's advantage.

2. *Ideological appeal.* The appeal of Ayatollah Ruholla Khomeini's teachings among the Arab population has threatened many regimes in the region. Unlike Iran, these Arab regimes draw on non-Islamic ideologies for their legitimacy, such as Ba'ath socialism in Iraq and Syria (of the Takriti and Alawite varieties respectively), or have appropriated Islam and turned it into an official establishment ideology without popular content, as in Saudi Arabia. As a result, "revolutionary Islam as a movement has great potential for popular mobilization in these countries—a lesson driven home by the Iranian example."[6]

3. *Political ambitions.* Unlike the shah, who settled with the Iraqis once his aspirations for Gulf hegemony were recognized, the Khomeini regime hopes to fashion an Iranian zone of influence throughout the Middle East and possibly beyond. For Iran to succeed, Saudi Arabia and the Gulf states, for example, must not only throw off U.S. protection but also have nonmonarchical, populist Islamic regimes like Iran's, dominated by the clerical establishment.[7]

4. *Psychological impact*. Iran's crazy image has contributed to its position in the region. Historically vindicated by such regimes as Nazi Germany, the country has a distinct advantage over its rivals. Utterly convinced of the rightness of its ends, Iran has forsaken ordinary inhibiting scruples in its choice of means. Consequently the United States and Israel have found it difficult to respond to the onslaught of Khomeini's followers in Lebanon, indirectly affirming the seriousness of the Iranian challenge.[8]

By mid-1982 the new constellation of forces in the region crystallized enough for some Arab scholars to warn of a new crisis threatening the Arab world. Specifically, the moderate Arab system, said to have dominated Arab politics since the 1973 war, was now seen as on the verge of collapse because of two almost simultaneous events. In the Gulf war Iran had scored major victories that all but cleared its soil of the Iraqi invaders and transferred the fighting into Iraqi territory. These Iranian successes were closely followed by a display of near impotence among conservative and radical Arab rulers alike in the face of the Israeli invasion of Lebanon. As one scholar wrote, "the point must have been driven home that there was something so radically wrong about the political structures over which these [Arab] regimes preside that it prevented their combined potential strength—in demographic and economic terms—from being translated into actual political and military capabilities."[9] With the rise into regional dominance of both Israel and Iran, the Kuwaiti *Al-Anba* on October 27, 1987, concluded: "We are living in the worst age of Arab tragedies."

Future Dynamics

Will the Arab strategic decline continue in the 1990s? Will bipolarization still be the main aspect of the Middle East conflict system in the next decade? What effect, if any, would the new constellation of forces have on strategic stability in the Levant? How will local players and the superpowers respond to regional transformation? These are the major issues to examine.

Some may argue that the preceding analysis, though essentially accurate, is nothing but a synopsis of short-term developments. In the case of Israel, for example, the long-term trend is precisely opposite to the country's present dominance. A small country such as Israel cannot hope to beat the objective determinants of national power in the end. Likewise Iran's superiority over the Arabs cannot continue for long. Time, so the argument goes, is on the Arabs' side.

The point cannot be entirely ignored. In fact, at least one leading Israeli analyst has begun talking about an erosion in the country's strategic lead.[10] But a reverse trend is unlikely in the Middle East in the next decade for several reasons. First, Israel will use its operational and strategic edge to prevent such a reversal. Second, the argument is based on a tacit fallacy of a unified Arab threat, assuming a near-total pan-Arab commitment to the fight against Israel and/or Iran. Third, even a decline in Israel's military might would not necessarily mean the loss of its strategic superiority over the Arabs. What matters most is the *relative* positions of the antagonists. Fourth, until now the Arab numerical superiority (in terms of population) has frequently been a source of weakness rather than strength. Fifth, critical processes in the Arab countries spell continued if not accelerated decline. For example, even the small-population countries in the Gulf (like Saudi Arabia) and Libya, overwhelmingly dependent on oil exporting, face mounting economic difficulties. At the same time the Egyptian and Syrian economies are faltering.[11] Finally, as far as the determinants of Arab power are concerned, the long term is probably not the 1990s. But the more remote the cutoff date, the less relevant it becomes for policy making. As John Maynard Keynes once said, "In the long run we are all dead."

Still, significant factors could drastically alter the trend in the region, although they have little to do with the power of Arab countries. Both Israel and Iran face potential *internal* constraints that could undermine their regional dominance. Israel faces possible civil war, at least in the West Bank and Gaza.[12] The cohesion of its population is in danger as the struggle over the country's national ethos continues.[13] The Israeli economy is a constant source of concern. Combined, these weaknesses could produce a frail-Samson syndrome whereby internal turmoil threatens the country's strategic predominance. The process could also lead Israel to adopt militant foreign and defense policies.

In addition to paying an increasing price for maintaining a war economy, Iran faces the problem of succession. The passing from the scene of the Ayatollah Khomeini sometime in the 1990s, if not before, is a near certainty. Thus the power struggle reputed to be under way in Iran may come into the open and endanger the country's integrity. At the least, Iran's political stability is likely to suffer. Consequently Tehran may be forced to turn inward, to Arab (and possibly Israeli) advantage.

If these difficulties are overcome, however, continued bipolarization of the Middle East conflict system is likely. The Ayatollah Montazeri, Khomeini's heir apparent, is believed to be much more anti-Semitic than his mentor. He has often stated that Jewish money controls the world and in his hatred for the Saudi royal family has declared that it is descended from Mecca Jews.[14] If the *Pasdaran* (Iran's Revolutionary Guards) seizes power, hostility toward Israel is bound to become more active, and the verbal-ideological struggle might turn into an actual military fight against Israel. Even if a nationalist opposition takes over after a civil war, Iran may prefer moving closer to the Arabs to renewing even limited relations with Israel. In turn, the stronger Iran's hostility toward Israel—that is, the more polarized the Middle East becomes between its two power centers—the less severe will be the consequences for the Arabs of their strategic decline.

However, Israeli-Iranian dynamics are only one determinant of the Arab position. More important is the future of the Iran-Iraq war. As Iraq weakens, Arab concerns will mount and the quest for effective solutions will intensify. Politically a revival of pan-Arabism may be expected. In fact, the Amman summit's anti-Iran resolutions and the reestablishment of relations with Egypt indicate that the trend has already begun. There is talk of an emerging moderate axis in the Middle East, comprising Egypt, Jordan, Saudi Arabia, and Iraq. Further, Syria may also be on the verge of breaking with Iran, and Libya's Moammar al-Khadafy has amended his stand toward the Gulf war, or so he claims.[15]

The problem for the Arabs of pursuing this path is twofold. First, the more unified and effective the Arabs become in their opposition to Iran, the greater Iran's incentive to dampen its hostility toward Israel. As Iran's reaction to the Amman summit indicates, the Arab response itself plays a role in deciding the relative distance between Tehran and Jerusalem. Second, a more unified Arab world implies a growing threat to Israel, especially if the Arab-Israeli conflict remains unresolved. The reemergence of pan-Arabism in the Levant could thus be the harbinger of the next Arab-Israeli war, since the process increases the chances of an eventual Arab assault and/or Israeli preemptive strike.

Realignment is another political option some Arab countries may try, particularly if pan-Arabism proves illusory again. The stronger Iran becomes, the greater the incentive for Arab regimes in the Gulf to accommodate Iranian interests.[16] But Iran's price may be too high, namely, the removal of what it calls these countries' agent regimes. In this regard the Israeli option may be the lesser of two evils. Despite Arab propaganda, Israel—unlike the Islamic Republic—cannot hope to fashion a zone of influence in the region. In the wake of the 1982 war in Lebanon, Israelis have learned that being the region's superpower does not mean having limitless power. It became evident that Israel cannot hope to impose peace on the Arabs. Thus for the Arabs to settle with Israel now, without fear of coercion, may free their resources to confront the more acute danger of Khomeinism and Iran. For example, Egypt's President Hosni Mubarak reportedly disclosed that King Fahd of Saudi Arabia has "encouraged him to strengthen the peace with Israel."[17] Meanwhile many Israelis now doubt the wisdom of the country's traditional support for Iran. Instead, some suggest the time is ripe for striking a deal with Iraq.[18] A leading Israeli commentator wrote: "What is needed to take advantage of [the transformation in the region] is an intellectual revolution in our strategic concept. No more strategies based on taking advantage of the split in the Arab world . . . But rather we must attempt to integrate with the moderate Arab camp."[19]

However, Iran's threat to Israel depends on winning the Gulf war and sweeping the Arab world with its brand of revolutionary Islam. Iraq needs no such victory to be viewed in Jerusalem as a potential partner in an Arab coalition that will confront Israel after the conflict with Iran is over. Nevertheless, Foreign Minister Peres plainly stated that Israel has no intention of hampering the moderate Arab countries in their struggle against Khomeini's Iran. Israel, he said, "cannot want to become a tiny island of freedom and prosperity in an ocean of fundamentalism and poverty."[20] Consequently Tehran has charged that an Arab-Israeli alliance against Iran is in the making.[21]

The Arab search for a superpower guarantee, another political alternative, has been in progress since the early 1970s. In a bid to counterbalance Israel's superiority, Syria has sought a Soviet defensive umbrella and is likely to adhere to its 1980 friendship treaty with Moscow. At the same time, in view of the deterioration in the Arab strategic position caused by Iran's rise, the quest for a superpower commitment is likely to extend to other areas of the Arab world. Kuwait, for example, had already experimented with Soviet naval escorts before the U.S. reflagging operation and is currently pushing for an even larger U.S. security role in the region.[22] Saudi Arabia has quietly extended military facilities to U.S. warplanes.[23] And Bahrain's prime minister, Sheikh Khalifah ibn Salman Al Khalifah, recently emphasized the existence of "mutual interests" between the inhabitants of the region and the West. Therefore, he said, "the West should participate in backing efforts to maintain stability" in the Gulf.[24]

Still, the Arab embrace of this option is likely to be lukewarm. The problem is how to publicize the security guarantee for deterrent purposes while keeping it inconspicuous to avoid provoking Iran or stirring internal nationalist and Muslim fundamentalist forces opposed to a foreign, especially Western, presence. The pace of the linkage process will be determined not by Arab preferences but by Iranian actions.

Three additional observations of strategic nature may be ventured. First, Arab resort to subconventional means of struggle, such as terrorism, will grow in frequency the greater their strategic decline becomes because of the increasing unattractiveness of the conventional option vis-à-vis both Israel and Iran, and the ability of the former to escalate to nuclear means in extremis. Furthermore, Shia extremism may eventually lead to widespread

Sunni fanaticism, as in Lebanon, both to compete for political power and to repulse the encroachments of the "infidels."

Second, the Arabs' search for a mass-destruction option will intensify. The recent introduction of chemical weapons into the Syrian arsenal ostensibly to achieve "strategic parity" with Israel is a case in point.[25] Nor can the potential relevance of Pakistan's "Islamic bomb" be overlooked in this regard.[26] But the traditional rationale of countering Israel's nuclear monopoly is reinforced by the Arabs' need to deter Iranian expansionism. Although a mass-destruction option would be irrelevant against Iran's mainly subversive threat, certain Arab rulers may view it as a political means to restore Arab standing in the Levant and to reclaim lost prestige. In turn, Iran's interest in a mass-destruction, especially nuclear, option will increase. Tehran is likely to view such weapons as the Islamic revolution's ultimate life insurance, as a means to break Israel's nuclear monopoly, and as the supreme challenge to the "arrogance" of the superpowers.

Both developments are likely to test Israel's tolerance. Intensified terrorism may lead to an Arab-Israeli war, since Israel is likely to respond to the source of such attacks. At the same time Israel will probably preempt any credible Arab effort to challenge its strategic supremacy, especially its nuclear monopoly.

Finally, there could be a change in the regional military balance if the Iran-Iraq war came to an end. Two alternative futures—a negotiated settlement or an Iraqi military collapse—seem at the moment possible. The consequences of the first would be felt mainly by Israel. Iraq will be the Arab country with the largest army—some forty divisions—rich in combat experience. Its high- and low-level commands will be combat-tested and its equipment sophisticated and diverse. "If freed of the war what will confront Israel is not just a large and experienced power, but a power with the ability to stand fast," one Israeli paper warned.[27]

But in the wake of the war Iraq will face an immense reconstruction task. The demobilization of a large portion of the army will follow. Another large segment will be permanently deployed to cover the Iranian front. Further, Baghdad's enthusiasm for another military adventure could not be too great in the wake of the Gulf war, especially since a confrontation with Israel can end in defeat. After all, the Iraqi army's performance far from its home base left much to be desired in both the 1973 and the Gulf wars. Still, on paper at least, the combined Arab conventional and chemical military option would look more impressive vis-à-vis Israel.

If the war ends with an Iraqi military collapse, the consequences will be felt primarily in the Arab world, especially in the political and ideological spheres. Defeat would aggravate the Arab security problem but would also intensify the bipolarization of the region between Israel and Iran.

Nevertheless, Arab woes could be compounded by such players as Turkey and the region's restive minorities, such as the Kurds. Whether or not Iraq disintegrates, these forces are likely to use the occasion to promote their own interests. Ankara has even thought about securing its energy needs if Baghdad falls under Tehran's influence, including suggestions to capture the Mosul and Kirkuk oil fields of Iraq as a precautionary measure.[28]

The United States: Dilemmas and Opportunities

Even if the basic nature of the Middle East as a conflict system were unlikely to change into the 1990s, an important transformation is under way in the region that could alter the strategic equation. Moreover, a new Soviet foreign policy is energetically seeking to address the changes in order to benefit from the emerging constellation of forces. Because the area will continue to hold important U.S. and Western political, security, and economic interests, both regional and global forces present the United States with new dilemmas and potential new opportunities.

The rise of Iran, especially its vehement anti-Americanism, has openly challenged U.S. power and regional interests. Still, Tehran has little strategic incentive to confront the United States directly, not only because of the risk of a forceful U.S. reprisal but also because a U.S.-Iranian conflict would play into the hands of Iraq. Such a confrontation will also contradict the Khomeini regime's disinclination to be forced into the Soviet embrace. From an Iranian perspective it is quite all right to play the Soviet card as long as Iran benefits through trade and deterrence of the United States. However, it is an entirely different matter for a theocratic government like that of Iran to contemplate a long-term alliance with Moscow. As long as Islam remains the cornerstone of the Iranian regime, this reality will continue to hold true.

Moreover, Tehran is aware that, unlike the United States, geostrategic circumstances rule out an off-the-horizon Soviet presence. Although Moscow has to a degree drawn Iran toward its orbit, the two countries' strategic objectives do not always coincide. As long as both superpowers are reluctant to confront Tehran for fear of forcing it into the rival's sphere, Tehran will enjoy room to maneuver. The establishment of an Iranian zone of influence depends partly on maintaining this superpower stalemate. Thus as long as Khomeini's vision of Iran's role in the world and the Middle East persists, a marked change in Tehran's present practice of neither East nor West is unlikely. In the final analysis, for Iran's new dominance to continue to be in the Soviet interest, Tehran must not only remain anti-imperialist but also turn pro-Soviet. Otherwise Moscow may find itself competing for regional influence not just against Washington but increasingly against Iran as well.[29]

On the global level, therefore, a decreased U.S. military presence in the Gulf would further reduce Iran's motives for a strategic link with the USSR. Moreover, for the Soviets to switch their support to the Arab side might yield little while putting Moscow on a collision course with the strategic trend in the region. Avoiding this collision is the primary Soviet rationale for courting Iran in the first place. Finally, a U.S. disengagement of sorts could contribute to improving the United States' image in Tehran, even if marginally.

The problem for Washington is to square the responses to the Soviet challenge with U.S. regional concerns and vice versa. Thus as Iran's dominance over the Arabs grows, calls for U.S. protection will increase. In turn Washington may be able to exact higher prices for its friendship, including the establishment of military bases in the region. But even if the United States were in principle ready for a large-scale commitment here, such a step may not further U.S. or local interests. A permanent U.S. military deployment in the Gulf would come at the expense of U.S. commitments elsewhere—for example, in the Pacific. Such a presence, especially on the ground, could endanger the domestic stability of Kuwait, Oman, and even Saudi Arabia and in the long run would be counterproductive. Strategically speaking, the greater Iran's superiority, the stronger the U.S. rationale to align with it—provided Tehran remains outside the Soviet orbit—and the less the incentive to commit to Arab defense. To act otherwise may well invite an Iranian challenge to the United States. Indeed, an increasingly pro-Arab tilt in U.S. policy would push Iran further from the United States and improve Moscow's chances to exploit the possible post-Khomeini turmoil.

But shunning Arab appeals for help could also be costly, endangering pro-Western Arab regimes and thus U.S. interests in the area. And it might open the door to the Soviet Union in the Arabian peninsula, especially if Moscow were eventually rebuffed by or fed up with Iran. It could also damage U.S. credibility worldwide while only marginally improving the chances of a rapprochement with Tehran. Hence for the foreseeable future the United States will have to perform a delicate balancing act in the Gulf to keep its options open with the Arab countries and with Iran after Khomeini. For example, the United States should avoid permanent military commitments in the region but be visibly ready to rush to the aid of its friends there. In time this course may lead Iran to accept a modus vivendi with the United States in the Middle East.

The United States' increasing difficulties in the Middle East and Israel's rise to prominence guarantee that U.S.-Israeli strategic relations will grow in importance in the 1990s. The notion that under the new circumstances the United States could reduce its military support to Israel is therefore improbable. Indeed, the United States has no interest in encouraging Israel to rethink its current policy of downplaying the nuclear option—a move that could be triggered by a substantial cut in conventional arms aid. Nor would the United States stand to gain if, as a consequence of such a cut, Israel were more inclined to preempt Arab military preparations.

Although Israel will continue to depend on the United States for political, economic, and military support,[30] its rise in the area and in U.S. eyes could diminish Washington's leverage over the country. The more precarious the Arab position becomes in the Middle East, the greater the value Israel has for the United States. Given its strategic supremacy, Israel could thus enjoy extra room to maneuver in the future, possibly in contrast to U.S. interests. However, the greater Israel's perceived freedom of action, the stronger its deterrent image in both Arab and Soviet eyes, in line with U.S. goals. Moreover, even if the U.S. brakes on Israel weakened, Israel is likely to continue to observe the unwritten limitations on its operational freedom vis-à-vis the Arabs. The uncontrolled exercise of Israeli power against Arab countries could further erode the U.S. standing in the Middle East, contrary to Israel's objectives. After all, if the United States loses all its positions in the area save Israel, it is unlikely to stay in the Middle East.

Although Arab efforts to counter Israel's superiority are likely to continue, Israel's enhanced deterrent image can help prevent another all-out Arab-Israeli war. The projected strengthening of the U.S.-Israeli alliance will also contribute to this end. Together these developments could lead to limited strategic stability in the Arab-Israeli conflict.

Given Iran's rise as a revolutionary power and the growing predicament especially of the moderate Arab regimes, not to mention Moscow's new activism in the region, the prognosis for the United States in the Middle East is not encouraging. But the prospects of an Arab-Israeli settlement may grow brighter the more Arab rulers are preoccupied with Iran and the less they are inclined to test Israel's power. In the 1990s the promise of this future may become strong enough to warrant another U.S. diplomatic try.

Although it is impossible to detail here the precise elements of such an initiative, it should be guided by the following strategic considerations:

> 1. Israel's advantageous position in the Middle East conflict system should allow it greater diplomatic flexibility. Such a posture would also be conducive to its regional standing, since the retaining of a growing and increasingly radicalized Arab population under its control could affect Israel's favorable strategic position and its alliance with the United States.

2. For the Arabs to stick to their maximum demands vis-à-vis Israel is increasingly unrealistic given the prevailing trends. The question for Arab leaders is not how to achieve at the negotiating table what was unattainable on the battlefield but rather how to promptly contain the consequences of their strategic slide. They should also be concerned lest growing Palestinian restiveness hasten the emergence of a militant majority in Israel. Given Israel's growing strategic advantage, such a political transformation could spell trouble for Jordan, for instance.

3. For the United States, prodding both Arabs and Israelis should become easier. In principle, Jerusalem should find U.S. diplomatic overtures toward the Arabs less objectionable given the country's improved strategic status, especially if the United States continues to cement its strategic ties to Israel. Such an approach will also tend to compensate for the U.S. balancing act in the Gulf, aimed at keeping the doors to Iran open, which rules out a pro-Arab tilt there. Further, given the growing Arab strategic predicament and the increasing need for U.S. support, Washington's leverage over the moderate Arab countries is likely to increase.

If the U.S. initiative leads to an Arab-Israeli settlement, an improvement in the U.S. position in the Middle East could be expected, since any agreement is likely to involve U.S. political, economic, and security assets. An Arab-Israeli diplomatic breakthrough would also deal a blow to radicalism in the Middle East, especially Palestinian radicalism, in line with U.S., Israeli, and moderate Arab interests. Equally important, however, such an outcome would contribute to Israel's (and by implication the United States') long-term objective of preserving the strategic advantage in the region. After all, the main challenge to this Israeli goal is now internal, given the erosion in the Arab strategic position in the Levant.

Notes

1. See, e.g., King Hussein of Jordan's opening speech at the November 1987 Arab summit meeting in Amman; *Al-Ray* (Amman), November 10, 1987. See also Saudi King Fahd, quoted in *New York Times*, December 28, 1987.

2. Fouad Ajami, *The Arab Predicament: Arab Political Thought and Practice Since 1967* (London and New York: Cambridge University Press, 1986), pp. 12–13; Emannuel Sivan, *Radical Islam: Medieval Theology and Modern Politics* (New Haven: Yale University Press, 1985).

3. Central Intelligence Agency, "Memorandum: Prospects for Further Prolifera-

tion of Nuclear Weapons," September 4, 1974, p. 1. See also Avigdor Haselkorn, "Israel: From an Option to a Bomb-in-the-Basement?" in Robert M. Lawrence and Joel Larus, eds., *Nuclear Proliferation: Phase II* (Lawrence: University of Kansas Press, 1974), pp. 149–82.

4. Shlomo Aronson, *Conflict and Bargaining in the Middle East: An Israeli Perspective* (Baltimore: Johns Hopkins University Press, 1978).

5. Israeli Defense Minister Yitzhak Rabin recently said: "We can see that Israel's position has improved. Eight years of peace with Egypt have discouraged the formation of an Arab coalition against us and have reduced the risk of an Arab-Israeli war" (*Liberation* [Paris], June 20–21, 1987, pp. 14–15).

6. Mohammed Ayoob, "Between Khomeini and Begin: the Arab Dilemma," *The World Today*, July–August 1983, p. 259.

7. R. K. Ramazani, *Revolutionary Iran: Challenge and Response in the Middle East* (Baltimore: Johns Hopkins University Press, 1986), esp. chaps. 2 and 3; Robin Wright, *Sacred Rage: The Wrath of Militant Islam* (New York: Simon & Schuster, 1985); Shaul Bakhash, "Iran and the Americans," *New York Review of Books*, January 15, 1987, pp. 10–13.

8. See Gary Sick, "Iran's Quest for Superpower Status," *Foreign Affairs* 65, no. 4 (Spring 1987): 714. On the impact on Syria of these Iranian successes in Lebanon, see Christopher Dickey, "Assad and His Allies: Irreconcilable Differences?" *Foreign Affairs* 68, no. 1 (Fall 1987): 66–67.

9. Ayoob, "Between Khomeini and Begin," p. 260; Fouad Ajami, "The Shadows of Hell," *Foreign Policy* 48 (Fall 1982): 94–98.

10. Ze'ev Schiff, *Israel's Eroding Edge in the Middle East Military Balance*, Policy Paper no. 2 (Washington, D.C.: Washington Institute for Near East Policy, 1985).

11. Eliyahu Kanovsky, "The Rise and Fall of Arab Oil Power," *Middle East Review* 18, no. 1 (Fall 1985): 5–10; "Saudi Arabia's Dismal Economic Future: Regional and Global Implications," occasional paper, Dayan Center for Middle Eastern Studies, Tel Aviv University, April 1986; *Economist* (London), June 27, 1987, pp. 13–14, 78. On Syria's economic crisis, see *Al-Alam* (Rabat), June 17, 1986.

12. Ze'ev Schiff, "The Spectre of Civil War in Israel," *Middle East Journal* 39, no. 2 (Spring 1985): 231–45.

13. Mordechai Nisan, "The Search for an Israeli Ethos," *Global Affairs* 2, no. 3 (Summer 1987): 147–66.

14. *Ha'aretz* (Tel Aviv), November 8, 1987, citing Israeli "veteran scholar on Iran," Menashe Amir.

15. On Syria's possible break with Iran, see *Financial Times*, October 31, 1986; *Los Angeles Times*, July 8, 1986; *Al-Tadamun* (London), November 21, 1987, pp. 7–8; *Al-Wafd* (Cairo), December 28, 1987. On Khadafy's apparent change of heart, see *Al-Khalij* (Al-Shariqah), September 28, 1987; BBC World Service, *FBIS* (NES), December 29, 1987, p. 14.

16. For example, Saudi interior minister, Prince Naif ibn Abudulaziz, "indi-

rectly" confirmed that his government had an agreement with the leaders of the Iranian delegation to the 1987 *hajj* celebrations, or pilgrimage, that gave the Iranians "at least tacit" approval to stage an anti-American demonstration (*Los Angeles Times*, August 26, 1987).

17. Information relayed by Israeli Energy and Infrastructure Minister Moshe Shahal after talks with Mubarak (*Al-Hmishmar* [Tel Aviv], November 17, 1987).

18. See, e.g., *Ha'aretz*, November 2, 1987; *Khadashot* (Tel Aviv), November 13, 1987; *Jerusalem Post*, November 15, 1987. See also *Wall Street Journal*, October 19, 1987.

19. Yehoshua Ben-Porat, in *Yedi'ot Aharonot* (*Le Shabat* supplement), November 20, 1987, p. 5.

20. *Le Monde*, November 20, 1987. See also *Jerusalem Post*, November 18, 1987; *Ha'aretz*, November 22, 1987.

21. See Iran's President Ali Khameini's reaction to the Amman summit meeting, in Tehran Domestic Service, *FBIS* (NES), November 20, 1987, pp. 49–50; Sheikh Muhammad Hussein Fadlallah, spiritual leader of the *Hizballah* (or Party of God) in Lebanon, Voice of Lebanon, *FBIS* (NES), November 23, 1987, p. 35.

22. See Kuwait Domestic Service, *FBIS* (MEA), July 21, 1987, p. J9.

23. *Washington Post*, September 3, 1987. See also ibid., August 22, 1987.

24. *Uman* (Muscat), November 7, 1987.

25. On the Syrian chemical warfare capability, see Israel's chief of military intelligence, Maj. Gen. Amnon Shahq, in *Ha'aretz*, December 23, 1987. On Libya's construction of a plant for producing chemical weapons, see *New York Times*, December 24, 1987. On Egyptian-Argentinian cooperation in the production of a "long-range battlefield missile," see *Financial Times*, December 21, 1987. On Iraq's development of a 650-km-range missile, see *Ha'aretz*, November 17, 1987. On reports that the USSR had provided Iraq with the SS-12 *Scaleboard* SSMs with a 900 km range, see *Washington Post*, June 8, 1984.

26. See Steve Weissman and Herbert Krossney, *The Islamic Bomb: The Nuclear Threat to Israel and the Middle East* (New York: Times Books, 1981).

27. *Ha'aretz*, November 17, 1987.

28. *Hurriyet* (Istanbul), *FBIS* (WEU), March 27, 1987, p. T3; *Milliyet* (Istanbul), *FBIS* (WEU), February 5, 1987, pp. T1–T2; *Los Angeles Times*, August 23, 1987. For a Kurdish perspective, see the interview with Amin Nushirwan, general secretary of the Patriotic Union of Kurdistan, in *Le Monde*, April 16, 1987.

29. For example, Iran's *Majlis* Speaker, Hashemi Rafsanjani, recently stated: "The Russians tell us frankly that because we support the Afghans, they give weapons to Iraq. If we stopped helping Afghanistan, the Russians would be prepared to cut off their arms supplies to Iraq. But we remain loyal to our principles" (*Die Welt*, August 10, 1987).

30. See Gerald M. Steinberg, "Indigenous Arms Industries and Dependence: The Case of Israel," *Defense Analysis* 2, no. 4 (December 1986): 291–305.

ROBERT WESSON

Latin America and the Caribbean

Neighbors and Friends?

♦ Latin America is the sector of the less-developed world closest to the United States culturally, economically, and politically as well as geographically. It is a major trading partner and should be a much better one. People of Latin American background are well on the way to becoming the biggest minority in this country. Latin America is also the chief purveyor of narcotics to U.S. markets. Even more significantly, it shares our political values.

Latin America is the region for which the United States rightly feels most responsibility. Historically it has been considered a sphere of influence of this country. This concept is dated, but the United States continues to be the power to which the republics of the south look for assistance or that they blame for problems. Latin America is also a testing ground of democracy and the ideals of freedom, where they at the same time have great promise and are threatened by economic and social problems and political tensions. It is the area above all others where the outcome is in doubt and may be influenced by American policies. If the United States can wisely fulfill its responsibility, its neighbors should be friends and partners.

The need for new initiatives becomes ever more acute. Although the president of Mexico was the first Latin American leader with whom President-elect Reagan met, the chief U.S. policy toward Latin America has been neglect of everything except the threat of communism in and around El Salvador and Nicaragua. It is not surprising, then, that most of the region has become more alienated from this country than at any time since the 1920s. A few years ago it would have been inconceivable that the Central American nations would agree on a peace plan without consulting the United States and in disharmony with its wishes, as they did in August 1987. As another token of dissatisfaction the presidents of eight principal countries met in Mexico in December 1987 to underline Latin Americanism in contrast to Pan-Americanism in the first such summit meeting ever to exclude this country. Their most important proposal was contrary to U.S. policy: that Cuba should be readmitted as a full member of the hemispheric community.

The needs of the region, of which the United States has failed to take serious notice, are extremely grave. Almost all the republics have suffered an economic setback at least comparable to the depression of the 1930s and in many cases worse. They are consequently subject to tensions that place moderate politics in doubt, and the democratic tide that seemed in recent years to be flowing briskly has halted or is turning back. For example, Brazil, which constitutes about one-third of Latin America in area, population, and economic strength, is in the severest chronic crisis of its history. President José Sarney, the first civilian president after 21 years of military rule, took office in 1985 buoyed by high expectations of freedom and democracy. But he has found himself unable to carry out significant reforms, unable to check the fiscal deficit, completely at a loss to manage the economy, bitterly at odds with the elected constituent assembly, and politically dependent on the military authorities who have theoretically surrendered power. Despite stern plans and austerity decrees, inflation is uncontrollable, reaching several hundred percent. There is little hope of a workable order of true democracy, and Brazilians have lost their congenital optimism. Brazil until recently was a land of opportunity to which people flocked; now increasing numbers of its citizens in desperation seek a better life abroad. Many mutter that things were better in the good old days of militocracy.

Mexico is hardly better situated. Inflation runs in triple digits. Real wages have sunk by about half since the debt crisis began in 1982—a condition people find hard to accept after decades of steady growth with almost no inflation. The monopoly of the governing party is worn out after six decades, and it resorts increasingly to electoral fraud, but there is no apparent way to replace it. If the border with the United States were not half-open, conditions would be much worse.

The third largest Latin American country, Argentina, is equally afflicted. President Alfonsín's election in 1983 was greeted with great enthusiasm, and the military governors were discredited by both the Falklands fiasco and the dirty war they had carried on by murdering thousands of real or supposed subversives. But the new regime brought no prosperity. Inflation has soared higher than ever, the standard of living has fallen, the army has reasserted itself as an autonomous power, and the doubtfully democratic Peronist party has regained considerable power. The road ahead is likely to be bumpy.

Colombia, which follows Argentina closely in population and GNP, has equally serious problems. The political system has been fairly stable since 1957, but guerrilla conflict is unending. Political murder is commonplace, and ordinary crime makes the streets hazardous. Narcotics traffic has rotted society; the judicial system has been crushed by bribery coupled with assassination; the government is paralyzed. Colombia is nominally ruled by an elected government, but it is more subject to the drug lords, criminals, and killers loosely associated with the military who drive from the country or kill not only political opponents but independently minded people. During the first nine months of 1987 there were more than a thousand assassinations and uncounted drug-related murders.[1] Such is the impotence or corruption of the state that not a single case has been prosecuted.

All the major countries of the region seek in vain to cope with depressed economies, unemployment, inflation, demoralization, and political conflict. Chile enjoys relatively good economic conditions but suffers a dictatorship overly prolonged and faces threats of increasingly violent social unrest. In Venezuela democracy is coming into question for the first time in many years. Peru is torn by the radicalism of the formerly popular President Alán García. In Ecuador president and congress are completely at loggerheads. Paraguay waits in trepidation for the dictator to die. All of Central America (except utterly impoverished Nicaragua) subsists, poorly enough, on an American dole of about a billion dollars per year that everyone knows cannot last forever. Hardly anywhere (except in small states such as Trinidad-Tobago and Costa Rica) can the democratic order be deemed reasonably successful. Although there are many more elected presidents than a decade ago, their tenure is insecure and the expectation that democracy would bring great improvement has died.

The most obvious reason for this dismal condition is the foreign debt, which is edging toward $400 billion. This implies interest obligations of about $40 billion yearly, not to speak of principal payments, which are always restructured. Some of the republics are much more indebted than others, but none is really unburdened. Various countries have paid out, net, 5 percent of their GNP for years; from 1985 through 1987 Latin America was making net transfers of capital to the richer countries of about $30 billion per year to cover interest without reducing the outstanding principal at all. Any effort to make transfers of such magnitude (to which must be added capital flight) weighs heavily on poorly functioning economies. One may imagine the costs if the United States were compelled to transfer to foreign countries, in their currency, something like $200 billion per year, or about 30 times more than total U.S. expenditures on foreign economic aid. Latin Americans no longer pay out more than they get with new loans; but when countries stop paying, the usual ills of inflation and capital flight do not disappear. Even if a debtor country actually transfers little or nothing to its creditors, the debt has devastating negative effects. Investment from both foreign and domestic sources disappears, the currency is distrusted, interest rates soar, and needed capital disappears.

Other problems beset Latin American economies. Commodity prices are generally weak, and they fall further if Third World producers try to increase output and exports to finance debt service. Both the United States and Western Europe are in a protectionist mood; when Latin American countries push new, especially manufactured, exports they encounter protests from producers in importing countries, and new barriers or countervailing tariffs arise. About half of Brazil's exports to the United States have to climb over tariff walls. Grain and beef are about all that Argentina can sell to pay its way in the world, and it cannot easily compete with the subsidized exports of the United States and the European Economic Community.

Exports of marijuana and cocaine, by contrast, flow all too freely. The corresponding dollars help the balance of payments of Colombia, Peru, Bolivia, Mexico, Ecuador, and Jamaica; but they mostly elude the governments, and they poison the economy as much as they build it up. The social and political effects are disastrous, vastly worse than the gangsterism that Prohibition spawned in the United States in the 1920s. Latin Americans generally blame this country for creating the demand, but they suffer too as addiction grips a growing sector of their people.

There are also political problems of more or less externally encouraged movements of radical violence. Guerrilla violence perennially heats the political pot in Colombia and Peru; even though the radicals do not seriously threaten to topple the government, they make all its tasks more difficult and challenge the competence of the democratic order. In Guatemala guerrilla warfare bubbles chronically; in El Salvador leftist extremists always keep up tension and sometimes half-paralyze the economy. In Nicaragua exguerrillas have brought their combative mentality and ideological commitment into the government. It is hard to expect great economic or political improvement while the guerrilla activity continues, but it is hard to foresee liquidation of guerrilla movements without economic and political improvement.

Even without extraneous causes of trouble, Latin America would have difficulties enough; stability has always been rare. Argentina has been going downhill, at least relative to world standards, ever since 1930, when a military coup put an end to six remarkable decades of growth and development and inaugurated prolonged misgovernment punctuated by disorder. Most countries of the region have shown a tendency to swing periodically between dictatorship and constitutional (although not very democratic) regimes. Neither kind has been efficient, and Latin American nations have been chronically subject to maladministration and corruption.

Many of these ills may be ascribed to an ingrained proclivity to statist intervention in the economy, a tradition going back to colonial days when the respective Iberian government regulated trade and production mercilessly to squeeze as much revenue out of the colonies as possible. A U.S. businessman who feels harassed by Washington or the state capital would be poorly prepared to deal with most Latin American countries' regulation of prices, labor relations, profits, lines of production, and perhaps even the choice of vendors or customers. Regulation, of course, implies staff and very likely payments to expedite paper handling or to obtain an exemption from requirements. An insidious form of corruption is an overstaffed and underproductive bureaucracy enjoying large political and economic power. This has been the biggest cause of the inflation that has plagued many countries with varying, usually increasing, severity for decades.

Yet the three decades after World War II were hopeful. They brought generally good growth and steadily rising per capita incomes to most countries. Latin America seemed finally on its way to joining the modern world, as it has long aspired and felt entitled to do. The first OPEC price shock in 1974 hit oil-importing countries badly, but an abundance of foreign loans kept prosperity around for another six or seven years. By 1982 debt service obligations overtook the ability of the countries to pay or of the banks to make new loans.

The irresponsible lending of the late 1970s has proved ruinous. One could not reasonably have expected needy Latin American politicians to decline billions so freely and generously offered; few in any country would be inclined to say, "No, thanks." Putting huge sums in the hands of governments in the golden years of recycling petrodollars, with little concern how they were to be used or misused, was a careless invitation to waste and consequent insolvency. No one should have been surprised that they were used to cover deficits, thereby encouraging fiscal laxity if not actually financing corruption. A large fraction was reexported by individuals with more foresight than scruples; nearly half of the amount of the debt became flight capital in the United States or other havens, much of it deposited with banks that had provided the money in the first place.

A secondary effect of careless lending policies was perhaps as bad as the draining of capital, namely, the swelling of the state sector. A large part, perhaps over half, of the loans went to state-owned enterprises—for general convenience the bankers preferred to lend to officially guaranteed borrowers. This policy made possible a great enlargement of the public sector, the losses of which fired up the uncontrollable inflation afflicting many countries and making economic calculations impossible. It also strengthened political interests opposed to liberalization and to the opening of the economy for greater productivity.

Official U.S. policy has contributed to statization. Although Latin American countries have been encouraged to reduce controls over the economy, to get away from overvalued exchange rates (which subsidize imports, penalize exports, and promote capital flight), to charge economic real interest rates, and so forth, and although many programs of the International Monetary Fund (IMF) have called for similar reforms, the U.S. government has strongly encouraged if not actually coerced banks to make new loans (as incentives and assistance for keeping up interest payments) to the same governments that misused previous ones. U.S. willingness to continue lending to the debtor regimes has been much more convincing than the exhortations and ignored conditions of the IMF.

A more pardonable failure has been the handling of the drug problem. Latin Americans complain that it has been thrust on them by the demand of U.S. (and to a much smaller degree European) consumers. If their law enforcement agencies were efficient and immune to temptations, they would still need the world's best ethical armor to resist the assault of billions of dollars. U.S. authorities would like to combat narcotics imports by getting at the sources in producing and processing countries, but this is futile except as a public relations exercise. If coca bushes are uprooted or killed in one district, they will be planted elsewhere. Peasants will not renounce a crop bringing in five to ten times as much as coffee or cassava without stronger incentives than anyone can afford to offer. A typical charade was the excursion of a company of marines to Bolivia in 1986. After destroying an insignificant acreage of coca plantations, the marines went home; but the Bolivians, like the Colombians, have to live with the drug gangsters. The sociopolitical order is thoroughly corroded by illegal wealth, and the situation seems hopeless short of hermetic border controls or a big change in the market in the United States.

Latin America is thus in critical condition, and its relations with the United States are certain to deteriorate unless this country can formulate and carry through farseeing policies to build a better hemispheric order. Above all, the rest of the region needs as much attention as Central America. Although Central America comprises only about 8 percent of the regional population and perhaps 5 percent of its economic potential, it has received nearly all aid funds and perhaps 80 percent of the planning time devoted to Latin America. Latin American diplomats who take their problems to the

Organization of American States complain that U.S. representatives only want to talk about Nicaragua.

As with the narcotics trade, American policy has failed to take into account the needs of the nations with which it deals. There have been words of encouragement for new democracies but no real help. The debt question has been treated entirely in terms of the lenders' short-term interests, with little consideration of the borrowers' needs and sensitivities. Trade matters have been handled separately from both political and financial questions. The most imaginative undertaking, the Caribbean Basin Initiative of 1982 (the key provision of which was free entry for twelve years into the U.S. market for Caribbean and Central American products), lost most of its impact because of qualifications and limitations imposed by protectionist causes.

There is probably not much near-term danger of widespread revolution because of the exemplary failure of Marxism-Leninism to improve the well-being of Cubans and Nicaraguans. Thus far leftist parties have gained little from exploitation of the debt issue, perhaps because it is far from the consciousness of the average citizen. But we must expect shapeless and purposeless violence (as practiced by the *Sendero Luminoso* in Peru and a host of both leftist and rightist groups in Colombia and other countries) to increase in the continuing economic slump. Institutions in most countries seem to be not developing but decaying.

The United States, still the power looming over the hemisphere, will receive more than its share of the blame. What is left of the hemispheric community is being undermined, as Latin Americans see their common interests opposed to those of the United States. We will not be able to count many friends in the region unless we turn away from policies of drift to do whatever possible to help them get back on their feet.

The Debt Problem

Unless the Americas not only manage the debt problem but do away with the burden, we can undertake hardly anything else. Managing the debt requires accepting the reality, which almost everyone recognizes in the abstract, that the debt is unpayable in terms of sending huge amounts of capital from the developing countries to the financial centers. Such a transfer of capital cannot be done, and it is not in the best interests of the United States or of other industrial nations to try to compel it. Given the political costs, it is remarkable that the debtor countries have actually paid huge amounts to their creditors at a high cost to their own economies.

The policy of temporizing with the help of new loans, especially from

1982 to 1987, had the virtue of enabling banks to keep more or less worthless paper on their books at face value while they set aside reserves; but it prolonged the suffering, aggravated the problem, and offered no solution. Its logical outcome could have been only more and more difficulties in payment and unilateral moratoriums—in effect, defaults. The worst blow was Brazil's suspension of payments on most commercial loans in February 1987; later that year nine debtor nations were paying little or no interest. By the end of 1987 the creditor banks and the U.S. government largely abandoned the pretense that the loans were repayable.

It is obviously in the interest of debtors and creditors to liquidate the debt problem as rapidly as feasible to get back to normal business relations. This liquidation has to be painful, because a great deal of money has been, in effect, lost. Ideally settlements should be managed by amicable negotiation without political conflict; the potential for political exploitation by the debtors, though large, has not been used much thus far because all parties have a strong interest in maintaining good relations. It is desirable for the creditors to get as much as they reasonably can without beggaring the debtors and to spread the losses over a considerable number of years; it is in the debtors' interest to relieve their burden as much as possible and to allow the resumption of capital flow. It is important for the debtors as well as for the world financial system to maintain, as far as possible in difficult conditions, the principle of payment and the validity of contract.

The debt problem of the 1930s, when nearly all Latin American countries defaulted their bonds, was liquidated by countries buying back their paper at about 20 to 30 percent of face value. Some form of repurchase is probably the means to handle the current debt load; not many countries are prepared simply to repudiate it. Repurchase takes different forms, of course, and it may be facilitated by the U.S. government both by regulatory measures and by assisting particular arrangements, such as Mexico's issuance of bonds backed by long-maturing U.S. Treasury bonds, enabling the banks to consider the principal guaranteed while they accept a percentage of write-off as negotiated. It is especially attractive for small and regional banks to unload their Latin American (and other Third World) loans in some such fashion. Money center banks, unhappily, are so deeply committed that they should be allowed to spread their losses over perhaps a decade.

At the same time, however, banks should renew lending to Latin America on a strictly commercial basis, not to governments and politicians but to productive businesses and entrepreneurs. The region is more than ever in need of capital, and loans well applied should be remunerative, assist the revival of the flagging economies, and make it feasible to pay more on the old debt. Banks loaned freely to governments largely because doing so was easy and convenient. It is much more trouble to make sure that money goes where it will do good, but loans simply placed at the disposal of political authorities encourage careless spending or worse. The unhappy experience of failure of sovereign lending should not discourage the useful practice of foreign financing of worthwhile enterprises, and this cooperation should be an important part of U.S.–Latin American relations.

Settling the debt question cannot be expected to bring an immediate economic upsurge (distortions run deep, and the state sector can at best be only gradually cut down), but it should permit a renewal of growth and save the new democracies.

A Free-Trade Area

American policy should be directed toward helping needy neighbors help themselves through production and exports. There is no good reason for any barrier to legal exports from any of the republics when we wish to help them out of their difficulties, except perhaps to have bargaining chips for reducing their barriers (usually much higher than ours). It is senseless to make the Dominican Republic an economic basket case by squeezing down the quota of its sugar permitted into the United States; it would be far better to allow the Dominicans to pay their way (and provide cheaper sugar for U.S. consumers) than to subsidize high-cost domestic producers while using economic aid to keep the Dominican economy and its fragile democracy alive. The cheapest way to make a dent in the narcotics traffic is to facilitate the legitimate exports of such countries as Colombia and Peru.

The U.S. imposition of penalty tariffs in response to Brazil's prohibition of imports competitive with its computer products makes little sense while Brazil is expected to generate a trade surplus to service its debt. Such action also convinces Brazilians that the United States jealously desires to impede their high-tech industrialization. The closure of the Brazilian market to U.S. computer products is regrettable but understandable; the United States has been known to protect industries considered of special importance. Perhaps the Brazilians can be persuaded that it is really in their best interests to permit more foreign access and cooperation with U.S. firms and might in fact lead to a more rapid development of their high-tech industry. It would be easier to convince them if the U.S. market were generally open. If they cannot be persuaded, we should accept that it is their economy to injure instead of pressing an issue on which nearly all Brazilians will join in an anti-U.S. position.

Any reduction of barriers to trade is welcome. But we should set sights higher. Complete free trade with Canada is desirable, and the recent agreement shows that it is possible to agree to it, with minor qualifications. It is equally desirable, and in some ways more necessary, to tear down barriers to exchanges with our Latin American–Caribbean neighbors. An invitation to join the U.S.-Canadian free-trade area should be extended to our southern neighbors, beginning with Mexico and going on to Argentina. This arrangement preferably should include free movement of capital. It would not, of course, be a customs union, which is more complicated and requires centralized decision making.

Probably no country would accept such an agreement immediately. The poor state of U.S.–Latin American relations would make those countries reluctant to become more closely associated with the United States. Latin Americans believe that the U.S. market should be open to them but that protectionism on their side is justified in the name of development; they have invested a great deal in industries able to compete only behind a wall of protection—to the harm of their economies.

But we might be able to convince them that mutual openness would be in their best interest, since the wage level in the less-developed countries would rise as surely as it has in the cumbersome facilities of the *maquiladora* plants along the U.S.-Mexican border.[2] In the long run economic integration makes leveling possible, except where one area suffers unproductive political or other institutions. Incentives might make acceptance easier. For example, countries entering a free-trade agreement with the United States deserve better terms on debt service on the reasonable assumption that their joining would ultimately improve prospects for repayment. This would seem at least as rational as the current policy of the IMF and the commercial banks to grant new loans accompanied by austerity conditions that promise hardships and usually remain on paper. Moreover, assistance in adjustments to more economic trade patterns would certainly be more rational than an unproductive dole.

Even if there were no quick acceptances, a generous and imaginative proposal would do the United States much good in the eyes of its neighbors. In time some of the smaller countries might see freer trade as a potential remedy for their parlous economic situation. If one or another did so and prospered thereby, others would inevitably follow. When the idea had taken hold broadly, it would be difficult for any to hold back.

There would be much to gain. A hemispheric free-trade area would go a long way toward creating confidence, encouraging investment and new lines of production, and stabilizing the economies of the republics. It would give security and probably reduce or end large-scale capital flight from Latin America. It would broaden opportunities for all competitive enterprises and strengthen market forces. It would conduce to sounder economic policies. It would reduce pressures for emigration. And it should create conditions for a better approach to the debt problem.

The way cannot be easy. The pact with Canada was under negotiation for two and a half years, and the complete document runs to a thousand pages of details, with provisions for special concerns, such as the Canadian entertainment, publishing, and broadcasting industries, coastal shipping, and the like. Implementation cannot be quick; the new arrangements with Canada become effective over a period of ten years.

But the idea of a broad free-trade area is no longer utopian. That the two nations of the world with the biggest volume of interchanges, Canada and the United States, can come together marks a major step. Another example is the free-trade agreement between the United States and Israel, which has worked satisfactorily since 1985. There has been some discussion of free trade with Mexico, and Uruguay has given some thought to it. The two biggest markets of South America, Argentina and Brazil, agreed in 1986 on a drastic reduction of trade barriers, and they have seen a large increase in bilateral trade. Taiwan[3] and South Korea have suggested free-trade agreements with the United States, as have some Southeast Asian countries.

It is probably desirable to enter into special economic relations with nations anywhere that wish to associate themselves with the U.S. market, but it is even more desirable to form an economic unit with our Latin American neighbors and friends. Economically, they are much more complementary with the United States than potential Asian free-trade candidates. No important U.S. industry would be destroyed by Latin American competition, and full access to their markets would be extremely beneficial.

Latin America and the Caribbean have special political significance for us. They comprise our area of particular responsibility and strategic interest, where we can best hope to see democratic ideals made effective. Their troubles, far more than Asia's, reflect on us; and nothing would do the U.S. world image more good than the shared prosperity of the hemisphere.

Economic integration cannot solve all problems, but it does imply a degree of political integration. It would stabilize democratic systems and shield them against military coups and radical violence while exerting strong pressure on authoritarian regimes to bow to the democratic norm. It would isolate the Marxist-Leninist states of Cuba and Nicaragua if they remained aloof. In their economic difficulties they might even be impelled to join. If they did so, they could not manage their economies in a communist manner.

In sum, the present troubled time for Latin America could represent an opportunity for a promising new beginning. There is no good reason for national boundaries in the Americas to impede the free flow of goods for the general enrichment; abolishing the barriers as fully and rapidly as possible would be a major victory for economic rationality, democracy, and freedom. For Latin Americans this move would offer the best hope of narrowing the gap between their economies and the developed world. For the United States it would assure that our neighbors are really partners and friends.

Notes

1. *Latin American Regional Report: Andean Group*, November 12, 1987, p. 6.

2. Sidney Weintraub, *Free Trade Between Mexico and the United States?* (Washington: Brookings Institution, 1984), p. 174.

3. Phillip M. Chen, ed., *Politics and Economics of U.S.-ROC Free Trade Area* (Taipei: Asia and World Institute, 1986), passim.

DENNIS L. BARK

◆ ─────────────── ◆

Europe
America's Heritage?

◆ It is perfectly obvious that the United States is not a European nation. But it is equally clear, and a matter of great consequence for the future of the world, that the United States, though not a European nation geographically, is in truth the next thing to it. For it would be a denial of the underlying reality and a disservice to civilized discourse to ignore that America is the daughter of Europe; so Charles de Gaulle, that most European of Europeans, described it, and few Americans would contest the wisdom and acuity of his perception. A close look at American society reveals a whole whose parts are assembled from every continent. The union of these parts depends on the heritage of Western civilization—on a belief in the enduring values of the civilized world of Europe contained in its thought and literature, its art and music, and its economic and political legacy. The responsibility for preserving these traditions is ours, as the primary spokesman and defender of the spirit of liberty and the value of freedom in the twentieth century. It is a heritage born in Europe but peculiar to the United States, and it marks for us the difference between savagery and civilization.

Out of the American Revolution grew a nation whose citizens took their values from both the example and the experience of their European forefathers. They developed a spirit of individualism and magnanimity, a conviction of grace and consecration, a pride in reaping what is sown and sharing generously with others. From the same source came the ability to combine the real and practical with the ideal and altruistic, the commitment to moral and ethical standards, and the belief in equality of opportunity, liberty, and peace. From these noble virtues and practical values arose also the U.S. commitment to defend freedom and preserve peace. Furthermore, the United States' pride in its institutions and in its acceptance of humane responsibilities in a world often rent by war, starvation, and misery—what the Romanian historian Mircea Eliade called the terror of history—gave hope to oppressed peoples throughout the world. The Americans' convictions, their courage, and the results of their endeavors earned not only the respect and admiration of countries abroad, but in Europe pride in the United States of America.

The United States in turn not only took pride in Europe but also valued the many merits of the Europeans as friends and allies, merits derived from their experience and versatility and also from their inquiries and reflective attitude toward life. In World War I, and again in World War II, Americans died defending ideals they shared with Europeans. But it was not only the defense of Europe in which Americans believed; it was also the importance of freedom. The conditions of extreme collapse on the continent in 1945 led to the creation of the North Atlantic Treaty Organization (NATO) in 1949 for the purpose of preserving, by alliance, the peace that had been won at great sacrifice. This U.S. commitment went hand in hand with the Marshall Plan in 1947, which, in the wake of widespread devastation, sought successfully to provide the Europeans with the economic help necessary to rebuild their lives and their countries. It was an example not only of magnanimity but also of the enlightened assertion of Western values. Only with the restoration of economic health to Europe would the continent's political institutions recover, and that was an interest in which we all shared.

Until the late 1960s Europe and the United States were not only allies but incontestable friends whose differences did not interfere with a sound and straightforward relationship based on heritage, mutual interest, and respect. Indeed, George F. Kennan described its nature well in a lecture to a British audience in 1957:

> When I see people in Europe indignant over the way we behave, I am moved to reflect that the way we behave is—when you stop to think of it—exactly the way one hundred and sixty million Europeans, or their descendants, would behave if they were to be put over into the New World and subjected to the influences, and the discipline of experience, that we have been subjected to. This, in fact, is precisely what has happened. When the European sees us as we are today, he ought really to say: "There, but for the grace of God, go I!" for it is only fortune, the merit, perhaps, of his forefathers but no merit of his, that has saved him from this fate.[1]

The decades of the 1970s and 1980s, however, saw if not a change in the nature at least a change in our perception of the relationship and its value. As we approach the end of the twentieth century, we of the United States must choose what kind of relationship we want to have with Europe—and Europe with us—in the future, how strong and solid it is, how much value we place on the friendship of our oldest allies. Essentially we must decide whether to acknowledge the European legacy and develop it or whether we feel that the legacy has lost its intrinsic value and has little to offer us, and that the postwar rationale for alliance with Europe vis-à-vis the Soviet Union or other potential adversaries has been passed by time and technology and is therefore unnecessary.

It will be a hard choice to make for a number of reasons, especially if one accepts *Washington Post* economic columnist Hobart Rowan's dubious observation that "America has a new role in the world and must recognize that interdependence and the need to cooperate are more important goals than a costly effort to contain Soviet expansion."[2] Memories fade with time, and in the 1990s it will be difficult for new generations of European and U.S. leaders to recall, half a century after World War II, the common interests that had unified the United States in its effort to defend freedom and liberty in Europe. New generations are less and less familiar with their own history and therefore are more prone to repeat the errors of the past; indeed, the passage of time obscures one of the lessons of the past: "economic power is important . . . [but] so is the means to protect it from those who would take it from you. It's not a question of one or the other. It's a problem of finding the right balance."[3] There is a growing movement to belittle the values and achievements of Western civilization by describing them as "racist, sexist and imperialistic"[4] and asserting an artificial parity between so-called wars of liberation in Afghanistan, for example, and efforts to promote freedom. This movement is a blatant attempt to equate totalitarian practice with democratic values. But there is, fortunately, a discernible difference between truth and falsehood. Indeed, we must insist on verifiable truth when discussing the values of Western civilization. Political relativism is intellectually dishonest, represents a specific political perspective, and ignores the truth that the activities of popes, presidents, and revolutionaries are not all of the same order.

If we choose to strengthen our relations with Europe—based on the foundation of a heritage impossible to deny—the resulting challenge will be to give that choice form and substance. But if we choose the other way, and the United States continues to lecture its European allies and turns its focus on a supposedly interdependent world while neglecting its European friends, the United States will find itself increasingly isolated in an envious and hostile world. The same argument applies, conversely, to the Europeans.

It is no secret that the Soviet government has sought for more than a generation to separate the United States from its European allies by seeking to undermine Europe's faith in the value of the alliance the United States maintains in NATO. Ironically this effort is aided by political relativists in the United States who neither respect the values of Western civilization nor possess the wisdom to defend them. If the value of our heritage is to be preserved and to represent an asset in the future, there should be no temporizing in the conduct of relations between the United States and Europe. That the United States and Europe share common interests should be self-evident, but as the decade of the 1980s draws to a close the validity of this conclusion, so long taken for granted, appears to be in doubt. The national security interests of the United States dictate an active role throughout the world. But these same interests also dictate a special relationship with the Europeans as friends and as allies.

Consider the purpose of NATO. It rests on the premise that we and our European allies share the values of freedom and liberty and the desire to live in a peaceful world. The bond that unites us is the common conviction that we can defend ourselves more effectively if we do so together. In determining what we do we rely on our united courage and will and on the greatly increased strength we possess when we work together. It would be impossible to exaggerate the importance of this common bond when committing all our political, economic, and military resources to preserving our way of life.

These last points seem self-evident. But not everyone considers the Soviet Union a potential political or military threat to peace. In fact, some argue that NATO has outlived its usefulness and that the Europeans are mature enough, four decades after the end of the war, to defend themselves while the United States goes home. But is that a realistic point? To protect our interests we need a credible defense. We have to convince a potential enemy that we will fight if we or our allies are attacked, that our allies will support us, and that jointly we can do so much damage that it would not be worthwhile for anyone to attack us.

Here the central issue is what kind of arms and strategic defense will serve to deter our adversaries. Paradoxically our country and two of our allies, France and Great Britain, maintain sophisticated nuclear forces under the assumption that we are prepared to use them and in the expectation that they will never be used. This situation leads to another paradox: we seem to be the victims of the very peace we have maintained so successfully. Since 1945 Western Europe has been free of war for the longest period of time since the birth of Christ. Thus we can conclude that the NATO alliance has been an overwhelming success. For it has done precisely what it was designed to do: it has preserved peace.

Yet at the same time a growing restiveness in Europe and in the United States has produced an increasingly urgent demand for disarmament, attired in various cloaks and colors. Disarmament advocates, but also assertedly responsible political figures, insist that NATO dismantle the very mechanism—the alliance—that has preserved peace on the assumption that the alliance is no longer necessary. Is NATO a victim of its own success? Only superficially. For it must not be forgotten that boredom and complacency are also forces in history. Unfortunately NATO's unequivocal success is breeding boredom and contributing to complacency at the very moment it faces Soviet military dynamism of an unprecedented nature; that is, during the most massive military buildup since 1945, voices in the United States are calling for a U.S. withdrawal from Europe and Europeans are questioning whether Soviet military force really poses a threat to European security.[5]

Primarily because the alliance has preserved peace, I would argue that the continued maintenance of the alliance is imperative—and that the efforts of those who seek to discredit the purpose for which we maintain arms might lead to the very conflict they wish to avoid. If in the eyes of our potential enemies we are unable to defend ourselves, we invite attack. Whether we shall continue to possess the means to defend ourselves successfully is entirely up to us.

The agreement signed by President Ronald Reagan and General Secretary Mikhail Gorbachev in December 1987 to eliminate intermediate-range missiles from Europe strikes the nerve of the question. It is a revolutionary step. For the first time two nations have agreed to destroy some nuclear missiles. It is a major achievement that peace activists have called for vociferously throughout the United States and Europe for more than a decade. Given the terrible threat posed by nuclear arms, rational men and women must welcome the courage of the decision as well as its purpose. But the decision poses also the most serious threat to the stability of and need for our alliance with Europe. Former Secretary of State Henry A. Kissinger calls it a "grave crisis of confidence . . . What is new about the current situation is that America is being doubted not by its traditional critics but by its oldest friends."[6]

The argument troubling many Europeans is this:

> The apparent change in a military doctrine pursued by the past five administrations places the predominant burden of nuclear defense on weapons based in the United States or at sea. This is occurring at a time when congressional budgetary pressures have put in doubt plans to develop new weapons necessary for a more flexible strategy.
>
> In the process, many Europeans are convinced, a gap is being created that in time will enable the Soviet Union to threaten Europe while sparing the United States. In technical terms, the defenses of the two sides of the Atlantic will be "decoupled."
>
> This fear is all the greater because the Soviet conventional superiority has not been reduced. Because of that imbalance, administration invoca-

tions of its horror of nuclear war send a shudder through the Europeans, who worry that America may recoil before its nuclear commitments.

. . . Some countries will be tempted to maneuver between East and West and to extend the administration's denuclearization rhetoric to battlefield weapons. Others will go in the opposite direction and seek to build up their own nuclear forces. In either case, the old pattern of American tutelage will end.[7]

If these last conclusions are perceived as a crisis in either Europe or the United States, the crisis will become a reality only if it is of our joint making. The strength of the alliance, through its conventional and nuclear defense, provides security but does not guarantee peace. We must ensure that our commitment to it remains unshaken, along with our conviction that there is no substitute for the maintenance of a credible defense.

Diplomacy remains critical to the task, for it refers not only to the skillful management of international relations but also to the art of discussing and considering possible alternatives rather than simply resorting to force. It is the art of dealing with a totalitarian regime in the Soviet Union that is politically ruthless, militarily powerful, and extremely dangerous: witness Afghanistan or the invasion of Czechoslovakia in 1968.

Diplomacy is the practical implementation of the recognition that, although sustained political confrontation with the Soviet Union may not be enjoyable, it is nevertheless a better alternative than sustained military conflict. Cowardice is neither a U.S. nor a European trait, but it has two near relatives: exaggerated caution and realism, in whose name self-deception can occur. When we Americans and Europeans deal with each other, prudence and pragmatism require us to discuss the issues that divide us as well as those that unite us, while avoiding the self-deceptive conclusion that peace in Europe no longer requires NATO.

Diplomacy will not solve all the problems or erase all the differences that divide Europe and the United States or the NATO alliance and the USSR. It can at least serve as the vehicle by which we communicate with friends and with enemies. This is why it is an essential part of preserving tranquillity and maintaining security. But if it is conducted with arrogance or excessive caution, with overconfidence or with condescension, confusion will result instead of consensus.

In the West, the longer Europe has been at peace, the more difficult it has become *to summon the will to maintain the mechanism that preserves it*. One source of trouble lies in the breakdown of unity among the democracies on the necessity of linking peace and freedom in a close and lasting union. For the democracies, this crucial matter concerns what peace truly means for democratic societies and what is demanded of those who wish to live in peace in the world as it is today.

The weakening of the will to preserve a peace capable of enduring—in other words, the wish to deny the threat posed by the military power of the Soviet Union—reflects a failure to understand what peace is and how it can be lost. Like freedom, peace is not an end in itself; its meaning depends on the circumstances. The value of both arises from what is done with them. There is peace that recognizes compromise as the strength of diplomacy while respecting the right of peoples everywhere to determine their own destiny. And there is peace that rests on dictatorship and on the denial of freedom and individual liberty, long familiar in history as *pax romana*.

To illustrate the point, consider the purpose of the Berlin Wall or of the mine fields dividing Germany and Europe. The freedom of the western sectors of Berlin has been preserved because French, British, and U.S. military forces, in cooperation with the West German government, have remained in Berlin for more than 42 years, since 1945. Reflect also that neither the Berlin Wall nor the division of Germany will remain forever. What we do not know is when or on whose terms the division will end. Although it is in the interest of Europe and the United States to end the division on terms of economic and political freedom, this end will occur only if we, as citizens of free societies, recognize that what happens in Germany—or what fails to happen there—must affect all of us.

What free people believe determines what they do, for at the heart of policy are values. Despite this age of magical technology and instant communication, mankind is not the measure of all things. In this century, as in the past, we are just as capable of beginning war, fomenting revolution, and promoting peace as we have ever been. Today the question of defense is just as critical and just as paradoxical as it has ever been. We remain subject to human weakness and human frailty and therefore capable of changing what we value. What we believe today is not necessarily what we will believe, or do, tomorrow. But undoubtedly what the United States and Europe do today and in the future is much more likely to be salutary and safe if it is done in concert.

Over two hundred years ago the United States was created as an act of will. If the free peoples of the world believe that the citizens of the United States still possess that will and the means to defend themselves, the chance of war will be significantly reduced. There must be no doubt that those who have enjoyed freedom will risk everything to retain it, provided there is a strong, free power with which they can ally themselves. There is no alternative in Europe or in the United States, therefore, but to preserve the will to defend what we believe is right while we are still free to adopt that course.

By the grace of God we are still free, and we may offer alliance to other free peoples as well as to those in bondage.

We need to remind ourselves, however, as free people of the West, that liberty is not cheap. It is costly but worth its price. It is a powerful idea dreaded by the enemies of free governments. Freedom is also a natural right, but it must be nurtured and respected if it is to prevail. Therefore we must decide whether our values are worth defending, whether we have the will to defend them, and whether we have the arms to do so. But we should not forget that no political development elsewhere has displaced the values of Western civilization with better ones. On the contrary, our adversaries attest their respect for these values by the lip service they constantly pay them, and also by the tentative movement away from totalitarianism being discussed in China and the Soviet Union.

The defense of Western civilization is the defense of the joint heritage of our societies in Europe and in North America. The day this heritage is forgotten and we fail to lend material and moral support to the maintenance of freedom—whether in divided Berlin or elsewhere—we place our future in jeopardy. If that occurs the outcome will only be a matter of time—but its form will be a foregone conclusion. But if we are willing to recognize "that Europe will seek new directions in the years ahead"[8] and that we have a responsibility, with Europe, to provide the framework for that direction, the future is not bleak. If we recognize that taking the initiative is preferable to inaction, that leadership is preferable to proclaiming self-fulfilling prophesies of doom, and that our actions are determined by our belief in the value we place on truth, freedom, and peace, then we remain free. And if that is the case, the design of the future becomes not a threat but a challenge.

The outcome rests on several propositions. One is to recognize that neither the Europeans nor the Americans can have it both ways. We need to pursue our individual and joint interests competitively and cooperatively, for, to paraphrase Benjamin Franklin, if we do not hang together we will most assuredly hang separately. Another is that the governments of Europe and of the United States are not infallible, nor are they always in possession of the truth. When Americans and Europeans think about each other, we should recall that different opinions about how to achieve the same goals are not necessarily a liability. If accorded respect, they have enormous value. In fact the Europeans are the strongest allies and best friends the United States has or could possibly have, and the reverse is equally true. But this relationship gives neither of them the license to preach to the other; rather, it entails for both the responsibility to listen.

There simply does not exist anywhere in the world a relationship that provides the same kind of strength and friendship as that between Europe and the United States. The United States is undeniably more powerful. Nevertheless, it is clearly not in the national interest of the United States to let its closest friends remain divided and weak. The United States must encourage its European allies to take their own individual and joint steps to foster their individual strengths. As the economist Melvyn Krauss has wisely concluded, "to help our allies become great again—not merely clever in the pursuit of their own national vested interests, but independent, proud, spirited, and generous—will require an act of creative statesmanship on our part, just as creative statesmanship was required at the end of World War II in response to increasing Soviet power and Western Europe's economic ruination." [9]

In my own view, however, this does not mean, as Krauss argues, that "we should have the wisdom to dismantle" NATO because it is harming our relationship,[10] for that would amount to throwing the baby out with the bathwater. Dismantling NATO is by no means as inconsequential as changing the arrangement of the living-room furniture. On the contrary, we should have the wisdom and courage to reassess frankly how the alliance serves the purposes for which it was designed and make adjustments accordingly.

Krauss's forceful analysis of NATO's weaknesses is of great value for both Europe and the United States. But NATO also offers strengths and opportunities, and it is the task of creative statesmanship to take advantage of them. Such statesmanship means encouraging Franco-German military cooperation and U.S. support of a European nuclear force. In addition, it means actively supporting Western European political and economic partnership, for it is only through this mechanism that the continent will develop the power it needs to compete in the international economic arena as well as the power to have the courage of its convictions instead of the courage to complain. Whether we call this a European identity, a European community, a European partnership, or a European alliance, the point is that Europe can be a force of potentially enormous power. That power is in Europe's interest, and it is in United States' interest. We both should welcome it.

If the Europeans are confident of their commitment to freedom and peace, the United States will have friends who command respect in their own right. Such friendship entails disagreement, but that is the way of the world. The important point is that friendship based on mutual respect is not only more admirable, it is also more durable and resilient.

To some these conclusions may seem elementary, but they are of vital importance and bear repeating. Yet both Europeans and Americans have failed to take positive steps to strengthen each other. It is much easier to carp, and there has been a substantial amount of that on both sides of the

Atlantic for the past decade. It is much more difficult to recognize and accept differences and to move from them to forge consensus where consensus is clearly needed.

The way we communicate, do business, and conduct our political, financial, economic, and military affairs is more rapid and more complex than ever before. What we face are choices. What we need to cope with these choices are friends as well as our own imagination, initiative, creativity, and commitment. To assert that we can go it alone would be not only a miscalculation of far-reaching import but a classic exercise in delusion; and these are luxuries we cannot afford. Without Europe we deny ourselves the irreplaceable foundation of common values we have built since the founding of our republic. Our changing world and the changes themselves make the firm alliance of Europe and the United States more, not less, compelling—in brief, not relatively but absolutely obligatory.

If there is any example in today's world where common heritage and common interests are reflected in common values, it is the friendship and alliance of the Europeans and the Americans. Historic examples abound. Equally numerous are future opportunities. The question is whether they will be seized jointly. If one stands out more than any other, it is that offered by strategic defense. The merits of the Strategic Defense Initiative, announced by President Reagan in March 1983, have been and will continue to be argued and debated. But if we accept the proposition that it presents a realistic hope of making the world a safer place by reducing the likelihood of the nuclear destruction of cities in Europe and the United States, then Europe and the United States must pursue it together, and decisively.

Raymond Aron, one of France's most distinguished political philosophers, wrote in the early 1970s that "what indecision teaches is not cynicism but Aristotelian prudence."[11] Aristotle's admonition to be prudent makes just as much sense in the United States today as it did in Europe more than twenty centuries ago. Prudence dictates the will to turn hope into reality. The ability to do so is in abundant supply in Europe and the United States. It remains only for us to make the right choice. Will we make that necessary transformation from hope to reality?

Notes

1. George F. Kennan, *Russia, the Atom and the West* (New York: Harper & Brothers, 1958), p. 104.

2. Quoted by Harry Summers, "A Lesson from the First Thanksgiving," *San Francisco Chronicle*, November 26, 1987.

3. Ibid.

4. As Sidney Hook observes in his straightforward discussion of the debate on the teaching of Western civilization at Stanford University, in "A Letter to the Senate of Stanford University," December 31, 1987.

5. See Thomas F. O'Boyle, "Gorbachev Sways German Missile Town," *Wall Street Journal*, January 7, 1988: "Only 24% of the German public view the Soviet Union as a military threat today, the lowest level in . . . 25 years . . . [T]he notion of peace through disarmament is more widespread. Half the German public favors unilateral disarmament as a way to achieve peace, up from 35% five years ago."

6. Henry A. Kissinger, "Kissinger: A New Era for NATO," *Newsweek*, October 12, 1987.

7. Ibid.

8. Ibid.

9. Melvyn Krauss, *How NATO Weakens the West* (New York: Simon & Schuster, 1986), p. 238.

10. Ibid.

11. Raymond Aron, *The Imperial Republic: The United States and the World, 1945–1973* (Englewood Cliffs, N.J.: Prentice-Hall, 1974), p. 329.

RICHARD V. ALLEN

◆ ———————————————————— ◆

The Pacific Basin

The Legacy

The final years of the Reagan presidency have been marked by serious divisions on major foreign policy issues and have culminated in an election campaign that helped focus the nation's attention on the proper role of the United States in the world.

There have been obvious setbacks, mistakes, and major blunders for which the administration will necessarily be held accountable, but after eight years as the chief steward of the nation's foreign policy and national security, Ronald Reagan can look back with substantial satisfaction at a number of solid achievements, all consistent with the policies and programs promised by the two political platforms on which he ran in 1980 and 1984.

Some of those achievements have been largely unheralded, leaving observers to wonder why the administration failed to claim its share of credit for the success. A central role in the stabilization of the entire Pacific Basin and the emergence of a clear vision of the long-range importance of the region to the United States, accompanied by a pragmatic and comprehensive policy, is certainly a case in point. No area of the world has benefited more from the eight years of the Reagan administration than the Pacific Basin; the security and well-being of the inhabitants of the region have been enhanced beyond even the most optimistic forecast. The engine of growth has gathered momentum in every vital sector, and change has come in a dynamic acceleration of modernization, economic growth, social change, and political evolution.

The cultural impact—some might say shock—of Asia has been felt throughout the world, but nowhere more directly than in the United States. The tragic experiences of the unsuccessful war from 1965 to 1975 in Vietnam, a bitter legacy for an entire generation of Americans, left this country in a mood to forget about Asia on purpose. In the late 1970s politicians stepped lightly around the issue of a future for the United States in Asia, choosing instead to concentrate on the more traditional areas of U.S. foreign policy, Europe and the Middle East.

As Reagan approached the presidency in 1981, few observers believed he could fashion credible foreign policy solutions to a series of pressing problems. How, for example, could he manage the crucial East-West relationship when his stance toward the Soviet Union was so implacable and untrusting? Would Reagan, a long-time proponent of dealing with the Soviets and other adversaries from a position of strength, try to force the Soviet Union into an arms race and therefore endanger the security of the entire world? In Asia, how could a man so thoroughly committed to defending the interests of the Republic of China on Taiwan come to terms with the People's Republic of China and continue the successful management of the delicate relationship inaugurated by his Republican predecessor in 1972? On many major issues critics were clearly braced for a series of problems resulting from the new president's lack of experience in major international dealings.

President Reagan did believe that the nation's defenses had been seriously weakened by more than a decade of underfunding. But he did not trust a policy of relentless rearming without direct linkage to foreign policy objectives. His overriding objectives were to maintain peace, to defend the interests of the United States and those of its major allies, and to lose no more territory to communist aggression.

Faced with serious situations on several fronts, the administration chose its priorities with care: restoring confidence at home and respect abroad by a long-term program of steady and purposeful rearmament, shoring up the near-disastrous situation in Central America, and taming the domestic economy by arresting runaway inflation and high interest rates.

First Steps in Asia and the Pacific

In the confusion surrounding the inauguration of a new president, few would expect an important foreign policy initiative to be undertaken; yet that is precisely what Ronald Reagan did in the first days of his administration. In so doing, he sent an important signal to all of Asia.

The issue was Korea and its future stability. Torn by internal dissent and still reeling from the instability characteristic of a government that experiences political transition by assassination, Korea was governed by a group of military officers who had seized power in the aftermath of the murder of President Park Chung Hee. The regime, headed by former General Chun Doo Hwan, was seriously considering executing Kim Dae Jung, a famous dissident and determined opponent of military rule who had been implicated, tried, and convicted in connection with an uprising in the southern city of Kwangju.

During the transition period from November 1980 to January 1981, the outgoing Carter administration had taken a public confrontational stance on the safety of Kim Dae Jung, threatening dire consequences for U.S.-Korean relations if the death sentence were carried out. Reagan, kept abreast of the developing situation, believed that confrontation would yield little and that the Koreans could be persuaded by a longer-term policy of persuasion, pressure, and cooperation. Playing for time to ensure that the sentence on Kim would not be carried out, Reagan sent signals that the future would be exceptionally troublesome for the Chun regime if it did not remove the threat to Kim. Then, the day after his inauguration on January 20, Reagan issued a low-key invitation to Chun to visit the United States. Ten days later Chun met with Reagan at the White House, where Chun made known his pledge to stay in office for one seven-year term.

The effect of Chun Doo Hwan's visit was important for all Asians; apart from a short working visit by Prime Minister Edward Seaga of Jamaica, Chun's invitation was a signal that the new U.S. president, a Californian with a natural Pacific orientation, intended to inaugurate a new era of attention to and engagement with the Pacific Basin. Although the Japanese were abashed that a nation of lesser stature had snared the first official invitation to Washington, they were also not oblivious to the opening that the Chun visit presented to them, and they lost no time in launching efforts to patch up the troubled Japanese-Korean relationship. These steps eventually led to an exchange of visits by Chun and Yasuhiro Nakasone, opening a new era of expanded cooperation and trade between the two countries.

On another potentially troublesome front, U.S. relations with the People's Republic of China (PRC), President Reagan chose a principled, firm approach. Dire threats and systematic denunciations emanating from Beijing throughout the presidential campaign and the transition period suggested that the new administration would not be able to sustain the relationship initiated by Richard Nixon and formalized by Jimmy Carter. Because of Reagan's strong support for Taiwan, Beijing feared the prospect of renewed diplomatic relations or an elevation of the unofficial relationship resulting from Carter's decision to break with Taiwan.

Reagan chose to ignore the barrage of criticism from Beijing and to focus on the essence of the relationship. On the one hand, he shared the view of some of his advisers that mainland China could be an important offset to the Soviet Union in the Pacific region, and he therefore believed that the relationship could and should be extended. On the other hand, he did not go so far as some in believing that the PRC could eventually become an ally of the United States, and so he eventually settled on a formulation that described the PRC as a friendly non-aligned country. But he also insisted that Beijing turn down the volume and the intensity of its verbal attacks on the United States as a condition for a more normal state of affairs between the two countries.

On the contested issue of the sale of F-5G fighters to Taiwan, seen by some as a key test for the direction of Reagan's policy, the new president was inclined to approve the aircraft but faced an intense opposition from Secretary of State Alexander Haig and his State Department bureaucracy, which was soon joined by Caspar Weinberger and his military advisers. Debated hotly but informally in the first months of the administration, the issue eventually withered away until the possibility of the sale was foreclosed by political and practical considerations, including the decision by the manufacturer to abandon the aircraft altogether.

It took nearly two years, a new policy statement on arms sales to Taiwan (known as Shanghai II, after the original Shanghai communiqué), and a new secretary of state, George Shultz, to bring essential stability and calm to the relationship with the PRC. After eight years relations are cordial, if not warm, and in the atmosphere of change permeating modern China, Ronald Reagan leaves office profoundly satisfied with his management of a relationship that could easily have turned sour. At the same time, he obviously takes comfort from his basic adherence to the provisions of the Taiwan Relations Act, a totally unique legislative infrastructure that regulates relations between the United States and the Republic of China on Taiwan. No other nation can boast of a *legislative* basis for its relationship with the United States. On the negative side of the ledger, the damaging impact (to Taiwan) of Shanghai II cannot be overlooked. Many observers believe that the language of the communiqué is overly restrictive on the subject of defensive weapons sales to Taiwan and hence runs counter to the underlying Taiwan Relations Act.

Since the administration deliberately assigned first priority to domestic policy, given the need to pass the president's economic package and a significant tax cut designed to stimulate domestic economic activity, foreign policy initiatives were not emphasized, except for the administration's determination not to permit El Salvador to be taken over by the Cuban- and Soviet-backed Sandinista revolutionaries in Nicaragua.

Japan was eager to establish close ties with the Reagan administration, and Prime Minister Zenkō Suzuki paid an official visit in the spring of 1981.

From this visit emerged an important new stage in the U.S.-Japan relationship: the Japanese agreed to expand their role in the defense of the Pacific and to take specific steps to increase the range of their patrol activities to safeguard the Pacific sea-lanes to a distance of 1,000 miles. The decision to reaffirm Japan's defense alliance with the United States caused political heartburn for the Suzuki government back in Japan but was a bold stroke for the Reagan policy of nudging Japan into a more active role in the Pacific Basin.

These policies were continued and elaborated by the government of Prime Minister Yasuhiro Nakasone, whose close relationship with the United States and with President Reagan marked a high point for post–World War II relations between the two countries. Under Nakasone and stimulated by the United States, Japan first penetrated the artificial barrier of limiting defense spending to 1 percent of gross national product (GNP); still more rapid growth in this sector must be the target of the 1990s, although Japan must exercise caution and restraint with respect to the type and quality of its defense activities because of the sensitivity of neighboring Pacific nations with unhappy memories of the Great East Asian Coprosperity Sphere of the 1940s. As the Reagan administration leaves office, the overall political relationship has never been better, but the approaching storm clouds of severe trade friction generated by a huge trade deficit and clearly unfair Japanese trade practices cast a lengthening shadow across the Pacific.

The Reagan administration also stressed relations with Australia and New Zealand, traditional and important allies in the South Pacific. Surprisingly relations with Australia solidified even after the election of Labourite Robert Hawke. Reagan forged close ties with Hawke, and a steady stream of Cabinet-level traffic flowed between Canberra and Washington. But the Americans suffered a setback in relations with New Zealand, which chose a different path from the country's traditional support for the ANZUS treaty when it elected David Lange prime minister. Lange's nonnuclear preferences soon led to a confrontation with the United States over the issue of armaments aboard U.S. vessels visiting New Zealand ports, and Lange was given an ultimatum to face up to New Zealand's obligations under the treaty. He demurred, and the U.S. nuclear umbrella was removed from New Zealand, leaving relations tense and strained.

The Next President:
Opportunity and Challenge in the Pacific

Oddly the first to notice the Reagan administration's new emphasis on the Pacific Basin were the Europeans. In the doldrums during the 1980s and plagued by huge deficits and a dose of so-called Europessimism or Euro-fatigue, our Atlantic partners began to worry that they would soon be abandoned by the United States, which viewed its destiny and its interests in the Pacific Rim as more attractive and more economically rewarding. First over the threshold to mainland China, the United States was, according to many Europeans, positioning itself to cash in on the huge market there. In reality the huge market did not materialize, and by the late 1980s the Europeans learned what many Americans before them knew, namely, that China is not the boundless market opportunity that some have depicted.

Moreover, given the dynamism of Japan, Korea, Taiwan, and the six members of the Association of Southeast Asian Nations (ASEAN), in which the United States had a clear edge and the Europeans virtually no postwar experience, the appeal of the expanding Asian marketplace to the United States seemed only logical and natural. Then, too, many Europeans argued, Reagan was a native Californian understandably oriented toward the emerging opportunities in the Pacific Basin. Since the United States could not deal with two parts of the world at the same time, the Europeans felt justified in their pessimism.

These fears subsided as the final year of the Reagan administration got under way. The successful conclusion of the intermediate-range nuclear forces (INF) treaty with the Soviet Union, two visits by Reagan to Europe (including a Moscow summit with the Soviets), the new popular and political attraction of analyzing Gorbachev and his policies of *glasnost'* and *perestroika*, and the continuing problems in the Middle East assuaged the Europeans' bruised feelings about being ignored completely. By the late 1980s Europeans themselves had begun to organize for competition in the Pacific, although trade and investment prospects for Europeans in the area will be handicapped by the high cost structures in their own economies and the relative attractiveness of U.S. products to Asian buyers.

The president who takes office on January 20, 1989, will quickly conclude that the Pacific Basin remains an area of enormous opportunity and growth. He will also see that the United States retains important responsibilities in the region, especially in security commitments. The United States has much at stake in Asia in the immediate future, and if we handle the area well there will be great rewards for Asians and Americans. Mishandled or driven by narrow and counterproductive nationalist goals, U.S. policy toward Asia could well lead to spectacular failures in the next decade.

It may seem contradictory to herald the success of one political era in its policies toward Asia, claiming that an extraordinarily solid foundation has been laid for the future, and then promptly warn that the foundation could simply be destroyed. But that prospect looms, given the increasingly difficult problems in our economic relations with Asia and the potential for such problems to spill over into political and security affairs.

Trade Frictions: A Major Threat to U.S. Interests

The boom years of the last decade have permitted Asian modernization to progress at breathtaking speed. Given the renewed U.S. commitment to Asia during the 1980s and, with notable exceptions, freedom from the burdens of maintaining effective military deterrent forces, Asian nations have reaped great dividends. The standard of living has shot upward, the quality of life has greatly improved (although large pockets of poverty persist, especially in Southeast Asia), and the future appears bright.

The capitalist ethic, almost second nature to Asians, has combined with a dedication to hard work long since gone from the industrialized West. Some in the West even criticize the Asians for working too hard, and the fabled hard-working Japanese, now on the verge of being able to afford to work less, glance nervously over their shoulders at the hard-charging Asian competitors from Korea, Taiwan, and other countries.

In the United States this Asian dynamism, once a source of wonder and admiration, is increasingly seen as a key ingredient in the chronic U.S. trade deficit. In a politically charged atmosphere, we hear of growing concern about so-called unfair trading practices (widely attributed to Asian countries), which result in a loss of jobs at home and, if we are to believe the more strident politicians, the permanent decline of the U.S. living standard "unless we do something about it now." In practice, this is a demand for quick solutions, always political in nature and almost always protectionist in practice.

Frustration with Japan is at the center of the argument—a frustration fueled by Japan itself. If any nation can be singled out as the beneficiary of the protection and the generosity of the United States in the past four decades, it is this wartime enemy. Japan's climb to success and riches is unarguably the result of sacrifice and hard work on the part of Japan's greatest and only abundant resource, the Japanese people. Highly educated, highly motivated, and totally dedicated to achieving excellence in their own society and in the world, the Japanese have created a special society. That special character is also the source of much of Japan's trouble in the world today, especially in the United States, where anti-Japanese sentiment is growing rapidly.

Because the Japanese consider themselves a special, even a superior, society, their society has become exclusionist. Despite all the trappings of the most modern high-technology society and a certain cosmopolitanism reflected in Japan's international outlook, the Japanese way of thinking has not kept pace with the nation's economic development. Interdependence, by now an article of faith in the industrialized world, has a separate meaning for Japan and is at the root of rising anti-Japanese sentiment abroad. This ill feeling perplexes and frustrates the Japanese, who consider demands from abroad that they change their ways rude and impertinent.

By the end of the 1980s it is abundantly clear that Japan does not play by the same rules on international trade that govern other industrialized nations. Access to lucrative Japanese markets is restricted by a combination of societal and governmental traditions and rules whose effect is to establish nearly impenetrable barriers to products from other nations, with the exception of highest-quality consumer goods. This attitude bespeaks the Japanese demand for excellence, incorporated in nearly everything produced in that country, and accounts for the extraordinary demand for its products.

Above all, Japan is a formidable competitor in the world; indeed, the relentlessness of Japanese competition angers other countries and their producers. In case after case, country after country, the drive and singlemindedness of Japanese firms to penetrate markets, secure market share even at the cost of long-term losses, and then drive out all competition has led to rules and legislation designed simply to exclude Japanese firms.

Whether U.S. businessmen fail in the Japanese marketplace because they are excluded, or, as many Japanese argue, because their goods are inferior in quality and unsuited to Japanese tastes, or because they are not interested in developing the market on a long-term basis, the results are reflected in the U.S. bilateral trade deficit. Unless that deficit is reduced steadily and substantially by the beginning of the 1990s, drastic protectionist measures will become irresistible in the United States.

Collateral damage results from the burgeoning trade imbalance with Japan. Other nations, such as Taiwan and Korea, have also achieved trade surpluses with the United States, and they are much more vulnerable than Japan to pressures for immediate redress. But the Japanese trade surplus problem incites anger about *any* additional surplus problems, no matter how large or how recent. Thus in U.S. domestic politics the important differences between smaller nations and Japan are judged only in dollars, not on the basis of qualitative differences. In this sense, Japan's enormous trade surplus with the United States aggravates the minor problems of Taiwan, Korea, Hong Kong, and Singapore. Those nations also run deficits with Japan, but there would be no significant domestic debate in the United States about trade deficits if Japan's surplus were substantially smaller.

With the dramatic appreciation of the Japanese yen in 1987–1988, U.S. hopes for a sharp decline in the trade deficit rose. By means of highly intelligent manufacturing techniques, increased efficiencies, and reduced profits, and thanks to a decline in the price of raw materials, including petroleum (all denominated in dollars), Japanese producers managed to remain competitive in the U.S. market. Clearly the benefits from the depreciation of the overvalued dollar fell far short of Washington's expectations.

Other important trading partners, such as Taiwan, Korea, and ASEAN, will have to be handled much more skillfully in the future. For them, trade relations are equivalent to policy relations, and trade frictions could rapidly turn into political problems. Of course, each nation in the region will have to be handled differently, because the circumstances of each are different. In this respect the challenge to the new U.S. administration will be especially significant, because political pressures for protectionist measures have until now reflected the inability or unwillingness of many politicians and interest groups to distinguish among Japanese, Koreans, Taiwanese, mainland Chinese, and others. To many Americans all Asians represent a threat to U.S. jobs and hence to our long-term economic security.

This difficult situation becomes a nightmare when one contemplates the prospect of a modernizing China harnessing the energies of a billion people, opening to fundamental structural change in the economic system, and emerging as a serious competitor in world trade. This is certainly not a short-term prospect, but if the pace of change toward free enterprise should accelerate, by the mid-1990s China's role in the regional economy could become very important indeed.

A major task for the new U.S. leadership will be to enhance our economic ties with ASEAN and the other smaller states of the Pacific area. Faced with substantial internal and external problems, these traditional friends of the United States can progress only by growing economically. It is of vital importance that these countries maintain access to the U.S. market; if it is closed off in a spasm of protectionism, their internal stability will be adversely affected—a development that runs directly counter to our vital interests. Too much effort has been invested in stabilizing these important countries in the post-Vietnam era to place their futures at risk because of momentary distress in our trade balance.

That the United States will be the loser in any sustained trade conflict with our Pacific Basin trading partners ought to be obvious to the president and the Congress leading the United States into the 1990s. Managing the trade policy of a new administration may become the new president's most challenging task, and nowhere will the application of intelligence, hard work, and a completely integrated trade policy be more important than in the Pacific region.

The future president should use his authority to enter into a free-trade area (FTA) agreement with Taiwan and, if possible, Korea. Under a bilateral

FTA arrangement, the parties negotiate a gradual transition until all tariffs are removed and trade between them is completely free. The United States has already negotiated similar agreements with Israel and Canada, and the FTA concept is ideally suited to the resolution of persistent trade imbalances.

To accomplish an FTA agreement, and to serve the president more efficiently, the next administration should establish a more effective trade policy mechanism. Under the present system, responsibilities for trade are scattered widely, with dozens of agencies competing for a share of the policy-making authority. In theory, principal responsibility rests with the secretary of the Treasury, who also heads the Economic Policy Council, and with the U.S. special trade representative, who must be equally responsive to the president and the Congress.

The United States needs an international economic and trade policy council in the White House, situated at the elbow of the president and equal in status to the National Security Council. As president, Richard Nixon heeded the recommendations of a special presidential commission and established the Council on International Economic Policy (CIEP) in 1971. CIEP quickly became a high-powered and effective integrator of policy, a friend in court for the numerous competing factions seeking a share in policy formulation. Unfortunately it eventually fell victim to turf battles, and because it was viewed as a threat to the traditional areas of jurisdiction of the Departments of State and Treasury, two powerful Cabinet secretaries combined forces to reduce its importance. By the time Jimmy Carter entered office, he decided to eliminate CIEP (along with the president's Foreign Intelligence Advisory Board!) as an economy measure at the very moment that its value and importance could have been restored. In 1981 the incoming Reagan administration unwisely rejected suggestions that CIEP be reestablished in some form. In retrospect, much of the disorganization in the administration's policy-making machinery could have been avoided had there been a White House agency with enough stature and clout to enforce discipline in international economic and trade policy matters. Moreover, such an instrument would have involved the president more directly and systematically in such matters.

Security Considerations for the 1990s

U.S. security interests in the Pacific Basin will clearly be an issue of principal importance throughout the coming decade. In January 1989 a new president and a new Congress will face important choices as resources are allocated to fulfill the nation's global security responsibilities. Having pursued

U.S. interests in the Pacific throughout the 1980s with a comprehensive and clear-headed policy and a determination to achieve specific objectives, the United States should move to consolidate the gains by encouraging the nations of the region to assume greater responsibility for their own defense. This encouragement is especially needed in Japan, now fully capable of spending a much larger share of its enormous GNP on self-defense and on the defense of the collective interests of Pacific Basin nations.

Of all the countries in the region, only Australia, Korea, and Taiwan spend realistically for their own defense and ours. In view of the increasing regional presence of the Soviet Union, it is clear that the United States will continue to bear the main burden. To accomplish that task, we will need all the help we can get, and more.

The 1980s brought significant changes for the better in the political stability of several key countries in Asia. The Philippines ousted the Marcos dictatorship and started, somewhat uncertainly, on the path to democracy. The Aquino government confronts a serious, growing challenge from the communist New People's Army, and trouble is brewing over the ability of the United States to retain its two most important bases in the entire South Pacific, Clark Field and Subic Bay Naval Station. The importance of these irreplaceable facilities is magnified by the increased Soviet presence at Cam Ranh Bay in Vietnam. If access to the U.S. bases were denied, and if they eventually fell into Soviet hands, the entire Asian strategic balance would change.

Korean President Chun Doo Hwan presided over a turbulent and dangerous period of political instability but made good on his commitment to leave office on schedule, thus facilitating the first peaceful transition of political power in that country. His successor, President Roh Tae Woo, campaigned on a platform that all but repudiated the seven years of Chun and committed himself to the realization of full democracy as soon as possible. Few doubt that the Korean people, 98 percent literate and intent on securing their future, would permit a return to autocratic rule. Without the clear policy pronouncements of Reagan administration officials, the outcome could have been different.

North Korea, a heavily armed police state that brazenly engages in international terrorist acts against South Korea, remains a special problem. Some have suggested that the passing of Kim Il Sung, the aged dictator who has ruled in Pyongyang since the end of World War II, will presage a new era of pragmatic leadership. Unfortunately the planned succession of Kim's son, Kim Jong Il, to the presidency would be the first dynastic succession in a communist country and bodes ill for the South, since the younger Kim is even more irrational and dangerous than his father. The danger to peace in Northeast Asia posed by the strange and aggressive regime in the North is more than adequate justification for the continued presence of U.S. troops in the South.

In the 1990s, as South Korea restructures its military forces and achieves military superiority over the North, it will be able to project its military presence beyond the peninsula. Since Japan's capabilities will be similar, a new challenge for the Koreans and the Japanese will be to address the sensitive issue of regional security cooperation.

In Taiwan the passing of President Chiang Ching-kuo marked the beginning of a new era in the political life of that country. The transition to a new president, Li Teng-hui, a native Taiwanese, and his elevation to the chairmanship of the ruling Nationalist Party strengthened the trend toward political liberalization inaugurated by President Chiang and promises continuing political stability in the island nation. In its developing relations with mainland China, Taiwan has begun to dismantle the barriers to trade and family contacts—a reflection of Taiwan's confidence in its future and its belief in the demonstrated superiority of its system over the harsh repression that continues to characterize life in the PRC.

Making It Work

Fortunately for the new U.S. president the major elements of his Asian policy are already in place. No major repair work is needed in the immediate future, and he does not face the task of reintroducing Americans to Asia. That much was accomplished for him by Ronald Reagan and the outstanding people that made up his Asian policy team at the Department of State, the Pentagon, and the National Security Council.

But the new president must be prepared to resist the advocates of trade barriers against our Asian partners. Special measures, constant pressure, and a good deal of determination will be necessary to convince Japan to abide by the rules of international trade and to facilitate access to its markets, but the problem with Japan differs markedly from those posed by other countries in the Pacific Basin.

Certainly the new Congress will seek greater authority in the field of international affairs, a demand the president must resist. By the same token, the president will face a new reality in international economic and trade policy, since the political dynamics clearly signal an erosion of executive authority. The future of U.S. interests in the Pacific Basin is linked directly to the new president's ability to lead, constructively and pragmatically, the nation and Congress to support a clearly articulated policy to defend those interests.

PETER DUIGNAN
L. H. GANN

◆ ——————— ◆

Hope for Africa

◆ Black Africa embarked on the road to independence after 1957 in a mood of confidence and anticipation. The end of empire was supposed to usher in peace, prosperity, and new dignity. Academics, policy makers, and experts in the West and in Africa alike were optimistic. The beneficent combination of central planning, state intervention, foreign aid, massive education campaigns, and industrial development would create a new prosperity—or so most intellectuals believed.

By contrast, few politicians or experts before or during the independence struggle predicted the plethora of coups and ethnic dissensions, the administrative venality, the economic crises, the tyrannical rule that so often succeeded colonial domination. Those who did (including ourselves) were roundly criticized as supporters of colonialism.[1] Liberal observers such as Gwendolen Carter, a doyenne among Africanists in the United States, were convinced that single-party governance of the kind adopted in Guinea and elsewhere would benefit the people. The mass party would stand as "the purveyor of plans and precepts, the stimulator of new projects, the educator of the young, and of the peasants, and the emancipator of women." The mass party would strive for "the liberation . . . from poverty, illiteracy, and apathy." Given the beneficence of these objectives, Africans could hardly be faulted for rejecting "disagreement or divided effort."[2]

The optimism of earlier decades has since given way to pessimism and loss of hope. Hunger stalks the land; droughts continue; disease spreads (especially acquired immunodeficiency syndrome, or AIDS); the deserts advance; the forests recede. Tyrants rule in 21 states; civil wars rack Angola, Mozambique, and Ethiopia; race war looms in South Africa; blood flows without end; refugees abound (half the world's refugees are in Africa). This pessimism finds sophisticated expression in World Bank reports, studies put out by public agencies, and academic inquiries written from contrasting political perspectives. As a well-known French author put it, "Africa got off to a bad start." [3]

Failures and Successes

To start with, a good deal did go right with Africa, even in the face of physical and political obstacles (28 of the world's poorest states are in Africa). Africa remains politically divided. Most of the new states owe their existence to European colonizers and are ethnically diverse; national consciousness remains elusive. Even a generation after independence the new states are short of people with managerial, technical, and entrepreneurial skills. Much of Africa suffers from a difficult climate, poor soil, irregular rainfall, few natural resources, and a weak communications network. African cultivators must cope with numerous diseases and parasites, deficient transport and marketing systems, and rapacious governments. In a global context the African economies have suffered gravely from circumstances beyond the new African rulers' control, especially the sharp drop in the world price of many African raw materials and the sharp rise in the price of essential imports such as oil.

Nevertheless, most of the newly independent countries initially achieved modest progress up to the mid-1970s. Some attained striking economic expansion. For example, the Ivory Coast's economic expansion during the 1960s and early 1970s was one of the world's most rapid (with growth rates of 8 percent in the 1960s and 6.7 percent in the early 1970s). Nigeria, Cameroun, Gabon, Zaire, Malawi, Botswana, and Kenya all did well. The economy of South Africa prospered the most even though writers kept predicting imminent revolution.

Some African countries have also made political progress. Not all African states are run by ideologues, soldiers, or gunmen. Botswana, for example, has a deserved reputation for efficiency and probity in government. Senegal has been styled the Costa Rica of Africa for the moderation of Senegal's multiparty government, which abides by constitutional rules and neither practices torture nor sends political opponents to concentration camps. After independence Africa significantly improved its literacy rate (to

28 percent) and life expectancy (from 39 to 47 years) and lowered the death rate of children (from 39 per 1,000 to 25 per 1,000). University and secondary education expanded rapidly in most states. African growth rates were positive between 1960 and 1972 even though birthrates were high—2.5–4 percent. Independence unleashed energy and propelled a fierce drive for modernization and development. People felt pride and enthusiasm in the new governments; social mobility increased, and Africanization proceeded in government and the economy.

Unfortunately success in Africa has been outweighed by failure. During the 1950s, except for the Mau Mau rebellion in Kenya, there were no African wars or coups, but many parts of Africa are now in fact worse off than they were at the end of the colonial era. What went wrong? There were fundamental constraints on development: "undeveloped human and material resources, difficult climate and geography, rapid population growth, alien unassimilated political institutions and insecure political legitimacy."[4] If Africa is to improve its performance in the 1990s, these constraints must be overcome.

Ever since independence African governments have lacked educated, skilled, and experienced people and have had to depend too often on bad advice from outside experts. These counselors came in many guises— academics, United Nations commissioners, officials attached to aid-administering agencies, and so forth. They preached a secular gospel of modernization replete with once-fashionable jargon such as "stages of growth," "planning," "accelerated development," and "mass mobilization." Many, if not most, of Africa's foreign advisers at the time promoted a peculiar variety of *Vulgar-Keynesianismus* that called for the "primitive accumulation of capital" at the expense of the rural sector, state planning and state intervention in the economy, import substitution industries, an expanded state machinery, and an unbalanced budget. (Africa's external debt was expected to reach $200 billion at the end of 1987—almost 440 percent of its total export earnings.) The foreign experts' advice, whether in terms of Keynesianism or Marxism, conformed to the material interests of a new African governing elite. Western-educated, urban in orientation (though not necessarily in descent), and widely dependent on state employment, state patronage, and state contracts, the elite generally neglected the rural sector at the expense of urban interests.

The new creed of development laid special stress on education and foreign aid. Education became one of the largest and fastest-growing industries in Africa. (By the early 1970s Nigeria had more teachers than manufacturing and commerce workers.) But too many graduates emerged for the economy to absorb; hence postcolonial governments came under constant pressure to expand the size of state and party bureaucracies to provide positions for the new diploma-bearing elite.[5]

Foreign aid also had unintended effects. Like education, it benefited many lobbies in the developed as well as the undeveloped world. Development aid, by contrast, was designed to transform the entire social and economic structure of backward countries. For this purpose foreign aid was ill designed. There was little or no accountability; vast sums were wasted or diverted into illegitimate channels. Aid was given inconsistently, often for contrasting purposes. For a long time foreign aid went exclusively to governments, not to private enterprise. It thereby strengthened the bureaucratic sector within African states, promoted specific bureaucratic lobbies, and encouraged copious state expenditure rather than public thrift. Too little was done to help agriculture—a widespread failing in postcolonial Africa.[6] U.S. food aid in fact has at times depressed agricultural production and prices abroad. All too often project designs did not fit local needs and could not work because they used inappropriate techniques and machinery.

The new Africa has suffered from other ills easy to analyze but hard to cure: widespread instability, the decline of political legitimacy, the growth of one-party states and of military rule, a crushing burden of foreign debt, and a long legacy of financial irresponsibility, ethnic divisions, and civil wars. During the colonial era Africa fed itself and produced crops for the world market. Between 1960 and 1987, however, sub-Saharan Africa as a whole suffered from a striking decline (25 percent) in the index of per capita food production during a period of rapid population increase (an average of 3 percent).[7] Some regions (such as the Sahel and the Horn of Africa) suffered from endemic famines.

To make matters worse, statism became the dominant ideology of the postcolonial era at a time when the power of the state was also expanding in all former colonial motherlands. Statism in Africa came in many ideological guises—through African humanism in the Zambian fashion, African socialism of the Tanzanian variety, and later an Africanized version of Marxism-Leninism. But in general independence accelerated the growing power of the former colonial state through such bureaucratic devices as central planning or collectivization, nationalization of major industries, and so on. These assumed reforms bloated state administrations, state corporations, and ruling parties. Bureaucracies three or four times larger than the previous colonial establishments impeded economic growth.[8] The new states' military establishments often vastly exceeded the strength of the peacetime colonial forces. Above all, the widespread failure of leadership and growing corruption far surpassed the worst venality displayed in the colonial era.[9]

What Needs to Be Done?

Africa's future need not be as bleak as its past. The African continent has great natural riches in minerals, hydroelectric potential, and other resources. Above all, there is the potential wealth of its peoples—black, brown, and white. In solving Africa's problems, foreigners can play only a modest role. But foreign counselors and aid givers can at least avoid giving bad advice.

More scope should be left to voluntary private organizations, church groups, and charities that are not politicized and that commonly know more than Western governments about local conditions. The West, including the United States, can best contribute to Third World development by lowering trade barriers against Third World exports. Such barriers restrict markets, impede foreign contracts, inhibit productive investment, exacerbate unemployment, and restrict the spread of skills. Far from succumbing to protectionist pressures, the United States should resist them. When proffered, U.S. aid should take forms that make it possible to identify costs and benefits. The United States must insist on full accountability. Aid should not be in untied cash grants. The so-called multilateral approach should be avoided. U.S. aid should favor governments that promote a free-market economy and eschew central planning and state ownership. Aid moreover should be confined to specific projects and should reward balanced budgets, not deficit spending.[10]

The fact remains that public enterprise has performed poorly in Africa in nationalized industries, marketing, and agriculture alike. By contrast, academics and public planners have consistently underestimated the indigenous African entrepreneur. For example, a detailed sociological study of Zambian businessmen has shown that small African merchants in Zambia have a much higher rate of profit than state trading corporations.[11] Hence even dedicated African communists such as the leaders of Mozambique have been forced to adopt an African variant of Lenin's New Economic Policy. The late President Samora Machel denationalized retail trade, and a 1981 ten-year development plan sensibly gave first priority to agriculture, a policy already pursued with some success by neighboring Malawi.[12]

Governments do, of course, have a part to play in economic development. They have a vital role in promoting research and in providing transport facilities, health, and education; above all they must concentrate on protecting person and property. African governments have to reacquire legitimacy and earn the trust and obedience of their people. But the state needs to place more trust in the private sector. The privatization of public enterprise will have to be encouraged through large inflows of private foreign investment.[13] In sub-Saharan Africa as a whole, however, investment opportunities by the end of the 1980s were limited by the fear of political instability, the cost of corruption, infrastructural weakness, and the loss of markets.

Although the privatization of public enterprise has become part of the political agenda, political barriers remain. Privatizing a state-owned enterprise usually means cutting bloated payrolls and thereby occasioning unemployment—at least in the short run. Governments will have to risk popular wrath by selling off important national assets to foreigners. Privatization is nevertheless workable. Since 1986 at least 28 African countries have embarked on a series of limited reforms: price incentives to promote agricultural development, improved internal distribution, and more investment in agriculture. Subsidies to public enterprises have been reduced and market investment codes liberalized. But these measures are only a start.

Reforms are needed particularly to increase agricultural production and improve marketing, which has become a government monopoly in many African countries. Marketing boards are inherently unsuited to large-scale bureaucratic organizations—especially under African conditions. Policy makers who wish to protect peasants from real or imagined exploitation by private traders can best achieve this goal by allowing competition between public and private agents. "Monopoly—private or public—is the breeder of inefficiency."[14] Key agricultural services can likewise be privatized.

The United States, with the most productive agriculture in the world, can teach African farmers a great deal about soil reclamation, dry farming, natural farming (without expensive artificial fertilizers and insecticides), improved breeding methods, and better seeds. The state should provide extension services and research and should free farmers and herders from the state's exactions. To improve African agriculture and to make it scientific, the U.S. agricultural-college model (technical training in agricultural science and research in agriculture) should be adapted by every African state. An equally strong case exists for supporting private agriculture, whether carried out by large-scale entrepreneurs (such as white farmers in Zambia and Zimbabwe) or by African smallholders. African communal land holding and common grazing customs will have to give way to encourage production through individual ownership, as in Zimbabwe. This process of emancipation should be encouraged by U.S. advice and technical assistance.

Above all the West has to help African governments regain their legitimacy and end instability, disorder, violence, and unconstitutional governance. At the least, however, the United States should not overestimate its influence but should quietly provide counsel, aid, and expert advice when asked for. Stable governments are crucial, but Africa also needs entrepreneurship, hard work, thrift, and other traditional economic virtues. African societies therefore have to build up their social and human capital, whereas economic infrastructure can be developed in partnership with Western countries. But the key to African development is the agricultural sector. The World Bank has predicted a 0.1–0.5 percent decline in per capita product for the next ten years and a population growth of between 3 and 4 percent a year. These numbers spell disaster unless African governments reform and get external assistance. The West should help with aid and training, but it can help best by ending import duties for agricultural products from Africa.

The United States can also encourage private investment. Africa has islands of widely scattered potential wealth awaiting further development. (The continent is a major producer of petroleum, coal, uranium, copper, iron, gold, diamonds, platinum, chrome, nickel, and many other minerals.) But foreign skills and foreign capital are essential to the exploration and extraction of this wealth and may be in short supply in the 1990s. Hence African governments will have to encourage foreign investment if they are to develop. Africa's mineral industry has developed thus far largely because of foreign investment. More needs to be done to encourage agricultural and mineral processing and to develop the industrial sector. With plentiful hydroelectric power and vast amounts of mineral wealth scattered through the continent, parts of Africa could follow the pattern of the economic development of South Africa, Zambia, Zimbabwe, and even Zaire and Ghana (until Sese Seko Mobutu and Kwame Nkrumah partially ruined their respective economies).

Economic development requires enhanced commerce not merely between Africa and the West but also between adjacent African countries. The United States should therefore encourage Africans to rebuild former associations developed during the colonial era; for example, the East African Federation and the two former federations of francophone Africa. Interterritorial cooperation, planning, and free trade will assist economic development, avoid wasteful duplication, and overcome the handicap of small markets.

There remains the apparently insoluble problem of South Africa. We dissent from the policy pursued during the last years of the Reagan administration by Secretary of State George Shultz and Congress. We agree that South Africa's regime is harsh and undemocratic, but sanctions, disinvestment, and recognition of the African National Congress (ANC) will not bring about a just society. We favor a free-market economy in which men and women of any color can vote, buy land where they please, and run their business enterprises as they wish.[15]

South Africa is a great deal stronger than many critics assume. Revolution, in our view, is not around the corner and will not succeed against white rule during the 1990s. South Africa's economy is the most productive, the most diverse, and the most resilient on the African continent. (South Africa in the 1980s accounted for an estimated 70 percent of Africa's GNP). South Africa dominates all eleven states of southern Africa and supplies the bulk of its own capital (85–90 percent). The foreign stake in South Africa's economy amounts only to a small minority holding. The disinvestment campaign in fact has merely accelerated the Afrikanerization of the South African economy, an ongoing process that, in Marxist terms, has strengthened the South African national bourgeoisie at the expense of international capital. But sanctions have also retarded the growth of the economy, leading to unemployment for hundreds of thousands of black graduates each year. An economic slowdown in South Africa will also impede the economic development of the entire region of southern Africa. This development is not in the U.S. interest; hence the U.S. policy of sanctions and disinvestment should be discontinued.

Instead of withholding capital and goods from South Africa, the United States should reestablish former links. The United States can only benefit from strengthening a pro-Western power that occupies both an important geostrategic location in the South Atlantic and the southern part of the Indian Ocean and a strong position in the international metals trade. More investment, not disinvestment—more trade, not less—should therefore be the U.S. policy for the 1990s. Trade and economic growth will help end racial discrimination in South Africa.

South Africa can become the engine for development of all of southern Africa in the 1990s. Instead of trying to lessen the dependence of surrounding states on South Africa, the United States should encourage cooperation and joint development. South Africa holds a key position in agriculture, transportation, capital investment, and technical skill. It provides a market for men and goods from the neighboring states; it collects customs revenue for Swaziland, Lesotho, and Botswana; it feeds many people and provides capital, mining, equipment, and manpower to develop hydroelectric schemes in Angola and Mozambique. Integration, not disintegration, should be the West's goal for southern Africa in the 1990s. South Africa is an African country and should be judged by the much lower standards of Africa, not by Western standards. It has much to give to the rest of Africa in a common effort to solve problems that in future will loom much larger than purely political issues—underdeveloped economies, a lack of skilled people, pollution, scarce water supplies, desertification, and unchecked population growth.

Other Seeds of Hope for the 1990s

The United States needs to counter Soviet efforts in Africa and defeat the so-called liberation fronts ruling Ethiopia, Angola, and Mozambique so that peace and stability can return to the Horn of Africa and southern Africa. This brief essay cannot provide detailed advice on how to channel increased funds and arms to the guerrillas (to pressure Marxist-Leninist governments to form coalitions with the forces fighting them) except to reiterate the sound principle that, other things being equal, the enemies of our enemies should be regarded as our friends, the friends of our enemies as our enemies. By a judicious exercise of realpolitik, the Cold War can perhaps be ended in Africa in the early 1990s, and economic and social development can improve the material well-being of the continent's people.

The United States should encourage nonformal participation by Africans in voluntary organizations to reduce the role of authoritarian regimes. These organizations can give citizens a greater sense of participation in the political life of their state and encourage the growth of a civic culture. African governments also need to be decentralized and local government expanded by locally elected officials. Limiting the state can also foster the growth of the bourgeois and entrepreneurial classes.[16]

The executive branch of governance should be checked by granting more power and authority to the legislature and the judiciary. Federal or confederal systems should be built; administrative decentralization should go hand in hand with electoral reforms and more civic education to develop a democratic political culture.

The United States needs many different African policies appropriate for the 45 African countries. We should aim at flexibility and realism. Our policies should promote peace and economic development. We should give aid directly, rather than channel funds through international bodies, and should control, with U.S. technicians, most funded projects. Arms and security programs should be instruments of diplomacy in Africa. The military and police of many African states need to be properly trained and inculcated with professionalism and national pride to make them loyal citizens who protect the state rather than threaten it.

We should continue to encourage Nigeria to end military rule and to promote domestic development. We should stress the advantages of private over state enterprises and of trade over aid. It is also in the interest of the United States to continue to secure Kenya as an ally and to help that state remain a stable democracy. The United States should be equally concerned to promote close relations between the states of East Africa (Kenya, Tanzania, and Uganda) in diplomacy, commerce, and technology.

During the 1990s the United States should supply enough arms and training to Somalia to prevent Ethiopia from expanding its territory at Somalia's expense. U.S. food aid programs must be modified to encourage, rather than discourage, Somalian farmers by not selling food at below-market prices and by not giving food away. Dissident forces in Angola and Mozambique should be trained and armed to force a negotiated peace in those states as well.

We should assume the offensive in the war of words against the communist regime of Ethiopia, a brutal and repressive client of the Soviet Union. We should likewise help the Eritreans in their war with Ethiopia, thus placing additional strain on Ethiopia while helping to improve U.S.-Arab relations. Just as we have armed the Afghan rebels, we should arm the rebellious ethnic groups savagely treated by the Ethiopian government and work to rebuild Ethiopia as a multiethnic confederation. We should seek the withdrawal of Cuban troops and Soviet advisers from the Horn of Africa and Angola, two strategically important areas. And we should control the distribution of food relief everywhere (as Herbert Hoover did in the Soviet Union in the 1920s) so that the Ethiopian and other African governments cannot use it for political purposes.

Given Zaire's enormous potential wealth, its strategic position in the heart of Africa, and the absence for the moment of an effective alternative to Mobutu's authority, the United States must support Mobutu despite his poor record. A policy of patient persuasion along with foreign experts to run government, business, and industry can improve the performance of the regime. The United States, France, and Belgium should retrain the military and police and educate a new class of efficient administrators to reduce corruption and to reestablish administrative control in the provinces of this vast state. The transportation system has to be rebuilt and expanded so that the peasant farmer's security can be guaranteed and agricultural production restored. Zaire needs to decentralize its government so that the provinces basically rule themselves while depending on Kinshasa for foreign affairs and defense matters.

Zambia is another important state that requires many reforms; it needs to support agriculture more, cut down on its bureaucracy and state-owned corporations, and encourage private investment to develop its vast mineral wealth. The best service the United States can render Zambia (and all other African states) is to keep our tariffs low, buy more, sell more, and encourage international commerce by all means at our disposal.

The policy of U.S. harassment of South Africa will certainly fail and will cost us a good market for our exports and investments and for needed strategic minerals. The United States should therefore use its diplomatic and commercial leverage (a leverage diminished since the 1986 antiapartheid law imposing further sanctions on South Africa) to follow a policy of moderate persuasion and selective engagement designed to bring about reform in South Africa—not revolutionary change. We should extend rather than diminish academic, cultural, athletic, diplomatic, and economic contacts with South Africa. We should point out to liberation fronts such as the ANC that it is in their interest to end Marxist-Leninist domination of their organizations. Only if they do so should the United States collaborate with them to assist the growth of democracy and economic development.

Sanctions, boycotts, and disinvestment have always failed; they have not brought an end to white rule, but they have reduced U.S. influence, hardened white resolve, and led blacks to unrealistic expectations. To date sanctions have only slowed the rate of growth of the South African economy and caused massive black unemployment; no major reforms have been enacted lately. So why continue sanctions?[17] Ending sanctions, pressing quietly for change, ending apartheid, increasing educational and job opportunities for blacks, expanding self-government for urban blacks, devising a system of consociation (proportional representation, joint veto power, coalition building)—these are attainable goals in the 1990s. Pretoria will only stop attacking its neighbors when it feels secure. When the Soviets and Cubans withdraw from Angola there can be a realistic chance for Namibian independence and for a southern African association that will profit both South Africa and all adjacent countries.

In sum, during the 1990s the United States should amend Lenin's dictum to "All power to the moderates." We do not want to recolonize Africa; we do not want to be paternalistic. We share neither the exaggerated optimism of yesteryear nor the excessive pessimism of today. We look at Africa's problems in terms of enlightened U.S. interest. We are convinced that Americans and Africans have a common stake in political stability, peace, and development. Moreover, we do not want to exaggerate the influence that the United States can exert in Africa. U.S. influence can best be exercised by quiet advice and pressure, by the judicious allocation of aid and technical assistance, and by a restrained diplomacy that emphasizes mutual interests. The U.S. political model of constitutionalism and congressional democracy cannot be exported in toto, but Africans can learn from our experiences. U.S. actions in Africa in the 1990s should therefore be modeled after our successful efforts in rebuilding and democratizing our friends and enemies after World War II, especially through the Marshall Plan. Officials did not force or impose reforms; they suggested and cooperated in writing constitutions, reshaping governments, and restructuring industry and agriculture. These efforts brought about the recovery of Western Europe and Japan and the modernization of Taiwan. There is still hope for Africa if we can rediscover the idealism and realism of U.S. occupation policies and the

Marshall Plan. The future of Africa will best be served during the 1990s not by statism and revolution but by revisionism, reconciliation, and reform.

Notes

1. See Peter Duignan and L. H. Gann, "The Case for the White Man," *New Leader*, January 2, 1961, pp. 16–20.

2. Gwendolen M. Carter, ed., *African One-Party States* (Ithaca, N.Y.: Cornell University Press, 1961), p. 9.

3. René Dumont, *L'Afrique est mal partie* (Paris: Seuil, 1978). See, e.g., World Bank, *Toward Sustained Development in Sub-Saharan Africa: A Joint Program of Action* (Washington, D.C.: World Bank, 1984); Peter Duignan and Robert H. Jackson, eds., *Politics and Government in African States, 1960–1985* (Stanford: Hoover Institution Press, 1986); Gwendolen M. Carter and Patrick O'Meara, eds., *African Independence: The First Twenty-Five Years* (Bloomington: Indiana University Press, 1985).

4. See *Accelerated Development in Sub-Saharan Africa: An Agenda for Action* (Washington, D. C.: World Bank, 1981), p. 9.

5. See Alan Rufus Waters, "A Behavioral Model of Pan-African Disintegration Again," *African Studies Review* 14 (September 1971): 300. For a critique of Waters's view, see Kalonji Ntalaja, ibid., pp. 292–97. See also Arthur T. Porter, "University Development in Africa," *African Affairs* 71 (January 1972): 74.

6. For a classic critique of foreign aid, see P. T. Bauer, *Dissent On Development: Studies and Debates in Development Economics* (Cambridge, Mass.: Harvard University Press, 1972). For a critique of U.S. programs, see Peter Duignan and L. H. Gann, *The United States and Africa: A History* (Cambridge, Eng.: Cambridge University Press, 1984), pp. 314–24.

7. *Accelerated Development*, p. 15.

8. See Duignan and Jackson, *Politics and Government*.

9. Victor T. Le Vine, *Political Corruption: The Ghana Case* (Stanford: Hoover Institution Press, 1975), p. 113. For official investigations, see, e.g., Republic of Kenya, *Review of Statutory Boards: Report and Recommendations of the Committee Appointed by His Excellency the President* (Nairobi: Government Printer, 1979); Republic of Zambia, *National Assembly: Report of the Committee on Parastatal Bodies* (Lusaka: Government Printer, 1978–1981), 3 vols.

10. P. T. Bauer, "Foreign Aid and The Third World," Peter Duignan and Alvin Rabushka, eds., *The United States and Africa in the 1980s* (Stanford: Hoover Institution Press, 1980), pp. 559–83.

11. See Andrew A. Beveridge and Anthony R. Oberschall, *African Businessmen and Development in Zambia* (Princeton: Princeton Univesity Press, 1979), esp. pp. 212, 219.

12. Thomas H. Henriksen, "Lusophone Africa: Angola, Mozambique, and Guinea-Bisseau," in Duignan and Jackson, *Politics and Government*, p. 391.

13. Elliot Berg, "The Potential of the Private Sector in Africa," *Washington Quarterly* 8, no. 4 (Fall 1985): 73–83.

14. Ibid., p. 75.

15. L. H. Gann and Peter Duignan, *Why South Africa Will Survive* (New York: St. Martin's Press, 1981).

16. See Larry Diamond, "Introduction: Roots of Failure, Seeds of Hope," in Larry Diamond, Juan J. Linz, and Seymour Martin Lipset, eds., *Democracy in Developing Countries: Africa* (Boulder, Co.: Lynne Riener Publishers, 1988), pp. 25–29. See also Duignan and Gann, *The United States and Africa*, pp. 284–300; and L. H. Gann and Peter Duignan, *Africa South of the Sahara* (Stanford: Hoover Institution Press, 1981).

17. See Peter Duignan, "The Case Against Disinvestment," *Orbis: A Journal of World Affairs* 31, no. 1 (Spring 1987): 6–19.

RICHARD F. STAAR

◆ ———————————————— ◆

The Soviet Union Abroad

◆ Ever since the Bolshevik Revolution the foreign policy of the USSR has been guided by principles enunciated in a basic party document. Only three times since 1917 have congresses issued such programmatic statements. The most recent one, binding at least through the year 2000, includes the following under "CPSU [Communist Party of the Soviet Union] Tasks in the International Arena":

- ◆ Cooperation with socialist states
- ◆ Strengthening relations with liberated countries
- ◆ Relations with capitalist states: the struggle for lasting peace and disarmament
- ◆ The CPSU in the world workers' and communist movement[1]

How have Soviet leaders pursued these objectives in practice, and how are they likely to do so in the future?

The Socialist Commonwealth

Soviet ideologists have arrogated to themselves the word *socialist*, which actually means communist and has little in common with genuine labor or social democratic political movements in the West. The so-called socialist commonwealth now has twelve members: Bulgaria (which joined the Council for Mutual Economic Assistance [CMEA] in 1949), Czechoslovakia (1949), Hungary (1949), Poland (1949), Romania (1949), the USSR (1949), East Germany (1950), Mongolia (1962), Cuba (1972), Vietnam (1978), Cambodia (observer status), and Laos (observer status). The Soviet Union hopes to bring in the other communist-ruled states as well: Albania, mainland China, North Korea, and Yugoslavia (an associate CMEA member).

The USSR probably expects Albania and Yugoslavia to rejoin the bloc in the 1990s. It may even hope that a future Chinese leadership will draw closer to Moscow. Although relations with North Korea remain ambiguous, the number of Soviet delegations visiting Pyongyang has increased over the past several years.

The main instrument of USSR control over the socialist commonwealth includes the military divisions stationed throughout the northern tier (East Germany, Poland, Czechoslovakia) and Hungary. Other leverage centers on CMEA, which has been used on occasion to coerce member governments in Central Europe. These regimes import 70 percent of their iron ore, 93 percent of their coal, and 68 percent of their petroleum requirements from other CMEA countries. By 1990, however, they will be forced to purchase half of their energy needs from outside the bloc,[2] so this economic instrument may diminish in importance.

Per capita gross national product (GNP) growth in Central Europe has declined steadily from 1970–1975 (4.9 percent) through 1975–1980 (2.0 percent) to 1980–1985 (1.2 percent), with the distinct possibility that the bloc is becoming a greater economic burden to the Soviet Union. One estimate suggests that trade subsidies, credits, and economic aid during one recent year cost the USSR the equivalent of U.S. $10–15 billion.[3] Another problem involves the hard-currency debt, which surpassed $100 billion for all of Central Europe (including Yugoslavia) and reached $36.7 billion for the Soviet Union itself.[4] Moscow has assets in Western banks of about $15 billion. Other bloc governments (especially Poland, the largest debtor) continue to hope that the World Bank and/or the International Monetary Fund will come to their rescue.

Certain trends within the Central European countries adjacent to the Soviet Union portend change in the 1990s. However, the client states remain bound politically, economically, and militarily to their metropole. Transitions in local communist party leadership should be peaceful, since an heir apparent has been selected for most regimes. However, opposition political parties are out of the question as long as the indigenous satraps can rely on the USSR for support and protection.

CMEA binds the Central European regimes to a system that may never catch up with the computer revolution now sweeping the rest of the industrialized world. Even before launching its recent economic reforms, the USSR had allowed diversity in Hungary and Poland. But change like that attempted under Alexander Dubček before June 1968 in Czechoslovakia will be resisted.[5]

During the 1990s the people, though not the regimes, of Central Europe will be less willing to accept Soviet domination. Moscow probably anticipates and fears future revolutionary outbreaks and/or the spontaneous development of Solidarity-type labor unions. Allowing greater autonomy is not a solution, because it would permit closer contacts with Western Europe and the United States. In an address to the Tenth Congress in Warsaw of the ruling Polish United Workers' Party, Soviet leader Mikhail Gorbachev drew the line at fundamental systemic change when he reiterated the Brezhnev doctrine by implicitly threatening military intervention.[6]

The armed forces in the northern tier of Central Europe might not willingly fight against the West. After the complete elimination of intermediate- and short-range nuclear missiles in early 1991, however, the overwhelming conventional superiority of the Warsaw Pact could change that attitude to one of support for the Soviet Union.

The Liberated Countries

If most of Central Europe can be called the contiguous empire of the USSR, then certain Third World states comprise the extended empire.[7] These less-developed countries (LDCs) are endowed with reserves of strategic raw materials and are near 23 of the 31 maritime choke points, or channels of water essential for international trade. To Moscow the most important among the LDCs are those with a so-called socialist orientation.

In 1978 a Soviet official listed only 9 countries in this category; less than a decade later, another one gave the number as 40.[8] Despite past setbacks (Indonesia, Egypt, Somalia), Soviet influence has steadily expanded. The CPSU program emphasizes cooperation with "revolutionary-democratic parties."[9] Also known as vanguard parties, these represent an intermediate stage between national liberation movements and a recognized communist party.

National liberation movements comprise organizations fighting to overthrow governments in power. For example, the African National Congress (ANC) is directed against the Republic of South Africa and the South-West African People's Organization (SWAPO) against the regime in Namibia. Another such movement, the People's Front for Liberation of Sakiet al-Hamra and Rio de Oro (Polisario) remains active in the Western Sahara against Morocco. The Palestine Liberation Organization (PLO) operates against Israel, although its headquarters are in Tunisia. The Association of Revolutionary Organizations in Guatemala and the Farabundo Martí National Liberation Front (FMNLF) in El Salvador belong to the same category. All are supported by the Soviet Union. Although armed opposition may not flare up throughout the USSR's contiguous empire of Central Europe, several of the active insurgencies in its extended empire should continue into the 1990s. There are approximately 500,000 insurgents fighting against Soviet-supported regimes throughout the Third World.[10]

Despite the absence of any recognized African communist party in power at this time, the USSR has attained considerable influence throughout Africa since the breakup of the Portuguese empire. Angola and Mozambique are ruled by Marxist-Leninist vanguard movements, whereas Guinea-Bissau has a socialist orientation. Praise is lavished on these client states, all of which rely on Soviet assistance. Moscow's greatest gains have come in Ethiopia, however, where several thousand USSR and Central European technicians have been guiding the ruling workers' party and its armed forces to develop Marxist-Leninist politico-economic structures.[11]

The Arab-Israeli conflict and the Iran-Iraq war complicate USSR relations in the Islamic world. Despite Gorbachev's support for Iraq, preceded by $2.5 billion in arms on credit, the U.S. Department of State reported that Central European regimes were selling weapons to Iran.[12] Meanwhile the Soviets have directly committed 120,000 troops to a debilitating war in Afghanistan since December 1979. Already about 4.5 million Afghans, one-fourth of the population, have fled to Iran and Pakistan. The Kabul regime's armed forces have declined from 80,000 to 30,000 under four consecutive puppet rulers. Gorbachev recently indicated he would like to withdraw from this no-win situation by the end of 1988.

Only one Middle Eastern country, the People's Democratic Republic of [South] Yemen, has a vanguard party in power. The Soviets reestablished influence there after thwarting a coup attempt in 1986. Although India considers itself neutral, it signed a friendship treaty with the USSR in 1971 (see Table 1). Arms transfers from Moscow to Delhi between 1981 and 1985 totaled $4.2 billion.[13]

Cambodia appears to be in the process of establishing a coalition government, with Prince Norodom Sihanouk as a figurehead and symbol of reconciliation. USSR-supported Vietnamese occupation forces should then be able to exterminate the resistance, which has relied on mainland China for weapons in the past.

The USSR has made substantial inroads also throughout the Western Hemisphere. During the mid-1980s Soviet economic assistance to Cuba averaged $4.6 billion per year, or about one-fourth of Cuba's GNP.[14] The island in return provides ground, naval, and air facilities for its benefactor.

Table 1
Treaties and Declarations of Friendship
and Cooperation in the Third World

Country	Date	Place	Duration (years)	Abrogated
Egypt	May 27, 1971	Cairo	15	March 15, 1976
India[a]	August 9, 1971	New Delhi	20	
Iraq	April 9, 1972	Baghdad	15	November 13, 1977
Somalia	July 11, 1974	Mogadishu	20	
Angola	October 8, 1976	Moscow	20	
Mozambique	March 31, 1977	Maputo	20	
Vietnam[a]	November 3, 1978	Moscow	25	
Ethiopia[a]	November 20, 1978	Moscow	20	
Afghanistan[a]	December 5, 1978	Moscow	20	
South Yemen[a]	October 25, 1979	Moscow	20	
Syria	October 8, 1980	Moscow	20	
Congo	May 13, 1981	Moscow	20	
North Yemen	October 9, 1984	Moscow	20	
Mali[b]	July 18, 1986	Moscow	—	
Burkina Faso[b]	October 12, 1986	Moscow	—	
Benin[b]	November 25, 1986	Moscow	—	

[a] The World Bank ranked these five countries in the lowest annual per capita income category at the time these treaties were signed (*Washington Post*, May 14, 1978).

[b] These declarations on further development of friendship and cooperation may lead to formal treaties.

SOURCES: *Pravda*, May 28, 1971; August 10, 1971; April 10, 1972; July 13, 1974; October 9, 1976; April 2, 1977; November 4, 1978; November 21, 1978; December 6, 1978; October 26, 1979; October 9, 1980; May 14, 1981; October 11, 1984; July 20, 1986; October 13, 1986; November 28, 1986. "Egypt Breaks Off Soviet Pact," *Facts on File, 1976,* p. 193; "Somalia Expels Soviets, Cubans," *Facts on File, 1977,* p. 874.

Cuban mercenaries also function as surrogates for Moscow in several African countries.

A second Soviet foothold has been established in Nicaragua. The formula for success, devised by Fidel Castro, included unification of the extreme left, a coalition with noncommunist elements, isolation of the right, and "fraternal" assistance from abroad.[15] About 15,000 Bulgarians, Cubans, East Germans, Libyans, Soviets, PLO members, and other terrorists serve as advisers. All five top Sandinista leaders received training in Havana, and one of them (planning chief Henry Ruiz Hernández) spent two years at the USSR's Patrice Lumumba University. By 1995 the Sandinista armed forces will total 600,000 or more men.[16] The enormous quantities of weapons shipped to Nicaragua suggest that the USSR is using the country for stockpiling military equipment in anticipation of a protracted struggle throughout Central America and the Caribbean.[17]

Relations with the United States

The CPSU claims that it follows the "Leninist principle of peaceful coexistence with countries that have different social systems."[18] Peaceful coexistence, or détente, provides a relatively safe framework within which support for wars of national liberation in the Third World, on the one hand, and so-called active measures within the developed countries, on the other, can be pursued. It also serves as a useful slogan for mobilizing Western public opinion in support of Soviet foreign policy.

USSR allocations for defense from 1978 through 1987, however, were one-third higher than those of the United States and produced nine times as many artillery pieces, five times as many surface-to-air missiles, over three times the number of tanks, and twice as many fighters, helicopters, and submarines.[19] Soviet military spending continues to absorb 15 to 17 percent of GNP.

The USSR buildup has taken place since the first strategic arms limitation treaty (SALT I) was signed in 1972, during negotiations for and following the signing of SALT II in 1979, and in the course of talks that finally led to the intermediate-range nuclear forces (INF) treaty in December 1987. None of these diplomatic activities seems to have affected Soviet military expansion.[20]

The INF agreement will not slow down this momentum. In fact, the treaty specifically states that each side's nuclear warheads and guidance elements will be removed intact. Only the missile, launch canister, and launcher itself are to be destroyed or cut into pieces as specified.[21] Nothing prevents the USSR from using warheads and their guidance systems from dismantled SS-20s in the new SS-25s. The INF treaty may well leave a modernized Soviet nuclear strike force confronting a Western Europe stripped of U.S. intermediate- and short-range nuclear weapons after 1991.

If the INF agreement will be difficult, a strategic arms reduction treaty (START) may be impossible to verify. The question remains whether the Soviets have ever intended to abide by any arms control obligations. President Reagan has submitted six reports on USSR noncompliance with such agreements since 1972. The bipartisan General Advisory Committee on

Arms Control and Disarmament prepared a classified study on Soviet violations that went back a quarter of a century.[22]

Despite the USSR's growing strategic superiority, the open supply of weapons to Marxist-Leninist regimes in the Third World, the invasion of Afghanistan, the suppression of Solidarity in Poland, and noncompliance with past agreements, U.S. and NATO officials have apparently decided to renew détente. This change in attitude may have something to do with Soviet public relations.

The USSR probably spends over four billion dollars each year on propaganda activities. Many of them are conducted through such international front organizations as the World Peace Council (WPC), which mobilizes public support abroad for Soviet foreign policy. A WPC-staged world parliament of peoples for peace in Sofia, Bulgaria, reportedly attracted 2,260 carefully selected delegates from 134 countries who unanimously approved a pro-Soviet "charter of the peoples for peace."[23]

Although a large number of indigenous communists belong to the Campaign for Nuclear Disarmament in Britain and the KGB's *Novosti* Press Agency ran an entire peace movement in Switzerland,[24] the rank-and-file members unwittingly serve the cause of Moscow. Since their influence on government policy is limited, the Soviet propaganda machine years ago began to target Western businessmen, lawyers, intellectuals, and government officials.

High-level conferences and international meetings continue under the auspices of the Pugwash group, founded by the late Canadian industrialist Cyrus Eaton. A smaller operation, restricted to USSR and U.S. personalities, started at Dartmouth College and alternates sessions between the two countries. A specialized organization, International Physicians for the Prevention of Nuclear War, was cofounded by Drs. Bernard Lown of Harvard University and Evgenii I. Chazov. Now health minister, Chazov had denounced Andrei Sakharov in a letter to *Izvestiia*.[25] Gorbachev's separate meetings with businessmen and intellectuals during his December 1987 visit to Washington, D.C., followed this pattern.

The World Revolutionary Process

This last objective of Soviet foreign policy encompasses communist parties, the national liberation movement, and the left wing of Western socialist and labor parties, all of which were represented at the Twenty-seventh CPSU Congress in Moscow: 84 communist parties from capitalist countries or administrative units, such as Puerto Rico and West Berlin; some 33 revolutionary democratic parties and national liberation groups; about 23 left-socialist and social democratic or labor parties; and the Congress and Center parties from India and Finland, respectively.[26]

Communist or workers' parties recognized by the CPSU rule 16 regimes and form part of the opposition in 80 other countries throughout the world. The latter group comprises just under 4.7 million from a total claimed world membership of 82 million communists (including 46 million members of the Chinese Communist Party).[27]

The Soviets find it impossible to influence all of these communist parties. For example, neither the Albanians nor the Chinese attended the Twenty-seventh Congress. No serious attempts have been made since 1969 to organize an international meeting of communist parties, and even Gorbachev has suggested that such a conference would be inappropriate.[28]

USSR support for national liberation movements, as an aspect of the world revolutionary process, has concentrated more on Africa and Asia than on Latin America, which has a relatively developed capitalism and a strong working class as well as communist parties in almost all countries. Of course the Soviets also help Latin American movements, such as the Marxist-led insurgency in El Salvador. The local communist party leader represented the FMNLF on trips to Cuba, Vietnam, Ethiopia, the USSR (twice), Bulgaria, Czechoslovakia, Hungary, and East Germany. All eight regimes promised to supply weapons, ammunition, and uniforms.[29]

The most important vehicle by which the Soviets influence moderate socialists, especially in Western Europe, has been the Socialist International (SI), which includes 75 national organizations and about 20 million members. At least 15 of these groups have representatives on the World Peace Council, the best known among all CPSU-controlled international communist front organizations.[30]

Only a few days after the Soviet invasion of Afghanistan, SI president Willy Brandt of West Germany proclaimed that the world still suffers from too little détente. The following month (January 1980), without mentioning Soviet aggression, an SI disarmament commission was established under the late Olof Palme of Sweden. Subsequent interviews with moderate socialist leaders throughout northern Europe indicated a definite move toward Moscow's position on arms control.

It is possible that only left-wing socialists are consciously in tune with the world revolutionary process. Less reliable, although even more useful to the USSR on occasion, have been people like Brandt and the late Palme or the late Indira Gandhi because of their international influence. They do not seem to have been Moscow-controlled and probably reached their relatively pro-Soviet outlook independently.

In conclusion, one should anticipate that the training, supply, and coordination of armed forces in Marxist-Leninist and communist-ruled client states overseas—especially those near the southern borders of the United States and in Asia—will be more important than ever in the 1990s for the USSR. Recruits from Angola and Nicaragua will join Cubans and Vietnamese in the Soviet foreign legion. The main operations at that time may well concentrate on Central America.

Moscow could face possible turmoil among its allies in the coming decade, although the most distant Soviet armed detachments will make sure that factional infighting does not diminish Moscow's influence. Such prepositioned combat units for special designation (*spetsnaz*) already exist and would provide insurance for highly speculative politico-military ventures far from home.

Investments in proletarian internationalism, however dangerous, could pay large dividends. Once an active front is opened along the southern border of the United States, for example, the U.S. role in the world will end—assuming the United States does not strike back at the source of its troubles, namely, the USSR. Such a decision would depend on the correlation of strategic forces between the United States and the Soviet Union. By 1995 the latter may have good reason for confidence that the military balance has shifted decisively in its favor, unless future U.S. presidents remember that "the most significant threat to U.S. national interests remains that posed by the Soviet Union."[31]

Notes

1. Communist Party of the Soviet Union, *Programma Kommunisticheskoi Partii Sovetskogo Soiuza* (Moscow: Politizdat, 1986), pp. 60–74 (hereafter cited as *CPSU Program*).

2. Richard F. Staar, *USSR Foreign Policies After Détente*, rev. ed. (Stanford: Hoover Institution Press, 1987), p. 163.

3. Charles Wolf, Jr., et al., *The Costs and Benefits of the Soviet Empire* (Santa Monica: Rand Corp., 1986), R-3419-NA, table 14, p. 35.

4. Central Intelligence Agency, *Handbook of Economic Statistics, 1987* (Washington, D.C.: Directorate of Intelligence, 1987), CPAS 87–10001, tables 33 and 51, pp. 60, 75 (hereafter cited as *CIA Handbook*).

5. Speech by Miloš Jakeš, newly elected general secretary of the Communist Party of Czechoslovakia, summarized by *Pravda*, December 19, 1987, p. 4.

6. "Speech by Comrade Gorbachev, M.S.," *Pravda*, July 1, 1986, p. 1.

7. Henry S. Rowen and Charles Wolf, Jr., eds., *The Future of the Soviet Empire* (New York: St. Martin's Press, 1988), esp. chap. 13, pp. 279–324.

8. Evgenii M. Primakov, "Certain Problems in the Developing Countries,"

Kommunist, no. 11 (July 1978): pp. 81–82; Karen N. Brutents, "Liberated Countries and the Anti-Imperialist Struggle," *Pravda*, January 10, 1986, p. 3.

9. *CPSU Program*, p. 65.

10. Commission on Integrated Long-Term Strategy, *Discriminate Deterrence* (Washington, D.C.: Government Printing Office, 1988), p. 14.

11. *CIA Handbook*, p. 126, gives the number of military technicians.

12. Cited by the *New York Times*, October 2, 1986.

13. U.S. Arms Control and Disarmament Agency, *World Military Expenditures and Arms Transfers* (Washington, D.C.: Government Printing Office, 1987), table 3, p. 146.

14. *CIA Handbook*, table 86, p. 116.

15. U.S. Department of State and U.S. Department of Defense, *The Challenge to Democracy in Central America* (Washington, D.C.: Government Printing Office, 1986), pp. 17–36.

16. Dispatch from Managua in the *New York Times*, December 16, 1987, pp. 1, 5, quoting the Nicaraguan defense minister.

17. A similar communist operation on a much smaller scale had been planned for Grenada. The combined U.S.-Caribbean landing force expelled all Bulgarians, Cubans, East Germans, Libyans, North Koreans, and Soviets. U.S. Department of State, *Lesson of Grenada* (Washington, D.C.: 1986), publication 9459, analyzes captured documents.

18. *CPSU Program*, p. 67.

19. Commission on Integrated Long-Term Strategy, *Discriminate Deterrence*, p. 28.

20. Richard F. Staar, ed., *Arms Control: Myth Versus Reality* (Stanford: Hoover Institution Press, 1988), paperback ed., esp. chap. 1, "The Arms Control Record," by William R. Van Cleave, pp. 1–23.

21. *Treaty Between the United States of America and the Union of Soviet Socialist Republics on the Elimination of Their Intermediate-Range and Shorter-Range Missiles* (Washington, D.C.: Government Printing Office, December 1987), pp. 4–11.

22. General Advisory Committee on Arms Control and Disarmament, *A Quarter Century of Soviet Compliance Practices Under Arms Control Commitments, 1958–1983: Summary* (Washington, D.C.: Government Printing Office, 1984), pp. 15; unclassified.

23. Vladimir Bukovsky, "Peace as a Political Weapon," in Sidney Hook et al., *Soviet Hypocrisy and Western Gullibility* (Washington, D.C.: Ethics and Public Policy Center, 1987), p. 18, citing *Pravda* and *Izvestiia*.

24. Ibid., p. 22.

25. Cited in Staar, *USSR Foreign Policies*, pp. 72–74.

26. Ibid., p. 9.

27. N. F. Shumikhin, ed., *Sotsializm i sovremennyi mir* (Kiev: Vyshcha shkola, 1987), pp. 20–21; *Pravda*, October 25, 1987, p. 4.

28. See his interview with *L'Unita* (Milan), May 22, 1985.

29. U.S. Department of State, *Communist Interference in El Salvador* (Washington, D.C.: Government Printing Office, 1981), Special Report no. 80.

30. The Socialist International is considered part of the international workers' movement by V. V. Zagladin et al., *Mezhdunarodnoe rabochee dvizhenie* (Moscow: Politizdat, 1984), pp. 72–106; Wallace Spaulding, "Communist Fronts," *Problems of Communism* 37, no. 1 (January–February 1988), pp. 57–68.

31. Ronald Reagan, *National Security Strategy of the United States* (Washington, D.C.: White House, 1988), p. 26.

CASPAR W. WEINBERGER

◆ ——————————————————————— ◆

National Defense in the Next Decade

◆ The perennial question of how much and what kind of national defense we need—now or in the next decade, or indeed in any decade—should take us back to the most basic question of all: Why do we need any national defense?

The amount of defense spending, and what it is spent for, should be determined by one yardstick only. What are the threats to our freedom and our peace, and what must we do to preserve our peace and freedom in a world inhabited also by the Soviet Union, with its strong military capability and its unchanging goal of world domination?

Our national defense in the 1990s, as in the 1980s, must be strong and effective enough to convince the Soviets that any attack against us or our allies could never be successful or yield them any advantage.

Translating this defense requirement into dollars is always difficult. The equations of deterrence are always hard to calculate and quantify. But the margin of error allowed our military planners is exceedingly small. We know only two things for certain: (1) we can easily afford to do what we have to do to stay free, if our freedom is still important to us; (2) if we do not do enough, we will never know it until it is too late.

The amount of defense spending we require in any given year cannot be a unilateral decision but will rise and fall depending on the nature of the Soviet threat or other threats that may develop.

In the past—throughout the 1950s and the 1960s with full prosperity— we have spent nearly twice as large a percentage of the gross national product on defense as we do now. In fact, as recently as 1974 we were spending a larger portion of our annual federal budget on defense than we do today.

Of course, we cannot and should not carry the full burden ourselves. We must have strong allies for our own security, just as they need us to preserve their own freedom. Alliances must be completely interdependent and mutually supportive relationships. The United States, the North Atlantic Treaty Organization (NATO), Europe, Japan, Korea, China, the Association of Southeast Asian Nations (ASEAN)—indeed all the free nations of the world—must work together. We are best able to defend the United States from forward-deployed positions held by our forces and those of our allies. If Europe should fall, or Japan or Korea or Australia or any of the others, then the defense of the United States would be infinitely more difficult, and probably impossible. *We cannot afford the wrongheadedness, the selfishness, and the inherent folly of isolationism, economic or military.*

It is now the rage to predict the downfall of the very fiber of the West—in the economic, military, and moral spheres. Some postulate that the power and influence of the United States is destined to shrink. These doomsayers argue that the West in general, and the United States in particular, is entering a preordained era of decline. The new guru of this group is Paul Kennedy, author of a current best-seller, *The Rise and Fall of the Great Powers*.[1] His thesis is that the United States will inevitably collapse like the profligate empires in sixteenth-century Spain and eighteenth-century France, and indeed all prior civilizations. Such predictions evoke memories of the Club of Rome's dour and quite wrong forecasts in the 1970s about overpopulation, environmental Armageddon, and the exhaustion of the world's resources. Today's doomsayers argue that the United States is reeling from imperial overstretch and must drastically scale back its role in today's world. These arguments represent a return to Fortress America. Some Democratic presidential candidates have argued for a form of neoisolationism in the area of trade. The fundamental problem with these flawed analyses is that if enough people accept them at face value, they could well become a self-fulfilling prophecy.

Isolationism represents a great and recurring threat to the United States and our allies. It has the potential to damage alliances, hurt our economy, and ultimately threaten the security of the West. Fundamentally isolationism is the demagogic and seductive offer of permanent peace without effort. Maintaining the power and strength of our ideals and keeping our freedom *does* require a major effort. But it does not require constant intervention in combat. It requires nothing more than we can easily accomplish.

The use and commitment of U.S. combat forces to battle should be approached with caution, but this cautiousness is *not* isolationism. Our forces must be so strong that our capability to intervene militarily around the world is unquestioned. But the real question is, When and under what circumstances *should* U.S. forces intervene—and how can our intervention be effective?

In the increasingly complex world of the 1990s, this question becomes more difficult. But I think the answer can be found if we apply six tests. Before committing our forces to combat, the U.S. government should first determine that all of the following are true:

1. Our vital interests are at stake.
2. The issues involved are so important for the United States' and our allies' future that we are prepared to commit enough forces to win.
3. We have clearly defined political and military objectives, which we must secure.
4. We have sized our forces to achieve our objectives.
5. We have some reasonable assurance of the support of the American people.
6. U.S. forces are committed to combat only as a last resort.

In the past we have demonstrated that when our vital interests or those of our allies are threatened, we are ready to use force, and use it decisively. We should continue to do that. Our policy is not and never can be isolationist. In the future our society needs to think more about the variety of threats we face and the need to employ the varieties of our power available—to respond to some of those threats with covert action, for example, and to others with force. All of these considerations are consistent with the principle that we must have a clear mission—the success of which is vital to our nation—and that we must apply all the force necessary to achieve these vital objectives.

Our plans for the use of U.S. military forces and other elements of national power must recognize, as they do, that the United States, as the world's defender of freedom, has a difficult role. It is the fate of defenders, who have no aggressive plans or agendas, that they cannot choose the time, place, or method of attack. We must be better prepared than in the past to meet a wider range of contingencies, and we must also be able to choose the level and the means with which we will face the inevitable threats that confront us. Seeking to contain the level of potential conflict requires, among other things, active measures of aid, assistance, and training for our friends that will help deter conflict. That is how we make deterrence credible at all levels of conflict. And in choosing those active measures, we should seek to reduce the causes of conflict—political, economic, and social—before they lead to armed conflict.

To meet these threats successfully in the future, we must make more sophisticated use of the many elements of U.S. power we have at our disposal. These elements of power—such as diplomatic, economic, and even moral tools—can support and complement the application of military force under particular circumstances.

In the Third World in the 1990s, it will be increasingly vital to respond to future instability with the political and economic instruments of U.S. national power. It will be critical to seek out the root causes of instability and conflict *before* they lead to, and require, armed combat and the involvement of U.S. troops. Small increases in economic aid, training, security assistance, and other so-called nation-building activities could pay long-range dividends for the growth of democracy, world stability, and peace. But year after year Congress practices the false economy of cutting our requests for these funds as well as our requests for needed military spending so that they can continue increasing spending for politically popular domestic programs.

We have entered an era where the dividing lines between peace and war are less clearly drawn than ever before, and this trend is likely to accelerate in the 1990s. We and our allies now face a spectrum of threats from overt military attacks to a variety of lesser but equally dangerous threats—including covert action, internal subversion, pressure, intimidation, and terrorism. To protect our security and interests against these threats, we must be prepared to respond appropriately. The six tests mentioned earlier offer a way to frame possible responses.

In the decades ahead we must also make the most of the West's resources, playing to our strengths. The United States and the West have many inherent strengths—our superior technology, our economic prowess, and our political allies, among others. An initiative I began at the Pentagon, called competitive strategies, holds great promise as a creative means to make the most of Western strengths while exploiting Soviet weaknesses in the European theater. It may hold part of the solution to our future defense challenges, particularly in Europe after an intermediate-range nuclear forces (INF) agreement.

An intelligent and imaginative use of competitive strategies can even multiply the effectiveness of our defense funds and achieve a more effective force. Most important, it will enable us to maintain a robust deterrent without matching the Soviets plane for plane, ship for ship, and tank for tank. We have profited from such an approach in the past, and we can apply those lessons to even greater benefit in the future. Consider, for example, how our shift to low-level penetration bomber operations together with air-, surface-, and sea-launched cruise missiles capitalized on our technological strengths to prompt a huge Soviet investment in air defenses to protect its territory. This move diverted some resources that the Soviets could otherwise have invested in offensive forces capable of striking Americans and our allies.

A similar result was achieved in antisubmarine warfare (ASW). Our ASW capability reinforced the Soviet navy's defensive orientation, forcing the Soviets to keep their highly prized ballistic missile submarine fleet closer to home—thus reducing somewhat the threat to the sea-lanes and protecting our own shores.

As we seek to capitalize on these competitive strategies, we must continue to exploit such new developments as Stealth technology. Using U.S. technology to reduce the effectiveness of massive Soviet investments in air defense will force another diversion of Moscow's now apparently strained defense resources away from the offensive capabilities that threaten us. Another example of new competitive strategies is the unmanned Tacit Rainbow missile, which can help us compensate for our quantitative conventional inferiority vis-à-vis the Warsaw Pact. Tacit Rainbow can linger over targets, such as enemy radar systems, waiting for them to be turned on so that the missile can hunt them down. It attests to the value of selected advanced standoff technologies as force multipliers in countering the threat of massive Soviet numbers.

Competitive strategies must continue to be given the funding and priorities needed to bring the program to full fruition. The first competitive strategies task force (which examined mid- to high-intensity conventional conflict in Europe) concluded that the West should focus on technologies and tactics that can exploit Soviet and Warsaw Pact weaknesses. These areas include countering Soviet air operations, countering Soviet penetration of NATO forward defenses, stressing the Warsaw Pact troop control system, and countering Soviet global and multitheater operations. These will be programs of the 1990s. All four share some characteristics. Other technologies that the West should capitalize on include various unmanned systems, such as surface-to-surface, precision standoff, air-to-surface, and cruise missiles; drones; and remotely piloted vehicles, area munitions, various extended-range tube-launched projectiles, rapidly emplaceable barriers, precision penetrator warheads, and smart submunitions. Also we should take advantage of our advances in automatic data processing, intelligence fusion, and electronic miniaturization.

We need to recognize that such technologies are critical to the West's defenses and are made possible by our democratic system. We must protect our advanced technology from the Soviet Union, which is engaged in a constant effort, by purchase and by theft, to acquire what they thus far have not been able to develop for themselves.

Some in Europe see Mikhail Gorbachev's *glasnost'* through the same lens they used to view Brezhnev's détente fifteen years ago. They echo Soviet rhetoric about removing the "technological curtain" that divides Europe. They talk about ending "economic warfare" that dates back to the Cold War and that they say is now outmoded.

Such prophecies are both false and dangerous. They repeat the errors of the 1970s. At that time U.S. and West European political leaders hoped that an expanding East-West trade would strengthen those groups in Soviet politics associated with consumer goods and would weaken their military–heavy industry complex.

Instead, expanded trade between East and West helped fortify the position of the Soviet military establishment. High technology imported from the West went overwhelmingly to the military and space sectors. This choice of priorities indicates that, when faced with the Western openness of the 1970s, Soviet leaders chose to emphasize strategic and political competition rather than commercial cooperation in their relations with the West.

Through Gorbachev's *perestroika*, a Soviet offensive to promote the transfer of key Western technologies to the East has been taking shape. For example, Soviet economics ministries are pressing for joint ventures with Western firms that produce sensitive technologies. The USSR believes that it can establish close enough commercial and legal relations with selected Western firms to allow it to draw off technologies that have great military potential and are now controlled through proprietary, national, or Coordinating Committee on Multilateral Export Controls (COCOM) regulations.

The Toshiba-Kongsberg sales to the Soviets have shaken the Western alliance more than any export control case in recent memory. All those who wish to encourage legitimate East-West trade must be disturbed by this Soviet penetration of reputable European and Japanese companies. Since the Soviets see Western firms as a source for the theft of high technology, every corporate executive interested in the Soviet and East European market must concentrate as much on preventing espionage as on promoting sales. That is one of our vital defense priorities for the 1990s.

The importance of stemming the hemorrhage of Western technology to the Soviet Union could not be more clear. Soviet military leaders are counting on advanced technology—as much as possible from the West—to help them overtake whatever qualitative advantages in conventional weapons and equipment we still have. Soviet leaders state explicitly that advanced technology is critical to what they call the military-technical competition with the capitalist world. It is also clear that the military establishment supports Gorbachev's program of economic reform because they believe it will contribute to military modernization. The Central Intelligence Agency

(CIA) has stated publicly that "most signs" point to "broad-based military support" for economic modernization.[2]

Soviet leaders know that they are successfully challenging NATO's lead in many areas of conventional-arms technology. The West in turn is counting on new weapons systems to strengthen our defenses both in Europe and through the Strategic Defense Initiative (SDI). These conventional-force technologies will become even more important for NATO as U.S. intermediate-range nuclear forces are withdrawn from Europe. But they are expensive, and the savage cuts in requested military investment that Congress began reimposing in 1987 and 1988 put us at much greater risk than we should or need be. Another of the priorities of the 1990s should be to reverse those cuts and allocate the resources necessary to give us at least a 3 percent real growth in defense investment.

SDI must also play a central role in our defenses in the 1990s. It provides a far safer way to keep the peace, moving the world away from the threat of mutual assured destruction and toward a greater reliance on defensive systems. The critics of SDI have created a straw man argument. They say that a perfect defense cannot exist and therefore SDI is a waste of technical and financial resources. But the value of SDI must be viewed in phases. Deterrence, strategic stability, and arms reductions all would benefit from a first SDI phase. It would offer an important element of protection for all the West. It could, for example, provide significant protection from limited strikes from the Soviet Union and other countries. Additionally the first phase could protect us from an accidental launching of a part of an aggressor's ballistic missile force by shooting the missile or missiles down. By deploying SDI, we also greatly complicate the calculations of Soviet planners weighing the costs of an attack. Above all, SDI opens the way to deep reductions in offensive nuclear weapons with a margin of safety. That opportunity could be missing if we rush to give up nuclear weapons too soon or if any future president should yield to Soviet blandishments and agree to give up our SDI, leaving them free to pursue theirs, as they have, and they will.

If we have defenses in place, the Soviets have less incentive to cheat on any arms reduction agreements. If the United States and the Soviet Union agreed to destroy a portion of their ballistic missiles as they deployed defensive systems, they would be sending each other signals that neither side was seeking a strategic advantage.

We must also recognize that we are not alone in pursuing strategic defense. It is a serious misperception that the United States *alone* is involved in strategic defense. It is time to shed a little *glasnost'* on projects Moscow prefers to shield in secrecy: the USSR is deeply involved in its own strategic defense initiative and has been for nearly two decades. The Soviets are doing advanced work on laser weapons, involving ten thousand scientists and engineers and costing about $1 billion a year. The Soviets have already constructed at least one ground-based laser capable of damaging our satellites. Overall, the Soviet Union has spent $150 billion on all forms of strategic defense in the last ten years alone while purporting to adhere to the antiballistic missile treaty and loudly decrying any effort we make to acquire defenses against their missiles. In contrast, in 1987 the United States spent $3.6 billion on SDI, slightly more than 1 percent of the U.S. defense budget. And Congress threatens to cut this back even further in the future.

The technological developments making SDI possible will continue to move forward. The only question is whether the United States will sustain the funding and the will and the clarity of vision necessary to strengthen our security through SDI. A world in which both we and the Soviets come to rely more on defenses against nuclear attack and less on the mutually suicidal threat of massive retaliation would be a far safer place.

The most important challenge we will face in the 1990s and beyond is the same challenge we have faced since our country's inception. We must persuade the public, and thereby our Congress, that we must make the investments necessary to preserve peace with freedom. It is the fate, the paradox, and possibly the ultimate destruction of free, open democratic societies that they are frequently unwilling to spend the amounts necessary to keep themselves free.

Alexis de Tocqueville recognized this dilemma. The problem of sustaining the consensus for defense spending is much broader than just concerns about the deficit. It is basically an unpopular endeavor for a democracy. De Tocqueville more than 150 years ago pointed this out:

> The ever-increasing numbers of men of property who are lovers of peace, the growth of personal wealth which war so rapidly consumes, the mildness of manners, the gentleness of heart, those tendencies to pity which are produced by the equality of conditions, that coolness of understanding which renders men comparatively insensible to the violent and poetical excitement of arms, all of these causes concur to quench the military spirit [in a democracy].[3]

Whenever we fail to make and keep our military strong enough to preserve us and our allies from attack, we invite aggression. In the words of President Reagan, "We tempt tyrants." The same temptation is offered when congressmen and senators, who have come late to worrying about deficits, conclude that less politically popular programs such as defense spending can be more easily cut than domestic spending, always perceived as politically more popular. The inevitable result is that defense budgets must be constructed with no real consideration of the most basic question: How much do we need to deter attack?

Easy and generally wrong rationalizations are offered:

♦ "I am for a strong defense, but there are not enough votes in it."

♦ "There is waste in the Pentagon, so it is all right to vote for deep cuts."

♦ "We cannot afford to be in so many parts of the world. We need to give up these broad commitments" and presumably concentrate on defending the United States alone because we are doomed by historical imperatives to ultimate collapse anyway. This is the Paul Kennedy thesis, which gives isolationism much false ammunition and pleases a Congress bent on defense cuts and domestic spending increases.

♦ "The Soviets have changed and genuinely want to reduce armaments, and so should we. We can trust this nice Mr. Gorbachev."

♦ "Reduced expenditures will be all right, because they will mean a leaner, better prepared, albeit smaller force"—even though the Soviets continue to add to the massive conventional lead they already have over us.

Indeed, there is no end to the various ways defense reductions can be rationalized. The ultimate false rationalization is Professor Kennedy's: the United States is doomed, by the rhythm of history, to decline and lose power and influence—so let us retreat and enjoy it as we become weaker.[4]

There is one major difficulty with all these canards. None of them changes or reduces the threat from the Soviet Union, with its great superiority in most forms of arms, with its aggressive intentions, and with its autocratic system that allows huge military investments without challenge by public opinion. This Soviet threat must continue to drive our defenses in the 1990s, as it has in the past. We must continue to cast for new creative ways to keep peace with freedom. (SDI and competitive strategies hold some of the answers.) But above all, we must sustain the consensus for spending the amounts for defense that are required to deter our adversaries. Our way of life and the freedoms we enjoy depend on it.

Notes

1. Paul M. Kennedy, *The Rise and Fall of the Great Powers* (New York: Random House, 1987).

2. CIA statement to the Congressional Joint Economic Committee, Subcommittee on National Security Economics, September 14, 1987.

3. Alexis de Tocqueville, *Democracy in America*, trans. Henry Reeve (New York: Vintage, 1945), 2:279.

4. See Kennedy, *Great Powers*, p. 515.

◆ PART II ◆

International Economic Issues

CHARLES WOLF, JR.

The Rise of Market Forces

The Dramatic Effects of Gradual Change

♦ Major changes in the international environment can come about through two different processes: the gradual accumulation of small changes or abrupt and sharply discontinuous events. The gradualism of the first process often belies the depth and breadth of the accumulated changes. The rise of market forces around the world in the past decade has illustrated this phenomenon. We might more accurately describe the phenomenon as the rediscovery of the power and value of market forces, because market forces held sway in the industrialized world from the end of the eighteenth century until the growth of Marxism, Fabian socialism, and social democracy in the mid-twentieth century. The gradual revival of interest in and recognition of market forces has made the international economic landscape of the 1990s fundamentally different from that of prior decades.

Markets and Governments in the Allocation of Resources

Before reviewing the altered role of market forces, considering their future prospects, and reflecting on what U.S. policies toward them should be, we should dispel certain myths and acknowledge certain truths about market forces and the relative roles of markets and nonmarkets (or governments) in influencing the allocation of economic resources.

The cardinal policy issue facing modern economic systems concerns the appropriate roles and relative scale of government and markets. The choice is not clear-cut between perfect governments and imperfect or inadequate markets, or between perfect markets and imperfect or inadequate governments. The real choice is among imperfect markets, imperfect governments, and various combinations of the two. Thus the cardinal economic choice concerns the degree to which markets or governments—with their respective flaws—should determine the allocation, use, and distribution of resources.[1]

This issue pervades the U.S. political and economic scene. Disagreement about how to resolve it is one of the two principal differences between the Republican and Democratic parties. (The other is in their views of the Soviet Union—its objectives, the goals of its leadership, its prospects for fundamental systemic reform—and how the United States should conduct relations with it.) The market-versus-government issue also divides the business and financial communities (generally pro-market) from the media and academic communities (generally pro-government). To be sure, these divisions are often blurred by the willingness of protagonists on both sides to adjust their principles to more immediate and practical considerations of self-interest.

Thus the U.S. business and financial communities, which typically extol the virtues of the market and contribute to the Republican party, are often in the forefront of lobbying activities favoring the protection of domestic markets against foreign competition. Similarly the academic and media communities, which typically extol the virtues of government intervention and contribute to the Democratic party, complain if the government intervention and assistance they generally favor is tied to standards or criteria pertaining to their own activities. For example, these latter groups plump for government aid to education but oppose having it conditioned on standards of performance established and evaluated by the government.

Milton Friedman has aptly commented on this familiar subservience of principle to self-interest by observing that pro-market advocates in industry seem to favor the market's free operation with regard to other industries while seeking government help for their own. In contrast, pro-government advocates in academia favor freedom from government restraint for their own activities while advocating government intervention to regulate the activities of others.

The real world has neither perfect markets nor perfect governments. Both are abstractions, useful for analytic purposes but dubious, if not dangerous, if extended too far or applied too rigidly. In the real world the markets-versus-government issue relates to the preferred degree of reliance on one or the other mode in allocating resources for the economy as a whole as well as for particular sectors. If the preferred choice favors the market, a significant role for the nonmarket will and, because of the pervasiveness and inevitability of market failure, *should* remain. This role relates especially to the production of so-called public goods such as defense and national security, to establishing and maintaining the legal and other environmental conditions for the effective functioning of markets, and to the provision of appropriate redistributive services and programs constituting an acceptable safety net for society and reflecting the standards of "distributive justice" with which that society is, as Jacob Viner put it, "tolerably content." [2]

But if the preferred choice favors allocative decision making by nonmarket means, a significant role for the market may and, because of the extent and inevitablility of nonmarket failure, should also remain. [3] This role relates especially to the production of private goods in amounts that comport with demand for them and to production methods that reflect the relative scarcity and productivity of production factors.

The genuinely striking change in the international economic landscape and in the agenda of economic policy discussion around the world in the past decade has been the sharp tilt toward greater reliance on market mechanisms and away from nonmarket mechanisms in the allocation, use, and distribution of resources.

Market-Oriented Policies in the Three Worlds

Although the trend toward greater reliance on markets has been global, its manifestation in the so-called First World (the industrialized and capitalist democracies of North America, Western Europe, and Japan) represents a resuscitation and renewal, whereas in the so-called Second World (the communist countries) and the even less aptly named Third World (the developing countries) [4] the trend is, for the most part, a genuine innovation that is largely unprecedented.

In the First World the expanded attention to market forces marks a midcourse adjustment, or at least a slowing down, in the rate of government expansion into market domains in the three or four preceding decades, when the welfare state and the programs of social democratic parties were growing. In contrast, among communist and developing countries the rise of market forces is largely a first-time reconsideration and restructuring of the centralized statist premises on which their economic policies have generally been based.

In the First World the reorientation toward market forces has been led by Ronald Reagan's administration in the United States and Margaret Thatcher's Conservative government in the United Kingdom. From its inception in the 1980 campaign, the Reagan administration has stressed incentive-oriented tax reductions and reform, the deregulation of business (notably in airlines, other transportation, and banking), a reduced role for the federal government in housing, transportation, and welfare, and a moderate commitment to privatizing government assets (for example, in the sale of Conrail and of certain small parts of the government's loan portfolio).

It is significant as well as sobering that, despite the strong commitment of the Reagan administration to greater reliance on market forces, the share represented by federal government spending in the U.S. gross national product (GNP) is slightly larger (about 25 percent) in 1988, the last year of the Reagan administration, than it was at the end of the preceding administration in 1980. Although this change is in part due to a slight increase in the percentage of GNP devoted to defense, it also reflects that outlays for social and other programs, representing resource allocations through nonmarket processes, have grown apace with GNP. The rise of market forces in the United States should not be misconstrued: federal government programs and the additional 11 percent of GNP represented by the expenditures of the 50 state governments remain large and vigorous.

In Britain the rekindling of market forces has been the central tenet of three successive Thatcher governments, preceding the Reagan administration in the start of their market-oriented policies by two years. Since 1979 Thatcher has privatized thirteen major companies in the telecommunications, airline, aerospace, automotive, and transportation industries, representing more than $11 billion in state assets returned to the private market sector. With Thatcher's renewed mandate in 1987, she will certainly pursue plans to transfer other government-owned companies and several public services in the next few years. In particular the British Steel Corporation, newly returned to profitability, is a prime candidate for privatization. In Britain privatization has been the focus of market-oriented policies, whereas tax reduction as a stimulus to the market sector has played a secondary role.

French market-oriented policies under a mixed socialist-conservative government have included the denationalization of several large firms in electricity, glassworks, banking, and other industries that had been nationalized by the previous socialist administration. These policies also include ambitious plans to denationalize 65 companies representing $30–50 billion in state-owned assets, although the implementation of these plans was delayed by the October 1987 stock market crash. Besides privatization, the turnaround in French economic policies has accorded an enhanced role to market forces in other areas by invoking market standards for determining industrial wage rates and opening the state-owned television industry to competition by private television stations.

Market-oriented policies have also waxed, though to a lesser extent, in

Germany, Japan, and Italy. In Japan these policies are reflected in the privatization of the huge Nippon Telegraph and Telephone Corporation and in the loosening of restrictive regulation in banking and finance. Of course, one reason for the more limited extent of new market-oriented policies in Japan in recent years is the predominance of such policies all along. In West Germany denationalization measures have been an important adjunct of efforts to reduce the government's budget deficit and cushion the initial revenue effects of tax reform. Italy's market-oriented policies have included privatization by the large state-owned industrial reconstruction holding company (IRI) of 26 enterprises, including Alfa Romeo, between 1983 and 1987.

Within the First World one contrast between the United States and the others is worth noting. In the United States, where labor markets are freer and more competitive, employment increased by more than 13 million between 1981 and the start of 1988, and the unemployment rate fell from 7.5 to 5.8 percent. In Western Europe, where labor markets are much more tightly regulated by government and labor union restrictions, total employment remained nearly unchanged, whereas average unemployment rates rose to 10 or 11 percent, about twice what they had been a dozen years ago.

Although the First World has accorded market forces an enhanced and pervasive role, the point should not be carried too far. In the United States, Western Europe, and especially Japan, the agricultural sector remains protected from market forces by far-reaching, complex antimarket subsidies, tariffs, and import restrictions. Moreover, in the 1980s the average government-spending share of gross domestic product for the European countries in the Organization for Economic Cooperation and Development (OECD) continued at about 47 percent. If so-called off-budget expenditures are added, the resulting share is over 50 percent (compared with 36–37 percent in the United States).[5]

In the Second World the pace-setting, innovating country with respect to market-oriented policies has clearly been China under the leadership of Deng Xiaoping, beginning in the late 1970s. Following the turmoil of the Cultural Revolution, Deng's aim has been to advance China's Four Modernizations—of agriculture, industry, technology, and defense—at least in part through market-oriented reforms. These reforms involve the decentralization of economic decision making partly guided by market prices in agriculture, in the small-scale production of consumer goods, and more extensively in China's special economic zones, while maintaining centralized resource allocation in large-scale industrial and infrastructure sectors. Although there may be a fundamental conflict between these two directions—partial market orientation in agriculture (which remains heavily influenced by large government subsidies as well as price controls) and small-scale industry, on the one hand, and centralized resource allocation in heavy industry, on the other—in the past decade China has achieved impressive rates of real economic growth, averaging better than 6 percent per annum, largely attributable to the working of market forces.

Following in China's path with a lag of seven or eight years, the Soviet Union, under Mikhail Gorbachev's leadership, has embarked on a much-publicized program of economic restructuring (*perestroika*) that purports to accord a more active role for market forces in this planned socialist economy. Gorbachev has described the reasons for *perestroika*—stagnation in the Soviet economy from the late 1970s through at least the mid-1980s, resulting in constant or perhaps even declining rates of growth in per capita Soviet GNP—with disarming candor:

> In the latter half of the 1970s . . . the country began to lose momentum. Economic failures became more frequent . . . [E]lements of stagnation began to appear in the life of society . . . [T]he gap in the efficiency of production, quality of products, scientific and technological development began to widen . . . thus a sizeable portion of the national wealth became idle capital . . . [T]here are glaring shortcomings in our health services . . . and there were difficulties in the supply of food-stuffs, housing, consumer goods and services.[6]

Perestroika involves a series of reforms that include an enhanced role for market forces: legalizing service enterprises, extending permission and encouragement to agricultural collectives to produce for the market, full-cost accounting to be applied in agricultural and industrial enterprises, and promulgating the rule that "profits will be directly proportionate to efficiency."[7] These reforms, embodied in formal decrees and legislation by the Central Committee and by government regulations, represent a surprising recognition by a communist state of the need to rely more on market forces.

Nevertheless, the results of *perestroika* should not be exaggerated. Thus far, nearly three years after Gorbachev assumed leadership, an enormous gap remains between the rhetoric of marketization and decentralization, on the one hand, and actual movement in these directions, on the other. Moreover, even the rhetoric of *perestroika* abounds in ambiguities and inconsistencies, as in Gorbachev's statement that "we do not want to weaken the role of the center, because otherwise we would lose the advantages of the planned economy."[8] Gorbachev's reiterated intention to strengthen and revitalize the role of the party and the center, while relying more on market forces and decentralized incentives, smacks of the dialectical contradiction that Marxism-Leninism attributes to political and social systems other than its own.

In fact the contradictions inherent in efforts to reconcile centrally planned socialism with a considerably expanded role for market forces are serious. For example, if market-determined outcomes are allowed in some sectors (such as agriculture, consumer goods, and services), while central planning is maintained in others (such as heavy industry and high technology), grey or black markets will construct a bridge between them. As a result, capital and labor will gravitate away from the controlled and toward the market-oriented sectors. If central allocation is maintained in these input markets, then grey or black markets will arise again, and the economy will return to the unsatisfactory situation Gorbachev so candidly described. Nevertheless, over the past decade market-oriented reforms have become more important in most communist countries, either antedating the Soviet restructuring (in Hungary and Poland) or following upon it (perhaps even in Vietnam and North Korea).

The rise of market forces in the multiple other worlds that we conveniently, if inaccurately, refer to as the Third World has been hardly less surprising. Economic development theory since the 1940s was never particularly sophisticated, realistic, or practicable in part because until a dozen years ago the field was dominated by the economic ideas associated with Raoul Prebisch, Rosenstein-Rodan, and the Cambridge economists. Their ideas focused on the predominant developmental role of goverment, central planning, foreign aid, and other nonmarket processes. At least until the mid-1970s the economic development field had a distinctly antimarket orientation in which prices, competition, and incentives played second fiddle to centrally planned government investment, planning, and control for industry, agriculture, and infrastructure.

This orientation was reflected in the policies not only of most Third World governments but also of the national and international agencies concerned with economic development—namely, the World Bank, U.S. and other developed countries' foreign aid agencies, and the Overseas Development Council. As a result, most developing countries have resolved the cardinal choice in favor of government, rather than market, determination of major allocation decisions.

The exceptions to this generalization are a small number of Third World members, including South Korea, Taiwan, Hong Kong, Malaysia, and Singapore. Despite occasional setbacks, these newly industrialized countries (NICs) were the only successful instances of sustained economic growth in the Third World during the 1970s and early 1980s. Their success was marked by a more prominent role for market forces and competition, especially competition in international export markets, in resolving the cardinal economic policy choice. Generally government policies in these countries encouraged rather than hindered the market's role. That their policy makers were disposed and able to depart from the usual statist pattern followed by most Third World countries in the 1960s and 1970s is not easy to explain. In South Korea the influence of Japan's market orientation surely was part of the explanation. In Taiwan the Kuomintang leadership evidently learned what not to do from its unhappy mainland experience, and Taiwanese entrepreneurship responded remarkably to the new environment. In the other three instances, the explanation probably lies in some combination of the legacy of a market-oriented, British-trained civil service together with the entrepreneurial zeal of expatriate Chinese.

Until recently these countries were exceptions to the prevalence of anti-market forces and limited growth in most of the Third World. In the mid- and late 1980s, however, the prominence of market forces increased markedly. Price competition, competitive exports as a leading growth sector, the privatization of state enterprises, and incentive-oriented tax reform have become prominent, though not necessarily dominant, items on the policy agendas of many Third World countries. Significant policy changes along these lines have begun in Brazil, Chile, and Turkey, and to a lesser extent in Mexico, Argentina, the Philippines, Indonesia, Nigeria, Kenya, Senegal, and Tanzania.

These policy changes in Third World countries have been associated with corresponding changes in the concerns of the international and national agencies involved in economic development and technical assistance programs, notably the World Bank, the U.S. Agency for International Development (AID), and the development agencies of the West European countries and Japan. For example, in 1986 AID convened an international conference on privatization attended by participants from 40 countries. At the meeting AID officials stressed that "privatization is a major priority of the Reagan administration, and certainly of AID," and Secretary of State George Shultz observed: "Privatization is not just a device to cut back the size of government; rather, it is a policy to improve the delivery of services people are now getting—energy, housing, transportation . . . and it is central to the solution of a lot of the problems we see around the world."[9] Although such pronouncements are hardly synonymous with the implementation of market-oriented policies, the changes they imply should not be underestimated. Such statements were beyond the bounds of the Third World's economic development dialogue a decade ago.

The Rise of Market Forces: Reasons and Prospects

In sum, the past decade has witnessed a remarkable global recognition of the importance of market forces in contributing to sustained economic growth, and this recognition has been conspicuously manifest in all of the three so-called worlds in which the globe is sometimes divided. Although the trend has been pervasive, its strength and durability are less certain.

Pointing toward its continuance are the basic reasons underlying the trend itself: the aspiration toward greater efficiency associated with the operation of market forces and the disenchantment with nonmarket mechanisms to govern the use of resources. There is substantial evidence that market forces—competitive prices, free and open markets, the mobility of capital and labor, and the wide accessibility of information about products, factors, and technology—are associated with allocative efficiency (the efficiency with which inputs are used to produce outputs of goods and services at a given time) and dynamic efficiency (sustained growth of output and productivity over time), although the evidence is controversial.[10]

With respect to allocative efficiency, one international survey of comparisons between private and public output in the United States, West Germany, Switzerland, Australia, and Canada found that in 40 of the 50 case studies reviewed, private (market) production was more efficient than public (nonmarket) production. In three of the studies (relating to electric utilities, veterans' hospitals, and garbage collection) nonmarket provision seemed less costly than market delivery. In five studies (dealing with Canadian railroads, refuse collection in the United States, electric utilities in various parts of the United States, and insurance sales and servicing in West Germany) the results showed no difference between public and private production efficiency, whereas in two of the studies the results were ambiguous.[11] A recent study by E. S. Savas of the record of privatization in the past decade and its prospects for the future further supports the greater efficiency associated with market-based operations.[12]

With respect to dynamic efficiency, the examples of Korea, Taiwan, Hong Kong, Singapore, and Malaysia indicate the growth-promoting effects of market forces. Other evidence is provided by empirical work done at the World Bank and at the Rand Corporation dealing with the economic growth of various countries in the 1970s and 1980s. Subject to a number of qualifications about the underlying data and other factors, this work strongly suggests that, in general and on the average, a larger and growing market sector is associated with higher economic growth, whereas a larger and growing nonmarket sector is associated with slower growth.[13]

To be sure, other factors have contributed to the rise of market forces; for example, the desire to reduce the role of government in areas that can be privatized so that government resources can be diverted to those that cannot, such as defense.[14] But the principal cause of the dramatic rise of market forces has been the desire to achieve greater efficiency and more rapid growth and to escape from the stagnating effect of nonmarket forces, regulations, and bureaucracies. These influences have contributed to the trend of the past decade and seem likely to sustain it.

Another major factor supporting this trend is the explosion of telecommunications technology, which has increasingly linked financial and commodity markets worldwide. The unprecedentedly rapid transmission of information about prices, costs, changes in tax policies and legislation, and investment opportunities has strengthened market forces throughout the world, partly by assuring that the financial markets are accessible 24 hours a day and partly by facilitating market-related responses to such information. Although the accelerated transmission of economic information can also be a source of instability—witness the speed with which the October 19, 1987, stock market crash in New York reverberated in the Tokyo and London exchanges—rapid and extensive information dissemination is generally a powerful contributor to the improved functioning of markets.

In the past decade the increased globalization of financial and commodity markets has both transcended and reinforced the separate factors contributing to the rise of market forces in each of the three worlds. This trend is likely to accelerate in the 1990s, providing momentum for the wider influence of market forces. International trade in the 1980s has been governed by flexible market-determined exchange rates, sometimes abetted and sometimes impeded by the monetary and fiscal policies of the major trading countries. In the future, exchange rates may be less flexible, but they are still likely to result primarily from the play of market forces.

Although there are strong reasons to expect market forces to continue to rise, some influences point to a slowing down or even a reversal of the pro-market trend. Two such influences are the rising tide of protectionism in the United States and Western Europe and the failure of Japan to open its markets fully to competition in imports of services and goods from other developed countries as well as the NICs. In addition, agricultural markets in the United States, Western Europe, and Japan are immured by a larger, more complex, and more expensive set of subsidies, quotas, and tariffs than ever before. These antimarket forces are as likely to remain or grow as to recede.

Another cause of a possible reversal of pro-market forces lies in a rising concern for equity, fairness, and social justice and criticism of the inequities and hardships accompanying market outcomes. Viner's comment of nearly 30 years ago still holds: "No modern people will have zeal for the free market unless it operates in a setting of 'distributive justice' with which they are tolerably content."[15] Efforts in majoritarian democracies to remedy the distributive injustices of the marketplace may, if not devised and managed with care, erode the mainsprings of investment, innovation, and growth, thereby curtailing if not reversing the rise of market forces. It is also true that these efforts, even when motivated by genuine concerns for distributive justice, may impair rather than contribute to it.

Whether the rapid growth, innovation, change, and flexibility associated with markets are viewed as desirable goals or as unsettling risks depends on the eyes, heart, and mind of the beholder. If less-rapid growth is preferred to more-rapid growth, restriction of the market sector may be preferred to its expansion. (In this respect, China's development plan for 1986–1990 deliberately opts for restrained growth rather than rapid growth). Also, in the communist world the surprising rise of market forces over the past decade—within the bureaucracy and among the leadership—will encounter stiff resistance as one of the inherent contradictions of such reform efforts becomes starkly evident; namely, the contradiction between decentralized decision making through markets and the central political control of the Communist Party and its ruling elite. In the Third World it is also possible that political and bureaucratic elites may curtail the growth of market forces to acquire and expand political power.

Policies and Implications

How the cardinal choice between markets and governments in the allocation of economic resources will evolve in the 1990s is as important as it is uncertain. In my view, the rise of market forces is likely to continue at a diminished rate in the Western democracies, especially in Western Europe but also in the United States; it is likely to continue at a sustained or even an increased rate in the Third World (despite the dangers of protectionism and the restrictive effects on the flow of private capital to the developing countries caused by the international debt overhang); and it will run into serious obstacles in the communist world, with a continued rise of market forces more likely in China than in the Soviet Union.

In U.S. public policy at home, the choice between markets and governments should not be posed so starkly that it obscures the crucial issue of identifying opportunities by which government and markets can each improve the operations of the other. For example, government efforts could improve the functioning of markets by revising and reducing regulations of labor markets, health care, pension funds, and anti-trust legislation.[16] By the same token, market forces could greatly improve the functioning of government in, for example, dual-sourcing defense procurements, providing educational vouchers for the public school system, taxing emissions of chemical or other pollutants rather than specifying precise levels of permissible emissions, and using "beneficiary charges" as a partial substitute for taxes to finance some public services.[17]

U.S. policy has limited leverage on the emergence and expansion of market forces in the rest of the world. Nevertheless, we should not underestimate the influence of precedent, advocacy, and negotiation, given the global repercussions of Reagan's and Thatcher's policy redirections.

Among the objectives U.S. policy should seek to advance within the First World is the gradual elimination, or at least reduction, of the network of complex and costly impediments to free trade in agricultural products in Western Europe, Japan, and the United States itself.

U.S. policy toward the communist world should encourage, pragmatically and without meddling, the further development of market forces for political as well as economic reasons. If communist countries genuinely move in the direction of decentralized market-oriented decision making, international trade can prosper, to mutual advantage. Moreover, market-oriented reform in the communist countries will contribute to economic pluralism and diversity, which are likely (though not certain) to promote political pluralism and perhaps a gradual transformation of communist systems. The pragmatic encouragement of market forces in the communist world should involve reducing barriers to free trade and developing joint ventures governed by commercial considerations of costs, prices, profits, and risks. However, U.S. policy should eschew all subsidies—whether in the form of subsidized credits, loan or investment guarantees, trade preferences, or any other measures—of economic reform in Marxist-Leninist systems, first, because providing subsidies would relieve or reduce pressures for genuine economic reform arising from economic stagnation and the inherent contradiction between command economies and efficiency; and second, because providing subsidies would reduce the operation of market forces and thereby encourage the very misallocation of resources that the operation of market forces is intended to remedy.

These arguments against unwarranted subsidies apply also to U.S. policies toward the Third World, with several qualifications. First, extending economic and technical assistance to these countries is justified by basic humanitarian considerations and by the formidable difficulty of escaping from the poverty trap. Second, many Third World countries face additional resource burdens because they need to maintain or enhance their security capabilities, thus straining the resources they can mobilize through market forces alone. Nevertheless, when the United States extends economic and technical assistance, it should arrange a clear but tactful discussion with recipients of the market-oriented policies such assistance envisages. External assistance should complement and reinforce market forces rather than work against them.

Notes

1. For an extended treatment of these and other ideas, see Charles Wolf, Jr., *Markets or Governments: Choosing Between Imperfect Alternatives* (Cambridge, Mass.: MIT Press, 1988).

2. Jacob Viner, "The Intellectual History of Laissez Faire," *Journal of Law and Economics* 3 (October 1960): 45–69

3. On nonmarket failure, see Wolf, *Markets or Governments*.

4. "Less aptly named" because this "world" is really not a single entity but rather multiple and heterogeneous ones whose diversity is much greater than that within the other two worlds.

5. See Wolf, *Markets or Governments*, p. 8; and Peter Saunders and Friedrich Klaw, *The Role of the Public Sector* (Paris: OECD, 1985).

6. Mikhail Gorbachev, *Perestroika: New Thinking for Our Country and the World* (New York: Harper & Row, 1987), excerpted in *U.S. News and World Report*, November 9, 1987, pp. 70–71.

7. Ibid., p. 72.

8. Ibid., p. 77.

9. Quoted in *New York Times*, February 20, 1986, p. A13.

10. See Wolf, *Markets or Governments*, pp. 137–48. See also E. S. Savas, *Privatization: The Key to Better Government* (Chatham, N.J.: Chatham House Publishers, 1987).

11. Thomas E. Borcherding et al., *Comparing the Efficiency of Private and Public Production: The Evidence from Five Countries* (Zurich: Institute for Empirical Research in Economics, University of Zurich, 1982).

12. See Savas, *Privatization*.

13. See Wolf, *Markets or Governments*, pp. 139–48.

14. This motive is most relevant to the United States and other First World countries.

15. Viner, "Intellectual History of Laissez Faire," p. 68.

16. See Wolf, *Markets or Governments*, pp. 158–65.

17. See ibid., p. 71.

NATHAN ROSENBERG

◆ ———————————————————— ◆

Technological Change Under Capitalism and Socialism

I

◆ In 1987 Mikhail Gorbachev enunciated a policy of *perestroika*—a series of economic measures aimed at a fundamental restructuring of the stagnating Soviet economy. A central component of that policy is an intense focus upon the exploitation of sophisticated technologies to accelerate economic growth.

This focus suggests that now may be a good time for an intellectual stocktaking on the economic role of technology in a centrally planned economy. Soviet industrialization over the past 70 years has focused overwhelmingly upon the achievement of rapid economic growth through high rates of capital formation. This avenue now appears to be distinctly less promising than it once was, because recent evidence suggests that the Soviet economy derives far less growth impetus from a unit increment of capital than it did at an earlier stage in its history. In essence, with only a limited ability to make effective use of superior technology, the marginal productivity of capital has been declining to worrisomely low levels.

Ironically no one has ever articulated more forcefully than Marx the indispensable role technological change plays in generating economic growth. But Marx also believed that the bourgeoisie was the indispensable historical vehicle for introducing these changes in technology that so transform the productivity of human labor. As Marx and Engels stated in *The Communist Manifesto*, socialism becomes possible only after the bourgeoisie has performed its historic role of "constantly revolutionizing the instruments of production." Socialism was supposed to inherit a sophisticated technological system and to exploit it free of the inherent contradictions of capitalism. Instead the Bolsheviks found themselves in control of a backward economy in 1917. They moved this economy through the early phases of industrialization by relying upon central planning and a panoply of economic controls that was able to extract resources from low-priority sectors, especially agriculture, and to mobilize these resources in support of unusually high rates of capital accumulation. This process seems now to have exhausted itself.

For many years, then, the Soviet system has been far more successful at marshaling more resources to capital accumulation than at using more sophisticated technologies. Why has the centralized socialism of the Soviet Union been so inhospitable to the introduction and efficient use of such technologies? I propose to address that question after considering briefly the historical conditions that gave rise to rapid rates of technological progress in Western capitalist economies. I do not suggest, of course, that there is only one path to technological progress. Indeed, there are compelling reasons to believe that latecomers confront a set of opportunities distinctly different from those that confronted the pioneers. Nevertheless, a brief consideration of the past conditions that have been conducive to rapid rates of technological progress should at least help us deal with the question of Soviet inhospitableness and at the same time lend more depth to the evaluation of the prospects for a successful restructuring of the Soviet economy.

II

The central feature in the search for improved technologies is great uncertainty. This uncertainty has powerfully shaped the economic institutions that emerged within Western capitalism. Capitalism historically developed a cluster of novel organizational forms that reduced certain intolerable risks to more tolerable levels. These were the risks that were unavoidably associated with committing large amounts of financial resources to the search for technological improvements. These high levels of risk were inseparable from technological innovation because the outcome of the search for new technologies was extremely uncertain. Moreover, even if one did succeed in developing a new and clearly better technology, the prospect of making money out of it remained highly uncertain.

Marx himself recognized this uncertainty, although only in the third volume of *Capital*, published after his death and many years after the publication of the immensely influential first volume of *Capital*. In the third volume Marx called attention to "the far greater cost of operating an establishment based on a new invention as compared to later establishments arising *ex suis ossibus*. This is so very true that the trail-blazers generally go bankrupt, and only those who later buy the buildings, machinery, etc., at a cheaper price make money out of it."[1] This passage constitutes Marx's explicit recognition of the great vulnerability of the capitalist in his social role as a carrier of technological innovation. Had Marx given more attention to this vulnerability in volume 1 of *Capital,* he would have had to portray the capitalist in a distinctly different light. He would also have had to face up more candidly to the painful trade-offs that all societies must confront between greater equity and greater efficiency. But such an examination would have highlighted the weakness of capitalists, whereas Marx was intent on portraying their social power and their capacity to exploit others.[2]

The history of capitalism involved the gradual introduction of a large number of institutional devices that facilitated the commitment of resources to the innovation process by reducing or placing limitations upon risk. Among the most critical were new institutions, laws, and legislation that (1) limited the liability of an investor in any particular enterprise, (2) provided for the easy marketability of ownership shares, (3) established stock markets that were essential for ready marketability, (4) reduced risk by the fundamental technique of insurance, and (5) defined the obligations between principals and agents.[3]

The emergence of business firms with limited liability for their owners and readily marketable ownership shares was central to facilitating investment in risky undertakings. From the point of view of the individual investor, a limited-liability corporation made it possible to convert a long-term risk involving large amounts of capital into a short-term risk that could be limited to small amounts of capital. Marketable assets and ready markets for the sale of these assets meant that owners were not undertaking commitments as long-lived as their capital assets. On the contrary, they could realize financial gains or cut financial losses whenever doing so seemed expedient. In this way a capitalist proprietor's long-term risk was eventually converted into an investor's short-term risk. At the same time, the ownership of the firm's assets was effectively divided into two levels: first, those of the corporation as an ongoing entity and, second, those of the shareholders who supplied the firm with its capital. The first-level risks remained as great as they had always been, but the second-level risks were of a different order and were much more readily acceptable. This division of risk bears a close analogy to the redistribution of risk that takes place between a property owner and an insurance company.

Although Marx had a profound appreciation for the technological dynamism of capitalism,[4] he did not appreciate the extent to which this was due to institutional measures that reduced risk and thereby encouraged the extensive experimentation that made innovation so commonplace under capitalism. The willingness to undertake experiments in both the social and technological spheres depends upon limiting the negative consequences for the individual if the risky enterprise should fail, as it frequently did. The great technological achievements of capitalism have been inseparable from the system's success in reducing risk to more tolerable levels while at the same time offering the prospect of huge financial rewards if the risky enterprise should succeed.

These technological achievements were thus based upon capitalist legal institutions and property rights that legitimized the right to experiment with new organizational forms as well as with new technologies. The final arbiter of whether something new was socially desirable was not a government authority or the religious clergy or the guild members or the merchants whose personal interest might be threatened by innovation. Rather, the final arbiter was the impersonal marketplace. Capitalism legitimized innovation only if it could pass a stringent market test. It was, as Marx recognized, the first form of social organization in which economic life was dominated by groups whose economic interests caused them to threaten the status quo.[5]

III

The freedom to conduct experiments in turn required that yet other conditions be fulfilled. In particular the economic sphere had to attain a higher degree of autonomy from external forces, especially freedom from arbitrary and unpredictable interventions by government authorities.

A critical aspect of this increasing autonomy was the emergence of new political institutions that reduced the risk of arbitrary exactions and appropriations (or even expropriations) by a powerful ruler. The rise in Western Europe of parliaments in control of government financial purse strings was an essential part of this story. So was the emergence of new legal concepts, precedents, and institutions for the enforcement of contracts and property rights. In this respect the bourgeois political revolutions of the seventeenth and eighteenth centuries were central to the later economic achievements of capitalism.

The freedom to conduct experiments required not only a high degree of autonomy but also a large number of decision makers; in other words, decentralization and also the inability of the experimenters to influence the outcome of the market evaluation of the new product. In fact some of the most decisive failures of twentieth-century socialism flow from the failure to allow experimentation and from the resulting failure to benefit from observing the outcome of such experiments.

The need to expose investment decisions to the risk of being proved wrong implies the decentralization of decision-making authority, since any central authority will have a strong motivation for withholding financial support from those who are bent on proving that the central authority has made a mistake. The costs and risks of a new investment might well render it worth financing from society's point of view, but the costs and risks *to centralized decision makers* might well be prohibitive.

Historically one of the distinctive features of capitalist economies has been the practice of decentralizing authority over investments to substantial numbers of individuals who stand to make large personal gains if their decisions are right, who stand to lose heavily if their decisions are wrong, and *who lack the economic or political power to prevent at least some others from proving them wrong.* Indeed, this particular cluster of features constitutes an excellent candidate for the definition of capitalism. Its importance for Western economic growth turns on the point that the choice of capital investments includes the selection of the proposals for innovation that are to be funded. The diffusion of authority to select programs for capital expenditure and the diffusion of authority to select projects for innovation thus cover much the same ground.[6]

The historical outcome of the freedom to conduct experiments under capitalism has been the Western economies' extraordinary organizational diversity. This diversity may be considered the end result of a process of social evolution in which a wide range of organizational forms has been introduced and in which firms have been allowed to grow in accord with underlying conditions of technology, location, market size, range of products, and so on. The particular outcomes of size of firm, pattern of ownership, product mix, and so on, have been essentially determined by a market process in which the underlying conditions of different industries have generated patterns of survival reflecting their own special conditions, rather than some a priori notion of a single best model to which they were expected to conform.

It is common to stress the importance, indeed the predominance, of large firms in Western capitalist economies. This perspective has been particularly common among Marxists (although by no means confined to them), who have seen the trend toward bigness and greater industrial concentration as part of the inner logic of capitalism. According to this view the emergence of monopoly capitalism not only reflects the pervasive advantages of bigness; it also conveniently facilitates the transition to socialism through the simple expedient of nationalizing the giant firms. But the commitment to this view has long served as an easy substitute for the more serious task of examining and accounting for the remarkable institutional complexity of contemporary capitalist societies. For example, although large firms are the predominant employers of capital, small firms are the predominant employers of labor. Further, organizational structures not only differ immensely among the agricultural, manufacturing, public utilities, and services sectors, but great differences exist within each of these sectors. Giant corporations play an important role, but so do millions of self-employed individuals. Any perspective that sees only giant corporations misses the most impressive feature of Western economies: the great subtlety with which organizational modes have been adapted to, and modified by, the particularities of products and markets.

Consider the manufacturing sector, generally regarded as the home of bigness and the basis for most sweeping generalizations about the nature or the structure of the U.S. economy. This sector actually employs less than 20 percent of the U.S. labor force. The largest U.S. manufacturing corporations (measured by value of sales) are in the petroleum and automobile-manufacturing industries. Yet according to the Bureau of the Census, in 1982 there were 282 companies in petroleum refining, 284 in motor vehicles and car bodies, 2,000 in motor vehicle parts and accessories, and 566 in automotive stampings. Further, in almost all industries that included the largest firms, there were a large number of smaller firms. Thus the aircraft industry in 1982 had 139 firms; the electronic computing equipment industry, 1,520; and photographic equipment and supplies, 723.[7]

IV

This discussion of organizational diversity as the outcome of prolonged experimentation leads us to consider some of the economic problems of contemporary socialist societies. The failure of these societies to permit experimentation has been compounded by a strong commitment to the economic advantages of bigness—a commitment that had its origins in Marx's writings. The reluctance to tailor organizational size and structure to the specific needs of different economic activities has been combined with an incentive system that is pervasively hostile to risk taking. This combination goes a long way toward explaining one of the most fundamental and perhaps surprising difficulties of contemporary socialist societies: their failure to take full advantage of superior technologies.

It is not immediately clear why hostility toward experimentation and risk taking should have created such serious obstacles to exploiting better technologies. After all, in a world where technologically advanced capitalist economies already exist, a socialist economy has the invaluable option of acquiring such technologies from abroad. There are no compelling reasons why foreign capitalist economies cannot serve as sources for the more sophisticated technologies that socialist economies are unable to develop.

Of course, to a considerable extent such technology transfers are precisely what has happened. Since the 1920s the Soviet Union has been a large-scale importer of Western technologies. Its inability to generate the incentives or to provide the social space and opportunity for experimentation has been at least partially offset by imports of technology from the capitalist West, which has made its technologies universally available. Indeed, all industrializing countries have managed to grow more rapidly by borrowing foreign technologies. This pattern has been true of Japan in the twentieth century, and it was also central to the United States' rapid industrialization in the nineteenth century, which built upon British technologies of metallurgy, power generation, railroads, and textiles.

Although twentieth-century socialist societies did not have to develop their own technologies from scratch, their mode of economic organization limited the economic benefits they could derive from imported technologies. Technology transfer is never simply a matter of shipping hardware from one place to another. Rather, such borrowing presupposes a large cadre of engineers, technicians, and managers to modify, adapt, maintain, and repair such technology. These in turn imply a competent infrastructure of skills, organization, and facilities. Unless these major preconditions are fulfilled, the prospects for successful technology transfer are poor.

But there are more fundamental systemic considerations at issue. Central planning and the negligible freedom of action of plant managers under the Soviet system have been deeply hostile to the introduction of new technologies. Such technologies disrupt established routine. Although they promise long-term improvements in productivity, they exact a short-term cost in the time and effort involved in installing new equipment, teaching different skills, establishing new work routines, working out bugs in product design and process technologies, developing new arrangements with unreliable suppliers (or arranging to bypass them), and so on. In fact the entire central-planning apparatus is geared to short-term goals. The success of a plant manager has been based relentlessly upon his ability to fulfill the central planners' annual output quota. Although there have been numerous attempts to introduce greater flexibility into this system, the incentive problems have proven intractable. In its present form, the system severely penalizes the plant manager who fails to fulfill his annual output goal but gives only a small reward for fulfillment or overfulfillment. A new technology that offers the prospect of huge productivity improvements in four or five years, but at the expense of disrupting target fulfillment in the next year or two, is a distinctly unattractive risk to a plant manager. Thus risk aversion with respect to new technology is endemic to the incentive system.

Indeed, since the setting of annual targets is based upon the central planners' estimate of a plant's productive capabilities, it is distinctly dangerous to the plant manager to reveal a capability much higher than the most recent annual target. Since cost considerations and the size of the wage bill are not major concerns, the hoarding of labor is widespread. The plant manager has a strong incentive to underrepresent his capabilities to keep his future targets low and therefore easily attainable.

This managerial risk aversion and dissimulation is powerfully reinforced by a huge, well-entrenched Soviet bureaucracy. Drastic reforms toward greater managerial discretion and flexibility would threaten both the power and the perquisites of that bureaucracy. Decentralization would carry with it a devolution of power to the regions and to the plant managers. For these reasons, a greater reliance upon the associated apparatus of markets and market-determined prices is likely to remain anathema to planners and bureaucrats. In other words, *perestroika*, if successful, will entail a massive redistribution of political and economic power within the Soviet state.

In addition, the systematic neglect of the consumer has further weakened the incentive at the plant level to improve products. Within the perpetual seller's market that the Soviet system has created, selling a product is never a problem. As a result, the effort involved in improving a product, or the disruption involved in changing the productive apparatus to introduce an entirely new product that would be more attractive to consumers, has a zero, if not a negative, payoff to the plant manager. With long queues of patient buyers outside shops in response to mere rumors of imminent deliveries of the old product, the plant manager need not concern himself excessively with product improvement or innovation. His continual preoccupation is not with the marketing of his product but with the unreliability of his suppliers in providing the inputs essential to quota fulfillment.[8] Here again the system provides no incentive to innovation.

The limited supply of goods in the shops is the most pervasive of all disincentives in the Soviet Union. The absence of sizable financial rewards for effort and risk taking, combined with the sheer unavailability of goods that one might acquire with higher incomes, reinforces the weak incentive system at the heart of the present restructuring efforts. It is difficult to see how the Soviet Union can strengthen individual incentives without enlarging the flow of consumer goods.

V

The failure of socialist societies to benefit from experiments has been most conspicuous in the so-called giantism in Soviet central planning: the uncritical belief in indefinitely continuing economies of large-scale production.[9] Its intellectual antecedents undoubtedly lie in Marx's admiration for the large-scale technologies of the British Industrial Revolution. In Marx's words: "The battle of competition is fought by cheapening of commodities. The cheapness of commodities depends, *caeteris paribus*, on the productiveness of labour, and this again on the scale of production. Therefore, the larger capitals beat the smaller." [10]

Marx was one of the first economists (along with Charles Babbage and J. S. Mill) to call attention to the economic significance of large-scale production. He appreciated the importance of indivisibilities and pointed to numerous cases (especially in the capital goods sector) where economic advantages derived from doing certain things on what he called a cyclopean scale.

As a perceptive observer of the industrial scene, Marx might not have advocated the indiscriminate giantism pursued in the Soviet Union. Indeed, evidence suggests that Stalinist giantism reflected a determination to emulate certain large U.S. establishments that were believed to be highly efficient, such as those in the steel industry. [11] Moreover, as a matter of administrative convenience, central planners undoubtedly found it simpler to deal with a small number of large plants rather than a large number of small ones. Bigness clearly served the interests of the central bureaucracy. This was most apparent in the disastrous experience in agriculture, the sector where bigness was least appropriate. However inefficient the large collective farm may have been in the productivity of agricultural inputs, it served as a powerful organizational device for collecting an agricultural surplus that could then be made to serve the interests of rapid capital accumulation and industrialization.

Ironically, whereas Marx predicted that bigness would emerge from the competitive process under mature capitalism, employment in industrial firms is far more concentrated in the Soviet Union than it is in the United States or Japan. Data for the 1960s suggest that 24 percent of Soviet enterprises had more than 500 employees. In the United States only 1.4 percent were so large, and in Japan a mere 0.3 percent. At the other extreme, only 15 percent of Soviet enterprises had fewer than 50 employees, whereas 85 percent of U.S. firms and 95 percent of Japanese firms had fewer than 50 workers. [12] Obviously the larger size of Soviet firms has been imposed by deliberate government policy and is not the outcome of historical experience or of socialist experimentation.

The purpose of experimentation, of course, is to provide useful information for answering certain kinds of questions. But Marxism, at least in some of its most influential twentieth-century forms, has been unwilling to admit that the answers to some questions were in doubt. This unwillingness has often taken the form of simply asserting the priority of ideological purity over technical expertise. In China both the Great Leap Forward and the later Cultural Revolution denied the role of technical expertise in an efficient industrial society. Chairman Mao further claimed that a new socialist man would pursue economic efficiency and embrace an ideal of hard work merely from a sense of commitment to socialism without any strong material rewards. Mao's followers made important technical and economic decisions without reference to technical specialists. Ideology was the litmus test for important managerial and technical positions. It is fair to say that these episodes set back the industrialization of China by at least a generation.

Curiously the Great Leap Forward may be said to have involved experimentation of a perverse sort: the attempt to set up backyard blast furnaces and chemical plants involved a test of the nonexistence of economies of large-scale production in precisely those sectors of the economy where they are known to be of critical importance! The essential point, in both China and the Soviet Union, is the absence of competitive forces in judging the *outcome* of economic experiments.

Socialist giantism, especially in the Soviet Union, is hostile to technological innovation in another fundamental way. Some of the disadvantages of bigness are minimal in a highly stable environment, but where technology is changing rapidly or might be made to change more rapidly, bigness can be a more serious handicap. Many experiments are easier and less costly to conduct on a small scale. It is inherently difficult to introduce numerous and frequent small changes in a large hierarchical organization requiring permissions and approvals from a remote central authority.

The history of industries that have recently been undergoing rapid technological change, such as electronics and biotechnology, suggests that the flexibility of small firms may be highly advantageous to experimentation and exploration. Large firms, operating through layers of management with rigid rules, are ill suited to rapid changes and the need for frequent on-the-spot decisions.[13]

Soviet giantism has even pervaded research and development (R and D) activities within each of the ministries that has planning responsibilities for major sectors of the economy. Among other consequences, this organization has isolated R and D from managerial decisions relating to production planning and has thus intensified the difficulties of introducing new technologies.[14] It also further isolates the findings of Soviet science from possible industrial applications—a consideration of great significance. Improving the links among the separate components of the R and D process is crucial to successful innovation in all industrial economies.[15] In the case of the Soviet Union the cost of poor links is undoubtedly great, since much basic Soviet research meets the highest international standards.

I have argued that a peculiar strength of capitalism historically has been its ability to accommodate the special needs of the innovation process. I have also argued that the failure to provide for such accommodation in organization and incentives has been responsible for the persistent failure of Soviet socialism to generate new technologies or even to adopt and to exploit more effectively technologies that already exist. Obviously this discussion does not exhaust all the significant things one might say about capitalism and socialism as alternative ways of organizing economic activity. But as recent developments in Eastern Europe and China have emphasized, it is extremely difficult to make socialist societies more amenable to technological change without at the same time making them more capitalist.

Notes

1. Karl Marx, *Capital* (Moscow: Foreign Languages Publishing House, 1959), 3:103.

2. Insofar as Marx may be said to have dealt with the trade-off between equity and efficiency, he did so by assigning to capitalism the historical role of providing efficiency and to a later socialism the role of delivering equity.

3. These and related matters are discussed in detail in Nathan Rosenberg and L. E. Birdwell, Jr., *How the West Grew Rich* (New York: Basic Books, 1986), esp. chaps. 4–8.

4. See Karl Marx and Frederick Engels, *The Communist Manifesto*, in *Selected Works* (Moscow: Foreign Languages Publishing House, 1951), 1:37.

5. See ibid., p. 36.

6. The last two paragraphs derive from Rosenberg and Birdwell, *How the West Grew Rich*, pp. 234–35.

7. U.S. Department of Commerce, Bureau of the Census, *Statistical Abstract of the U.S.* (Washington, D.C.: Government Printing Office, 1987), p. 729.

8. One important by-product of supplier unreliability is an incentive to vertical integration to achieve greater control over the supply of inputs and thereby to reduce dependence upon others. This translates, of course, into another incentive to increase the size of the firm.

9. See Leon Smolinski, "The Scale of the Soviet Industrial Establishment," *American Economic Review Papers and Proceedings* 62 (May 1962): 139–40.

10. Karl Marx, *Capital*, Modern Library (New York: Random House, n.d.), p. 686.

11. Smolinski, "Soviet Industrial Establishment," p. 141.

12. Joseph Berliner, *The Innovation Decision in Soviet Industry* (Cambridge, Mass.: MIT Press, 1976), pp. 33–34. Large enterprises are also characteristic of Yugoslavia and Hungary but not of South Korea, which strongly resembles Japan. Mainland China has few large firms, reflecting the government policy of encouraging the rapid development of small- and medium-size rural industry.

13. For a suggestive analysis of the role of firm size in innovation, see Kenneth Arrow, "Innovation in Large and Small Firms," in Joshua Ronen, ed., *Entrepreneurship* (Lexington: D. C. Heath, 1983), chap. 1.

14. See Herbert Levine, "On the Nature and Location of Entrepreneurial Activity in Centrally Planned Economies: The Soviet Case," chap. 9 in Ronen, *Entrepreneurship*, pp. 249–50.

15. See Masahiko Aoki and Nathan Rosenberg, "The Japanese Firm as an Innovating Institution" (Paper delivered at the International Economic Association Roundtable Conference, Tokyo, September 15–17, 1987).

ROGER W. ROBINSON, JR.

Financing the East Bloc

◆ The year 1988 will bring the most intense period of negotiations between the United States and the Soviet Union in the eight years of the Reagan presidency. On the table are not only an array of arms control issues
but also regional disputes and Soviet human rights practices. Looming behind these discussions are the major unresolved issues of economic cooperation and competition between the free world and the East Bloc. Specifically
the Soviets intend to use their economic relations with the West to avoid the
prospect of falling irreversibly behind the technology curve. In addition, continued depressed levels of Soviet hard-currency earnings, enduring systemic
rigidities in the economy, and an empire that drains rather than generates
scarce capital are accelerating Moscow's efforts to tap Western economic
and financial resources. Clearly time is not on Mikhail Gorbachev's side.

This and previous administrations have linked the economic, human
rights, and foreign policy aspects of U.S.-Soviet relations. A careful look at
the possibilities for forward movement in the U.S.-Soviet negotiations on
other issues is therefore warranted before any conclusions can be drawn
about the future of our bilateral economic relations.

In the regional talks now under way, the Soviets seem to be striving for
a clear win over the United States. The most striking characteristic of the
current Soviet proposals for settling the conflicts in Afghanistan, Nicaragua,
Angola, and Cambodia is their remarkable consistency. In each instance
Moscow expects the Soviet-backed government to be permitted to remain,
even though some elements of the political opposition might be coopted

into the administration. Whereas the United States and its allies would be expected to terminate all assistance to the anti-Marxist resistance, the Soviet Union and its allies would be free of similar constraints. The dead hand of Leonid Brezhnev, not the much-heralded energy and imagination of Mikhail Gorbachev, seems to be guiding Soviet negotiators.

Such a tough-minded stance on regional disputes does not augur well for a major expansion of U.S.-Soviet trade; neither does continued Soviet reluctance to fulfill their obligations under the Helsinki accords. Despite some widely advertised claims that a new human rights breeze is blowing from the Kremlin, actual Soviet accomplishments have fallen far short of expectations. Soviet emigration figures in the 1980s are poor compared with those of the late 1970s, and official harassment of independent religious institutions has increased. Gorbachev's advisers—usually well informed on Western attitudes—are mistaken if they believe that the posthumous rehabilitation of Nikolai Bukharin will greatly improve the Soviet Union's human rights image abroad.

Only in the area of arms control is a breakthrough possible that would add to the momentum of improving relations between the superpowers. The odds are better than even that an understanding will be reached at the upcoming Reagan-Gorbachev summit to reduce the size of each side's strategic nuclear arsenal. However, initial euphoria within the North Atlantic Treaty Organization (NATO) over the arms control process is gradually giving way to a sober-minded assessment of NATO's limited options in future negotiations on reducing conventional, chemical, and short-range nuclear forces. The harsh reality is that the Soviet Union has invested much more heavily in defense modernization in past years and so can negotiate from a position of strength. Defense Secretary Frank Carlucci's fiscal 1989 annual report to Congress puts the Soviet net investment advantage at $510 billion from 1970 to 1985. Pressure to reduce the federal budget deficit could lead to as much as a $200 billion reduction in future U.S. defense programs, largely erasing the progress achieved in the Reagan years, which prevented the USSR from gaining overall strategic superiority and increasing its negotiation leverage.

NATO members, led by West Germany, have called for a comprehensive review of alliance arms control and force modernization objectives. The growing discord within NATO over modernization of the aging Lance missiles indicates that no solid consensus on a future course of action will soon emerge that adequately protects U.S. interests.

What does all this mean for U.S.-Soviet economic and financial relations? To a great extent, the Western Alliance looks to the United States for a clear sense of direction on economic and financial policy, consistent with members' national interests. U.S. opposition in 1981–1982 to the martial-law crackdown in Poland and our reluctance to see the USSR eventually capture a commanding share of West European natural-gas markets helped catalyze a new allied consensus on the strategic aspects of East-West economic relations. Alliance agreements in 1982–1983 on strengthened multilateral export controls, the elimination of subsidized interest rates on government-backed credits, and the accelerated development of secure Norwegian gas supplies for Western Europe to substitute for Soviet supplies constitute a major contribution to East-West economic security.

The Soviets can be expected to make strenuous efforts throughout the 1990s to overturn Western coordination of the East-West economic security policies achieved during the Reagan administration. The USSR has consistently sought to put economic and financial ties on a separate track from other issues, hoping that such ties with Western countries can be expanded even while the Soviet military buildup, Third World adventurism, and violations of the Helsinki accords continue. Unfortunately there are also calls from the U.S. side to decouple East-West security, human rights, and economic issues. For example, the president of the U.S.-USSR Trade and Economic Council recently predicted a sevenfold increase in U.S.-Soviet trade but neglected to note the political obstacles that would hinder such a major expansion.

Western efforts to grapple with the international debt crisis add another complication. The growing competition in the 1990s between the East Bloc and developing countries for access to Western markets, capital, and technology will force the governments of the Organization of Economic Cooperation and Development (OECD) to examine more closely the implications of expanded East-West economic and financial relations. The question, in simple terms, is which high-debt countries deserve our priority attention—the centrally planned economies of the Warsaw Pact or the democratic free-market nations of the South?

Predictions for the 1990s

In a rapidly changing policy environment, predictions are hazardous. Nevertheless, they can point out potential opportunities and dangers. By the end of the next administration, we could witness the following developments:

♦ The volume of U.S.-Soviet trade will probably remain at modest levels ($2.5–4 billion annually, far below the possible $10–15 billion predicted by the U.S.-USSR Trade and Economic Council). The Soviets will probably try to use the slight warming in bilateral political relations to have the administration and some U.S. Jewish leaders press for a one-year waiver of the Jackson-Vanik and/or Stevenson amendments to the Trade Act of 1974, which currently inhibit Soviet access to equal tariff treatment and U.S. Export-Import Bank credits respectively. Such a request is likely to coincide with a Soviet Jewish emigration figure of about 15,000, up from fewer than 10,000 exits in 1987. This waiver will probably face stiff opposition in Congress.

◆ The ambitious Soviet strategy to recruit Western joint-venture partners will probably fall short of Moscow's expectations because of differing goals among the participants, the political risk perceived by Western firms, problems with profit repatriation and quality control, and management bottlenecks within the USSR itself. The Western partners will focus their attention on unfettered access to some four hundred million East Bloc consumers, access Moscow is unlikely to provide. The public surfacing of important and costly new cases of diverted strategic technology to the Soviet Union, through third countries or directly, will foster substantial congressional skepticism about the merits of large new joint ventures, whether economically and technically justified or not. Foreign joint ventures with the USSR will also be increasingly scrutinized by Congress and the media.

◆ Trade with the East is likely to remain only a marginal part of overall OECD trade (approximately 2–3.5 percent), largely because of depressed East Bloc hard-currency earnings and the lack of competitive goods for export to the West. The East Bloc will probably try to offset this negative trend in the 1990s by demanding the artificial stimulation of East-West trade through, for example, subsidies of industrial as well as agricultural exports from the West and preferential access to Western markets for East Bloc products. In addition, the East Bloc will continue to push Western government and private creditors for preferred terms on debt reschedulings and refinancings, as in the cases of Poland and Hungary.

◆ The Soviets will also continue to press for entry into the General Agreement on Tariffs and Trade, the International Monetary Fund (IMF), the World Bank, the Asian Development Bank, the Multifiber Arrangement, and other Western economic and financial institutions as a way of boosting trade and financial ties with the noncommunist world. Soviet efforts to join these organizations will be impeded by the lack of a proven track record of economic reform, the fundamental incompatibility of a large centrally controlled economy with the market-oriented philosophy underpinning these institutions, and inadequate human rights improvements.

◆ The high-debt developing countries will probably outperform East Bloc debtor nations in structural economic adjustment and export competitiveness. Accordingly, barring radical economic reforms throughout the East Bloc, developing countries will have greater success in growing out from under their respective debt burdens and re-entering the global economy. Congressional resistance to East Bloc credit drawdowns from multilateral development banks is likely to increase significantly.

◆ Controversy in NATO countries and Japan will grow more intense over any expansion of East-West financial relations. In particular, bipartisan U.S. congressional concern over continued untied general-purpose lending by Western commercial banks (which averaged about $1.6 billion per month in 1986) will increase. The Soviet Union's recent entry into the international securities markets (through the issuing of Eurobonds) will exacerbate this concern. The damage to Western security interests from Moscow's easy diversion of the proceeds of Western untied loans could grow significantly, barring policy reforms by Western governments. It is therefore likely that an alliance consensus, led by the next U.S. administration, will establish greater voluntary discipline and transparency in Western lending to potential adversaries. Japan and the United States, which together constitute roughly 45 percent of the total annual volume of Western loans to the East Bloc, may proceed with such an initiative before Western Europe.

◆ Congress, the executive branch, and some key allies will likely focus on both unilateral and multilateral economic and financial security policies, particularly those supported by compelling commercial arguments, as compensatory measures for inadequate Western public support for sustained high levels of defense spending. The notion that billions of dollars in annual defense-related savings are achievable over time by increasing alliance discipline in its economic and financial dealings with Warsaw Pact countries and client states will become more widely accepted as a strategic doctrine. Japan may respond early to U.S. policy initiatives in this area to help offset domestic and regional constraints on sufficient defense burden sharing. Given the enormous cost of bolstering allied conventional forces and maintaining a global military base structure, the West's current inordinate economic and financial underwriting of Soviet global operations will increasingly be viewed as unaffordable.

◆ The Western Alliance consensus achieved during the first term of the Reagan administration on three key security aspects of East-West economic relations is likely to be reaffirmed. These three areas, known as the strategic trade triad, involve stemming the flow of militarily relevant Western technology, limiting Soviet natural-gas deliveries to Western Europe to 30 percent of total European gas supplies, and eliminating subsidized credits to the USSR. Aggressive Soviet efforts to overturn the International Energy Agency Agreement of May 1983 (reinforced by the Williamsburg Summit Declaration of May 1983 and the NATO Ministerial Communiqué of June 1983) and expand gas deliveries to Western Europe will probably fail.

The above predictions illustrate that economics and finance have emerged as central underpinnings of the East-West competition. This major development is consistent with the rapidly growing stature of international economic and financial considerations in overall foreign policy and national security decision making by Western governments. As mentioned earlier, the importance of these issues was reflected in the intense controversy during the Reagan administration over economic sanctions against Poland and the USSR in 1982, the OECD dispute over subsidized terms on credits to the USSR, and the huge Siberian natural-gas pipeline to Western Europe. This controversy stimulated a positive new alliance consensus in the areas of energy trade and finance.

The United States and its allies will continue their activist stance in this area for several reasons: (1) economics and finance occupy the large middle ground between diplomacy and military action and hence are often the most flexible responses to international developments adverse to Western security interests; (2) economic and financial security policies will probably be among the most effective in balancing trends toward reduced reliance on nuclear weapons in Western Europe and the lack of Western public support for adequate levels of defense spending; (3) economics and finance are the East Bloc's greatest weakness and the West's greatest strength; and (4) they offer substantial leverage with which the West can advance human rights objectives.

Although NATO and Japan will support the continuation and even expansion of nonstrategic East-West trade, the real policy action and potential controversy will still revolve around the issue of how strategic and nonstrategic trade are defined within the alliance. Even though the Reagan administration made substantial progress in achieving an allied consensus on the strategic dimensions of East-West economic relations, more policy work remains to be done, particularly in the area of financial security.

Untied General-Purpose Lending

Over the past few years the Soviet Union and its East European allies have borrowed heavily on Western financial markets. The trend toward securitization of most international borrowing and the current dearth of creditworthy sovereign borrowers have contributed to the eagerness of Western banks to lend to the East Bloc. According to Treasury Department figures, total East Bloc borrowing from the West in 1986 jumped to roughly $24 billion, or an average of about $2 billion per month. PlanEcon Inc. estimates total Western financial flows to East Bloc borrowers for 1986 at roughly $38 billion, but this figure reportedly includes short-term credits. The total amount of East Bloc debt increased to about $127 billion by the end of 1987. The types and sources of borrowing have changed markedly over the past decade.

In the 1970s most East Bloc borrowing was under Western government guarantee programs. These loans were tied to the exports of the respective Western countries as a precondition for access to often below-market terms on government-backed financing. After a year of steady effort, the Reagan administration in July 1982 achieved an agreement within the OECD that discourages subsidized terms on government-backed credits to the USSR.

Because of this development and the finer terms offered by Western commercial banks, the Eastern Bloc moved its borrowing activity strongly in the direction of the commercial banks. For example, in 1985 and 1986 the share of total East Bloc borrowing from private banks was about 90 and 85 percent respectively. Another important but unfortunate characteristic of this new East Bloc borrowing pattern was the shift away from tied specific-purpose loans (such as those in direct support of trade transactions and projects) to untied general-purpose loans by Western banks, which can be used for any purpose at the sole discretion of the borrowing country. The primary rationale for untied syndicated lending is that such loans are somewhat cheaper and easier to process for both the lenders and the borrowers than, for example, individual trade financing. The disadvantage of this development, however, has commercial, national security, and human rights dimensions.

On the commercial side, untied general-purpose lending to sovereign borrowers was one of the principal underlying causes of the current trillion-dollar international debt crisis, along with the collapse of commodity prices, disinflation, and capital flight. The large syndicated balance-of-payments loans by commercial banks during the 1970s were not verifiably linked to specific productive purposes, such as the creation of export-oriented industries or other growth-producing enterprises. For this and other reasons, over

30 countries have thus far declared repayment problems since 1982 on an estimated $650 billion in total debt.

In recognition of this harsh lesson of the last decade, the Washington-based Institute for International Finance (IIF), whose members include 170 of the world's leading commercial banks, recommended in a June 1987 report that banks should phase out untied general-purpose loans to sovereign borrowers in favor of traditional specific-purpose lending. The fundamental difference between tied and untied loans is further underscored by recent decisions by several large U.S. regional banks to write off or substantially increase loan loss provisions against only their nontrade, or untied, loans. There is relatively little 1970s-style untied lending by commercial banks to sovereign borrowers today, with the notable exception of the USSR and Eastern Europe.

The fact that the debt crisis still grips Eastern Europe and that East Bloc countries are having serious difficulties implementing major structural reforms reinforces the IIF's recommendation for greater prudence. For example, Poland and Hungary, with combined debt of over $50 billion, are likely to seek drawdowns under IMF standby arrangements sometime in 1988, reflecting the deep economic problems of these countries. Soviet client states such as Cuba, Nicaragua, Vietnam, Syria, Mozambique, and Ethiopia are also currently drawing scarce resources from the East Bloc and experiencing repayment difficulties on their Western credit obligations.

From a national security perspective, it is fundamentally unwise to provide the Soviet Union or other potential adversaries with untied loans, which are simply cash that can be flexibly diverted for purposes inimical to vital Western security interests. A hard-currency cash flow analysis of the USSR shows that in 1986 between 80 and 90 percent of total Soviet hard-currency income derived from the export of only four items: oil, gas, arms, and gold. Moscow is now encountering obstacles to enhanced earnings in all four areas. All of the USSR's hard-currency income in 1986 (approximately $29 billion) could have been used just to purchase imports from the West and to service debt. If one assumes that Soviet hard-currency earnings were earmarked for these purposes, nearly all of Moscow's global commitments requiring hard currency were funded on Western financial markets. Of the estimated $24 billion loaned by the West to East Bloc borrowers last year (not including short-term credits and interbank deposits), over $19 billion, or about 80 percent, is estimated to have been in the form of untied cash credits.

Admittedly the fungibility of money makes it difficult to trace the ultimate destination of untied Western borrowings. Nevertheless, undisciplined and at times nontransparent commercial bank lending of this kind to potential adversaries has assumed strategic importance in East-West relations and requires corrective allied action. To underscore this concern are the following plausible scenarios: (1) some of the proceeds of untied syndicated credits to East European borrowers could be skimmed and downstreamed to Soviet client states or to the USSR itself; (2) Western bank deposits in Soviet-owned banks in the West could be moved through the inter-German financial corridor or certain Middle East countries into Moscow without being detected by current Western statistical reporting procedures (such as the Bank for International Settlements); (3) certain projects in the USSR could be double-financed, with the Western equipment required for the project purchased by natural-gas or other resource deliveries while Moscow simultaneously attracts large-syndicated loans for ostensibly the same purpose; and (4) Western bank six-month deposits in Soviet-owned banks could be repeatedly renewed by Soviet traders and used as an unobserved, untied reserve checking account at almost the cost of funds for a range of purposes harmful to Western security interests. Similarly West European bank deposits in the Libyan Arab Foreign Bank could be downstreamed to help fund terrorist groups in Lebanon or elsewhere. In sum, Moscow and client state flexibility to use these and other methods to divert borrowed funds for purposes damaging to Western security would be reduced significantly by more vigilant and prudent lending practices by Western banks.

The Soviets also wish to expand significantly their access to untied Western borrowings as inexpensively and nontransparently as possible. Moscow's likely plan to accomplish this objective is to enter the international securities markets, which they did for the first time in January 1988. Besides the untied nature of these funds, other advantages to the Soviets of this development could be (1) recruiting major new Western institutions as lenders to the Soviet Union, such as securities firms, pension funds, insurance companies, corporations, and even individuals; (2) evading current Western statistical reporting, which today only records the credit exposure of banks to other banks, not the claims of nonbanks such as securities firms and pension funds; and (3) creating vested interests on the part of this new group of influential Western creditors to support continued economic, political, and financial concessions to the USSR. Over the past year and a half, several Western experts urged that high-level alliance consultations be held on the commercial and security implications of this strategic development before this threshold was crossed.

Finally, there is the issue of promoting greater transparency in East-West financial relations. The confusion in this area comes largely from misleading Soviet data and the way the Soviets have structured their banking network in the West. For example, Western bank deposit and loan exposure to 100 percent Soviet-owned banks in Western financial centers—estimated at $5–10 billion—is today not included as part of the total indebtedness of the USSR. Inter-German financial flows are also not reported to the Bank for International Settlements.

In short, the West does not have an adequate accounting of East Bloc access to Western financial resources or a clear idea of how the proceeds of Western credits and deposits are being used. Although the OECD cannot fully track complex fungible financial flows any more than the Coordinating Committee on Multilateral Export Controls (COCOM) can stem the flow of all militarily relevant Western technology to the East, major improvements in reporting can be made.

Recommendations

1. The president should use the next economic summit to propose a multilateral voluntary initiative to strengthen the discipline and transparency of Western lending practices toward potential adversaries, citing solid commercial, national security, and human rights arguments. The OECD could be tasked by the heads of state to supervise and monitor this allied policy initiative. On at least three previous occasions the OECD has successfully accomplished similar undertakings. Specifically Western banks should be urged to verify as far as possible the uses of borrowed funds by tying their loans to equipment exports, commodity transactions, or tightly structured projects. Maturities on loans should be strictly matched against the duration of the underlying trade transactions. A documented effort should be made to ensure that the proceeds of loans for the project or joint venture are genuinely dedicated to the project or joint venture in question. Western bank deposits in all Soviet-owned banks, including those in the West, should be aggregated and reported to bank regulators.

2. Present gaps in Western statistical reporting should be closed so that Western analysts can more precisely estimate the total amount of credits and deposits available to Warsaw Pact countries and their client states at any one time. Western banks and governments should demand much greater data disclosure from East Bloc borrowers. Inter-German financial flows should be reported in full to the Bank for International Settlements. The quality of Soviet hard-currency loans to Eastern Europe and the Third World, which according to PlanEcon total roughly $65 billion, should be more carefully examined.

3. Ministerial-level OECD consultations should be convened immediately on the security aspects of Soviet entry into the international securities markets. The Soviet Union should be denied expanded access to the international securities markets because of the untied and

largely invisible nature of the funds raised in these markets, unless mitigating adjustments can be made. Maintaining as far as possible Western banks and governments as the only holders of Soviet debt would greatly improve Alliance monitoring capabilities, which will be crucial if the containment policies of the 1990s and beyond are to be affordable and successful.

4. The new strategic field of East-West economic security should be institutionalized in the executive branch by the next administration. Accordingly new positions and groups should be established, such as a new under secretary of defense for international economic security (with emphasis on East-West relations), who would act as a counterpart to the new Commerce Department under secretary for export administration. A standing Cabinet-level group should manage these issues under the auspices of the National Security Council, as in the first term of the Reagan administration. The intelligence community's resources in the area of economic and financial security should be bolstered substantially.

5. The 1990s may witness increased friction between industrialized countries, debtor and creditor nations, and industrialized countries and the Third World. Differences among democratic nations over trade and financial issues should not compromise a security-minded perspective on East-West economic and financial relations. Many socialist countries have embarked on a largely uncharted course of economic reform. A multiyear wait-and-see attitude is prudent before integrating these economies further into Western economic and financial institutions, particularly if the interests of the export-oriented developing countries are jeopardized. Before sitting down with the Soviets to discuss short-range nuclear arms reductions, the administration and Congress should seek a comprehensive NATO (plus Japan) economic and financial security policy toward Warsaw Pact countries and client states.

6. The United States and our allies should continue to support nonstrategic East-West trade to build incentives for greater geopolitical cooperation, but without subsidies or other artificial support. The widespread availability of certain Western technologies should be recognized, and the list of items inhibited by COCOM should be trimmed to only those items that could harm Western security interests. The COCOM list review should be accelerated so that older technologies can be freely sold to the East Bloc. The funding of COCOM as an institution should be sustantially increased from today's inadequate levels.

Conclusion

Sensible Western economic and financial security policies should be fully integrated into our overall strategic analysis of East-West relations. Creative policy proposals in this area warrant close attention by policy makers to compensate for continued conventional force imbalances in Western Europe and the erosion of adequate levels of Western defense spending to counter the Soviet threat. The West should reject the current East Bloc economic agenda, designed to revitalize those economies without making meaningful foreign policy and human rights concessions. Alliance partners should be able to craft prudent East-West economic and financial policies that permit unsubsidized nonstrategic trade to proceed unimpeded. Such policies should limit the acquisition of militarily relevant technology by Warsaw Pact countries, the undisciplined cash underwriting of Soviet global operations by Western banks, and Moscow's command of West European natural-gas markets. To do so would make sound commercial sense and would greatly advance our broader national security and human rights objectives.

LAWRENCE J. BRAINARD

◆ ─────────────────────────────────── ◆

Trade, Debt, and National Security

U.S. Security: Economic and Military Dimensions

◆ Americans have traditionally worried about military security but have taken economic security—the preservation of economic liberties and the well-being of our citizens—for granted. During the postwar era the U.S. economic system provided unquestioned economic prosperity at home and supremacy in international economic matters. There seemed little reason to worry about economic security.

During the 1980s the foundations of U.S. national security changed significantly. The military was strengthened as the Reagan administration responded forcefully to the post-Vietnam deterioration of U.S. military power around the world. At the same time, however, divergent economic changes raised new questions about economic dimensions of U.S. national security. The administration's tax reforms and other economic policies boosted economic growth. But unexpected international developments pushed the country's trade deficit to record levels, and foreign borrowing expanded dramatically.

Will international economic changes threaten U.S. national security in the years ahead? If the next administration diagnoses these problems correctly and makes appropriate changes in policy to deal with them, the United States need not sacrifice its hard-won achievements in either military or economic security. But the issues are complex, and the penalties for mistaken policies could be substantial.

U.S. Indebtedness and National Security

In the 1970s debt creation centered on the Third World, culminating in the 1982 debt crisis in the less-developed countries (LDCs). During the 1980s debt creation shifted to the United States. As trade deficits grew, the U.S. international investment position steadily deteriorated, and the country joined the ranks of net international debtors for the first time since World War I.

With the rising level of U.S. borrowings from abroad during the mid-1980s, consumption exceeded production at all levels—the federal government, businesses, and individuals—and contributed to the rising U.S. trade deficit. But apart from a reluctance (some would say an inability) to bring expenditures in line with income, especially on the federal level, U.S. economic performance was strong. As Herbert Stein has reminded us, the budget deficit reflects a collective lack of will, not U.S. economic weakness.[1] Whatever the cause of these problems, though, they clearly challenge future U.S. economic policy.

Measures of the value of the U.S. net debt position ranged from $100 billion to over $400 billion at the end of 1987. As a rough order of magnitude, the cumulative U.S. current account deficit during 1983–1987 totaled nearly $500 billion, suggesting the scope of the deterioration in the country's net investment position over these five years. The counterpart to this rising indebtedness was a growing positive net international asset position for Japan and Germany, the two principal surplus countries. Japan's net international assets totaled an estimated $340 billion at the end of 1987, up from only $11 billion in 1981. Germany's net surplus at the time was more modest but still substantial, an estimated $150 billion.[2]

How will the United States manage its trade and debt? Will dollar depreciation and increased inflows of foreign investment bring trade and debt more into line by decelerating the debt buildup and boosting trade? Or will the rising U.S. indebtedness lead to financial instabilities, provoking further sharp falls in the dollar and eventually a serious world recession?

Part of the U.S. trade problem derives from overseas protectionist barriers to our exports. Examples include subsidies to domestic producers, especially to agriculture in Japan and Europe, undervalued currencies in South Korea and the Republic of China, and restrictive bidding practices for public contracts in many countries. There is common agreement that U.S. policy should vigorously seek changes in such practices.

Experts appear divided, however, on how to deal with the broader issues of global trade and debt imbalances. Some economists believe that market-driven adjustments are both feasible and desirable. But others worry that financial instability and dollar collapse are more probable. It is important, then, to diagnose the problem carefully to understand both points of view.

Even if standard market-based mechanisms can accomplish much of the required adjustment, success here could nonetheless erode U.S. national security. Unless appropriate policies are designed and implemented to anticipate such developments, a solution for our economic problems would come at the expense of our military security. To explore the implications of this dilemma, we start with an assessment of the changing role of trade and capital in the international economy.

Trade Flows and Capital Flows

During the past two decades the relative roles of trade and capital in the international economy have undergone a gradual but steady reversal. Trade was the driving force behind global economic growth from postwar recovery into the early 1970s. International capital flows mirrored these trade flows, since financing was typically tied to the stream of exports from industrial countries.

With the oil price hike in 1973, a worldwide pattern of trade surpluses and deficits emerged overnight. Worried about the potential implications of the energy crisis on the economies of the oil-importing countries, policy makers in industrial countries reordered their priorities. Banks were encouraged to lend to finance these trade imbalances, especially for the developing countries. It seemed desirable to facilitate the needed economic changes by spreading the adjustment over several years. The choice of the financing option opened the international economy to a set of new and unpredictable forces. The previous link between trade and capital was broken as the growth of financing took on a life of its own, independent of trade and production flows.

Two important earlier developments set the stage for the spectacular growth in international capital markets that continues to this day. One was an innovation of the late 1960s, the Eurodollar rollover loan with its variable interest rate, which facilitated long-term bank lending by reducing the risks of interest rate fluctuations. A group of neophytes—the commercial banks—engaged in large-scale foreign lending. Unlike earlier periods when they had acted primarily as underwriters distributing bonds to nonbank investors, the banks were now lending on their own account.

The second development was the 1971 breakdown of the Bretton Woods arrangements followed by a transition to floating exchange rates two years later. The new system facilitated the accommodation of diverse economic policies among the major countries through variations in capital flows and fluctuations in exchange rates and interest rates. The link between balance-of-payments disequilibrium and pressures for real adjustments in production and trade weakened. At the time this development seemed welcome, given the perceived rigidities of the fixed-rate system. But increasingly capital flows—not flexible exchange rates—began to dominate trends in the real economy.

This was the era of recycling. Financing was in; adjustment was out. Awash with deposits from the oil-exporting countries, banks scrambled to relend these funds in ever larger syndications mostly to sovereign borrowers, who used the proceeds to cover their balance-of-payments deficits. Cutthroat competition among banks undermined traditional credit discipline as loan maturities lengthened and credit standards were compromised.

In the inflationary environment of the mid- and late 1970s, it was easy for the LDCs and other sovereign borrowers to lose sight of the need for fundamental balance-of-payments adjustment. Exports were rising rapidly, and debt ratios were stable or were rising only moderately. Many believed that economic growth—led by expansion in the United States and other locomotive economies—was the answer to world economic problems. Moreover, nobody seemed in charge of the overall stability and integrity of the international financial system.

When Federal Reserve Board Chairman Paul Volcker decided to tackle the U.S. inflation problem in October 1979, he hardly considered that tightening monetary policy might fuel an LDC debt crisis. Indeed, many considered the LDCs' debt and economic performance in the late 1970s basically sound. No one recognized that their apparent success in trade and economic growth, driven by a boom in global capital flows, was not sustainable. As sharp declines in growth ensued in 1980–1981, banks restricted international lending, triggering the LDC debt crisis.

By the early 1980s international capital had assumed several new roles. Policies to manage the LDC crisis, for example, emphasized the provision of involuntary new money from the banks and increased disbursements from multilateral agencies such as the World Bank. This approach reflected complexities of the debt itself. No mechanism could determine and allocate the implicit losses among the diverse creditors—including hundreds of banks, First World governments, and multilateral agencies. And radical changes in debtors' economic policies, including the conversion of debt into the equity ownership of state companies, were ruled out. Instead of conforming existing claims to underlying trade and production realities, official policy artificially sustained private and official capital flows, whose excesses had caused the problem in the first place.

Substantial shifts in capital flows associated with the LDC debt crisis also contributed to the substantial overvaluation of the dollar in 1983–1985. Because of the wave of LDC defaults in late 1982 and early 1983, outflows of capital associated with U.S. bank lending abroad dried up overnight. Private bank capital outflows of nearly $50 billion in 1982 turned into net inflows of $20 billion a year later. The overvalued dollar in turn contributed to the deterioration in U.S. trade, producing relatively sudden shifts in the flow of international capital toward Japan and Germany, the new surplus countries.

The Dynamics of Capital Markets

In the short space of twenty years capital has moved onto center stage, with significant effects on growth and change in the international economy.[3] This transformation has been facilitated and strengthened by policy changes in the industrial countries, by new technologies, and by financial innovation that together have created a global integrated capital market characterized by large asset volumes, rapid shifts in assets, and complex relations among various markets.

Financial deregulation and privatization in the United States and other major industrial countries have contributed to the globalization of capital not only in banking but also in the securities business. A competitive element has sustained these changes as countries have pursued deregulation in order not to lose capital-market business to other countries. New telecommunications technologies permitted the worldwide instantaneous linkage of financial markets, amply demonstrated in the October 1987 stock market crash. Computers have meanwhile facilitated the tracking and management of individual banks' risks in capital markets, thereby reducing costs and supporting an expansion of transaction volumes in capital markets. Financial innovations have improved the efficiency of markets by offering a new array of instruments for borrowing and hedging interest rate and foreign-currency exposures.

Financial globalization, though, has also changed the rules of the international economy. Rapid financial innovation and deregulation have accelerated debt while reducing the credit quality of the debt obligations. Complex new financial instruments have also masked their underlying risks. These factors have reduced financial discipline and increased the vulnerability of the system to shocks and loss of confidence. And with market confidence the operational rule of the global marketplace, increased volatility is inevitable.

Stability and Capital Markets

In considering how the United States will manage its trade and debt problems, we should not fear that the accumulation of international capital in Japan and Germany will be used to protect and expand these countries' comparative advantage in trade. The importance of technology to competitive advantage is indisputable. But there is little evidence that the accumulation of foreign financial assets is critical to generating new technologies. What matters is past investment in human capital, management, entrepreneurship, effective incentives for innovation, and (in isolated cases) government subsidies. Japanese companies are increasingly effective in generating new technologies because they are learning how to put these critical elements together, not because they derive special advantages from large foreign-asset holdings. And although capital resources are obviously needed for investments in research and development, U.S. firms have few difficulties securing such funds.

Growing Japanese and German asset holdings do permit increased investment in the United States. But that is exactly what is needed to reduce the debt overhang. By creating jobs, reducing imports, or increasing exports, such investments strengthen the U.S. economy and provide the income to service the dividends sent abroad—though if past U.S. experience in foreign direct investment is a guide, most of the earnings will likely be reinvested. It is essential, however, for U.S. policy to provide safeguards for U.S. companies in security-related fields.

Whereas U.S. policy should clearly seek to remove protectionist barriers to our exports, we should not worry that Japan and Germany's accumulation of foreign assets will by itself sustain current trade and debt imbalances. Foreign investment in the United States should be encouraged. A more relevant concern is how the capital markets themselves will react to the rising level of U.S. debt. The increased liberalization of domestic and international capital flows has helped finance the U.S. deficit, but these developments also make the economy vulnerable. Stability requires that debt created within a financial system be tied to production or underlying asset values—as reflected, for example, in a company's cash flow or a country's export revenues.

U.S. economic policies to support domestic growth, increased productive investment, and expanded exports are therefore essential to the stability of the adjustment process. The markets are looking for reassurance that increased debt will be associated with a general strengthening of U.S. exports and growth.

The issue of the budget deficit must be assessed in this regard. Reducing the deficit will contribute to market stability only if the reduction is seen to strengthen economic growth prospects. Such a reduction is clearly desirable, but not all approaches to deficit reduction have this goal. The best way to cut the deficit is to shift taxes from investment to consumption and to cut government consumption-related spending. The introduction of incentives for savings and investment associated with a longer-term growth-oriented strategy are also desirable.

A related issue concerns the market's perception of U.S. monetary policies. Erratic swings in Federal Reserve policy in recent years have undermined the confidence of international markets. To take advantage of the current competitiveness of U.S. goods by increasing new investments, manufacturers need confidence that interest rates and the foreign exchange rate of the dollar will not be subject to wide swings up and down. Monetary policy can best promote the long-term investment process by aiming for stable and consistent monetary management.

The essential debt problem facing the United States is that international capital markets could cause financial instability and recession. But there are also opportunities to manage the problem without causing economic calamity. A consistent set of long-term economic policies aimed at stimulating productivity, investment, and increased private savings will reduce the risks of possible capital-market instability.

Implications for National Security

Even with the best domestic adjustment policies, the United States will find its opportunities to expand and enhance U.S. interests abroad increasingly circumscribed by the past accumulation of debt, the continuing trade deficit, and the decline in the dollar's value. Appropriate security-oriented policies are needed, therefore, to complement the package of domestic adjustment measures recommended above. There are three areas of concern: sharing the military burden with our allies, East-West relations, and the LDC debt crisis.

Sharing the Defense Burden

Without new burden-sharing arrangements on defense, the U.S. policy of dollar depreciation only increases the disparity between our defense commitments abroad and our lack of resources. The decline of the dollar raises military expenditures and—in an era of budget stringency—undermines our ability to meet our foreign military security commitments.

Current arrangements on burden sharing with Japan and Germany are inappropriate for a world in which the United States is one among several *coequal* partners. The United States, the indebted coequal, provides military security for all partners and pays most of the cost. Germany and Japan pay far less than they can afford, while devoting their energies to preserving and extending their competitive economic and technical advantage. A more equitable sharing of the West's common defense burden is needed. Whether this adjustment will involve pulling U.S. troops out of Europe and Asia depends on how the allies define their defense requirements and how much they are willing to pay.

East-West Relations

Burdened with inefficient economies and outmoded industrial plant, the Soviet Union and other socialist countries face severe economic adjustments in the years ahead. Their survival strategies will likely focus on engaging the West in an interlocking set of agreements in the military, political, and economic spheres. Although relations in the military sphere will focus on the United States, economic initiatives will be directed elsewhere.

In their search for capital the Soviet Union and Eastern Europe will target Germany, the primary European surplus country, whereas China will likely target Japan. Given the sharp appreciation of their respective currencies, Germany and Japan will find offers of new export markets hard to resist. The surplus capital to finance such exports is already at hand.

A new strategic perspective on the role of capital in East-West transactions is essential. The transfer of untied financial resources and technology by our allies to the East imposes large security costs on the United States. The allies should agree on policies to ensure that such East-West transactions are nonstrategic and that the socialist countries make available essential economic data.

The LDC Debt Crisis

Failure to manage the LDC debt crisis would clearly threaten U.S. interests if it led to political instability in Latin America. But debt relief for middle-income countries able to implement economic reforms is not the answer because it would jeopardize their access to trade and undermine bank financing of trade in other countries thought likely to follow the path of forgiveness. Forgiveness also leads to a loss of confidence by potential domestic and foreign investors in the debtor countries, thus reinforcing the cycle of low investment and low growth.

Experience shows that the only way for debtor countries to gain access to new capital inflows is through the restoration of confidence resulting from sound economic policies and reforms. Restoring the confidence of those supplying the capital has been a key element of the Reagan administration's debt strategy. Despite the chorus recommending debt relief, nothing has changed that would alter this aspect of the strategy.

New initiatives, though, are both desirable and feasible. Mechanisms such as the conversion of debt into equity investments and other voluntary market-oriented programs deserve support. Such programs provide effective cash-flow relief to the debtor. In addition, other voluntary market-based mechanisms are desirable to allow smaller banks to get out of the forced new money exercises—at a cost.

Conclusion

The evolution of international capital over the past two decades has transformed the international economy. But policy makers have been slow to grasp how these dynamic changes affect U.S. economic prosperity and national security interests. As the next administration looks to the 1990s, it faces the risk that international capital will control the country's destiny, leading to disarray in financial markets, loss of confidence, and inevitably recession and a serious erosion of U.S. national security. The option to control our own destiny as a nation, however, is also clear. It lies in promoting productivity, increased competitiveness, and savings.

Notes

1. Herbert Stein, "Lack of U.S. Will Isn't Economy's Fault," *Wall Street Journal*, January 20, 1988, p. 28.

2. Data on net international investment positions are published periodically in official sources: the *Survey of Current Business* in the United States, the *Monthly Report* of the German Bundesbank, and the *Balance of Payments Monthly* of the Bank of Japan. Estimates of the U.S. net international investment position differ because some use stock estimates, which assess U.S. foreign investment at book value and hence understate U.S. foreign assets, whereas others use net flows of interest and other factor payments, which suggest that the United States became a net debtor in mid-1987. To derive the end-1987 estimates, the 1986 data are adjusted by the estimated 1987 current account positions of each country.

3. For a similar argument including specific examples of foreign direct investment, see Peter F. Drucker, "From World Trade to World Investment," *Wall Street Journal*, May 26, 1987, p. 30.

MELVYN KRAUSS

◆ —————————————— ◆

Foreign Aid, Protectionism, and National Security

◆ The Soviet Union has substantially extended its influence in the poorer countries of the world in the past two decades. Angola, Ethiopia, South Yemen, Vietnam, Laos, Cambodia, Afghanistan, Nicaragua, Syria, Libya, Madagascar, and Congo have all fallen into the Soviet orbit. In the Western Hemisphere the problem of growing Soviet influence—first in Cuba, then in Nicaragua—has been particularly disconcerting. Achieving social and political stability in countries such as Haiti, Guatemala, El Salvador, and Honduras is clearly of paramount importance to U.S. national security interests.

The preferred tactic of liberals in the U.S. Congress and foreign service professionals in the State Department has been to increase economic aid. But if we really eschewed protectionism and opened our borders to our neighbors' exports, our hemisphere would realize the economic prosperity and political stability we seek but fail to attain with economic aid. This essay argues that trade, not aid, is the way to defeat the communists in the Third World.

Copycatting the Soviets

The Soviets have certainly had some success in using economic aid to influence, and sometimes to control, aid recipients. If the Soviets do it, why shouldn't we? Indeed, because of our greater wealth, Washington should have a comparative advantage over Moscow in this area. But just because we are richer than our adversary does not mean that U.S. leaders have fewer economic resource constraints than do Soviet leaders. That the United States is a real democracy works to our disadvantage in the use of economic aid for strategic purposes.

In both the United States and the USSR there is a trade-off between the amount of resources that can be put into economic aid and that available for other uses—for example, the satisfaction of consumer needs and social services. In a totalitarian system resources are allocated by a small group of men operating in secret. If a consensus exists among these men to put resources into imperialist adventures, no one can stop them. The amount of resources the U.S. government can divert to combat Soviet imperialism, however, is limited by public tolerance of the anti-imperialist measures. Historically public tolerance for economic aid in this country has been low. Thus even though our economy is more productive, U.S. leaders may work under more severe economic resource constraints.

Our democratic institutions put the United States at a comparative disadvantage to the Soviets in another, more important, respect. When, for example, economic aid is given for strategic reasons, its purpose is to make the aid recipient dependent on the donor and hence amenable to manipulation. The United States' potential to manipulate aid recipients, however, is limited by the influence that the recipients' friends can have on Congress and the White House through the democratic process. The relationship between Israel and the United States is a case in point. The United States gives more economic aid to Israel than to any other country. There is also a wealthy, politically active, well-organized Jewish community in the United States that has made economic aid to Israel something of a sacred cow. The politician that dares oppose it faces certain and substantial retribution.

This situation has not been good for the United States or for Israel. From the U.S. point of view, our economic aid to Israel has not given us the leverage over Israel's foreign policies we would like to have. From Israel's, the economic aid has allowed successive Israeli governments to follow ruinous economic policies. A country that spends almost 50 percent of its public budget on defense cannot afford the elaborate welfare state Israel has been able to finance because of the economic aid it receives from the United States. Instead of making Israel's economy strong, U.S. economic aid has made Israel the Sweden of the Mediterranean.

Does Cuba have the same political clout in Moscow that Israel has in Washington? It is highly unlikely that the Cuban tail wags the Soviet dog. As noted above, in the decentralized political system of the United States, a client state can exert an influence over the most important decision makers by appeals to public opinion and the media. In a totalitarian system, these avenues of influence do not exist.

Moreover, Castro's ideological base is so intrinsically anti-American that he has no real bargaining power with the Kremlin. Can anyone seriously imagine Castro trying to hold up the Soviets for more economic aid by threatening to adopt pro-American policies? Yet U.S. clientele in the Third World consistently threaten the United States that if it does not give—and give generously—they will turn to the other superpower for assistance. For example, in 1985 several noncommunist Latin American countries were reported to be warming up to Castro, who, in an interview with a Mexican newspaper in March 1985, said that the Latin American foreign debt of $360 billion cannot be paid and must be canceled by U.S. banks. The message the debt-ridden Latin American governments were—and to some extent still are—sending Washington is obvious enough: unless you bail us out with economic aid on favorable terms, we will tilt our foreign policies toward Havana and Moscow. Because the ideological orientation of these countries is not intrinsically anti-Soviet, their threat to change political color has a credibility in Washington that Castro lacks in Moscow.

Sometimes, of course, U.S. clients in the Third World are so implacably anticommunist that any threat on their part to defect to the other side would be equally incredible. But even in these cases, buying the allegiance of foreign leaders with money that often finds its way into numbered Swiss bank accounts is fraught with danger. The United States had Marcos of the Philippines in its pocket; the same can be said of Somoza in Nicaragua, the shah in Iran, and Batista in Cuba. But our close identification with these former heads of state guaranteed that their successors would be anti-American. True, U.S. foreign aid bought the allegiances of these former leaders for a time. But now the United States must face the unenviable prospect of dealing with Ortega in Nicaragua, Khomeini in Iran, and Castro in Cuba.

The Food Aid Deception

Even in cases where economic aid is given for humanitarian reasons—food aid, for example—more often than not it props up an incompetent government or winds up in the pockets of corrupt public officials. Rarely does it reach the poor people for whom it is intended. As Peter Bauer writes: "Food aid does not in fact go to the pitiable figures we see on aid posters, in aid advertisements, and in other aid propaganda in the media. It goes to the governments, that is to the rulers, and the policies of the rulers who receive aid are sometimes directly responsible for conditions such as those depicted."[1]

A 1981 story in the *Wall Street Journal* confirms that food aid often winds up being used by the governments of poor countries to subsidize elites and keep themselves in power:

> No wonder the effectiveness of food aid around the world is under suspicion in the United States. Some critics have concluded that this low-cost food is merely a device for keeping elites in power by propping up foreign-government budgets and feeding influential middle classes. Food aid has discouraged food production, these analysts say, and has failed to address the basic challenge of helping the poor earn enough to buy the food already available.[2]

In Bangladesh, for example, food aid meant for starving people never reaches them because the government uses the food to buy votes. "Governments typically sell the food on local markets and use the proceeds however they choose. Here, the government chooses to sell the food in cut-rate ration shops to members of the middle class."[3]

The Bangladesh case of misused food aid is by no means isolated. Indeed, compared to the recent tragedy in Ethiopia, it is distinctly minor. No doubt many of us remember the heart-breaking pictures and television reports of starving adults and children in that poverty-stricken North African country. People were dying a horrible death before our eyes as we sat in the comfort and security of our living rooms watching their cruel fate on television. Who was not moved to give generously to famine relief in the face of such calamity?

It goes without saying that U.S. television assured its viewers at the time that the deaths they were viewing were due to famine—a natural, not man-made, calamity. But according to a group of concerned physicians, Doctors Without Borders, "more Ethiopians were dying as a result of the policies of their Government than as a result of famine." As many as 300,000 people are likely to die in the forced relocation from north to south, a death rate of 20 percent. The group calls the relocation program "one of the most massive violations of human rights we have seen" and notes that it is "being carried out with funds and gifts from international aid."[4]

Some days after Doctors Without Borders released their report, the *Wall Street Journal* published the following editorial:

> French relief workers were touring Washington last week with awful news that had already been reported by eyewitnesses from the U.S. Agency for International Development. The Ethiopian government's year-old "relocation program," now greatly stepped up by the military Dergue, or junta, and its Russian patrons, has already claimed the lives of 20 percent of its targets, a death toll of some 100,000. It shapes up as a mass extermination

in the order of the Khmer Rouge killing fields and the deportation of Armenians, in 1915, with the added horror that *it would not have been possible without the aid and silence of Western famine relief.*[5]

Time quoted Britain's *Economist*:

Aid will strengthen the dominion of Ethiopia's ignorant rulers. The weather is the only calamity not directly caused by Colonel Mengistu . . . and his cronies. Their Russian advisers have taught them to run vast state farms that produce no food. Imitating Stalin's anti-kulak terror, they have shot "hoarders and saboteurs" prudent enough to store grain . . . Help for the starving may make some of them suffer more, and reinforce the grip of the government that caused them to starve.[6]

Unhappily, the Ethiopian case is not the only one where food aid financed government persecution of innocent peasants. According to Peter Bauer, "without large-scale external aid [Tanzanian President Nyerere] would not have been able to persist for so many years with *forced* collectivization and large-scale removal of people into so-called socialist villages. These policies not only involved brutality and hardship but had devastating effects on food production and distribution, and on economic conditions generally."[7]

The Ethiopian case shows that food aid helps bad governments do bad things to their own people. Such bad things, of course, are not always as extreme as forced deportation and collectivization. Food aid may simply facilitate classic policy errors in recipient countries, which make poor countries even poorer. From a public policy point of view, it is better to do nothing than something if something only makes matters worse.

A specific example where food aid facilitated bad general economic policy is India, where the strategy of its second and third five-year plans focused on import-substituting industry, particularly heavy industry. It is generally agreed that India could not have pursued its misconceived strategy, which transfers domestic resources from high- to low-productivity uses, without generous food aid from abroad, particularly from the United States. Even friends of foreign aid, such as liberal economists Paul Iserman and Hans Singer, blame food aid: "Food aid supported and facilitated the [import substitution] strategy, primarily by enabling the Indian government to maintain large subsidized distribution programs while, in the eyes of most analysts, not adequately addressing some basic questions of food grain production and distribution."[8]

Import substitution artificially transfers resources out of agriculture and into industry. This transfer reduces agricultural production—which raises the price of food unless food can be imported from abroad. Without imported food, import substitution would cease, particularly in a democratic country like India where the government would respond to popular discontent over food shortages and high food prices. The example of India illustrates the food aid trap: The demand for food aid in Third World countries indicates severe economic mismanagement. Yet satisfying that demand only perpetuates the economic mismanagement responsible for poverty in the first place.

So far, attention has focused on the role food aid plays in facilitating bad or foolish policies by bad or foolish governments. We turn next to the so-called disincentive effects of food aid—the direct role food aid plays in damaging local agriculture in recipient countries.

By increasing the amount of food available for domestic consumption, food aid depresses the price of agricultural products in recipient countries. Such price reductions in turn depress agricultural output, so that what the recipient country gains in food aid it loses to some extent in domestic output. When the offset in domestic output equals the food aid, the marginal effect of food aid on food supply is zero. In this case food aid fails to increase the recipient's domestic supply of food. The marginal effect is greater than zero but less than unity when the offset of domestic supply is less than the food aid. And it is even theoretically possible for the domestic supply offset to be greater than the food aid, in which case the marginal effect of food aid is negative.

Whatever the marginal effect of food aid on total food supply, however, it can clearly have a negative effect—sometimes devastatingly negative—on domestic food production. For example, from 1953 to 1971 wheat imported to Colombia under food aid rose from 50 percent to about 90 percent of total wheat consumption. In that same period the price for wheat declined by about half while wheat production declined sharply to about one-third its original level.[9] Note the direction of causality. Food aid did not result from low food production; low food production resulted from food aid.

Moving down the supply curve is not the only consequence of price changes induced by food aid. There are also the income transfer effects of price changes to consider—and these too tend to reduce agricultural production in aid-receiving countries. Income transfer effects relate to the changes in the distribution of income caused by price changes. When, for example, the price of agricultural commodities declines because of food aid, income is redistributed from local producers to local consumers. Whatever the ethics of such redistribution, it is likely to reduce agricultural production by reducing the means by which agricultural investment, either to extend the margin of cultivation or to improve productivity through technological progress, can be made. When investment suffers, so must production.

This analysis of food aid—which applies to general economic assistance as well—has an important message for the U.S. public. Although many of us assume that food and other forms of aid create goodwill for the United States abroad, the truth is often the opposite. In recipient countries, the aid may be seen as propping up defunct and corrupt governments whose incompetent and exploitative policies are responsible for their citizens' poverty in the first place. The oppressed and exploited come to identify U.S. aid with the oppressors and exploiters. Sometimes we are not entirely innocent of this charge. In our attempt to keep the communists out, we can and sometimes have aligned ourselves with some pretty nasty fellows. But often we are victims of our own naiveté. We think we are doing good when in fact we do harm—both to ourselves and to others. Fortunately other avenues for helping poor people do not suffer from the substantial liabilities that burden economic aid.

Playing to Our Strength

Those who argue that the United States' comparative advantage over the Soviets in the Third World lies in economic aid are correct in only one respect: that our economy is our strength. This country must learn to turn its enormous economic strength to its strategic advantage if it is to impede the spread of communism among the poorer countries. Unfortunately the United States has probably spent too much time and too many resources containing communism, and too little time and too few resources spreading capitalism. The marketplace is this country's strongest institution, and the United States must learn to use it to help poorer countries develop a vested interest in the capitalist system. Once capitalism spreads, communism will contain itself.

The best way the United States can spread capitalism is through deeds, not words. The poor countries of the world have already had too many lectures about the benefits of free trade and too few examples of it. Access to the vast U.S. market is what these countries need—and should get—to build their allegiance to a capitalist system. Over the long run, protectionism is as subversive to U.S. security interests as Castro and Ortega.

That access to the U.S. market is preferred to U.S. aid by at least one of our most important allies was recently made clear by Turkish Prime Minister Turgut Ozal. One look at the map reveals Turkey's strategic importance to the United States. Not only does it guard frontiers with the Soviet Union,

Bulgaria, and the straits from the Black Sea into the Mediterranean, but it also shares borders with Iran, Iraq, and Syria. According to the *New York Times*, "Mr. Ozal said Turkey was 'not fairly treated' [by the U.S.] in comparison with the two top beneficiaries of American military aid, Israel and Egypt, the only countries that receive more aid than Turkey." The Turkish prime minister, however, is not seeking additional military aid; instead, he is asking that U.S. protectionism be relaxed. "Mr. Ozal . . . said protectionism limited the export of such Turkish products as textiles and steel goods. He also said that Turkey received little help in reducing a trade deficit of $800 million with the United States."[10]

"We are spending a lot for our armed forces," Mr. Ozal said. "This affects our economic development. We have the poorest per capita income in NATO." The Turkish prime minister's comments demonstrate the link between increased U.S. imports on the one hand and the fight to contain communism on the other. Many U.S. allies would prefer trade to aid but settle for aid because that is what the U.S. government offers them. When Secretary of State Shultz, for example, traveled to Turkey in March 1986, influential Turks told him to "assist us not by aid, but by facilitating our export performance."[11] Indeed, Turkey explicitly linked the renewal of U.S. military-base rights to major trade concessions by the United States.

National Security and Protectionism

If capitalism is to be encouraged abroad, protectionism must be discouraged at home. We ask Third World countries to reject communism. Yet our protectionist policies drive them into the communists' lap by restricting Third World exports to the most important market. To make matters worse, the products whose entry we restrict—textiles, clothing, sugar—are the very ones our neighbors in the Western Hemisphere can produce efficiently. Because the poorer nations of the world economy are endowed with relatively large amounts of labor compared with other factors of production, they tend to export labor-intensive products. But labor in the United States wants protection from cheaper labor abroad—and by lobbying Congress and the White House, it has achieved many of its protectionist goals. Unfortunately neither public officials nor the public fully realize the national security implications of yielding to self-serving protectionist interests.

No doubt the fires of protectionism have been fanned in this country by the record U.S. trade deficits run up during the Reagan years. Moreover, mercantilists reason that the U.S. record trade deficit is proof that the U.S. economy is sick. But the truth is the opposite. In fact we have a large trade deficit because of record capital inflows to this country. The promise of Reagan's early years in office attracted capital to this country from all over the world. This flow can be considered a vote of confidence in the Reagan agenda by international capitalists. But as record amounts of capital came into the United States, the dollar was bid up in foreign exchange markets. The high dollar in turn made it difficult for our exports to compete abroad and easy for imports to compete with U.S. import substitutes. The result was record U.S. trade deficits. When interpreted properly, the record trade deficits show that capital from all over the world wants to invest in the United States—a sign of health, not sickness.

But even in healthy economies not all industries prosper. And in the U.S. economy during Reagan's first term some domestic industries suffered disproportionately from the high dollar—agriculture, automobiles, farm machinery, steel, and so on. Not surprisingly these industries led the protectionist charge in Washington.

The protectionist agenda has been (1) to reduce the international value of the dollar and (2) to impose trade restrictions on U.S. imports. Unfortunately the Reagan administration has accommodated the protectionists on both points. On the first, although the dollar probably would have come down anyway, its descent was accelerated and exacerbated by U.S. Treasury Secretary James Baker's statements that it was official U.S. policy to get the dollar lower. On the second point, Reagan has effected numerous trade restrictions—on automobiles, semiconductor chips, sugar, motorcycles, textiles, clothing, electronics, and so on—though he claimed, as he signed successive pieces of restrictionist legislation, that he was pushed into his increasingly protectionist stance by an even more protectionist Congress. The president's rhetoric continues to espouse free trade, but his record is more protectionist than Jimmy Carter's.

A U.S.–Caribbean Basin Common Market

Instead of playing a game in which the Soviets can compete effectively— buying foreign leaders with economic aid—we should play one in which the Soviet disadvantage is so great that it guarantees a U.S. victory. The USSR simply could not match the economic impact of the United States' granting unlimited access to its vast market. We could use trade against the Soviets as they use aid against us. Let the United States declare war on communism in Central America, for example, not by sending in troops but by forming a common market with all countries in Central America who want to participate. As Irving Kristol asks:

> How can the U.S. achieve a reasonable measure of social and political stability in Central America? The power of example clearly does not work, nor does economic aid, while military occupation goes against the American grain. Is there really nothing the U.S. can do? . . . There is indeed a way by which the U.S. can offer its client states—many of them, at least—the benefits of economic growth and political liberty while maintaining adequate stability. And that way is economic integration.[12]

The United States should agree to eliminate all obstacles to imports from any Central American country that agrees to reciprocate by removing all obstacles to U.S. exports. A common market with the Caribbean Basin countries would help fight communism in at least four important ways: (1) it would increase the exports and economic well-being of the Central American countries; (2) it would create an allegiance to capitalism in a part of the world where the economic process has been dominated by the political process for too long; (3) it would improve the efficiency of the Caribbean Basin economies by imposing more liberal trade policies; and (4) it would place Uncle Sam in a new light.

A common market with the Caribbean Basin would help alleviate resentment against the United States by showing the region that the United States practices the competitive ethic it preaches. Economic aid merely reinforces our enemies' image of Uncle Sam—a rich bully all too willing to use its enormous wealth to manipulate others for its own selfish reasons.

Conclusion

In countering Moscow's moves in the Third World, Washington must develop tactics and strategies appropriate to U.S. institutions, values, and strengths—not simply imitate the tactics of our rivals. Our strong suit is our economy, and we must learn to use our enormous economic power to improve the material standard not only of our own citizens but of all those who live with us in the Western Hemisphere. Other things being equal, the better off our neighbors, the more secure they—and we—will be.

Notes

1. P. T. Bauer, *Reality and Rhetoric: Studies in Economic Development* (Cambridge, Mass.: Harvard University Press, 1984), p. 49.

2. Barry Newman, "Bangladesh Provides Plenty of Ammunition for Critics of Food Aid," *Wall Street Journal*, April 16, 1981, p. 1.

3. Ibid.

4. Clifford D. May, "Moving Ethiopians Causes a Dispute," *New York Times*, January 28, 1986, p. 1.

5. *Wall Street Journal*, January 27, 1986, p. 26 (emphasis mine).

6. "Does Helping Really Help?" *Time*, December 21, 1987, p. 44.

7. Bauer, *Reality and Rhetoric*, p. 50.

8. Quoted in L. Dudley and R. J. Sandilands, "The Side Effects of Foreign Aid: The Case of PL480 in Colombia," *Economic Development and Cultural Change* 14 (January 1975): 325–36.

9. Ibid., p. 328.

10. Henry Kamm, "Turkey Seeking Changes in U.S. Aid," *New York Times*, August 4, 1985, p. 3.

11. Ibid.

12. Irving Kristol, "Now What for U.S. Client States?" *Wall Street Journal*, March 3, 1986, p. 18.

D. GALE JOHNSON

Paradoxes in
World Agriculture

◆ Of the two important and interrelated paradoxes of agriculture, the one that most commonly comes to mind is the paradox of hunger in a world with plenty of food. Large stocks of grain, butter, dry skim milk and meat in the industrial market economies testify to the abundance of world food supplies. Even more relevant than the large stocks, the real international prices of foods that account for most of the calories consumed by poor people are at historic lows for the twentieth century.

The other paradox is that industrial market economies subsidize farmers while many of the low-income developing countries discriminate against them by taxes and low prices. Indeed, the richest farmers in the world—the large commercial farmers in Western Europe, North America, and Japan—are heavily subsidized, with the costs of farm price and income support programs to consumers and taxpayers equal to or exceeding net farm operator incomes in the 1980s. The farmers who receive most of the subsidies have much greater wealth than the average family in their countries and also receive annual family incomes significantly above average nonfarm family incomes. By contrast, in low-income countries farm people are, on the average, poorer than urban people; yet the urban population has access to low-cost food through government subsidies and/or low farm prices. In a number of countries with a significant potential for agricultural growth, per capita food production declined during the 1970s and 1980s. Fortunately in some instances the misguided exploitive policies have been changed, and farmers have responded to the positive incentives as expected.

World food production per capita is at its highest level in human history. Stocks of grain (the major source of calories for two-thirds of the world's population) at the beginning of the 1987 crop year were at their highest level in the past two decades, equal to more than 23 percent of consumption during the year.[1] International market prices of grain and other food products generally are at the lowest real levels this century; adjusted for inflation, they are lower than during the Great Depression of the 1930s. Yet despite this global cornucopia, some people don't have enough to eat at least part of the year, and some may face actual starvation or diseases associated with famine.

Before looking ahead to the 1990s, let us review significant changes in the world food situation over recent decades. Although much remains to be done to eliminate hunger and malnutrition among the world's poor, much more has already been accomplished over the past half-century. The evidence is clear: famines due to shortfalls in food production have been nearly eliminated. And, as I shall argue, it is possible to eliminate famine and most forms of hunger in low-income countries by the end of this century if the governments of these countries follow constructive policies for agriculture. Even now, the primary source of famine and extreme hunger is not nature but man's inhumanity to man.

A World Food System

An effective world food system is now possible. At the end of World War II only visionaries would have made such a statement, but enormous strides have been made during the past four decades. More can and will be done by the end of this century to realize the potential of a system that has been created by the world's farmers, agricultural scientists, marketing agencies, processors, input suppliers, and land and water transport systems.

In a world food system, food that can be transported at reasonable cost and produced anywhere in the world is actually or potentially available to any person with the means to purchase it.[2] Most of what is required for a world food system now exists. Further improvements and extensions could mean that by the end of this century only a few million of the world's nearly six billion people would not have access to the system. Just four decades ago people throughout the world could not draw on the available supplies of staple foods, regardless of where these foods were produced or located. With minor exceptions, grain produced in North America, Australia, Argentina, and France would now be available to most of the world's population if governments did not get in the way. Governments intervene either by prohibiting their citizens from importing food they are willing and able to pay for or by preventing their farmers from exporting food others are willing and able to pay for. Farmers in India, for example, are not permitted to export rice or wheat even when foreign prices are higher.

The substantial improvements made during the past half-century in the cost and speed of transportation and communications have helped form the basis of a world food system and have added immeasurably to food security for the world's poorest people. It is impossible to exaggerate the importance of this system to tens of millions of people each year. We need only recall that in the last quarter of the nineteenth century as many as 25 million people died of famine conditions in China and India primarily because food that was available elsewhere in the world could not be delivered.[3]

In some isolated parts of the world, primarily in Africa, where communication is limited and transport is slow and expensive, a small percentage of the world's poor are genuinely outside the world food system. But inappropriate policies, corruption, the absence of civil order, and genocide are more responsible for the human disasters in East Africa, especially in Ethiopia, than the absence of roads. Unfortunately governments have prevented their citizens from having access to food that the world food system could provide, letting their people starve for political and ideological objectives. The studies of the Stalin period that General Secretary Mikhail Gorbachev has said are under way may for the first time document the enormous unnecessary loss of life caused by famine in the USSR during the early 1930s. The great famine in China in 1959–1961, when 20–30 million may have perished, was caused primarily by Mao Zedong's policies, not by adverse weather.[4]

Improvements in the World Food Situation

The access to food under normal or continuing circumstances has clearly improved over the past several decades in Asia and Latin America. Even in Africa food supplies may not have deteriorated, because food imports have increased significantly since 1970.

Because agriculture is heavily subsidized in industrial countries, more is produced than would be without such subsidies. However, many developing countries, including some of the most populous ones, subject farmers to heavy taxation. Returns to many farmers are significantly below world market levels because of export taxes, low procurement prices, and overvalued exchange rates.[5] In addition, most developing countries have an urban bias and provide farm people with inferior education, poor roads and communications, and limited access to health care. In fact, the exploitation of farm people through low farm prices pays for much of the superior urban facilities.

Political power rests primarily with the minority urban population in developing countries. Governments respond to the urban areas to prevent riots and to preserve tranquillity. And, of course, most government officials and bureaucrats live in urban areas. Even though farmers are in the vast majority (80 percent of the poor people in developing countries live in rural areas), they have neither the ability nor the resources to organize to present their needs forcefully and persuasively.

But even with all the adverse factors affecting farmers in developing countries, world food production has grown rapidly since 1950. From 1952 to 1986 world agricultural production grew at an annual rate of 2.8 percent. For the developing countries the growth rate was even higher, at 3.1 percent. The growth in agricultural trade, at 5.3 percent, was nearly double the rate of output growth. From 1952 to 1986 world food production increased by 154 percent, and world food trade increased by more than 300 percent.[6]

World trade in grain increased threefold from 73 million tons in 1960–1961 to 219 million tons in 1984–1985.[7] Those 219 million tons represent more than 50 kilograms for each of the world's 5 billion people. If equally distributed, which of course it is not, it would provide more than 450 calories per person per day, or nearly a fifth of the daily per capita calorie consumption in low-income developing countries.

Two kinds of evidence indicate an improved food situation in low-income countries. One is the remarkable increase in life expectancy at birth and the sharp reduction in infant and child mortality since 1950. The other is the data on per capita food production and supplies. Because of trends in international trade, available food supplies can differ from trends in food production and may do so in the case of Africa. Data on changes in life expectancy and infant mortality are presented in Table 1, with particular emphasis on Africa. Data on per capita incomes are given for comparison.

The substantial increases in life expectancy at birth cannot be attributed solely or even primarily to improved food supplies and nutrition. Many factors have been involved: improved sanitation, safer water supplies, vaccinations, the elimination of small pox, and the reduction in the incidence of malaria. But since children suffer most during periods of food stringency, the large declines in infant and child mortality presumably could not have occurred if nutritional conditions had worsened.

As of 1985 average life expectancy in low-income countries with per capita incomes of less than $390 was 52 years, if China and India are excluded.[8] In only a quarter-century, life expectancy at birth increased 12 years. Even in Africa the increase in life expectancy has ranged from a low

Table 1

Life Expectancy at Birth, Infant Mortality Rate, and Child Death Rate

Country or income group[a]	Life Expectancy at Birth		Infant Mortality Rate[b] (under age 1)		Child Death Rate[b] (ages 1–4)		GNP per capita (in $U.S.)
	1960	1985[c]	1960	1985[c]	1960	1985[c]	1985[c]
Low-income economies							
China	42	69	165	35	26	7	310
India	43	56	165	89	26	11	270
Other	43	52	163	112	31	19	200
Average	42	60	165	72	27	11	270
Africa							
Low-income							
Semi-arid	37	44	203	151	57	34	218
Other	39	49	158	112	37	22	254
Average	38	48	164	117	40	24	249
Middle-income							
Oil importers	41	50	159	111	37	21	670
Oil exporters	39	50	191	113	51	21	889
Sub-Saharan	—	49	170	115	42	23	491
Middle-income economies	51	62	126	68	23	10	1,290
Lower-middle income	46	58	144	82	29	13	820
Upper-middle income	56	66	101	52	15	6	1,850
Industrial market economies	70	76	29	9	2	—	11,810

SOURCE: World Bank, *World Development Report, 1987*.

[a] Income designations are based on per capita income (in 1985 U.S. dollars): low income, $390 or less; lower-middle income, $400–1,600; upper-middle income, $1,600–7,420.

[b] Rates are per 1,000.

[c] Data for Africa are for 1982.

of 7 years to a high of 11 years for the four groups of countries in Table 1. (However, African data on population and child and infant mortality are less reliable than those of other low-income countries and should be viewed with caution.)

To put these data in perspective, note that persons born in the United States in 1920 had an expected life span of 55 years, a figure now equaled by India, Burma, and Haiti (three of the world's poorest countries) and exceeded by a decade or more in Brazil, Mexico, and South Korea. Infant mortality in the lowest-income countries fell by half between 1960 and 1982. A comparable drop was achieved in the United States between 1900 and 1920, when the infant mortality rate per 1,000 births fell from 160 to 80.

For the low-income countries with half or more of their population engaged in agriculture, data on food supplies are subject to substantial error and need to be interpreted with caution. Table 2 gives such data for the developed market economies, for several groups of developing countries, and for the world. The small improvements in per capita food supplies for

Table 2
Per Capita Daily Calorie Supply

	CALORIES PER CAPITA PER DAY		
Region or group	1961–1963	1969–1971	1979–1981
Developed countries	3,110	3,280	3,380
Developed market economies	2,080	3,260	3,370
North America	3,270	3,480	3,610
Western Europe	3,140	3,290	3,430
Oceania	3,190	3,280	3,150
Other	2,540	2,770	2,870
Eastern Europe and USSR	3,160	3,320	3,390
Developing countries	2,000	2,140	2,350
Developing market economies	2,080	2,170	2,330
Africa	2,130	2,180	2,260
Latin America	2,380	2,510	2,630
Near East	2,290	2,410	2,840
Far East	1,950	2,030	2,170
Other	1,950	2,190	2,310
Asian centrally planned economies	1,840	2,080	2,410
World	2,350	2,470	2,620

SOURCE: J. A. Mollett, "The Key Role of Food Imports in Dietary Improvement in Developing Countries—and Their Cost," *Outlook on Agriculture* 14, no. 1 (1985): 27–34 and table 1.

Africa came from a large net increase in food imports that more than off-set the decline in per capita food production. Between 1961–1965 and 1979–1981, per capita food production in Africa declined by 13 percent. In the early 1960s African food exports equaled about 5 percent of food consumption (both measured in calories). In 1979–1981, 16 percent of to-tal food supplies were imported. Thus the shift in net food trade more than made up for production declines. Unfortunately per capita food production declined a further 5 percent by 1984, but a significant recovery in food production in 1985 and 1986 returned food supplies to almost the 1979–1981 levels.

Falling Food Prices

During the early and mid-1970s numerous observers predicted that the world was on the verge of food shortages and that millions would starve. Such predictions are not unusual. In 1967 a book was published with the title *Famine 1975! America's Decision: Who Will Survive?* And at the end of the Carter administration a committee of experts and, alas, some propa-gandists produced *The Global 2000 Report to the President*, which included the outrageously inaccurate conclusion that "the real price of food is pro-jected to increase 95 percent over the 1970–2000 period, in significant part as a result of increased petroleum dependence."[9] That time period is now more than half over, and food prices in international markets have actually fallen. U.S. export prices for fiscal year 1987 (in constant dollars) were only 60 percent of the 1969–1971 average for wheat and 50 percent for corn. Real food and agricultural prices have declined since 1970, with little pros-pect of returning to 1980 levels until well into the 1990s, if then.

Hunger in the Midst of Plenty

Given the large surpluses of food in the industrial market economies, how can there be hungry, perhaps even starving, people in the world? Why isn't the surplus food in North America and Western Europe made available to hungry people in Africa, Asia, and elsewhere? Before answering these ques-tions we must realize that there is no way to count the number of persons whose lives are adversely affected by a lack of food or by malnutrition. The basis for estimates that 800 million are malnourished or that 15–30 million children die every year of famine conditions is very weak indeed.

The oft-repeated statement that half the children in low-income deve-loping countries die by the age of five is false (see Table 1). But it is far from obvious that a lack of food is the primary cause of infant and child death. A large percentage of the deaths may be nutrition-related because infants and children suffering from disease and parasites cannot make effective use of the food they consume. The United Nations International Children's Emergency Fund (UNICEF) estimates that 14–15 million children under five die each year, about 70 percent before their first birthday. Deaths attributed to preventable causes include 3 million from pneumonia, 2 million from measles, 1.5 million from whooping cough, 1 million from tetanus, and 5 million from dehydration caused by diarrhea.[10] Each of these causes of death has some primary source other than hunger or malnutrition. Deaths from dehydration are caused by diseases associated with unclean water or poor sanitation, but those who are hungry or malnourished are more susceptible to diarrhea and less able to withstand its ravages than those who are well fed. The incidence and severity of measles is greater among the ill-fed than the well-fed. Thus although poor nutrition or insufficient food may be a factor, it is clearly incorrect to attribute a large fraction of the deaths of infants and children to hunger or famine.

Food Aid

The frequent and obvious response to hunger problems is food aid. Two years ago entertainers in Great Britain and the United States raised tens of millions of dollars to provide aid for the hungry and starving in Ethiopia and refugees in Sudan and Somalia. Although these generous and well-meaning efforts may have helped relieve short-term distress, they have had no long-term positive effects. Once again, in 1987 and 1988, hunger and famine stalked Ethiopia.

Some argue that the massive response of the world community, both through government and private agencies, to the 1984–1985 Ethiopian famine has made it possible for the Ethiopian government to continue its misguided and repressive policies of collectivized agriculture, low farm prices, and the forced resettlement of hundreds of thousands of people. Food aid was used to attract hungry people to centers from which they were forced to resettle hundreds of miles from their homes. Adverse weather played only a minor role in the 1984–1985 famine; the confiscation of food stocks and heavy taxes took from the peasants the stores of food and livestock herds that had been their traditional means of coping with a harsh and variable nature. Only after the government destroyed these means did hunger and starvation emerge on such a huge scale.

One study of the Ethiopian famine of 1984–1985 concludes that governments and private humanitarian agencies made no attempt to understand the causes of the famine. The consequences are extremely serious:

> If the West is willing to feed the starving Ethiopians without asking how they came to be in that condition or evaluate whether Western assistance programs alleviate those conditions, they will face a monumental task in the future. The government of Ethiopia is establishing a social and economic system that will produce starving people for generations to come.[11]

The return of famine supports the view that the Ethiopian government has continued the policies that so devastated many rural areas just a few years ago.

Not all food aid goes to governments as despotic and inhumane as the Ethiopian. Clearly some uses of food aid have beneficial effects: food for pregnant women and children in families with low incomes, school lunch programs to provide nutrition and incentives for children to remain in school, and programs to meet emergencies resulting from natural disasters. Food aid may also be used beneficially for food-for-work programs, where the work creates and improves the rural infrastructure. But the amount of food aid that can be used for these directed objectives is limited by the capacities of the bureaucracies involved. A Food and Agricultural Organization (FAO) estimate indicates that the total that can be effectively used in targeted nutrition programs is about five million tons.[12]

Food aid may contribute to the uneconomic use of national resources. A case in point is Egypt, the largest recipient of U.S. food aid. U.S. food aid makes it possible to sell bread in Egypt for less than five U.S. cents per pound loaf—only a fraction of the production cost. The low bread price keeps the market price for wheat and other grains too low to encourage farmers to expand their output. Even with U.S. food aid, nearly 25 percent of total government expenditures in Egypt went to food subsidies in the early 1980s.[13]

From the perspective of international bureaucracies, the ideal food aid program provides a constant flow of aid at a high level (a minimum of ten million tons of cereals annually), with additional aid in emergency conditions. Since the amount of aid used for targeted nutrition programs is small, if food aid were available in a constant flow for several years, most of it would be sold on the market. The income from the sales would then become government revenue—without donors raising questions about how the food aid is used or how the sale of imported food on local markets affects farmers.

Although John Stuart Mill discussed the relations between a government and its own citizens, the paradox he raises applies equally to governments that become dependent on aid from other governments.

> In all cases of helping, there are two sets of consequences to be considered: the consequences of the assistance itself, and the consequences of relying on the assistance. The former are generally beneficial, but the latter, for the most part, injurious; so much so, in many cases, as greatly to outweigh the value of the benefit. And this is never more likely to happen than in the very cases where the need for help is most intense. There are few things for which it is more mischievous that people should rely on the habitual aid of others, than for the means of subsistence, and unhappily there is no lesson which they more easily learn. The problem to be solved is therefore one of peculiar nicety as well as importance; how to give the greatest amount of needful help, with the smallest encouragement to undue reliance on it.[14]

If the governments of developing countries believe they can rely on food aid, they have a clear incentive to neglect agriculture and to devote more resources to urban areas. They also have an incentive to use low-priced food to win the support of urban groups for the government in power.

Paradox Resolved?

Hunger in the midst of plenty seems to be a rousing call for action. But that action often runs counter to the real interests of the poor people of the world. The primary cause of malnutrition and insufficient food consumption is not a lack of supplies but low income or poverty. Thus the solution for most of the poorly fed is not to add to the supply of food but to raise the incomes of the poorest people so that they can buy the food that is available. For aid to work, it must be used to meet a temporary emergency situation in which some people have lost their sources of income or capital.

The most appropriate assistance increases people's productive power. For example, high-yielding grains, principally wheat and rice, were transferred to some of the most densely populated areas of the developing world and now add substantially to the food supply of many countries. But it is not only the contribution to output of the new seeds and the cultural practices associated with them that is important. The change in production methods has made both labor and land more productive in farm areas. And contrary to the gloomy projections before the introduction of high-yielding grains, the demand for labor has not declined. In many areas the demand for labor has increased, and higher wages have been necessary to meet that demand.

In some areas, such as India, most of the early increase in wage rates has been eliminated by the migration of workers to higher-wage areas. This outcome clearly supports the view that returns to labor in agriculture depend primarily on the value of labor in the rest of the economy. Although it is important to improve productivity in agriculture (and such improvements have been occurring in many developing countries), there will be long-run increases in the incomes of farm people only when real per capita income grows. But agriculture and farm people must also receive fair treatment from their governments, which must overcome an urban bias that assigns most of the benefits of economic growth to a small urban minority.

Even though the major industrial market economies produce more food than is justified by the market price, efforts to improve the productivity of agriculture in the developing countries should not be neglected. On the contrary, since most of the world's poor live in rural areas, one of the most important means of increasing their real incomes is to help them produce more agricultural products with less labor and land. Since expenditures on food account for a high percentage of total consumption expenditures, poor rural people gain even if market prices fall, because lower food prices reflect the increased productivity of their resources.

Both the industrial and developing countries can take measures to improve agricultural productivity and incomes in rural areas of developing countries. The industrial countries can reduce barriers to trade that adversely affect the exports of developing countries, especially for labor-intensive manufactured products such as textiles, shoes, and clothing, but also for farm products such as sugar, peanuts, processed foods, and rice. The industrial countries should also continue to support international agricultural research centers and to expand their efforts to help developing countries improve their national agricultural research systems.

I am optimistic about the future food situation for the world's poor. Substantial improvements have occurred during the past half-century, and I see no reason why further progress will not be made. I do fear that the world will miss several opportunities to achieve more rapid progress. In particular, developing countries need to move faster to remove the discrimination against agriculture and farm people, a process now under way in many countries. I believe that food aid plays a modest role in meeting shortfalls in food production due to natural causes and that the United States should stand ready to meet such needs. But a stable transfer of food without regard to the domestic availability of food is counterproductive except for restricted purposes such as school lunches and nutrition programs for women and children.

Most of what is necessary to eliminate poverty and hunger must be done by the developing countries themselves. And much of what is needed involves increasing the incomes and productivity of farm people. In the long run, of course, the incomes of farm people will depend on the growth of real per capita incomes in their countries.

Notes

1. U.S. Department of Agriculture (USDA), Economic Research Service, *Agricultural Outlook*, AO-135 (October 1987): 52. USDA, Foreign Agricultural Service, *Foreign Agriculture Circular: Grains*, FG-19–82 (June 15, 1982): 26.

2. Foods that can be transported at reasonable cost (including grains, sugar, and fats and oils) supply as much as 60–80 percent of the calories consumed by low-income families in developing countries.

3. *Encyclopedia Britannica*, 1970 ed., s.v. "famine."

4. An analysis of the 1982 population census resulted in an estimate of 29.4 million famine deaths from 1958 to 1961. Almost three-fifths of the deaths were estimated to have occurred at age ten or over. See Basil Ashton et al., "Famine in China, 1958–61," *Population and Development Review* 10, no. 4 (December 1984): 619. On China in the late 1950s and early 1960s, see Liang Wensen, "Balanced Development of Industry and Agriculture," in Xu Dixin et al., *China's Search for Economic Growth: The Chinese Economy Since 1949* (Beijing: New World Press, 1982), p. 60. On the loss of life during the famine in the USSR during the early 1930s, see Robert Conquest, *The Harvest of Sorrow: Soviet Collectivization and the Terror-Famine* (New York: Oxford University Press, 1986).

5. World Bank, *World Development Report, 1986* (Washington, D.C.: World Bank, 1986), chap. 1 and pt. 2.

6. Food and Agricultural Organization (FAO) of the United Nations, *FAO Production Yearbook* and *FAO Trade Yearbook* (Rome: FAO, 1952–1986). The rapid growth of trade in agricultural products since the early 1950s reflects the failure of agriculture in the socialist countries to expand production as fast as the growth in food demand as well as the effects of rapid population and income growth in the developing market economies during the 1960s and early 1970s.

7. USDA, *Agricultural Outlook*, p. 52.

8. World Bank, *World Development Report, 1987*, p. 202, for 1985 data; ibid., *1982*, p. 150, for 1960 data.

9. Gerald A. Barney et al., *The Global 2000 Report to the President* (New York: Penguin, 1982), p. 17.

10. UNICEF, *State of the World's Children, 1984* (Oxford: Oxford University Press, 1983), p. 10.

11. Jason W. Clay and Bonnie K. Holcomb, *Politics and the Ethiopian Famine, 1984–1985* (New Brunswick, Conn.: Transaction Books, 1986), p. 193.

12. Barbara Huddleston, *Closing the Cereals Gap with Trade and Food Aid,*

Research Report no. 43 (Washington, D.C.: International Food Policy Research Institute, 1984), p. 63.

13. Grant M. Scobie, *Food Subsidies in Egypt: Their Impact on Foreign Exchange and Trade*, Research Report no. 40 (Washington, D.C.: International Food Policy Research Institute, 1983), p. 12.

14. John Stuart Mill, *Principles of Political Economy* (London: Longmans, Green, & Co., 1920), p. 967.

• PART III •

Domestic Policy and National Purpose

JAMES M. BUCHANAN

Constitutional Imperatives for the 1990s

The Legal Order for a Free and Productive Economy

Introduction

◆ October 19, 1987! Black Monday indeed! The search was on for causes, and for scapegoats. The reaction should have been different. Why are we so vulnerable to the mobilization of the animal spirits? Why does the formation of economic values depend so critically on confidence in those persons and parties that hold, or may hold, political office? Ronald Reagan's legacy may be measured by a six-year demonstration that confidence in personal leadership matters. But the flip side of confidence is the lack thereof, and the events of late 1987 should prompt us to look not for signs of shifts in spirits but for ways to reduce our dependence on, and hence vulnerability to, such turns in attitudes. Black Monday should be seen as evidence of a failure in *constitutional structure* exhibited in an exaggerated dependence on personal sources of policy expectations. The very purpose of constitutional order is to offer insulation from the cult of personality on the one hand and the ravages of political irresponsibility on the other. Constitutional rules are meant to constrain politicians against adventurism, foreign and domestic. Particular economic adventures such as post-Keynesian deficits, the now and prospective resurgence of protectionism, the then and future inflation—these are but symptoms of dramatic constitutional-structural failure.

Failure is apparent along many dimensions, summarized by the over-reaching of modern politics, in the large and in the small. Everything seems politicized, despite the loss of the romantic image of politics and the state that dominated intellectual-academic attitudes for more than a century. We do indeed now see politics without romance, but we still live with politics supreme. And there seems to be no reversal to the long-continuing erosion of the constitutional wisdom embodied in the documents of our founders. How can we fail to despair when a legislative supremacist is nominated for our highest court and is rejected on grounds that his constitutional views are overly restricted? Where is the wisdom that understands the Constitution as a set of constraints on executive, legislative, and judicial intrusions into the lives of citizens?

Despite temptation, I shall not argue principles of political and legal philosophy here, although more attention must be paid to such principles by all concerned with a free society. My purpose is to evaluate and assess constitutional failures along the several economic dimensions: fiscal, monetary, regulatory, and distributional. Each of these separate dominions for political manipulation (and mischief) is related to the others through structural failure in the rules. The political-economic-legal order as it has functioned since World War II has not embodied the predictability that allows the productive potential of the economy to be realized. We have lived less well than would be possible under an eminently realizable political framework.

The next section briefly discusses the overall design of the constitutional regime of an economically viable and free society. The sections that follow examine the constitutional imperatives that the achievement of such a regime requires in the separate policy dominions. The prospects for reform vary over the set. Changes in fiscal and monetary regimes can be accomplished readily; changes in regulatory or distributional rules may require more fundamental modifications in attitudes toward the state. The final section offers an integrative summary of the whole argument.

The Economic Constitution of the Free Society

My title embodies the presupposition that a free society is a positive value that is widely, if not universally, shared. We might, of course, enter into a lengthy philosophical disquisition on the meaning of the terms *free* and *society*. But for present purposes it is sufficient to think about a political-legal setting in which persons remain free to pursue their own activities, whatever these may be, in voluntary association one with another, while legally protected in the use of several properties and in their voluntarily contracted obligations.

There exists no social, national, or public interest, objective, or goal in this construction. Only persons generate values. Specific objectives pursued by collective units or organizations, from the firm to the state, are made legitimate only because these objectives are shared among individuals who are members. Without such shared objectives, there could be no justification for collective action, including that taken by the politically organized unit, the state.

But to attribute net positive value to the game of politics, to assign value productivity to the political-legal arrangements that provide both the order within which persons interact and collective consumption or public goods and services, amounts to an acknowledgment that there do exist shared purposes available for achievement through a polity. The *constitution of the polity*—the set of rules defining both the organizational structure of governance and the range and scope of institutions within that structure—finds its *raison d'être* in the furtherance of the shared goals of citizens, which include protection of person and property against the intrusion of political as well as private predation.

The essential criterion for an economic constitution is the existence of positive-sum expected value for all participant member-citizens. It thus becomes imperative that the constitutional structure operate to insure individuals, and groups or classes of individuals, against both public and private exploitation, defined as a potential opportunity cost. Value-enhancing voluntary exchanges must be free from interference by special-interest and protectionist pressure groups. Value-reducing restrictions on voluntary exchanges must be effectively proscribed, whether instituted by private or by public agency. Further, there must be limits on the governmentally implemented transfers of value among persons and groups.

The constitution must facilitate the establishment of common standards that allow persons to contract one with another without undue uncertainty in the standards themselves. In particular, this imperative includes the elevation of monetary rules to constitutional status, with the value of the monetary unit assuming its place alongside such standards as ordinary weights and measures.

Finally, the constitution of any free society must act to limit government. It is critically important that we recapture the eighteenth-century wisdom of the need for checks and balances and that we shed once and for all the romantically idiotic notion that as long as processes are democratic all is fair game. The constitutional failure we now observe does not lie in a deficiency of democracy. On the contrary, democracy has overreached its own limits. In 1988 it is surely within the shared interests of all citizens to curb the excessive political exploitation that we mutually exercise against each other as members of overlapping and intersecting groups, each of which grabs for artificially created rents. Nearly all citizens participate in this set of activities and nearly all end up as net losers. There are few net gainers from what Anthony de Jasay has properly called the "churning state."[1]

Toward Tax Limits and Budget Balance

I have now sketched in broad outline the elements of an economic constitution for a free society. As I noted earlier, the separate elements of this constitution vary in their prospects for implementation. In this and the following sections I discuss these elements in rough order of descending proximity to realization. This order does not, of course, imply anything about relative importance.

This section addresses the fiscal constitution broadly defined, since it is here that prospects for genuine reform seem closest to realization. What must such a fiscal constitution include if it is to pass muster as one element in the more inclusive bills of economic rights for a free society? The first point to be noted is positive: we have in place some constitutional restrictions on the exercise of government's fiscal authority. Governments cannot arbitrarily discriminate among persons in the imposition of taxes. For example, a dominant majority coalition or party cannot exempt its own members from taxes while imposing coercive levies on members of the political opposition. The constitutional prohibitions are much less binding on the spending side of the budget, and, indeed, much of the resource wasting of modern governments takes the form of programs directed toward targeted beneficiary groups. Nonetheless, limits remain on arbitrary discrimination; for example, personally targeted benefits for partisan friends are the stuff of political scandal.

Perhaps the greatest constitutional anomaly lies in the total absence of restrictions on the absolute level of fiscal exaction that might be imposed on citizens generally. The Constitution protects horizontal equity in fiscal treatment, but there are no protections against exorbitant absolute levels of taxation as long as the horizontal requirements are satisfied. It would be unconstitutional for the government to levy, say, an 80 percent rate of tax on my income solely because I am an economics professor while leaving you, a business executive with the same income, with only a 15 percent rate. By way of dramatic contrast, there could be no constitutional challenge against the levy of 70, 80, or even 90 percent on *both* our incomes so long as the horizontal precepts of nondiscriminatory treatment are not violated. The absence of absolute limits on the taxing authority of government seems clearly to be a gap in our fiscal constitution that should be filled.

In this respect we must recognize the distinction between the ideal design of a constitution, a design on which persons might agree at some original formation of a polity, and the more limited design for reform or change in a long-existing and ongoing fiscal structure. In the second case, which is, of course, the only setting relevant for us, the introduction of absolute tax limits must pay heed to the status quo. In the United States of the 1980s the central government takes approximately 19 percent of the value of all product in taxes. In an idealized setting for the initial design of a fiscal structure, citizens choosing behind some veil of ignorance and/or uncertainty might agree to an overall limit of, say, 12 percent. But we start from where we are, and if we seek consensus on specific constitutional change, the existing 19 percent may become the effective proximate upper limit. To roll back taxes to some lower limit would require that a new majority impose its will coercively on those persons and groups who are possible net gainers in the overextended welfare state. Constitutional change becomes meaningless, however, unless it is accomplished by constitutionalist procedure, which, in the practical sense, means generalized assent on the part of most if not all citizens. Viewed in this light, the expectations described by the status quo become the effective benchmark for change.

Essentially the same logic applies to the observable and universally acknowledged flaw in the budget-making procedures of ordinary politics in the central government, a flaw that cries out for constitutional correction perhaps more urgently, if not more importantly, than the absolute tax limit anomaly. I refer, of course, to the proclivity of modern democracy to finance large shares of ordinary spending by debt rather than by taxes, generating thereby the observed regime of apparently permanent and accelerating deficits, with public debt principal and annual interest charges mounting cumulatively through time. This outcome of the working of ordinary politics post-Keynes is acknowledged to be grossly irresponsible and in need of correction even by those political decision makers who participate directly in the process. Such acknowledgment is demonstrated by enactment of the Gramm-Rudman-Hollings budget reform legislation first in 1985 and again in 1987, legislation that involves attempts by the U.S. Congress to impose binding constraints in advance on its own spending proclivities.

A more effective, long-lasting, and surely more credible correction would take the form of an amendment to the Constitution that would dictate budget balance, after some appropriate phase-in period and with an appropriately drawn escape clause for fiscal emergency. Such an amendment was widely discussed in the late 1970s and early 1980s; 32 of the required 34 states passed legislative resolutions calling for a constitutional convention, and the Senate passed one version of the amendment in 1983. Attention was diverted from constitutional to legislative remedy by the Gramm-Rudman-Hollings action.

It is difficult to construct any plausible argument against a constitutional rule for budget balance once the elementary facts of the matter are acknowledged. Why should dominant political coalitions in 1988 or 1990 be empowered to finance program benefits enjoyed by contemporary constituents through the levy of taxes (directly or via inflation) on citizens who will be around in the year 2000 and beyond? Such irresponsibility is grossly immoral and has been deemed so through the centuries. The half-century aberration we have witnessed stems from acceptance of the dangerous and fallacious Keynesian precept that repealed budget balance as a norm, a precept based on the incredible proposition that politicians will act contrary to their own interests. Indeed, before Keynes the moral norm against budget imbalance was strong enough to make formal rules unnecessary. Post-Keynes the natural proclivities of politicians have now emerged to plague us all; only formal constitutional checks can restore the fiscal responsibility necessary for the functioning of government in a free society.[2]

The Monetary Constitution

Article 1, section 8, of the U.S. Constitution empowers Congress "to coin money [and] regulate the value thereof." Through legislative enactment Congress has created a complex institutional arrangement presumably pursuant to this initial grant of authority. Nonetheless, the central feature of an effective constitutional regime is absent, namely, the guarantee of predictability in the value of the monetary unit, without which no economy can function effectively. Congress, either directly or through its agency, has never fulfilled the second half of its monetary mandate.

This jerry-built arrangement has gradually and more or less accidentally come to acquire powers of monopoly issue of fiat currency, with few constraints. The Federal Reserve system was designed and put in place early in this century to facilitate adjustments to regional credit crises within the overall operation of the international gold standard monetary structure. Over the ensuing decades, and especially from the 1930s through the 1970s, we totally divorced the monetary unit, the U.S. dollar, from any relation to gold or indeed to any other real-valued commodity or commodity bundle. During this half-century of demonetization of gold, the Federal Reserve came to acquire, residually and without express design or intent, powers of fiat issue that would never have been assigned to such an institution constitutionally or legislatively.

As with the absence of absolute tax limits and budget balance, no plausible argument could defend the existing monetary structure as a preferred part of a rationally designed constitutional order. It is difficult to imagine a regime that could embody *less* predictability than one that places discretionary authority over money issue in the hands of a multiperson board operating only under vague and incoherent guidelines. Professor Axel Leijonhufvud has called the existing U.S. structure a random-walk monetary standard, a description that accurately conveys its unpredictability.

Constitutional failure seems less apparent here than in budgetary imbalance only because, as it has operated over the 1980s, the monetary monopoly has not yet overtly succumbed to the ubiquitous pressures for inflation. This record offers little assurance, however, that the agency will operate with comparable restraint into the 1990s and beyond. And herein lies the problem. There is *no* insurance against irresponsible behavior. Participants in the national economy who try to make decisions on investment, saving, organizing firms, and entering markets remain vulnerable to shifts in the value of the monetary standard. Such vulnerability cannot be a part of a productive economy. All persons and groups can benefit by a move toward a regime that would insure greater predictability.

One of the encouraging signs in the 1980s has been the increasing academic attention to analyses of alternative monetary regimes and to potential changes in the effective monetary rules. A consensus is developing that current arrangements cannot be defended as elements of a preferred economic constitution. Economists have advanced various descriptions of alternative regimes. Some exploit the age-old mystique of gold and seek to reestablish a relation between gold and monetary value. Others, reading the history of the gold standard less favorably but recognizing the value of convertibility, suggest relating the monetary unit to some defined commodity other than gold or to some commodity bundle. Still others suggest that the modern miracle of instant electronics would allow government's role to be limited to the mere definition of the value of the dollar. Others prefer less dramatic shifts in the regime and propose the issue of more explicit directives to the existing authorities to fix either the quantity of the monetary base or the rate of its increase. My personal preference is to return to the suggestion of Irving Fisher and Henry Simons and to propose legislative dictation that would require the Federal Reserve to stabilize (within narrowly defined limits) the value of the dollar, defined by some specified index.[3] Such a change could be legislatively generated, although its effect would be genuinely constitutional.

Economists should agree, however, on the basic imperative for some change in the rules of the monetary game. Quarrels among proponents of different regimes must not by default allow the current set of arrangements to continue.[4]

The Regulatory Constitution

Any agenda for constitutional reform in the 1990s must place changes in fiscal and monetary rules high on the list of priorities, and it seems realistic to hope that such changes will take place. There is less reason to be hopeful about reform in regulatory and distributional rules, although these changes may be equally if not more important for the functioning of a productive economy. The difference lies in the difficulty of removing bad law from the constitutionally authorized set of permissible government activities—bad law that has long existed and that has been explicitly judged constitutional by the highest courts.

In the late twentieth century we observe many laws, federal, state, and local, that interfere with and prevent value-enhancing voluntary exchanges, such as price, wage, and rent control laws, licensing laws, zoning laws, and so on. Courts have held all such activities to be constitutionally within the regulatory authority of governments as long as majority coalitions in legislative bodies have approved the laws. Legislative majorities may, of course, repeal such laws in the same way. Soundly based economic policy proposals advanced within the workings of ordinary legislative politics would aim to roll back damaging economic restrictions on many fronts.

There is, however, a categorical distinction between securing, or hoping to secure, the repeal of economic protectionist law by forming majority legislative coalitions and reform in the prevailing constitutional interpretation that has allowed such value-reducing restrictions to be enacted and implemented at the behest of legislative majorities. Nothing less than a revolutionary shift in prevailing legal and political philosophy is required here, a shift that can only occur through the cumulative effects of an academic dialogue and discussion that has scarcely commenced.

For more than a century, and despite earlier constitutional understandings, judicial and public opinion has posed little or no constitutional challenge to increasing governmental intrusions into the economic liberties of citizens. This constitutional acquiescence occurred because political and legal philosophers, as well as citizens generally, were trapped in the romantic delusion that as long as democratic electoral procedures are in place, legislative majorities act to further the public interest. Modern public-choice theory has shattered this romantic delusion, if such delusion were not already demonstrably destroyed by the mere observation of modern political excesses. We now recognize that politicians in elected office will act to further their own interests by satisfying the interests of their constituents. This simple but realistic model of political behavior implies that deference to legislative majorities is not sustainable as constitutional principle.

These ideas are only beginning to gain adherents among law scholars and other academics. Reversal of a century of constitutional misunderstanding is unlikely during the 1990s. But perhaps, just perhaps, governmental intrusion into the economic activities of citizens is slowing down. With the romance of politics gone, rational constitutional discrimination between the legitimate and the illegitimate exercise of legislative authority may at last emerge.

The Redistributional Constitution

Much of the preceding discussion of the regulatory constitution applies equally to the redistributional, or transfer, activities of the modern state. Transfers make up an increasing share of total public outlays, and many of the transfer programs bear little or no relation to the redistributional objectives that might be summarized under any plausibly supportable welfare state rubric. The programs reflect, instead, the relative successes of politically organized interest groups competing for larger shares of taxpayers' dollars. We need only think of agricultural and maritime subsidies, geographically dispersed water projects, disguised subsidies to users of parks and other public facilities, and transfers to the aged, veterans, and other groups too numerous to mention.

The constitutionality of these transfer programs has rarely been challenged, and it seems unlikely that substantial support could be organized in the near future to impose constitutional limits on transfer activity generally. Nonetheless, as a more realistic and less romantic image of governmental and especially legislative processes comes to dominate both academic and public opinion, there will surely arise some increased willingness to consider constitutional limits on the types of transfers allowed. As scholars and citizens alike come increasingly to realize that much modern governmental-political activity involves persons and groups attempting to secure private profit from public sources, support for a redesigned economic constitution for the welfare-transfer state may build rapidly. But explanation and understanding come first, and the role for an academic-educational effort in this respect is self-evident.

The Constitutional Agenda for the 1990s

The economic constitution of the United States is in disarray in the late 1980s. The post-Keynesian era of continuing budgetary deficits is only the most visible and most newsworthy of the constitutional aberrations. The flaw in budget making is in procedure, not in policy; no amount of legislative responsibility will set matters aright. Alongside the deficit regime, we sit in fear of a post-Reagan resurgence of envy-motivated exploitative marginal tax rates on income. We are vulnerable precisely because we have no constitutionally defined limit on absolute levels of taxation.

The monetary rules (if we can call them that) are almost totally unpredictable: a single agency with no operating guidelines possesses monopoly power of fiat issue. The regulatory elements of our economic constitution have been in a shambles for all of this century. There is no constitutional-legal-judicial differentiation between value-enhancing and value-reducing economic transactions, and legislative interference proceeds willy-nilly as motivated by competing special-interest groups seeking something for nothing. Economic protectionism has again become the order of the day, and all who are decision makers remain hostage to the unpredictability inherent in the prospective post-Reagan political landscape. The failures of the Johnson Great Society programs for the extended welfare state were highly visible in the early 1980s, but the residues of these programs, in the form of still-increasing entitlements, remain to be dealt with in the 1990s and beyond.

Expectations for genuine reforms in the economic constitution must be tempered. A tax-limiting, balanced-budget amendment to the U.S. Constitution is possible, even probable, early in the 1990s, if not before. Supporters should not be distracted by apparent upsurges of responsibility reflected in possible temporary reductions in deficit sizes or by a hold-the-line policy on marginal tax rates. Constitutional limits, and only constitutional limits, can restore predictability.

Effective change in monetary rules can be constitutional in substance but legislative in form. Congress can readily mandate a targeted objective for the operation of the monetary authorities. Nothing prevents such action, even as early as 1988, except carryover support for discretionary intervention, which must act to insure unpredictability in the authorities' behavior and hence a guarantee of vulnerability for all those who deal in dollars, from households to high finance.

As I have noted, to get constitutional reform in regulatory and distributional elements of our economic constitution will take much longer. In the 1990s we can realistically anticipate an increasingly skeptical attitude toward politically orchestrated nostrums for alleged economic ills. The actors on the political stage will change in the post-Reagan theater, but there will be no return to the romance of the Kennedy Camelot. The citizenry will never again allow "the best and the brightest" from Eastern establishment universities to rule as benevolent despots. Politics post-Reagan offers both challenge and opportunity. Without the glitter of romantic delusion and with a hard-nosed understanding of the limits and the potential of ordinary politics, we may be able for the first time in more than a century to reinter-pret our Constitution and/or to redesign and reform it to exploit the full potential of a free people.

This prospect is based on possibility and on hope. My doomster coun-terpart suggests that with the romance gone special-interest groups will in-herit the earth. Such a scenario too is possible, but we can and must prevent its staging. And personally, I feel morally compelled to believe we can succeed.

Notes

1. Anthony de Jasay, *The State* (New York: Blackwell, 1985), pp. 232–43.

2. See James M. Buchanan and Richard E. Wagner, *Democracy in Deficit* (New York: Academic Press, 1977); James Buchanan, Charles Rowley, and Robert Tolli-son, eds., *Deficits* (Oxford: Blackwell, 1987).

3. See Irving Fisher, *The Purchasing Power of Money* (New York: Macmillan, 1911); Henry Simons, *Economic Policy for a Free Society* (Chicago: University of Chicago Press, 1948), chap. 7.

4. See Geoffrey Brennan and James Buchanan, *Monopoly in Money and Infla-tion: The Case for a Constitution to Discipline Government*, Hobart Paper 88 (Lon-don: Institute of Economic Affairs, 1981).

AARON WILDAVSKY

◆ ——————————————— ◆

If You Can't Budget, How Can You Govern?

◆ Budgeting has become the great issue of our time. Members of the House and the Senate spend as much time on taxing and spending as they do on all other matters put together. Not that they love budgeting; in fact they have grown to hate it. They spend endless amounts of time to discover that they no longer agree. What is it they disagree about? Nothing much, really: how much revenue should be raised, who should pay, how much should be spent and on what.

To some it appears that the great issue is the federal deficit. But the deficit hides its political significance from us. It appears that people are concerned solely about the size of the gap between spending and revenue. The real issue is different: what kind of government are we going to have, and therefore what kind of people are we going to be? Will we balance the budget at much higher levels of revenue and expenditure, or will we balance it at much lower levels of revenue and expenditure? The Democratic party now has as its dominant faction liberals whose main purpose in achieving power in government is to do good deeds with public money. The main purpose of the major faction of the Republican party is to assure a limited government; that is, their idea of a good deed is to let taxpayers spend their own money. These conceptions are fundamentally at odds.

This paper is a much revised version of my Dillon Lecture at the University of South Dakota, April 9, 1987.

Equality

Politicians like Hubert Humphrey and Henry Jackson—liberal Democrats who want a substantial welfare state and a substantial defense effort—no longer exist. Now defense policy is considered a domestic issue. Republicans look at it as an index of determination to support our institutions, as a sign of patriotism. Democrats look at it as a question of equality; more for defense means less for social welfare.[1] I recall Representative Barney Frank of Massachusetts saying the defense budget was immoral. To call it too big is one thing (so we compromise on a little bit less or more), but immoral—you don't have much room to go from there. Walter Fauntroy from Washington, D.C., said it would be unconscionable to provide so many billions for national defense while there was one homeless person in the United States; clearly he assumed that defense was not defending the people, just as Republicans no longer necessarily consider welfare programs part of the general welfare.

Americans are able to agree on the desirability of equality precisely because we all mean something different by it. Some believe in equality before the law so that different people can follow their different gender, income, class, or other destiny. Other people believe in equality of opportunity so that people can be different from each other and end up with more or less than others depending on their luck or talents. Still others believe in greater equality of results to reduce the power differences between men and women, blacks and whites, parents and children, and even animals and people. How could social movements that have transformed the lives of all Americans, like feminism and civil rights, fail to have an impact on the major priority-making machine of the public sector, the government budget?

Between Democrats and Republicans there is a big divide, with Republicans sticking to equality before the law and equal opportunity and Democrats moving more and more toward more equal results. Republicans talk about opportunity, about how wonderful the United States is because it enables people to be different; Democrats talk about how most people are left out of power—women, poor people, racial minorities, gays, the elderly. Only a few fat cats are left in. It is these fundamental differences about how people ought to live with one another—to secure more equal opportunity or more equal outcomes—that create irresolvable conflicts over budgeting.

Dissensus

In the last twenty years as a sign of dissensus (or fundamental disagreement) every relationship in budgeting has been radically transformed. From the early 1920s to the 1970s the starting point for consideration of the budget was the president's proposal. Today the phrase used to describe the president's budget when it gets to Congress is "dead on arrival."

Even more significant is the concept called the budgetary base. The past pattern of agreement maintained funding for programs at a level approximating what they got the year before. Instead of fighting the past over again in each year's budget, budgeters focused on incremental changes. Nowadays budgeters not only disagree on where the budget ought to go, they disagree on where it ought to start. Is the budgetary base what an agency spent last year? Maybe. Is it the current services budget (last year plus an inflation allowance)? Possibly. Is it the president's budget message? Unlikely. Is it the first Senate budget resolution? Perhaps. Is it the House budget resolution? Is it the first of a series of conference reports? Could be. Is it a continuing resolution, a new and exotic art form, which accommodates dissensus by providing for different levels of funding depending on how far along (subcommittee, committee, floor, conference) a bill has moved? Or is it the omnibus continuing resolution, that wrap-all package that puts everything together in a single bill? It is not easy for a president to veto the government. In recent years all of the above have been used by some of the participants some of the time as the budgetary base. None of the above has been used by most of the participants most of the time as the agreed budgetary base.

Disagreement about the base occurs not because Congress or the president is foolish or because they try to fool the people. These differences are driven by policy preferences: the starting point for additions or cuts helps determine how much will go to defense or welfare or other programs about which the participants differ. Public officials disagree about policy not because they cannot agree on the budget; they cannot agree on the budget because they are fundamentally at odds over policy.

The problem is not that our legislators are dumber than we are or that they lack good will. Any one of them alone could make a terrific budget. The problem is that legislators together cannot agree on a good budget.

Gramm-Rudman-Hollings (GRH) is more than a sign of dissensus; it also tells us what our politicians can agree about. It calls for cumulative proportionate cuts to reduce the deficit. Three types of programs are not subject to the dreaded sequestration (reduction of budget authority): major entitlements, poor people's programs, and veterans' programs. What can be cut fully is (1) defense and (2) general government. Consequently more than half the spending budget is outside GRH. Obviously entitlements are now the nation's number one priority whereas defense and the federal establishment are last. Our politicians can agree not to savage the poor (a good thing), not to harm huge numbers of voters (an expected thing), and to threaten each other with doing damage to government (a bad thing if one is supposed to govern).

The deficit-reducing provisions of GRH are deliberately unintelligent because the alternative, agreeing on an intelligent budget, is something that can't be achieved. Every year for the last eight years we have heard about the coalition of moderates that believes in budget balance, budget rationality, and budget intelligence. We keep hearing about them, but we never see them winning votes. Moderates do not win because they are outnumbered.

The disappearance of the annual budget made on time and followed for a whole year is caused by dissensus over public policy. Liberals want higher progressive taxes, lower defense spending, and more welfare programs. Conservatives want the opposite. Because the budgeters do not agree, they wait until the last moment only to discover that they are no better able to work out their differences at the end than they were at the beginning. Dissensus is now so deep that it extends beyond the issues of the day to the norms of proper action that used to guide and constrain budgetary behavior.

Norms

Once upon a time budgeters agreed on the old norms of balance, comprehensiveness, and annual review. Balance meant not only that revenue would be within hailing distance of expenditures (except for times of war and depression) but also that everyone acknowledged a limit on acceptable taxation so that they knew what total spending could add up to. Because they agreed on an acceptable range for total spending, they also knew that a lot more for one program meant a lot less for another. In other words, the participants in budgeting—agencies, appropriations committees, interest groups, politicians—all knew they were in this together. If one agency or program tried to break the bank, that money would be taken out of the hide of the others; therefore they exerted mutual discipline on one another. Now they don't. So what?

You do not stop the growth of budgets by turning people down. That is hopeless. There are so many of them and so few budget controllers. The rise of spending is stopped by inhibiting people's desire to ask in the first place. If kids choose to importune all the time, parents can rarely turn them down.

But if through some parental magic they have persuaded their children not to ask, then there is no need to turn them down.

Comprehensiveness died because we can no longer tell the value of different expenditures. In the old days most of the talk was about appropriations. Now appropriations are around 40 percent of the budget. Most of the money is in entitlements. The structure of the budget reveals the dilemma. Roughly 47 percent is in social welfare programs, legally mandated payments to individuals. Defense is 28 percent. With interest on the debt at 14 percent, that totals 89 percent. The rest, that bloodless category, is called nondefense discretionary. There are many types of spending, moreover, that barely existed in the early 1960s. Today over a trillion dollars in loans and loan guarantees is outstanding. These expenditures do not appear as one trillion dollars in the budget; only defaults, which are only three or four billion, appear in the budget. There are off-budget corporations. There are hundreds of billions of dollars in tax preferences. There is a marvelous institution called the Federal Financing Bank, which is capable of changing tens of billions of dollars from on- to off-budget. Thus it is impossible to say how much is being spent. What is the value of a loan versus a loan guarantee versus money for an off-budget corporation versus several hundred billion dollars in tax preferences, like fringe benefits or various subsidies for housing? The desire to spend from different spigots (I haven't mentioned imposing costs on the private sector through regulation) has overwhelmed the old budget process.

Historically the United States has never made a formal decision on how much revenue it should raise or how much it should spend. The norms of balance and comprehensiveness served as informal safeguards. A lot of trouble was avoided by not voting on matters that might become contentious, such as how much should be taxed and spent. According to the Budget Act of 1974, all that was changed. From the new budget resolutions came decisions on the total amount of taxing and spending. There is only one problem: although everybody agrees legislators should stand up and be counted, nobody agrees on what they ought to stand up for. That is the basic reason the budget has not been passed on time in the last fifteen years.

Deficits

Delay is one thing; huge deficits are another. One would think that if you had disagreements there would be just stalemate. What happened?

President Reagan thought of budgets as political instruments. As he saw it, Democrats were using spending to create constituents. As they addicted these constituents to federal largesse, they got more votes. Tax and spend and elect was their accomplishment; Reagan feared if this went on for too long the public would dominate the private sector. To prevent this Reagan brought in his children's allowance theory, namely, that the way to stop spending was not to issue endless admonitions but to cut down on the allowance. If you took the tax money away, Congress wouldn't have it to spend. Believing the budget was about political economy, not just economic economy, the president radically reversed the conventional wisdom, which held that spending had to be cut before taxes could be lowered.

The reverse happened. Income tax rates were cut 23 percent over three years. But, of course, it didn't happen exactly the way Reagan thought. What he wanted was prosperity to show that increasing economic incentives worked. What he got (the result of the Federal Reserve's efforts to stop stagflation) was recession.

Reagan had two choices. One was to give up everything he believed in, to do exactly what Mondale would have done, that is, to raise taxes, thereby erasing differences between Democrats and Republicans. Instead Reagan accepted large deficits in preference to the alternative of strengthening the Democratic party and its egalitarian vision of the United States.

In considering the components of the deficit, we cannot know whether, if income tax rates had gone up, the economy might have slowed down, leading to a still worse situation. We do know that higher defense spending contributed to the deficit. But that ended by 1984. Since then defense budget authority (the right to spend into the future) has declined substantially. What does contribute to the size of the deficit? When the Federal Reserve slammed on the monetary brake in 1981–1982, the resulting recession not only caused spending to go up and revenue to go down, which increased the deficit, but it also pushed prices down a lot faster than anyone had thought possible. This severely reduced bracket creep, which raised the deficit still further.

A good half of the deficit is caused by the lasting effects of the recession of 1981–1982. When one adopts a version of what the British call the public sector borrowing requirement (in the United States that means including state surpluses), the deficit that matters for economic purposes declines. Adjusting for inflation makes the deficit go down further.

When one considers that economic data fail to support the notion that large deficits are necessarily harmful, one wonders why Democrats reversed their long-standing liking for deficits. This rationale is more important than a desire to remind Republicans of their previous opposition to deficits.

Consider the Law of Political Compound Interest: interest on the debt drives out future Democratic programs. A large deficit does two things: it works as the only powerful instrument to keep spending down that we have had in half a century, and it drives out future Democratic programs. Ask also, in the older tradition of institutional political economy, to whom is the debt owed? It's owed to the constituents of the Republican party. If the deficit didn't exist, on whom would the money be spent? On the constituents of the Democratic party.

The Law of Political Compound Interest accounts for the Democratic born-again commitment to budget balance. What the party would like, especially its mainstream liberal faction, is to raise taxes substantially from the richest segment of the population to support larger social programs. There is nothing new in this. But then President Reagan cut them off at the pass again. If he could wed much lower tax rates to much lower tax preferences, he could make it difficult for Democrats to raise income taxes. Any time the Democrats say they want to raise taxes, they will be accused of breaking their compact (lower preferences for lower rates) with the people. Yet without new money, the Democratic party may self-destruct.

Realignment

Liberals cannot live with perpetual cuts in social programs. The devotion of Democrats to reducing inequalities through governmental action is now so great that they will not be able to tolerate doing less. Therefore their main need is for money. Where is that money going to come from? Before Jimmy Carter's time the government took something like 18 percent of GNP in revenues. Jimmy Carter took that figure to 20 percent. And he also left the nation a present: there were built-in tax increases—bracket creep through inflation, Social Security, and windfall taxes on energy—amounting to about 4 percent of GNP. Left alone, the tax code would have produced about 22 percent of GNP in revenues. What Reagan did was not to lower the tax take but to bring it back to traditional levels. Reagan took away the increment that Democrats would have used to fund their programs.

That is why I believe the value-added tax or some related consumption tax will be the next great issue of our time.[2] A value-added tax is a turnover tax, a sales tax at different stages of production. It is a giant revenue raiser. Experience from Europe is uniform: in no country has the value-added tax replaced the income tax. In every country that adopted the value-added tax the proportion of GNP spent by the government has gone way up. Thus the question of whether the United States will remain capitalist or go semisocialist will be decided on the question of the value-added tax. And with the nature of the regime will go the character of the party system.

If the Democrats don't get their money, I believe they will split. Left liberals will form their own party so that they can at least advocate what they would like, even if they can't get the government to do it.

Economic individualists support the Republican party because it brings limited government. But if Republicans move toward higher taxes, individualists in the party will see no reason to support it. Then they might well form their own libertarian party.

Reform

With budgeting becoming equivalent to governing, while dissensus makes it difficult to do either, the aims of recent budgetary reforms come into clearer focus. The balanced-budget amendment, which limits federal spending to the last year times the increase in GNP, aims to restore by formal action what was previously accomplished by the informal workings of budgetary norms. A formula provides the limits that hitherto welled up spontaneously as balance, comprehensiveness, and annual review. Consensus is to be restored by altering the formal rules of the game.[3]

The amendment encapsulates a macro and a micro political theory. The macro theory expresses a political preference: the public sector should not expand into the private sector. This philosophy is supported by the provision that spending cannot exceed the percentage growth in national income. The micro theory seeks to create incentives for limiting expenditure by making it in the interest of program advocates to restrain their demands. Imposing a global limit means that increases for one program or agency above the percentage increase in national income have to be accompanied by equivalent decreases in others. Budgeting by addition, in which program costs are piled on top of each other to be paid for by tax increases or debt, would be replaced by budgeting by subtraction, in which desired increases would have to compete within the limits of economic growth.

The grand purpose of constitutional revenue and expenditure limitation is to increase cooperation in society and conflict in government. As things stand, program advocates within government have every incentive to raise their spending income while reducing their internal differences. How? By increasing their total share of national income at the expense of the private sector. Why fight among their public selves if private persons will pay? Thus conflict is transferred from government to society.[4]

Once limits were enacted, however, the amendment's advocates believe that the direction of incentives would reverse: there would be increasing cooperation in society and rising conflict in government. Citizens would have a common interest in growth, whereas the sectors of policy—housing, welfare, environment, defense—would plunge into conflict. This change in the pattern of perceiving interests would come about because society would be united in increasing productivity and government would be divided over the relative shares of each sector within a fixed limit. Organizations interested in income redistribution to favor poorer people would come to understand that the greater the increase in real national income, the more there will be for government to spend on their purposes. Instead of acting as if it didn't matter where the money came from, they would have to consider how they might contribute to enhanced productivity. Management and labor, majority and minorities, would be thinking about common objectives, about how to get more out of one another rather than about how to take more from the other.

Until now the arguments on both sides have been hypothetical. The opposing view goes from the ridiculous—the Constitution contains no economic provisions (try reading it and stop after ten such provisions), or there will be a runaway convention creating a wholly new, radically revised Constitution (imagine economic libertarians and social conservatives agreeing beyond the preamble) ⁵—to the unanswerable: people will find ways around every provision. These arguments come from people who in other contexts pride themselves on the punctilious observation of constitutional dictates.

Fortunately a lesser known provision of GRH involves a real-life test of the theory behind the amendment. For the last two years the Senate has operated under GRH's offset provisions. Essentially this means that within every large appropriations account any effort to increase spending must be accompanied by either a spending cut or a revenue increase elsewhere, subject to a 60 percent vote against a point of order prohibiting the proposed increase. This provision results in far fewer proposed increases because of the difficulty of finding offsets. Friends of one kind of spending keep other spending down by refusing to provide offsets. Defense contractors scrutinize welfare spending while its defenders examine the military budget. Spending interests guard each other.⁶

Governing

The lateness, confusion, and obfuscation surrounding the budget; the proliferation of gimmicks designed to hide increases; the failure to agree on substantial deficit reduction measures; the experience of budget, budget, budget, apparently to little purpose—all these have limited the capacity of Congress and the president to govern the nation. This is the view not only of external critics of Congress but also (and more importantly) of leading members. The resignation from the Senate of Democrat Lawton Chiles, chair of its Budget Committee, is but one of many such signs of the times.

Yet experience under the Senate offset provision (the liberal majority in the House has so far refused to adopt it) offers hope for demonstrating

Congress's ability to govern. If Congress refuses to support the amendment, it could still rescue its self-respect by using the offset provision to demonstrate a capacity to govern.

Once both houses, by legislation or by rule, adopt offset provisions, elected officials will not only govern but be seen by themselves and observers to be governing. They will face fewer demands because demanding increases will cease to be an unalloyed good. The costs not only for the deficit, and hence future programs, but for other desired expenditures will immediately be apparent. Demands will be countered by other spending interests that are thereby threatened with loss. Soon enough there will be fewer importuners around. Instead, the special interests will have to go to the politicians because they are the only ones who can make the hard trade-offs in which X, Y, and Z give something to support A, B, and C. The genuine mediating skill of politicians will become apparent as soon as resource addition, for which no help is needed, gives way to resource subtraction, for which political mediation is essential.

It is said that the growth of government has led to inflated currency and inflated expectations. Certainly it has led to inflated rhetoric. What we have not realized is that getting government to grow and grow inflates political capital as well. The first few generations of politicians who practice budgeting by addition get inflated reputations. After a few decades have passed, however, politicians are disparaged either because they (1) give in to special interests or (2) fail to give in. For politicians, at least, this is ultimately a losing game.

For the federal government, ultimately is now. Those who disagree about taxing and spending may still wish to see the political vocation valued in our democracy. But if politicians are to be important, they must be concerned with more than giving away and giving in.

Trends

One obvious trend for the future is a gradual but pronounced growth of government. As government grows so will the Democratic party, expanding its semipermanent majority in the House to the Senate and winning the presidency more often. Another trend would be maintenance of a smaller government. Republicans would be able to compete not only for the presidency and the Senate, as they do now, but for the House as well.

For either of these trends to take place, the general public would have to change its voting patterns. Realignment on ideological grounds, so far restricted to the South, would have to expand to the rest of the nation. Supppose, however, that the people continue to give inconsistent results, on the one hand, while their elected officials, on the other, show signs of deep dissensus? Then politicians will have to decide whether their capacity to govern is more important to them than their differing ideologies. My crystal ball clouds over, but so far ideology appears to be winning.

Notes

1. See Aaron Wildavsky, "No War Without Dictatorship, No Peace Without Democracy: Foreign Policy as Domestic Politics," *Social Philosophy & Policy* 3, no. 1 (Autumn 1985): 176–91. Also in Ellen Frankel Paul et al., eds., *Nuclear Rights/ Nuclear Wrongs* (Oxford: Blackwell, 1986).

2. See Aaron Wildavsky, "The Unanticipated Consequences of the 1984 Presidential Election," *Tax Notes* 24, no. 2 (July 9, 1984): 193–200.

3. My reasons for believing that the item veto will be inefficacious in overcoming ideological dissensus are found in Aaron Wildavsky, "Item Veto Without a Global Spending Limit: Locking the Treasury After the Dollars Have Fled," *Notre Dame Journal of Law, Ethics and Public Policy* 1, no. 2 (1985): 165–76. For a powerful argument that the federal budget, unlike that in most states, does not lend itself to the item veto, see Louis Fisher and Neal Devins, "How Successfully Can the States' Item Veto Be Transferred to the President?" *Georgetown Law Journal* 75, no. 1 (October 1986): 159–97.

4. I recapitulate here my argument in *How to Limit Government Spending* (Berkeley and Los Angeles: University of California Press, 1980).

5. See Aaron Wildavsky, "The Runaway Convention or Proving a Preposterous Negative" (Paper prepared for the Taxpayers' Foundation, 1983), pamphlet ISBN 0-911415-10-5.

6. For a fuller account, see Aaron Wildavsky, *The New Politics of the Budgetary Process* (Glenview, Ill.: Scott, Foresman; Boston: Little Brown, 1987).

JOHN F. COGAN

The Federal Deficit in the 1990s

A Tale of Two Budgets

♦ The problem of reducing the federal budget deficit is the single most important domestic challenge confronting the next president and other political leaders of the 1990s. Although deficit spending has been characteristic of federal government fiscal policy making since the 1930s, the current and projected future deficits, because of their magnitude, persistence, and underlying causes, have far more severe consequences for the economy and policy making than deficits in earlier years.

From the experience of the last five years' economic recovery it should be clear that the federal budget deficit is structural; that is, economic growth alone will not produce enough revenues to finance federal programs at their current level. The present economic recovery, the longest since World War II, has raised the federal government's *annual* revenue intake by more than $300 billion (50 percent) since 1983. However, the budget deficit still remains at $150 billion, far higher than even the recession-driven 1982 budget deficit of $127 billion. Because of the spending momentum built into the budget, closing the revenue-expenditure gap in the 1990s will require at a

I am indebted to my assistant, Mary Farrell, and my colleague John Raisian for their valuable comments and suggestions. A note of acknowledgment is due to David Stockman, who recognized the emerging revenue-expenditure imbalance between the trust funds and the general fund as early as 1984, for suggesting the title to this paper in one of his Office of Management and Budget graduate seminars on budget policy.

minimum a major restructuring of the laws underlying these program expenditures.

The failure to shrink radically the size of the deficit is likely to have profound economic consequences. To the extent that government deficits crowd out private investment, the structural deficit reduces the rate of long-term economic growth. Recently, however, the wide swings in the dollar's value relative to currencies of other major industrial nations, the abrupt stock market decline in October 1987, and the market's ensuing volatility suggest that large and persistent deficits may also have short-term consequences for economic stability.

Correcting the imbalance between federal revenues and spending will receive top priority in the early 1990s. This essay documents an increasingly important dimension of the structural deficit problem: the growing revenue-expenditure mismatch in the federal budget's trust funds and general fund. Since 1984 the trust fund component of the budget has been building an ever-increasing surplus. At the same time, the general fund has been sinking deeper into deficit, continuing the postwar trend. Without a radical change in budget policy, these two opposing trends will continue well into the 1990s.

The large general fund deficits together with trust fund surpluses point to the role congressional budget procedures have played in producing the total budget deficits and the increasing political difficulty of reducing these deficits. The next section of this essay presents the total budget deficit picture for the early 1990s, documents the growing revenue-expenditure mismatch in the trust and general funds, and describes the role each plays in producing the overall budget deficit. The second section examines the role of the congressional committee system in generating persistent general fund deficits. The third section assesses the extent to which trust fund revenues and expenditures, which now constitute almost 40 percent of all government revenues and expenditures, can help shrink the budget deficit. The final section outlines budget process reforms that would greatly facilitate deficit reduction efforts.

General Fund and Trust Fund Imbalances

Budget experts have reached a broad consensus that without significant changes in economic performance compared with the past few years, and without sharp changes in tax and spending policies, the federal budget deficit will not decline appreciably during the next five years. Nearly all major forecasts of budget deficits throughout the first part of the 1990s project current-policy deficits in the range of $150–200 billion.[1] In all major forecasts, the expenditure growth built into the budget through previous decisions offsets the increase in revenues resulting from the anticipated growth in nominal gross national product (GNP).

A conventional forecast of federal budget deficits into the early 1990s is provided in Table 1. Though based on the administration's fiscal year 1989 (FY89) budget, this forecast assumes a less-optimistic growth rate in real GNP and assumes that interest rates remain at their current levels rather than decline.

For the purposes of this essay, the federal budget may be viewed as two separate budgets: a budget for trust fund programs and a budget for general fund programs.[2] Trust funds are an accounting device enabling Congress to dedicate revenues from a particular source or sources to finance a specific expenditure. Expenditures from trust funds can only be made if the designated revenues have been raised to finance the expenditures, although trust funds have been permitted to borrow from the general fund temporarily to alleviate a revenue shortfall. The trust fund is required to repay such loans, usually within a short time and always with interest. Trust fund revenues cannot be used directly to finance general fund expenditures, such as defense expenditures or food stamp benefits, although surplus revenues from trust funds may similarly be borrowed to finance general fund activities in lieu of borrowing from the public.

The general fund differs from the trust fund in that general revenues, mostly income and corporate taxes, are pooled to finance activities ranging from national defense programs to migrant health centers to education benefits. In addition to the accounting distinction, there is an important legislative difference between the two types of funds. Jurisdiction over trust fund expenditures is lodged in a single committee, whereas jurisdiction over general fund expenditures is divided among more than a dozen committees in both the House and the Senate.

The overall budget deficit picture described in Table 1 masks the disturbing structural imbalance within the general fund and the trust fund budgets. The direction and magnitude of this imbalance is shown in Table 2.[3] Throughout the early 1990s, as the total budget deficit remains in the $160–170 billion range, the surplus in the trust fund budget will grow rapidly from $40 billion in FY88 to over $80 billion by FY93. In contrast, the deficit in the general fund will increase from about $200 billion to more than $240 billion. Since both the trust fund surplus and the general fund deficit have already reached historically high levels, the projected future increases would create an imbalance between the two funds unprecedented in U.S. fiscal history.

One might argue that the division of the federal budget into a general fund budget and a trust fund budget creates a distinction without a dif-

Table 1
Federal Budget Projection
(in billions of dollars)

	FY89	FY91	FY93
Revenues	945	1,050	1,179
Expenditures	1,105	1,218	1,343
Deficit	− 160	− 168	− 164

SOURCE: Author's computations and the *Budget of the United States Government, Fiscal Year 1989* (Washington, D.C.: Government Printing Office, 1988).

Table 2
Projected Revenues and Expenditures
for Trust Funds and General Fund
(in billions of dollars)

	FY89	FY91	FY93
Trust Funds[a]			
Revenues	379	442	501
Expenditures	337	376	419
Surplus	42	66	82
General Fund			
Revenues	566	608	678
Expenditures	768	842	924
Deficit	− 202	− 234	− 246

SOURCE: Author's projections, based on the *Budget of the United States Government, Fiscal Year 1989*.
[a] Trust funds include only the eight largest trust funds (see n. 3).

ference because only total federal budget taxes and spending affect the economy. A dollar in tax revenue entered as a receipt to a trust fund could be portrayed as having the same impact on the economy as a dollar in revenue entered as a receipt to the general fund. Likewise, one could argue that a U.S. government check debited against a trust fund account and a check for the same amount debited to a general fund account have identical consequences for the economy. But the legislative spending process for programs in the general budget differs from the process for programs in the trust fund budget. These differences have important implications for assessing the causes of the deficit, the increasing political difficulty of reducing it, and reforms in the congressional process that would help bring it down.

General Fund Deficits

It should be clear from the preceding discussion that in an accounting sense the causes of the structural deficit in the 1980s are rooted in the general budget. More important, the general fund has been the source of the total federal budget deficit since the deficit emerged as a persistent phenomenon in the 1930s.[4] Table 3 illustrates the close relation between total and general fund deficits since the Korean conflict. Clearly since the general fund budget deficit accounts for the entire deficit since World War II, an explanation for the total budget deficit must lie in the general fund and should rely on forces affecting the general fund but not the trust funds. One likely candidate is the congressional committee structure and its role in budgetary decision making.

Beginning in 1932 and continuing through the mid-1970s, Congress has systematically spread jurisdiction over expenditures to an ever-increasing set of committees. It has not done so with trust funds. For each trust fund a single committee has primary jurisdiction over expenditures.

The problem with divided spending jurisdiction is that it produces incentives for each committee, acting independently of all other committees, to spend more than it would if committees cooperated. Consequently the combined expenditures exceed what all committees acting in concert would spend.

When many congressional committees have spending jurisdiction, no individual committee has any incentive to control its spending commitments. In fact the opposite incentive operates. Competition develops among committees as each strives for greater recognition and a larger share of resources for the programs under its jurisdiction. Each committee in turn be-

Table 3
Total and General Fund Deficits as a Percent of GNP

	1955–59	1965–69	1975–79	1985–89
Total budget deficit	0.5	0.9	3.0	4.1
General fund deficit	0.3	1.0	3.0	5.0

SOURCE: *Special Analysis Budget of the U.S. Government*, annual publications, FY55–89 (Washington, D.C.: Government Printing Office, 1954–1988).

comes a focal point for the special interests that benefit from the committee's expenditures. Soon each committee becomes a special pleader instead of weighing the merits of its program against the merits of others and the limited availability of revenues. Thus the congressional spending process becomes dominated by special interests. The process also precludes political accountability: since no single committee is responsible for the total level of spending, no one can be blamed for the excess.

The proliferation of committees with spending jurisdiction inevitably increases government expenditures. This is precisely what has occurred in the general fund budget since the committee proliferation began in the 1930s. Between 1932 and 1987 general budget expenditures rose from less than 1 percent of GNP to 16 percent of GNP.[5]

Deficits have not plagued the trust funds because jurisdiction over expenditures is centralized. Jurisdiction over Social Security, disability insurance, Medicare hospital insurance, and unemployment insurance resides exclusively with the tax-writing committees: the House Ways and Means Committee and the Senate Finance Committee. For each of the remaining trust funds jurisdiction over expenditures resides primarily with a committee other than the tax-writing committee. But in each case a single committee and the tax-writing committees have joint jurisdiction to review proposed expenditure limits to ensure the trust fund's solvency.

Shifts in taxation have also played an important role in contributing to the general fund deficit. Since the mid-1930s the total tax burden relative to the size of the economy has been remarkably stable. Taxes as a percent of GNP have fallen outside the 17.5–19.5 percent range only three times since 1955 and never in two consecutive years. But within this constant tax burden, the tax-writing committees in each house have continuously substituted trust fund taxes for general fund taxes. As a result trust fund taxes have risen from about 2 percent of GNP to almost 7 percent since the mid-1950s, while general fund taxes as a proportion of GNP have fallen almost 4 percentage points.

Tax policy in the 1980s brings this substitution of trust fund taxes for general fund taxes into sharp relief. From 1981 to 1983 nearly all federal government taxes dedicated to financing major trust funds increased through legislation. In 1981 the railroad retirement payroll tax increased by almost one-third and the coal tax for black-lung benefits doubled. Each of these tax increases was necessary to forestall the imminent bankruptcy of the trust funds they support. The 1982 Tax Equity and Fiscal Responsibility Act (TEFRA) almost doubled the airline ticket tax and tripled fuel taxes to increase support for the Airport and Airway Trust Fund. Also in 1982 the wage base and the payroll tax rate that finance the federal share of unemployment benefits rose, and the federal gasoline tax that supports the Highway Trust Fund doubled. In 1983 the railroad retirement payroll tax rose again, and major legislation restoring the solvency of the Social Security fund was enacted. The Social Security Amendments of 1983 raised taxes that support all four major federal Social Security programs: the old-age pension program, disability insurance, Medicare hospital insurance, and unemployment insurance.

General fund taxes, however, were sharply reduced. The reductions achieved in the 1981 Economic Recovery Tax Act (ERTA) were only partially offset by the subsequent tax increases in TEFRA, the 1984 Deficit Reduction Act, and other later tax legislation. To highlight the stark contrast between the 1980s tax policies for the general budget and those for the trust fund budget, we can compare the income tax provisions of the 1981 ERTA with the payroll tax provisions of the Social Security Amendments of 1983. Income tax rates were lowered each year from 1981 to 1983, and tax brackets were indexed starting in 1985 to prevent automatic future tax increases through inflation. The opposite policies were pursued for Social Security. The 1983 amendments raised payroll tax rates in successive stages; the first take effect in 1984 and the last in 1990. The 1983 amendments also established a tax on Social Security benefits for those with incomes over $25,000. This income threshold was not indexed, and thus the tax burden rises with inflation.

The observed substitution of trust fund taxes for general fund taxes may well stem from the different incentives facing members of the tax-writing committees. To committee members, raising taxes is painful. When they raise general fund taxes, they do so from a sense of duty to finance the general expenses of government. Committee members have little control over how the general revenues will be spent. But for over 90 percent of trust fund expenditures, the tax-writing committees also have jurisdiction over spending. Because of this, raising trust fund taxes is less painful than raising general fund taxes. The result is an institutional bias that favors trust fund taxes over general fund taxes.

Some Implications of Trust Fund Surpluses for Deficit Reductions

Experience with trust fund tax and spending policies strongly suggests that it would be difficult for trust fund revenue and spending policies to be used to reduce the overall budget deficit in the 1990s. Trust fund benefits historically have been reduced through structural reform only in response to a financial crisis that immediately threatens the solvency of the trust fund. For example, in the post–World War II history of Social Security, structural reforms that reduced benefits have only been enacted twice, in 1977 and in 1983. In both instances the benefit reductions were part of a package of reforms designed to prevent the impending bankruptcy of the fund. Railroad retirement benefits have been reduced only twice in the program's history, both times in an effort to avoid bankruptcy. The same holds true for benefit reductions for the black-lung program. In the Social Security disability program, calls to stem the rapid growth in outlays and to correct widespread abuses went unheeded for years until the trust fund faced financial insolvency. Benefit reductions to alleviate a general fund financial problem occasionally occur, as the experience with Medicare during the 1980s has demonstrated. But these occasions are rare and usually do not involve the structural reform of underlying statutes.

The pay-as-you-go financing rule invariably results in tax increases only when the trust fund faces a financial crisis or when a revenue increase is needed to finance a specific benefit expansion. Since World War II all legislated increases in Social Security taxes have been justified on the basis of one of these two considerations. From 1946 to 1976 twelve separate pieces of legislation raising Social Security taxes were enacted. In 1977 and 1983 the tax increases were enacted to ensure the solvency of the trust fund. In the ten other instances the legislation directly linked the tax increase to an increase in benefits. An unanticipated deficit in the Highway Trust Fund led to the 1959 gas tax increase. The 1982 gas tax increase was to finance the renovation of the nation's roads and bridges. Moreover, federal unemployment taxes were raised in the 1970s and early 1980s with the express purpose of financing additional weeks of extended or supplemental unemployment benefits.

Also because of the pay-as-you-go rule, trust fund surpluses usually do not persist for long. In many instances the surplus comes from a revenue increase enacted along with a *future* commitment to spend additional resources. Such was the case with many of the Social Security coverage expansions during the 1950s and 1960s, and more recently with the 1982 increase in Highway Trust Fund revenues. When trust fund surpluses do arise, pressure groups that are the direct beneficiary of expenditures invariably exert pressure to spend excess funds. This was the case with the Social Security benefit hikes of the late 1960s and early 1970s and is currently the case with the Airport and Airway Trust Fund.

These considerations strongly suggest that the expenditure-revenue mismatch between the trust funds and the general fund during the 1990s exacerbates the political difficulty of balancing the overall budget. The political problem of reducing trust fund benefits or raising trust fund taxes when these funds are running historically high surpluses should not be understated. Indeed, in the face of these surpluses, simply holding the line on trust

Table 4
Difficulty of Balancing Total FY93 Budget
(projected deficit: $164 billion)

	Across-the-board policy	General budget policy
Revenues	$1,179 billion	$678 billion
Increase required to balance budget	14%	24%
Expenditures	$1,123 billion	$704 billion
Reduction required to balance budget	15%	23%

fund spending would represent a significant break from past congressional practices.

The increased difficulty of balancing the total budget because of the fiscal imbalance between trust funds and the general fund is quantified in Table 4. The table compares opposite cases using the budget projections for 1993. In both cases the objective is to balance the 1993 budget by either tax increases or spending reductions—although the example applies equally well to deficit reduction efforts of any size. The across-the-board policy ignores the distinction between general fund programs and trust fund programs. In this case all taxes would be available for possible increase and all programmatic expenditures (that is, all expenditures except interest payments on the debt) would be available for possible reductions to balance the budget. The general budget policy assumes that trust fund surpluses cannot be used to reduce the deficit. Thus only general fund taxes can be raised, or general fund expenditures reduced, to eliminate the total budget deficit.

In the first case, a 14 percent across-the-board increase in taxes or a 15 percent across-the-board reduction in spending would be required to eliminate the $164 billion FY93 budget deficit. Although the second case requires the same magnitude of deficit reduction, revenue increases or expenditure reductions must come from a smaller base of taxes and expenditures. The general budget revenue increase or expenditure reduction required to eliminate the deficit amounts to 23 percent when trust funds are excluded—approximately twice the proportionate change required by the across-the-board policy. As expected, removing the trust funds from the chopping block proportionately increases the size of the tax increase or spending decrease required to eliminate the deficit—but the size of the proportionate increase is eye-opening.

Policy Implications

The preceding examination of the two components of the budget suggests several important policy ideas to eliminate the structural total budget deficit. For a solution to the structural deficit problem to last, the problem must be approached in two ways. A permanent or long-term solution requires correcting not only the imbalance between total expenditures and total revenues but also the imbalance between spending and revenues within the trust fund and general fund budgets. To correct the former problem without addressing the latter would make only a temporary and illusory fix. Either mounting trust fund surpluses will eventually lead to irresistible pressure to spend them, or, if the pressure is resisted, the demographic forces that drive the bulk of trust fund expenditures will eventually eliminate the trust fund surplus and thereby expose the general fund deficit.

The foregoing analysis also has an important implication for the timing of deficit reduction efforts. Although the total budget deficit seems to have stabilized, the revenue-expenditure gap in the trust funds and in the general fund widens each year. Thus reducing the structural deficit becomes ever more difficult. Further delay will only worsen the problem as the mounting trust fund surplus generates additional pressures for increased trust fund expenditures.

Ultimately the solution to the deficit problem depends on balancing the general fund budget. This outcome is unlikely, however, without reforming the congressional spending and taxing process. The preceding analysis suggests some process reforms to help break the budget stalemate.

One such reform would combine all spending authority for general fund programs into a single committee. In making spending decisions on individual programs, this committee would have to weigh the merits of each program against the merits of all other programs, thus improving the system of checks and balances on spending decisions. This process would impose greater political accountability and would curtail the excessive influence of special interests. Although this reform might be difficult to achieve, there is a precedent for it. Just before World War I many Americans were concerned about the extravagance of congressional spending. Political leaders of both parties recognized that part of the problem lay in the multiplicity of congressional committees with jurisdiction over expenditures, a situation that had prevailed since the 1880s. The 1916 Democratic party campaign platform called for the House of Representatives to combine all appropriations authority in a single committee—a practice the House had used throughout the first 93 years of the nation's history. The 1916 Republican party platform, though less specific, urged the consolidation of spending authority.

Under the pressure of these party platform planks, the House in 1919 and the Senate in 1922 consolidated spending into a single committee.

The analysis also suggests that some mechanism be introduced to attenuate the bias of the tax-writing committees, which favor raising trust fund taxes for programs over which they have spending jurisdiction rather than raising general fund taxes. One approach would be to strip the tax-writing committees of their authority over expenditures. Again, there is a precedent for such a change. In 1865 the House stripped the Ways and Means Committee of its jurisdiction over expenditures, a jurisdiction it had held since the beginning of the republic. The committee remained without spending authority for the next 70 years, until the Great Depression led to the reinstatement of spending authority in the 1930s.

Notes

1. Current-policy deficit projections assume that no changes occur in the laws underlying entitlement programs or revenues and that discretionary programs are funded at a rate that enables the same level of services to be provided over time.

2. The federal budget also contains several other types of funds, such as revolving funds and public enterprise funds. These funds are financed primarily by general fund contributions and therefore are treated as part of the general fund in this essay.

3. The individual trust funds included in this essay's trust fund budget differ from the official list of trust funds defined in the U.S. Budget Accounts. This essay includes only the eight individual trust funds that derive their principal source of revenue from taxes levied on the public: Social Security Old-Age and Survivors Insurance Fund, Social Security Disability Insurance, Medicare part A, the Railroad Retirement Trust Fund, the Black Lung Trust Fund, the Unemployment Trust Fund, the Highway Trust Fund, and the Airport and Airway Trust Fund. Individual trust funds excluded from the trust fund budget are those financed jointly by general revenues and dedicated revenues. Such funds include Medicare part B and the military and civilian retirement programs.

4. See John F. Cogan, *The Congressional Committee Structure and the Federal Budget* (forthcoming).

5. Throughout the 1920s, when all spending jurisdiction resided in one committee in each house, federal spending as a percent of GNP declined slightly. See Cogan, *Congressional Committee Structure,* for similar evidence in the nineteenth century.

CHARLES E. McLURE, JR.

◆ ——————————————————————— ◆

Tax Policy for the 1990s
Tending to Unfinished Business

Introduction

◆ The United States is likely to enter the 1990s with a seriously flawed federal tax system, despite the historic Tax Reform Act of 1986. The 1986 act retained far too many loopholes that undermine the fairness, economic neutrality, and simplicity of the law. Conversely it deals too harshly with some forms of income, again resulting in inequities, economic distortions, and complexity. Most important, the tax system simply does not yield enough revenue to pay the bills.

This essay examines some of the most important defects of the federal tax system and discusses proposals for their solution. It concentrates entirely on the federal income tax and measures that have been suggested for its improvement, replacement, or augmentation. It does not address the financing of Social Security, other areas of federal finance in which action would be appropriate, or questions of state and local government finance in which the federal government arguably has a stake.[1]

Tax policy is commonly judged according to the criteria of equity, neutrality, and simplicity.[2] To be equitable a tax system must impose comparable burdens on similar families with the same income. The relative burdens that should be imposed on families with different incomes cannot be known with scientific precision, being a matter of individual taste that must ultimately be settled by social consensus. Most observers probably agree, however, that regressivity (tax burdens that fall relative to income as income rises) should be avoided, and many favor at least some degree of progressivity. Economic neutrality is an attractive feature of a tax system because a neutral tax does not interfere with economic decisions made in response to market forces. Like equity, it is furthered by taxing all real economic income consistently, regardless of its source or its use. Simplicity in tax policy has several dimensions. Clearly a simple tax system would not impose onerous burdens of record keeping and preparation of tax returns. Perhaps equally important for many, a neutral tax system would also be simple because it would not interject tax considerations into economic decision making.

Some observers include economic growth and international competitiveness as explicit goals of tax policy. I believe that growth and competitiveness would take care of themselves if only the tax system were more neutral (rather than biased to support the pet projects of politicians and their influential supporters) and if the federal government would substantially reduce the budget deficit (rather than borrowing scarce capital and drawing in funds from abroad, which inevitably lead to a current-account deficit).

Income Tax Reform

The Tax Reform Act of 1986 substantially improved the federal income tax by broadening the tax base, lowering marginal tax rates, and reducing opportunities for tax shelters. As a result the tax system is more equitable and more neutral than it was a few years ago. Yet many of the most important reforms recommended to President Reagan in the Treasury Department's 1984 report *Tax Reform for Fairness, Simplicity, and Economic Growth* (hereafter Treasury-I)—and others excluded from that report for political reasons—were left on the cutting room floor.[3] Moreover, and partly because of this inaction, the federal income tax is far more complicated than it needs to be.

Broadening the Tax Base

The most important remaining omissions from the income tax base involve provisions that most Americans might not consider loopholes, much less causes for concern. Among these are the deduction for mortgage interest, the exclusion of employer-provided health insurance and other fringe benefits, and the deduction for state and local income and property taxes. Massive amounts of revenue, as well as inequities and distortions, are at stake in these three areas. Of course, reform is also needed in many other areas.

Under the tax law prevailing before 1981, when the top marginal individual income tax rate was 70 percent, governments in effect paid as much as 70 percent (or more) of the mortgage interest expense of home owners. It is thus not surprising that too much investment was made in owner-occupied housing and too little in plant and equipment, even leaving aside other important tax breaks for home ownership.[4] The reduction in marginal rates has reduced the maximum government subsidy to home ownership through the tax system to only 36 to 40 percent for those subject to the top marginal rates.[5] But there is still a substantial inducement for overinvestment in housing. Moreover, these benefits are worth more, per dollar of mortgage interest, to taxpayers with high incomes than to those with low incomes. Thus the continuation of this deduction undermines both the neutrality and the equity of the income tax.[6]

Much the same can be said about the tax treatment of employer-provided fringe benefits, the most important of which is health insurance. Given subsidy rates of the magnitude just described, together with the moral-hazard problems that inevitably affect insurable risks, it is hardly surprising that medical care takes a high and rising fraction of national output. Equity is also compromised, since those with the highest incomes receive the most generous fringe benefits.

In the deduction for state and local income and property taxes there is an additional twist to the problems of inequity and distortion. Not only is there a tax-induced tendency for overexpansion of state and local spending and an inequitable favoritism for high-income taxpayers; there is also senseless geographic discrimination. Overexpansion is favored most in jurisdictions populated by high-income taxpayers. By comparison, the federal subsidy hardly exists for poor areas, where many residents pay no income tax or do not itemize deductions. Finally, allowing a deduction for only income and property taxes discriminates against residents of states that choose other means of finance, most notably sales taxes, and inappropriately creates federal intrusion into state and local fiscal decision making.[7]

The remedy for these problems is straightforward, at least in broad outline.[8] Home mortgage deductions should be capped, if not eliminated. Employer-provided medical benefits above some fairly generous amount should be either included in the employee's taxable income or disallowed as an employer's deduction. State and local income, sales, and property taxes should all be treated equivalently, preferably by disallowing deductions for a high fraction (if not all) of them.

Such suggestions are usually considered politically naive because vested interests oppose them. Opposition could probably be reduced by the provision of reasonable transition rules. If, for example, the disallowance of mortgage interest deductions began only ten years after enactment and phased in over the following ten or twenty years, the present value of the resulting windfall losses would be trivial. An alternative transition strategy that builds on the 1987 budget compromise would disallow some fraction of mortgage interest deductions in excess of a fairly high figure and then reduce that figure over time. A further reason for carefully crafted transition rules is the geographically differentiated impact of these reforms. High-tax states, states with high housing costs, and heavily unionized states would be hit harder than other states and thus would oppose these reforms vigorously.

Adjusting for Inflation

The tax system of the United States is built on the implicit assumption of a stable price level. The interaction of such a tax system with inflation creates inequities and distortions. Depreciation allowances that would allow the tax-free recovery of capital in a period of stable prices are inadequate in the face of inflation. Deductions for nominal interest expense are too generous, and the inclusion of nominal interest receipts in taxable income is overly harsh. The result is an incentive to borrow and a disincentive to save and lend. Finally, tax is paid on nominal capital gains that are not real, and tax may even be due where the taxpayer has experienced a real loss.

Various ad hoc techniques are commonly used to avoid some of the most pernicious effects of the failure to adjust for inflation. In particular, depreciation is accelerated, an investment credit has been allowed, and part of long-term capital gains has been excluded from taxable income. Unfortunately each of these ad hoc techniques is appropriate for one rate of inflation at most; at any other rate it is either too generous or not generous enough. Moreover, hardly any adjustment is ever made for interest income and expense. Inequities and distortions occur, and the advantages of tax shelter opportunities are aggravated.

Treasury-I contained a comprehensive set of proposals intended to prevent inflation from distorting the measurement of income from business and capital. Depreciation allowances based on the best available estimates of economic depreciation would have been adjusted for inflation, the inflation component of interest income and expense would have been disregarded for purposes of calculating taxable income, and the basis used for calculating capital gains and losses would have been adjusted for inflation.[9]

The reasons these proposals were not adopted are worth considering. First, critics argued that the rate of inflation was too low to justify the complexity of inflation adjustment. This argument is analogous to arguing against the purchase of fire insurance because the house is not ablaze. Indeed, there is much to be said for adopting an inflation-adjusted system when inflation is low, especially if, as is likely, inflation will return.

Second, inflation adjustment appears to lose a substantial amount of revenue. The net effect on the federal budget is almost certainly overstated, however, since we would expect indexation to result in a reduction in interest rates, including those paid on the national debt. Moreover, failing to improve the tax system simply because it would lose revenue is not one of the more widely respected canons of taxation.

Finally, interest indexing was opposed by those who would be adversely affected by it, particularly if it were implemented too rapidly. This line of argument has substantial merit. It is essential for both political and economic reasons to provide fair and orderly transition rules that would avoid imposing large windfall losses on debtors or bestowing large windfall gains on creditors.[10]

Dividend Relief

The United States is one of the few advanced countries that does not provide relief from the double taxation of corporate dividends. Consequently U.S. tax law discriminates against use of the corporate form and against economic activity that requires the corporate form, encourages reliance on debt finance rather than equity, and treats shareholders inequitably.[11] The conceptually preferred means of dealing with this problem, attributing corporate-source equity income to shareholders whether distributed or not, has generally been considered infeasible.[12] The advent of business organizational forms combining many attributes of corporations with the tax treatment of partnerships suggests that this conclusion should be reexamined.

The most common means of providing relief from double taxation of dividends is a shareholder credit for income tax paid by the corporation on income deemed to be distributed. A substantially simpler approach would allow a corporate deduction for dividends paid. This alternative was proposed in Treasury-I despite the conventional wisdom that no country would unilaterally grant the benefits of dividend relief to tax-exempt organizations and foreigners.

Providing relief from double taxation for all dividends creates windfall gains for existing shareholders, who presumably invested expecting double taxation to continue. The government sees these windfall gains as substantial losses of revenue. If it could make dividend relief available only on new issues of stock, it could achieve all the allocative and distributional advan-

tages of the more traditional approach without entailing substantial windfall gains or revenue losses.[13]

Complexity

The hallmark of the Tax Reform Act of 1986 is its complexity. This
problem occurred largely because Congress was unwilling to eliminate certain tax benefits—such as immediate deduction for intangible drilling costs
in the oil and gas industry, deductions for home mortgage interest, and
exclusion of interest income on state and local obligations—and yet wanted
to limit the predictable abuse of these benefits. In many instances the complexity was accentuated by the absence of inflation adjustment of interest
expense.

This essay can only hint at the complexity of the 1986 act.[14] There are
at least four types of income from business and capital (active, passive, investment, and exempt) and at least seven types of interest expense. Moreover, there is an alternative minimum tax on a different base from that of
the regular income tax. Following the clean route to tax reform proposed
in Treasury-I—the taxation of all real economic income—would eliminate the need for most such line drawing, make the alternative minimum
tax redundant, and thereby simplify both the tax code and economic decision making.

A Consumption-Based Direct Tax

In recent years considerable attention has been devoted to the possibility of
substituting a system of direct (personalized) taxation based on consumption for the existing income taxes.[15] (A direct tax would be levied on individual taxpayers and thus, like the existing income tax and unlike the indirect taxes on consumption considered in the next section, could
accommodate personal exemptions, itemized deductions, and graduated
rates.) Economists commonly tout the intertemporal neutrality of such a
tax; that is, unlike the income tax, a consumption-based tax does not artificially discourage saving and encourage consumption. Businesspeople also
like this form of taxation because it allows immediate expensing (first-year
write-off) for all investment; they are generally less enthusiastic about (if
not ignorant of) another necessary feature of such a tax, the disallowance
of deductions for interest expense.[16]

These advantages of a consumption-based direct tax are not its primary
attraction. Implementation of a tax on real economic income is invariably
complicated for at least two reasons. The inflation adjustments described

and espoused earlier inevitably add complexity to the income tax. Moreover, the accurate measurement of economic income requires satisfactory answers to a large number of timing issues, which would make the construction of a satisfactory income tax complex even in a world of stable prices. Many changes in value that constitute income or expenses do not occur at a readily identifiable time, so it is necessary to gear tax liability to identifiable events or to employ arbitrary schedules.

Perhaps the best example of a timing issue involves depreciation allowances. An asset bought at a given price eventually becomes worthless. To measure income accurately it is important to know the time pattern of the decline in value of the asset, since deductions for depreciation should track actual loss of value as closely as possible. Since the decline in value is generally unknown, tax laws employ schedules of depreciation allowances.

Other well-known timing issues include accrued interest on discount bonds, amortization, depletion, intangible drilling costs, and inventory accounting. The 1986 act brought increased attention to additional timing issues, including recognition of income from installment sales and long-term contracts, capitalization of construction period interest and expenses of inventories, and limits on the cash method of accounting. These are among the reasons businesses, especially small ones, howled about the complexity of the 1986 act.

The primary advantage of a consumption-based direct tax is its simplicity. Taxation of business income would be based on cash flow. Hence inflation adjustment would be unnecessary because all magnitudes relevant for tax purposes would be measured in dollars of the current accounting period. Timing issues do not arise since income is recognized when cash is received and deductions are allowed when cash is disbursed. Since a deduction is allowed for the entire purchase price of depreciable assets in the year of acquisition, there is no need for depreciation allowances, and the issue of adjusting them for inflation cannot arise.

Under the most attractive method of implementing a consumption-based tax, the treatment of dividends and of interest income and expense is also simple.[17] Rather than allowing a deduction for interest expense and taxing interest income, as under the income tax, a consumption-based tax would exclude interest from taxable income and allow no deduction for interest expense. Dividends would be treated the same way.

This approach has several advantages over existing practice under the income tax. Administration and compliance would be vastly simpler. It would not be necessary to ensure that the millions of recipients of interest and dividends include them in taxable income. Arbitrary line drawing at the business level between interest and dividends would be avoided. The equality of tax treatment of interest and dividends also means that current-law discrimination against equity finance would be eliminated. Finally, issues of parity and discrimination between tax-exempt organizations and taxpaying individuals and business would be eliminated by making the receipt of both interest and dividends tax-exempt for all.

Proposals for a consumption-based direct tax are often criticized as unfair because in present-value terms income from business and capital is effectively excluded from the tax base. Since income from such sources increases as a fraction of total income as income rises, critics say that a consumption-based tax system violates both vertical and horizontal equity. One response to such objections is that any degree of progressivity can be achieved simply by modifying the graduated rate structure. This response detracts, however, from a more basic line of argument.

If amounts received as gifts and bequests are included in the tax base of both recipients and donors, we can characterize the consumption-based tax as one on lifetime endowments (the present value of lifetime command over resources, including gifts and bequests as well as earned income). Many would argue that this is a better measure of taxpaying ability than either annual income or annual consumption. Seen in this light, the consumption-based alternative may actually be preferable to the current income tax on both horizontal and vertical equity grounds.

Raising Revenue

The discussion to this point has implicitly stayed in the context of revenue neutrality; that is, we have assumed that any change in the tax base resulting from the suggested income tax reforms or from the switch to a consumption-based direct tax would be offset by changes in tax rates that would leave revenues unchanged. Many readers may wonder whether this is the most relevant context for a discussion of tax policy for the 1990s. After all, many recognize that it is unwise and irresponsible for the United States to continue to incur federal deficits as big as those of the last decade; since reducing the deficit by cutting expenditures remains unlikely, many would argue that revenue enhancement is a more appropriate context for a discussion of tax policy. The remainder of this essay asks how the United States might best go about raising substantially more federal revenue, if that course should be thought appropriate.[18]

Aside from nickel-and-dime approaches such as excise taxes, user fees, and the sale of assets, we could raise additional federal revenues in three major ways: expanding the income tax bases, raising income tax rates, and introducing a broad-based sales tax.

As we noted above, gaping holes remain in the definition of taxable income, even after passage of the 1986 act. Thus substantial amounts of revenue could be raised simply by taking the first alternative: curtailing existing tax preferences such as those for state and local taxes, municipal bonds, employer-provided fringe benefits, and owner-occupied housing. In addition, smaller amounts could be raised by closing loopholes enjoyed by the politically powerful who largely escaped damage under the 1986 act, including oil and gas and timber. All things considered, further base broadening may be the best way to raise additional revenue in the long run.

This approach to deficit reduction has formidable shortcomings. First, not all tax reforms result in higher revenues. It would be inappropriate to enact only those that would raise revenues without also enacting those that would lose some, including especially inflation adjustment and dividend relief. Second, this approach involves a frontal attack on precisely the tax preferences that survived the 1986 act. There is little reason to expect greater success next time. Finally, it would be inappropriate to implement reform of this type suddenly. Thus it may not be possible to raise additional funds from these sources quickly, even if that goal could be achieved with appropriate transition rules. In short, if revenue is needed during the early 1990s, we may be forced to look elsewhere.

The second alternative would be to increase rates on the existing income tax base. This would be a real mistake, aggravating disincentives and economic distortions. Many believe that the promise of substantially lower tax rates greased the skids of tax reform that made the 1986 act possible. If so, the threat of substantially higher rates might well cause the miraculous tax reform we have accomplished to unravel.

The third alternative may be the best and most likely means to deal with the continuing budget problem. A broad-based indirect tax on consumption, such as a value-added tax (VAT), would probably yield at least $20 billion for each percentage point of the tax rate. Thus a 5 percent VAT might yield $100 billion per year. This is either the good news or the bad. Those who fear the growth of government view with horror the prospects of putting a VAT money machine in the hands of Congress and would seek a constitutional amendment to restrict the ability to use VAT revenues to expand federal spending. Those who support a larger role for government view the same prospect with delight.

To understand the likely economic effects of the VAT, we need only consider the effects of a similar tax, the retail sales tax (currently levied by all but five states). We can then agree quickly that (1) the tax would burden some low-income families and would be regressive, (2) it would be relatively neutral in its impact on economic decision making, (3) it would favor saving more than the income tax does, (4) it would have no appreciable effect on international competitiveness, and (5) it would preempt the sales tax field, which has historically been the fiscal domain of state and local governments. Since all of these propositions are important, and at least one may be surprising, they deserve further elaboration.[19]

The base of the VAT would be consumption. Since consumption constitutes a decreasing fraction of income as income rises, the VAT would be regressive. More to the point, it would take a substantial share of the income of low-income households. This is perhaps its primary disadvantage, aside from the money machine argument. The method many states use to reduce the regressivity of their sales taxes, the exemption of food and other necessities, is not cost-effective. It might be necessary to introduce an expanded system of income maintenance to offset the burden on low-income households and to avoid the regressivity of a VAT.

Unless shot through with exemptions and zero rates, the VAT would be relatively neutral in its impact on economic decision making. State sales taxes generally are not neutral because they commonly exclude many services. One of the advantages of the value-added technique is that exclusions would be less likely.

A federal sales tax would favor saving more than the existing income tax does. This advantage is easily overstated, however. After all, it is easier to increase national saving by reducing the federal deficit than by using structural tax policy to influence the level of private saving.

One claim commonly made for the VAT is that it would increase the international competitiveness of the United States because it would apply to imports and be rebated on exports. This line of argument is simply wrong. Imported goods would pay the same tax as domestically produced goods but no more; similarly, exports would enter world markets free of tax but without a subsidy.

The issue of intergovernmental fiscal relations is particularly troublesome. There is no good answer to the crucial question of how best to mesh a federal sales tax with the existing sales taxes imposed by state and local governments.[20] Along with the money machine and equity concerns, this is an important problem of using a broad-based sales tax as a source of additional federal revenues.

A final plea is necessary before leaving the discussion of the VAT. The technique used to implement a federal sales tax is not a matter of indifference. Whether it should be via a retail sales tax (RST) similar to those levied by the states or via a VAT is a close call on which informed observers might reasonably disagree. The VAT is more neutral and has administrative advantages, but the RST is much more familiar to U.S. business. The choice between a conventional VAT of the type used in roughly forty countries and the business transfer tax (BTT) that has been discussed in both the United States and Canada is not a close call. Under the conventional VAT, tax is levied on sales and credit is allowed for tax paid on purchases. Under the BTT, tax is applied to the difference between purchases and sales. This small difference has crucial implications for the politics, administration, and economic effects of the two taxes. For those reasons the BTT approach should not be considered.[21]

Conclusion

Much remains to be done in the area of tax policy. If the income tax continues to be the flagship of the federal fisc, it should be improved and simplified along the lines spelled out in Treasury-I. Improving the income tax is an attractive, though perhaps slow, way to increase revenues without raising rates. Raising rates on the existing income tax base would be less attractive than introducing a general sales tax. An alternative to both the income tax and a sales tax, a personal tax on consumption, deserves consideration since it is far simpler than the income tax.

Notes

1. See the following by Charles E. McLure, Jr.: "U.S. Tax Policy in the 21st Century: Sharks, Reefs, and Quiet Pools," in Herbert Stein, ed., *Tax Policy in the 21st Century* (New York: John Wiley & Sons, 1988); *Economic Perspectives on State Taxation of Multijurisdictional Corporations* (Arlington, Va.: Tax Analysts, 1986); and *The State Corporation Income Tax: Issues in Worldwide Unitary Combination* (Stanford: Hoover Institution Press, 1984).

2. For further discussions of these criteria, see any textbook on government finance. See also Charles E. McLure, Jr., "Rationalizing the U.S. Tax System," in Geoffrey Brennan, ed., *Taxation and Fiscal Federalism: Essays in Honour of Russell Mathews* (Canberra: Australian National University Press, forthcoming).

3. For further analyses of the Tax Reform Act of 1986, see Charles E. McLure, Jr., "Where Tax Reform Went Astray," *Villanova Law Review* 31 (November 1986): 1619–63; and Charles E. McLure, Jr., and George R. Zodrow, "Treasury I and the Tax Reform Act of 1986: The Economics and Politics of Tax Reform," *Journal of Economic Perspectives* 1, no. 1 (Summer 1987): 37–58.

4. Patric H. Hendershott and James D. Shilling, "Capital Allocation and the Economic Recovery Tax Act of 1981," *Public Finance Quarterly* 10 (April 1982): 242–73.

5. This is the range calculated by adding to federal marginal tax rates of either 28 or 33 percent the product of 1 minus that rate and 11 percent, the highest state tax rate.

6. I have argued that continuing this deduction also makes meaningful income

tax reform almost impossible; see Charles E. McLure, Jr., "The Tax Treatment of Owner-Occupied Housing: The Achilles' Heel of Tax Reform?" in James R. Follain, ed., *Tax Reform and Real Estate* (Washington, D.C.: Urban Institute Press, 1986): 219–32.

7. See Charles E. McLure, Jr., "Tax Competition—Is What's Good for the Private Goose Also Good for the Public Gander?" *National Tax Journal* 39 (September 1986): 341–48.

8. Much of what follows is simply the conventional wisdom, long recognized by tax experts, as encapsulated in U.S. Department of the Treasury, *Tax Reform for Fairness, Simplicity, and Economic Growth*, 3 vols. (Washington, D.C.: Government Printing Office, 1984).

9. Ibid., vol. 2, chaps. 8 and 9.

10. Though Treasury-I discussed the need for a fair and orderly transition, its actual transition proposals were far too harsh. See U.S. Department of the Treasury, *Tax Reform* 1:19, 229–43.

11. See Charles E. McLure, Jr., "Integration of the Personal and Corporate Income Taxes: The Missing Element in Recent Tax Reform Proposals," *Harvard Law Review* 88 (January 1977): 532–82.

12. See Charles E. McLure, Jr., *Must Corporate Income Be Taxed Twice?* (Washington, D.C.: Brookings Institution, 1979).

13. For discussions of this proposal, see William D. Andrews, "Tax Neutrality Between Equity Capital and Debt," *Wayne Law Review* 30 (1984): 1057–71; William Warren, "The Relations and Integration of Individual and Corporate Income Taxes," *Harvard Law Review* 94 (February 1981): 717–800.

14. For further analysis, see Charles E. McLure, Jr., "U.S. Tax Reform," *Australian Tax Forum* 4 (1987): 293–312.

15. See David F. Bradford, *Untangling the Income Tax* (Cambridge, Mass.: Harvard University Press, 1986), and references cited there.

16. The aggregate tax base is consumption because expensing frees capital goods from tax. The disallowance of interest deductions is required to prevent the tax base from falling short of consumption. For further elaboration of this point, see ibid.

17. For more on the issues discussed in this section, see George R. Zodrow and Charles E. McLure, Jr., "Alternative Methods of Taxing Consumption in Developing Countries" (World Bank, photocopy).

18. This section draws heavily on Charles E. McLure, Jr., *The Value Added Tax: Key to Deficit Reduction?* (Washington, D.C.: American Enterprise Institute, 1987).

19. See ibid.

20. For further discussion of this crucial issue, see ibid., chap. 9, and Charles E. McLure, Jr., "State and Local Implications of a Federal Value-Added Tax," *Tax Notes* 38, no. 13 (March 28, 1988).

21. See McLure, *Value Added Tax*, chap. 6.

ROBERT E. HALL
ALVIN RABUSHKA

◆ ———————————————————— ◆

An Efficient, Equitable Tax for the 1990s

◆ The 1980s saw remarkable changes in the U.S. tax system (and in those of many other nations as well). Legislation enacted in 1981 phased in tax rate reductions that instantly cut the top marginal rate from 70 percent to 50 percent, cut rates 25 percent across-the-board during the next three years, eliminated inflation-induced bracket creep, and injected a number of business investment incentives into the tax code. The net effect of these changes lowered federal income tax revenue from 11.9 percent of gross national product (GNP) in 1981 to 10.6 percent in 1986. Tax reform in 1986 cut maximum tax rates even more aggressively—from 50 percent to 28 percent for individuals and from 46 percent to 34 percent for corporations. The 1981 act improved incentives to work, save, and invest through lower marginal rates, but it largely left the tax structure unchanged. However, federal income tax revenue (excluding social security) fell in relation to national income. The 1986 tax reform, in contrast, extended the reach (broadened the base) of the tax system so that its large reductions in tax rates resulted in no loss of revenue in relation to national income. Both the president and Congress accepted the goal that the 1986 act be revenue neutral.

Many commentators are pessimistic about making further progress in improving the tax system in the 1990s. Merely defending the 1986 tax rates against pressures to raise federal revenue would be an important accomplishment, they say. Some financial advisers even recommend that individuals cash out of retirement plans and other tax-advantaged investments in

1988 or 1989 to take advantage of current low tax rates. These advisers foresee tax hikes intended to reduce the anticipated fiscal deficits of the 1990s.

In December 1981 we published an article in the *Wall Street Journal*, followed by two books in 1983 and 1985 along with a spate of academic and popular articles, advocating a complete revision of the federal tax system from the ground up. Under our proposal businesses and workers would each file a return that fits on a postcard. All income would be taxed only once, at a 19 percent rate on all income over an exemption level of $15,400 for a family of four. The idea of a simple flat tax is not new. It was practiced in nineteenth-century Britain and has been advocated by such distinguished economists as Milton Friedman. What is new is that we developed a detailed, practical, workable plan that would eliminate a morass of forms, calculations, and paperwork. From 1981 through early 1986 we were considered hopeless visionaries, proponents of an ivory-tower tax reform that could never get anywhere in a Congress dominated by special interests. Tax rates would always remain at levels of close to 50 percent for higher incomes because the special interests defending tax shelters and other sources of untaxed income were so strong. Other critics of our flat tax vehemently argued that steep graduation in tax rates was an essential feature of a fair system—rich people should appear to pay a sharply increasing fraction of each dollar earned in taxes.

The Tax Reform Act of 1986 confirmed our dogged optimism. We proposed a reduction of 31 percentage points in the tax rate imposed on the incomes of the most successful Americans, from 50 percent to 19 percent. Congress enacted legislation that actually lowered the tax rate by 22 percentage points, over two-thirds of what we had proposed. This is one of the rare instances in modern U.S. political history in which the general interest of the public at large prevailed over special interests.

We remain optimistic about the prospects for further improvements in the federal income tax system. Although the 1986 tax reform made a number of key improvements, most notably the large reduction in the tax rates applied to the incomes of successful people, we believe that there are important further reforms that should and will be made. First, we believe that the 9 additional percentage points in lowering the top marginal tax rate are an appropriate goal. The 19 percent overall tax rate in our original proposal is still consistent with the revenue requirements of the federal government, provided the trend toward increasing discipline in federal spending continues. Second, we believe that the largest remaining category of untaxed income—fringe benefits—should be brought into the tax system in a politically sensible way. Third, we fault the 1986 tax reform for wiping out tax incentives for investment and would favor a rationalization of investment and saving incentives into a single powerful incentive.

All the improvements we propose can build on the important progress achieved with the Tax Reform Act of 1986. Enormous simplification and greater efficiency remain attainable goals. We do not believe that the nation should be reluctant to reopen tax issues in the 1990s for fear of slipping back from the major achievements of the 1986 act.

The Continuing Problem of Leakage

All tax reformers—certainly including the authors of the 1986 tax reform—recognize the problem of leakage in the tax system. Leakage (or tax base erosion) occurs when categories of economic income are excluded from taxable income. Some leakage is desirable; for example, almost all tax systems excuse some exemption level of income from taxation to limit the burden of taxes on the poor. But when tax rates are applied to a measure of income that falls far short of total national income, significant distortions occur. Those types of income singled out for taxes bear high rates, and people face a strong incentive to shift income from taxed to untaxed types.

The U.S. tax system suffers from three significant types of leakage:

1. *The underground economy.* Some types of business activities involving cash sales are invisible to the Internal Revenue Service (IRS). Many are perfectly legal except for tax evasion—moonlighting plumbers and the like. Others, notably the making and selling of drugs, would be illegal even if income were reported to the IRS. The IRS has numerous programs to bring businesses above ground. We do not have any surefire answers to the continuing problem of the remaining underground sector. But the payoff to remaining underground is measured by the tax rate. When tax rates fall, the underground economy shrinks simply because lower rates reduce the benefits of evasion in relation to penalties that may be imposed on those caught violating the law. Reduced leakages from the underground economy are one of the benefits of further reductions in tax rates.

2. *The long chain of business income.* A large amount of business income is taxed only after changing hands a number of times. The part of business income paid out as interest is not taxed at the level of the business—both corporations and noncorporate businesses are allowed to deduct interest payments when computing taxes. The recipient is supposed to declare the interest income as taxable income in certain cases. Enforcement of taxation of interest income has improved recently through the ponderous apparatus of over a billion Form 1099s that trace the movement of interest through the economy. But a great

deal of interest escapes taxation because it is paid to nontaxpayers such as pension funds.

3. *Fringe benefits.* Workers in the United States receive over a hundred billion dollars of untaxed fringe benefits each year. Medical benefits are the biggest single element of untaxed fringes, but life insurance, sick pay, country club memberships, company cars, and numerous other perks add to the leakage from taxable income. It is important to understand that taxation of these fringes would make it possible to cut tax rates on other types of income and need not add to the burden on the typical taxpayer. The enormous rise in untaxed fringe benefits over the past thirty years is clearly a response to high tax rates. The existence of fringe-benefit leakage stimulates wasteful consumption of the types of goods and services permitted as tax-deductible fringe-benefit payments by employers.

Adverse Incentives of the New Tax System

Though the reductions of tax rates to 28 percent on the highest personal incomes and 34 percent on corporations is a landmark achievement, the tax system created by the 1986 legislation has some significant incentive problems. Most acute are the severe penalties for risk taking. Consider an entrepreneur who builds a successful corporation by combining a good idea and a lot of hard work. The fruits of the success are primarily the buildup of the market value of the corporation, not the salary paid to the entrepreneur. The corporate income tax takes 34 percent of the buildup, because 34 percent of the corporation's income is collected by the IRS before it is capitalized in the market. When the entrepreneur chooses to make use of the value built up, either by paying dividends or by selling shares at a capital gain, an additional tax at 28 percent is due. The combined tax rate is 52 percent. The federal government takes over half the value created by the risk-bearing entrepreneur; many states take another 5 to 10 percent as well. Even with the seemingly low tax rates of the new tax system, entrepreneurial success is strongly discouraged.

The inefficiencies and distortions from excessive taxation of entrepreneurial activities affect many sectors of the economy. Talented individuals considering whether to become entrepreneurs at a 52 percent tax rate or to become lawyers or investment bankers at a 28 percent tax rate will usually choose the latter. And even within entrepreneurial activities, there is a serious distortion in favor of partnerships, where the income is taxed only at the personal rate. The tax system favors real estate and other businesses with highly marketable assets where the partnership form of business organization is not a serious impediment. But in areas where a new business has an innovative product or process, the corporate form of business is essential. The 52 percent total tax on value created in corporations is a significant barrier to this form of expansion of the economy.

The 52 percent tax rate we have attributed to the new tax system does not apply in all cases. For one thing, the personal tax rate is actually 33 percent over a range of income from about $100,000 to $220,000. An entrepreneur who happens to fall in this range pays a combined tax rate of 56 percent in federal income tax. But there are ways to achieve lower taxes as well. An entrepreneur who chooses not to cash in capital gains gets the advantage of deferral of the capital gains tax. Most important, if the deferral lasts until the entrepreneur's death, the capital gains tax is never collected because the heirs pay tax only on the gain that occurs after the death. However, the trapping of the value reduces the incentive to create the value in the first place, so we cannot pretend that the capital gains tax does not exist.

The new tax system has also been faulted for its adverse impact on capital formation in established businesses. Under the new system, when investment is financed by equity (usually retained earnings), the total tax rate is roughly the same as the 52 percent falling on entrepreneurs. Again there is a substantial disincentive, with attendant inefficiencies and distortions. Corporations face a severe penalty for investing their equity capital in new plant and equipment. But the disincentives are not nearly as severe for borrowed capital. When a corporation finances a new plant by borrowing from a pension fund, the income from the plant is in effect not taxed by the corporate tax because the interest payment to the pension fund is tax deductible. The only tax is the one paid ultimately by the pension recipients, which may be at an average rate of only 15 percent. The distortions from that rate are far smaller than from the 52 percent rate on equity.

Two key investment incentives of the earlier tax system were ripped away by the reform of 1986: the investment credit and accelerated depreciation. Restoration of these incentives would not be a good solution to the problem of incentives for capital formation. Restoration would reduce the burden of taxation of equity-financed investment, which would be an improvement in efficiency. But it would also turn the taxation of debt-financed investment into a subsidy, one of the prime defects of the old tax system. In other words, restoration of investment incentives of the old type would bring back tax shelters. Subsidies are even more inefficient than taxation. An important accomplishment of the Tax Reform Act of 1986 was the taming of tax shelters. Further tax reform needs to preserve that step forward.

Complexity

The public's number-one complaint about income taxes is their sheer complexity. Middle-income home-owning taxpayers have to fill out a dozen or more pages of tax forms. High-income taxpayers with business interests, portfolio transactions, and the like may easily file fifty pages or more. The 1987 Form 1040 kit is even longer than its immediate predecessor. Each page involves complex rules, alternative calculations, and other features that require the advice of expensive expert advisers. And even those experts make frequent mistakes. The mere process of filling out tax returns is a tremendous psychological burden. More and more higher-income taxpayers are deferring filing from April 15 until August to postpone the grief of preparing returns (the law permits taxpayers to defer submitting the returns but not the payment, which has to be made in April).

The complexity of the current tax system has two causes. First, the taxation of business income at the destination (the individual taxpayer) rather than at the source (the business where it was generated in the first place) requires a complicated tracking process with Form 1099s and full reporting at the individual level. Source taxation of business income, widely used in other countries, makes individual tax reporting far simpler. Second, the tax system has grown by historical accretion. Essentially the same taxes could be collected from the same taxpayers with a vastly simpler system if it were redesigned from scratch, as we proposed in 1981.

The authors of the 1986 tax reform lost the opportunity to make many important simplifications. For example, rather than come to grips with the full problem of interest deductions and taxation, they chose the stopgap solution of restricting certain types of personal interest deductions. The result was hideous additional complexity for taxpayers who may be in danger of deducting more home mortgage interest than is permitted by the new law. The only important simplifications achieved in the new tax law were the collapse of the tax schedule from over a dozen tax brackets to three and the drop in tax rates, which make tax shelters less attractive. But this simplification has little practical value when the calculation of taxable income that goes into the tax schedule requires scores of pages.

Ideas for the Next Round of Tax Reform

The principles of an improved tax system are implicit in our earlier discussion of the defects of the current system. First, the tax system should control leakage by applying to a broad measure of income. Second, it should put a uniform low rate on all types of income rather than discouraging entrepreneurial effort and encouraging debt-financed investment. In this connection, it should provide a single uniform incentive for capital formation. Third, the system should be dramatically simplified. Fourth, it should not make any important change in the distribution of tax burdens; it should retain the important feature of the current system that the poor are excused from income taxes and the highest-income families pay the largest fraction of income as taxes.

The tax returns for a tax system with all of these characteristics could both fit on postcards (though to retain confidentiality, we suggest they be mailed in sealed envelopes). The two returns together constitute an airtight comprehensive tax at a uniform rate of 19 percent. All income is divided into two categories: wages and salaries, taxed on Form 1; and business income, taxed on Form 2. Before we explain the logic of each form, we need to stress that the two forms together constitute a tax system; it would not make sense to have one of the forms without the other. Moreover, there is no analogy between our Form 1 and the existing Form 1040; many of the components of income taxed on Form 1040 would be taxed on Form 2 (interest, dividends, and partnership income, among others).

Form 1 just taxes the wage and salary part of income. The great majority of families would file only Form 1. It puts a uniform tax of 19 percent on all earnings and pensions above a generous exemption level of $15,400 for a family of four, indexed to inflation. Other than the exemption, no deductions would be permitted. Relative to existing provisions, the main discontinued deduction is for state and local income and property taxes. Allowing the deduction of these taxes essentially creates untaxed forms of consumption through government. Our proposal is simply an extension of the process that eliminated the deduction for sales tax as part of the 1986 tax reform legislation. Another deduction we would eliminate is charitable contributions. We do this mainly for consistency and simplicity. Continuation of existing provisions for deduction of contributions is a politically attractive alternative and would have little effect on revenue; however, its retention would invite other special interests to argue that their deductions are equally meritorious and put the simplicity of our proposal at risk.

Note that mortgage interest is not a deduction on Form 1. There is no change in the substance of taxation in our proposal, however. Changes in the taxation of interest income on Form 2 have the net result of giving home owners the same benefit they currently receive from mortgage deductions on their Form 1040s.

Form 2 is the complement of Form 1—it taxes all forms of income not taxed on Form 1. All businesses, including corporations, partnerships, and proprietorships, would file Form 2. The basic idea is to capture all income the moment it is generated in the business, rather than wait for it to make

Form 1	Individual Wage Tax		1990
Your first name and initial (if joint return, also give spouse's name and initial) Last name		Your social security number	
Present home address (Number and street including apartment number or rural route)		Spouse's social security no.	
City, Town or Post Office, State and ZIP Code	Your occupation ◆		
	Spouse's occupation ◆		

1 Wages and Salary	**1**	. . . .	. . . . . .
2 Pensions	**2**		
3 Total (*line 1 plus line 2*)	**3**	. . . .	
4 Personal allowance			
(a) ☐ $11,000 for married filing jointly	**4(a)**	. . . .	
(b) ☐ $5,500 for single	**4(b)**		
(c) ☐ $9,800 for single head of household	**4(c)**		
5 Number of dependents, not including spouse	**5**	. . . .	
6 Personal allowances for dependents (*line 5 multiplied by $2200*)	**6**	. . . .	
7 Total personal allowances (*line 4 plus line 6*)	**7**	. . . .	
8 Taxable wages (*line 3 less line 7, if positive, otherwise zero*)	**8**	. . . .	
9 Tax (*19% of line 8*)	**9**	. . . .	. . . . . .
10 Tax withheld by employer	**10**	. . . .	
11 Tax due (*line 9 less line 10, if positive*)	**11**	. . . .	
12 Refund due (*line 10 less line 9, if positive*)	**12**	. . . .	

its way to households. Form 2 plugs multiple leaks in the tax system. It starts at the top of the long chain of business income. It taxes fringe benefits in the only politically practical way: the cost of fringe benefits is not allowed as a tax deduction for businesses. It offers the hope of progress in taxing the underground economy because of its low tax rate of 19 percent.

Form 2 completely solves the incentive problems laid out earlier in this essay. On the key issue of entrepreneurial incentives, it puts a tax rate of exactly 19 percent on the fruits of success. The successful corporation built by an entrepreneur pays a tax of 19 percent on the business income it generates. No further tax applies to the value created by the entrepreneur. If the corporation pays dividends, those dividends are from after-tax income and incur no further tax. If the entrepreneur sells appreciated shares, the appreciation is the capitalization of after-tax income, and no tax is imposed on the capital gain. The tax rate on entrepreneurship drops from 52 percent to 19 percent.

The problem of low taxation of debt-financed business is equally solved by Form 2. Since all business income is taxed at the same 19 percent rate, there is no preferential treatment of interest over dividends. The bias in favor of partnerships and the ownership of marketable assets endemic in the current tax system disappears completely.

Form 2 provides one simple coherent investment incentive. On line 2c a business subtracts its purchases of plant, equipment, and other capital assets. The economic effect of this first-year write-off is to bring the effective tax rate on the earnings of capital to zero. Another way to express the economic effect of the tax is to call it a consumption tax. Consumption taxes are widely supported by economists for providing the correct incentive for investment. Note that the tax base for the combination of Form 1 and Form 2 is total private income less investment, which equals consumption. Hence the flat tax is a consumption tax.

Under our tax system all interest would be paid after tax. For example, the interest payments by a corporation on its bonds would be paid out of income that had been taxed on Form 2, which has no deduction for interest payments. The recipient would not have to pay any more tax on the interest because the corporation would have paid the tax already. By contrast, under present tax principles, interest is always before-tax income. The payer takes a tax deduction for the interest and the recipient has to pay tax. With other forces held constant in the economy, interest rates would be lower under the after-tax principle we favor than under the before-tax principle in current

Form 2	**Business Tax**	**1990**
Business Name		Employer Identification Number
Street Address		County
City, State and ZIP Code		Principal Product

1 Gross revenue from sales	**1**	
2 Allowable costs.		
(a) Purchases of goods, services and materials	**2(a)**	. . . .
(b) Wages, salaries and pensions	**2(b)**	. . . .
(c) Purchases of capital equipment, structures,		
and land	**2(c)**	. . . .
3 Total allowable costs (*sum of lines 2(a), 2(b), 2(c)*)	**3**	
4 Taxable income (*line 1 less line 3*)	**4**	
5 Tax (*19% of line 4*).	**5**	
6 Carry-forward from 1989	**6**	
7 Interest on carry-forward (*6% of line 6*)	**7**	. . . .
8 Carry-forward into 1990 (*line 6 plus line 7*)	**8**	
9 Tax due (*line 5 less line 8, if positive*).	**9**	
10 Carry-forward to 1991 (*line 8 less line 5, if*		
positive)	**12**	

use. Consequently the actual burden of interest on the borrower would be the same under our principle as it is today, even though the taxpayer would no longer get a tax deduction for interest payments.

Prospects

Our 19 percent universal flat tax was called visionary until 1986. Having achieved two-thirds of our goal for the tax rate applied to earnings, we believe additional progress is easily within the nation's grasp in the 1990s. Even without the adoption of a flat 19 percent rate, important structural reforms with lower effective tax rates for entrepreneurial activities could be achieved. We could keep the current three-rate tax rate schedule but move to the principle of source taxation of business income. This step alone could reduce the critical 52 percent rate on entrepreneurial success to 28 percent. At the same time the problem of leakage in business income could be solved, with tremendous savings from eliminating the process of tracking a billion Form 1099s. Less leakage permits lower rates, which would give the economy an additional supply-side kick. Economic growth is always the critical consideration in the design of any tax system and in the long run will generate higher, not lower, tax receipts.

We see the elimination of penalty taxation of entrepreneurial success as a central tax issue of the 1990s. Those calling for cuts in capital gains taxation are dealing with only a fraction of the problem. Far better would be the adoption of a completely coherent tax reform that puts a low uniform rate on all income. In addition, a truly simple tax system promises greater compliance and billions of dollars in savings in preparing tax returns. As the full benefits of the lower rates enacted in 1986 take hold in 1988, we hope that Congress and the executive can work together to make a low, simple flat tax a reality.

THOMAS J. SARGENT

The Role of Monetary Policy Under U.S. Institutions

◆ The job of monetary policy is to manage the portfolio of debts owed by the federal government. Popular discussions impute great power for producing good or bad economic effects to the government officials who administer monetary policy. In truth, monetary policy is much less powerful than is often depicted, because its administrators are constrained by economic forces beyond their control. Most important, the monetary policy authorities do not control the size of the portfolio of government debts that they must manage.

In the United States responsibility for determining the total size of the government debt is separated from responsibility for determining the financial composition of that debt, whether it takes the form of noninterest-bearing debt (currency and bank reserves) or interest-bearing debt of various terms to maturity. The total amount of debt at any time is the cumulative result of past federal government deficits, which are determined jointly by Congress and the president. Given the total debt, responsibility for determining its composition is assigned to the Federal Reserve Board. The Federal Reserve Board continuously conducts open-market operations, equal-value trades of one form of government debt for another. By executing these trades, the Federal Reserve alters the composition of the government debt owned by the government's creditors while leaving the total value of that outstanding debt unchanged at a point in time. "Monetary policy" or "open-market policy" or "debt management" are three phrases used to describe the responsibilities of the Federal Reserve. "Fiscal policy" is the phrase used to describe the activities of the president and Congress that generate the stream of government deficits that have to be financed.

Although the United States has decentralized authority for making fiscal and monetary policy across distinct and nominally independent institutions, it would be possible and perhaps even desirable to distribute responsibility in different ways. Indeed, the nominal independence of U.S. monetary from fiscal institutions is fictitious because the arithmetic of the government's budget constraint requires interdependence. The force of U.S. economic policy institutions is to leave that interdependence implicit, and therefore to leave the procedures for coordinating monetary and fiscal policy to be worked out haphazardly through the interactions of the succession of personalities that happen to occupy economic policy-making positions.[1] Milton Friedman's long-standing proposal that monetary policy be executed according to a simple rule that increases the monetary base a constant percentage (close to zero) each year ought to be interpreted as one device for removing this haphazardness and for making explicit and predictable the terms according to which monetary and fiscal policies are to be coordinated.[2]

This essay describes limitations, possibilities, and suitable goals for monetary policy within the existing pattern of institutional responsibilities. A discussion of limitations and possibilities is necessary as a prolegomenon to any discussion of proper goals for monetary policy. Limitations on what monetary policy can accomplish are determined by the arithmetic of the government budget constraint and by the behavior of the parties who demand the U.S. government debt that the Federal Reserve markets.

My starting point for describing the limitations and possibilities of monetary policies is Milton Friedman's celebrated 1968 article "The Role of Monetary Policy."[3] Friedman's theme is that we should not expect too much from monetary policy. He warned that monetary policy could not be counted on to accomplish some of the goals that were then being advocated for it, such as controlling the paths of unemployment, output, and interest rates. He argued that the structure of the economy is such that monetary policy can have no permanent effects on the levels of unemployment, GNP, or real interest rates. Friedman did maintain that monetary policy can be used to control the time path taken by the price level.

In the light of the twenty years' research on macroeconomics that has occurred since this article, I would like to reexamine, re-present, and lengthen Friedman's list of limitations and possibilities for monetary policy. Subsequent research has reinforced the cautionary notes Friedman sounded. My discussion will center on six propositions governing the role of monetary policy.

1. Monetary policy cannot be used to influence unemployment.

Friedman's 1968 article contained an early version of the natural un-employment rate hypothesis, formulated independently by Friedman and Edmund S. Phelps.[4] Friedman and Phelps sought to interpret the Phillips curve, the inverse correlation between inflation and unemployment traced out by U.S. and U.K. data in the first two decades following World War II. Paul Samuelson and Robert Solow had earlier interpreted that correlation as a stable relationship confronting the macroeconomic policy authorities with a trade-off between inflation and unemployment.[5] According to this interpretation, by running larger government deficits and incurring higher rates of currency expansion, the policy authorities can engineer a reduction in the average unemployment rate. In the late 1960s many macroeconomists recommended that the government accept this trade-off and run a high-inflation, low-unemployment policy.

Friedman and Phelps described a theory that explained the inverse cor-relation between inflation and unemployment in the postwar data but that also implied that the correlation would not endure in the face of an attempt permanently to exploit it. Friedman and Phelps reasoned that at a given level of their expectations about future rates of inflation, labor suppliers' behav-ior would cause unemployment to vary inversely with the current rate of inflation. However, if workers' expected rate of inflation were to increase, Friedman and Phelps reasoned that the terms of the apparent trade-off be-tween inflation and unemployment would worsen. Indeed, it would worsen so much that no decrease in unemployment would accompany an increase in actual inflation that was just matched by a corresponding increase in people's expected rate of inflation. This theory, constructed by analyzing the factors underlying workers' decisions to supply labor, implies that there is no permanently exploitable trade-off between inflation and unemployment. Unemployment is interpreted as responding only to the part of inflation that is surprising or unexpected, a part that cannot be permanently set to a value other than zero. This theory is known as the natural unemployment rate theory.

Friedman used this theory, together with a theory that people's ex-pected rate of inflation was formed as a moving average of actual rates of inflation (the so-called adaptive expectations theory), to conclude that monetary policy cannot be used permanently to influence the unemploy-ment rate. With adaptive expectations, people eventually eliminate any dis-crepancy between actual and expected sustained rates of inflation, and hy-pothetically monetary policy's effects on the unemployment rate are entirely mediated through that discrepancy.

Whereas Friedman's formulation denied the possibility of any permanent effects, it left open extensive possibilities for dynamically intricate temporary effects of monetary policy on the unemployment rate.[6] These effects could be achieved by subtly manipulating private agents' errors in forecasting future rates of inflation. However, subsequent research has strengthened Friedman's argument by eliminating or greatly weakening even these temporary effects. This modification has resulted from replacing Friedman's hypothesis of adaptive expectations (the weakest part of his theory in relation to economic motivation) with the hypothesis of rational expectations.[7] We can motivate the idea of rational expectations by noting that in Friedman and Phelps's model the people made worse forecasts of future inflation than did the government, which owns the economists' model. The model showed how to make better forecasts of inflation than those made by the simple moving-average schemes attributed to people by Friedman and Phelps. The idea of rational expectations is to remove this asymmetry between the forecasting ability of the person who owns the model and the agents who live in the model by positing that the agents in the model forecast at least as well as the outsider (the government) who owns the model.

Attributing rational expectations to private agents substantially strengthens the limitations on the ability of monetary policy to influence the unemployment rate. There is no systematic monetary policy capable of influencing the unemployment rate even temporarily. Monetary policy affects the unemployment rate only by inducing surprises, and there is no systematic (that is, predictable) way to manipulate those surprises. As for the likely distribution of unemployment rates, monetary policy can do no better than to use a constant growth rate rule such as the one Friedman recommends.

2. Monetary policy cannot be used to influence real interest rates.

As a corollary of the natural-rate hypothesis, it follows that monetary policy cannot be used to influence real rates of interest. A version of this principle was stated in Friedman's 1968 article, and subsequent research has strengthened his statement by replacing his assumption of adaptive expectations with the assumption of rational expectations.

That real interest rates are beyond the influence of monetary policy follows from two features of the economic environment. The first feature, embodied in Irving Fisher's famous theory, is that at given tax rates, real interest rates are determined once the levels of aggregate employment and national product are determined.[8] Thus, given a time path for national product, real interest rates are determined by the marginal productivity of capital along that path. The second feature is the natural-rate hypothesis, which makes the expected path of employment and national product independent of the choice of a monetary policy rule.

According to Friedman's principle the monetary policy authority could exert no permanent influence on real interest rates because it could not permanently influence the unexpected component of inflation. Under the adaptive expectations system assumed by Friedman, the monetary policy authorities still had the power to influence real interest rates temporarily by inducing sequences of errors in private agents' forecasts of inflation. Again, research subsequent to Friedman's has strengthened his result by replacing the assumption of adaptive expectations with that of rational expectations, a replacement that withdraws from the monetary policy authority the superior wisdom and forecasting advantage that would permit it to manipulate private agents' forecast errors.[9]

3. Monetary policy can be used to influence the time path of the price level (assuming that the monetary authority's powers are augmented by sufficient powers to levy taxes).

Proposition 3 embodies the main possibility left open to the monetary authority in Friedman's analysis, with my parenthetical qualification. This qualification was implicit in Friedman's treatment, but subsequent research has emphasized its importance.

The ability of the monetary authority to influence the price level rests on two aspects of the economic structure: (1) the demand schedule for government-issued currency (currency and bank reserves, so-called high-powered money) and (2) the intertemporal sequence of government budget constraints. The amount of government currency demanded varies proportionately with the price level, a doubling of the price level leading to a doubling of the amount of money demanded. This proportionality reflects the idea that the economic demand is for a "real" quantity of money, the nominal amount deflated by the price level. The real amount of money demanded also depends partly on the levels of real output and real interest rates (which propositions 1 and 2 state are outside the influence of the monetary authority) and on the path of future price levels expected by private agents. A demand schedule for money with these features implies that by making the supply of government-issued currency follow a path with a steady and low growth rate, the price level will also follow a fairly steady path with a growth rate comparable to that of the path of the currency stock. This is a version of the quantity theory of money. According to this theory, subject to exceptions caused by disturbances in the demand for currency, monetary policy can choose a stable and low-inflation likely time path for the price level by executing an open-market strategy that sets a path of government-issued currency along which currency is growing slowly and steadily. But is it feasible for monetary policy to select such a path for the stock of currency? This question brings us to the second condition required to validate proposition 3, the part alluded to in the parenthetical qualifier.

The government has an intertemporal sequence of budget constraints. In each period the real value of government expenditures plus interest payments on government debts plus retirements of outstanding debts must exactly equal the sum of three components: tax collections, proceeds from issues of new interest-bearing government debt, and the change in government-issued currency divided by the price level. The last term on the receipts side, sometimes called seigniorage, is under the control of the Federal Reserve. Government expenditures and tax collections are formally under the joint control of Congress and the president. (Legally the parenthetical qualifier behind proposition 3 is not met. But for proposition 3 to hold, we shall see that it must be met at least implicitly and informally.) The preceding argument states that the monetary policy authority would be able to control the path of the price level if it could permanently control the path of the rate of growth of currency. But it follows from the government budget constraint that if the rate of growth of currency is controlled with an eye toward stabilizing the price level path, then other elements of the government budget constraint must be adjusted to assure that it is always satisfied. To take the simplest case, suppose that monetary policy is executed according to Friedman's k percent growth rule, with k equal to zero so that no growth in currency is ever permitted by the monetary authority. For this to be feasible, fiscal authorities must manage their affairs so that government expenditures plus interest payments equal tax collections plus the net proceeds from new issues of interest-bearing debt.[10] One way to accomplish this is to freeze the level of outstanding interest-bearing government debt and to set government expenditures plus interest payments equal to tax collections period by period. This is a balanced-budget rule for fiscal policy, with the gross-of-interest government deficit for each period being equal to zero. This rule is one of many that set the net-of-interest government surplus equal in present value to the outstanding stock of interest-bearing government debt. In general, supporting the no-seigniorage, 0 percent growth rule monetary policy requires a fiscal policy satisfying the condition that the present value of the government's net-of-interest surplus always equal the current stock of interest-bearing government debt. This fiscal rule instructs the government to behave like a firm (one without a printing press) and to balance any current deficits with the credible prospect of future surpluses sufficient to service debt created by those deficits.

For the monetary authority permanently to influence the price level path, a mechanism must be in place for coordinating monetary and fiscal policies that gives the monetary authority the power permanently to withhold a flow of seigniorage from the fiscal authority.[11] To support a no-seigniorage monetary policy, the government budget must be in balance in the present-value sense just described.

To emphasize the importance of the qualifier in proposition 3, it is useful to focus on the assumptions used to rationalize neutrality-of-money experiments in textbook models representing the quantity theory of money.[12] These experiments imagine that the monetary authority engineers a once-and-for-all decrease in the stock of currency by open-market sales of government interest-bearing bonds to the public. This operation increases the stream of interest payments that the government must pay to its creditors. To finance these payments, the textbook experiments assume that the open-market sale of bonds is accompanied by an increase in the stream of taxes just sufficient to service the higher interest payments resulting from the sale. This experiment illustrates the way tax adjustments are required to support the monetary policies that control the price level.

Under current institutional arrangements in the United States, the monetary authority does not have the authority assumed in the qualifier to proposition 3. It is an open question whether it can acquire that authority by engaging in a "game of chicken" with the fiscal authorities, as described by Neil Wallace.[13] In any event, under U.S. institutional arrangements the following proposition, which can be viewed as a corollary to proposition 3, is actually pertinent.

4. Monetary policy cannot permanently prevent inflation (given a fiscal policy implying a stream of net-of-interest government deficits).

Proposition 4 follows from the same premises underlying proposition 3. Assuming that fiscal policy is managed to create a permanent stream of net-of-interest deficits, it follows arithmetically that monetary policy must supply a permanent stream of seigniorage sufficient to make up the shortfall in the budget. This is an aspect of the "unpleasant monetarist arithmetic" explored by Sargent and Wallace.

The economic forces underlying propositions 3 and 4 also produce a fifth proposition that characterizes the ability of monetary policy to influence the value at which U.S. currency exchanges for the currencies issued by foreign governments.

5. Monetary policy is incapable of determining the rate of exchange of domestic currency for foreign currencies (unless supported by an appropriate fiscal policy).

This principle follows from adding to propositions 3 and 4 the logic of purchasing-power parity: the rate of exchange of a domestic for a foreign currency equals the ratio of the foreign price level to the domestic price level. For example, given a constant British price level, a 25 percent rise in the U.S. price level is predicted by purchasing-power parity to be associated with a 25 percent depreciation in the value of the dollar in exchange for pounds. Purchasing-power parity is a particular application of the law of one price. Although there can be substantial transitory deviations from the value of exchange rates predicted by the principle of purchasing-power parity, for sizable and sustained divergent movements in price levels across different countries exchange rates tend to adhere to the paths predicted by the principle.

Bonding the logic of purchasing-power parity with that of propositions 3 and 4 immediately produces proposition 5. By propositions 3 and 4, the monetary authority cannot permanently set the domestic price level along a noninflationary path unless it is supported by an appropriate fiscal policy. Given time paths for foreign price levels (determined by the operation of principles 3 and 4 in foreign countries), it follows that domestic monetary policy cannot affect the time path of foreign exchange rates unless it is supported by the same fiscal policies consistent with the required domestic price level paths.

Proposition 5 leaves open the possibility of operating a monetary regime keyed to stabilizing a foreign exchange rate. The international gold standard is one example of a regime under which principle 5 is respected by all participating countries and the foreign exchanges are stabilized. A gold standard regime is a set of rules for running monetary and fiscal policies designed to stabilize rates of exchange of foreign for domestic currencies for all participating countries. Under a gold standard each participating government borrows only by issuing promises redeemable in gold. Government debt in the form of currency assumes the form of a note for a given amount of gold, payable to the bearer on demand. Under this system a British pound is an immediate claim on x units of gold, whereas a U.S. dollar is an immediate claim on y units of gold. The exchange rate between pounds and dollars must be x/y.

To adhere to a gold standard, a government has to back its debts with gold or other assets that are themselves as good as gold. In practice as well as in theory, it is unnecessary to hold stocks of gold equal in value to the entire stock of a government's liabilities. Instead, it is sufficient to back debts by sufficient prospects of future government surpluses. By accepting a gold standard rule, a government in effect agrees to operate its fiscal policy by a present-value budget balance rule. Under this rule government deficits can occur, but they are necessarily temporary and are accompanied by prospects for future surpluses sufficient to service whatever debt is generated by the deficit.

Thus a gold standard is as much a fiscal regime as it is a monetary regime. Indeed, during the high tide of the gold standard in the late nineteenth century, most of the central banks of Europe faced rules imposing a low ceiling on the amount of government loans they could purchase. The central banks were permitted to issue bank notes on the security of gold, foreign exchange, and safe evidences of short-term commercial indebtedness. Such rules well capture the spirit and structure of the gold standard as a fiscal institution supported by monetary arrangements that deny the fiscal authority access to the printing press as a source of finance.

During the period of the gold standard, the role of lender of last resort began to be assigned to the central bank. A tradition developed to guide the central bank's behavior during periods of unusual stringency in credit markets. The central bank was supposed to lend as freely as possible (albeit at a high interest rate) to forestall what threatened to be contagious defaults on commercial banks' liabilities, in the form of either suspension of convertibility into central bank notes or outright bankruptcy.[14] Feasible practical limits on the range of such operations were imposed, first, by the commitment of the central bank to keep its notes convertible into gold at par and, second, by the limited capital of the central bank. In acting as a lender of last resort during bad times, the central bank was conducting open-market operations by paying out good assets (central bank notes) in exchange for bad assets (commercial loans originally owned by the banks in jeopardy). Such operations would impair the central bank's capital and, if conducted without limit, would destroy the central bank's ability to honor its commitment to convert its notes into gold on demand. Under some constellations of threats to the commercial banks, the central bank simply could not act as a lender of last resort and also honor its commitment to manage its portfolio according to the rules of the gold standard.

The lender of last resort ultimately acts as an insurer of banks' liabilities. In the absence of deposit insurance, requiring a central bank to act as a lender of last resort amounts to setting up an underfunded insurance scheme. For a lender-of-last-resort scheme to be feasible and also consistent with gold standard commitments, it must be properly funded. Alternative ways of funding such a scheme are either explicitly to charge sufficiently high and sufficiently risk-indexed fees for deposit insurance or to commit the general taxing authority of the government as a funding source. In the

Great Depression central banks failed to be lenders of last resort because they lacked such funding.

These considerations indicate how under a gold standard regime the provision of a lender of last resort to the banking system is a matter for fiscal policy. Though somewhat less obvious, it remains a matter of fiscal policy under the fiat standard with which we live today, which is not anchored by the commitment to convert government debt into any bundle of physical assets. Under a fiat standard a central bank's commitment to pursue price level stability limits the amount of seigniorage it can supply to the fiscal authority, thereby requiring discipline on the part of the fiscal authority. In a fiat system, commitment to price level stability constrains the actions of the monetary authority just as it does under the gold standard. If the central bank is not bound by a commitment to price level stability, it acquires some ability to act as a lender of last resort. By giving up the constraints imposed on its actions by price stability, the central bank in effect acquires a set of taxing powers (it controls an inflation tax) that enables it to reallocate resources between borrowers and lenders. These taxing powers are strongest when loan contracts are denominated in nominal terms and when loans have long terms to maturity.[15]

The preceding discussion can be summed up in the following proposition, which can be interpreted as another corollary to proposition 3.

6. Monetary policy cannot insure bank deposits by acting as a lender of last resort while simultaneously managing the central bank's portfolio in a way designed to assure price stability.

Note that proposition 6 does not deny that monetary policy can in some circumstances play an important role in bailing out threatened banks. But without support in resources from the fiscal authority, monetary policy will at times have to sacrifice price stability to prevent failures of commercial banks. This is the meaning of the old adage that "the role of monetary policy is to convert bad loans into good ones."

Conclusion

The first two propositions describe limits placed on the monetary authorities by an economic system in general and by the way monetary policy impinges on the opportunities (budget constraints) available to private economic agents in particular. The last four propositions describe limits placed on the potential accomplishments of monetary policy by the arithmetic of the government's own budget constraint. These propositions provide concrete meaning to an old maxim in central-banking circles: with a tight fiscal policy that hands the monetary authority a small portfolio of government debt to manage, it is easy to run a noninflationary monetary policy; but under a deficit-spending policy, it is *impossible* to run a noninflationary monetary policy. These propositions are especially relevant for U.S. monetary policy in the late 1980s and the 1990s because the fiscal policy of recent years has given the U.S. monetary authorities a large portfolio of debts to manage.

Notes

1. On the coordination problems facing the monetary and fiscal authorities, see the following by Thomas J. Sargent: "Reaganomics and Credibility," chap. 2 in *Rational Expectations and Inflation* (New York: Harper & Row, 1985); "Interpreting the Reagan Deficits," *Federal Reserve Bank of San Francisco Review*, Fall 1986; *Dynamic Macroeconomic Theory* (Cambridge, Mass.: Harvard University Press, 1987). See also Thomas J. Sargent and Neil Wallace, "Some Unpleasant Monetarist Arithmetic," *Quarterly Review* (Federal Reserve Bank of Minneapolis), Fall 1981.

2. See Milton Friedman, *A Program for Monetary Stability* (Bronx, N.Y.: Fordham University Press, 1960).

3. Milton Friedman, "The Role of Monetary Policy," *American Economic Review* 58 (March 1968): 1–17.

4. Edmund S. Phelps, "Phillips Curves, Inflation Expectations, and Optimal Employment Over Time," *Economica* 34, no. 3 (August 1967).

5. Paul A. Samuelson and Robert M. Solow, "Analytical Aspects of Anti-inflation Policy," *American Economic Review* 50, no. 2 (May 1960): 177–94.

6. These effects are analyzed formally in Phelps, "Phillips Curves."

7. See John F. Muth, "Rational Expectations and the Theory of Price Movements," *Econometrica* 29, no. 3 (1961): 315–35.

8. See Irving Fisher, *The Theory of Interest* (New York: Macmillan, 1930).

9. Thomas J. Sargent, "Rational Expectations, the Real Rate of Interest, and the Natural Rate of Unemployment," *Brookings Papers on Economic Activity* 2 (1973): 429–72 (correction in ibid., vol. 3 [1973]).

10. For formal analyses, see Sargent and Wallace, "Some Unpleasant Monetarist Arithmetic," and Sargent, *Dynamic Macroeconomic Theory*.

11. In "Some Unpleasant Monetarist Arithmetic," Sargent and Wallace describe what will happen if the monetary authority tries to control the price level when no such mechanism is in place.

12. See Sargent, *Dynamic Macroeconomic Theory*, chap. 5.

13. For a description of Wallace's game of chicken, see Sargent, "Reaganomics and Credibility," and Sargent, "Interpreting the Reagan Deficits."

14. See Walter Bagehot, *Lombard Street: A Description of the Money Market* (1873; London: Smith, Elder & Co., 1915).

15. For further analysis, see David Beers, Thomas Sargent, and Neil Wallace, "Speculations About the Speculation Against the Hong Kong Dollar," *Quarterly Review* (Federal Reserve Bank of Minneapolis), Fall 1983.

THOMAS GALE MOORE

Regulation, Reregulation, or Deregulation
The Issue for the 1990s

◆ The 1990s will see an increasingly competitive world. The United States, which for most of the post–World War II period has been the dominant economy, experienced a real loss of competitiveness in the first half of the 1980s. Over the last twenty years Japanese industry has become known worldwide for its quality and innovativeness. In addition the rise in the value of the dollar from 1980 to 1985 and the growing perception that U.S. goods may not embody the most up-to-date technology have reduced the U.S. share of world trade.

With the reversal in the value of the dollar in the second half of the 1980s, it became apparent that U.S. manufacturing was still highly competitive. In fact the evidence from 1983 on was of a vibrant, strong economy, which despite a large trade deficit was employing more people and generating more jobs than any other economy in the world. Europe, in contrast, enjoyed a large and growing trade surplus but failed to reduce its unemployment or add jobs. Only in Great Britain, which adopted a policy of privatization and of encouragement of business, was economic growth vigorous.

The United States followed two policies in the 1980s that strongly con-

The views expressed in this paper are the author's and do not represent the views of the Council of Economic Advisers, the U.S. government, or the Reagan administration.

tributed to superior economic performance. The Reagan administration led a successful effort to reduce marginal tax rates to the lowest levels since the 1920s. The top individual marginal tax rate, which was 70 percent in 1980, was reduced through two major tax acts to 28 percent in 1988. The corporate rate was lowered from 46 to 34 percent.

The other factor contributing to U.S. economic performance was the low and decreasing level of government control over markets. During the 1960s and first half of the 1970s U.S. government regulation had been growing, but this trend slowed and in important aspects reversed around the middle of the 1970s. In much of the rest of the world, however, governments continued to believe that they could do better than competitive markets. Recently a number of other countries have been following the U.S. lead in deregulating such industries as airlines and telecommunications.

From the mid-1970s to the mid-1980s the federal government carried out a remarkable bipartisan program of reducing economic regulation of many industries. Starting with commissions on stock transactions, air freight, and airlines, deregulation was extended to motor carriers, railroads, oil prices, intercity buses, long-distance telecommunications, and interest rates on savings accounts. In the anti-trust area, during the Reagan administration the Department of Justice took actions to revise and clarify merger guidelines, encourage productivity-enhancing joint research and development efforts, and, by dismissing the IBM case, remove the implicit condemnation of bigness per se. In the main this deregulation did not extend to environmental, safety, or social regulation, although the Reagan administration did slow the growth of government intervention in these areas. Even for economic regulation the agenda is incomplete. Financial markets remain under strict controls, although less regulated than in 1975; motor carriers are still subject to Interstate Commerce Commission (ICC) regulation; only a portion of natural gas sold at the wellhead is free from federal restrictions.

Nevertheless, the partial deregulation of the U.S. economy has worked to improve the competitiveness of our industry. Transportation, banking, and communication costs have declined. The growth and partial freeing of financial markets have lowered the cost of capital. Over the last seven years inflation has reduced the extent to which the minimum wage prices low-skilled labor out of the market. The United States has also been fortunate in not following Europe's example of regulating the labor market through rules designed to protect jobs. Laws that inhibit layoffs inhibit hiring; laws that mandate health benefits impose higher costs and less flexibility on labor markets; attempts to protect jobs in one industry cost jobs in another.

Partly as a consequence of deregulation and resisted efforts to extend regulation, productivity in U.S. manufacturing has increased at an annual rate of 5 percent since 1982. Overall employment has grown by about fifteen million.[1] With only a modest growth in wage rates, unit labor costs in 1986 and 1987 (through the third quarter) actually declined in manufacturing. Adjusted for the sharp 1986 appreciation of foreign currencies, Japanese and Western European unit labor costs rose about 20 to 40 percent.[2]

But there is significant room for improvement. Except for reduced control over broadcasting content, a speedup of Federal Drug Administration new drug approvals, and an increased use of trade-offs in the control of air pollution, there has been little movement toward making safety, environmental, or social regulation less burdensome. In fact legislation has been enacted limiting the energy requirements of most household appliances. Although controls on natural gas uses have been eliminated, federal restrictions on the fuel efficiency of new cars have continued despite declining petroleum prices.

Progress on Deregulation

Airlines

Pressure is growing for reregulation of many of the industries deregulated in whole or part in the earlier period. Some claim that abolishing the Civil Aeronautics Board (CAB) was a major mistake, whereas others point to the huge benefits for consumers.[3] Nevertheless, the evidence clearly shows that decontrol reduced fares, increased competition, and improved the frequency and availability of individual flights.[4]

A Brookings Institution study concluded that airline passengers gain about $6 billion a year in 1977 dollars (or about $11.5 billion in 1988 dollars) from deregulation.[5] Contrary to the predictions of those who opposed deregulation, most small towns have more service now than before decontrol.[6] Airlines have improved efficiency and thus can offer more and deeper discounts while making a good return on their investment. Of course not all airlines are in the black, but in any competitive industry some firms will do worse than others. Safety has continued to improve in the decade since airline deregulation started.[7]

Decontrol, however, has brought problems. The very success of the experiment has led to a tremendous burgeoning of travel. The number of passengers has risen 74 percent since 1977 and the number of flights, 30 percent.[8] Unfortunately this rapid growth, together with the illegal air traffic controllers' strike in 1981, the subsequent firing of the strikers, and the slow rebuilding of the system, has led to increased congestion and concern about safety. There is little reason for concern about decreased safety as a result of deregulation, but there are real problems with congestion and delays.

Some have suggested bringing back the CAB. Legislation has been introduced to prevent airlines from buying and selling operating rights. The most likely prospects include legislation to require that airlines compensate passengers for lost or delayed baggage, report on-time performance, and have the Federal Aviation Administration (FAA) limit takeoffs and landings at certain airports. These requirements, if enacted, would move the airline industry back toward regulation. The result would undoubtedly mean higher fares, lower capacity, and less-frequent service. Thus the benefits of greater competition would be sacrificed to reduce congestion and delays.

A more promising solution would be to introduce variable landing fees. Higher charges for landing and taking off at peak times would push those more flexible about their travel time away from the most congested periods. Another promising change would be to privatize part or all of the air traffic control system. Currently air traffic controllers are government employees whose job security limits the FAA's ability to assign them where they are most needed. Moreover, an airport wishing to expand capacity cannot be sure that the FAA will increase tower personnel and equipment enough to accommodate the increase in traffic. Privatization of airways and airports would be a natural sequel to airline deregulation.

Railroads and Trucking

Not only are there efforts to increase regulation of the airlines, but a coalition of coal shippers, grain firms, and power companies is trying to amend the Staggers Act, which partially freed the railroad industry from ICC control. This move would be a major mistake. Deregulation of the railroad industry has provided major benefits for the railroads, for shippers, and for taxpayers and has contributed to the profitability and sale to the private sector of Conrail, a government-operated freight railroad. Railroads are now free to market their services rather than to follow the dictates of the ICC. The Staggers Act eliminated maximum rate regulation on all railroad traffic except for service to captive shippers. Thus nearly two-thirds of all railroad traffic can now be managed like a business.[9]

The railroads have used this new freedom aggressively to pursue traffic diverted to trucks or water carriers. Despite increased competition from motor carriers, the share of freight traffic carried by rail, which had fallen for 60 years, has stabilized. For some special commodities such as fresh fruits and vegetables rail freight actually increased.

In 1980 Congress reduced controls on entry into the interstate trucking industry; new operating authority was readily granted. Although trucking firms were still required to file tariffs with the ICC, they could change rates to meet market conditions. The ICC routinely approved lower rates, allowing vigorous competition among motor carriers.

Adjusted for inflation, rail and trucking freight rates have declined as shippers have benefited from deregulation. Between 1979, the year before deregulation, and 1984, the latest year for which we have trucking data, truck rates fell 14 percent in real terms and rail rates fell 13 percent. Rail rates continued to decline after 1984 and were down 23 percent from 1979 levels by 1986. Thus shipping costs and the cost of inventories, warehousing, customer service, and distribution have declined significantly. One study concluded that in 1985 such logistics costs, including shipping costs paid by manufacturers and distributors, were approximately $56 billion lower than before deregulation.[10] This reduction reflects the ability of business to carry lower inventories (because of prompter transportation services and lower shipping charges) but not changes in interest rates to carry these inventories. Although not all of the savings are attributable to deregulation, their size suggests significant benefits from it.

Deregulation of the motor carrier industry, however, is far from complete. Rates must still be filed with the ICC, must not be discriminatory, and are subject to challenge, and entrants must apply for certificates of public convenience and necessity. Although the ICC has been reasonably permissive about granting new operating rights and allowing rate flexibility, the remaining controls are burdensome and in the hands of a more regulation-prone ICC could significantly reduce competition. One estimate of the gain from completing deregulation was $28 billion in 1990.[11] Given this potential gain and the possibility that much of the savings already achieved might be lost in the future, it is important to complete deregulation and abolish the remaining controls over the motor carrier industry.

Energy

Regulatory reform has also benefited the energy industry, though the benefits are hard to quantify. The decontrol of oil prices in 1981 and the removal of most controls on natural-gas pricing has freed the energy market. Costs and prices have come down, and the Organization of Petroleum Exporting Countries (OPEC) has found it increasingly difficult to set prices. The collapse of energy prices in 1986 and at the end of 1987 was at least partly caused by the deregulation of U.S. energy markets.

Unfortunately Congress does not appear to understand this lesson and has resisted removing the remaining controls on natural gas. Given the present gas surpluses, decontrol would more likely result in lower rather than higher prices. Removing the ceiling on the price of some gas that has been controlled for many years (old gas) would allow producers to invest more to secure the energy. More gas would be produced now, and some gas that would never be recovered under price controls would be marketed. The Department of Energy has estimated that decontrol would produce 15 percent more gas in the future.[12] Thus from an energy conservation point of view, decontrol would save on the use of other fuels and add to total supplies.

Telecommunications

Less well known is the success of the 1984 divestiture of the Bell operating companies from AT&T. Despite advance planning, there were initial difficulties with the quality of service and other adjustment problems. Now, in 1988, most of these problems seem to be behind us, although there is considerable pressure to modify the conditions limiting the activities of the regional Bell operating companies. Although no one has done a rigorous assessment, service quality appears to be as good as it ever was. Since the decree breaking up AT&T, competition in the industry has greatly increased. At least four new long-distance companies offer nationwide service for residential and business customers, and a handful of others provide service exclusively for business. Some five hundred interexchange carriers, providing connections between exchanges, compete with AT&T. Together they have installed nearly twice as many circuit miles as Ma Bell.[13] Consequently interexchange rates have declined over 30 percent since divestiture.[14] The long-distance companies have been competing by offering new services for residential and business users.

The manufacturing market has also become much more competitive. Before the decree Western Electric had most of the market to itself. Six large new international firms and over a hundred new smaller firms now offer residential telephones, key systems, private branch exchanges, central office switches, and transmission equipment. Prices have dropped sharply, and many innovative products not previously offered are now available. The former assistant attorney general for antitrust, William Baxter, estimated that "the per-line price of key telephone systems would decrease by 25 percent in 1985 alone, at the same time as technological advances made such systems more versatile than ever before. In the market for telecommunications equipment, the per-line price of certain central office switching equipment has been cut in half."[15]

Regulatory Reform Agenda

It is vital in the 1990s to maintain the gains that have already been achieved from deregulation. Reregulation of transportation, communication, or energy would be a tragedy. Where regulation is incomplete, such as trucking and natural gas, it should be perfected. In addition, regulatory reform should be extended to Corporate Average Fuel Economy (CAFE) standards, financial institutions, and environmental regulation.

CAFE Standards

Among the least known but most pernicious regulations are the CAFE standards. These regulations, intended to reduce fuel consumption, have required automobile manufacturers to sell cars that on average meet or exceed a specific mileage-per-gallon standard. For the last few years the CAFE standard has been 27.5 miles per gallon. If the average vehicle sold failed to meet that standard, the manufacturer would be fined $5.00 per tenth of a mile under for each car sold. Thus if a producer sold a million vehicles and missed the standard by 0.2 miles per gallon (that is, its cars averaged 27.3 miles per gallon), it would be fined $10 million. This standard applies separately to domestically produced and imported vehicles.

Whether the CAFE standards have had much effect until recently is questionable. During most of the period since their implementation, gasoline prices alone have been high enough to encourage consumers to demand fuel-efficient vehicles. But the drop in oil prices in the last few years has reduced gasoline prices to consumers considerably, and many are purchasing bigger, more comfortable, safer cars with lower fuel efficiency than smaller vehicles. General Motors (GM) and Ford have had trouble meeting the current standard and have successfully petitioned the National Highway Traffic Safety Administration to reduce it, though only temporarily. The auto companies are in danger of having to pay heavy fines in the future.

When firms exceed the standard, they get credit toward years when they fall short. Most Japanese companies, which sold mainly fuel-efficient small cars in the past, have built up considerable mileage credits and are now in an excellent position to import large cars to the U.S. market without CAFE constraint. By contrast, to meet the CAFE standard GM and Ford must offset sales of large cars with sales of small ones by raising and lowering prices respectively. Thus the CAFE standard acts as a tax on domestic manufacturers of large cars, a market where the United States has a comparative advantage, and favors Japanese imports. It may be undesirable to discriminate against imports, but it is certainly not sensible to discriminate against U.S. producers and in favor of imports.

Financial Markets

On October 19, 1987, the Dow Jones Average on the New York Stock Exchange plunged 22.6 percent, the second largest fall in history (a collapse in 1914 was larger). The next day the stock market in Tokyo fell 15 percent, the London market dropped 12 percent, Sydney plummeted 25 percent, and Hong Kong closed for the week. If before the debacle the public did not understand that we operate in a world capital market, it did afterward. The same firms operate in each of the major capital markets and trade around the clock and around the globe. Banks, securities firms, investment bankers, insurance companies, and individual borrowers and lenders buy and sell in all these markets. Foreign currency and gold can be bought 24 hours a day, and many other securities can be purchased in one market and sold in another after the first has closed.

The worldwide integration of capital markets has increased competition between markets, between government regulations in various countries, and between individual players in the markets. An early example of this competition was the development of the Eurodollar market in the late 1950s and early 1960s, created primarily to avoid U.S. interest rate ceilings and reserve requirements.

Interest rate ceilings have now been eliminated, but U.S. firms are handicapped by considerably more controls than exist in many of the most competitive markets worldwide. Restrictions on interstate banking in the United States have led to the balkanization of financial firms. Whereas elsewhere banks can operate throughout a country, in the United States until recently a bank was confined to its state of origin and sometimes to its original location. Consequently many U.S. banks do not compete directly with each other. The economies of very large size have been denied to all but a few U.S. banks in New York and California. Banks in other states are unable to achieve sufficient scale to compete adequately in world markets.

Although federal law still permits states to exclude or control competition from out-of-state banks or even to limit or prohibit branching, many states are opening their markets to either regional or nationwide banking. This trend is likely to continue, and ultimately U.S. banks will be permitted to operate throughout most of the country. As a result our institutions will gain a much stronger deposit base to compete in world financial markets.

Under the Glass-Steagall Act, passed in the 1930s as a consequence of the banking collapse, commercial banks are prohibited from entering the investment banking field and other financial markets. Conversely investment bankers, brokers, insurance companies, and other such institutions are barred from commercial banking. Similar restrictions exist in some other international markets, but not in such major ones as London or Frankfurt.

There are legitimate concerns about banks entering other markets. Because of deposit insurance, which protects depositors from losses, creditors of the banks (depositors) have little interest in whether the bank is soundly managed. Banks typically have only a small equity position compared with their liabilities (deposits). If bad management or ill luck take a bank's equity toward zero, managers face a strong temptation to make risky loans. If such loans are profitable, the firm can rebuild its equity base. If the loans lose value, the taxpayers, who have implicitly guaranteed the bank, must cover the losses.

The problem resulting from the deposit guarantee is inherent and cannot be totally eliminated by regulation. If the bank is permitted to enter other lines of business, regulation to protect the government (taxpayer) guarantee becomes much more difficult. This is why most proposals to abolish Glass-Steagall have required noncommercial banking activity to be carried out in a separately incorporated subsidiary. This precaution would most likely provide adequate protection for the taxpayer and prevent reckless behavior.

Environmental Regulation

A clean environment is high on nearly everybody's agenda, yet there is considerable dissatisfaction with current controls. The costs of the controls are high and the results meager. Although the nation's air and water have been getting cleaner, Congress's utopian objectives have in almost all cases been postponed.

A more significant problem has been the unwillingness of Congress to allow environmental regulation to have a significant impact on important interest groups. Basically it has attempted to secure a cleaner environment without making any existing identifiable group pay the cost. Congress has been willing to throw money at pollution and to prescribe costly standards for *future* investments where no existing interest is hurt but not to impose costs on known participants.

Nevertheless, private expenditures on pollution abatement have been costly. In 1984, the latest year for which there are data, total expenditures on abatement ran to $51.6 billion (in 1982 dollars).[16] In addition, environmental regulations have also reduced measured productivity in U.S. industry.[17] Moreover, the air pollution laws and their amendments have effectively discouraged the construction of new heavy industrial facilities or power plants and have made it more expensive to build such facilities in areas of the country that are in compliance with the ambient air pollution standards. Since clean-air laws also require the use of expensive scrubbers to remove sulfur from smokestacks but give no credit for burning clean coal, coal-mining jobs are preserved at high economic and environmental cost.

Because of these restrictions, U.S. industry is less efficient and uses older plants. Power companies refrain from building new cleaner plants and simply maintain the existing ones, which must meet much less stringent standards.

Complicating the issue is the ongoing debate over the harm various pollutants cause. For example, acid rain is identified with the acidification of lakes, the deterioration of forests, and the impairment of agriculture. The National Acid Precipitation Assessment Program (NAPAP) released an interim report in September 1987 on the effects of acid rain. The report identifies three subareas where acidic deposition has contributed to acidification of between 2 and 12 percent of lake areas and concludes that "overall, the number of historical trends analyses in the United States documenting loss of fish populations as a result of acidic deposition is low."[18]

On the effect of acid rain on forests, the report concludes that "results to date suggest negligible impact from acid rain on the foliage of plantations and low-elevation forests." The report also finds that "at current deposition levels, there is no detectable effect of acidic deposition on crop yield; however, there may be a net fertilizer benefit from nitrogen deposition on the order of $100 million per year."[19]

Even when there is a documented problem, many regulations appear excessively stringent. For example, medical evidence indicates that ozone levels above fifteen parts per billion can cause damage to exercising individuals with respiratory problems. The Environmental Protection Agency has set the ozone standard at twelve parts per billion. Although such a standard might be prudent, compliance requires that no monitor in a city measure more than twelve parts per billion for more than three periods of one hour each over a three-year period. Thus a city could have twenty measuring stations, nineteen of which show not one hour in a three-year period in which the level of ozone exceeds eleven parts per billion; but if the twentieth station registers four one-hour periods over the limit during three years, the city is considered not in compliance.

Conclusion

In the long run the only way to maintain a vibrant, strong economy that can compete in the world is to preserve its flexible markets. The lessons of other countries that have experimented with market intervention and the lessons that the United States has learned from regulating and then deregulating industries are that free and uncontrolled markets work best. Regulation may be necessary in some situations—to protect the environment, to provide safe working conditions and safe products, and to protect against financial fraud and manipulation. But it is important to be cautious and ensure that the cure is less harmful than the disease. The beneficiaries of regulation and of regulatory regimes are often special interests rather than the general public. The deregulation of transportation, energy, telecommunications, and some financial services has lowered costs, benefited consumers, and made the U.S. economy more competitive, but it is still incomplete. The 1990s will be the critical decade for maintaining these gains and accomplishing what remains to be done in the automobile industry, banking and finance, and the environment. Continuing the trend toward deregulation is critical to U.S. jobs and to the U.S. position in world markets.

Notes

1. *Economic Report of the President* (Washington, D.C.: Government Printing Office, 1988).

2. Ibid.

3. See Hobart Rowen, "Airline Service Has Gone to Hell," *Washington Post,* July 23, 1987; and Brock Adams, "Contemporary Issues in Surface Transportation: Economic Pressures and Safety Priorities" (Paper delivered at the Transportation Deregulation and Safety Conference, Northwestern University, June 22–25, 1987).

4. Thomas Gale Moore, "U.S. Airline Deregulation: Its Effects on Passengers, Capital, and Labor," *Journal of Law & Economics* 29, no. 1 (April 1986): 1–28; Steven Morrison and Clifford Winston, *The Economic Effects of Airline Deregulation* (Washington, D.C.: Brookings Institution, 1986); E. E. Bailey and D. P. Kapalan, *Deregulating the Airlines* (Cambridge, Mass.: MIT Press, 1985).

5. Morrison and Winston, *Airline Deregulation,* p. 1.

6. Jerzy Jemiolo and Clinton V. Ostor, Jr., "Regional Changes in Airline Service Since Deregulation," *Transportation Quarterly* 41, no. 4 (October 1987): 569–86.

7. Thomas Gale Moore, "Deregulation and Safety" (Paper delivered at the Transportation Deregulation and Safety Conference, Northwestern University, June 22–25, 1987).

8. *Air Transport 1987: The Annual Report of the U.S. Scheduled Airline Industry* (Washington, D.C.: Air Transport Association of America, 1987).

9. Thomas Gale Moore, "The Record on Rail and Truck Reform," *Regulation Magazine* 7, no. 6 (November–December 1983): 34.

10. Robert V. Delaney, "The Disunited States: A Country in Search of an Efficient Transportation Policy," *CATO Institute Policy Analysis,* no. 84 (March 10, 1987): 9.

11. Ibid., p. 15.

12. U.S. Department of Energy, *Energy Security: A Report to the President of the United States* (Washington, D.C.: Department of Energy, 1987), p. 127.

13. John D. Zeglis, statement on behalf of AT&T before the Committee on Com-

merce, Science, and Transportation, U.S. Senate, 100th Cong., 1st sess., December 10, 1987.

14. Ibid.

15. Douglas H. Ginsburg, statement before the Committee on Commerce, Science, and Transportation, U.S. Senate, 99th Cong., 2d sess., S. 2565, *The Federal Telecommunications Policy Act of 1986* (Washington, D.C.: Government Printing Office, 1987), p. 95.

16. *Statistical Abstract of the United States, 1987,* 107th ed. (Washington, D.C.: Department of Commerce, Bureau of the Census, 1986), table 341.

17. Wayne B. Gray, "The Cost of Regulation: OSHA, EPA and the Productivity Slowdown," *American Economic Review* 77, no. 5 (December 1987): 998–1006.

18. *NAPAP Interim Assessment: The Causes and Effects of Acidic Deposition,* vol. 1, *Executive Summary* (Washington, D.C.: Government Printing Office, 1987), pp. I-30 to I-32.

19. Ibid., p. I-9.

RITA RICARDO-CAMPBELL

◆ ─────────────────────────────────── ◆

Aging

Social Security and Medicare

───────────────────────────────────

◆ The United States is an aging society. This is true for all nations of the world that are experiencing greater life expectancy and lower birth rates. The developing countries have a much younger average age and do not usually provide compassionate but expensive government programs for the aged because families support those who become too old to work. In the industrialized countries, where higher national incomes provide increasingly better nutrition, health care, and other factors that prolong life, an increasing proportion of the population lives beyond the commonly accepted age of an economically rewarding working life. At age 65 men in the United States can anticipate 14.8 more years of life and women, 18.6 years. Even at age 75 additional years of life average 9.1 and 11.8 respectively.[1] The baby boom generation, those born from 1946 through the mid-1960s, will start to retire about 2006. Because they have few children, the future number of workers entering the labor force will decline, and our population will age faster than now.

The United States, like almost all industrialized nations, has government programs to protect its aged from the risks of lower incomes and higher expenses of ill health. The U.S. Social Security system is a government program that covers income for retirees, survivors, and the permanently disabled and, under its Medicare provisions, some health expenses for those 65 years and older. The costs of Social Security are met by taxes paid by the working population.

Who Are the Aged?

The aged in most industrialized countries are defined as persons 65 years and older, but increasing life expectancy is calling this formal demarcation line into question. Indeed, the U.S. Social Security system was changed in 1983 in partial recognition of this increase, so that by 2009 entitlement to a full retirement benefit will require attainment of 66 years; by 2025, 67 years. But the United States still pays reduced retirement benefits at 62 years and derivative (from the worker) widow and widower benefits at 60. No wonder the average age at retirement in the United States, now 62, has continuously declined since the passage of the Social Security Act in 1935.

In Japan, where 45 percent of men 65 years or older were working in 1980,[2] compared with 18.5 percent in the United States, and where life expectancy is the highest in the world, many persons view age 70, not 65, as the current old-age marker. A 1987 Japanese survey asked adults, "How old do you think an 'old person' is?" Of those polled, 48 percent (the most frequent response) stated "70" and 30 percent "65." Of those under age 64, 52 percent said they "wish to continue working after 65;" 43 percent replied they would not.[3] The Japanese government predicts that by 2000 those 65 and older will compose 19 percent of the population of Japan,[4] compared with 11 percent today. Not until 2010 does the U.S. government predict that even 14 percent of the U.S. population will be 65 years and older, compared with 12 percent in 1987. Japan is aging faster than the United States.

The "old, old"—those 85 years and older—will continue to increase even more rapidly in the United States than those 65 years and older. From 1950 to 1980 the number of persons 65 years and over doubled, and by the year 2000 the common projection is that their numbers will have tripled. But from 1950 to 1980 the number of persons 85 years and older quadrupled, and by the year 2000 their number is expected to be ninefold the 1950 count of 590,000, or over five million people.[5] Can the United States afford to continue its Social Security policy of encouraging individuals to retire at 62, paying male workers benefits averaging 18 more years (and female workers even longer), and paying each of their surviving spouses[6] benefits averaging an additional four years? Older people still working do not receive benefits without substantial penalty until they reach age 70.

Other U.S. government policies encourage older persons to work beyond 61 years. Congress has virtually eliminated any mandatory retirement age and also requires, for older workers, employer continuation of pension accruals in tax-qualified plans. Already many state laws do not permit persons below 70 years to be forced to retire solely because of age. However, large companies may integrate their pension plans with Social Security benefits to encourage retirement at earlier ages when productivity is perceived to peak. Generous company pensions may make up the reduction in Social Security benefits received prior to age 65 and thus reinforce the Social Security system and the effect of an apparent increasing value of leisure, defeating a goal of later retirement.

The Social Security System

The U.S. Social Security system, with its generous benefits indexed to the cost of living, has greatly favored older workers, covered earlier, over younger generations not yet retired. It also favors one-worker families over two-worker families and single workers with no dependents. The major problem of the Social Security system is that it taxes on an individual basis but pays out on a family basis. The system assumes a one-worker family. Times have changed.

The revenue from Social Security, or Old-Age, Survivors, Disability, and Hospital Insurance (OASDHI), taxes continues to rise annually even when the tax rates stay the same because the maximum earnings base to which the rate applies is indexed to average wage increases. In addition, earnings of new workers, immigrants, and previously noncovered federal employees are added each year.

Overlooked is the indirect effect of high rates on first dollar of earnings (7.51 percent in 1988; 7.65 percent in 1990—each matched by employers) on the birthrates among young workers, who include 70 percent of all women of childbearing age, and their husbands. Young people, who average lower per capita incomes than those 65 years and over, perceive that they have little chance of acquiring a home, a new car, and household capital goods unless both husband and wife work. Women who work have fewer children than women who do not. The U.S. fertility rate, now 1.8 children born to a woman over her lifetime, has fallen steadily for the past 200 years. Unless immigration makes up the shortfall, the U.S. population will begin to shrink once the baby boomers are beyond their childbearing years. The number of workers whose earnings can be taxed will also shrink and make vulnerable the payments of benefits to the baby boomer retirees.

The Social Security actuaries project under their most commonly used intermediate II-B assumptions that by 2010, less than 25 years hence, the taxable payrolls will have quadrupled,[7] and although the two major trust funds, Old-Age, Survivors, and Disability Insurance (OASDI), peak about 2015, they then are gradually drawn down, becoming in deficit about 2050. It is a policy question of how much to tax now and for the next 20 years to build up a trust fund balance to pay out monies beginning 25 years hence and for nearly 50 years following. This matter is discussed further in the policy section below.

Financial Status of the Aged

The incomes of the aged (65 years and over) in 1983 were "99.1 percent of the all-persons level." When one takes into account the much greater degree of underreporting of pensions and interest, rents and royalties, compared with wage and salary income, "adjusted per-person mean income for elderly-headed households would be 126 percent of the figure for all households. If one went further and sought to estimate after-tax adjusted per-person household income, the ratio would be even higher: about 145 percent for 1982."[8] The average income per capita of all aged is greater than that of families headed by persons 20–44 years, who are the parents of our future generations. In such families 70 percent of wives work, compared with 50 percent 20 years ago. Working and having children are a difficult combination, and many working women opt to have no children, or no more than one or two.

By 1984 the lowest incidence of poverty of any age group was among families headed by a person aged 65 or older. There has been "a significant shift between 1977 and 1983 in the age-distribution of financial wealth toward older households," resulting in their "higher-than-average net worth."[9] There are large numbers of poor among the aged, as there are large numbers of aged who are well-off. On average the older aged are poorer than the younger. Individuals 85 years and over, especially those who do not live in family units, are on average much poorer than individuals 65–74 years of age, who have the highest net worth of any age group.[10] Families headed by persons 65–74 years old had median incomes of $17,798 in 1983, and those headed by persons 85 years and older had median incomes of $11,988.[11] But in 1983 the number of persons 85 years and older was 2.6 million—and some of those are wealthy—whereas the number 65–74 years of age was 16.5 million. The younger aged can pay for their own wants and needs, and their numbers create new opportunities for private businesses. This is also true for the near-aged, 55–64 years, whose average per capita income is the highest of any age group.

The millions of higher-income younger aged are potential purchasers of ordinary housing, mobile homes, and apartments as well as housing in retirement communities, travel packages, video cassette recorders, stereos and personal computers, adult education courses, new cars, household furnishings and household equipment to replace worn-out and outdated appliances, expensive wines, and clothing. The travel business is well aware of this large lucrative market, but only recently have advertisements for many other products and services been pitched to the aged. The new Mature Market Institute, organized by large companies such as AT&T, banks, and airlines, is providing data and ideas to reach the relatively high-income market of persons 60 years and older. Insurers have been slow to tap this large market for long-term nursing-home care policies.

Some banks are offering reverse annuity mortgages and low-interest lines of credit based on home equity that permit older home owners to have access to cash as needs dictate. For example, on house equity valued at $200,000, a $125,000 line of credit might be offered to the 80-year-old owner. By varying the credit line with age and permitting variable annual drawdowns, the cash ceiling could be set so that amounts lent, plus nominal interest, could easily be repaid when the house is sold upon death of the borrower or when the borrower voluntarily moves (for example, to a retirement home).

Such plans are especially workable where housing prices have risen in an extraordinary fashion, as in Boston and San Francisco. However, the house equity need not be that high to finance the long-term health care needs of most people. There is considerable literature on conversion of home equity into cash flow for the elderly. Although many elderly own "homes of modest value, such owners are most likely to be widowed or among the 'old, old,' characteristics that allow for RAM [reverse annuity mortgage] payments from each $1,000 of equity available. At the same time, these individuals are at the greatest risk of need for long-term care; hence the overlap between the profile of risk and the profile of opportunity to convert home equity" that makes this approach workable. Further, "fifty-six percent of all high-risk single elderly homeowners could generate more than $3,000 per year (to start) from their home assets." [12] This amount could pay for some home nursing and homemaker visits to supplement Medicare's provisions. If coupled with the purchase of insurance against the much lower risk of the necessity to enter a nursing home, it could provide substantial protection. Home equity converted to cash flow can be used to pay the premiums, which may be high. High premiums are mainly a result of self-selection by those more likely to enter a nursing home. However, the relatively low risk among *all* aged—only 5 percent are in nursing homes—should enable an insurance market for such policies to develop.

In 1980 American Homestead Mortgage Corporation pioneered open-term reverse mortgages that assure monthly payments until death. That company had several years of experience with fixed-term reverse mortgages in six states. In those states that do not exclude such income from Medicaid's income eligibility level, fewer aged may be interested in equity conversion. However, the real opposition to home equity conversion stems from the children of the aged, their potential heirs.

Medicare

In 1986 Medicare paid for less than half the health bills of the aged. Yet government planners initially stated that "health insurance should be covering somewhere in the neighborhood of 90 percent of all consumer expenditures for health care."[13] The criticism levied against private health insurance coverage in 1960 can today be applied to Social Security's Medicare because it also pays primarily only costs of hospitalization (part A of Medicare) and surgery. Costs of physician care are running out of control, as did hospital costs prior to the recent form of price regulation, diagnosis-related groups, where payments to hospitals are set in relation to a diagnosis regardless of the number of hospital days and/or resources used. Medicare's part B costs (primarily for physician care) rose during the first six months of 1987 by 22 percent over the same period of 1986. Two-thirds of the increase was due to higher utilization—more visits and more procedures—and one-third to higher prices. But over the past ten years, two-thirds of the rise in total expenditures for *all* personal health care was due to price increases. Government subsidies of medical care seem to be self-defeating because they foster overutilization and inflation.

Unforeseen were the extraordinary increases in life expectancy at age 65—two additional years for men and five for women—that have occurred since 1940. Also largely unforeseen were the effective but costly medical technologies such as organ transplants that have helped drive up the demand for and the cost of medical care and also the development of so many effective drugs that support but do not cure persons with chronic disease. The acquired immunodeficiency syndrome (AIDS) epidemic was clearly unpredicted and has also increased costs of medical care for all by absorbing scarce resources. In addition, some of the increase in the use of medical services is unwarranted, as the sizable variations by states in the number of specific operations per 1,000 illustrate. An estimated $50 billion annually is spent on tests that have accuracy ratings of less than 80 percent. The life-extending value of costly coronary bypass operations, which now number 200,000 annually (compared with 25,000 in 1973), continues to be questioned. New drugs provide alternative and, in a substantial number of cases, preferable treatment to this expensive procedure, often paid for by Medicare.

The expansion of Medicare to cover the limited acute catastrophic health expenses not now paid by Medicare before effective restraints on costs are in place can be seriously questioned; yet this was one subject of the 1987–1988 congressional debate. Health costs absorb 11 percent of GNP, and federal government expenditures on health under Medicare and Medicaid (for the poor) are growing faster than all other areas of the budget. Physician fees, influenced by guildlike arrangements, continue to grow faster than inflation; physician incomes in the United States are a higher multiple of the average of earnings of all U.S. workers than in most other countries. Medicare's part B so-called premium covers at most only one-fourth of the program costs; the other three-fourths is met by general revenue taxation. Thus taxes on personal and corporate incomes rise to support Medicare part B. If individuals and business have to pay an increased percentage of their earnings in taxes, they may risk less in investment because the potential after-tax gain has decreased.

The most pressing national health care problem created by our aging population will be the greater incidence of chronic disease among the aged—who themselves are aging—and the concomitant higher costs of their health care. Although in 1984, 28 million individuals were 65 years and older and 2.6 million 85 and older, by 2000 these numbers will be 35 million and 5 million respectively.[14] Because "males and females 85 and older are four times more likely to be disabled than those age 65 to 74,"[15] the impact of increasing life expectancy on the delivery and financing of health care is substantial. For example, heart disease per 1,000 persons over 64 years has been increasing rapidly as more people (from 274 to 305 per 1,000, over the six-year period 1979–1985) with these (and other) chronic diseases are kept alive by newer, more effective drugs that support but do not cure. Demand and therefore costs of medical care rise. The average annual number of physician visits increases with age: from 6.1 visits per capita for those 45–64 years, 7.4 visits for those 65–74, to 8.4 visits for those 75 and over.[16] Similarly hospital discharge rates (expressed per 1,000 persons) increase with age: 208 for those 55–64 years, 320 for those 65–74, and 591 for those 85 and over.[17] Although only 2 percent of persons aged 65–74 are in nursing homes, that figure rises to 16 percent of persons 85 years and over. The percentage of all elderly in nursing homes, which has remained stable at 5 percent for many years,[18] will start to rise as the older population itself ages.

Policy

By 1990 the annual costs of all federal government entitlement programs, primarily Social Security, will be about 50 percent of total federal spending.

The federal government can no longer consider Social Security and other cost-of-living adjusted (COLA) retirement programs off-limits for political reasons.

The public is largely uninformed about Social Security, civil service retirement, and other government COLA plans that are largely supported by tax money, not by dollars paid in by the recipients. However, politicians have been frightened by their opponents' political rhetoric. Even an across-the-board freeze on 1986 COLAs, agreed upon by the Senate in 1985, was unacceptable to the House, and in the final deadlocked hours a swap was made by the White House for defense moneys.

The 1983 so-called reform legislation succeeded politically because it balanced gains and sacrifices among the major groups involved. The already retired sacrificed a one-year COLA increase while Social Security tax rate increases on current workers were imposed earlier than scheduled. The experience of the 1980s has made clear that politically no changes in the system can be made without a package deal.

For 50 years there have been no trust funds "to fully finance [the] benefits promised" to future retirees.[19] For 50 years benefits have been paid from taxes on earnings of current workers. There never has been a true trust fund. In no year after 1961 was the balance of the OASDI trust funds equal to even one year's payout of only the Old-Age and Survivors Insurance (OASI) benefits.

Why is the federal government now so concerned that trust funds should accumulate so that, under Social Security's II-B intermediate assumptions, they will peak at 23 percent of the GNP in 2030? What is sacrosanct, after 50 years of pay as you go, about a need to accumulate sizable trust funds when Medicare will need dollars to pay for its hospital benefits and when current workers need lower taxes on earnings in order to pay day-to-day bills? The answer probably lies in the large number of knowledgeable baby boomers who are approaching retirement age and the misinformation held by current retirees who fear that their benefits may be cut.

Although I believe that the long-run financial imbalance, primarily created by the long-run demographic imbalance of the baby boomers (who have relatively few children), is worse than that officially projected,[20] this essay addresses only what probably can be done in the 1990s. Radical reform of the Social Security system, such as my "Two Tier or 'A plus B,'" proposed in 1983, is in the long run preferable to continual tinkering to balance the system's inequities. "This plan would award everyone at a given age who has proof of U.S. residence for 40 years a monthly benefit, without a means test. This is the first tier or A of the two-tiered system used today in some countries . . . and to this would be added a strictly earnings-related amount, or B."[21] I do not foresee that this or other radical proposals will be legislated in the 1990s.[22]

First, I would roll back the existing 7.51 percent tax rate, matched by employers, to the December 1987 level of 7.15 percent. These rates include the Medicare hospital insurance part A rate of 1.45 percent. The 1988 and 1990 increases are not needed at this time because the trust funds will grow steadily without them until 2015. Well before that date a national commission to review the actuarial status of the trust funds should be appointed. The legislatively required quadrennial Advisory Council on Social Security is mandated to be tripartite, representing employers, employees, and the public. The 1988 council has not yet (February 1988) been appointed. Congress may wish to reconsider the mandated makeup of this four-year council. The nominal scheduled tax rate increase of 1990 may be so irritating to young workers as to preclude future larger increases that are not scheduled and will be needed closer to the retirement of the baby boomers. To build up huge balances so early will tempt Congress to spend them, possibly unwisely; if not spent they will eventually equal about one-fourth of GNP.

In addition, I propose that persons with high incomes receive an annual COLA minus 1 percent until the suggested review commission evaluates carefully the demographic and economic assumptions behind the projections for 25 years and later, when the baby boomers will retire. This would restrain the growth of total benefits and favor low- and middle-income individuals. The COLAs would be reduced only for the well-off; no one's current benefit would be reduced.

Already enacted is a tax on Social Security benefits paid to individuals whose gross adjusted income is above $25,000, or $32,000 for couples (note the incentive for divorce!). I believe that a reduction in the COLA is preferable to the tax because the other, increasingly expensive, entitlement programs primarily financed by general taxation (such as the civil service retirement system) also have COLAs, and this approach might be carried over to restrain their future costs.

Legislation in 1983 extended the age of entitlement to a full benefit to age 67 by 2025. To complete this recognition of greater life expectancy, entitlement to a reduced benefit should be gradually increased to age 64 by 2025. Disability benefits would still be available for those whose health at ages 62 and 63 warrants retirement. The initial selection of ages 62 and 65 for the reduced and full benefits was arbitrary, and gains in health as well as life expectancy make working through age 63 reasonable.

I also reiterate, with considerable simplification, my 1983 proposals to help working women. "Working married women and dependent men (Social Security is now sex-neutral) on retirement may add part of their earned benefits to their derivative benefits, the total being capped by 125 percent of the earned benefit, or three-fourths rather than one-half of the spousal benefit, whichever is higher."[23] Because women are increasingly receiving a retirement benefit based on their own earnings,[24] the long-run costs of this proposal are minimal, well below 0.5 percent of payroll, and will decline over the years.

"The surviving spouse may add 25 percent of an earned primary benefit to the spousal benefit, the total being capped by 133 percent of the earned benefit or 125 percent of the spousal benefit, whichever is higher . . . An integral part of my recommendation is to allow two years of earnings credit for each child born, at a cost of 0.07 percent of payroll. Similar provisions are in Social Security programs in other countries."[25] The U.S. fertility rate is below replacement, and this earnings credit is at least minimal recognition for childbearing women. It would increase many women's primary benefit because it decreases the number of years in which there are no covered earnings.

Because the average lifetime earnings of women are in almost all cases below the average lifetime earnings of their spouses, it is the rare woman who receives any increase in Social Security benefits because of the taxes that she and her employers pay. Most people are ignorant of the complexities of the system, and many young widows, divorced women with children, and others take jobs in the belief that they will be adding to their Social Security benefits. They usually do not, because the rule is that everyone receives only *one* benefit, whichever is the largest. One unchallenged estimate, made in 1982, is that this "has saved the Social Security system about 3.5 percent of long-run payroll" taxed to support the system.[26]

When Social Security was enacted only 25 percent of women worked. Today 70 percent of women 20–54 are working, and over 90 percent of women by age 62 have worked the ten years that would qualify them for a benefit. Over 80 percent of women are or have been married, most of them the ten years or more to one person that would qualify them for a derivative benefit based on their husband's earnings. (Derivative benefits are commonly justified on welfare grounds.)

Medicare Policy

I would restore the personal income tax deductibility for payments to individual retirement accounts (IRAs) that presumably, upon retirement, could be used for any purpose, including the medical expenses of old age. New net savings were created by the IRA policy,[27] and these are beneficial to the nation's economy even though low-income and low-middle-income persons did not, and many could not, take full advantage of them. The annual tax revenue loss is estimated to be about $9 billion for 1988–1992.[28] Direct earmarking of IRA savings, while one is employed, to pay premiums for long-term care insurance in old age should be considered. The federal government cannot support a new extraordinarily expensive government-financed program of long-term care because of the existing large federal deficit. Employers should be able to take tax deductions for contributions made during their employees' working years to pay for retirement health care coverage.

IRAs need redesigning if they are to be successful sources of nursing-home expenses. The denial of deductions for payments to an IRA after 70.5 years and the mandated distribution beginning at that age do not jibe with the late age (75–80 years) of usual nursing-home admissions.

Like many other economists, I support taxing the premiums of the private medigap insurance policies. Their coverage of Medicare's deductibles and copayments defeats the hope of restraining demand by increasing out-of-pocket payments. Seventy percent of the aged are covered by medigap insurance. The current government policy is contradictory, and its annual costs to the government are about $8 billion.[29] This estimate assumes that such policies increased the use, and therefore the costs, of all Medicare-covered services by this amount in 1987.

A tax on the premiums to yield revenue as close as possible to the externality cost of $8 billion should be imposed. Because it is likely that insurers will adjust to the tax, it is hard to estimate potential yield. Alternatively medigap policies could be required to cover only payment of items not covered by Medicare, such as nursing-home care excluded by Medicare's strict rules, which in practice have resulted in its paying less than 5 percent of the total nursing-home bill.

Because of the expansion of employer's retiree health benefit plans, the middle- and high-income worker will have less incentive to purchase medigap insurance than earlier. In large-and medium-size companies, 57 percent of employees are now covered for retiree health benefits.

For those whose incomes, even during working years, do not permit such options as purchasing private nursing-home insurance coverage, Medicaid for the poor must be maintained. For those whose incomes are marginally too low for even tax-deferred put-aways to appeal over the exigencies of everyday expenses and whose income in old age will not allow Medicaid entitlement, new financial incentives need to be created. Here reverse annuity mortgages and low-interest lines of credit based on home equity hold great promise.

Over the long run the best hope to contain the costs of medical care will continue to lie in the provision of information to consumers. Nationwide, large employers use comparative utilization and price data to audit large hospital bills and to help the company and employee select prepaid per capita options. This has been cost-effective. Information about prices of physician visits and hospital days and anticipated benefits from medical interventions is being made available to employees and those retirees covered by company policies. They are becoming informed purchasers who increase meaningful competition. It is hoped that this approach might control the extraordinary increase in utilization and can be largely a private effort, not a governmental one.

Massachusetts has banned balance billing (that is, billing amounts above the Medicare reimbursement level) to Medicare patients. Other states are likely to follow. This practice contains costs for Medicare but increases them for other buyers. Disseminating the names of physicians who accept Medicare reimbursement as full payment is preferable.

It was debated during 1987 and 1988 whether the federal government should considerably expand Medicare's coverage of health care bills because the aged have higher per capita costs for medical care than other age groups. Among other changes, it was proposed that Medicare cover prescription drugs. The financial status of the aged and the twenty-year history of Medicare suggest that expanding Medicare is not the best policy. Medicare provides an illuminating example of the failure of a well-intentioned government program to reduce the economic uncertainty of ill health among the aged.

Public Awareness: Social Security and Medicare

The public is not well informed about Social Security. Part of the problem is that the Social Security Administration and its trustees continue to talk and write required reports using the word *contributions* for *taxes*. No wonder over the years economists have been concerned with income taxes and have ignored the steady increase in Social Security rates. It is time to call a spade a spade. News commentators and others who emphasize that Social Security entitlements must not be cut misrepresent the issue. No one suggests cutting existing benefits.

Notes

1. Metropolitan Life Insurance Company, "Women's Longevity Advantage Declines," *Statistical Bulletin* 69 (January–March 1988): 19.

2. Long-Term Outlook Committee, Economic Council, Economic Planning Agency, *Japan in the Year 2000* (Tokyo: Japan Times, 1983), p. 119.

3. Survey of 2,290 adults conducted by Yomiuri Press in July 1987, as reported in *World Opinion Update* 10, no. 10 (October 1987): 114.

4. Long-Term Outlook Committee, *Japan in the Year 2000*, p. 120.

5. U.S. Bureau of the Census, *Demographic and Socioeconomic Aspects of Aging in the United States*, Current Population Reports, series P-23, no. 138 (Washington, D.C.: Government Printing Office, 1984), p. 15.

6. Ten years of marriage are required except for the current wife; no one may collect more than one benefit.

7. Harry C. Ballantyne, "Long-Range Estimates of Social Security Trust Fund Operations in Dollars," *Actuarial Note*, no. 130, Social Security Administration Publication no. 11–11500, April 1987, p. 3.

8. Stephen Crystal, "Measuring Income and Inequality Among the Elderly," *Gerontologist* 26 (1986): 57, 58.

9. Randall J. Pozdena, "Inflation, Age, and Wealth," *Economic Review* 1 (Federal Reserve Bank of San Francisco, Winter 1987): 28.

10. Ibid., p. 22.

11. U.S. Senate Special Committee on Aging, in conjunction with the American Association of Retired Persons, the Federal Council on Aging, and the Administration on Aging, *Aging America, 1985–1986* (Washington, D.C.: Government Printing Office, 1986), p. 44.

12. Bruce Jacobs and William Weissert, "Using Home Equity to Finance Long-Term Care," *Journal of Health Politics, Policy and Law* 12 (Spring 1987): 90, 83.

13. Wilbur J. Cohen, "Next Steps for Voluntary Health Insurance," in *Private Health Insurance and Medical Care: Conference Papers*, Office of Research and Statistics, Social Security Administration, U.S. Department of Health, Education, and Welfare (Washington, D.C.: Government Printing Office, 1968), p. 92.

14. U.S. Senate Special Committee on Aging et al., *Aging America*, p. 12.

15. Ibid., p. 87.

16. Ibid., p. 101.

17. R. Havlik et al., *Vital and Health Statistics*, National Center for Health Statistics, Health Statistics on Older Persons, United States, 1986, series 3, no. 25 (Washington, D.C.: Government Printing Office, 1987), p. 61.

18. U.S. Senate Special Committee on Aging et al., *Aging America*, p. 97.

19. John C. Hambor, "Economic Policy, Intergenerational Equity, and the Social Security Trust Fund Buildup," *Social Security Bulletin* 50 (October 1987): 13.

20. See Rita Ricardo-Campbell, "U.S. Social Security Under Low Fertility," in Kingsley Davis, Mikhail S. Bernstam, and Rita Ricardo-Campbell, eds., *Below-Replacement Fertility in Industrial Societies* (Cambridge: Cambridge University Press, 1987), pp. 300–305.

21. Rita Ricardo-Campbell, "Social Security Reform: A Mature System in an Aging Society," in John H. Moore, ed., *To Promote Prosperity* (Stanford: Hoover Institution Press, 1984), p. 116.

22. The most common of these proposals would permit individuals now covered to opt out and invest amounts equivalent to their forgiven Social Security taxes in IRAs. Low-income persons do not have IRAs, and the younger the worker, the more likely he or she will opt out of the system, leaving older workers to provide benefits to current workers and also for their own old age.

23. Ricardo-Campbell, "Social Security Reform," pp. 91–123.

24. Upon retirement a worker receives a 100 percent primary benefit; the derivative benefit is 50 percent of the spouse's benefit. At the worker's death a surviving spouse who meets the rules receives 100 percent of the primary benefit. Benefits to divorced spouses are not included in the 175 percent family cap that applies to parents, children, and current spouse.

25. Ricardo-Campbell, "Social Security Reform," pp. 115–16.

26. Rita Ricardo-Campbell, "Social Security: The Working Woman's Burden," *Washington Post*, September 20, 1982.

27. Steven F. Venti and David A. Wise, "Have IRAs Increased U.S. Saving? Evidence from Consumer Expenditure Surveys," Hoover Institution Working Paper in Economics, no. E-87-13, p. 36.

28. Joint Committee on Taxation, "On Estimates of Federal Tax Expenditures for Fiscal Years 1988–1992," prepared for the Senate Finance and House Ways and Means committees (JCS-3-87), February 27, 1987, table 1, as published in *Daily Tax Reporter*, March 2, 1987, p. J-1.

29. Sandra Christensen, Stephen H. Long, and Jack Rodgers, "Acute Health Care Costs for the Aged Medicare Population: Overview and Policy Options," *The Milbank Quarterly* 65, no. 3 (1987): 412–13.

JUNE O'NEILL

Poverty

Programs and Policies

Introduction

◆ A compassionate and humane society is naturally concerned about poverty and feels committed to alleviating it. "A decent provision for the poor," said Samuel Johnson, "is the true test of civilization." [1] As a practical matter, however, the implementation of public policies to help the poor involves complex problems with no satisfactory solutions. Even the preliminary questions—Who is poor? What is a decent provision?—are not easily resolved. The fundamental issue, however, and the one that has generated the greatest controversy, concerns the actual effectiveness of measures to help the poor.

The basic dilemma of poverty policy is that the provision of income to those who meet the poverty standard is bound to weaken the incentive to be self-supporting. This change in incentives may in time lead to a permanent underclass of individuals dependent on the state. As Gertrude Himmelfarb has reminded us, the conflict between the most humanitarian motives and unintended and undesired outcomes has been noted by astute commentators for as long as poverty policies have been implemented. [2] Having observed the system of relief for the poor in nineteenth-century England, Alexis de Tocqueville wrote in 1835: "I am deeply convinced that any permanent, regular, administrative system whose aim will be to provide for the needs of the poor, will breed more miseries than it can cure" and "will deprave the population that it wants to help and comfort." [3] Charles Murray, writing in the 1980s, has made much the same point, assigning to the expansion in the poverty programs of the late 1960s and 1970s a role in many troubling social trends, including the dissolution of families, declines in educational achievement, and increases in crime.[4]

Since the early 1970s no major changes in poverty programs have been enacted. Two recent developments, however, have generated renewed interest in antipoverty policy. One is a rise in measured poverty in the 1980s; the other is the priority given to welfare reform by President Reagan in his 1986 State of the Union address, which may have been an unwitting Pandora's box. A flurry of legislative proposals has emerged. Because of the strong impact of the writings of Charles Murray and other critics of poverty policy, most recent proposals contain rhetoric about the responsibilities of welfare recipients to become self-supporting. This emphasis has led to much talk about a new consensus on welfare policy. Despite the rhetoric, however, there is still considerable disagreement about the extent to which income support for the poor should be made more generous, more uniform, and more universal.

Defining and Measuring Poverty

The U.S. government did not develop an official measure of poverty until the War on Poverty was launched in the mid-1960s and a need arose for an estimate of the number of persons who might be served by the ambitious new programs. The official measure of poverty used by the Census Bureau and other government agencies is based on a poverty standard devised in the Social Security Administration by Mollie Orshansky in 1964.

Although the official poverty definition may seem like a scientific concept, it is not at all scientific. To determine who is poor is an exercise in value judgment. As Ms. Orshansky has written, "Poverty lies in the eye of the beholder."[5] Differences in the definition of poverty, however, can cause substantial differences in the perceived size of the poor population, giving this definition considerable political and budgetary significance. In addition, the income and other data available to implement the definition are also subject to judgment and interpretation.

Definitions

The foundation for the Orshansky poverty threshold is a food budget developed by nutritionists in the Department of Agriculture in the early 1960s. The food budget was intended to represent amounts needed to purchase a low-cost but nutritionally adequate diet with adjustments for families of various sizes. To derive nonfood needs and the total income that constitutes the poverty threshold, Orshansky multiplied the food budget by three, since the *average* family was found to spend one-third of its income on food.

Although the food component of the poverty measure has not generated much controversy, the decision to use a multiplier of three has been highly controversial. As Rose Friedman pointed out in a study contemporaneous with Orshansky's, it is more logical to base the poverty threshold on the income of those families that actually spend the equivalent of the nutritionally adequate diet.[6] Such a family would have a lower income than the average family, and food would make up a larger share of its income, resulting in a multiplier less than three. Evidently Orshansky made a value judgment that low-income families who could afford an adequate diet would be unable to purchase what she believed to be adequate amounts of nonfood items (shelter, clothing, and so on).

Orshansky's arbitrary decision to use a multiplier of three led, of course, to a higher poverty threshold and a higher estimate of poverty than the method suggested by Friedman. The number of poor Friedman counted was roughly half the number found using the Orshansky method. At the time, however, the nation was embarking on the War on Poverty, which called for a target substantial enough to be a real challenge. Yet if the poverty count had been much larger—such as the numbers claimed by Michael Harrington and other advocates for the poor—the formidable budgetary implications might have discouraged any effort.[7] The Orshansky measure suited the political needs of the period.

As it is, the concept of poverty embodied in the official poverty measure clearly is not hunger and destitution. Few in the United States today would be poor by such a definition. In 1986 the poverty threshold was $11,206 for a family of four, or 38 percent of the median family income. By comparison, the U.S. poverty threshold is roughly equal to the average income in the Soviet Union.[8]

The official definition has been criticized for various reasons. One argument points out that it is an absolute measure adjusted only for increases in inflation. Therefore as real income rises the poverty threshold falls relative to the average income and the number of persons below the poverty line declines. This property of an absolute standard permits us to chart the progress of the economy in reducing poverty over time. But some critics argue that poverty should be defined in relation to the overall standard of living. Peter Townsend, for example, advocates a definition of poverty based on the concept of "relative deprivation," a lack of "resources to obtain the types of diet, participate in the activities and have the living conditions and amenities which are customary, or are at least widely encouraged or approved, in the societies to which [people] belong."[9] Townsend takes relativism to an extreme, however, and includes in his poverty measure such indicators as a lack of holidays away from home, Sunday roasts, hot breakfasts, and evenings out for entertainment.

If poverty were defined in relative terms, the poverty threshold would be a moving target, increasing with the real level of income. Under a relative measure, poverty would show little or no decline, even during periods of great gains in prosperity, unless there were a significant decline in the inequality of the income distribution. For this reason relative definitions of poverty are likely to be popular among those who advocate policies to redistribute income.

The official U.S. poverty measure has been fixed in real terms since Orshansky developed it in 1964. It is relative in that it reflects present-day value judgments of what a minimum acceptable standard should be and not the judgments of a century ago or of a Third World country. As average income rises over time, however, the poverty threshold will eventually become irrelevant and obsolete. Some believe that this point has already been reached. Orshansky, for example, has called for a "technical update" of the poverty threshold based on the observation that the multiplier is now larger than three (because as income has increased, the proportion of the average family's income spent on food has declined well below one-third). But the multiplier of three was never an objective technical requirement of the poverty definition. Moreover, as Friedman pointed out, it was set too high to be internally consistent with the methodology.

Interestingly, using two different methods, a recent study to measure basic needs in Wisconsin suggests that the official poverty standard is useful for defining present-day needs.[10]

Because poverty is a judgmental concept, an official poverty measure should reflect the views of the public. Any major changes in the poverty measure should not be relegated to technicians but should be openly debated so that the public is aware of the subjective choices involved.

Measurement Issues

The actual measurement of poverty requires data on the consumption patterns of the population. The official income data used by the Census Bureau to approximate a family's command over goods and services are deficient in several well-known respects. Income is measured for a given year, but under atypical circumstances it may be temporarily low or high for that year and therefore does not reflect the family's true ability to consume. Indeed, considerable turnover has been found in the poverty population. One study found that about one-third of the poverty population in one year is not poor in the following year.[11]

Other drawbacks in the income data include the use of gross income because of the difficulty of obtaining data on tax payments, the omission of a value assigned to unpaid work in the home (particularly relevant for full-time homemakers), and the underreporting of income from such sources as welfare benefits. Some of these considerations would likely have a significant effect on the number counted as poor.

Two additional factors known to have important effects on the measurement of poverty are the omission from income of noncash benefits (such as food stamps and housing subsidies) and the use of a flawed adjustment for inflation. These issues are discussed below since they are areas where data have become more available and could be used to improve the official measure of poverty.

Noncash benefits. Over the past fifteen years, a growing share of government transfer payments intended for the poor has been provided in the form of noncash benefits. In 1970 about half of means-tested benefits took the form of noncash benefits; by 1986 this proportion had grown to two-thirds.

The Census Bureau has been collecting data on the receipt of noncash benefits and experimenting with various ways of measuring the value of these benefits. Although the valuation of some noncash benefits (such as food stamps) is straightforward, it is exceedingly difficult to determine the value of others, particularly medical benefits. Medicaid, for example, provides complete first-dollar coverage of health expenditures. If such a policy were sold as health insurance on the private market it would be extremely expensive. The Census Bureau estimated that the market value of Medicaid for a single parent with two children would have been about $1,900 in Texas in 1986.[12] But some question whether a $1,900 health insurance policy is worth that much to a low-income family, and if not, what it is worth. The answers are not easy to determine.

The Census Bureau now provides two alternative estimates of noncash benefits. One estimates the market value of the benefits; the other aims to measure the utility of the benefit to the recipient. The problems associated with determining utility to the recipient, however, are much more formidable than those associated with measuring market value.

The inclusion of noncash benefits as income has a substantial effect on the number counted as poor. Census Bureau estimates for 1986 show that when noncash benefits are priced at market value, the number of persons counted as poor falls by 11 million—a 34 percent reduction. When valued by an estimate of the utility to recipients, the number of poor falls by 4.8 million—a 15 percent reduction. For various reasons the value-to-recipients measure is likely to underestimate noncash benefits.[13] But the reduction in poverty is substantial even using the lower valuation of benefits. Noncash benefits are clearly too important to be excluded from the definition of income used to measure poverty.

Another similar improvement in the measurement of poverty would include estimates of the value of fringe benefits in the definition of income. Although such an adjustment would undoubtedly raise the measured incomes of higher-income individuals, it would also be likely to affect the poverty rate of the working poor.

Adjustment for inflation.   Another measurement problem is the choice of a price deflator for adjusting the poverty threshold for inflation. The official Consumer Price Index (CPI) has been used, yet the CPI is known to have overstated inflation during the 1970s and early 1980s. The CPI methodology was changed to correct the problem starting in 1983, but the change was not made in the official measure for the years before 1983, when the discrepancy was actually at its peak. The adjusted CPI measure is available for these earlier years, however, and should be used to revise the official poverty (and income) statistics. It shows greater income gains and a smaller rise in poverty than are presented in the official data.[14]

Trends in Poverty and the Economy

Changes in the incidence of poverty in the United States have been driven by changes in the economy. The strikingly close relation is depicted in Figure 1. In 1949 an estimated 34 percent of the population had incomes below the official poverty threshold. During the next two decades poverty declined steadily, reaching 22 percent in 1959 and 12 percent in 1969. These two post–World War II decades were years of remarkable economic growth that steadily raised real earnings (measured by real compensation per hour in Figure 1) and thereby lifted more and more families and individuals out of poverty.

During the 1970s the rate of productivity growth in the economy slowed sharply. In addition the level and volatility of unemployment rose through a series of recessions, the deepest of which started after 1979, hitting an unemployment peak close to 10 percent in 1982 and 1983. These developments are clearly mirrored in the poverty rate, which fluctuated around a plateau in the 1970s and rose and then fell in the 1980s with the changes in unemployment.

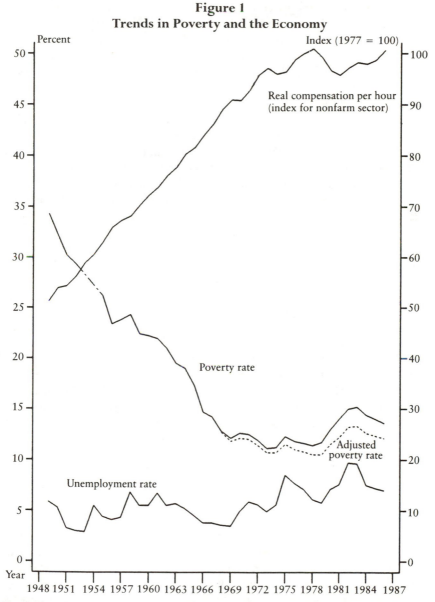

Figure 1
Trends in Poverty and the Economy

Percent
Index (1977 = 100)

Real compensation per hour
(index for nonfarm sector)

Poverty rate

Adjusted
poverty rate

Unemployment rate

Year
1948 1951 1954 1957 1960 1963 1966 1969 1972 1975 1978 1981 1984 1987

NOTE: The adjusted poverty rate (dotted line) is based on a poverty threshold indexed by an alternative CPI that uses a different methodology to measure housing costs.

SOURCES: *Economic Report of the President,* January 1987, tables B-35 and B-43 (unpublished data for real compensation for 1984–1986); U.S. Bureau of the Census, *Current Population Reports,* series P-60, no. 157 (Washington, D.C.: Government Printing Office, 1987).

In 1986 the official poverty rate was 13.6 percent, still above the level of the 1970s. The poverty rate adjusted with the alternative CPI (represented by the dotted line in Figure 1) is not as much above the 1970s level as the official measure, but it still shows a failure of poverty to return to prerecession levels. This observation has caused much handwringing in the nation's editorial pages over growing income inequality and persistent poverty that is resistant to economic growth.

One plausible and more hopeful explanation is that the period 1983–1986 reflects a recovery from a deep recession exacerbated by severe but transitional structural changes. Increases in unemployment are typically associated with increases in income inequality, since the reduction in weeks and hours worked is not uniformly spread over the labor force but is concentrated among certain industries (such as manufacturing and construction) and certain workers (usually those who are younger and less skilled). During the recovery stage following the 1982–1983 recession, the usual problems may have been compounded by sectoral shifts associated with the trade imbalance and the low demand for U.S. export goods as well as shifts in relative prices and industry demand for certain products, such as farm goods and oil. Workers tied to industries and geographic regions that experienced employment declines did not, of course, fare as well as those in regions and industries experiencing strong demand (such as financial services).

The U.S. economy has always been remarkably resilient. The unemployment rate in 1987 fell to 6.2 percent from 7 percent in 1986. The poverty rate in 1987 probably again declined significantly. For the future, however, further declines in poverty will not approach the progress of the 1950s or 1960s unless the pace of economic growth increases.

The Role of Transfers

Expenditures on transfers have increased enormously since the start of the War on Poverty in the mid-1960s, and it is natural to expect this increase to have reduced poverty significantly. Poverty did decline between 1965 and 1970, but this was a period of great economic expansion. Poverty stopped declining around 1970 when economic growth slowed, despite the continued rise in transfers: defined in terms of total social welfare expenditures, transfers rose from 14.7 percent of GNP in 1970 to 18.5 percent in 1980 (see Table 1). At least superficially, transfers do not appear to have had a significant impact on overall poverty rates.

There are several reasons why the apparent relation between transfers and poverty is not stronger. One is that many social welfare programs are not intended for the poor exclusively. For example, Social Security (includ-

Table 1
Growth in Public Social Welfare Expenditures, 1950–1984

FISCAL YEAR	EXPENDITURES PER CAPITA (in constant 1984 dollars)			EXPENDITURES AS PERCENT OF GNP		
	All social welfare programs	Social insurance	Public welfare	All social welfare programs	Social insurance	Public welfare
1950	630	133	75	8.2	1.7	1.0
1960	984	346	94	10.3	3.8	1.0
1965	1189	432	119	11.2	4.1	1.1
1970	1773	660	229	14.7	5.5	1.9
1975	2424	1026	389	19.0	8.1	2.9
1980	2671	1243	454	18.5	8.6	3.1
1982	2733	1388	424	18.9	9.6	2.9
1984	2801	1424	434	18.2	9.3	2.8

SOURCE: Ann Kallman Bixby, "Public Welfare Expenditures, Fiscal Year 1984," *Social Security Bulletin* 50, no. 6 (June 1987), tables 2 and 4.

NOTE: Social insurance includes all Social Security programs, including Medicare, unemployment insurance, public employee retirement, workers' compensation, and other similar programs. Public welfare consists mostly of means-tested programs, including cash public assistance, Medicaid, Social Security Income (SSI), food stamps, low-income energy assistance benefits, public housing, and child nutrition. Other social welfare expenditures included in all social welfare programs but not in the social insurance or public welfare categories include health and education expenditures and veterans' programs.

ing Medicare), which accounts for 36 percent of all social welfare expenditures, is based on age and retirement, not poverty status. Although it contributed to a reduction in poverty, clearly a large portion of Social Security has always benefited the nonpoor.

Expenditures on programs targeted specifically on the poor (designated as public welfare expenditures in Table 1) make up only 15 percent of all social welfare spending. However, this component followed much the same pattern of growth as total transfers, nearly doubling in real terms (on a per capita basis) between 1970 and 1980. Moreover, such expenditures account for about 3 percent of GNP. An expenditure of $434 per capita amounts to an income supplement of more than $3,000 for each person in poverty, or $9,000 for a family of three.

Of course, to have an effect on measured poverty, benefits must be included in income. As noted, noncash benefits for the poor are not counted as income. Yet they have grown much more rapidly than cash benefits and now comprise about two-thirds of means-tested benefits. When noncash benefits are counted as income, the decline in poverty from 1964 (when noncash benefits were negligible) to 1986 is much more substantial than the official data would indicate, particularly for groups likely to receive benefits in kind. As indicated in Table 2, the official poverty rate declined by only about 5 percentage points from 1964 to 1986, while the rate adjusted for noncash benefits (at market value) declined by 10 percentage points. Among families headed by women, the official poverty measure shows only a small decline (from 44 percent to 38 percent); adjusted for noncash benefits, the poverty measure for this group declines by almost half (from 44 percent to 24 percent).

The elderly who receive the largest share of cash benefits also receive a substantial share of noncash benefits. The poverty rate of persons aged 65 and older falls from 29 percent in 1966 to 3 percent in 1986 (instead of 12 percent) when noncash benefits are included as income. In sum, taking noncash transfers into account reveals a much more substantial decline in poverty than the official statistics show.

The objection raised to transfer programs does not deny that they have brought some relief to those in need. Clearly many poor families have had their incomes increased by both cash and noncash benefits. What is at issue is that transfers give rise to more complicated offsetting effects, since they create incentives for people to reduce their work effort or to change their behavior in other ways to qualify for benefits.

Thus far welfare policy in the United States has been restrained by apprehension about the potentially counterproductive consequences of extending aid to young able-bodied individuals. We have come close to adopting a national guaranteed income policy several times, starting with

Table 2
Percentage of Persons in Poverty,
by Demographic Group, 1964 and 1986

Persons	Official measure 1964	Official measure 1986	Adjusted for noncash benefits[a] 1986
All	19.0	13.6	9.0
White	14.9	11.0	7.4
Black	49.8[b]	31.1	19.8
Hispanic	—	27.3	18.7
Living in female-headed family	44.4	38.3	23.5
Living in married-couple family	14.6[c]	7.1	5.0
Age 65 and over	28.5[d]	12.4	3.0
Under age 18	22.7	20.3	13.8

SOURCE: U.S. Bureau of the Census, *Current Population Reports,* series P-60, no. 102 (Washington, D.C.: Government Printing Office, 1976), table 1; U.S. Bureau of the Census, Technical Paper 57, table 1.

[a] This adjustment uses the market value of noncash (in-kind) benefits.

[b] The 1964 figure refers to all nonwhites, since data on blacks were not tabulated separately for that year. The black rate was probably about 3 percentage points above the nonwhite rate.

[c] The 1964 figure includes the small percentage of persons living in male-headed single-parent families.

[d] The poverty rate shown is for 1966, since the rate for this age group was not tabulated for 1964 or 1965.

President Nixon's proposed Family Assistance Plan and with its successors—President Ford's Income Supplementation Plan and President Carter's Program for Better Jobs and Income. Concern that a guaranteed income would in time erode individual efforts for self-support have combined with budgetary worries to prevent the enactment of such a plan. The income support programs that have been enacted are targeted on groups for whom self-support is viewed as a less-pressing issue, such as the elderly and the disabled. Even so, many studies suggest that the rise in Social Security benefits has significantly accelerated the retirement of the older and disabled populations.[15] But the resulting reduction in work effort has evidently not been viewed as a social problem.

Welfare and the Female-Headed Family

The one group of young able-bodied adults who have been recipients of large-scale income transfers is unmarried women heading families. The program synonymous with welfare—Aid to Families with Dependent Children (AFDC)—is intended to help such families. The AFDC program was initiated in the 1930s as a supplement to the Social Security system. Unlike Social Security, the program is administered by the states, and funding is shared with the federal government. States set their own benefit levels and establish income and asset criteria for eligibility, subject to federal limitations. Benefits vary widely among the states.

The main purpose of the program has always been to provide for children who are caught unexpectedly in deprived circumstances because of the loss of support by the father, who 50 years ago was likely to be the family's sole financial provider. The underlying reasons for nonsupport by the father, however, have changed radically. In the early days of the program 75 percent of the children covered by the program had fathers who were deceased or severely incapacitated. By the 1980s fewer than 5 percent of the fathers were in this category, whereas close to half had never been married to the children's mother, with most of the remainder divorced or separated. About half of the states now provide AFDC benefits under certain circumstances to families in which the father is present but unemployed; such families make up only about 6 percent of all AFDC families.

Criticism of the AFDC program has grown in recent years. The changing character of the caseload is one factor, as a birth out of wedlock is viewed as a more voluntary route to becoming a single parent than death, disability, or desertion by the father. Another is the dramatic change in women's work participation among those who are not on welfare. More than 60 percent of married women with children under the age of 18 now work (as do 54 percent of those with children under age 6). Among all women who are single parents, work participation is on average even higher. Yet women on AFDC have reported work participation that over the years has not exceeded 15 or 16 percent. The discrepancy in work effort between welfare mothers and other women is bound to raise the ire of taxpayers. Perhaps the biggest cloud raised by the program, however, is the extent to which it is implicated in the rise in out-of-wedlock childbearing, the disintegration of the family, and the seeming persistence of an underclass population. Although several studies have attempted to address these issues, no one has yet provided conclusive evidence about the role of AFDC, leaving room for disagreement over the true effects.

The basic facts about growth in the program are shown in Table 3. The

Table 3
Trends in AFDC Families and Benefit Levels

Year	Number of AFDC families[a] (in thousands)	Number of female-headed families with children (FHFC)[b] (in thousands)	AFDC families as percent of FHFC	FHFC as percent of all families with children	Combined AFDC and food stamp benefits[c] (in constant 1986 dollars)
1964	992	2,833	35.0	10.0	6,949
1968	1,400	3,190	43.9	11.0	7,501
1972	2,784	4,077	68.2	13.3	9,359
1976	3,426	5,119	66.9	16.3	9,133
1980	3,501	6,035	58.0	18.6	7,877
1984	3,438	6,622	51.9	20.2	7,314
1986	3,488	6,892	50.6	20.6	7,519

SOURCES: *Social Security Bulletin,* various issues; Committee on Ways and Means, U.S. House of Representatives, *Background Material and Data on Programs Within the Jurisdiction of the Committee on Ways and Means* (Washington, D.C.: Government Printing Office, 1986); U.S. Bureau of the Census, *Poverty in the United States, 1985,* series P-60, no. 158 (Washington, D.C.: Government Printing Office, 1987), table 3.

[a] Average monthly number of recipients in calendar years 1964 and 1968, fiscal years 1972–1986. Excludes families with unemployed fathers.

[b] Refers to March of each year. Includes single-parent families only.

[c] Weighted average across states of annual combined AFDC and food stamp benefits for a family of four with no other cash income.

pattern of participation in AFDC over time corresponds closely to the change in the benefit level. Between 1964 and 1972 the average real benefit (for a family of four with no other income) increased by 35 percent. (The increase in the AFDC benefit level in the 1960s was spurred largely by the federal government, which in 1966 offered to pay at least half of a state's total AFDC payments to states that agreed to provide Medicaid.) This increase does not reflect the introduction of Medicaid or the expansion of public housing, school meals, and other programs and services that added significantly to the value of the welfare package. Even without these add-ons, the AFDC cash benefit combined with food stamps provided an annual income of close to $9,400 in 1972 (for a family of four without other income, expressed in 1986 dollars). This income was tax-free and required no hours of work away from home or work expenses. It may well have appeared an attractive alternative for a woman with few labor market or marriage options.

During this period of rapid benefit increases, the number of female-headed families on AFDC tripled—marking a doubling in the percentage of female-headed families participating in the program (from 34 to 67 percent) and a 50 percent rise in the number of female-headed families. After 1976 the total AFDC benefit package began to erode as states failed to raise AFDC cash benefit levels to keep pace with inflation. When benefits stopped rising and then fell, the AFDC caseload stopped rising and the percentage of single mothers participating in the program fell. Following the changes introduced in the Omnibus Budget Reconciliation Act of 1981, which somewhat restricted program eligibility, the caseload declined slightly despite rising unemployment.

These basic data on program trends support the commonsense expectation that welfare participation is related to the financial attractiveness of the program.[16] More sophisticated studies of the determinants of welfare participation also support such a relation.[17] Such studies typically also find that women whose alternative income streams are expected to be low are more likely to participate in AFDC or to stay in the program longer. For example, women with low levels of education, low prior work experience, and a large number of children are more likely to be program participants.

Although the case that welfare participation among single parents is related to the relative attractiveness of the program is quite well established, it has proven much more difficult to determine the effect of welfare on the decision to become a single parent—to marry, divorce, or have a child out of wedlock—since these are exceedingly complex behaviors to study. The level of welfare benefits is but one of several factors likely to affect such decisions.[18] The decision to be married or not must in some sense result from a balancing of the gains from and opportunities for marriage, on the one side, with the attractiveness of marriage alternatives, on the other. Welfare is one alternative form of support, but the woman's level of earnings and potential level of child support are also likely to be important factors. It is difficult to obtain data on all the ingredients for a study that would enable us to sort out the effect of welfare. None that I know of has done so.[19]

With reference to the trends shown in Table 3, note that up to 1976 the incidence of female-headed families increased with the rise in benefit levels. After 1976, however, the number of female-headed families continued to rise for a time, while the percentage on welfare fell. This finding by no means negates the hypothesis that welfare is an important factor affecting marital decisions. During the 1970s women's labor market opportunities began to expand and women's earnings (particularly among those under age 35) began to rise relative to men's. Rising women's earnings would have made it easier for women to become financially independent and may well have provided the impetus for the continuing growth in single-parent families. The growth in female-headed families has slowed considerably in the 1980s, however, as has the divorce rate.

Policy Implications

We are tempted to deplore the jumble of cash and in-kind programs that comprise the transfer "system" in the United States. By contrast, a single cash transfer program that would supplement the incomes of the poor based solely on need may seem much more efficient. Such reasoning has motivated radical welfare reform proposals over the years, including the negative income tax once favored by many economists as well as the various versions of a national guaranteed income.

What such plans fail to consider, however, is the complexity of human behavior in response to a simple plan and the intractable problems of trying to counter such behavior once it is encouraged. *Need* is not simply an unavoidable lack of income but also a consequence of voluntary decisions on work, marriage, and fertility. The extent of need, therefore, is not a fixed number but is susceptible to incentives. Although researchers differ in their estimates of the magnitude of the disincentive effects of transfers, even those who favor redistributive programs concede that such disincentives do have measurable effects.

There is some wisdom in the current system of providing aid on a categorical basis, roughly related to the extent to which disincentives would be regarded as a problem. Thus the elderly and disabled receive the most generous transfers, whereas able-bodied males and their families are eligible for few benefits (the main exceptions being unemployment insurance, food stamps, and veterans' benefits). Moreover, poverty among able-bodied males is low. In 1986 the poverty rate for married-couple families in which the head was under age 65 was 4 percent for whites and 8 percent for blacks. Further reductions in unemployment and productivity gains in the economy will continue to reduce poverty for these groups.

Welfare reform efforts at present focus on the AFDC program and single-parent families. This is an appropriate emphasis in view of both the large percentage of the poor in female-headed families (57 percent of poor children are in such families) and the criticisms of the program. Although positive proof on these subjects is lacking, many believe the program has fostered a life-style where people do not take responsibility for their own support or their children's. For example, women on the program are increasingly those with children born out of wedlock, corresponding to the surge in their share of all births. Among blacks 26 percent of all births were out of wedlock in 1965 and 60 percent in 1985. (Among whites these percentages were 4 percent in 1965 and 14.5 percent in 1985.) The birthrate has fallen sharply among both black and white teenagers, but the share of births to nonmarried girls soared to 90 percent for black teenagers and 45 percent for white teenagers in 1985. It is hard to imagine that parents would continue to be as permissive with their daughters and that the daughters would find such a life-style appealing if government aid and benefits were unavailable.

It is difficult if not impossible for the government to demand responsible behavior from recipients of welfare grants. However, a number of initiatives may help along these lines. One is greater vigilance in requiring fathers to contribute to the support of their children, including those born out of wedlock. Such efforts may have a significant long-run payoff if they encourage more responsible behavior among parents.

The AFDC program has itself become an anachronism as more and more women work. The idea that being on AFDC is an acceptable life-style is encouraged by the nearly unlimited duration allowed on the program (until the youngest child reaches age 18). Providing a time limit on the program for able-bodied women would convey the message that the program is intended to be temporary, like unemployment insurance, with the purpose of enabling women who find themselves in an emergency situation to find employment.

Any time the issue of welfare reform is raised, someone is bound to propose that benefits be made more generous, particularly in states with low benefits. Raising benefits would undoubtedly increase the welfare caseloads and reduce the work effort of women heading families. Moreover, it would be unlikely to reduce poverty in the long run. AFDC benefit levels have always been much lower in the South than in the North. Yet poverty rates among women heading families are actually lower in the South.[20] (Welfare receipt is lower in the South and work participation higher.) Similarly, frequent proposals suggest mandating the AFDC program for unemployed fathers in all states to prevent family breakups. Again, Southern states have not extended benefits to two-parent families where the father is unemployed. Yet the female headship rate is lower in the South than elsewhere.[21] Given the risks involved, making AFDC more generous is not a prudent course to follow.

Because of the large number of possible policy changes and the variation in circumstances among states, states should be allowed to experiment with policy changes. The Reagan administration has been active in endorsing this approach. Finally, we should not forget that preventive measures to build skills, such as improvements in basic education, may ultimately be the most fruitful way to reduce welfare dependency.

Notes

1. Cited in Gertrude Himmelfarb, *The Idea of Poverty: England in The Early Industrial Age* (New York: Alfred Knopf, 1984).

2. See ibid.

3. Cited in ibid., p. 151.

4. Charles Murray, *Losing Ground* (New York: Basic Books, 1984).

5. Mollie Orshansky, "How Poverty is Measured," *Monthly Labor Review* 92 (February 1969): 37.

6. Rose D. Friedman, *Poverty: Definition and Perspective* (Washington, D.C.: American Enterprise Institute, 1965).

7. Michael Harrington, *The Other America: Poverty in the United States* (New York: Penguin, 1964).

8. Gertrude E. Schroeder, who has made detailed studies of Soviet consumption patterns, estimates that per capita consumption in the USSR was 34 percent of U.S. consumption in 1975–1976, roughly the same ratio that the U.S. poverty threshold has to the U.S. average income. See Gertrude E. Schroeder, "Soviet Living Standards in Comparative Perspective," in Horst Herlemann, ed., *Quality of Life in the Soviet Union* (Boulder and London: Westview Press, 1987), table 3.1, p. 15. See also Mervyn Mathews, "Aspects of Poverty in the Soviet Union," in ibid.

9. Peter Townsend, *Poverty in the United Kingdom: A Survey of Household Resources and Standards of Living* (Berkeley and Los Angeles: University of California Press, 1979), p. 31.

10. Maurice MacDonald, "Evaluating Alternative Approaches to Measuring Basic Needs," in *Wisconsin Basic Needs Study: Final Report to the Social Security Administration* (University of Wisconsin–Madison, Institute for Research on Poverty, 1984, Mimeographed); summarized in *Focus* 8, no. 1 (Spring 1985).

11. Greg J. Duncan and Saul D. Hoffman, "Welfare Dynamics and the Nature of Need," *Cato Journal* 6, no. 1 (Spring–Summer 1986).

12. U.S. Bureau of the Census, *Estimates of Poverty Including the Value of Noncash Benefits, 1986*, Technical Paper 57 (Washington, D.C.: Government Printing Office, 1987), table 2.

13. As noted by the Census Bureau (see Technical Paper 57) a computer error was found in the measure of recipient value that leads to an underestimate in the number removed from poverty by this method. See also Barry R. Chiswick, "Evaluation of Census Bureau Procedures for the Measurement of Noncash Benefits and the Incidence of Poverty," in U.S. Bureau of the Census, *Proceedings of the Conference on the Measurement of Noncash Benefits* (Washington, D.C.: Government Printing Office, 1985), vol. 1.

14. The overstatement resulted from an improper use of the mortgage interest rate to measure changes in the price of housing. See John Weicher, *Mismeasuring*

Poverty and Progress (American Enterprise Institute, Washington, D.C., 1986, Mimeographed).

15. Among many studies tying the dramatic decline in the labor force participation of older men to the rise in Social Security benefits, see *Economic Report to the President* (Washington, D.C.: Government Printing Office, 1976), pp. 111–16; and Michael Boskin, "Social Security and Retirement Decisions," *Economic Inquiry* 15 (January 1977).

16. Note that benefits also rose relative to women's earnings during this period.

17. See Robert Moffitt, *Work and the U.S. Welfare System: A Review* (Paper prepared for the Heller Graduate School, Brandeis University, May 1987), p. 18. For evidence of the effect of AFDC benefits on welfare duration, see June E. O'Neill, Laurie J. Bassi, and Douglas A. Wolf, "The Duration of Welfare Spells," *Review of Economics and Statistics* 69, no. 2 (May 1987).

18. For a theoretical and empirical analysis of marital dissolution, see Gary S. Becker, Elisabeth M. Landes, and Robert T. Michael, "An Economic Analysis of Marital Instability," *Journal of Political Economy* 85, no. 6 (1977): 1141–85.

19. On the deficiencies of the various studies, see Saul D. Hoffman, *Marriage, Divorce, and Dependency: An Empirical Review* (Study prepared for U.S. Department of Health and Human Services, Hudson Institute, Alexandria, Va., 1987, Mimeographed).

20. June O'Neill, "Transfers and Poverty: Cause and/or Effect?" *Cato Journal* 6, no. 1 (1986): 72, 73.

21. See ibid.

EDWARD P. LAZEAR

◆ ——————————————————— ◆

The Labor Market and International Competitiveness

◆ In the dynamic U.S. economy, change is rapid and success comes only to those who can adapt quickly. Women have replaced older men as a source of labor, and part-time work has increased. The industrial mix has changed drastically since 1940, and even the last six years have witnessed significant industrial shifts. There is an increasing tendency for women to work at home, reversing the long-term trend toward centralized work. Unionization rates have declined dramatically, while unemployment rates have risen, especially for black teenagers. Business welfarism is on the rise, with increases in the proportion of pay that comes as health benefits and child care. The government has overseen an erosion of the doctrine of employment at will, made most concrete by legislation and court rulings on unfair dismissal.

This essay begins with a brief summary of labor market trends of the past decades. It then presents a few examples of counterproductive government policies and goes on to offer general and specific policy recommendations for the 1990s. The main point is that the government should be reluctant to take actions that diminish the economy's ability to adapt rapidly to change. Specifically government's role should be restricted to enforcing private contracts and, to a lesser extent, to providing information.

Recent Trends

A higher percentage of women are participating in the labor force, both overall (52 percent) and in almost every age group. As late as the 1970s, fewer women 25–34 years old held jobs than did younger and older women. In the late 1980s labor force participation during childbearing years shows no decline, and older women are working longer. Careers for women are longer because of their choice of occupations and educational levels. Many more women are professionals today, with salaries that match those of their male counterparts.[1] Gaps in promotion rates between males and females are likely to continue to narrow in the 1990s. More private firms are providing assistance in child care without the pressure of legislation.[2]

The increase in female workers has been somewhat offset by a decline in male participation rates. Younger males are studying longer and hence working less. Older men are retiring earlier, partly in response to Social Security and pension incentives.[3] More people, especially women, are working part-time.[4] Some of the increase derives from a shift toward industries where more part-time work is available. But even within given industries, part-time work has increased.

The composition of jobs in the United States has changed as well over time. Jobs have moved away from manufacturing and toward services. Government jobs have increased by almost 50 percent since 1940, accompanied by growth in the importance of finance, insurance, and real estate and a modest decline in trade. One of the more dramatic changes, the increase in the average unemployment rate, is not a specifically U.S. experience. In the United States, females have fared best and black teenagers worst in this regard—a problem that labor policy should address.

Unionization has declined significantly in the private sector and increased in the public sector in recent years. Part of the private-sector decline reflects changing employment patterns, with workers moving from heavily unionized industries to less-unionized ones. Overall unionization rates are not much more than half of what they were in 1950, having declined steadily in all industries except services, agriculture, and government, perhaps because of a shift of production from union to nonunion firms within each sector.

In industrial relations much attention has been paid to worker involvement in corporate decision making, best exemplified by the GM-Toyota NUUMI plant in Fremont, California. But there is little evidence that workers are sharing a larger part of the risk with stockholders. Norma Carlson reports that of 47 manufacturing industries, only 5 increased the proportion of workers who received some kind of incentive pay rather than straight-time rates.[5]

Employment at Will

In both Europe and the United States, government control of labor markets has generally increased. This trend marks an erosion of employment at will, the principle that the worker serves at the pleasure of the employer. Under this principle no valid reason need be given for dismissal. The job is not the property of the worker but is better thought of as owned by the firm, to do with as the owner sees fit. Employment at will characterized labor relations until the 1930s, when the National Labor Relations Act established rules that firms had to follow. Firms were required to negotiate in good faith and could not engage in unfair labor practices. The National Labor Relations Board (NLRB) was established to process complaints against firms. Although the NLRB's scope was limited, the power it was given marked a major break with the past.

The United States and Europe differ considerably in what is euphemistically called industrial democracy. Denmark, France, Germany, and the Netherlands have compulsory work councils in firms with over a small number (say, 50) of workers. Swedish law requires that at least two seats on each company's board of directors go to labor. A 1982 agreement provides for joint consultation even on day-to-day operations. By European standards, the governments of Belgium and the United Kingdom have kept out of issues involving labor's role in firm operations. In the United States, the major pressure for worker involvement comes through the National Labor Relations Act, which requires that firms bargain in good faith. But this requirement is much weaker than European practices.

In the United States, experience-rated unemployment insurance deviates from employment at will. Since employers are forced to pay into the unemployment pool when they lay workers off, the unemployment insurance system penalizes termination.[6] Some states, notably California and Minnesota, regulate an employer's ability to terminate a worker without cause. In California from 1979 to 1983, of 74 jury verdicts on unjust dismissal cases, 48 favored the employee.

Discrimination law is also a significant break with employment at will. Title VII of the Civil Rights Act of 1964, the Equal Pay Act, and the Age Discrimination in Employment Act all limit an employer's discretion over hiring, firing, and promotion. The importance of these limitations increases with demographic changes that move a larger proportion of workers into the protected categories. More women workers, the growing Hispanic population, and the aging work force all raise the number of protected individuals. Women, Hispanics, and males 40 and over, among others, are protected. The Employee Retirement and Income Security Act (ERISA) of

1974, a response to pension abuses by some firms and union pension plans, established requirements on the funding of pension plans and vesting rules.

The Effects of Government Action in the Labor Market

Examples of government action in labor markets are readily available. The minimum wage reduces employment, especially of youth.[7] Affirmative action policies, which act like minimum wage laws by raising the required payment to protected groups, may also adversely affect those the law intends to protect.

Many countries have adopted job security provisions, presumably to reduce turnover and unemployment. A job security rule penalizes an employer for laying off a worker in some cases, even with cause. These laws reduce the probability that an incumbent will be terminated but also reduce the likelihood that a new worker will be hired. In theory, the effect on unemployment is ambiguous. In practice, job security laws have had serious adverse effects on employment.

France, Italy, and Portugal have greatly increased severance pay to terminated workers. At the same time, unemployment rates have risen substantially. In countries with a small increase in unemployment, such as Switzerland, Norway, Greece, and Japan, there has been no increase in the amount of severance pay.[8] I estimate that if the United States required three months' severance pay, it would cost about 1.3 million jobs and raise the unemployment rate from 6.0 to 6.75 percent.

Severance pay requirements, which apply primarily to permanent full-time workers, turn full-time jobs into part-time ones. Employers can evade the law by hiring part-time temporary workers, generally not covered by the provisions. A shift from zero to three months of required severance pay would change about three million U.S. jobs from full-time to part-time.

Severance pay exacerbates the very problem it was intended to eliminate. But other cases of government involvement in labor markets have undesired effects less directly related to the original reason for the intervention. These cases may be more dangerous because they are more difficult to spot. Among the most important examples for the United States is the Social Security system, instituted to provide insurance for old age. How well the system has performed this function is debatable; more important are other, unintended, effects. The Federal Insurance Contributions Act (FICA) tax structure has implications for income distribution. The ceiling on taxable income adds a regressive element to the entire tax structure. Of course, the same is true in reverse for payments. Wealthy individuals receive higher benefits than lower-income individuals, but not in proportion to their wealth advantage. The pay-as-you-go structure of the system, however, means that payments and receipts are linked only in the roughest sense. Thus unintended redistribution results. Further, the Social Security earnings test discourages older workers. And the Pension Benefit Guarantee Corporation, which insures workers' pension benefits, creates incentives for firms to default on pension plans.

Protective legislation frequently penalizes the group it seeks to help. For example, the Coal Mine Health and Safety Act was meant to ensure that mines would be safe. In fact the act forced many small mines out of business, so that workers who were to be protected lost their jobs altogether.[9] Rather than dwell on what past policy has done to labor markets, let us turn to the future and the main theme of this essay.

The Government in a Dynamic Economy

To organize effectively, to ensure a mobile and responsive labor force, and to encourage rapid growth in labor productivity in a changing economy, public policy must work to promote rather than hinder the efficient functioning of labor markets. The government should limit its intervention into the labor market to those areas where it has an advantage—specifically, to enforcing private contracts and providing information.

Basically two kinds of rigidities can be created by law. The first is the rigidity of generality. Legislation, by definition, covers many economic agents and so must be general enough to apply to all.[10] Just as one-size-fits-all garments could be renamed one-size-fits-none-well, a general law fits few actual situations. The minimum wage is an example of a general law that fits no one situation well. Assume for the sake of argument that a minimum wage is desired. Suppose $4.25 per hour is the minimum. That number means different things in different places. For example, wages and prices are lower in the South and in rural areas. Thus a $4.25 minimum is a tighter constraint in the rural South than it is in the urban Northeast. It also affects some industries and occupations more than others. In particular, retailing and other industries where a large proportion work part-time are affected more directly. The minimum wage hits harder in a recession, when wages are low, than in an expansion, when wages are high. Of course, differences by region, industry, and time could be (and sometimes are) brought into the legislation. But such tailoring never results in a perfect fit.

The second kind of rigidity results not from the generality of the law but from the actual content of the legislation. Some laws prevent markets from adjusting smoothly—for example, laws that require employers to award severance pay. Layoffs are discouraged and new hiring made more costly. As a result, employment adjusts sluggishly to changing business conditions. Another example is the change in the Age Discrimination in Employment Act that makes it illegal to use mandatory retirement. Even if both worker and firm agree that both can be made better off by the inclusion of a mandatory retirement provision at, say, age 65, current law precludes the use of such provisions. Preventing an employer and a worker from entering freely into a labor contract in this context lowers productivity.[11]

The argument that the government should make it cheap to enforce private contracts not only makes common sense but is consistent with modern economic theory. Economists who advocate intervention into labor markets usually presume the failure of the competitive market to reach socially desirable outcomes. Failure occurs, by definition, when some trades that would make society better off do not occur. Government action to reduce enforcement and negotiation costs improves the chances that socially efficient trades take place. In the same vein, improving the information available to trading parties also helps trade.

A non–labor market example is provided by California real estate transactions. California house sales usually occur without either side employing lawyers. There are two reasons: First, realtors use so-called standard contracts. The word *standard* signifies that it has been used by the vast majority of buyers and sellers and conveys information about the reasonableness of the contract's terms. Second, the disputes are settled more quickly and cheaply by binding arbitration, a less costly courtlike procedure. There is no evidence that the outcomes are any worse in California, and real resources are saved on legal services. The institutions need not be governmental; the government should involve itself in these activities only if it has an absolute advantage. The coercive power of the state may provide the advantage in enforcement.

Some worry that labor is at a bargaining disadvantage when dealing with management. Labor must be protected because of the inherent asymmetry of loss that accompanies job termination. There are two answers to this argument. First, protective legislation, as will be shown below, generally protects some workers at the expense of others; management does not bear the full cost. Second, labor loses from termination only when the current employer is paying the worker more than he can obtain elsewhere. But then there must be something special about the current employment relationship, which means that the firm is as likely to lose from the termination as the worker. And labor is not always at a disadvantage in such circumstances. Consider a lawyer who knows a great deal about a law firm's most important client. The lawyer's decision to leave may cost the firm far more in future profit than it costs the lawyer in future wages.

In addition, there is a distinction between the government provision of information and government regulation. Many arguments for regulation are actually arguments for information. Consider safety regulations. The government does not prevent citizens from skydiving, rock climbing, hang gliding, or scuba diving, all of which have higher death rates than almost any work activity. There is no reason why the government should prevent workers from taking risky jobs as long as workers are aware of the danger. Rather than establishing absolute standards, the government should rate the risks, thus providing information rather than regulation.

The Labor Market of the 1990s

As documented above, the U.S. work force is moving away from the unions. Some consider this trend a problem, reflecting a transfer of power from labor to capital. Another interpretation is consistent with the data: unionization may make U.S. industries less competitive than their foreign counterparts. The decline in manufacturing in the United States reflects in part a change in consumption patterns, but it also reflects a substitution of foreign-produced durables for U.S. ones. Automobiles and electronics are obvious examples where foreign competition has made significant inroads. The U.S. industries that have gained ground have been the least unionized, whereas those that have lost ground are the most unionized. Manufacturing had about a 45 percent unionization rate during the 1970s, and services had about a 10 percent rate. The decline in employment in manufacturing since 1940 closely matches the growth of employment in services. Even within specific industries, nonunion firms or plants have generally grown more than union ones during the past decade. Unions may cause industries or firms to be less competitive if they raise the price of labor and force the use of less-than-ideal production technologies.

Unions cannot be held culpable without additional clarification. After all, Japan's manufacturing sector is heavily unionized. But the U.S. union movement has historically espoused business unionism. The goals and successes have been economic rather than political. U.S. unions, with their emphasis on wages, may affect costs more directly than foreign unions do. In Japan, where company unions are more common, they are more closely associated with industrial democracy than with direct wage demands. In Britain wildcat strikes and the push for higher wages and better working conditions appear to have harmed British competitiveness. In recent years some U.S. unions, notably the United Auto Workers, have renegotiated contracts when the survival of the employer was threatened. Others have de-certified the national union rather than stick with its tough negotiating policies.

If unions deserve some of the blame for the woes of U.S. manufacturing, why have unions created problems only recently? One possibility is that unions and change interact in a negative way. The unions' charge to represent incumbents makes unions inflexible. Featherbedding and other make-work arrangements are inefficiencies created by a union's desire to protect the existing work force. Business unionism exacts a higher price in the form of increased costs when an economy must respond rapidly to changing conditions.

There is a lesson in the rise and fall of U.S. unions. Government can mimic the operations of a union. Legislation that dictates wages, working conditions, and layoff penalties substitutes for a union. Care should be taken to avoid doing by fiat what the market is in the process of undoing. Much proposed labor legislation attempts to establish by national decree what labor unions have tried unsuccessfully to win through the bargaining process. Some examples follow.

1. Notice of plant closings.   H.R. 1122, a bill debated in the House in 1987, would require firms to give 60 days' advance notice of plant closings so that workers would have time to relocate. Although this law seems innocuous, it would reduce flexibility by penalizing firms that use layoffs to respond to changing market conditions. Many European countries have such laws. Their main effect is to induce firms to hire part-time and temporary workers, who are generally exempted from notice requirements.[12] Of course, nothing prevents firms from voluntarily including 60-day notice provisions in the employment contract. The law should be used to enforce these voluntary arrangements rather than mandating them for all firms. In some industries and occupations, where firm-specific human capital is minimal and workers can move easily from firm to firm, notice requirements would be socially detrimental. Imagine an extreme case of requiring 60 days' notice for migrant farm workers. Since the cost of employing those workers would be prohibitive, farms would alter their harvest techniques to get around the law.

2. Mandated leave with or without pay.   With more women in the labor force, pressure has been mounting for more generous leave policies, especially maternity (and sometimes paternity) leave, with or without pay. The costs of leave vary by industry and firm. In some industries a six-month absence is only a minor disruption; in others it can be devastating. Rather than requiring all firms to give leave, the government should allow employees to negotiate leave arrangements with employers. Women or men who would like to take time off to raise a child should be steered by market forces toward industries where time off imposes small costs on both employer and worker. A general law that forces all employers to provide for leave, like H.R. 925, hinders the market's direction of workers toward the firms for which they are best suited and makes firms less anxious to hire women of childbearing age.

The leave policy is worth more to some workers than to others. Single and older workers would rather receive the value of child care leave in some other form, such as longer vacations or better health benefits. If the government restricted its role to enforcing private labor contracts, workers could negotiate the kind of benefits they prefer. Firms that catered to workers' tastes would find hiring easier and could produce at lower cost.

3. Child care. With more women in the labor market, more firms are offering assistance in child care. This trend has led some to advocate state or federal laws requiring firms to provide such care. The suggestions take two forms. The most extreme would require that each firm above a minimum size provide on-site child care. Few favor this version, since it means that firms that are best at producing autos must also learn the baby-sitting business. The more reasonable alternative would require firms to pay some portion of their employees' child care expenses. Only those who have young children benefit, and the cost of employing them would increase. Child care, like leave, can be provided as a benefit choice, and it is likely that more firms will choose to offer it in the future as competition for young workers increases.

4. Labor market discrimination. The Civil Rights Act of 1964 makes it illegal to discriminate by race or sex in hiring, promotion, or wage determination. Supplemented by the Age Discrimination and Employment Act and the Equal Pay Act, this act forms the main body of discrimination law. The enforcement of the law depends largely on its interpretation by the executive branch. For example, some have argued that these laws imply the doctrine of comparable worth, which claims that different jobs of so-called equal value should be paid the same wages. Value is determined by external criteria, usually including some required skill level and work conditions. Courts have been unreceptive to discrimination suits based on comparable-worth arguments, usually because of inherent measurement problems. The better argument against comparable worth is that if wages are low in a female-dominated occupation, then women should exit that job and join a male-dominated one. As they do, wages in the female job will rise. Of course, women may be prevented from entering the male occupation. If so, the source of the problem is a barrier to entry into the male occupation, which is a clear violation of Title VII.[13] A restricted interpretation of that law to eliminate employment and promotion barriers is the best way to remove discrimination in the labor market without inducing additional distortions. This interpretation makes comparable-worth studies, such as the one proposed in H.R. 387, undesirable and unnecessary. If women's jobs are paid less, women should be free to enter those government jobs that pay more. Competitive pressures will then force the government to raise the wages of jobs for which they are unable to recruit. The sex ratios of jobs is then irrelevant.

    5. Benefits.   Senator Edward Kennedy has proposed that employers be required to provide health insurance to all employees who work at least 17.5 hours per week. The problem with mandated benefits is that those workers who derive less value from the particular benefit cannot trade it off, implicitly or explicitly, for other benefits or higher wages. In two-earner households, one member may receive family coverage from his employer that renders redundant additional coverage by the spouse's employer. The requirement also penalizes small firms that cannot obtain per-worker coverage as cheaply as large firms because of group benefit payment structures. Similar arguments apply to other mandated benefits, especially pensions. Here, however, laws like ERISA can be defended on the grounds that they reduce the worker's concern by reducing the cost of obtaining information on the solvency of private pension funds. This argument meets the information test for government intervention but fails on other scores. A better-designed ERISA could avoid some of the negative effects. For example, ERISA could be modified to replace funding and vesting requirements with requirements that information on plan solvency and vesting be provided to workers. This information would allow workers to trade off higher wages today against less-secure pensions in the future. Again, the government can provide information—the basis for favoring much labor regulation—without constraining the transacting parties.

    6. Minimum wages.   Many economists have argued against the minimum wage, so I will be brief. But since Congress is considering raising the hourly minimum from $3.35 to $4.65, a few points are relevant. First, the best evidence suggests that minimum-wage legislation increases the wages of low-wage workers who continue to work. Second, the continued pressure by organized labor to increase minimum wages, which affects no union workers directly (since their wages exceed the minimum), suggests that there are indirect effects on union workers' wages. Third, there is evidence that the employment of low-wage workers declines as a result of minimum wages. Finally, the adverse employment effects cannot be trivial because those groups most likely to be affected, such as young workers, frequently push to be exempted from the minimum wage.

If not eliminated, minimum-wage constraints should be amended to allow employers to pay below the minimum as long as the worker signs an acknowledgment that the wage is subminimum. A better solution would be to replace minimum wages altogether with a requirement that the employer report the average wage of production workers (supplied by the Bureau of Labor Statistics) at the time of hire. Then the government fulfills its information role without imposing the employment costs of the minimum wage.

7. Protection from displacement by international competition.   Some workers lose their jobs through no fault of their own. Temporary layoff due to poor business conditions is one example; another is permanent dismissal after a U.S. company has failed to compete successfully with a foreign one. One response has been a call for general trade protection so that the inefficient firms can survive. Another is special assistance and retraining for displaced workers. Though seemingly innocuous, such programs give firms and workers the wrong incentives. First, workers should be discouraged from entering declining industries and making investments in skills that are becoming less marketable. If workers are insured against adverse business conditions, they enter the wrong industries with impunity. Second, firms and workers are too anxious to call it quits when government assistance is available. The government should not, and for the most part does not, insure capital against international competition. There is no obvious reason why the government should provide such insurance to labor.

8. Work sharing.   A number of researchers have found that U.S. wages are more stable but employment more variable than in other countries, most notably Japan and the United Kingdom.[14] Thus when business is bad U.S. firms are more inclined than their foreign counterparts to lay off workers. Workers are kept during downturns either by reducing hours per worker or simply by labor hoarding. Other countries (Germany and Austria, recently) have taken steps to spread the work around in the hope of reducing unemployment, usually shortening the work week by legislating large overtime payments for time worked in excess of, say, 35 hours. This approach assumes that there is a fixed amount of work to be divided up. But imposing constraints on hours of work implicitly increases the price of labor and lowers the amount of labor demanded. These constraints not only reduce overall employment but also have adverse effects on costs and international competitiveness.

Profit sharing to smooth out employment during recessions has been endorsed by some governments. Nothing is wrong with profit sharing as part of a private contract, but the government should not push it. It has obvious disadvantages. Some risk is shifted from stockholders to workers, who may be in a worse position to bear short-run variations in their incomes. Profit sharing also distorts the employment decision. More is paid to workers during good times and less in bad times, but movements in compensation do not accurately reflect movements in productivity. Again the role of government should be restricted to ensuring that the parties comply with the terms of privately negotiated profit-sharing arrangements.

Positive Moves

Most government intervention in labor markets reduces competitiveness and distorts decisions. The government should be reluctant to take actions that diminish the economy's ability to respond to change. But there are some positive actions the government should take in the labor market:

1. Licensing.   The government should consider legislation that facilitates labor mobility. For example, states set up licensing for occupations ranging from physician to barber. Most economists interpret licensing as an attempt by members of a trade to capture monopoly profit. Because licensing limits labor mobility, eliminating it would be beneficial under most circumstances. Short of elimination, I favor an interpretation of the constitutional guarantee of free interstate commerce to include requirements that state licenses carry reciprocity. Then a barber licensed in Illinois could cut hair in California. (We can live with the fear that hairstyles may differ by region of the country.) It makes little sense to allow a doctor in Los Angeles to write a prescription that can be filled four hundred miles away in San Francisco but to prohibit one in Reno, Nevada, from prescribing drugs to a patient in nearby Truckee, California. Of course, reciprocity requires that states have the same standards or that they relinquish the right to regulate professionals within their jurisdictions. But this conflict is surmountable. For example, it might be resolved by having national exams but allowing states to set their own standards for passing grades. Reciprocity would mean that only those Nevada-licensed physicians who scored above the California minimum would be permitted to write prescriptions in California. This limitation preserves California's right to set standards but reduces constraints on mobility across state lines. The administrative burden of this variant would be no greater than that under current law. A Nevada physician would be authorized at the time his license was issued to practice in other states in which he met the standard. Those states could be notified when his Nevada license is issued.

2. The NLRB.   The NLRB should be modified to play two primary roles: arbitrator and fact finder for all workers. First, it should act as the arbitration board that decides all labor disputes (rather than only those covered by collective bargaining) over privately negotiated contracts. Second, it should act as a better business bureau of labor relations, reporting on the number of unfair labor practices found against each firm.

A third modification in NLRB procedures concerns collective bargaining. Unions are certified when a majority of workers in the bargaining unit vote in favor of the union. Decertification is rare (although becoming less so), since it requires that a grass-roots organization of workers launch an effective campaign against an organized, established group of coworkers. A union elected by a majority can impose high costs on a minority of workers by voting for strikes or negotiating changes that adversely affect, say, older workers with limited mobility. As a result, certification and continued representation should be made more difficult by requiring a two-thirds majority vote of the bargaining unit. Additionally minority interests should always be permitted to present their case to the NLRB when the union has violated a preexisting contract between the workers and the firm. The NLRB should have the power to redress such grievances.

3. Unionization in the public sector.   Since state and local governments have given public-sector unions more power to negotiate contracts and to strike, public-sector unionism has grown.[15] But the effects of higher wages for public employees do not show up in lower profits, so international competition cannot discipline the local government that awards too much to its workers. Taxpayers suffer nonetheless. States and localities should be extremely reluctant to award greater bargaining power to their unions, since other constituencies do not have an equal voice in labor negotiations with governments.[16]

Conclusion

The role for government in the labor market is to ensure smooth operation by enforcing private contracts and by providing information to uninformed parties in those circumstances where the government has an advantage in information provision. Most other government intervention into labor markets is detrimental and should be avoided.

Notes

1. Edward P. Lazear, "Male-Female Wage Differentials: Has the Government Had Any Effect?" in Cynthia B. Lloyd, Emily S. Andrews, and Curtis L. Gilroy, eds., *Women in the Labor Market* (New York: Columbia University Press, 1979).

2. See Renée Yablans Magid, *Child Care Initiatives for Working Parents: Why Employees Get Involved*, American Management Association (AMA) Survey Report Series (New York: AMA, 1983).

3. Nancy Brandon Tuma and Gary D. Sandefur, "Trends in the Labor Force Activity of the Elderly in the United States, 1940–1980," in Rita Ricardo-Campbell and Edward Lazear, eds., *Issues in Contemporary Retirement* (Stanford: Hoover Institution Press, forthcoming 1988).

4. An analysis of the data from the 1/100 sample of the U.S. census, 1940, 1950, 1960, and 1980, reveals the trend toward increasing part-time work.

5. See Norma W. Carlson, "Time Rates Tighten Their Grip on Manufacturing Industries," *Monthly Labor Review* 105, no. 5 (May 1982): 15–22.

6. A perfectly functioning labor market can undo the penalties imposed by the unemployment system just as side payments from renters to owners can counteract the effects of rent control. But few believe that such transactions are costless.

7. See, for example, Robert H. Meyer and David A. Wise, "The Effects of Minimum Wage on the Employment and Earnings of Youth," *Journal of Labor Economics* 1, no. 1 (January 1983): 66–100.

8. See Edward P. Lazear, *Job Security and Unemployment*, Working Paper in Economics, no. E-87-47 (Stanford: Hoover Institution, 1987).

9. See George R. Neumann and Jon P. Nelson, "Safety Regulation and Firm Size: Effects of the Coal Mine Health and Safety Act of 1969," *Journal of Law and Economics* 25, no. 2 (October 1982): 183–99.

10. Even the most detailed tax code is general when applied to individual cases. Whether the part-time pro's deduction for golf shirts is allowable as an employee business expense is only generally discussed by a very specific tax law.

11. See Edward P. Lazear, "Why Is There Mandatory Retirement?" *Journal of Political Economy* 87 (December 1979): 1261–64.

12. See Lazear, *Job Security and Unemployment*.

13. As Fischel and I have argued elsewhere; see Daniel R. Fischel and Edward P. Lazear, "Comparable Worth and Discrimination in Labor Markets," *University of Chicago Law Review* 53, no. 3 (Summer 1986): 891–952.

14. See Robert J. Gordon, "Why U.S. Wage and Employment Behavior Differs from That in Britain and Japan," *Economic Journal* 92 (March 1982): 13–44; and Linda A. Bell and Richard B. Freeman, *Does a Flexible Industry Wage Structure Increase Employment? The U.S. Experience*, NBER Working Paper no. 1604 (Cambridge, Mass.: National Bureau of Economic Research, 1985).

15. See Richard B. Freeman, "Contraction and Expansion: The Divergence of

Private Sector and Public Sector Unionism in the United States," *Journal of Economic Perspectives* (forthcoming 1988); and Melvin W. Reder, "The Rise and Fall of Unions: The Public Sector and the Private," ibid.

16. On the problems of interest group relations to a government body, see George J. Stigler, "The Theory of Economic Regulation," *Bell Journal of Economics and Management Science* 2 (Spring 1971): 3–21; and James M. Buchanan and Gordon Tullock, *The Calculus of Consent: Logical Foundations of Constitutional Democracy* (Ann Arbor: University of Michigan Press, 1962).

GERALD A. DORFMAN
PAUL R. HANNA

◆ ──────────────── ◆

Can Education
Be Reformed?

◆ Education has soared to near the top of the U.S. political agenda during the 1980s. With every candidate for president and political leaders from the national down to the local level lavishing attention on education, it will almost certainly be a major issue into the next decade.

Education has drawn so much attention in recent years because it is a central part of a wider discontent about the condition of our nation. We are dissatisfied with our educational system because we believe that it is not producing skilled, informed, and effective citizens for the future. The United States seems to us to be slipping, and education is a natural target when we ask why this has happened.

We are now about five years into the educational reform movement, and there is no shortage of proposals for change. Every state and the federal government, as well as a multitude of private foundations and corporate organizations, have sponsored intensive studies of our educational system. Each has offered comprehensive proposals, and government at every level has been pressing forward with a great deal of new spending and legislation.

What is going largely unattended in the midst of all this activity is the broad question of how we can make sure that all these recommendations, attention, and activity produce effective and lasting reform. This is no small problem in the United States. Much of our deep disappointment about the condition of our nation that causes the current interest in education is bound up in our unhappiness about the performance of our public policies.

The purpose of this essay is to broaden the debate about educational reform to include attention to the formidable difficulties that stand in the way of making effective change. If our next U.S. president is to deliver on his promises to give strong leadership in building educational excellence, then he will need to deal with this aspect of the problem as well.

Trouble in Our Schools: The Problem

As we look at our schools today, we are dismayed because at one time most local communities in this nation had good common schools. During the last three decades our educational system seems to have deteriorated. This malady has infected elementary and secondary schools as well as the institutions preparing schoolteachers.

The signs of educational difficulties are painfully obvious. Pupil test scores, both in absolute terms and comparatively between the United States and other developed nations, have declined significantly during the last several decades. Youth disaffection is shown in increasing drug and alcohol addiction as well as school vandalism by undisciplined youngsters. School attendance is down, and the dropout rate is up. In numerous ways society voices its dissatisfaction. The loss of support by disgruntled voters is lately expressed in a much higher failure rate for school bond issues. A small percentage of citizens even advocate that we abandon public education and turn the task of schooling over to the private sector.

Our Founding Fathers believed that our republic could not survive without education to prepare us for self-government. They avoided making the national government responsible for schools, since they assumed that parents would provide for the training of their own children. Parents generally accepted this responsibility and either taught their children themselves or joined with neighboring families in employing a schoolmaster to tutor youngsters in the rudiments of reading, writing, and arithmetic. Virtues and values were taught by the family elders or by the religious leaders in the local community.

As labor became more specialized and the family unit less able to spend time nurturing the minds of the young, teaching tasks were assumed by private schools and academies. The private academy became the accepted door through which one entered a profession or prepared for a leadership position in early America.

By the mid-nineteenth century some citizens recognized that the private schools and academies were too diverse, for no common curriculum assured the preservation and improvement of a national democratic society to hold our diverse subcultures together in support of common causes. Horace

Mann, the leading U.S. educator of the period, advocated a "common school" by which he hoped all children and youth would develop an understanding of and loyalty to the United States of America. Mann's persuasion resulted in the widespread support of public schools in local communities by labor unions, businessmen, and farmers. These common and public schools were to be supported by tax levies and universally attended by children who would be taught a common core of skills, concepts, and virtues.

The high expectations of Horace Mann and parents for the common public schools were realized increasingly for more than a century. Then came two world wars and much more rapid technological, social, and demographic changes. More and more the schools seemed inadequate to perform the new tasks.

The rate of this decline has accelerated over the last thirty years, mirroring the tumult that has ravaged and tested our political and economic institutions. The consecutive shocks of political assassinations, racial and ethnic conflict, the Vietnam War and its attendant social upheaval, Watergate and a multitude of political scandals, and the force of economic crisis have harshly affected the schools. As our society reeled from these successive shocks, it called on the schools repeatedly to shift priorities and meet new goals and objectives. These demands have, in turn, revealed and exacerbated some serious shortcomings in our educational system.

Trouble in Our Schools: Possible Solutions

The April 1983 report of the Gardner Commission appointed by Secretary of Education Terrel Bell and the subsequent issuance of a number of reports by state committees, private foundations, business organizations, and individuals during the following two years launched the reform movement in earnest.[1] The federal report *A Nation at Risk* has been most influential as an energizing force. The weight of the other reports together finally brought the discontent about the educational system into sharp relief.

Although the reports differ in a number of respects, a synthesis of their recommendations provides a good basis for significant changes if reforms can actually be implemented. The most valuable general recommendations follow.

> 1. Schools must do more to provide students with the necessary and relevant knowledge and skills to become productive citizens. They must place greater emphasis on science and math as well as the invaluable communication skills of speaking and writing. Moreover, the

school curriculum needs to be more conscious of the job market, the needs of industry, and especially the imperative that the United States be more competitive in the world marketplace.

This task is not simple. The United States is slipping in more than price competitiveness. We cannot return to a condition of dynamic growth by simply training students in skills that allow them to find more efficient ways to produce the same products other nations are manufacturing so successfully. The challenge is to train students to be literate in the new technologies so that they might create new kinds of production and therefore entirely new markets. Just to focus on a straightforward improvement in technical skills will leave us with little dynamism because our competitor nations are not standing still. They are working hard to train their young people to hold their newly won competitive edge and also to create new markets and better ways to serve them.

2. The teaching profession is in sad shape. The way teachers are selected and trained must change if schools are to perform better. The intellectual quality of the teaching profession is inadequate; teachers must have a higher status in society as well as better pay. This status can be accomplished by attracting brighter students into the profession and by making their training in undergraduate work more content-oriented. The best teachers need to be identified, rewarded, and used in leadership roles as models for the profession at large.

Teacher education colleges too often depend on gross enrollment figures for state financial support and consequently admit some applicants whose capabilities do not assure competence as future teachers. Once admitted, the promising and not-so-promising candidates eventually graduate and are certified without a careful examination of their knowledge of the subject matter they will teach. Teacher training has too long stressed the techniques of teaching over the substance of the material they will teach. This will become an even more destructive practice as our nation attempts to do a better job in training our young people to be dynamic and innovative thinkers able to meet the challenge of a competitive world. Our teachers must be up to the task of imparting highly complex knowledge and powerful new tools for effective analytical reasoning.

3. Schools must do more to educate for democratic citizenship. Although Americans have been and are increasingly a diverse people, with many religious, racial, and ethnic groups within our population, we do have a common political heritage. We are committed to liberty, justice, and equality as embodied in our Constitution and in the fabric and underpinnings of our political life. We must better educate our

young people in this commitment, in part by building allegiance to democracy in general as well as to our particular U.S. political institutions.

The history of this century soundly demonstrates the importance of this educational effort. Democracy does not exist widely or easily in this world. We obviously cannot take it for granted because we must constantly struggle with many authoritarian governments and ideologies. Therefore the teaching of civic education in the United States is as important to the future of the nation as the teaching of the skills that will make us economically competitive.

4. One aspect of the recommendations and action that is unlikely to be effective is the current move to have students spend more time in school, both during each day and over the school year. State legislatures have taken up this recommendation with particular zeal because it is easily susceptible to rapid implementation and review by law. By itself this measure is unlikely to produce much because more time spent in an unproductive school environment will not be beneficial. Rather, the challenge for better education is to create more effective teaching.

5. There is no doubt that discipline in the schools must be restored and maintained. This difficult problem contributes to lower achievement, higher truancy, and a serious increase in the dropout rate.

A main source of the problem and therefore the focus for improvement is the family. Many families neglect to rear their children with discipline, with socially acceptable behavior, with democratic values, and with incentives to study seriously to acquire knowledge and skills. The family must inculcate children with the spirit of responsibility for their own behavior and achievement. Until most families accept these parental duties, our educational system alone cannot effectively contribute to individual and social well-being. Our local and national leaders must vigorously stress the crucial and positive role families play in laying the foundations not only for the success of their children in school but for the survival of our society.

Winning Effective Reform

Taken together and effectively implemented, these recommendations for reform could produce the kinds of changes we are seeking. But how do we implement them? In this section we will point out some of the important obstacles the next U.S. president will confront when he constructs a much-needed strategy to implement educational reforms.

Changing national policy for any issue is obviously difficult. The nation is so large and pluralistic that every aspect of the process of change encounters serious setbacks. Even the most compelling reform enjoying the widest support faces formidable obstacles that erode and weaken its original purpose and detail.

Changing education is even more difficult than changing most other issue areas, especially when the educational system is a key focus of public attention. In the best and most normal of circumstances, educational policy is politically charged. Just about everyone feels personally involved with education, with an interest in its conduct and effectiveness. Even when education is not at the top of the national political agenda—as it is now—it is always near the top of the state and local agendas, where the costs and delivery of education are handled.

Education thus enjoys, as well as suffers from, continuous high-energy interest-group activity. Schools face competing demands that produce a nearly constant state of negotiations about the direction of education. Responsiveness, manipulation, and sometimes obstructionism are well known in the politics of education. Although they are part of the public's relationship with education, which is as old as our public schools themselves, they have become destructive in recent decades. The successive crises of the last thirty years—from the shock of Sputnik to the consequences of Vietnam and then the economic and political traumas of the 1970s—have spilled over into our schools in a number of ways, with consequences that have now raised additional obstacles to change.

We do not suggest that it is wrong for schools to adapt to society's contemporary contexts and goals. On the contrary, schools should respond to society's needs, especially in a democracy. But schools suffer when the society suffers, as both have in recent decades. Schools also suffer when our political system and our leaders lose credibility and legitimacy.

During each new societal crisis, we have demanded that our schools respond by reforming immediately. This pressure has caused considerable dislocation and confusion; hence each new wave of reforms has been ill planned and poorly implemented. The whole process has also been dispiriting. Society's demands that schools change have accompanied severe criticism of previous educational methods and policies—as if the next round of hastily formulated reforms would be panaceas. Thus reform has acquired a bad name.

Just as society has become cynical about change, so too have teachers and school administrators. When taking the lead for educational reform, the next president must recognize that increasingly defensive educators have begun to work against reform. Educators have learned a clever trick: they seem cooperative and even enthusiastic while working in many ways to trivialize or deflect reform. They have learned, in fact, how to mask their cynicism about change by making change an objective in itself. They try anything and everything, are enthusiastic about experimentation (and certainly about excellence), but take experimentation and change and refashion it in familiar styles—tailoring reforms to old ways in new clothes.

This familiar bureaucratic defensive maneuver occurs most often when the stress of innovation and change is most intense. In the case of teaching, one clear signal that this process is occurring has been the turning inward by teachers across the land toward a more militant concern with their pay and working conditions rather than with the substance of their professional work.

Outside the schools other signs suggest that the legacy of these past decades is inhibiting future change. Although we are clearly in a new era, in which reforming our educational system toward excellence can flourish, we have not left behind the high level of cynical participation of our citizenry in government. We still do not trust our leaders. This distrust encourages us to press our interest in and criticism of the schools much more forcefully than in earlier eras. Since nearly everyone cares about and/or pays for the schools, nearly everyone demands a say. Negotiating and implementing reform in this context is obviously a difficult and uncertain exercise. We run the risk that interest-group rivalry will produce policies targeting the lowest common denominator or no change at all. If reform is achieved at one moment, it is likely to come under vigorous attack at the next.

Conclusion

These pessimistic observations do not suggest that the next national administration faces a hopeless challenge, nor do they point the way toward the adoption of some form of voucher system. Obviously it is tempting to react to these obstacles by taking government out of the equation and letting the public, through the free market, make decisions on the future of education by their actions.

But public schools are the prime instruments for providing our citizens with the common concepts, values, and skills essential for the survival and progress of our democratic society. Only government (local, state, and national) can provide the leadership to assure society that there will be community-held beliefs and the competence to hold a diverse society together. The free-market system is the preferred way to satisfy most human needs. But turning schooling primarily over to the private sector for profit would result in such a diversity of curriculum policy and pattern that the concept of a common loyalty to democratic society would be improbable, if not impossible. To us the voucher system would bring such confusion and rivalry in the content of schooling that it would sacrifice the fundamental purpose of education as set forth by Horace Mann.

Rather than abandoning our public school system, we should improve the policy process that has served us so poorly during these last decades. Our political leaders, and especially our next president, must begin to pay creative attention to the problems of leading effective change in education. It is no longer enough for leaders to talk about new initiatives in policy simply to appeal for voter support. We now have a full plate of good ideas for reform that need to be implemented despite the obstacles mentioned above. The next president can make a great difference in the progress toward educational excellence. But he is going to need to rebuild confidence both within the communities in this nation and within the educational profession so that the new path will be carefully and effectively developed over a long period of time—and so that the participants in the process will have a stake in its success rather than in its destruction.

Note

1. National Commission on Excellence in Education, *A Nation at Risk: The Imperative for Educational Reform* (Washington, D.C.: Government Printing Office, 1983); Ernest L. Boyer, *High School: A Report on Secondary Education in America* (New York: Harper & Row, 1983); College Board Educational Equality Project, *Academic Preparation for College: What Students Need to Know and Be Able to Do* (New York: College Board, 1983); Commission on International Education, *What We Don't Know Can Hurt Us: The Shortfall in International Competence* (Washington, D.C.: American Council on Education, 1983); Education Commission of the States Task Force on Education for Growth, *Action for Excellence* (Denver: Education Commission of the States, 1983); John I. Goodlad, *A Place Called School: Prospects for the Future* (New York: McGraw-Hill, 1983); National Science Foundation, *Educating Americans for the 21st Century: A Plan of Action for Improving Mathematics, Science and Technology Education for All American Elementary and Secondary Students So That Their Achievement Is the Best in the World by 1995* (Washington, D.C.: National Science Foundation, 1983); Twentieth Century Fund, *Making the Grade: Report of the Twentieth Century Fund Task Force on Federal Elementary and Secondary Education Policy* (New York: Twentieth Century Fund, 1983); U.S. Department of Education, *Meeting the Challenge: Recent Efforts to Improve Education Across the Nation* (Washington, D.C.: U.S. Department of Education, 1983); U.S. Department of Education, *The Nation Responds: Recent Efforts to Improve Education* (Washington, D.C.: U.S. Department of Education, 1984).

ANNELISE ANDERSON

◆————————————————————◆

Immigration Policy

◆ The Immigration Reform and Control Act of 1986 is the most important immigration legislation enacted since 1965. Unlike earlier immigration legislation that wrestled with how many and whom to admit legally, the 1986 act sought to limit illegal immigration. Proponents of the legislation claimed that we had lost control of our borders; the number of undocumented border-crossers was a flood, a rising tide, a startling surge. "The first duty of a sovereign nation," said Senator Alan Simpson, "is to control its borders."[1] This was a reminder, perhaps, of Adam Smith's statement in *The Wealth of Nations*, first published in 1776, that the sovereign's first duty is that of "protecting the society from the violence and invasion of other independent societies."[2]

Adam Smith was not, of course, talking about people crossing a border looking for work; but Alan Simpson was. The solution of choice was to make it harder for undocumented workers to find jobs, specifically by establishing penalties—fines and ultimately prison sentences—for employers who hired anyone not eligible to work in the United States. The law lists documents that employers can check to verify identity and citizenship or immigration status to determine whether individuals are deemed eligible by the government to work. The law has the effect of encouraging employers to comply by discriminating against those who look or sound foreign; it tries to counteract this effect by forbidding discrimination on the grounds of alienage. To avoid deporting people who entered illegally, have been here for some time and may own houses, have children who are U.S. citizens, and are important in the U.S. labor force, a general amnesty—an opportunity to legalize one's status—was also made part of the law, as was a more specific amnesty for agricultural workers to address the need for an adequate labor force for agriculture. In addition, the law provides for a review of worker identification provisions and the establishment, if necessary, of a more secure system of identification.

Obviously more is at stake in immigration policy than numbers and national origin. Because immigration policy is an enormously complex issue, it will be helpful if we first consider the standards by which it might be judged and then look at some facts that must be considered in its formulation.

There are three basic values or objectives by which we can judge any immigration policy. These are peace, prosperity, and liberty. Immigration policy should be consistent with, and even contribute to, the national defense and foreign policy objectives of the United States. Prosperity is the economic issue, the search for an immigration policy that contributes to economic growth, jobs, and competitiveness. The third issue, usually given less attention than the others, is the issue of liberty, the extent to which the policy contributes to, or threatens, the rights of individuals with respect to the powers of government.

The Facts

A number of facts on which observers generally agree should be taken into account in evaluating any immigration policy. The potential list is endless, but here are some major and salient points:

1. The United States shares a border with a large and growing Third World country, Mexico. In this regard it is unique among major countries in the free world. The population of Mexico was 80.5 million in 1986, with a doubling time of 28 years.

2. The U.S. population was 241 million in 1986. It is increasing, but the birth rate is below replacement, as is that of Canada, Japan, and Western Europe.

3. Legal immigration to the United States has increased in the last several decades and become increasingly Asian and Hispanic. From 1951 to 1960, 2.5 million people were admitted, 28 percent Asian and Hispanic; 3.3 million were admitted in the next decade, 48 percent Asian and Hispanic; and an estimated 5.7 million immigrants will be admitted in the years 1981–1990, of whom over 75 percent will be

Asian and Hispanic. Between 1970 and 1980, the percentage of the population that was foreign-born (half of whom are citizens) increased from 4.8 percent to 6.2 percent but was still half of what it was in 1910.[3]

4. Markets are becoming increasingly international, and it is this international marketplace in which the United States needs to compete successfully.

5. The estimated number of illegal immigrants in the United States as temporary workers, cyclical workers, or permanent immigrants is far lower than many of the guesses presented to the public during debates on the legislation, and these estimates are sounder than is commonly believed. Estimates based on the 1980 census place the undocumented resident population at 2.5–3.5 million persons; this number may be increasing at 100,000–300,000 per year (though perhaps not at all in some years). Temporary workers are not included in these estimates.[4] These numbers are lower than many higher, speculative estimates, which experts have found to have no basis in any available data.[5]

6. As of 1983 eleven states (California, Connecticut, Delaware, Florida, Kansas, Maine, Massachusetts, Montana, New Hampshire, Vermont, and Virginia) and Las Vegas had employer sanctions legislation on their books but had chosen not to enforce these laws. The Illinois and New Jersey legislatures had considered and rejected such legislation.[6]

With these facts in hand, we can proceed to consider the objectives that should be considered in immigration policy.

Peace

The United States shares the North American continent with Canada and Mexico. It is obviously in our long-run interest to have good relations with Mexico as well as Canada, close enough that Mexico will always see its interests allied with those of the United States. The history of our border patrol efforts makes it clear that we are unwilling to police this border with lethal means, and the country is there and growing. It is in our interest that the Mexican government be in action if not in rhetoric pro-Western and therefore that our policies support economic growth and democracy there. Analysts are less confident of Mexico's political stability than they were before its economic problems became apparent in August 1982.[7]

Canada, the United States, and Mexico—the North American continent—should be sufficiently cohesive in their interests to be economic and political allies. The way to achieve this cohesion is through negotiation leading eventually to free trade, the free movement of capital, and free access to labor markets in all directions—in the words President Reagan used in his 1988 State of the Union message, "a North American Accord." The United States took a step in this direction with the October 1987 trade agreement with Canada and a more tentative step in November 1987 with the framework agreement with Mexico.

Prosperity

Prosperity, the economic issue, raises the question whether immigration, legal and illegal, contributes to U.S. economic growth and competitiveness. The answer of economists on this issue is a near unanimous yes. No one tries to estimate the optimum number of immigrants, but most studies demonstrate, in one way or another, increases in output and increases in average income for all income groups. Immigration contributes to the well-being of native Americans as well as the immigrants themselves, because often immigrant labor increases rather than reduces native employment; studies show a minimal effect on the earnings of native workers resulting from an increase in immigration. Immigrants do, however, compete with those who are most like them, generally other immigrants. Thus for some people wages may be lower—at least temporarily—than they would be otherwise.[8]

One of the recent good studies is that of the Rand Corporation on the effects of Mexican immigration on California. It found that Mexican immigrants have stimulated total employment, increased economic competitiveness, lowered some prices to consumers, and had a minimal effect on labor markets, possibly somewhat lowering wages for native-born Hispanic workers. (Hispanics were not found to have been competing directly in labor markets with either whites or blacks.)[9] Another study, based on a unique data file on illegal immigrants, concludes that "the illegal alien labor market appears to be well-functioning; that is, it is competitive, fluid, and flexible, and provides opportunities for economic advancement and job mobility even for low-skilled foreign-born workers in this country illegally."[10]

Immigration policy is affected by special-interest groups, one of which is of course labor. The AFL-CIO has long supported more restrictive immigration, perhaps because it would at some point protect the earnings of its members from competition from immigrant labor, or perhaps because amnesty, an adjunct to employer sanctions, might provide a larger pool of potential recruits. Given protectionist pressures, it is likely that the number of immigrants admitted through the political process is less than the number that would be desirable from the overall perspective of economic growth and competitiveness. Indeed, the members of the 1978–1981 Select Commission on Immigration and Refugee Policy supported the idea of closing the back door—illegal immigration—while opening the front door and increasing the number of immigrants admitted legally. Although the Immigration Reform and Control Act of 1986 attempted to achieve the first of these purposes, the second was dropped; restriction was its purpose.[11]

The other part of the economic question is the demands immigrants— and their children—place on government services. The outcome of the studies in this area is that immigrants receive less in social services, except for the cost of educating their children, than they pay in taxes. This is the case both for temporary workers, who stay away from social service agencies, and for permanent legal immigrants, who are eligible for social services and make greater use of them but also pay more taxes.

The cost of educating the children of immigrants, who are usually U.S. citizens, is, on the whole, an additional cost not covered by taxes paid. The Rand Corporation's study notes especially the concentration of California's Hispanic immigrants in Southern California and thus the burden of the children of immigrants on specific communities.[12] This burden should perhaps be shared by taxpayers nationwide or at least statewide, which in fact it is in California. Of course, this sort of burden is also being shared on behalf of other groups.

Finally, demographers are concerned about population decline in the industrialized democracies, given birthrates below replacement. In the United States, at current levels of immigration, the number of people in the labor force in relation to the number of retired persons will decline, the population will age, and payroll taxes or general revenue taxes on those employed will need to increase to fund retirement and health programs for the elderly. Immigration is an alternative to bribing people to have more children with favorable tax rates, child allowances, and the like. The West and East European evidence is that such bribes need to be quite large to have any effect, and of course the cost of educating the children must be paid in any case.[13]

Liberty

Liberty is the third overarching policy concern and refers, as I use the term, to rights held by the people that cannot or should not be infringed by the government. It includes due process of law and equal protection under the law and therefore encompasses equal opportunity.

In this regard we should question whether placing employers in the position of determining whether people in the United States are or are not permitted by the government to work is desirable. To provide evidence of a good-faith effort to comply with the law, employers must ask for documents proving identity and citizenship (or legal resident alien status) and must do so for all those who might be hired in order not to be charged with discrimination on the basis of citizenship or noncitizenship. In fact there are a great many different kinds of documents that might be offered—50 state driver's licenses, green cards for legal resident aliens, foreign passports stamped with temporary work permits, and so forth. In large businesses with transient labor forces—such as hotels and motels, construction, and restaurants—the screening process is continual, and the expenses are considerable. To reduce costs, such employers may come to support a simpler system: a single national means of identification—one card for each person with a unique identifying number that can be fed into a computer that will respond with an answer, permitted to work or not permitted to work.

In supporting the 1986 act, both the Reagan administration and many members of Congress opposed the concept of a national identity card. Under the law the president is, however, required to monitor the so-called employment verification system and implement (with Congressional approval) such changes as may be necessary. A new system, if proposed, "must be capable of reliably determining whether a person with the identity claimed . . . is eligible to work, and . . . is claiming the identity of another individual . . . If the new system requires that a document be presented to or examined by an employer, the document must be in a form which is resistant to counterfeiting and tampering." [14]

Penalties for employers who knowingly hire illegal aliens are intended to make it impossible to work in the United States without government-approved identification demonstrating the right to work. They thus make it much more difficult for any person to avoid the control of the authorities. In other countries—such as West Germany—individuals also require residence permits to rent housing, thus giving the government further means of keeping track of people. The development of a more reliable system of identification than currently exists, with the support of major employers, is a definite possibility. It is, of course, likely that such a system would come to be used for purposes other than employment—to deal with terrorism, gun control, civil disturbance, tax evasion, draft evasion, failure to pay child support, voter fraud, welfare fraud, spies, communicable diseases, and multiple drug prescriptions. There is, then, a major threat to liberty in employer sanctions legislation.

Finally, liberty encompasses the desire to maintain, in its broad outlines, our existing political-economic culture. Available studies support the idea that new immigrants, including Hispanics, are adapting to U.S. society and progressing economically and in their acquisition of the English language just as other groups have done at other times.[15] The United States is, by its historical origins and current political institutions, the world's specialist at developing citizens. Except for American Indians, all of us are Americans by virtue of relatively recent immigration, either our own or that of our ancestors. Also, our current political party system is unusual among advanced industrialized democracies in holding widespread contested primary elections and in the openness of these primaries. Legal immigrants can start taking part in this process as soon as they become citizens, and the major parties have incentives to recruit them as members. In the event we are dissatisfied with the knowledge of the English language or of U.S. economic and political institutions that our new citizens possess, we can of course increase the requirements for citizenship.

Is the New System Better than the Old?

Are employer sanctions working? More broadly, is the 1986 legislative package as a whole—employer sanctions, the identification of eligible workers, and the amnesty for those who came here illegally before January 1, 1982—working? The question implies that it will be good if it works. Unfortunately it may be bad if it works and bad if it doesn't. Although the law is too recent to judge its effects quantitatively, here are the observations it is possible to make at this point:

1. Many employers of large casual labor forces—such as operators of hotel and motel chains and restaurants—are attempting to comply with the law. They are training employees to screen applicants for eligibility to work and setting up record-keeping systems, tasks a good deal more complicated, given the wide variety of acceptable documents and the risk of liability for discriminating against someone eligible to work, than originally expected. The judgment of some experts in immigration law who are counseling corporations attempting to comply is that in the interest of both compliance and cost control, employers are likely to become a major constituency for a simplified means of identification, such as a national identity card.

2. There is some evidence that foreigners with work permits are finding difficulty in the labor market that they had not encountered before—simply, an unwillingness to hire that is apparently the consequence of employers' concerns about staying on the right side of the law. (Having the right to appeal on grounds of discrimination, which the law provides, is not a substitute for simple nondiscrimination.)

3. Public officials are already saying what Europeans have long

said: employer sanctions are not working but will work if the penalties are increased and greater efforts are made to enforce the law (including efforts to control the increased use of fraudulent documents). This conclusion is consistent with the experience of other countries that employer sanctions are ineffective in the absence of a homogeneous population and rigorous identification schemes.[16] Dual labor markets could develop, one comprising employers who are determined to comply, the other comprising employers willing to overlook the law. If those who overlook have lower costs than those who comply, it will become difficult for those who comply to compete.

4. The amnesty is proving more complicated and attracting fewer people than expected. It will, of course, increase the cost of social services, which was one of the complaints about immigration, legal and illegal, to begin with.

5. If employer sanctions are effective, labor costs are likely to increase, and there is some anecdotal evidence that this is occurring. The cost of goods and services to the U.S. public is also likely to increase. Exporters will find themselves less competitive. Mexico will have lost its flexible access to U.S. labor markets. In some industries (such as the garment industry in Los Angeles) employers are experiencing labor shortages and turning down contracts.

An Ideal System?

The problem of immigration puts us in a messy world: there may be no set of policies that meets all the objectives or embodies all the values we would like to achieve.

In pursuit of peace, our immigration policy should favor the economic integration of the North American continent and can justifiably treat Mexico and Canada differently from other countries. Employer sanctions—to the extent they are effective—increase Mexico's economic problems, and providing Mexican citizens greater access to our labor markets may be something we can negotiate for more open movement of capital. It is also in the interests of peace that the industrialized democracies establish immigration policies that will maintain their populations and avoid the stresses of too large a proportion of the elderly relative to the working-age population.

In the pursuit of economic growth and competitiveness, more immigrants, probably closer to 800,000 people a year rather than 400,000 (after deducting annual emigration of about 160,000 a year), are desirable, especially if we are to prevent a population decline in the next century.[17] The prevention of illegal immigration across our southern border, if successful, leaves this decision in the political realm, where it is more subject to special-interest forces and less responsive to the economics of the marketplace. Moreover, legal immigrants acquire rights to public benefits that illegal immigrants, usually men arriving without dependents, do not acquire.

In the pursuit and protection of liberty, employer sanctions should be repealed. This peculiar approach to limiting immigration—by making it impossible to get a job without proper documentation—arose during the years when the U.S. baby boomers were entering the labor market and increased Asian and Hispanic immigration, primarily legal, made us more aware of foreigners among us. Politicians claimed that we had lost control of our borders, and the press took up the cry. But employer sanctions do not control the border; they threaten, instead, control of the U.S. population.

Notes

1. Christopher Simpson, "Flood of Illegal Aliens Threatens Immigration System, Simpson Says," *Washington Times*, September 12, 1985. Anti-immigration rhetoric has been typical of the U.S. media, as Rita Simon shows in *Public Opinion and the Immigrant: Print Media Coverage, 1880–1979* (Lexington, Mass.: D. C. Heath, Lexington Books, 1985).

2. Adam Smith, *The Wealth of Nations* (New York: Random House, 1937), p. 651.

3. Annelise Anderson, *Illegal Aliens and Employer Sanctions: Solving the Wrong Problem*, Essays in Public Policy (Stanford: Hoover Institution, 1986), pp. 9–11, 14.

4. *Economic Report of the President, 1986* (Washington, D.C.: Government Printing Office, 1986), pp. 217–19.

5. Donald B. Levine, Kenneth Hill, and Robert Warren, eds., *Immigration Statistics: A Story of Neglect* (Washington, D.C.: National Academy Press, 1985), pp. 226, 235–38.

6. Carl D. Schwarz, "Employer Sanctions Laws: The State Experience as Compared with Federal Proposals," in Wayne A. Cornelius and Ricardo Anzaldua Montoya, eds., *America's New Immigration Law: Origins, Rationales, and Potential Consequences*, Monograph Series 11 (San Diego: Center for U.S.-Mexican Studies, University of California, San Diego, 1983), pp. 83–85, 96.

7. Brian Latell, *Mexico at the Crossroads: The Many Crises of the Political System*, Essays in Public Policy (Stanford: Hoover Institution, 1986).

8. For a summary of some of the evidence and an excellent discussion of the issues, see Pastora San Juan Cafferty et al., *The Dilemma of American Immigration: Beyond the Golden Door* (New Brunswick, N.J.: Transaction Books, 1983); and George J. Borjas and Marta Tienda, "The Economic Consequences of Immigration," *Science* 235 (February 6, 1987): 645–51.

9. Kevin F. McCarthy and R. Burciaga Valdez, *Current and Future Effects of Mexican Immigration in California* (Santa Monica: Rand Corporation, 1986), p. 53.

10. Barry R. Chiswick, "Illegal Aliens: A Preliminary Report on an Employee-Employer Survey," *American Economic Review* 72, no. 6 (May 1986): 257.

11. Public Law 99-603, 99th Congress, November 6, 1986, 100 STAT. 3359. Legislation moving through Congress in 1988 was, however, directed toward increasing somewhat the number of immigrants and providing for increased entry on the basis of education, skills, and proficiency in English.

12. McCarthy and Valdez, *Mexican Immigration*, p. 52.

13. See Kingsley Davis, Mikhail S. Bernstam, and Rita Ricardo-Campbell, eds., *Below-Replacement Fertility in Industrial Societies: Causes, Consequences, Policies* (New York: Cambridge University Press, 1986); and Ben J. Wattenberg, *The Birth Dearth* (New York: Pharos Books, 1987).

14. PL 99–603, Sec. 101 (d).

15. McCarthy and Valdez, *Mexican Immigration*, p. 66.

16. *Illegal Aliens: Information on Selected Countries' Employment Prohibition Laws*, GAO/GGD-86-17BR (Washington, D.C.: U.S. General Accounting Office, 1985).

17. For one estimate, see Wattenberg, *Birth Dearth*, pp. 25–26.

SEYMOUR MARTIN LIPSET

◆ ━━━━━━━━━━━━━━━━━━━━━━━━━━━━━━━━━━ ◆

Vote for the Other Guy

The Counterintuitive Character of Recent U.S. Politics

◆ Winston Churchill once noted, "Democracy is the worst form of govern-ment except for all those other forms that have been tried."[1] This fre-quently quoted statement is usually cited as an amusing reference to failings of autocratic regimes. But the first part of the statement, Churchill's con-clusion that democracy itself has major failings, is at least as important as the second.

The larger problem of democracy as a decision-making system is ex-emplified by Robert K. Merton's emphasis on "the unanticipated conse-quences of purposive social action."[2] This aphorism may be illustrated most strikingly by reference both to outcomes of major efforts to transfer power, such as revolutions, and to the postelectoral effects of regime changes in democracies.

Apart from the American one, most revolutions rarely establish the kind of government or society their ideological program calls for. Mao Zedong noted with sadness how little impact the revolution he led had on the basic traits of Chinese society.[3] Many made in the name of democracy or equality resulted in autocratic and severely inegalitarian social and po-litical systems. This is true not just of communist or Third World revolu-tions. The classic first democratic revolution, the French, is the epitome of this phenomenon. Robespierre, the subsequent leader of the Terror, pro-

I am grateful to Nicholas Orum and Janet Shaw for research and editorial assistance.

posed that the death penalty be abolished in 1789. During the height of the Terror in 1793–1794, well over one hundred thousand were killed.[4] As Eugen Weber notes, "Terror once past, its spies and policemen survived, its totalitarian aspirations continued to rise like vomit in French throats."[5] The revolution led to Napoleon and the eventual loss of two million lives.

Unanticipated consequences may also describe the results of more moderate efforts to reform stable democratic societies, such as those designed to aid the poor, to balance national budgets, or to create a more democratic polity—that is, those in which the citizenry has more direct control over government policies. But as Daniel Patrick Moynihan has noted, "much is counterintuitive in our politics."[6]

Counterintuitive Outcomes

The best examples of counterintuitive politics in modern U.S. history are the contrasts between the rhetoric of Franklin Roosevelt's campaign in 1932 and the subsequent New Deal, and between Richard Nixon's preelection image as a strong conservative and his liberal domestic and détente foreign policies. As a candidate Roosevelt followed Democratic tradition in attacking Herbert Hoover for deficit spending and enlarging the scope of government, but once in office he did the opposite. Nixon's counterintuitive dealings with China and the Soviet Union are well known. As striking are his domestic policies: wage and price control, a family assistance plan, the Occupational Safety and Health and Environmental Protection agencies, extension of unemployment insurance from 26 to 65 weeks, the Supplemental Security Income program, liberalization of the food stamp program, strict enforcement of school desegregation, affirmative action quotas, and more than tenfold increases in funding for intellectuals in the budgets for the endowments for the arts and humanities.

The Reagan record has been cited as one that followed campaign policies more consistently than other postwar administrations. But as the efforts to reach arms control agreements with the Soviets in the president's last two years in office indicate, he too can act counterintuitively. Equally noteworthy are the effects of his policies on the national budget. As Martin Tolchin emphasizes:

> Long committed to balanced budgets and fiscal integrity, Mr. Reagan has overseen the creation of more new debt than the combined deficits of all previous Presidents. He assailed Jimmy Carter's $73.8 billion deficit in the 1980 campaign, but the deficit reached $220.7 billion in 1986 . . . While Mr. Reagan was committed to reducing the size and scope of the Federal

Government, the Federal civilian work force increased during his Presidency by 150,000 growing to more than 3 million.[7]

Two articles in the *National Review* by Evans and Buckley pointed out that Reagan's practice with respect to budget policies for defense as well as domestic spending "is much closer to the Carter trend than to goals repeatedly affirmed by Reagan."[8]

Welfare reform, which remains on the agenda of both major political parties, is a continuing example of the inability of politicians to control results. Administrations from the 1930s through the 1970s tried to improve the situation of the poorest sector of the population by increasing expenditures, transfer payments, for them. There is much debate over the consequences, but the most noteworthy is that poverty, while declining overall, has increased greatly among children. Poverty rates are twice as high among preschool children (22 percent of the group) as among adults over age 65 (12 percent) and those 22–64 (10 percent).[9] The growing number of children living below the poverty line is linked to the increase in families headed by single mothers. Such families are eligible for federal assistance through Aid to Families with Dependent Children. Critics allege that this extensive program of government financial assistance has played a major role in encouraging the growth of illegitimacy in the population, since it assures mothers of support.

Counterintuitive outcomes occur on the level of public opinion as well as policy. Shortly before taking office in 1981, Reagan expressed concern about the "steady decline in public confidence in business" in the opinion polls, which he blamed on the growth of an "adversary relationship between the federal government and business" stimulated by his predecessor in the White House.[10] Ironically the improvement in the economy, reduced inflation, and lower unemployment during his administration greatly increased faith in public institutions, as reported in the polls, but did little to reduce the high level of distrust in major nongovernmental organizations, including business. In effect, the president served as a public relations man for government, demonstrating, like Franklin D. Roosevelt before him, that Americans respond well to a sense of leadership. A major unintended consequence of Reagan's presidency prior to the Iran arms scandal was that he managed to restore the public's faith in government as an agent of change. But no one was saying that business was doing especially well, and there was no Reagan-like figure to stimulate faith in the private sector.[11]

Although most Americans liked Ronald Reagan and gained confidence in government as a result, they did not moderate their suspicion of private power or accept the president's views on most issues. Senator Paul Laxalt, a close friend of the president and general chairman of the Republican National Committee, called attention to "the strange phenomenon" in the opinion polls that most Americans approved of Ronald Reagan but opposed much of what he supports: "People have deep differences with his policies. But they still have trust in him." [12]

Democratic Reform

The changes in U.S. politics during and since the 1960s provide case studies of the ways social action can accomplish some goals while producing circumstances quite different from those intended by the principal actors. The rise of single-issue mass movements during the 1960s, beginning with the civil rights struggle, which broadened into mass efforts to secure equal rights for minorities and women, proved to be part of a major drive to further democratize the United States. This drive was accompanied by measures to make the electoral process more responsive to the will of a participatory electorate.

These movements accomplished important changes in harmony with their objectives. The civil rights struggle opened doors for blacks in employment, education, and public life. It changed the voting patterns in the South so that blacks, who had largely been disenfranchised in many Southern states, obtained the ballot and have since had considerable impact on elections. The feminist movement has secured increased rights for women, particularly middle-class women, both in the economy and in social relations.

But apart from the increase in black voting, efforts to democratize the polity and increase participation and mass control of the political process must be included in the record of counterintuitive politics. Progressive, liberal, or left political forces in the United States have long sought to reduce the influence of established groups, party bosses, corporations, and the wealthy. They have been particularly successful in weakening the power of party leaders and organizations. Earlier changes included replacing patronage with merit civil service examinations as the main vehicle for job placement in government service and establishing tenure in government employment for all except a small group of high-level political appointees. A second major reform weakening the power of the party organization or machine has been the primary system. The movement to nominate candidates in primary elections started in the late nineteenth century, sponsored by the Populists and progressives.

Party organizations continued to play a major role in designating candidates through convention or caucus mechanisms until after World War II.

The 1968 Democratic convention, in which Hubert Humphrey defeated the forces of Eugene McCarthy and the assassinated Robert Kennedy (these two having won most of the primaries), proved to be a turning point in the expansion of the primary system. After that convention the Democratic party established the McGovern-Fraser reform commission, which changed party rules to prevent future party leaders from selecting a presidential nominee against the wishes of party members. The new policies assured citizen participation in delegate selection in all states and called for demographic representativeness in delegations to presidential conventions. They left state parties with two delegate selection methods, the participatory convention (or open caucus, as in Iowa) and the primary.[13] The regulations also encouraged multiple candidates by requiring proportional representation, the assignment of a proportion of delegates to candidates based on the percentage of votes they received above a cutoff point.[14]

The reformers were also concerned with reducing the power of the wealthy in the nomination and electoral processes. Limits on campaign contributions by individuals were reduced during the 1970s so that no one can contribute more than $1,000 to a given candidate in primary and general elections. This legislation also provides for federal financing of presidential campaign expenses. Most of the moneys have to be given to the candidate, not the party.[15] Demands of the student movement of the 1960s eventually led to a constitutional amendment lowering the voting age from 21 to 18. By the mid-1970s the major structural supports of party ability to nominate candidates and to control funding had been eliminated. Almost all restrictions on voting by people 18 and over were gone. And the rich could apparently no longer contribute large sums to those running.

Most liberals and leftists, however, would agree that the reforms of the last twenty years have not worked out well for them. The Republicans have won four out of the last five presidential elections. The Democrats have remained in control of the House for almost the entire period, but this control in part reflects the increased reluctance of the electorate to vote against an incumbent congressman, a clearly unanticipated development. The advantage of incumbency has increased greatly from the late 1960s through the 1980s.[16] In 1986, 98.4 percent of sitting members running for relection were returned. Only six were defeated.

The spread of the primary system has severely reduced the influence of party organizations on the nomination process, particularly to high office. This result was intended, but nominees are now designated by an activist minority that is frequently more interested in being right ideologically than in choosing candidates that can win in the general election. The proportion of the eligible population voting in presidential primaries has been around

25 percent.[17] This segment comes from the better-educated and more ideologically committed (as well as the most consciously self-interested) sections of the parties, those who do not have to be mobilized by party organizations. As Moynihan has put it: "Only the innocent assume that the more persons who are involved in a process, the more democratic it is. Power gravitates to the special and organized, as against the general interest."[18]

As the situation in 1987–1988 shows, the primary process also encourages a large number of candidates. It permits the nomination and even election of candidates who, like Jimmy Carter, have had little or no experience in national politics. The advantage to ideologues has shown up not only in the presidential nominations but also in the choice of congressional candidates for open seats.

The effects of restrictions on contributions have differed from those anticipated by the reformers. Those concerned with raising money for political candidates and with affecting their policies now form political action committees (PACs), a technique that, ironically, was first popularized by the trade union movement. Most of the money now raised by PACs goes to conservative and pro-Republican groups. There is no direct estimate of the totals contributed by ideology and party, but according to Herbert Alexander the ratio in favor of the Republicans over the Democrats was five to one for the totals received by the party national, senatorial, and House campaign committees in the 1970s and 1980. The Republican advantage has declined in the mid- and late 1980s to about two and one-half to one. As noted, the current legislation restricts the amount of money individuals can give to any one candidate, but each person can contribute to many candidates across the country. A wealthy person can contribute $500,000 by giving $1,000 to candidates in 500 constituencies. Affluent acquaintances can exchange donations by giving to each other's favorite candidates. They can and do run parties that raise half a million dollars or more. In effect, the big donor has been replaced by the big solicitor.

The restrictions on campaign contributions were modified by a Supreme Court finding that, ironically, may recreate a millionaires' Senate, as that body was once satirically dubbed. The court ruled that the right to freedom of speech means that individuals cannot be restricted from spending money to advance their personal points of view. A person therefore may spend as much money as he desires on his own campaign. If a multimillionaire runs for office, he is considerably advantaged over other candidates. John D. Rockefeller's 1986 campaign for U.S. Senator from West Virginia spent $12 million, of which $11 million was from his own fortune. There are increasing numbers of wealthy people holding public office, particularly in the Senate. The court's free-speech ruling also means that the rich can spend as much money as they wish supporting candidates by putting up billboards, paying for television programs, and setting up get-out-the-vote campaigns. The only restriction is that they may not have any formal connection to the campaign of the candidates they support.

All these changes, as political scientists like Nelson Polsby, Austen Ranney, and Byron Schafer have stressed, have so weakened the parties that, in Ranney's words, "presidential politics has become, in substance if not in form, something closely approaching a no-party system." [19] The absence of party has forced candidates to rely increasingly on expensive political professionals, such as campaign consultants, media specialists, fund-raisers, and pollsters. The overall costs have skyrocketed from $1.8 billion in 1983–1984 to an estimated $2.5–3 billion in 1987–1988.[20] Hence by reducing party influence, liberal reformers have strengthened the power of those with money or those who know how to raise money, including special-interest groups.

Party atrophy has particularly disadvantaged the Democrats. Since their support is still disproportionately drawn from the less-privileged and less politically active segments of the population, the Democrats require more organization, more ability to spread information, and more intense efforts to get people registered and to the polls than do the Republicans. As Gary Orren has noted, the reduction of the influence of blue-collar workers and trade unions among the Democrats, and the increase since the 1960s of the college-educated among them, has meant that ideologically committed people have become important in determining Democratic party nominations.[21] In the days when party organizations could determine nominations, party leaders sought candidates who were electable, who seemed to appeal to the largest segment of the population. Ideologically motivated primary voters look for nominees who agree with them, regardless of whether they can be elected or not.

Although more black voting in the South has clearly strengthened the Democrats (as well as greatly increasing the number of black officials), the same has not been true for the extension of the vote to 18-year-olds. The younger the eligible electorate, the less likely they are to register and go to the polls—patterns that are particularly true for the 18- to 21-year-old group. Only one-third of them voted in the 1984 election.[22] Ironically in recent years opinion polls indicate that the Republicans rather than the Democrats have gained from this small enlargement of the suffrage.

The deterioration of party has occurred in tandem with the ascendency of television. It may be argued that if party had remained stronger, television would not have gained as much power as it has, particularly in party primaries. With the decline of party and the lack of identifying labels in nomination contests, television has become crucial to candidates. The greater use of television is, of course, part of the reason campaigns have become so much more expensive.

The combination of the decline of party, the diffusion of primaries, and the increased influence of the media has made for prolonged political campaigns. Candidates start running long before the first primary, since they have to become known, build a personal organization, and raise money. In the presidential race, campaigns have been extended to practically the entire four-year period between elections. Jimmy Carter began running in 1974 and was preparing his strategy in 1972–1973. The Iowa caucuses, which occur in February, have become a major media event giving the 10 percent of the state electorate who participate a major role in nominating presidential candidates. During the two- or three-year-long campaign, journalists must cover all prospective candidates. Inevitably a great deal of attention is paid to the personalities and backgrounds of the candidates, and anything negative in their background is made public. As Moynihan notes, the primary is an "endless, debilitating ordeal that denies dignity to the defeated and somehow even diminishes the stature of the victorious."[23]

The prolonged election season may also contribute to the reduced rate of participation, possibly reflecting increased boredom with politics. It is noteworthy that voting in presidential elections fell roughly 10 percent, from about 63 percent in 1960 to 53 percent in 1984. Balloting in nonpresidential-year congressional contests has declined from 45 percent in 1962 to 33 percent in 1986.[24] This falloff may be linked to the decline of party commitment, as evidenced by the increase in split-ticket voting. In 1960 only 9 percent voted for candidates from different parties for the House and the Senate. The figure for 1986 was 28 percent.[25]

Some have sought to explain the lower level of participation in the United States compared with most European countries and Canada as a function of the U.S. emphasis on populism and the greater frequency of elections in this country. About 490,000 offices must be filled over every four-year cycle. Americans in many states are called on to vote every four years for president, in the intervening four years for state governors, every two years for Congress and the state legislature, and often the year in between for municipal and county officials. Beyond these are the expanded primaries, making close to one million elections in each quadrennial period.

The record of reform in politics since the 1960s is a classic case of unanticipated consequences to efforts at purposive social change. The reforms have been accompanied by a decline in participation. They cannot easily be turned around, since U.S. history indicates "that it is not possible to change our arrangements with the avowed intention of making them less democratic. The obvious course is to establish that our present ones, however well intended, have of late become closed and, well, undemocratic."[26]

Conclusion

Commenting on the counterintuitive character of some recent political events, Norman Podhoretz facetiously observed, "if you want something, vote for the other guy." No one, certainly not I, would draw this conclusion from an analysis of unanticipated consequences. Clearly conservatives and liberals in office behave differently, as the 1988 vote on aid to the Contras demonstrated. Lyndon Johnson, with the help of a large Democratic majority in Congress, pressed successfully for civil rights legislation. Important parts of the Reagan program—tax cuts, tax reform, increases in military spending—were carried through. But as David Stockman documented, much was not.[27]

Counterintuitive policies and outcomes may actually be what their policy makers intended even if they violate their public posture, ideology, or electoral mandate. Richard Nixon was concerned with gaining the support of those who opposed him. His support for policies he opposed on the hustings was logical from this perspective. Similarly Ronald Reagan's interest in reducing tensions with the Soviet Union at the end of his second term may involve a concern for his historical image. Presidential behavior often reflects that they run for reelection in their first term and for the verdict of history in their second.

Sophisticated awareness of the counterintuitive character of U.S. foreign policy may affect the actions of the communist powers. Mao commented in 1971 that he preferred Republicans in power.[28] In 1984 a leading analyst of the Institute for the Study of the USA and Canada, the major Soviet center for policy advice on North America to the Soviet leadership, told me that he and others (though not all) in the institute preferred Reagan to Mondale in the upcoming election. He noted that the Soviets had done better with Republican Presidents Eisenhower, Nixon, and Ford than with Democrats Kennedy, Johnson, and Carter (after the Afghan invasion). The Democrats were too ideological or, in Mao's terms, sentimental. My Soviet acquaintance believed that in the first term Reagan had acted to keep the support of the hard right, but that once reelected he could and would ignore their pressures.

Political decision making is inherently problematic. In democracies, particularly in the United States with its built-in checks and balances, no officeholder can command most of the factors affecting outcomes of any complex event. Presidents cannot control Congress. House and Senate leaders are often frustrated by their followers. Jimmy Carter was horrified that interest groups could block legislation he regarded as in the public interest.

Unanticipated consequences are inherent in complex social systems, dictatorships, and private organizations as well as democratic polities. There is no solution, given the multivariate causal process underlying all social actions.

Notes

1. Robert Rhodes James, ed., *Winston S. Churchill: His Complete Speeches*, vol. 7, *1943–1949* (London: Chelsea House, 1974), p. 7566.

2. Robert K. Merton, "The Unanticipated Consequences of Purposive Social Action," *American Sociological Review* 1 (1936): 894–900.

3. Henry Kissinger, *White House Years* (Boston: Little, Brown, 1979), p. 1063. For Lenin's concerns, see Karl A. Wittfogel, *Oriental Despotism: A Comparative Study of Total Power* (New York: Vintage Books, 1981), pp. 399–400.

4. The estimate has been raised recently by the findings in a recent Sorbonne doctoral dissertation by Reynald Secher, which "demonstrated that the inhabitants of the Vendée region, after they surrendered to the Republican armies in 1793, were systematically exterminated in 1794 by order of the convention led by Robespierre. About 117,000 civilians—including women and children—were massacred." For summaries, see Laurent Ladouce, "Was France the Fatherland of Genocide?" *The World and I* 3 (January 1988): 686–690; and David A. Bell, "All the King's Men," *The New Republic*, January 18, 1988, pp. 36–38. The study is Reynald Secher, *Le Genocide franco-français: La Vendée venge* (Paris: Presses Universitaires de France, 1987).

5. Eugen Weber, "A New Order of Loss and Profit," *Times Literary Supplement*, January 15–21, 1988, p. 51.

6. Daniel Patrick Moynihan, *Family and Nation* (San Diego: Harcourt Brace Jovanovich, 1986), p. 79.

7. Martin Tolchin, "Paradox of Reagan Budgets Hints Contradiction in Legacy," *New York Times*, February 16, 1988.

8. M. Stanton Evans, "How Jimmy Carter Won the Battle of the Budget," *National Review*, November 29, 1985, pp. 26–29; and William Buckley, "Ring in the New," *National Review*, February 5, 1988, p. 65.

9. U.S. Bureau of the Census, *Money, Income and Poverty Status of Families and Persons in the United States: 1986*, Current Population Reports, series P-60, no. 157 (Washington, D.C.: Government Printing Office, 1987), p. 30.

10. Ronald Reagan, "Government and Business in the 80s," *Wall Street Journal*, January 9, 1981, p. 18.

11. Seymour Martin Lipset and William Schneider, "The Confidence Gap in the Reagan Years," *Political Science Quarterly* 102 (Spring 1987): 1–23. See also Lipset and Schneider's *The Confidence Gap: Business, Labor and Government in the Public Mind*, rev. ed. (Baltimore: Johns Hopkins University Press, 1987).

12. Jack Nelson, "Despite High Popularity, Reagan Faces Tough Race," *Los Angeles Times*, September 25, 1983.

13. Byron Schafer, *Quiet Revolution: The Struggle for the Democratic Party and the Shaping of Post-Reform Politics* (New York: Russell Sage Foundation, 1983), pp. 197–201.

14. Nelson Polsby, *Consequences of Party Reform* (New York: Oxford University Press, 1983), pp. 54–62.

15. Austin Ranney, "The Political Parties: Reform and Decline," in Anthony King, ed., *The New American Political System* (Washington, D.C.: American Enterprise Institute, 1980), pp. 241–42.

16. John R. Alford and David W. Brady, "Personal and Partisan Advantage in U.S. House Elections, 1946–1986" (Department of Political Science, Stanford University).

17. Gary Orren, "The Linkage of Party to Participation," in Alexander Heard and Michael Nelson, eds., *Presidential Selection* (Durham, N.C.: Duke University Press, 1987).

18. Daniel Patrick Moynihan, "Our 'Succession Crisis': Why More Reform Means Less Democracy," *Newsweek*, February 1, 1988, p. 27.

19. Polsby, *Consequences of Party Reform*, pp. 75–81, 139–41; Schafer, *Quiet Revolution*, pp. 530–31; Ranney, "Political Parties," p. 243.

20. Herbert E. Alexander and Brian H. Haggerty, *Financing the 1984 Election* (Lexington, Mass.: D. C. Heath, Lexington Books, 1987).

21. See Orren, "Linkage of Party to Participation."

22. U.S. Bureau of the Census, *Voting Registration in the Election of November 1984*, Current Population Reports, series P-20, no. 359 (Washington, D.C.: Government Printing Office, 1985), p. 5.

23. Moynihan, "Our 'Succession Crisis,'" p. 27.

24. Norman J. Ornstein, Thomas E. Mann, and Michael J. Malbin, *Vital Statistics on Congress, 1987–1988* (Washington, D.C.: Congressional Quarterley, 1987), p. 16.

25. Figures from Martin Wattenberg's analysis of the University of Michigan's SRC/CPS National Election Studies. For earlier data, see Martin Wattenberg, *The Decline of American Political Parties, 1952–1984* (Cambridge, Mass.: Harvard University Press, 1985), p. 151.

26. Moynihan, "Our 'Succession Crisis,'" p. 27.

27. See David Stockman, *The Triumph of Politics* (New York: Harper & Row, 1986).

28. Kissinger, *White House Years*, p. 1061.

ANDREW YOUNG

◆ ──────────────── ◆

Thinking About Cities in the 1990s

◆ Cities are exciting. Cities are fun. Cities are frightening. They are the most challenging political entity because they are where the action is. In cities you can make things happen. You can try, you can fail, and the morning paper and hundreds of constituent phone calls will let you know immediately that "that dog won't hunt." So it's back to the drawing board with staff, council, and community and business leaders. In cities there's no place to hide behind long-range theories or legislative guidelines. Cities are the free market of politics.

Urbanization is one of the most revolutionary phenomena in today's world. The population shifts from agrarian and small-town or village environments to urban and suburban metropolises are a global phenomenon. With these massive movements of people come massive problems. People come to the cities essentially for economic reasons because life competing against the vagaries of weather, disease, and boredom is too hard or too unstable.

The city is a new life of economic, cultural, and educational opportunity. But almost always the growth in population exceeds the growth in jobs and opportunity. Therein lies the challenge to urban leadership: stimulating economic opportunity, developing social and educational systems to integrate the migrants who come ill-prepared for modern urban life, and providing the safety and security for meaningful human relationships. Even in the United States, but especially in the cities of the Third World, a simple move of several hundred miles may also mean a move across a century of developmental progress.

U.S. cities are caught in a peculiar vacuum in the 1980s. After a half-century of federal government assistance in the building and maintenance of infrastructure, our cities now face a difficult transition with little or no federal help. Without the direct involvement of the federal government in revenue sharing, grants for the construction of low- and moderate-income housing, and Environmental Protection Agency grants for water, sewer, and solid waste disposal, and with serious cutbacks in community development block grants, cities have been forced to go it alone in the face of mounting problems with diminishing resources.

The budget deficit of the 1980s, the move into a post-industrial era, and the absence of any coherent national urban vision will force the cities into new approaches if they are to survive.

Atlanta: A Case Study

Atlanta, Georgia, is one of the U.S. cities that has managed to thrive in the 1980s despite all the problems usually associated with urban deterioration. An in-depth look at Atlanta may provide some sense of what is required of urban America as we approach the twenty-first century.

Atlanta has never been a rich city. It has the second highest poverty rate (27.5 percent) in the nation, after Newark, New Jersey. The Atlanta metropolitan area is almost equally divided racially between black and white, with a small but growing population of Hispanic, Asian, African, and Caribbean immigrants. The city was almost totally destroyed by General Sherman during the Civil War and has been rebuilding from the ashes ever since.

Leadership

In the 1950s and 1960s two major decisions launched the city into the present era. Both can be attributed to the leadership of Mayor William B. Hartsfield. First, he directly confronted the race problem that then plagued the South by proclaiming that Atlanta was "a city too busy to hate"; and second, he launched the city into the air transportation business.

Hartsfield purchased an old racetrack twelve miles from the center of the city for $90,000 for an Atlanta airport and then proceeded to lure Delta Airlines from north Louisiana by offering them the land at $1 per year for 50 years. His vision and courage moved the city to the head of the pack in both air transportation and public-private partnership. Delta Airlines now employs 33,000 people in the Atlanta area, and the airport, named for

Hartsfield, is the largest and busiest in the world, averaging 2,278 flights per day in 1987.

Communication and Public-Private Partnership

Mayor Hartsfield's decisions established a pattern that has served the city well into the 1980s and helped us prepare for the devolution of President Reagan's new federalism. As federal funds gradually declined, Atlanta moved easily to greater participation in the private money markets. Our long tradition of public-private partnership made this transition possible.

In the Atlanta of the 1950s, this partnership was easier to achieve. The business and political leaders were all white. They attended the same schools and churches. They lived in the same neighborhoods. The primary differences were class insecurities, which were also easy to bridge in a booming economy when everyone was seeking upward mobility.

With the 1960s came the emergence of black voting strength, and a new and difficult dimension was added to the political equation. No longer was there a single agenda based on a heritage of trust and common interests. Instead a legacy of distrust, exploitation, and oppression threatened to reign. It was very difficult for black political leaders to convince their constituents that major public-private partnerships could address the needs of the black poor by promoting general welfare.

Fortunately Atlanta had developed a pattern of organized and regular dialogue. Under the leadership of Coca-Cola chief executive officer J. Paul Austin, the top ten executives of corporate Atlanta and ten black leaders from business, academic, and civil rights organizations (excluding elected officials) gathered for monthly off-the-record Saturday morning shirtsleeve sessions in which all made an honest attempt to understand the city's needs from different racial and class perspectives. At these privately held meetings no minutes were kept, no press conferences were held, and no public statements were issued, yet the Atlanta Action Forum, as it became known, established the personal relationships and trust that made possible the development of a truly workable racial partnership and an emerging social contract.

The development of MARTA, Atlanta's gleaming rapid rail system, was made possible by the type of communication practiced in the Action Forum. Atlanta has always been proud of its reputation as a transportation center. As a meeting place of two railroads, the converging point of three interstate highways, and home to a modern airport, Atlanta was anxious to build a mass transit infrastructure to accommodate its anticipated growth. To accomplish this goal, Atlanta's leaders took advantage of what may be the last of the big federal government projects, the urban mass transit funding of the late 1960s and early 1970s. To qualify for this federal funding for mass transit development, local governments were required to provide a matching share of 20 percent. Atlanta's leaders hoped to raise the required 20 percent share through a 1 percent sales tax, which under Georgia law required a local referendum.

After failing in one referendum attempt hastily put together in 1969, the city came back under the leadership of Mayor Sam Massell, the city's first Jewish mayor, and Jesse Hill, Jr., then actuary of Atlanta Life Insurance, one of Atlanta's oldest and most successful black businesses, to negotiate a successful formula. The agreement guaranteed the black business community 30 percent of new jobs in the system and 20 percent of all design, engineering, and construction contracts, and it reduced the fare from 50 cents to 15 cents for the seven-year construction period to compensate the poor for the regressive nature of the sales tax. The referendum passed, and Atlanta began to build a modern mass transit system a full decade ahead of its regional competitors in the South and the Southwest.

The MARTA system was conceived as both a capitalist development tool and a method of moving people around the city. Atlanta was the first city in the world to implement planning and encourage development around rapid transit stations, with appropriate stations being the nucleus for high-density, mixed-use development. These new towns channel growth and protect existing healthy neighborhoods. We have already seen millions of dollars of development around MARTA stations, with more sure to come.

The secondary functions of MARTA—creating a rational growth system, generating development and jobs, and connecting citizens with jobs and public facilities—have been at least as important as its primary function of moving people. The creative dialogue and the courageous consensus leadership that have made this type of project possible in Atlanta have proved well worth the time and effort required. They make it possible for a major metropolitan area to function as an extended family despite racial, cultural, and economic diversity. Indeed, the obvious diversity becomes a challenge and an asset in the process of urban development.

There are always differences of values, interests, and ego needs in any human environment. Because these differences had the obvious and explosive character of race, the business and civic leaders of Atlanta accepted the challenge to avoid the disastrous consequences they had observed in Little Rock, Birmingham, New Orleans, and Miami.

Cities must learn to thrive on adversity and diversity if they are to succeed in the 1990s. Problems will continue to mount as the pressures of a global economy and national indecisiveness increase. Successful cities have the leadership to pull together in a free and competitive spirit, to accept the challenge as an extended family, and to work for the common good. We can see examples of this leadership in postwar Tokyo, in the frozen cities of Helsinki and Göteborg facing the monstrous energy costs of the 1970s, and in Austin, Dallas–Ft. Worth, and El Paso struggling back from declining oil prices in the 1980s.

Leadership, public-private partnership, and compassionate communication between the diverse elements of society provide a social climate that encourages business investment, the growth of new companies and new ideas, and a wholesome, confident optimism that is essential for expanding urban opportunity.

The Importance of Education

In the early 1980s, just as Atlanta completed its new billion-dollar airport and began breaking all records in attracting new investment from home and abroad by averaging $10 billion per year from 1983–1987, the city received a shocking setback. IBM, Bell South, and AT&T had all proposed massive new expansions totaling several billion dollars in new investment, and we were certain that we would be the undisputed high-tech capital of the South. We had moved about as far and as fast as our outstanding infrastructure could take us when we began to compete for a research and development facility proposed by a consortium of twelve high-tech firms. If we could attract the facility, its $250 million annual research budget would mean a constant stream of new jobs and new companies for Atlanta.

Atlanta is used to winning these competitions, but in this instance we came up short behind Austin, Texas, of all places. It would be easy simply to say we were outbid—and we were, by Austin's offers of subsidized mortgages and numerous perks for the employees of the facility—but behind the loss lay a frightening revelation that the one area in which we did not quite measure up was education. Cities in the 1990s must be involved with an advanced research university in an academic environment that encourages its faculty and students to be involved in economic development and problem solving in the urban environment.

Immediately after losing the competition to Austin and the University of Texas, Georgia Governor Joe Frank Harris launched a Quality Basic Education Act through the state legislature, and Georgia Tech and the University of Georgia stepped up efforts to secure private endowments for additional academic chairs in high-tech and biomedical research. Both universities launched advanced technology development centers to spin off new business ventures from university research. The six historically black colleges in Atlanta, which have graduated black students from all over the world for over one hundred years, were also given new support as potential sources of leadership in world and domestic markets.

Businesses entered partnerships with local public schools, and the mayor's office launched an annual Dream Jamboree, introducing Atlanta's high school students to scholarship, employment, and job training opportunities that now result in 62 percent of our public high school graduates continuing their education. With the help of IBM, the Writing to Read computer-based literacy program was introduced in all city first-grade classes and city-sponsored day care centers for four- and five-year-olds. Such aggressive initiatives in education will be required of every city that hopes to survive and thrive in the 1990s.

Metropolitan Areas as Economic Units: Consolidation

Historically cities have always grown as trade and market centers. Dr. Jane Jacobs, in her book *Cities and the Wealth of Nations*, advances the thesis that economic growth derives largely from the free and competitive attempt to solve local problems through import substitution and innovation, which are then exported to other cities with similar problems.[1]

In Dr. Jacobs's view, the city is more of an economic unit than a political entity. When cities limit themselves and their long-range planning to their political geography, they soon find themselves swamped by problems such as poverty, racial tension, homelessness, and crime, which refuse to correspond to geographic political boundaries. But the economic entity, which has flexible boundaries, provides a total environment for economic growth and development and can deal with social and economic problems. The inner-city, suburban, and downtown neighborhoods and the surrounding agricultural and recreational spaces must somehow share a unified vision of the future.

These realities are leading to a new regionalism. The expansion of city boundaries—as in North Carolina cities; Jacksonville, Florida; Nashville, Tennessee; and Indianapolis, Indiana—are all attempts to create workable political and economic units out of total metropolitan areas.

The minority community of these cities has felt, however, that the true rationale behind consolidation was the dilution of minority voting strength and has usually opposed the expansion of boundaries. The suburbs, meanwhile, naively fear involvement with the central cities, as though artificial political lines can stop the spread of problems.

The extension in 1982 of the 1965 Voting Rights Act for 25 additional years assures that any such changes in jurisdictional lines cannot be used to diminish minority voting strength or the right to elect representatives. With this assurance the black community is looking more favorably toward enlarging boundaries, especially in places like Atlanta that have moved toward racial balance in the entire metropolitan area.

A close analysis of Cleveland, Ohio; Miami–Dade County, Florida; and Detroit, Michigan, gives a clear picture of the dangers of attempting to isolate the inner city and maintain suburban affluence. Inevitably investment declines and the suburbs begin to experience problems without a healthy central core city.

Regional Resource Planning

In Atlanta we have been able to foster regional cooperation through regional planning commissions. Transportation, water resources, sewage disposal, and solid waste management are all becoming too costly to handle separately in each political jurisdiction. The compromise in the 1990s will be that schools and police remain locally controlled, whereas other aspects of infrastructure and planning are accomplished regionally.

Atlanta's new water treatment facility is being built jointly with the government of Fulton County. The two governments established a joint authority for the single purpose of constructing and managing the $64 million facility. Cooperation on sewage treatment is occurring informally between Atlanta and DeKalb and Gwinnett counties. Fortunately Atlanta has been able to expand its existing plants to help accommodate the rapid growth in two of the nation's fastest-growing counties.

The most successful cities are able to find ways to help their region function as a cooperative economic unit beyond the limitations of political categories. Often the Chamber of Commerce can provide the economic cohesion for a region even when there is friction and hostility between local governments. The Atlanta Chamber of Commerce has promoted this metropolitan region for decades. The first Forward Atlanta campaign, launched in the 1960s, was a four million dollar effort built around Mayor Hartsfield's theme, "a city too busy to hate." Each decade since then, there has been a similar coordinated campaign involving the chamber and all of the metropolitan governments.

The City as a Trade Center

Cities have always been places to which surrounding citizens and neighboring villagers come to trade and market their crafts and services. In the twenty-first century cities will even more consciously and deliberately become centers for marketing services, produce, and inventions. With the birth of trade and market centers, new wealth is created and new economic development spreads throughout a region. Most often these things happen without being planned. They grow out of what Dr. Jacobs calls "drift." "In its very nature, successful economic development has to be open ended rather than goal-oriented, and has to make itself up expediently and empirically as it goes along," Dr. Jacobs writes, quoting MIT Professor Cyril Stanley Smith.

> Metallurgy itself began with hammering copper into necklace beads and other ornaments before useful knives were made out of copper and bronze ... The first successful railroad in the world was an amusement ride in London.
>
> Major economic initiatives tend to grow from innovative esthetic and often playful uses. Today's light weight carbons and plastic composites first were used in tennis rackets, golf clubs and fishing rods, and only later began to replace metals in automobiles and aircraft.[2]

The city as a place of entertainment and recreation often gives rise to invention and innovation, which then become the basis of development and trade.

The modern city has expanded this informal process into an aggressive market system designed around conventions and trade shows. The convention and visitor industry in Atlanta, along with the market center concept of architect John Portman, have placed Atlanta in the forefront of development and trade. The convention hotels and the Georgia World Congress Center hold trade shows on a regular basis. These conventions and trade shows bring 1.8 million people to Atlanta annually and account for 81,000 jobs in the hotel, taxi, air transportation, design, and marketing industries.

World trade begins with people coming regularly to cities to buy and sell their services and inventions, and expansion of that trade offers the U.S. economy its best hope of coping with its present enormous trade deficit.

The evolution of the Atlanta Market Center is a classic example of the importance of the marketplace and trade center role of successful cities. What began as a facility for a few small gift shows grew to a 2.6 million square foot Merchandise Mart, which then spun off a 2.2 million square foot Apparel Mart and a half-million square foot Decorative Arts Center. The center is now adding the 1.5 million square foot Inforum, a marketplace for the high-tech products of the information economy.

Future urban growth and development depends on this kind of creative marketing by a vibrant private sector. Government's role is merely to provide the supportive environment that makes successful business and a quality life-style possible.

Privatization

The successful city in the 1990s will find itself growing so rapidly and confronting such a broad array of challenges that limited resources force some serious choices. Housing low- and moderate-income citizens has traditionally been a federal responsibility, but budget deficits at the national level make that a rapidly diminishing option. States are feeling the pressure of abandoned small towns and rural areas, so there is not much help for cities from state governments either.

But as problems mount and the demand for local government action grows, citizens cry against more taxes while at the same time demanding that local leaders address the problems and come up with efficient solutions. This dilemma has sent local officials scurrying to the bond markets and the private sector in search of new ways to marshal funds for the common good.

Homelessness and hunger are a blight on any city's landscape. They represent the first signs of economic failure. They soon become the hiding place for crime and a forecast of the disintegration of the economic environment.

Fortunately for Atlanta, the problem of homelessness is being managed by 51 churches and synagogues that feed and house our city's homeless. They provide the much-needed love and concern that prevents alienation from degenerating into hostility, hatred, and violence. But although religious institutions aid in a temporary crisis, it remains the task of government to promote domestic tranquility by addressing the systemic nature of such crises. This sense of urgency and the explosive character of city problems too long deferred are forcing urban administrators to look at privatizing many city tasks and assets. This move will free city staff to address other problems, release city funds, and in rare cases even produce new revenues.

Privatization must be seen from several distinct perspectives. First, there are those services subsidized by the general public that serve the interests of only a few people, such as golf, tennis, and other specialized recreational facilities. These services represent a community investment that can be converted from a subsidized service to an income generator through private management.

The maintenance and management of City of Atlanta golf courses has been contracted to private firms, and a service that formerly cost the citizens several million dollars in taxes now generates income for the city while still maintaining a high standard of upkeep and continuing a free junior development program for youth under 16. Similar successful management leasings have been profitable in our public tennis centers, all without any major increases in the fees paid by users of these facilities.

Second, there are proposals to convert water, sewer, and waste management systems to private contracts. Some cities have succeeded in turning garbage collection, waste management, and water and sewer maintenance functions over to private companies, just as the Tennessee Valley Authority became private through regulated enterprise. To date, however, the City of Atlanta has decided to continue managing these systems as a public administrative responsibility, since they are vital services required by all citizens and since the employment and pensions provided to city workers would be difficult to guarantee. There is also the high cost of reentering the business should the private arrangement prove unsatisfactory.

It seems preferable in waste management, water, and sewer infrastructure projects to enter into regional arrangements that produce efficiencies of scale. Long-range, high-volume contracts between the political jurisdictions of the metropolitan Atlanta region seem to be the direction for our cities in the 1990s. In Atlanta the plans are already under way for water and sewer treatment facilities. Since all our regional governments depend on the same rivers and lakes for their supply, regional cooperation is necessary to conserve and maximize precious natural resources.

Waste management without pollution is certain to be an expensive high-tech process involving hundreds of millions of dollars in a metropolitan region. For both financial and environmental reasons, regionally planned strategies must emerge if we are to deal effectively and efficiently with this approaching problem.

A third aspect of privatization concerns those things that government can assemble and guarantee in their high-risk phase and then sell at a profit once they become established and profitable. Industrial parks that acquire land, develop streets and utilities, and create jobs in depressed economic areas are a good example of the use of government powers to finance development through tax-exempt bonds guaranteed by the city's good faith and credit. Once these projects are in place there is no need for government to remain as an owner.

The Atlanta Economic Development Corporation, the Urban Residential Finance Authority, and the Underground Atlanta Festival Development Corporation are examples of joint ventures between the public and private sectors that have successfully taken on tasks perceived as either too risky or too difficult to attract financing by a private entrepreneur acting alone. These public-private corporations have successfully developed industrial parks, moderate-income housing, and retail complexes that meet an important and well-defined public purpose.

A dramatic example of public-private cooperation is the Atlanta Hartsfield Midfield Air Terminal, where the city and the major airlines jointly developed the world's largest and busiest airport, servicing more than 250 destinations in 24 countries daily. The recent sale of Gatwick and Heathrow airports near London has raised the possibility of privatizing Atlanta Hartsfield. The appraised value and the revenue stream of this successful joint venture make it an extremely attractive property for a long-term, secure investment with a guaranteed flow of revenue as long as airplanes keep flying.

Privatizing such a facility would mean a great windfall for Atlanta's taxpayers. After paying off the debt, a private corporation could reimburse the citizens of Atlanta with a $500–700 million trust fund. Such a fund, properly invested at rates similar to the city's pension funds, could provide 10–14 percent interest, which could be used to fund the city's ongoing operations.

A city with a trust fund in excess of half a billion dollars could then roll back real estate taxes, build much-needed low- and moderate-income housing for sale to individual owner-occupiers, and provide the city with an educational trust fund to guarantee each high school graduate of the Atlanta public schools an opportunity for further training or higher education.

Privatization can guarantee a service while returning to the citizenry a profit on the resources invested and on the risk they originally sustained on behalf of the venture. Given the surplus of capital in the markets of the free world and the budget deficits now sustained by the governments of the United States, the United Kingdom, Japan, and Germany, it is likely that more privatization will and should occur.

Japan is currently generating $1.1 billion per day in its private sector while the Japanese government runs a deficit. Similar profits are being recorded by U.S. and European companies. The private sector must find secure and profitable investments for their surpluses or they will create inflationary effects on the market, which is already proving to be dangerous in Japanese real estate.

The infrastructure of U.S. cities and the housing needs of the American people are two worthwhile and profitable investments, but these will absorb only a portion of the surplus capital market of the free world. The pattern of government guarantees for private investment in the public purpose offers some hope for projects in the developing world as well. Money loaned to governments directly has produced an international debt crisis, but money invested in privately conceived and managed projects in the public interest offer new hope for global development and the expansion of the world's free market.

The City as a Spiritual Entity

Cities can not only generate wealth; they can also be the testing and proving ground for new ideas and values. The successful cities of the future will provide not only economic growth and a purposeful infrastructure but also a sense of meaning and vision for the life of each citizen. In the final analysis, cities possess much more than just fiscal and physical dimensions. The city is a place of culture and values. It is a place that imparts meaning to its citizenry and a vision to society as a whole.

In U.S. cities we have seen how the people rally to a victory by their sports team, whether it is the Washington Redskins' Super Bowl victory, the high school basketball championship in the State of Indiana, or the Little League World Series victory in Marietta, Georgia. We derive a spiritual pride and meaning from our life together as an extremely diverse and extended family.

In Atlanta that meaning is a result of the religious life and values taught in our churches and synagogues, our mosques and shrines. The religious values of family, work ethic, and civic responsibility are part of our total social and corporate life. They mean an honest and hard-working work force. They mean serious, dedicated students in our schools and universities. They mean a sense of competitiveness and a desire to freely explore the human potential.

The cities of the 1990s must also emphasize the values, the spiritual resources, that have brought us together in one place and that will enable us to live together in unity despite our tremendous diversity and our boundless desire for freedom. Crime and drugs are at bottom spiritual problems. They represent a failure of society to share meaning, communicate skills, and transmit values. Great cities will also address the questions of life's meaning and our vision of life together in the present and the future.

But the enormous amounts of money involved in drug trafficking and related crime are in danger of creating a counter-economy that threatens to undermine the security, stability, and domestic tranquillity of entire cities. Working with the police, community leaders must fashion new approaches to crime and crime prevention to meet this challenge.

Atlanta has embarked on a Partnership Against Crime involving the police and 76 active neighborhood groups, but the challenge of drug-related crime is too big for any business-as-usual approach. There is an organization and sophistication in this level of crime that far surpasses the Prohibition era and is even more brutal and violent. Drug-related crime is hard to deal with in today's cities because it involves so many young people and so much money.

Ultimately the cities are going to require a national and international approach to solving the drug problem. In the meantime, strong and determined leaders from the business community, neighborhoods, politicians, and the press must wage a legal battle against these criminal forces.

The family will also need support in the 1990s as its roles are redefined by the education and employment of both sexes and the growing freedom of all ages. Senior citizens, as the city's elders, must be structured into the wisdom equation. Values that develop in the transitional pop culture of each age must be challenged and tempered by the experience of those who have lived through many generations of pop culture, from the Charleston and black bottom through the jitterbug and bebop, and on to gospel, blues, rock and roll, and rap.

The city is exciting in its conflict. It is challenging in its chaos, for chaos constantly creates a new and vibrant order of things. In the meantime, as we work and plan for the future of the cities of the United States and the world, let us join with the prophet Jeremiah "and seek the peace of the city whither I have caused you to be carried away captives and pray unto the Lord for it; for in peace thereof shall ye have peace."[3]

Notes

1. See Jane Jacobs, *Cities and the Wealth of Nations: Principles of Economic Life* (New York: Random House, 1984).

2. Ibid., p. 222.

3. Jeremiah 29.7.

EDWIN MEESE III

◆ ——————————————— ◆

Criminal Justice
A Public Policy Imperative

◆ Five years ago a leading collection of essays on crime and public policy began with the statement "Today crime is a pervasive problem that leaves few Americans untouched." [1] As we approach the 1990s that observation is even more significant, because on average one major criminal offense occurs every two seconds in the United States. [2]

Elsewhere in this volume James Q. Wilson discusses the subject of crime as it relates to public policy and personal character, with an emphasis on influencing the human personality and individual behavior. This essay will focus on future developments in the criminal justice system and how governments at various levels can do a better job of carrying out their primary responsibility: the protection of the lives and property of their citizens.

In the United States today, we hear much discussion of the quality of life. Whether that phrase pertains to social, ecological, or economic conditions, it describes a value sought by most citizens of this country. Nevertheless, seldom do public policy discussions, budget priorities, or research agendas adequately reflect the influence that crime—and its corollary, crime prevention and control—have on the conditions of life and the vital decisions that people make in determining their own affairs.

For example, crime has a definite effect on where people choose to live, as indicated by the flight from the cities during the 1960s and 1970s as urban crime escalated. [3] The depopulation of large central cities and declining population growth in the metropolitan areas around those cities was one of the major demographic changes in the United States during that era. [4]

Crime also has a major impact on education. Too many schools have become sites of such offenses as assaults, larcenies, and robberies directed against both students and teachers.[5] Obviously quality education cannot take place in an environment of predatory crime.

The economic effect of crime can be illustrated both by property loss and real estate values. In 1986 the nation suffered a total estimated loss of $323 million from robberies, $3.1 billion from burglary, and $2.9 billion from larceny-theft (pocket picking, purse snatching, shoplifting, thefts from buildings and vehicles, and so on).[6] These losses, borne by individuals, families, and businesses, have an adverse impact on personal economic situations and on the investment potential of a community. For example, it has been estimated that a 3 percent decline in crime rates in the Boston metropolitan area would increase property values by 5 percent.[7] Obviously safer cities offer greater economic opportunities.

Even the public's choice of transportation is conditioned by the fear of crime. An analysis of mass transportation in New York City estimated that the crime increase there from 1978 to 1982 influenced 150,000 households to take taxis rather than buses or subways.[8]

These examples suggest that crime conditions have significantly affected social and economic conditions, even though traditional sociological theory posits that the reverse effect is true. It would follow then that in thinking about the United States in the 1990s, criminal justice policies and practices, as well as their interrelationship with other public policy issues, cannot be overlooked.

In analyzing the current crime situation and trends for the future, it is important to recognize the past quarter century as a turbulent period for criminal justice in the United States. The most significant phenomenon during these years has been a dramatic increase in crime throughout the nation. After a general decline in crime during the 1950s, the offense rate suddenly began to accelerate during the 1960s, leveled off during the early 1970s, and then began a precipitous increase that peaked in 1980. In that year the rate of crimes reported to police was 143 percent over the rate for 1965. The rate of violent crime increased some 198 percent during the same 15-year period.[9] Following that record year, crime generally occurred at lower levels during the 1980s, decreasing from 1981 through 1983 and then beginning to rise again in 1984 through 1986.[10] Although the crime rate in 1986 was still 8 percent lower than the peak year of 1980, it represented an increase of 124 percent over 1965. This unacceptably high incidence of crime, accompanied by the narcotics problem discussed below, poses a major challenge for policy makers at all levels of government.

To review the developments of the past 25 years, three other topics deserve attention. First, a series of court decisions, beginning in 1961, imposed major changes in criminal procedure that generally expanded the rights of criminal defendants and placed additional restraints on police and prosecutorial practices.[11] The new rules involved searches and the seizure of evidence, police interrogation, the taking of confessions, comments by prosecutors on the failure of defendants to answer police questions or to testify at their trials, and other similar issues focusing on collateral matters of investigation conduct rather than the more fundamental questions concerning the guilt or innocence of the accused.

Although it is difficult to calculate the precise effect these decisions have had on the crime rate, scholars have argued that the social costs of such rules—particularly those that exclude worthwhile, valid evidence—are extremely high.[12] The most demonstrable result, however, has been the additional time required for judicial hearings and trials as well as the significant drain on the already overtaxed resources of the courts.[13]

Second, a movement to improve the treatment of crime victims by the criminal justice system was begun in several states during the 1960s and 1970s by grass-roots service providers and victim advocates. A national Task Force on Victims of Crime was established in 1982 to study this serious problem and develop recommendations to improve the treatment of crime victims. Based on this effort, the Victim/Witness Protection Act of 1982 and the Victims of Crime Act of 1984 were enacted. The federal-state partnership in this legislation enabled states to expand and improve victim assistance and victim compensation programs. Equally important has been the improvement in the attitude of law enforcement officers, prosecutors, and judges toward victims of crime. This rekindled concern for victims as individuals who have suffered has sparked many of the reforms in the criminal justice process during the last several years and will provide continuing incentives to improve the system for the benefit of actual and potential victims.[14]

Third, an unusual situation occurred in the field of sentencing and corrections during the twenty years from 1960 through 1980. As serious crime increased during those two decades, the chances of a convicted felon going to prison dramatically decreased.[15] The cause of this change was an increased emphasis on rehabilitation and nonprison alternatives in sentencing. The extensive use of probation, short sentences followed by parole, halfway houses, and other community treatment programs were the dominant themes in correctional policy. During this period almost no new prison facilities were constructed. Therefore when a reemphasis on incarceration began in the late 1970s and the 1980s, the nation experienced extreme overcrowding in both state and federal correctional institutions.

Perhaps the most significant phenomenon during the past quarter century, which will profoundly influence crime in the United States for the foreseeable future, was the growth of drug abuse as a major social problem. Although in 1960 there was concern about the use of drugs, primarily heroin and the increasing experimentation with marijuana, a small and isolated segment of society was involved in such conduct. Most citizens were affected only by the crimes, such as burglary and theft, that drug users committed to support their habits. However, during the days of rebellion and social unrest of the 1960s and early 1970s, the illegal use of drugs spread to every segment of society. As Dr. Mark S. Gold has described it:

> First, young college students began to experiment with drugs they redefined, calling them 'recreational drugs'—primarily marijuana and psychedelic substances like LSD. The counterculture movement, which sprang up as part of this era . . . , embraced mind-altering drugs and their use spread across the country. Adults imitated students and young people, who were the trend setters in the 1960s.[16]

As these drug users grew older, the use of cocaine became more frequent, particularly among young professionals. By 1985 an estimated 36.8 million Americans had at some time in their lives been involved in the use of illegal narcotics and some 23 million were current users.[17] Although heroin and marijuana use has leveled off in recent years, cocaine use has become an epidemic.[18] In a recent survey, 98 percent of American adults sampled considered illegal drug use an important national problem and 73 percent described drug abuse as "one of the most serious problems facing the country."[19]

Whereas narcotics consumption is a social and health problem by itself, evidence of the close relation between drugs and crime continues to mount. Urinalysis testing of arrested persons in several cities throughout the United States revealed that as many as 75 percent of those arrested tested positive for illegal drugs, with the highest results among those charged with robbery and burglary.[20] Further, National Institute of Justice studies show that addicts committed four to six times more crime during periods of heavy drug use than when they were relatively drug-free. A particularly ominous finding is that drug abusers are at least as violent as, and perhaps more violent than, criminals who have not used drugs.[21] This confirmation of the link between drug abuse and criminality, and the new evidence of an increase in the degree of drug use found among arrested suspects, indicates further reason for additional efforts to reduce both the supply and the demand for illegal narcotics.

In determining the strategies and programs that might be initiated to deal with the challenges and opportunities chronicled above, the first step should involve a better definition of the relative roles, responsibilities, and relations among the various levels of government involved in law enforcement and the administration of justice. Throughout our history as a nation, most matters pertaining to law enforcement and crime control have been the province of state and local governments under our system of federalism. However, during the past quarter century, an increase in federal involvement in public safety policy and funding has paralleled the centralization of influence and initiative recorded in other areas of traditionally local government.

The establishment of a variety of new federal programs and projects, such as the President's Commission on Law Enforcement and the Administration of Justice in the mid-1960s, the Omnibus Crime Control and Safe Streets Act of 1968, the Law Enforcement Assistance Administration (LEAA), and the National Advisory Commission on Criminal Justice Standards and Goals in 1971, has involved a new relationship between the national government and the states on funding, the setting of requirements, and the monitoring of results. There has been much debate about the efficacy of this increased federal activity, and ultimately the LEAA program was phased out in the late 1970s. Those federal initiatives, including some subsequent programs, have blurred the traditional distinctions between the federal and state/local roles in protecting public safety, causing some confusion about the responsibilities at various levels of government for the funding of the criminal justice system. This confusion is manifest today in much political finger pointing and a continuing debate over the extent to which the federal government should tax the public and then return these funds in grants to state and local governments for police, court, and correctional expenditures. Also the vagaries of the federal budget system often work against long-term planning and consistent funding patterns from year to year.

Nevertheless, a definite federal role should complement the crime control efforts of state and local governments and private organizations:

1. Only federal law enforcement agencies can deal effectively with international and interstate criminal activity.

2. Comprehensive research, statistics, and information dissemination programs must be conducted on a national basis.

3. A nationwide system of identification records, with the related capability of timely processing and communication of data, is necessary for effective police investigation and the prompt apprehension of suspects as well as appropriate judicial decision making.

4. The provision on a national basis of scientific and other technical

investigative assistance, advanced training, and technological experimentation is cost-effective and maximizes scarce resources.

5. The federal government should support regional intelligence networks and similar multistate or nationwide activities.

At the same time, the basic funding for state and local criminal justice systems should derive from the public treasuries at those levels of government. The responsibility for levying taxes, determining priorities, allocating resources, and supervising expenditures and operations should be combined in the same governmental entity to ensure accountability and responsibility.

Within these parameters, I propose that the federal government initiate and/or support innovative programs in several priority areas appropriate to national solutions.

Science and Technology

The same technological research that has spurred new products and increased productivity in industry and the military establishment can be applied to expand policy options, reduce costs, and improve the entire criminal justice system as it moves toward the twenty-first century. Scientific means to dramatically improve our ability to detect and identify criminals will serve as a major deterrent to illegal activity. Quicker and more reliable identification will not only aid in the solution of more crimes but will encourage offenders to admit their guilt and thus conserve scarce prosecutorial and court resources.

A particularly promising technology to aid conclusive identification is the use of the DNA code present in every human cell. This technique, sometimes referred to as genetic fingerprinting, can use the DNA properties found in blood, body fluids, and hair to link evidence such as blood stains or other specimens to a specific individual. Another profitable area for research is the computer-assisted voice identification system. Voice identification, in a manner sufficiently reliable to be used as evidence in court, has great potential in dealing with crimes such as kidnapping for ransom, bomb threats, and terrorism. Other productive areas for research include developing less-than-lethal weapons to assist police in subduing violent or deranged persons without resorting to firearms or other deadly force; improved methods of detecting weapons, drugs, and explosives; microcomputer-based expert systems for automated investigation support; and portable computers to provide better police reporting and electronic linkage to data bases for officers in the street.

Narcotics Prevention and Control

The federal government should lead and support a major international effort to eliminate the cultivation and production of illegal narcotics in the source countries. Many of the countries in which drugs destined for the United States, and now the European Community, originate have the political will to contend with narcotics producers and traffickers, particularly when they understand the damage to their own nation in corruption, addiction, and political instability. But many of these same countries lack the financial, technical, and law enforcement resources to take effective action. An international effort, perhaps organized through the United Nations Fund for Drug Abuse Control (one of the most worthwhile, mission-oriented organizations of the United Nations), funded primarily by those nations currently or potentially involved in drug consumption, could take enforcement action to destroy production facilities and interdict trafficking while supporting economic development and crop substitution in the source countries. Preventing the cultivation and manufacture of narcotics in the countries of origin is much more cost-effective than trying to prevent drugs from being smuggled into or distributed within the United States.

In support of expanded worldwide drug enforcement, an international network of intelligence centers should be developed for the exchange of data on suspected traffickers as well as their planes, boats, and other means of transportation. A prototype for such an intelligence center has been established in the Dominican Republic to correlate information about clandestine air, land, and sea movements that could be involved in drug smuggling. Experience shows that most major drug seizures and the arrest of high-level drug traffickers depends on accurate intelligence.

The drug use forecasting program pioneered by the National Institute of Justice should be extended to courts in all jurisdictions. Based on urinalysis testing of arrested persons for drug use, this technique enables a judge to know whether a criminal defendant has used drugs during the two or three days prior to his or her arrest. Having such information available would contribute to better judicial decision making on such matters as pretrial release, the sentencing of convicted persons, and the revocation of probation or parole. A further refinement of this technique is being explored by the National Institute of Justice to determine if analysis of a few strands of hair can be used as an alternative to urinalysis to detect and monitor drug use.[22]

Law Enforcement Professionalization

Dozens of communities throughout the United States are developing creative programs to improve police department operations.[23] Known as team policing, community policing, basic car plans, or problem-oriented policing, these new approaches have been developed as alternatives to the traditional practice of routine patrolling and responding to calls for service. This new philosophy is described as "a pro-active, decentralized approach, designed to reduce crime, disorder, and by extension, fear of crime, by intensely involving the same officer in the same community on a long-term basis, so that residents will develop trust to cooperate with police by providing information and assistance to achieve those three crucial goals."[24]

A basic principal of this new manner of policing involves getting the officer out of the squad car and in direct communication with people in the community that he or she serves. It requires the officer to perform a variety of services, from educating citizens on crime prevention and organizing neighborhood groups to serving as a direct representative of city government and transmitting to city hall public requests for services from other municipal agencies.

If the new mode of policing is to realize its full potential in crime control and community service, police departments must attract highly educated persons with broad life experience and an expanded perspective on their position of public service. The U.S. Department of Education now distributes a large amount of public funds in grants and loans for higher education, most of which require no obligation of public service. A portion of these grants and loans should be allocated to young men and women willing to enter the police service, or to those already serving in police departments, who seek higher education. Loan funds could be disbursed with the understanding that repayment would be forgiven if the individual served two years in the police service for each year of college education. Grants and loans should also be available for veteran officers to pursue advanced degrees, with a requirement of three additional years of service for each year of graduate education.

In addition to this plan for expanding educational opportunities for individual officers, the United States also needs a police command college like Bramshill, the educational institution for senior police officers in the United Kingdom. Although the Federal Bureau of Investigation (FBI) provides an excellent series of training programs through its National Executive Institute and the Law Enforcement Executive Development course, the educational opportunities for top police executives would be considerably enhanced by having a residential institution offering a broad curriculum combined with a center for research and scholarship. The federal government, in collaboration with a public or private institution of higher learning, should establish such a command college, perhaps on the campus of the FBI academy.

Sentencing and Corrections

A number of recent studies have found that a small number of criminals commit a disproportionately high number of crimes and that incarcerating such persons would have a significant effect on the incidence of crime.[25] The difficulty lies in identifying potential career criminals at an early stage and reserving scarce prison space for criminally active defendants. A related problem involves holding criminals placed on probation accountable when they violate the terms of their suspended sentence by committing new crimes. In such cases the individual should not only receive the penalty for the new offense but should be required to serve the sentence that had been conditionally withheld for the previous crime. To fulfill these objectives, the criminal justice process needs to improve decision making at all stages. Training programs, improved criminal history information, and better comparative statistical data on sentencing practices would contribute greatly to the ability of prosecutors, judges, and correctional officials to make the critical decisions that determine the handling of each case. The National Institute of Justice and the Bureau of Justice Statistics should collaborate with the National Center for State Courts, the State Justice Institute, and other research and training institutions to develop an exemplary program for criminal justice decision making. At a minimum, such a system would provide key officials with the following information: (1) reliable criminal history information, juvenile records, and urinalysis test results (to indicate whether the defendant was on drugs at the time of arrest); (2) immediate information when a person on probation has been arrested for another offense so that the individual can be immediately returned to the judge who originally suspended his or her sentence; and (3) comparative data for prosecutors and judges on charging and sentencing decisions made by their peers within the same jurisdiction. Another feature of such a project could include periodic reports to judges on the persons they have sentenced so that they could evaluate the future conduct of such individuals in relation to the sentences imposed.

These modest suggestions indicate the rich opportunities for innovation and creativity in the field of criminal justice. The ability to make major changes in the crime situation, and thus to improve the quality of life in our communities, depends on the willingness of government and the private sector to work together—each sharing its unique capabilities—and to embark on new ventures that expand the horizons of law enforcement and the administration of justice.

Notes

1. James Q. Wilson, ed., *Crime and Public Policy* (San Francisco: ICS Press, 1983), p. xi.

2. Federal Bureau of Investigation (FBI), *Crime in the United States, 1986* (Washington, D.C.: U.S. Department of Justice, 1987).

3. During 1980, the peak year for reported criminal offenses, cities with populations over 250,000 had an index crime rate more than double that of cities under 10,000 and suburban counties, and quadruple the rate of rural counties. An index crime falls in one of eight categories established by the FBI. See calculations from *Uniform Crime Reports, 1980*, cited in Wilson, *Crime and Public Policy*, p. 17.

4. Wilson, *Crime and Public Policy*, p. 18.

5. See U.S. Department of Health, Education and Welfare, *Violent Schools—Safe Schools: The Safe School Study Report to the Congress* (Washington, D.C.: Government Printing Office, 1978).

6. FBI, *Crime in the United States, 1986*, pp. 18, 25, 29.

7. Joel L. Naroff, Daryl Hellman, and David Skinner, "The Boston Experience: Estimates of the Impact of Crime on Property Values," *Growth and Change* 11, no. 4 (October 1980): 24–30.

8. William W. Greer, "What Is the Cost of Rising Crime?" *New York Affairs* 8 (January 1984): 6–16.

9. FBI, *Crime in the United States, 1975*, p. 49; *1980*, p. 41; *1986*, p. 41.

10. Ibid., *1986*, p. 41.

11. See *Mapp v. Ohio*, 367 U.S. 643 (1961) (exclusion in state court proceedings of probative evidence by improper search and seizure); *Massiah v. United States*, 377 U.S. 201 (1964) (effectively barring the use of normal methods of undercover and informant investigation in relation to an indicted suspect); *Griffin v. California*, 380 U.S. 609 (1965) (barring judicial and prosecutorial comment regarding inferences from a defendant's failure to testify); *Miranda v. Arizona*, 384 U.S. 436 (1966) (exclusion of voluntary confessions given without a prior reading and explicit waiver of rights); *Doyle v. Ohio*, 426 U.S. 61 (1976) (requiring concealment at trial of a suspect's failure to answer questions following *Miranda* warnings); *Brewer v. Williams*, 430 U.S. 387 (1977) (effectively barring noncoercive police efforts to obtain information concerning an offense from the suspect without a waiver of counsel, following the initiation of judicial proceedings); and *Booth v. Maryland*, 55 U.S.L.W. 4836 (1987) (requiring concealment in a capital sentencing proceeding of the impact of the crime on the murder victim's family).

12. See Steven R. Schlesinger, "Criminal Procedure in the Courtroom," in Wil-

son, *Crime and Public Policy*, pp. 194–97; Dallin Oaks, "Studying the Exclusionary Rule in Search and Seizure," *University of Chicago Law Review* 37 (1970): 665; *The Effects of the Exclusionary Rule: A Study in California* (Washington, D.C.: National Institute of Justice, 1982); Malcolm Richard Wilkey, *Enforcing the Fourth Amendment by Alternatives to the Exclusionary Rule* (Washington, D.C.: National Legal Center for the Public Interest, 1982).

13. Comptroller General of the United States, *Impact of the Exclusionary Rule on Federal Criminal Prosecutions*, report CDG-79-45 (Washington, D.C.: U.S. General Accounting Office, 1979).

14. The extent of criminal victimization and the estimates of the likelihood that a person will become a victim of crime during his or her lifetime are analyzed by the U.S. Department of Justice in *Criminal Victimization, 1986*, in *Bureau of Justice Statistics Bulletin* (Washington, D.C.: U.S. Department of Justice, 1987); and *Lifetime Likelihood of Victimization*, Bureau of Justice Statistics Technical Report (Washington, D.C.: U.S. Department of Justice, 1987).

15. Edwin W. Zedlewsk, *Making Confinement Decisions* (Washington, D.C.: National Institute of Justice, 1987).

16. Mark S. Gold, *The Facts About Drugs and Alcohol* (New York: Bantam Books, 1987), p. 5.

17. See National Institute on Drug Abuse, *National Household Survey on Drug Abuse: Population Estimates, 1985*, NIDA-DHHS-(ADM)87-1539 (Washington, D.C.: Government Printing Office, 1987). "Current use" is defined as the use of narcotics at least once in the 30 days prior to the survey.

18. Mary G. Graham, *Controlling Drug Abuse and Crime: A Research Update* (Washington, D.C.: National Institute of Justice, 1987), p. 1.

19. National Institute on Drug Abuse, *Highlights of Attitude Survey of Drug Abuse* (Washington, D.C.: Government Printing Office, 1986), p. 2.

20. Graham, *Controlling Drug Abuse and Crime*, pp. 1–2.

21. Ibid, p. 2.

22. See Eric D. Wish, *Drug Use Forecasting: New York, 1984 to 1986* (Washington, D.C.: National Institute of Justice, 1987); and Graham, *Controlling Drug Abuse and Crime*.

23. See Robert Trojanowicz and David Carter, *The Philosophy and Role of Community Policing* (East Lansing: National Neighborhood Foot Patrol Center, School of Criminal Justice, Michigan State University, 1988); George L. Kelling, *Police and Communities: The Quiet Revolution* (Washington, D.C.: National Institute of Justice, 1988); and John E. Eck and William Spelman, *Problem-Solving: Problem-Oriented Policing in Newport News* (Washington, D.C.: Police Executive Research Forum and National Institute of Justice, 1987).

24. Trojanowicz and Carter, *Community Policing*, p. 17.

25. See Peter W. Greenwood, *Selective Incapacitation* (Santa Monica: Rand Corp., 1982).

◆ PART IV ◆

Philosophical Perspectives
Peace, Prosperity, Liberty

SIDNEY HOOK

◆ ──────────────── ◆

A Philosophical
Perspective

◆ Contemporary philosophy has abandoned the quest for an explanatory foundation of our knowledge of the world. It has renounced this grandiose project and returned to the more modest quest for wisdom in pursuing resolutions of the successive problems of mankind. This trend represents a fruitful convergence of interests with those engaged in the policy sciences of today, which by nature tend to be interdisciplinary.

When we speak of a philosophical perspective, we cannot intelligibly speak of a point of view bearing on all the problems of mankind. To be sure, many of them are interrelated and come in clusters, but the clusters are ineradicably pluralistic. Nonetheless, in facing the future we cannot make the bland assumption that all our problems are of equal significance or urgency. Despite foreign policy developments in recent years, the most important problem confronting mankind—as measured by the intrinsic weight of the values involved and by the number of other problems that depend on its resolution—is whether the free and open society of the West, which has blossomed in a comparatively brief period of recorded history, will survive or whether it will be overwhelmed by some form of secular or religious totalitarianism. Although the current threat from communism or secular totalitarianism is far greater than from any forms of religious fundamentalism, it certainly is not the only challenge to the survival of the free society.

What adds to the hazards of any analysis of our current problems and their probable resolution is the danger of an easy extrapolation of the historical and economic tendencies observable in the past and present. In past centuries the prophets of doom and gloom as well as of joy and peace have been exposed by unexpected developments in the historical process they relied on to confirm their predictions. There is a sobering moral in the parable of a political prophet in Munich in 1928

> who was asked to prophesy what would be happening to the burghers of his city in five, fifteen, twenty and forty years' time. He began: "I prophesy that in five years' time, in 1933, Munich will be a part of a Germany that has just suffered 5 million unemployed and that is ruled by a dictator with a certifiable mental illness who will proceed to murder 6 million Jews."
>
> His audience said: "Ah, then you must think that in fifteen years' time we will be in a sad plight."
>
> "No," replied the prophet, "I prophesy that in 1943 Munich will be part of a Greater Germany whose flag will fly from the Volga to Bordeaux, from Northern Norway to the Sahara."
>
> "Ah, then you must think that in twenty years' time, we will be mighty indeed."
>
> "No, my guess is that in 1948 Munich will be part of a Germany that stretches only from the Elbe to the Rhine, and whose ruined cities will recently have seen production down to only 10 per cent of the 1928 level."
>
> "So you think we face black ruin in forty years' time?"
>
> "No, by 1968 I prophesy that real income per head in Munich will be four times greater than now, and that in the year after that 90 per cent of German adults will sit looking at a box in a corner of their drawing rooms, which will show live pictures of a man walking upon the moon."
>
> They locked him up as a madman, of course.[1]

The moral is not that anything is possible and that we should give credence to any wild surmise about the future but that the natural assumption that the future will always be inferable from the present is unavoidably risky.

As hazardous as predictions are, I am not venturing much in asserting that during the next few decades free Western society—where the term *Western* is not merely a geographical designation—will face a serious challenge to its survival. Some maintain that its survival is possible only if the external threats from its totalitarian enemies are eliminated. Others assert that these threats no longer exist in virtue of the gradual transformation of communist societies and the abandonment of their program of world domination in favor of genuine peaceful coexistence—once merely proclaimed as a propaganda slogan but now imposed by the stern necessities of economic hardship. I believe that both positions are questionable. The preservation of our free society does not require the elimination of all totalitarian societies, secular or religious. Nor has the threat to the Western world lapsed with the policies of *glasnost'* in the Soviet Union and the overthrow of Maoism in China.

What is indisputably true is that socialism as an economic system has failed in our time not only in the fully socialized economies of the communist states and the Third World but also in several of the semisocialized countries of Western Europe. As an economy, socialism in varying degrees has failed to solve the problem of incentive and to find a substitute for the free market to satisfy the needs of the consumer. But it is simplistic to assume that the failure of socialism as an economy necessarily spells the end of communism as a movement. For what is distinctive about communism as a movement in the twentieth century is that it has synthesized an economic program and a political program.

The more accurate designation of communism today is Leninism, not Marxism. The distinction is perhaps best expressed in the profound difference between the way in which Marx and Lenin understood the unfortunate phrase "the dictatorship of the proletariat," which appears peripherally in Marx's writings and centrally in Lenin's. For Marx the Paris Commune, governed by a coalition of political parties whose economic measures were reformist rather than revolutionary, exemplified the dictatorship of the proletariat. For Lenin the dictatorship of the proletariat could only be exercised through the absolute dictatorship of the Communist Party *over* society guided by no law or restraint save its own power. Leninism, not Marxism, governs every communist country of the world today. In the life of communist countries everywhere, all lesser figures may be criticized for mistakes or excoriated for crimes; only Lenin remains an icon.

The great historical paradox, beyond the grasp of those unfamiliar with the theory and practice of communism, is that the principles of Marxism as Marx understood them explain the failure of socialism in communist countries. Marx himself declared that any attempt to collectivize society in an economy of scarcity (actually, in economies like those found wherever communism has been introduced in our century) would result not in prosperity but in socializing poverty.[2] On this score Marx's analysis and prediction have been historically confirmed. He believed that the development of the forces of production to their highest available level was a necessary condition for the introduction of socialism. The extent to which countries under communist rule were able to build up the industrial infrastructure required for socialism depended on what they were able to buy or steal from the capitalist economies of the West. On this point, Marx was perfectly justified in predicting the failure of any attempt to skip what he regarded as a necessary phase in social evolution. Where he went wrong was in his failure to predict that the attempt would be made and in the horrendous social and political consequences of the resulting failure for the modern world. Marx's theory of history was refuted by the political victory of Lenin and Leninism even as the economic breakdown of Leninist society testifies to the historical validity of Marx's economic analysis on this point.[3]

The alleged new turn in recent Soviet economic policy represents a departure from Marx's notion of how a socialist economy should function. It does not represent an abandonment of the political philosophy of Leninism and its underlying strategy. It is the most ambitious tactic in a long series of efforts to induce the Western world both to lower its military defense and to share its advanced technology to make the economic life of the Soviet masses more acceptable, at least to the point where the Soviet class system and differential privileges within it become tolerable. That Leninists should make this effort, even if it involves a strategic retreat, is comprehensible and consistent with the history of Leninism since 1918, when it dissolved the Russian Constituent Assembly whose convocation Leninists had called for before seizing power in October 1917. That some credulous Western leaders and distinguished organs of public opinion should regard the adoption of some features of the free-market economy as an abandonment of Leninism is more difficult to explain as anything but a form of wishful thinking.

We need not explain this wishful thinking to recognize the importance of strengthening intelligent allegiance to the democratic faith of the West and its institutions.[4] That faith has been under attack not only from the agitation and propaganda agencies of the Kremlin but from irreconcilably alienated elements within the Western world who, professing an indifference or even hostility to the communist totalitarian states, concentrate their main critical fire against "the so-called free world," especially the United States. When I contrast the democratic faith or allegiance to the free society with the ideology of communism, I use the term *ideology* to mean the set of ideas and ideals that constitute the legitimizing rationale of a society one is prepared to defend, if only as the best of the available alternatives. I am not saying that great historical events and decisions can be explained by these ideological allegiances or that they always override considerations of practical survival or the advantages of compromise. Even during the era of fierce ideological religious wars, dynastic and nationalistic factors disrupted theological and ecclesiastical allegiances. Because ideology or one's fighting faith is not everything, it is not nothing. In some crucial periods of history it may play an important even if not decisive role, and our time is such a period.

When we ask ourselves what intellectual supports we can rely upon to strengthen the free world, we must note with sadness the transformation of the philosophy of American liberalism into the doctrines and practices of illiberalism. The philosophy of American liberalism is rooted in Jefferson and flowered in the philosophy of John Dewey. This philosophical hybrid accepts as its mandate of authority in social affairs the freely given consent of the governed, that such consent cannot be free unless there are guaranteed rights of dissent, that the locus of these rights is the individual (not the class or caste or group), that the arbiter of the inevitable conflict of human rights is the democratic process, that intelligence or the use of reason in social affairs functions best when there is a free market of ideas, and that truth and justice however defined are color-blind and have no gender. In the American liberal philosophy the individual, not individualism, is central and the community, committed to an equal concern for all individuals to achieve the fullest measure of their desirable potential, recognizes its responsibility to adopt measures that will further equality of opportunity, not equality of result.

If this is indeed the historical legacy of American liberalism, then it has been betrayed by those who have donned the mantle of liberalism in our generation. It would require a volume to do justice to the record, but I content myself here with two important manifestations of that betrayal.

The first and most persuasive evidence of the erosion of liberal political traditions is the retreat among professedly liberal individuals and groups from a position of judicial restraint to one of judicial activism. The genuinely liberal tradition in the United States is rooted in the position of Jefferson and Lincoln. Until recently judicial activism has been associated with the fear of legislative majorities, with a history that began with the Dred Scott decision and continued with the overthrow of the civil rights acts after the Civil War, with *Plessy v. Ferguson*, and with the invalidation of New Deal legislation in the 1930s. With the emergence of the Warren court, the power of the Supreme Court has increased immeasurably, aided by the reluctance of congressional authority to exercise its mandate. Indeed, beginning with the Warren court, federal court decisions have had a more profound influence on the daily life of the nation—especially in education, business, and labor relations—than explicit legislation. The judiciary has reinterpreted the text of congressional legislation and presidential executive orders and has disregarded the legislative history of the acts in question.[5] Never in the history of the Supreme Court have defenders of judicial activism made bolder claims for its jurisdiction. Not only do they defend the role of the court as the supreme defender of the basic freedoms of the people (although all branches of government are equally pledged to their defense), but they believe that the court is empowered to invoke rights and freedoms, even by a five-to-four decision, not explicitly recognized either in the text of the Constitution or by any previous court or branch of government.

The extent to which the traditional philosophy of political liberalism, with its faith in the legislative process to educate the people in the meaning of freedom and to preserve the rights of minorities while upholding majority rule, has been transformed into the current view that the courts are the chief defenders of our basic freedoms may be measured by contrasting Henry Steele Commager's position in 1943 with his views today and with those of Professor Laurence Tribe, who under the aegis of present-day liberalism led the attack against the nomination of Judge Robert Bork to the Supreme Court. The flavor of Commager's early book, written in defense of the views of Justice Felix Frankfurter, comes through in these representative citations:

> The real battles of liberalism are not to be won in any court. If we make constitutionality the test of civil-rights legislation we are pretty sure to lose our case. It tends to distract attention from the real issues, places an improper responsibility on the courts, and encourages government by litigation instead of government by political machinery. No, the place to meet, and to defeat, unwise or unconstitutional legislation is in the legislature or in the arena of public opinion . . .
>
> The impatient liberal, confronted with some example of legislative stupidity or of injustice, is eager for immediate action. The court may nullify the offensive legislation, but would not more be gained if the question were raised and agitated in the political instead of the judicial arena? The tendency to decide issues of personal liberty in the judicial arena alone has the effect of lulling the people into apathy towards issues that are fundamentally their concern, with the comforting notion that the courts will take care of personal and minority rights. It effectively removes these issues from the arena of public discussion . . .
>
> This is the crucial objection to the judicial nullification of majority will in any field: that "education in the abandonment of foolish legislation is itself a training in liberty."[6]

There is no reason to believe that the justices of the Supreme Court are more qualified to determine the meaning of the basic freedoms on which our democracy rests or to resolve the inescapable conflicts of rights, values, and interests posed by legislative measures than the duly elected representatives of the people. Our nation was founded in a revolution against the actions of the British Crown and the British Parliament that were not responsible to the interests and consent of the American people. To accept the judicial activism of U.S. liberals is to abandon the principles of democracy and both the letter and the spirit of the Constitution.[7]

The second area of contemporary life that reflects the transformation of the liberal philosophy is the systematic perversion by certain administrative government agencies and the courts of the language of the Civil Rights Act of 1964 and of the original text of Presidential Executive Order 11246, which formulated the principles of affirmative action. The plain language of both documents forbids discrimination against any individual on grounds of race, religion, sex, or national origin. This position of traditional liberalism is expressed in Justice Harlan's famous dissent in *Plessy v. Ferguson*. His statement "the Constitution is color-blind" became the slogan of the National Association for the Advancement of Colored People (NAACP) when Roy Wilkins was its national secretary. It presupposes that individuals, not groups or classes, are the locus of human rights.

Today even in situations and institutions with no history of discrimination against minorities and women, the principles of affirmative action have become the instruments of policies of reverse discrimination and preferential hiring. In practice, the required "numerical goals and time schedules" to guide hiring practices wherever the underutilization of women and minorities is alleged actually result in a quota system. The historical effects of the deplorable discriminatory practices of the past are thus countered not only by remedial measures to increase the numbers of qualified minority and female candidates but by another kind of invidious discrimination.

Professional sports were rampantly discriminatory until Jackie Robinson shattered the immoral color barrier. Today no sensible or fair person argues that numerical goals and time schedules regulating the composition of the teams should replace the principle that open positions should be filled by the best players regardless of the racial percentage distribution on the team compared with the ratios in the general population or the pool of candidates trying out for the position. Why should it be different in any other field, especially in the universities and professions? Obviously the quest for excellence in education cannot survive the perversion of the principles of affirmative action into anything resembling a quota system. Although the term *quota* is carefully eschewed by those who have perverted the original meaning of affirmative action, in every area of public life today, especially in education, race and sex are regarded as relevant criteria in decisions affecting the admission, promotion, and reduction of personnel. How far the departure has gone from the traditional principle of liberalism is indicated by a recent declaration of Roy Wilkins's successor at the NAACP, Benjamin Hooks. Asked what was wrong with a "color-blind" approach to civil rights that would bar all forms of discrimination including reverse discrimination or preferential hiring, he responded, "It's wrong because it's stupid." [8]

Of all the negative effects of the illiberal view of affirmative action, probably the most worrisome is its impact on the prospects for liberal education. It has led in many areas to an abandonment of the quest for excellence on the ground that this leads to an invidious emphasis on the achievement of the elite. Even an equal-opportunity employer's announcement of a competitive scholarship for the study of English literature with the caution "Only the Best Need Apply" has been deemed "inappropriate, insensitive and inconsistent" with the policies of affirmative action. The assumption that teaching personnel should reflect the proportion of women and minorities in the pool of potentially qualifiable candidates may before long be extended to the subject matter taught. Some university students and faculty have demanded that curricular offerings in standard courses on Western civilization or Western culture eliminate their alleged imperialist racial and sexual bias and reflect the hitherto unrecognized contributions of the cultures of the oppressed.

Our concern with the nature and quality of our educational system is decidedly relevant to the prospects of survival of a free society. Jefferson's conviction that only an educated and enlightened democracy can overcome the weaknesses of the popular rule of the past that succumbed to anarchy or despotism gains strength in the light of events in our century. Both the Old World and the new confirm Madison's observation that democracies "have been as short in their lives as they have been violent in their deaths." We may even argue that the very survival of our culture is at risk in our increasingly technological age unless we raise the level of general education and enhance the quality of higher education.

The current conditions of both are disquieting. Public education in large U.S. cities now turns out functionally illiterate students unable to cope with modern society. The courts have contributed to undermining the authority of teachers, who can no longer bar disrupters from the classroom. Everyone seems to have a vested interest in concealing the endemic violence in school systems where rape, robbery, and assault often occur. The lack of discipline in the schools is a major reason for the white flight that defeats plans for desegregation in city schools. Parents will endure hardships to avoid the expense and inconvenience of relocation. But once they perceive threats to the safety of their children, inferior educational programs, and disorderly classrooms, they will uproot.

Ironically, uncontrolled permissiveness defeats the aim of democratic education: to teach students to accept the authority of rational method in reaching conclusions. For without recognizing the importance of disciplined habits and the authority of the teacher over the process by which those habits are acquired, the educational experience cannot truly develop. It is nearly libelous to attribute the state of U.S. public education today to progressive education as John Dewey understood it.[9]

When we turn to U.S. higher education, the devastating consequences of the so-called student revolution of the 1960s are still apparent in the curricular chaos of most undergraduate campuses, where the requirements of a liberal education were abolished for a miscellany of unrelated general and vocational courses. But a far more serious development, sedulously concealed by administrative authorities, is that freedom to teach and learn in our major universities has in effect been abolished in certain disciplines. The winds of freedom no longer blow on U.S. campuses where foreign policy, race relations, affirmative action, feminist studies, and allied areas are concerned. Outstanding officials and scholars defending the foreign policy of the U.S. government in recent years, even when officially invited by university bodies, have often been unable to speak without organized disruption by extremist students immune from disciplinary action even when the guidelines of permitted dissent are clearly violated. The contrasting receptions accorded by campus audiences to Angela Davis, the notorious communist agitator, and to Jeane Kirkpatrick, former U.S. ambassador to the United Nations, symbolize the situation.

More serious in its long-term effect is the growing politicalization of the humanities and social sciences, where classrooms have become bully pulpits for anti-American sentiment. The history of the United States is commonly portrayed as the successive oppression of Indians, Chicanos, blacks, Chinese, European immigrants, and women without reference to the liberating aspects of the U.S. experience that attracted millions of the underprivileged and deprived everywhere, who found a better life for themselves and their offspring in the United States. It is perfectly legitimate to develop a critical attitude toward national pieties and complacencies about U.S. foreign and domestic policies. It is not legitimate to employ double standards, to judge the United States by its practices and failure to fulfill its ideals, and to contrast it with the professions and rhetoric of its enemies in a comparative evaluation that draws a moral equation between the free and open society of the United States and totalitarian communist regimes.

Classroom procedures of this kind, whether motivated by a desire to further capitalism or socialism, really violate the responsibilities of honest teaching incorporated in the principles of academic freedom. Academic freedom defends the rights of qualified teachers to investigate, discuss, publish, or teach the truth as they see it in the discipline of their competence, subject to no authority except the standards of professional ethics and inquiry. Academic freedom, the common law of U.S. university life, not only tolerates intellectual heresy but legally supports it. Even more remarkable, it provides complete immunity from institutional sanctions for the exercise of one's constitutional rights—an immunity not enjoyed by other fellow citizens. For example, I share a public platform with my physician, my attorney, my grocer, and my butcher from which we defend some highly controversial position on a burning issue of the moment. My fellow speakers may all pay a high price for the expression of their opinions—the loss of clients or the loss of trade—but only I, as a member of a university where academic freedom obtains, am absolved of the normal costs of unpopularity.

The community directly or indirectly (by tax exemption) underwrites the great costs of university education upholding the institution of academic freedom because it is in the common interest to do so. But clearly the right to academic freedom is correlative to certain duties and responsibilities flagrantly violated by the practices described above. The proper enforcement of these duties and responsibilities must be in the hands of the faculties themselves. Their reluctance to enforce these intellectual standards may undermine public support for higher education. Even private support may be affected. U.S. corporations contribute close to two billion dollars annually in support of higher education. If they refused to appropriate funds to institutions in open violation of the principles of academic freedom, faculties might take the necessary corrective measures. In extreme situations in which university administrations refuse to enforce the provisions of disciplinary codes established by joint student-faculty committees, the Civil Rights Act should be invoked on the ground that those in a position to enforce the laws are violating the civil rights of students and teachers victimized by organized violence or disruption.

The politicalization of our universities relates directly to our basic theme, the defense of the free world against the threats of totalitarianism. Unlike elementary education, where some form of indoctrination is inescapable even while the critical faculties of students are being developed, higher education has no need for it, if by *indoctrination* we mean "the process of teaching through which acceptance of belief is induced by non-rational or irrational means or both."[10] In higher education every position should be open to critical evaluation. Karl Jaspers notwithstanding, there is no need to make propaganda for the truth. Conflicting claims about the achievements of free and totalitarian societies and their costs should be examined as carefully as conflicting claims in any field of knowledge or policy. We need not fear the outcome of honest inquiry—that is, the commitment to an intellectual discipline that examines both sides of an issue and recognizes the difference between historical truth, however incomplete and inadequate, and historical fiction.

No formula or program available can provide reasonable hope for solving the multitude of problems confronting the American people in the coming decade. On the domestic scene it is safe to predict that Americans will settle for a mixed economy but are extremely unlikely to reach a consensus on how wealth is to be created and distributed. A recurrent fear among the philosopher-statesmen who founded the United States was that its citizens would be unable or unwilling to summon up the virtue necessary in times of crisis to subordinate private interest to the public good. The chronic identification of private interest with the public good can only end in chaos and national disaster. There is general agreement that the community must provide a safety net for those who through no fault of their own find themselves living beneath the level of a decent subsistence in a civilized society. But it is impossible literally to provide equality of opportunity for persons of disparate talents and wildly varying parental concern and capacities. All the greater therefore is the necessity for reducing the inequality of opportunity by social action that will provide all groups with a stake in the community and in the democratic process great enough to make them willing to defend it.

Whereas we realize that moral exhortation without institutional reform is empty, we must also recognize that institutional change without the acceptance of moral responsibility for one's individual conduct leaves us with another set of problems. Public outlays that end up with a permanent underclass cannot solve the problems of dependency, misery, and crime. Too much of our social and juridical thinking and the attitude of the victims of misfortune themselves reflect the view that human beings are so completely the creatures of circumstance that they are merely objects to which things happen. Such a view lacks coherence and contributes to the difficulty of resolving problems. It denies human beings responsibility for their own condition, despite the variation in behavior among persons in the same condition. At the same time it blames other human beings for permitting these conditions to exist, assuming in their case that they have moral responsibility, a human status, denied to others. But there is less to be said for this division between human beings, between those who are objects of the social process and those who are subjects, than for any division along national, religious, racial, or sexual lines. In effect such a view wipes out the moral difference between the criminals and their victims.[11]

A liberal jurist has recently protested against those like myself who have pointed out that we give far less attention to the rights of the victims and potential victims of crime than to the rights of the criminal defendants and potential criminal defendants. He regards the question of responsibility as either irrelevant or equally pertinent. "I am astonished," he writes, "by those who point to the docile deprived and say, 'Their conditions do not force them to break the law: why should those conditions force others to?'" Instead of answering the question, he evades it by telling us that we should be as alarmed by those who accept their conditions as by those who engage in criminal violence reacting against them. Strange doctrine for a jurist! We should, of course, be alarmed by both groups, but where those who accept their conditions become the victims of the criminal violence of those who do not, we should certainly be *more* concerned to protect the first group and punish the second. But according to our worthy jurist, the victims are responsible as well as the criminals. "What is amazing is that so many deprived Americans accept their lot without striking out," that is, without engaging in violent crime too.[12]

Can we abolish crime, reduce poverty, and bring new opportunities by social reorganization alone? We certainly cannot do so without social reorganization, but that is not sufficient without human beings accepting some responsibility for their lives within the organization—a proposition Karl Marx recognized in his scornful contrast between the proletariat and the lumpen proletariat both living in a deprived environment. By all means let us provide those tempted by the easy money available by violence and vice with meaningful job opportunities and with modern housing that makes possible a comfortable family home. But how can we expect them to appear at work on Friday and Monday, to have the proper work ethic on other days, and to take care of their housing without their acceptance of personal—yes, moral—responsibility for their own behavior? The history of social reform and its impact on the statistics of violent crime in the last 50 years demonstrate that any increase in social concern must be accompanied by an increase in personal moral responsibility by encouraging those in need to reduce their social dependency on agencies beyond their own powers of participation and influence.

As long as we are committed as a nation to the defense of free societies, we can live without a consensus on the shifting pressures and conflicts of domestic policy. All the more necessary therefore is a consensus on a foreign policy that puts freedom first. The gravest internal threat to our survival is the danger that out of arrogance or ignorance U.S. foreign policy will be made a football in the struggle for U.S. electoral victory.

A genuinely democratic consensus cannot be established by manipulation but only by discussion, debate, and rational persuasion. The capacity to engage in this process and the quality of thought displayed in the decisions that emerge from it will reflect the character of the education—especially the public education—Americans receive. That is why wherever we are and whatever else we do, we must begin by improving our public education.

Notes

1. General Sir John Hackett, *The Third World War* (London: Macmillan, 1979), p. 424. I owe this reference to my colleague, Lewis Gann.

2. Karl Marx, *Collected Works* (London: Lawrence & Wishart, 1976), 5:49.

3. See Sidney Hook, "Marxism Versus Communism," in *Marxism and Beyond* (Totowa, N.J.: Rowen & Littlefield, 1982).

4. See Sidney Hook, *Political Power and Personal Freedom* (New York: Criterion Books, 1959), esp. pt. 1.

5. A conspicuous illustration of judicial legislation in the guise of arbitrary re-

interpretation of the text of the Civil Rights Act is the case of *Kaiser Aluminum and Chemical Corporation v. Brian F. Walker et al.* (1979).

6. Henry Steele Commager, *Majority Rule and Minority Rights* (New York: Oxford University Press, 1943), pp. 72 ff.

7. On the general question of the relationship between democracy and judicial review, see Sidney Hook, *The Paradox of Freedom*, 2d ed. (Buffalo: Prometheus Press, 1987).

8. *New York Times*, May 30, 1983.

9. Cf. Thomas Main, "John Dewey and Progressive Education," *American Educator*, Fall 1987, p. 24.

10. See Sidney Hook, *Education for Modern Man: A New Perspective* (New York: Alfred Knopf, 1963), pp. 169 ff.

11. I believe I was the first to sound the tocsin in "The Rights of Victims," a 1971 commencement address at the University of Florida reprinted in Sidney Hook, *Philosophy and Public Policy* (Carbondale: Southern Illinois University Press, 1980).

12. Judge David L. Bazelon, quoted in *New York Times*, January 7, 1988.

MILTON FRIEDMAN
ROSE D. FRIEDMAN

◆ ──────────────────────── ◆

The Tide in the
Affairs of Men

There is a tide in the affairs of men,
Which, taken at the flood, leads on to fortune;
Omitted, all the voyage of their life
Is bound in shallows and in miseries.

Shakespeare, *Julius Caesar*

◆ Shakespeare's image is an apt text for our essay. There are powerful tides in the affairs of men, interpreted as the collective entity we call society, just as in the affairs of individuals. The tides in the affairs of society are slow to become apparent, as one tide begins to overrun its predecessor. Each tide lasts a long time—decades, not hours—once it begins to flood and leaves its mark on its successor even after it recedes.

How tides begin in the minds of men, spread to the conduct of public policy, often generate their own reversal, and are succeeded by another tide—all this is a vast topic insufficiently explored by historians, economists, and other social scientists.[1]

The aim of this brief essay is modest: to present a hypothesis that has become increasingly plausible to us over the years, to illustrate it with experience over the past three centuries, and to discuss some of its implications. The hypothesis is that a major change in social and economic policy is preceded by a shift in the climate of intellectual *opinion*, itself generated, at least in part, by contemporaneous social, political, and economic circumstances. This shift may begin in one country but, if it proves lasting, ultimately spreads worldwide. At first it will have little effect on social and economic policy. After a lag, sometimes of decades, an intellectual tide "taken at its flood" will spread at first gradually, then more rapidly, to the public at large and through the public's pressure on government will affect the course of economic, social, and political policy. As the tide in *events* reaches its flood, the intellectual tide starts to ebb, offset by what A. V. Dicey calls counter-currents of opinion. The counter-currents typically represent a reaction to the practical consequences attributed to the earlier intellectual tide. Promise tends to be utopian. Performance never is and therefore disappoints. The initial protagonists of the intellectual tide die out and the intellectual quality of their followers and supporters inevitably declines. It takes intellectual independence and courage to start a counter-current to dominant opinion. It takes far less of either to climb on a bandwagon. The venturesome, independent, and courageous young seek new fields to conquer and that calls for exploring the new and untried. The counter-currents that gather force set in motion the next tidal wave, and the process is repeated.

Needless to say, this sketch is oversimplified and excessively formalized. In particular it omits any discussion of the subtle mutual interaction between intellectual opinion, public opinion, and the course of events. Gradual changes in policy and institutional arrangements are always going on. Major changes seldom occur, however, except at times of crisis, when, to use Richard Weaver's evocative phrase, "ideas have consequences." The intellectual tide is spread to the public by all manner of intellectual retailers—teachers and preachers, journalists in print and on television, pundits and politicians. The public begins to react to the crisis according to the options that intellectuals have explored, options that effectively limit the alternatives open to the powers that be. In almost every tide a crisis can be identified as the catalyst for a major change in the direction of policy.

We shall illustrate the relevance of our hypothesis with the two latest completed tides as well as the tide that, as we put it in the title of the final chapter of *Free to Choose*, is turning.[2]

The Rise of Laissez-Faire (the Adam Smith Tide)

The first tide we discuss begins in the eighteenth century in Scotland with a reaction against mercantilism expressed in the writings of David Hume, Adam Smith's *Theory of Moral Sentiments* (1759), and above all Smith's *The Wealth of Nations* (1776).

The Wealth of Nations is widely and correctly regarded as the foundation stone of modern scientific economics. Its normative thrust and its influence on the wider intellectual world are of greater interest for our present purpose. Its rapid success in influencing the intellectual community doubtless reflected the seeds planted by Hume and others—the intellectual counter-currents to the mercantilist tide—as well as the early stages of the Industrial Revolution.

On the other side of the Atlantic 1776 also saw the proclamation of the Declaration of Independence—in many ways the political twin of Smith's economics. Smith's work quickly became common currency to the Founding Fathers. Alexander Hamilton documented that phenomenon in a back-handed way in his 1791 *Report on Manufactures*. He quoted Smith extensively and praised him profusely while at the same time devoting the substance of his report to arguing that Smith's doctrines did not apply to the United States, which needed not free international trade but the protection of infant industries by tariffs—an example of the homage that vice, even intellectual vice, pays to virtue.

Smith had no illusions about the impact of his intellectual ideas on public policy: "To expect that the freedom of trade should ever be entirely restored in Great Britain, is as absurd as to expect that an Oceana or Utopia should ever be established in it. Not only the prejudices of the public, but what is much more unconquerable, the private interests of many individuals, irresistably oppose it."[3]

His prediction proved false. By the early nineteenth century the ideas of laissez-faire, of the operation of the invisible hand, of the undesirability of government intervention into economic matters, had swept first the intellectual world and then public policy. Bentham, Ricardo, James Mill, and John Stuart Mill were actively engaged in spreading these ideas and promoting them politically. Maria Edgeworth was writing novels based on Ricardian economics. Cobden and Bright were campaigning for the repeal of the corn laws. Reinforced by pressures arising out of the Industrial Revolution, these ideas were beginning to affect public policy, though the process was delayed by the Napoleonic Wars with the accompanying high government spending and restrictions on international trade. Yet the wars also furnished the needed catalytic crisis.

The repeal of the corn laws in 1846 is generally regarded as the final triumph of Smith after a 70-year delay. In fact some reductions in trade barriers had started much earlier, and many nonagricultural items continued to be protected by tariffs until 1874. Thereafter only revenue tariffs remained on such items as spirits, wine, beer, and tobacco, countervailed by excise duties on competing domestic products. So it took nearly a century for the completion of one response to Adam Smith.

The other countries of Europe and the United States did not follow the British lead by establishing complete free trade in goods. During most of the nineteenth century, however, U.S. duties on imports were primarily for revenue, though protection did play a significant role, as rancorous political debates, particularly between the North and the South, testify. Except for a few years after the War of 1812, customs provided between 90 and 100 percent of total federal revenues up to the Civil War. And except for a few years during and after that war, customs provided half or more of federal revenues until the Spanish-American War at the end of the century.

Nontariff barriers such as quotas were nonexistent. Movement of people and capital was hardly impeded at all. The United States in particular had completely free immigration. In Europe before World War I "the inhabitant of London," in John Maynard Keynes's eloquent words, "could secure . . . cheap and comfortable means of transit to any country or climate without passport or other formality . . . and could . . . proceed abroad to foreign quarters, without knowledge of the religion, language, or customs . . . and would consider himself greatly aggrieved and much surprised at the least interference."[4]

Hamilton's success in achieving protectionist legislation in the United States reflects the absence of effective ideological commitment by policy makers to avoiding intervention by government into economic activity, despite the intellectual tide set in motion by Adam Smith, the French physiocrats, and their later followers. However, strong belief in states' rights meant that states, not the federal government, played the major role. Many states established state banks, built canals, and engaged in other commercial enterprises. The catalytic crisis that produced a drastic change was the panic of 1837, in the course of which many, perhaps most, government enterprises went bankrupt. That panic served the same role in discrediting government enterprise as the Great Depression did nearly a century later in discrediting private enterprise.

In the aftermath the ideas of Adam Smith offered both an explanation and an obvious alternative option; tariffs aside, near complete laissez-faire and nonintervention reigned into the next century.

Measuring the role of government in the economy is not easy. One readily available, though admittedly imperfect, measure is the ratio of government spending to national income. At the height of laissez-faire, peacetime government spending was less than 10 percent of national income in both the United States and Great Britain. Two-thirds of U.S. spending was by state and local governments, with about half for education; federal spending was generally less than 3 percent of national income, with half of that for the military.

A striking example of the worldwide impact of the Adam Smith tide—this time in practice, not in ideas—is provided by post-Meiji Japan. For centuries prior to the Meiji Restoration in 1867, Japan had been almost completely isolated from the Western world. The new rulers had no ideological understanding, let alone commitment, to laissez-faire. On the contrary, they attached little value to individual freedom, either political or economic. Their overriding objective was simply to strengthen the power and glory of their country.

Nevertheless, when the Meiji rulers burst into a Western world in which laissez-faire Britain was the dominant economy, they simply took for granted that Britain's policy was the one to emulate. They did not by any means extend complete economic and political freedom to their citizens, but they did go a long way, with dramatic and highly favorable results.[5]

The absence of a widespread ideological underpinning for these policies helps explain their lack of robustness. After World War I Japan succumbed to centralized control by a military dictatorship—a policy that led to economic stagnation, military adventurism, and finally Japan's entry into World War II on the side of the Nazis.

On a broader scale the tide that swept the nineteenth century brought greater political as well as economic freedom: widening rights and a higher standard of living for individuals accompanied increased international trade and human contact. It was heralded as a century of peace—but that is somewhat overstated. The tide did not prevent the U.S. Civil War, the Crimean War, the Franco-Prussian War, or other local conflicts. But there was no major widespread conflict between 1815 and 1914 comparable either to the Napoleonic Wars of the preceding years or to the world wars of the later years.

Despite occasional financial panics and crises, Britain and the United States experienced remarkable economic growth during the nineteenth century. The United States in particular became a mecca for the poor of all lands. All this was associated with—and many, including us, would say it was a result of—the increasing adoption of laissez-faire as the guiding principle of government policy.

The Rise of the Welfare State (the Fabian Tide)

This remarkable progress did not prevent the intellectual tide from turning away from individualism and toward collectivism. Indeed, it doubtless contributed to that result. According to Dicey, "from 1848 onwards an alteration becomes perceptible in the intellectual and moral atmosphere of England."[6] The flood stage, when collectivism began to dominate intellectual opinion, came some decades later. The founding of the Fabian Society, dedicated to the gradual establishment of socialism, by George Bernard Shaw, Sidney Webb, and others in 1883 is perhaps as good a dividing date as any for Britain. A comparable date for the United States is 1885, when the American Economic Association was founded by a group of young economists who had returned from study in Germany imbued with socialist ideas, which they hoped to spread through the association—a hope that was largely frustrated when the association shortly adopted a policy of "nonpartisanship and avoidance of official commitments on practical economic questions and political issues."[7] Confirming evidence is provided by the publication in 1888 of Edward Bellamy's socialist utopian romance, *Looking Backwards*, which sold over a million copies.

How can we explain this shift in the intellectual tide when the growing pains of laissez-faire policies had long been overcome and impressive positive gains had been achieved? Dicey gives one indirect answer:

> The beneficial effect of State intervention, especially in the form of legislation, is direct, immediate, and, so to speak, visible, whilst its evil effects are gradual and indirect, and lie out of sight . . . few are those who realize the undeniable truth that State help kills self-help. Hence the majority of mankind must almost of necessity look with undue favor upon governmental intervention. This natural bias can be counteracted only by the existence . . . , as in England between 1830 and 1860, of a presumption or prejudice in favor of individual liberty—that is of *laissez-faire*. The mere decline, therefore, of faith in self-help . . . is of itself sufficient to account for the growth of legislation tending toward socialism.[8]

A more direct answer is that two effects of the success of laissez-faire fostered a reaction. First, success made residual evils stand out all the more sharply, both encouraging reformers to press for governmental solutions and making the public more sympathetic to their appeals. Second, it became more reasonable to anticipate that government would be effective in attacking the residual evils. A severely limited government has few favors to give; hence there is little incentive to corrupt government officials, and government service has few attractions for persons concerned primarily with personal enrichment. Government was engaged primarily in enforcing laws against murder, theft, and the like and in providing municipal services such as local police and fire protection—activities that engendered almost unanimous citizen support. For these and other reasons, Britain, which went furthest toward complete laissez-faire, became legendary in the late nineteenth and early twentieth centuries for its incorruptible civil service and law-abiding citizenry—precisely the reverse of its reputation a century earlier. In the United States neither the quality of the civil service nor respect for the law ever reached the heights they did in Britain, but both improved over the course of the century.

Whatever the reasons, Fabian socialism became the dominant intellectual current in Britain, driving out, at the one extreme, radical Marxism, and at the other, laissez-faire. Gradually that intellectual current came to dominate first public opinion and then government policy. World War I hastened the process, but it was already well under way before the war, as is demonstrated by Dicey's prescient remarks in his 1914 preface to the second edition of *Law and Public Opinion*:

> By 1900, the doctrine of *laissez-faire*, in spite of the large element of truth which it contains, had more or less lost its hold upon the English people ... It also was in 1900 apparent to any impartial observer that the feelings or the opinions which had given strength to collectivism would continue to tell as strongly upon the legislation of the twentieth century as they already told upon the later legislation of the nineteenth century ... and this conclusion would naturally have been confirmed by the fact that in the sphere of finance there had occurred a revival of belief in protective tariffs, then known by the name of a demand for "fair trade" [echoes of 1987!].

Dicey lists "the laws which most directly illustrate the progress of collectivism," from the beginning of the twentieth century, starting with the Old Age Pension Act of 1908. In respect of a later act (the Mental Deficiency Act, 1913), he remarks that it "is the first step along a path on which no sane man can decline to enter, but which, if too far pursued, will bring statesmen across difficulties hard to meet without considerable interference with individual liberty."[9]

Clearly the seeds had been sown from which Britain's full-fledged welfare state grew, at first slowly in the interwar period and then with a final burst after World War II, marked perhaps by the adoption of the National Health Service and the panoply of measures recommended in the Beveridge report.

In the United States the development was similar, though somewhat delayed. After the popular success of Bellamy's utopian fantasy came the era of the muckrakers, led by Lincoln Steffens, Ray Stannard Baker, and Ida M. Tarbell, with their exposures of alleged corruption and malfeasance in municipal government, labor, and trusts. Upton Sinclair used the novel to promote socialist ideas, his most successful being *The Jungle* (1906), which resulted from an assignment by a socialist newspaper to investigate conditions in the Chicago stockyards. Sinclair wrote the novel to create sympathy for the workers, but it did far more to arouse indignation at the unsanitary conditions under which meat was processed. On a different level Louis Dembitz Brandeis criticized the financial community. His volume of essays, *Other People's Money and How the Bankers Use It* (1914), has been described as "a frontal assault on monopoly and interlocking directorates."[10]

"The Populist party, through which William Jennings Bryan rose to" the nomination for the presidency on the Democratic ticket in 1896, "called not merely for regulation of the railroads but for outright government ownership and operation." [11] The Interstate Commerce Commission, created in 1887, was shortly followed by the 1890 Sherman Antitrust Act and later by the 1906 Food and Drug Act, for which Sinclair's novel served as the catalyst. The modern welfare state was well on its way. World War I greatly expanded the role of government, notably by the takeover of the railroads. The postwar period brought something of a reaction, with the major exception of Prohibition.

As late as 1929 federal spending amounted to only 3.2 percent of the national income; one-third of this was spent on the military, including veterans' benefits, and one-half on the military plus interest on the public debt. State and local spending was nearly three times as large—9 percent of national income—with more than half on education and highways. Spending by federal, state, and local governments on what today is described as income support, Social Security, and welfare totaled less than 1 percent of national income.

The world of ideas was different. By 1929 socialism was the dominant ideology on the nation's campuses. The *New Republic* and *The Nation* were the intellectual's favorite journals of opinion and Norman Thomas their political hero. The impact of opinion on the world of practice, however, had so far been modest. The critical catalyst for a major change was, of course, the Great Depression, which rightly or wrongly shattered the public's confidence in private enterprise, leading it to regard government involvement as the only effective recourse in time of trouble and to treat government as a potential benefactor rather than simply a policeman and umpire.

The effect was dramatic. Federal government spending grew to roughly 30 percent of national income by the 1980s, or to nearly tenfold its 1929 level. State and local spending also grew, though far less dramatically, so that by the 1980s total government spending was over 40 percent of national income. And spending understates the role government came to play. Many intrusions into people's lives involve little or no spending: tariffs and quotas, price and wage controls, ceilings on interest rates, local ceilings on rents, zoning requirements, building codes, and so on.

The delayed impact of the intellectual climate of the 1920s illustrates one aspect of the influence of intellectual opinion—producing options for adoption when the time is ripe. Despite Norman Thomas's popularity on the campus, he received less than 1 percent of the popular vote for president in 1928 and only 2 percent in 1932. Nonetheless, we concluded that "the Socialist party was the most influential political party in the United States in the first decades of the twentieth century . . . [A]lmost every economic plank in its 1928 presidential platform has by now [1980] been enacted into law." [12]

Like the earlier tide, the Fabian tide was worldwide. It contributed no less to the success of the Russian and Chinese communist revolutions than to the welfare state in Britain and the New Deal in the United States. And it largely explains the adoption of centralized planning in India and other British and European former colonies when they achieved independence. A major exception was Hong Kong, one of the few British colonial possessions that remained under the control of the Colonial Office. It never departed from the Adam Smith tide and as a result was a precursor to the next tide.

The Resurgence of Free Markets (the Hayek Tide)

As in the preceding wave, the world of ideas started to change direction just as the tide in the world of practice was cresting.[13] Throughout the ascendancy of socialist ideas there had, of course, been counter-currents—kept alive in Britain by G. K. Chesterton, Lionel Robbins, Friedrich Hayek, and some of their colleagues at the London School of Economics; in Austria by Ludwig von Mises and his disciples; and in the United States by Albert Jay Nock, H. L. Mencken, and other popular writers; Henry Simons, Frank Knight, and Jacob Viner at the University of Chicago; and Gottfried Haberler and Joseph Schumpeter at Harvard—to mention only a few.

Hayek's *Road to Serfdom,* a surprise best-seller in Britain and in the United States in 1944, was probably the first real inroad in the dominant intellectual view. Yet the impact of the free-market counter-current on the dominant tide of intellectual opinion, though perceptible to those directly involved, was at first minute. Even for those of us who were actively promoting free markets in the 1950s and 1960s it is difficult to recall how strong and pervasive was the intellectual climate of the times.

The tale of two books by the present authors, both directed at the general public and both promoting the same policies, provides striking evidence of the change in the climate of opinion. The first, *Capitalism and Freedom,* published in 1962 and destined to sell more than 400,000 copies in the next eighteen years, was not reviewed at the time in a single popular American periodical—not in the *New York Times,* the *Chicago Tribune, Newsweek, Time,* you name it. The second, *Free to Choose,* published in 1980, was reviewed by every major publication (by some more than once), became the year's best-selling nonfiction book in the United States, and received worldwide attention.

Further evidence of the change in the intellectual climate is the proliferation of think tanks promoting the ideas of limited government and reliance on free markets. In a recent talk Ed Feulner, president of the Heritage

Foundation, could mention only four that existed three decades ago: the Hoover Institution, still here today; the Intercollegiate Society of Individualists, which has changed its name but kept the initials; an embryonic American Enterprise Institute; and the Center for Strategic and International Studies. He should also have included Leonard Read's Foundation for Economic Education (FEE).

By contrast, Feulner noted a long list of additional institutions currently devoted to developing and spreading the idea of limited government and free markets, plus a host of others trying to translate ideas into action. The same contrast is true of publications. FEE's *Freeman* was the only one he or we can think of that was promoting the ideas of freedom 30 to 40 years ago. Today numerous publications promote these ideas, though with great differences in specific areas: *The Freeman*, *National Review*, *Human Events*, *The American Spectator*, *Policy Review*, and *Reason*. Even the *New Republic* and *The Nation* are no longer the undeviating proponents of socialist orthodoxy that they were three decades ago.

Why this great shift in public attitudes? The persuasive power of such books as Friedrich Hayek's *Road to Serfdom*, Ayn Rand's *Fountainhead* and *Atlas Shrugged*, our own *Capitalism and Freedom*, and numerous others led people to think about the problem in a different way and to become aware that government failure was as real as market failure. Nevertheless, we conjecture that the extraordinary force of experience was the major reason for the change.

Experience turned the great hopes that the collectivists and socialists had placed in Russia and China to ashes. Indeed, the only hope in those countries comes from recent moves toward the free market. Similarly experience dampened, to put it mildly, the extravagant hopes placed in Fabian socialism and the welfare state in Britain and in the New Deal in the United States. One major government program after another, each started with the best of intentions, resulted in more problems than solutions.

Few today still regard nationalization of enterprises as a way to promote more efficient production. Few still believe that every social problem can be solved by throwing government (that is, taxpayer) money at it. In these areas liberal ideas—in the original nineteenth-century meaning of liberal—have won the battle. The neoconservatives are correct in defining themselves as (modern) liberals mugged by reality. They still retain many of their earlier values but have been driven to recognize that they cannot achieve them through government.

In this country the Vietnam War helped to undermine belief in the beneficence of government. And most of all, as Dicey predicted nearly 75 years ago, the rising burden of taxation caused the general public to react against the growth of government and its spreading influence.[14]

In both the United States and Britain respect for the law declined in the twentieth century under the impact of the widening scope of government, strongly reinforced in the United States by Prohibition. The growing range of favors governments could give led to a steady increase in what economists have come to call rent-seeking and what the public refers to as special-interest lobbying.

Worldwide the contrast between the stagnation of those poorer countries that engaged in central planning (India, the former African colonies, Central American countries) and the rapid progress of the few that followed a largely free-market policy (notably the Four Tigers of the Far East: Hong Kong, Singapore, Taiwan, and South Korea) strongly reinforced the experience of the advanced countries of the West.

Ideas played a significant part, as in earlier episodes, less by persuading the public than by keeping options open, providing alternative policies to adopt when changes had to be made.

As in the two earlier waves, practice has lagged far behind ideas, so that both Britain and the United States are further from the ideal of a free society than they were 30 to 40 years ago in almost every dimension. In 1950 spending by U.S. federal, state, and local governments was 25 percent of national income; in 1985 it was 44 percent. In the past 30 years a host of new government agencies has been created: a Department of Education, a National Endowment for the Arts and another for the humanities, EPA, OSHA, and so on. Civil servants in these and many additional agencies decide for us what is in our best interest.

Nonetheless, practice has started to change. The catalytic crisis sparking the change was, we believe, the worldwide wave of inflation during the 1970s, originating in excessively expansive monetary growth in the United States in the 1960s. That episode was catalytic in two respects: first, stagflation destroyed the credibility of Keynesian monetary and fiscal policy and hence of the government's capacity to fine-tune the economy; second, it brought into play Dicey's "weight of taxation" through bracket creep and the implicit repudiation of government debt.

Already in the 1970s military conscription was terminated, airlines deregulated, and regulation Q, which limited the interest rates that banks could pay on deposits, eliminated. In 1982 the Civil Aeronautics Board that regulated the airlines was eliminated. Though government spending as a fraction of national income has continued to rise, the rate of increase has slowed. No major new spending programs have been passed since 1981. The increase in nonmilitary government spending has been predominantly the effect of earlier programs.

As in earlier waves, the tides of both opinion and practice have swept worldwide. Britain went further in the direction of collectivism than the

United States and still remains more collectivist—with both a higher ratio of government spending to national income and far more extensive nationalization of industry. Yet Britain has made more progress under Margaret Thatcher than the United States has under Ronald Reagan.

Equally impressive are changes in the communist world. Even there it was impossible to repress all counter-currents, as Solzhenitsyn, Sakharov, and many other brave men and women so eloquently testify. But beyond the counter-currents, the economic reforms in Hungary, Solidarity in Poland, the widened resort to markets in China, the current reformist talk in the Soviet Union—these owe as much to the force of events and the options kept open by intellectual ideas as do the election of Margaret Thatcher and Ronald Reagan in the West. True, it is doubtful that such reforms will be permitted to go far enough to threaten the power of the current political elite. But that does not lessen their value as testimony to the power of ideas.

One interesting and instructive phenomenon is that freeing the market has been equally or more vigorously pursued under ostensibly left-wing governments as under ostensibly right-wing governments. Communist countries aside, one striking example is the U-turn in French policy effected by Mitterrand, a lifelong socialist. In Australia a Labour government replaced a conservative government and then moved sharply to widen the role of the market. New Zealand, under a Labour government headed by David Lange, first elected in 1984 and reelected in 1987, has gone further than any other country in dismantling government controls and economic intervention.

By contrast, Germany, though it owed its dramatic post—World War II recovery to the free-market policies of Ludwig Erhard, has steadily moved away from those policies first under a Social Democratic government and, more recently, under conservative governments. Can the explanation for this aberration be that the dramatic move to free-market policies was primarily the result of one man's (Erhard's) actions and not of a change in public opinion?

All in all the force of ideas, propelled by the pressure of events, is clearly no respecter of geography or ideology or party label.

Conclusion

We have surveyed briefly two completed pairs of tides in the climate of opinion and the "affairs of men" and one pair still in progress. Each tide lasted between 50 and 100 years. First came the tide in the climate of public opinion: toward free markets and laissez-faire from, say, 1776 to 1883 in Britain, 1776 to 1885 in the United States; toward collectivism from 1883 to 1950 in Britain, from 1885 to 1970 in the United States. Some decades later came the tide in the "affairs of men": toward laissez-faire from, say, 1820 to 1900 in Britain, 1840 to 1930 in the United States; toward collectivism from, say, 1900 to 1978 in Britain, 1930 to 1980 in the United States. Needless to say, these are only the roughest of dates. They could easily be set a decade or so earlier or later.

Two new pairs of tides are now in their rising phases: in public opinion, toward renewed reliance on markets and more limited government, beginning in about 1950 in Britain and 1970 in the United States; in public policy, beginning in 1978 in Britain and 1980 in the United States, and even more recently in other countries.

If the completed tides are any guide, the current wave in opinion is approaching middle age and in public policy is still in its infancy. Both are therefore still rising and the flood stage, certainly in affairs, is yet to come.

For those who believe in a free society and a narrowly limited role for government, that is reason for optimism. But it is not a reason for complacency. Nothing is inevitable about the course of history—however it may appear in retrospect. "Because we live in a largely free society, we tend to forget how limited is the span of time and the part of the globe for which there has ever been anything like political freedom: the typical state of mankind is tyranny, servitude, and misery." [15]

The encouraging tide in affairs that is in its infancy can still be aborted, can be overwhelmed by a renewed tide of collectivism. The expanded role of government even in Western societies that pride themselves in being part of the free world has created many vested interests that will strongly resist the loss of privileges that they have come to regard as their right. Everyone is capable of believing that what is good for oneself is good for the country and therefore of justifying a special exception to a general rule that we all profess to favor.

Yet the lesson of the two earlier waves is clear: once a tide in opinion or in affairs is strongly set, it tends to overwhelm counter-currents and to keep going for a long time in the same direction. The tides are capable of ignoring geography, political labels, and other hindrances to their continuance. Yet it is also worth recalling that their very success tends to create conditions that may ultimately reverse them.

Notes

1. A British constitutional-law scholar has written the most insightful book on the subject: A. V. Dicey, *Lectures on the Relation Between Law and Public Opinion in England During the Nineteenth Century*, 2d ed. (London: Macmillan, 1914).

2. Milton Friedman and Rose D. Friedman, *Free to Choose* (New York and London: Harcourt Brace Jovanovich, 1980), p. 283.

3. Adam Smith, *The Wealth of Nations*, Cannan 5th ed. (London: Methuen, 1930), bk. 4, chap. 2, p. 435.

4. J. M. Keynes, *Economic Consequences of the Peace* (London: Macmillan, 1919), pp. 6, 7, 9.

5. See Friedman and Friedman, *Free to Choose*, pp. 59, 61–62.

6. Dicey, *Law and Public Opinion*, p. 245.

7. A. W. Coats, "The American Economics Association and the Economics Profession," *Journal of Economic Literature* 23 (December 1985): 1702.

8. Dicey, *Law and Public Opinion*, pp. 257–58.

9. Ibid., pp. xxxi, xxxii, xxxiii, li.

10. *Encyclopaedia Britannica*, 1970 ed., s.v. "Brandeis, Louis Dembitz."

11. Friedman and Friedman, *Free to Choose*, p. 196.

12. Ibid., pp. 286, 287.

13. This section is based partly on Milton Friedman, "Where Are We on the Road to Liberty?" *Reason* 19, no. 2 (June 1987): 31–33.

14. "[I]f the progress of socialistic legislation be arrested, the check will be due, not so much to the influence of any thinker as to some patent fact which shall command public attention; such, for instance, as that increase in the weight of taxation which is apparently the usual, if not the invariable, concomitant of a socialistic policy" (Dicey, *Law and Public Opinion*, p. 302n).

15. Milton Friedman, with the assistance of Rose D. Friedman, *Capitalism and Freedom* (Chicago: University of Chicago Press, 1962), p. 9.

THOMAS SOWELL

◆ ———————————————— ◆

Preferential Policies

An International Perspective

◆ Preferential policies are not unique to the United States or to our times. There are preferences favoring Muslims in the Philippines, Lulua in Zaire, Central Asians in the USSR, Sinhalese in Sri Lanka, Maoris in New Zealand, Sephardim in Israel, Malays in Malaysia, and a long list of local and national groups in India—among many others in countries around the world.

Some countries have had such policies longer and have carried them further than the United States, while still others are following in our wake, watching what we do and how it turns out. Seeing the rationales and consequences of preferential policies in other societies may also help us to understand the logic of American efforts in this area, and how the outcomes here look against the background of international patterns.

Definitions

Preferential policies are defined here as *all* government-imposed group preferences, whether or not in the specific form of a quota, and whether imposed through legislative, executive, or judicial processes. Preferential policies are therefore distinguished from purely individual preferences, lacking the force of law. Preferential policies are also distinguished from policies mandating equal treatment of individuals, though these mutually contradictory policies are often lumped together in the United States under the general heading of "civil rights." The hope that one set of policies will eventually lead to the other does not mean that their differences can be defined away *a priori.*

By now we all know the rationales for preferential policies, their hopes, their expectations, their promises. What we know remarkably little about are their actual consequences, even in our own country, much less internationally. Much of what is cited as evidence in the United States consists of comparisons before and after the "civil rights" era, loosely defined to include both equal treatment and preferential policies.

Before proceeding to hard evidence, it may be useful to make one further distinction, between majority preferential policies and minority preferential policies. Historically, majority preferential policies came first in the United States, especially under the Jim Crow system in the South. Majority preferential policies have a longer history internationally as well, and remain the dominant form of official preferences. Gentiles were officially favored over Jews in a number of European countries, including a quota ceiling on the number of Jews in particular jobs or university admissions, during the period between the two world wars. There are also majority preferences today, from Fiji to Africa to the Caribbean and for a variety of local majorities in various parts of India.

Throughout sub-Saharan Africa, preferential policies for whites during the colonial era were succeeded by preferential policies for blacks during the post-independence era—aimed not so much at Europeans as at such minorities as the Lebanese in West Africa and people from India in East Africa. If "majority" is defined as the *political* majority, as distinguished from the demographic majority, then South Africa's dominant white population has long voted itself preferential treatment in every phase of the economy and society.

Minority preferences, such as those for untouchables in India or blacks and other racial minorities in the United States, are more recent in history, and remain the exception rather than the rule. Although majority preferences and minority preferences are different in concept, the extent to which they are similar or different in consequences is an empirical question.

Beneficiaries

In a number of countries, preferential policies—whether for a majority or a minority—have benefited, primarily or exclusively, the most fortunate segment of the groups designated as beneficiaries. In India's state of Tamil Nadu, for example, the highest of the so-called "backward classes" legally entitled to preferences, constituting 11 percent of the total "backward classes" population in that state, received almost half of all jobs and university admissions set aside for these classes, while lower castes—making up the bottom 12 percent of the "backward classes" population—received only 1 to 2 percent of the reserved jobs and university admissions.[1] A study of preferential programs in Malaysia concluded that "at most 5 percent" of the Malays were in a position to benefit from preferential policies.[2] In Sri Lanka, preferential university admissions for people from backward regions of the country appear to have benefited primarily students from affluent families in these areas.[3]

Such results have sometimes been discussed as a maldistribution of benefits. But much more than that is involved. The less fortunate members of designated beneficiary groups have often not only failed to share proportionately in benefits but have actually retrogressed during the era of preferential policies. While the statistical representation of Malays on corporate boards of directors in Malaysia rose under preferential treatment policies,[4] so too did the proportion of Malays among the population living below the official poverty level.[5] In India, while the proportion of untouchables among high-level government officials has increased substantially during the era of preferential treatment,[6] so too has the proportion of untouchables who work as landless agricultural laborers.[7] In the United States, while blacks with college education or substantial job experience have advanced economically, both absolutely and relative to whites of the same description, during the era of preferential "goals and timetables," blacks with low levels of education and little job experience have fallen further behind whites of exactly the same description during the same span of time.[8]

As in so many other areas of public policy, while advances are readily attributed to the policies in question, retrogressions are attributed to other factors. However convenient such conclusions may be for those who state them, that is no reason for anyone else to accept them.

Much of the evidence cited on the consequences of preferential policies is necessarily scattered and fragmentary, and therefore open to the charge of being "selective." But noncomprehensive evidence is not necessarily selective in the sense that counter-evidence was ignored. Unfortunately, one of the common patterns across nations with preferential policies is a failure to compile hard data on the actual consequences of these policies, much less to specify in advance what will be considered "success" or "failure."

Sectoral Data vs. National Data

Even in countries where nationwide data on the economic position of the designated beneficiary group show no overall improvement, nevertheless improvements in particular sectors may be dramatic. In Malaysia, for example, the Chinese have historically earned about double the income of

Malays and continue to do so after two decades of preferences for Malays.[9] Nevertheless, the rise of Malays in both government and government-related sectors has been dramatic.[10] Comparisons between sectors of the economy that are more closely tied to government and those that are not consistently show the rise of officially preferred groups to be greater in the government and government-related sectors—whether in Malaysia, India, Sri Lanka, or the United States.[11] Some advocates of such policies consider this to be decisive evidence of their effectiveness. But nationwide statistics for the very same groups over the very same spans of time often contradict this.

How is this possible? In an economy with a substantial private sector, the special demand for particular groups in government-related employment may result in considerable *transfer* of that group's employment—which is then seen as a dramatic *increase* in the areas to which they transfer. In the United States, for example, the employment of blacks by private employers without government contracts *declined* between 1970 and 1980,[12] while increases in black employment in various government and government-related sectors were being hailed as indicators of the general progress of blacks under affirmative action.

Conversely, a decline in government-related employment does not mean an overall decline. During the period from the beginning of the Woodrow Wilson administration to the beginning of the Franklin D. Roosevelt administration, the position of blacks in the federal civil service declined dramatically. The number of black postmasters was approximately cut in half and blacks were forced out of the military, and especially naval, forces as well.[13] Yet the occupational position of blacks nationally did not retrogress, and in fact advanced slightly.[14] We cannot generalize from what happens in government or government-related employment, or in any particular firm or sector.

Trends

Assessing the net effect of a policy on any group requires more than simple before-and-after comparisons. Much discussion of the effects of preferential policies proceed as if there were a stationary situation, to which "change" was added. This is especially misleading in the United States, where equal treatment policies were initiated some years before preferential policies, and where the economic rise of racial and ethnic minorities preceded both. It is an often-cited fact that the proportion of blacks in professional and other high-level positions rose substantially in the decade following passage of the Civil Rights Act of 1964. It is an almost totally ignored fact that the proportion of blacks in such occupations rose even more substantially in the decade *preceding* passage of the Civil Rights Act of 1964.

It is an equally ignored fact that the incomes of Asian Americans and Mexican Americans rose substantially—both absolutely and relative to that of the general population—in the years preceding passage of the Civil Rights Act of 1964.[15]

Similar patterns appear in other countries where it was precisely the rise of an educated and upwardly mobile class that led to demands for preferential treatment policies, benefiting primarily this class but promoted in the name of the disadvantaged masses. This pattern emerged largely after World War II in India, Sri Lanka, Malaysia, and various other newly independent Asian and African nations.[16] A very similar pattern emerged after World War I, in the newly independent nations of central and eastern Europe, such as Poland, Czechoslovakia, and Lithuania.[17]

Any assessment of the impact of a policy must take account of trends already in existence at the time the policy was initiated, rather than assume a static world to which "change" is introduced.

Losers

If there is a reluctance to collect official data on the actual impact of preferential policies on the intended beneficiaries, it is virtually unthinkable politically to document the losses of those sacrificed to these policies. But the same economic logic that would suggest that the more fortunate members of the preferred groups are likely to gain most of the benefits would likewise suggest that the least fortunate members of the nonpreferred groups are likely to suffer the greatest losses. Whether in jobs or college and university admissions, it is not the most outstanding performers who are likely to be displaced through preferential policies, but those who meet the standards with the least margin. A study of corporate executives in Bombay showed that the dominant group—the Gujaratis—experienced only a small decline, from 52 percent of all executives to 44 percent, after preferential programs brought Maharashtrians into the executive category for the first time. But the more modest proportions of Bombay executive positions held by people from South India—25 percent—was cut in half, to 12 percent.[18] Similar results appeared in the very different setting of prewar Hungary, where preferential policies for Gentiles had little effect on the Jewish financial and industrial elite but had much more impact on the Jewish middle class and lower middle class.[19]

In a country such as the United States, where members of various racial, ethnic, and other groups overlap in their economic positions, to benefit the top of one group at the expense of the bottom of another group need not ameliorate economic inequalities, and may even increase them.

Assumptions

However important it is to know the hard facts on what actually happens under preferential policies, it is perhaps even more important to reconsider the specific assumptions and general vision on which such policies are based. This seems especially important with laws and policies which put the burden of proof on the accused to show why his employment or other statistics do not conform to the presuppositions of others. No evidence whatsoever has been demanded of those who presuppose that an even distribution of groups would occur in the absence of discrimination. Such even distributions might be expected if human beings were random events. In reality, uneven distributions are commonplace in countries around the world, in the most trivial and in the most serious activities, in activities in which others might discriminate and in activities in which each individual makes his own decisions, such as choices of television programs or voting in a secret-ballot election.

Consequences

One of the relatively mild but corrupting consequences of preferential policies has been fraudulent identification as members of the preferred group. Both in Indonesia and Malaysia, the term "Ali-Baba enterprises" has been coined to describe the widespread practice of having an indigenous "front man" (Ali) for a business that is in fact owned and operated by a Chinese (Baba).[20] Anti-Semitic policies in Poland during the interwar years similarly led some Jewish businesses to operate behind Gentile front men.[21] Fraudulent "minority" enterprises are of course not unknown in the United States. In India, an examination of the backgrounds of 28 state legislators holding parliamentary seats reserved in Rajasthan for "scheduled castes" (untouchables) showed that 16 of them became scheduled caste members by adoption.[22]

A much more serious—sometimes deadly—consequence of preferential policies has been polarization, hostility, and violence. Riots over group preference policies took hundreds of lives in India in 1985 alone, and lethal eruptions over this issue have been recurring sporadically there for years.[23] "Backlash" violence against untouchables is more continuous and involves thousands of officially recorded "atrocities" annually.[24] Three of the ugliest civil wars of this generation have erupted in multiethnic societies whose official group preferences pitted one group against another, first politically and then militarily. This has been the story of the Biafran civil war in Nigeria, the civil war currently in uneasy truce in Sri Lanka, and the civil war still erupting sporadically in Lebanon.

Given the great heterogeneity of the groups receiving preferential treatment around the world, and the vast differences between the societies in which they live, the emergence of some common patterns is especially striking—and ominous.

Notes

1. Marc Galanter, *Competing Equalities: Law and the Backward Classes in India* (Delhi: Oxford University Press, 1984), p. 469.

2. Mavis Putchucheary, "Public Policies Relating to Business and Land, and Their Impact on Ethnic Relations in Peninsular Malaysia," in Robert B. Goldmann and A. Jeyaratnam Wilson, eds., *From Independence to Statehood: Managing Ethnic Conflict in Five African and Asian States* (London: Frances Pitner, 1984), p. 163.

3. Chandra Richard de Silva, "Sinhala-Tamil Relations in Sri Lanka: The University Admissions Issue—The First Phase, 1971–77," in ibid., p. 133.

4. Lim Mah Hui, "The Ownership and Control of Large Corporations in Malaysia: The Role of Chinese Businessmen," in Peter Gosling and Linda Y. C. Lim, eds., *The Chinese in Southeast Asia* (Singapore: Marzen Asia, 1983), pp. 281, 284, 308.

5. Putchucheary, "Public Policies," p. 158.

6. Galanter, *Competing Equalities*, p. 89.

7. B. Sivaramaya, "Affirmative Action: The Scheduled Castes and the Scheduled Tribes," International Conference on Affirmative Action, Bellagio Conference Center, Bellagio, Italy, August 16–20, 1982, p. 25.

8. Finis Welch, "Affirmative Action and Its Enforcement," *American Economic Review*, May 1981, p. 132.

9. Robert Klitgaard and Ruth Katz, "Overcoming Ethnic Inequalities: Lessons for Malaysia," *Journal of Policy Analysis and Management* 2, no. 3 (1983): 335, 341, 343.

10. Tai Yoke Lin, "Inter-Ethnic Restructuring in Malaysia, 1970–1980: The Employment Perspective," in Goldmann and Wilson, *From Independence to Statehood*, pp. 47–48, 51, 54.

11. Ibid., p. 51; Pang Eng Fong, "Race, Income Distribution, and Development in Malaysia and Singapore," in *The Chinese in Southeast Asia*, p. 317; Myron Weiner and Mary Fainsod Katzenstein, *India's Preferential Policies* (Chicago: University of Chicago Press, 1981), pp. 53, 123, 124, 125; S. W. R. de A. Samarasinghe, "Ethnic Representation in Central Government Employment and Sinhala-Tamil Relations in Sri Lanka, 1948–81," in Goldmann and Wilson, *From Independence to Statehood*, pp. 173–84; James P. Smith and Finis Welch, "Affirmative Action and Labor Markets," *Journal of Labor Economics*, April 1984, p. 297.

12. Smith and Welch, "Affirmative Action and Labor Markets," p. 282.

13. Thomas Sowell, *Race and Economics* (New York: David McKay Co., 1975), pp. 182–83.

14. Thomas Sowell, *Ethnic America* (New York: Basic Books, 1981), pp. 212–13.

15. Thomas Sowell, *Civil Rights: Rhetoric or Reality* (New York: William Morrow, 1984), pp. 49–56.

16. Donald L. Horowitz, *Ethnic Groups in Conflict* (Berkeley and Los Angeles: University of California Press, 1985), pp. 221–26; Weiner and Katzenstein, *India's Preferential Policies*, pp. 4–5, 132; Myron Weiner, "The Pursuit of Ethnic Equality Through Preferential Policies: A Comparative Public Policy Perspective," in Goldmann and Wilson, *From Independence to Statehood*, p. 78; K. M. de Silva, "University Admissions and Ethnic Tension in Sri Lanka 1977–1982," in ibid., pp. 125–26.

17. See Celia S. Heller, *On the Edge of Destruction: Jews of Poland Between the Two World Wars* (New York: Columbia University Press, 1987), pp. 16, 17, 107, 123–28. Ezra Mendelsohn, *The Jews of East Central Europe Between the World Wars* (Bloomington: Indiana University Press, 1983), pp. 99, 105, 106, 167, 232, 236–37.

18. Weiner and Katzenstein, *India's Preferential Policies*, p. 52.

19. Mendelsohn, *Jews of East Central Europe*, p. 122.

20. Horowitz, *Ethnic Groups in Conflict*, p. 666.

21. Heller, *On the Edge of Destruction*, p. 102.

22. Sivaramaya, "Affirmative Action," p. 12.

23. See, for example, William Claiborne, "Indian Castes Battle Over Quotas for Schools and Jobs," *Washington Post*, April 21, 1985, p. A21; "Solanki: Under a Cloud," *India Today*, July 15, 1985, pp. 18–21.

24. Dilip Hiro, *The Untouchables of India* (London: Minority Rights Group, 1982), pp. 11–12.

JAMES BOND STOCKDALE

On Public Virtue

◆ Those who study the rise and fall of civilizations learn that no shortcoming has been as surely fatal to republics as a dearth of public virtue, the unwillingness of those who govern to place the value of their society above personal interest.[1] Yet today we read outcries from conscientious congressmen disenchanted with the proceedings of their legislative body and totally disgusted with the log-jamming effect of their peers' selfish and artful distancing of themselves from critical spending cutbacks, much-needed belt-tightening legislation without which the long-term existence of our republic itself is endangered.

The sad fact is that today such artful dodging of controversial questions is the road to reelection. It is not that a conspiracy of the selfish engineered such a turn of events, but that an evolution of governmental practices over time has made it easier for a legislator to stay on the fence and appear faultless. In the articles about the current national deficit predicament, we read that an exponential rise in public relations opportunities and techniques, with the resultant lure of extremely valuable, career-enhancing personal video coverage, has had its effect. This first generation of politicians since Pericles actually to be seen by their electors, we are told, is hooked on upbeat and safe 30-second spots. But the stampede for self-advancement at the expense of the national interest is now with us in many matters other than the national deficit and concerns much more than personal publicity. Even the patriot with instincts to stand up and be counted for what he knows in his bones is right but unpopular has reason to ask himself why.

The press regularly covers what this swing portends for national solvency, productivity, and other domestic economic issues. I will address how the trend toward sitting tight and playing it cool affects my calling: the profession of arms and the conduct of war.

It is crucial for the United States in the 1990s to reverse civilian government officialdom's steady drift toward shirking its duties to civic virtue, public virtue, the habitual taking of personal responsibility, and the placing of the overall good of the body politic above personal ambition and gain.

Probably no character trait was so universally identified by our Founding Fathers as essential to the long-run success of the American experiment as selfless public virtue. In those days of decision, almost all of them were quick with pleas for its encouragement and institutionalization. For instance, John Adams, in a letter to his friend Mercy Warren, author and sister of revolutionary leader James Otis wrote: "Public Virtue cannot exist in a Nation without private, and public Virtue is the only Foundation of Republics. There must be a positive Passion for the public good, the public Interest, Honour, Power and Glory, established in the Minds of the People, or there can be no Republican Government, *nor any real liberty.*"[2]

The connection between liberty and public obligation probably occurred naturally to those who founded the United States. Many of them were exceptionally well read in political history and theory. The founders' debates were salted with easy references to Locke, Hume, Machiavelli, and Montesquieu as well as the ancients: Aristotle, Seneca, Marcus Aurelius, and that second-century Greek who was the great historian of the early Roman Republic, Polybius. That Roman Republic and its ethos, particularly during its first three hundred years, were a natural model for our founders' dreams. Like ours, their republic emerged from monarchy; like ours, the people of its early years were mostly free farmers. And although war had been the most dramatic feature of the life of the early republican Romans, their historians described how the development of Roman character was formed by institutions with which our revolutionary forebears could identify: the family, the religion, the moral code, and to a lesser degree the school, the language, and the literature of the society.

Polybius (who died when the republic was a mere 386 years old, before it had become corrupt) praised the Roman government as the best in the world and described the honesty of the Roman people as superior to that of his own countrymen. Their army, "the most successful military organization in history," never lost a war and brought a city-state a mere twenty miles square to the status of conqueror of the whole of the Mediterranean world.[3] So it might be considered natural that during the formation of our government, when constitutional issues were being debated, the famous and not famous on both sides of the issues wrote under Roman pseudonyms (Publius, Camillus, Brutus, Cassius). George Washington was so taken with the character of Cato the Younger in Joseph Addison's 1713 play *Cato* that he made the Roman republican his role model. He went to see *Cato* numerous times from early manhood into maturity and even had it performed for his troops at Valley Forge despite a congressional resolution that plays were inimical to republican virtue. Washington included lines from the play in his private correspondence and even in his farewell address. According to historian Forrest McDonald, the life-giving principle of both Cato and his country's government was public virtue.[4]

My central point is this: in late twentieth-century America the lack of the republican virtue that our Founding Fathers so strongly felt was key to national harmony and longevity is creating internal distrust, ineptitude, and frequent failure in our foreign affairs and military employments at least as serious as those in our long-term national solvency and productivity. This point was forcefully laid bare at a Paris conference to rethink Vietnam in which I participated in December 1987.

This Paris conference was a tripartite event to reflect on the French and U.S. Indochinese wars since World War II. It was held a block from the Arc de Triomphe in the International Conference Center, where Dr. Henry Kissinger signed the final agreement of January 1973 on the Cessation of War and Restoration of Peace in Vietnam. About two hundred people attended, all by special invitation. Fifty or so were designated speakers. Translator headphones could be set to French, Vietnamese, or English.

From the first session it was clear that the conferees were most interested in the Americans' war (1964–1973). It also immediately became clear to all in attendance that our conduct of that war (the topic of the first session) is still, even among Americans, a matter of considerable confusion and angry dispute. Most participants in the war feel betrayed by one force or another, and certainly none of the high-level participants who spoke at Paris showed any interest in putting the war behind them. There were just too many fundamental breaks in national integrity that deserve to be aired. And they all come down to one thing: we can't afford to fight any more wars without a thoroughgoing national commitment in advance.

We Americans on that first panel were a varied lot, but all quite knowledgeable. Two were high-government on-scene officials: William Colby, director of the Phoenix pacification program in Vietnam and a CIA official who later headed the agency, and Ambassador Robert Komer, former assistant to President Lyndon Johnson in charge of pacification in Vietnam in 1967 and 1968. One was a professor of political science and an author: Guenter Lewy, a student of the Vietnam War who writes on international legal aspects of the conflict. Three were senior combat participants in the war: Colonel (ret.) Harry Summers, a combat infantry veteran of the Korean and Vietnam wars and now an author, Clausewitz scholar, and syndicated columnist; Major General (ret.) Mike Healy, combat commando in World War II and Korea, founder and commander of the U.S. Army Special Forces, who served in Vietnam five and a half years; and myself, Vice Admiral (ret.) Jim Stockdale, in Vietnam as a combat aviator for two and a half years and prisoner of war in Hanoi for seven and a half years.

So far as I know, no person in this group had any prior grudges against any other, and each seemed to speak from the heart when he drove home points that had welled up inside him as he devoted the best years of his life to the all-out pursuit of his nation's aims as he understood them. Each made cogent points with which almost none of the others could agree. The war went on so long and through so many phases that each one's honestly held views had a lot to do with his vantage point in the Vietnam fighting and the era he represented. In brief, people came down on different sides of such basic issues as whether the nationally accepted route to victory was seen as (1) working on the local level as counterinsurgency instructors and fighters to get the South Vietnamese on their feet, (2) focusing on what Clausewitz called the center of gravity, the North Vietnamese army, while the locals worried about the guerrillas, or (3) using our technical advantage in an early, quick, and unconstrained conventional air and possibly amphibious assault on North Vietnam's power base. The conflict between the first two options brought us to the question whether we were there to fight a people's war or a soldier's war. One participant remarked: "In 1959 the Communists launched a 'people's war,' to which we Americans [incorrectly, he thought] replied with a 'soldier's war,' which our pacification experts, starting in 1967, tried to slowly transform into a 'people's war'—which found itself facing a North Vietnamese 'soldier's war' by the time Lyndon Johnson gave up and abandoned the cause."

This is not to say that victory would have been particularly difficult or that the problem lay in poor coordination of military efforts. What it does say is that since the United States has given up declaring war and started sending armies forward on what will obviously be a prolonged campaign without a national consensus behind them, things have not gone well. Those who believe that U.S. war-making procedures as they have evolved since World War II provide built-in restraint by fencing in our overseas commitments to those that the traffic will bear in a running constitutional battle between Congress and the commander in chief need only see one of these years-long conflicts laid out and analyzed at such a conference to be convinced that warfare by grudging compromise is a disaster. Our Constitution as written protected our fighting men from shedding blood in pointless exercises while a dissenting Congress strangled the effort. But what has evolved, apparently to everybody's satisfaction but those soldiers', affords them no such protection.

What the traffic will bear nowadays in an overseas threat to U.S. national interests is almost never the old-fashioned forthright military intercession of times past, when we appeared at our friends' gates as a volunteer fire department prepared to climb the hills to windward to cut fire lanes to protect their homes. Now our internal debates—and we must have internal debates every step of the way because we allow Congress to sit on the fence, ready to take individually advantageous positions ex post facto—take the form of a morality play. (As Dr. Kissinger asked at the Paris conference, "Can anybody think of a more absurd concept than humanitarian aid for guerrillas?") From the outset, U.S. support of the noncommunist side of area squabbles is usually cast in compassionate paternalism, which can come back to bite us. We immediately find ourselves in the hearts-and-minds business, at the grass roots, trying to help our friends help themselves. Suddenly we are partners in matters not directly connected with our national interest; we are mired down in our friends' internal affairs (Washington's bureaucracies quickly supplying organizations to meet these ill-considered obligations), and we find we are not the fire department but the rich uncle, ready to mind hearth and home and shoulder the blame for all that goes wrong.

The problem with sneaking into wars in dovish poses and getting off to a misleading start in missionary roles was illuminated on the last day of the conference in an event billed as a conversation with Henry Kissinger. Both my wife Sybil (herself a conference participant) and I have great respect for Dr. Kissinger. I owe my freedom to him and President Nixon. And Sybil, who was founder and chair of the National League of Families of American Prisoners and Missing in Southeast Asia during the war, had bimonthly meetings with him for years. Ever since she has spoken of him as "the most honest man in Washington" during those years. (He never told the wives of those listed as prisoner or missing falsehoods about the prospects of peace; whereas a misleading cheery optimism they knew to be false was standard fare for most politicians.)

On that December day in Paris, 1987, Dr. Kissinger took us back to the situation when President Nixon entered office and Kissinger became national security adviser in January of 1969, inheriting from the Johnson administration (1) 500,000 American troops in place in South Vietnam (1,200 of whom were killed in action during the first month of the Nixon administration), (2) a bombing halt that had been in effect for months, and (3) a fully organized activist U.S. antiwar movement. This last was an unusual problem because it was backed by the very members of Congress who were largely responsible for the ill-defined role of our armed forces in Vietnam. Dr. Kissinger explained his prolonged negotiations with the North Vietnamese representative, Le Duc Tho, particularly those parts that took place after our December 1972 B-52 bombings had brought Hanoi back to the conference table (to the very room in which Kissinger then spoke). Of their final agreement of January 1973, Dr. Kissinger said, "I believe it was not a glorious agreement, but it was one that could have been maintained."

Kissinger later solicited questions from the floor, "particularly from the Vietnamese in the room." (These Parisian anticommunist Vietnamese made up about a third of the attendees.) Their questions were shockingly rude. We Stockdales couldn't believe our ears because the questions (almost all asked by young Vietnamese women who read from printed slips handed to them by Vietnamese men just before the session) implied a U.S. responsibility for a final settlement among the Indochinese people that had never occurred to us in all the ten years of our total commitment to the venture. Moreover, the questions had a sharp personal edge to them, and it was clear that Dr. Kissinger was being targeted by an organized ad hominem assault that puzzled and offended us greatly. For example: "Dr. Kissinger, I was but a little girl during the war; I am a boat person. Please tell us why you delivered Vietnam over to the communists." "Mister Kissinger, do you think Vietnamese history will clear you? If yes, what kind of a man are you? If no, what have you been doing to alleviate the sufferings of your involuntary victims?"

Though wincing at first, Dr. Kissinger held on to his good humor and evinced no anger. "Free Vietnamese should have the right to ask unfriendly questions," he said. His voice was steady and cool as he half-jokingly said he did not know how to respond to questions he had already answered (it being obvious to all present that the writers of the questions had imperfectly anticipated his preliminary remarks). He continued, "The tone of what I am hearing reminds me of that which I listened to in this hall fifteen years ago [from Le Duc Tho]. It is not in the interest of free Vietnamese to use the arguments of those trying to destroy them."

The Vietnamese seemed to be saying that the United States owed them another war. As for Kissinger as the source of Vietnam's downfall, one must start with the Johnson administration; it had written off the whole effort as early as the summer of 1967.[5] McNamara, in a widely publicized statement years later, said that he had become convinced that the enterprise (as he was running it, one must assume) was hopeless over a year before that. His fundamental change of mind has been traced to August 1966.[6]

Nevertheless, President Nixon pressed the war from 1969 through 1972 despite gloomy prospects left by the destabilizing changes of pace it had undergone before he came into office, and then he had the courage to mine Haiphong harbor, bring the B-52s to Hanoi, and force the North Vietnamese, at least temporarily, to give up. Dr. Kissinger told the audience his only regret was in not doing the mining and bombing of 1972 immediately when he and Nixon came into office in 1969.

Dr. Kissinger calmly answered questions from the floor until they played themselves out and then candidly explained the events of early spring 1973 in which the Vietnamese seemed to find his betrayal of them. "We never had expectations that the North Vietnamese would respect the accords," he said, "but we judged that an agreement would rally a consensus in Congress. We never dreamt that we would be unable to enforce the agreement."

I was in the process of being released from prison in those days, returning to the United States with the rest of the U.S. combatants in Southeast Asia that spring. In early April 1973 President Nixon invited me to visit with him in the Oval Office. We spent an hour and fifteen minutes alone there during the late afternoon of April 9th. We of course discussed my prison experiences as leader of the underground, but in time the subject changed to his preoccupation with ongoing North Vietnamese violations of the agreement they had signed that January. The president said he was seriously considering reinstituting B-52 bombing, now that U.S. personnel were out. He asked if I would publicly support him if he bombed. I said yes, and I would have done so wholeheartedly for the man who had extricated us prisoners from seemingly hopeless circumstances. My notes made immediately after the meeting show surprise that he even asked.

Sybil and I had privately discussed these revelations from the president back in the spring of 1973, and they flashed back into our minds as Dr. Kissinger continued his talk in the Conference Center in Paris 15 years later: "We had scheduled a meeting in Paris with the North Vietnamese in May 1973, and we planned a full month of bombing in preparation for it" (that is to say, bombing the North Vietnamese to force them to keep the word they had given only four months before). He then explained that in the crucial month of April 1973, John Dean went to the federal prosecutor. Six weeks later President Nixon was effectively powerless and Watergate had sealed the fate of Vietnam.

And then came the most bitter pill of all. Kissinger brought up what he called the final error in his calculations: "I suffered from the illusion that this [January 1973] agreement would unify the American people, that the peace movement would be gratified that we had reached settlement and that others would be gratified that we had maintained honor. It did not occur to me that the people who opposed the war would have an interest in proving peace could not be maintained." On August 15, 1973, the Congress of the United States decreed that there would be no more funds for U.S. military action of any kind in Indochina. What made it impossible to enforce the peace settlement, said Kissinger, was what made it impossible to fight the war: a minority of vocal Americans who wanted the United States to lose the war.

Talk about a lack of public virtue! Our fighting forces in the Vietnam War were working against public apathy, congressional institutionalized indifference, and the self-righteous vindictiveness of a powerful group of demonic haters. Benjamin Rush, physician, political and social reformer, signer of the Declaration of Independence, pioneer in the treatment of the mentally ill, father of American psychiatry, had all the credentials to be correct when he scanned our 1787 Constitution as a member of its Pennsylvania Ratifying Convention. He noted that the drafters had worked hard to protect the American public from the tyranny of the government but perhaps not hard enough to protect us from the tyranny of each other: "In our opposition to monarchy, we forgot that the temple of tyranny has two doors. We bolted one of them by proper restraints; but we left the other open by neglecting to guard against the effects of our own ignorance and licentiousness." [7]

Is the United States to go down the tubes of paralyzing self-interest? So far, this has been the fate of the best of the world's civilizations—even Rome, though not until it had run out of enemies that kept forcing it back to unity, vision, and heroism.

The United States has plenty of challenges ahead, *glasnost'* or no *glasnost'*, and the chances are good that they will awaken our best natural impulses. My certainty here comes from my own intense personal experiences within a society under stress. In a microcosm of the United States a little group of U.S. pilots clandestinely organized a tightly wound society in a political prison. I'll never forget my panic when, as frequently happened, that society was rent with the jailers' purges that tore it apart. When you're left stranded, alone, with nothing to cling to, no friends, no culture, no protection, you develop some mighty warm feelings for the group you left behind and learn why it's in your best interest to maintain the unity of your society, your nation, as a value higher than your personal interest.

But it's unfair to our fighting men to wait for natural impulses to repair the gap left in the Founding Fathers' plan for national unity in time of prolonged combat. War declarations may be irrevocably passé and the War Powers Resolution too tight a tether on our president's maneuvering room. But some compromise that makes Congress go on record before years-long military campaigns start has to be put in place. There has to be a better solution than leaving the self-sacrificing soldier's peace of mind to the whims of Washington infighting. I've heard too many decorated veteran warriors from Vietnam say, "Our government better figure out some way to make it clear that they mean business next time, or I'm through with soldiering." They are sick of being told that their lives have to be provisionally committed to a half-baked plan because it's the only way the president can, in the national interest, get around adverse congressional sentiment.

These men were brought up pledging allegiance to the flag of a United States of America, which from its beginnings was committed to a separation of powers. From maturity they knew the strengths of this form of government, which balances the legislature against the presidency. But they also sensed, as did our Founding Fathers and the six generations that followed, that its weakness was a tendency to become fickle when the point of no return had passed, when the fat was in the fire and the troops were in the field. Over those generations a national confidence had grown up, particularly through those personal commitments documented by congressional declarations of war. Even without those declarations, there was a history within our government of a broad base of men of public virtue who would not permit blood to be spilled in vain. If in the post-Vietnam United States the soldier is just to be told that in modern times opinions change, that he should be prepared to have commitments dropped, that he should do his job in the field and never mind that he will be fighting for a government constantly doing a balancing act against nasty opposition from within, that fighting and dying as part of a sideshow to a Washington power struggle are de rigueur in these times, this simply will not do. He is entitled to demand: "Where is that republican virtue and its emphasis on liberty and justice for all that I thought was part of what I was pledging to all of those years?" Soldiers will march off to their deaths only so long as they don't feel they have to die alone for what will be abandoned causes.

Rome sets a precedent for such causes. Heed the letter from deployed soldier Marcus Flavinius, Centurion in the 2nd Cohort of the Augusta Legion, to his highly placed cousin, Tertullus at home in Rome:

> We had been told, on leaving our native soil, that we were going to defend the sacred rights conferred on us by so many of our citizens settled overseas, so many years of our presence, so many benefits brought by us to populations in need of our assistance and our civilization.
>
> We were able to verify that all this was true, and, because it was true, we did not hesitate to shed our quota of blood, to sacrifice our youth and our hopes. We regretted nothing, but whereas we over here are inspired by this frame of mind, I am told that in Rome factions and conspiracies are rife, that treachery flourishes, and that many people in their uncertainty and confusion lend a ready ear to the dire temptations of relinquishment and vilify our action.
>
> I cannot believe that all this is true, and yet recent wars have shown how pernicious such a state of mind could be and to where it could lead.

Make haste to reassure me, I beg you, and tell me that our fellow citizens understand us, support us and protect us as we ourselves are protecting the glory of the Empire.

If it should be otherwise, if we should have to leave our bleached bones on these desert sands in vain, then beware the anger of the Legions![8]

Notes

1. Forrest McDonald, *Novus Ordo Seclorum: The Intellectual Origins of the Constitution* (Lawrence: University Press of Kansas, 1985), p. 71.

2. Ibid., p. 72.

3. Will Durant, *The Story of Civilization, Part III: Caesar and Christ* (New York: Simon & Schuster, 1944), pp. 34, 71, 33.

4. "It was at once individualistic and communal: individualistic in that no member of the public could be dependent upon any other and still be reckoned a member of the public; communal in that every man gave himself totally to the good of the public as a whole. If public virtue declined, the republic declined, and if it declined too far, the republic died" (McDonald, *Novus Ordo Seclorum*, pp. 70–71).

5. Jim and Sybil Stockdale, *In Love and War* (New York: Harper & Row, 1984), pp. 276, 464 n. 1.

6. Lieutenant Colonel F. Charles Parker, "The Vietnam War and Mao's Struggle for Power," *The World and I*, April 1987, p. 615.

7. Benjamin Rush, "An Address," in Hezekiah Niles, ed., *Principles and Acts of the Revolution in America* (New York, 1876), p. 234.

8. Jean Larteguy, *The Centurions*, trans. Xan Fielding (New York: E. P. Dutton, 1962), preface.

JAMES Q. WILSON

Public Policy and Personal Character

Society cannot exist unless a controlling power upon will and appetite be placed somewhere, and the less of it there is within, the more there must be without. It is ordained in the eternal constitution of things, that men of intemperate minds cannot be free. Their passions forge their fetters.

Edmund Burke, *Letter to a Member of the National Assembly*, 1791

♦ Controls on will and appetite in the United States have been insufficient to maintain the minimum levels of order, amenity, and decency essential to maintaining a free society. Crime rates have begun to drop, but they remain at levels far higher than 25 years ago. The reported rates of robbery and assault in 1985 were three times greater than in 1962, the rate of burglary was over two times greater, and that of homicide 70 percent greater.[1]

The statistics barely hint at the harsh reality in some cities. Public housing projects in Chicago are terrorized by violent crimes and random shootings so pervasive that residents live in a state of siege. In south central Los Angeles youth gangs use automatic weapons to control territory, exact revenge, and protect their drug trafficking. So common has crime become in some neighborhoods that many serious offenses are simply not reported to the police.

Though heroin use has declined in recent years, cocaine use has risen dramatically. Urine tests showed that the proportion of inmates in the Manhattan Central Booking jail who had used cocaine shortly before their arrests rose from 42 percent in 1984 to 83 percent in 1986; the proportion using drugs other than marijuana rose from 56 to 85 percent. A similar increase was reported among inmates in the Washington, D.C., jail.[2] Studies show that the most serious offenders are those most likely to be heavy and consistent drug users. The typical high-rate serious offender is a young man "deeply enmeshed in a world of drugs and illegal activities" who early on developed a "flagrant disregard for a traditional life-style and an appreciation for chemically induced highs."[3]

Even before drug abuse became common, a remarkably consistent portrait of the high-rate criminal emerged from studies here and abroad. He was typically an impulsive young man who grew up in a discordant family where one or both parents had a criminal record, discipline was erratic, and human relations were cold and unpredictable. He had a low IQ and poor verbal skills. His behavioral problems appeared early, often by age eight, and included dishonesty and aggressiveness. Even in kindergarten or first grade he was disruptive, defiant, and badly behaved. He had few friends and was not emotionally close to those associates with whom he began stealing and assaulting. His police record began early; as a young adult his life consisted of petty crime, some of it vicious, accompanied by sporadic bouts of marginal employment, intervals in custody, and many days of drug- or alcohol-induced oblivion.[4] Although widespread drug abuse did not change these traits, it magnified their effects. It is idle to speculate whether drugs cause crime: those most likely to be high-rate offenders are also most likely to find drug use appealing. If one drug becomes scarce, they will switch to another, sometimes using several simultaneously. To fund their habit heroin addicts will commit more crimes than intermittent users, but even when drugs are unavailable, users will steal and lead disorderly and criminal lives. Moreover, supplying drugs at little or no cost to regular users does not eliminate criminal misconduct.[5]

Neither the rise in crime and drug abuse nor the individual traits and social circumstances contributing to these pathologies are unique to the United States. The prevalence of delinquency among men is about as high in London and Copenhagen as in Philadelphia. The association between impulsiveness, low IQ, and discordant families, on the one hand, and high-rate delinquency, on the other, is as strong in England and Scandinavia as in the United States, although the United States has a higher rate of nonviolent crime.[6] We cannot end crime by discovering and changing what is uniquely bad about this country; from the point of view of crime and its causes, the United States is hardly unique.

Nevertheless this country differs from other industrialized democracies in having an underclass that is not merely poor but has few chances of escaping poverty. The inner-city poor are isolated in areas where "not working is the norm, crime is commonplace, and welfare is a way of life."[7] Many who once agreed that the cause of poverty was a lack of money and the solution more money (in the form of a negative income tax or a family allowance) now admit that for the underclass the problem is not simply poverty; it is behavior—criminality, alcoholism, drug abuse, teenage pregnancies, and discordant or broken families. Indeed, criminality is part of a wide range of disorderly and threatening behaviors. Those most likely to commit crimes are also most likely to drive recklessly, be sporadically employed, drink to excess, and abuse women.[8]

Because the underclass is not a census category we cannot say how much crime and disorder it causes. We can examine racial differences in crime rates, but these differences must be interpreted carefully because among blacks, as among whites, only a small proportion cause a large amount of crime. Blacks are about six times as likely as whites to commit murder.[9] In other words, if black and white homicide rates were the same, we would have one-third fewer homicides in this country. Our murder rate would then be about equal to that of Luxembourg and not much higher than that of France.

We can achieve a decent society through external and internal controls. Contemporary opinion prefers the external to the internal. Liberals like attractive job opportunities; conservatives like tougher or more certain criminal penalties. But both want incentives that convince the would-be offender to obey the law.

I have argued since 1975 in favor of making both the sanctions for crime swifter and more certain, if not more severe, and the alternatives to crime more abundant and rewarding,[10] even though more certain sanctions may have a greater effect on behavior than more abundant economic opportunities.[11] I have argued in favor of external controls because at the time I began addressing the matter academics and politicians had unjustifiably rejected sanctions and embraced rehabilitation. What needed rehabilitation was not the criminal (we did not know how to change him) but the concept of deterrence. We knew how to change penalties, and changing them seemed to make a difference.

But I was not overly optimistic. I concluded *Thinking About Crime* with the observation that "a sober view of man requires a modest definition of progress."[12] If everything I recommended were done, the robbery rate might drop 20 percent, but that would still leave us with the highest rate of almost any Western nation. Some claim that much of what I and others recommended was in fact done and that many state criminal justice systems began to emphasize the more certain application of more equitable penalties. But whether the means employed (passing determinate sentencing laws, abolishing parole, curtailing probation) actually affected the probability that a given offender would be punished is largely unknown. Rising prison populations may merely reflect the growing number of offenders. Whatever the penalties on the statute books, the actual time served by the median robber or burglar was significantly lower in the 1980s than in the early 1960s.

The one change that may have increased the deterrent or incapacitating effect of the criminal justice system was the spread of intensive-supervision probation (ISP) programs in place of loosely supervised (or unsupervised) probation. The intensity comes from a combination of small caseloads, frequent contacts by probation officers, house arrest, obligatory community service, victim restitution, and military-style training during a brief period of shock incarceration followed by entry into ISP.[13] These are steps in the right direction, at least as alternatives to conventional probation rather than imprisonment, but so far we have little systematic evidence of their deterrent or incapacitating effect.

We now face a new state of affairs. With the low U.S. birthrate there will be fewer males in the most crime-prone age groups, and thus crime rates will probably drift down. But there is no evidence that the baby bust will reduce crime dramatically. Careful studies of the prevalence of crime among two groups of Philadelphia youths—those growing up during the 1950s and those growing up during the 1960s and 1970s—have shown that the more recent offenders committed far more crimes than their predecessors. A delinquent Philadelphia boy born in 1958 was five times more likely to commit a robbery than one born in 1945.[14] This startling increase in the age-specific crime rate gives small comfort to those who hope that an aging United States will be markedly safer.

And the United States will not continue to age. Though the number of males between the ages of 18 and 24 will decline by over three million between 1980 and 1995, it will then start to rise again in an echo baby boom—the coming-of-age of the children of the baby boomers. (The number of black males in that age group will start to rise even earlier.)[15] The echo baby boom will probably produce an echo crime boom. If external controls were unable, for whatever reason, to prevent a tripling of the violent crime rate between 1962 and 1980, they are unlikely to prevent another increase in crime in the late 1990s.

External controls appeal to citizens of a free society. By contrast, building internal controls means building character, and Americans of many political persuasions find that akin to making the government a national nanny. But relying on external controls means accepting indefinitely the existence of a large underclass with inordinately high rates of crime, drug abuse, teenage pregnancies, unwed mothers, and welfare dependency; accepting as inevitable a black homicide rate six times higher than that of whites; and accepting as unavoidable widespread drug abuse.[16]

Some argue that we should abandon certain external controls and legalize drug use so that addicts will not have to steal to feed their habits. If heroin and cocaine were freely available, their cost would be trivial, and so there would be fewer crimes. But the economics of drug abuse works two ways. Lower prices would lead not only to fewer crimes but to more drug consumption. In the fifteen years before 1968, when private physicians in Great Britain could prescribe heroin for addicts, the number of British addicts increased 40-fold.[17]

Studies of how drug abuse spreads indicate that first-time users are powerfully influenced by sheer availability: when the drug is hard to get, beginners quickly abandon the search.[18] A two-tiered drug distribution system—high prices for experimental users and low prices for confirmed users—would both deter experimenters from becoming addicts and dissuade addicts from criminal activity.[19] But no such markets could exist side by side without experimental users finding a way to enter the low-cost market. There is a similar flaw in the scheme to make drug purchases legal for adults and illegal for children. Under these arrangements children would get access to drugs as surely as they now get access to beer.

It is important to maintain and enhance, in a manner consistent with constitutional liberties, external controls on destructive behavior. We must provide good police protection, swift and fair trials, certain but equitable punishment, alternatives to prison for offenders who would otherwise be the object of inadequate community supervision, jobs and job training for people on the fringe of the labor market, welfare programs that discourage family breakups and reward work, and drug policies that make it difficult to abuse drugs and easy for abusers to get treatment—all goals we have pursued for two decades. We need to make a decentralized, complex, and underfunded system of external controls work a little better. A president can play only a modest role in this process: he is not the nation's chief of police, presiding judge, prison warden, or head social worker, and only within narrow limits is he the architect of labor market growth.

U.S. leaders must now support efforts to improve the internal controls on which human character, and ultimately human behavior, depend. There is certainly a connection between strengthening external and improving internal controls. Punished criminals may or may not repeat their crimes, but the rest of us are reminded that crime is wrong and ought to be punished and that punishment is shameful and ought to make those who risk it feel guilty. But internal control—character—also comes directly from familial, neighborhood, and educational processes affected, even if not directed, by public leaders.

Character formation is widely misunderstood. To those suspicious of conventional mores, character is a matter of choice, not indoctrination, and is best formed through self-discovery. The well-educated take for granted that their behavior will meet essential standards of propriety, and so they believe that they and their children should be free to develop and to express themselves without philistine social constraints.

To those deeply committed to conventional standards, character is not a matter of choice but of proper indoctrination. People are taught right conduct by precepts that have traditional justification and are supported by religious beliefs and other-worldly sanctions. Such individuals value religious teachings and worry about the secularization of schools and society. Many hope that prayer in public schools would improve character.

In fact, character—moral virtue—is the product neither of self-discovery nor of formal precept but of habituation. Aristotle observed that moral virtue is a temperament, not a passion or a faculty. An intellectual virtue, such as wisdom or prudence, "in the main owes both its birth and growth to teaching." But a moral virtue, such as temperance or courage, "comes about as a result of habit." (*Ethics* derives from the Greek *ethos*, meaning habit.) "We become just by doing just acts, temperate by doing temperate acts, brave by doing brave acts."[20] A good character comes about through the regular repetition of right actions, not through moral instruction or personal discovery.

Aristotle's insight has been confirmed by countless studies. Children who are neither wantonly hostile nor regularly devious have usually been raised in families where the bonds of affection are warm and strong and the pattern of discipline consistent and fair.[21] That pattern is important in the management not only of major forms of misconduct but of the most routine aspects of everyday life. Some families find it easier than others to establish bonds and to practice discipline. A few children may be so cold, impulsive, and disturbed that no family can manage them. But most children are sufficiently disposed to social life that parents of the most ordinary attainments and temperament can raise them well.

Perhaps the most dramatic evidence of the effect on child behavior of parental management of daily activities comes from close studies of families with children who were out of control and who, with proper guidance, have learned to reassert control. The work of the Oregon Social Learning Center, under the direction of Dr. Gerald Patterson, is perhaps the best-known example,[22] but there are others—the clinical work of Dr. Robert Wahler at the University of Tennessee, the parent-training program in Seattle led by Dr. David Hawkins and others at the University of Washington, Project Pryde in Pittsburgh, and the Children's House program in New Haven, Connecticut.[23] What most of these programs have in common is teaching social competency by a fundamental principle of behavioral psychology—simply, that behavior is controlled by its consequences. When right actions are regularly, promptly, and consistently followed by approval and rewards and when wrong actions are regularly, promptly, and consistently followed by disapproval and punishments, good behavior becomes more common and bad behavior less so. Indeed, the "results of these programs have been one of the few success stories in the treatment of conduct-problem children."[24] Many of the alternatives, such as counseling and psychotherapy, have had no proven effects; although they may alter how people talk or think, they do not alter how people behave on a daily basis away from the therapist's watchful eye.

Conservative critics of these programs dismiss them as social engineering and call instead for empowering parents by, presumably, getting the government out of their hair. Liberal critics attack these programs for instilling conformist and conventional habits, thereby frustrating the emergence of creativity and spontaneity. Neither charge is justified. Incompetent parents cannot simply be empowered because they do not know what to do with power. They are so erratic in their management of behavior, so baffled by the challenges presented by an impulsive child, that they alternate between ignoring routine misconduct or wreaking havoc on a child for minor misconduct. What competent parents instill is not conformity or conventionality but a sense of personal responsibility. Character consists of taking into account the future consequences of present actions and the interests and feelings of others. The absence of character is revealed by an impulsive obsession with immediate pleasure. Character is consistent with—indeed, a prerequisite for—the life of a priest, a soldier, an artist, or a reformer.

One aspect of the concern for character has already gripped the imagination of many public officials. People wishing to reduce delinquency, improve educational attainment, and produce a more reliable labor force have seized the results of a few studies of programs akin to Project Head Start that seem to show that a few hours a week in a preschool program for three- to four-year-olds will have important and lasting effects. The most frequently cited study—because its findings are so interesting and its evaluation so rigorous—is that of the Perry Preschool Project in Ypsilanti, Michigan. The study randomly assigned 123 children (mostly from low-income black families, half of them female-headed) to two groups; one enrolled in a special preschool program (twelve hours a week) and the other entered the local elementary school without preschool training. They were followed to age nineteen. Their elementary-school teachers later judged that those in the preschool program displayed better conduct in the classroom, were more likely to graduate from high school, were less likely to be arrested, and were less likely to have admitted in interviews to having committed offenses not known to the police.[25]

These impressive results have led many states to require preschool education for all children and many groups to press Congress for heavy federal funding of such efforts. But these actions are premature. Even the authors of the Perry study readily admit that we do not know what kind of child is most and least likely to benefit from such a program. Some children may even be better off at home. We do not know what the content of a preschool program ought to be, what kind of staff it needs, or whether there are enough competent teachers to run successful programs nationwide. The Perry program was an experiment enlisting the efforts of a gifted and dedicated staff. Whether thousands of teachers nationwide could do what a few did in Ypsilanti remains to be seen.

Nevertheless the Perry project at least shows that for some problem children early efforts to improve social competence and to help people function effectively in an institutional setting can bring long-term benefits—in short, that efforts to mold character can succeed.

The school's ability to shape character does not end at first grade. James S. Coleman and his colleagues have shown that students of similar backgrounds learn more in private and parochial high schools than in public ones not only because of the more rigorous curriculum and heavier homework load but also because of the disciplinary climate: there is less fighting, less truancy, less defiance of teachers. Moreover, the public schools with the highest educational attainment also have the best disciplinary climate.[26]

Michael Rutter and his colleagues reached much the same conclusion in their comparison of educational outcomes and teenage criminality in a dozen secondary schools in a working-class area of London.[27] The more effective schools emphasized and praised achievement and encouraged the early identification and control of disruptive students. The good classroom functions like the successful family: "praise is freely given and disciplinary actions are few but firm."[28]

Secretary of Education William J. Bennett has identified the key factor in achieving a productive school ethos:

> [Successful] schools have outstanding principals who lead and inspire and bring out the best from a dedicated, motivated teaching staff. These schools reach out to parents and establish an alliance among the parents, the community, and the school: an alliance dedicated to the nurture, protection, and education of children. These schools concentrate on the basics—the basics of good behavior and the basics of academic achievement.[29]

But as Coleman and his colleagues suggest, the political constraints on public schools—rigidities in the selection, assignment, and discharge of teachers, in the freedom of schools to punish or expel unruly children, in the ability to concentrate resources on the most important endeavors—inhibit them from creating the proper ethos except where extraordinary principals manage to overcome these constraints. At the Brookings Institution Terry M. Moe and John E. Chubb surveyed teachers and administrators in many of the public and private schools Coleman studied. What they learned led them to doubt that the political controls on public schools would permit the changes necessary to improve educational attainment and youthful behavior:

> If public schools are to develop the organizational qualities that most research indicates are essential for real improvements in education, it may be necessary to emulate the system of control that governs the private schools . . . [E]ffective control over schools would be transferred from government to the market. Government would still set minimum requirements. It would also provide funding, likely in the form of vouchers allocated to parents. But virtually all the important decisions about policy, organization, and personnel would be taken out of the hands of politicians and administrators and given over to schools and their clients: the students and their parents.[30]

The educational establishment will bitterly resist such changes in public education. Many false charges will be levied against the market model, not least the claim that it would produce racial and economic segregation in education. The charge is false; as Coleman and others have shown, private and parochial schools actually produce *more* contact within the school between blacks and whites, and between poor and well-off children, than do public schools. The public school is rapidly becoming the most segregated educational institution.[31]

I began this essay on the subject of crime and drugs and have moved to the training of parents and the management of schools. Once such matters were considered wholly different subjects, but times have changed. The study of crime and drug abuse cannot be separated from the study of families and schools any more than the problem of economic growth can be seriously discussed without reference to the individual propensity to save and the sources of entrepreneurship. The harder problem is to identify the federal role in these issues. By and large, Washington should not manage or direct; the crucial decisions must be made locally. Even there it is as important to encourage private and voluntary efforts as to revamp governmental ones. But the federal government can set the tone, help with the funding, and encourage the testing of pilot projects.

Specifically, the federal government should take seven actions:

1. Fund more careful tests of alternative preschool education programs operated by both private and public agencies.

2. Design and test parent training programs for both teenagers (as part of the school curriculum) and parents who cannot cope with troubled children (as part of a clinic for families under stress).

3. Encourage the development and testing in schools of drug education programs that teach students to resist peer pressure. Examples of such programs include the Drug Awareness Resistance Education (DARE) in the Los Angeles public schools and the SPECDA program in the New York City schools.

4. Revive, expand, and evaluate programs using tuition grants, education vouchers, or the like, so that parents can choose the school their child attends.

5. Modify welfare laws to require work as a condition of aid for as high a proportion of recipients as possible and to require family support payments from every father.

6. Support long-term studies of how high-risk children grow up. High-rate criminals tend to begin as high-rate delinquents, and high-rate delinquents tend to display serious conduct disorders at an early age. We do not yet understand the causes of these disorders; they may well include biological factors (low birth weight, perinatal stress, and metabolic or neurological deficiencies), early childhood experiences, the presence of toxins (such as lead) in the environment, and stress in the transition from home to school. The justification for such research and the forms it might take have been set out at length elsewhere.[32]

7. Set a moral tone emphasizing the importance of character to a free society. Though character is formed mostly by habituation, there is still a role for moral instruction.

Some educated people who have benefited from their families' character-forming processes come to view them as stultifying or even repressive. Young adults often display this view by celebrating the virtues of self-expression over those of self-control. What they preach is less important (at least for them) than the habitual civility and self-control they take for granted. But such preaching has a profound and unhappy effect on those who for whatever reason lack the inclination to take into account the distant consequences of present actions. They hear from the prophets of self-expression a message extolling pure self-indulgence.

Public leaders cannot pretend that their statements have no moral content. Statements that dwell on injustice, the need for a fuller extension of rights, and the obligations society has to the individual will lead some to believe that such pervasive injustice justifies any form of rebellion, that the exercise of rights is more important than the performance of duties, and that the individual has no obligation to society. In a free nation our dependence on internal controls increases as our reliance on external controls decreases. Thus character becomes important precisely in those social circumstances that most threaten the legitimacy of the processes of character formation. Public officials, by their conduct and public statements, can help maintain those precarious processes.

Notes

1. *Uniform Crime Reports* (Washington, D.C.: Federal Bureau of Investigation, various years).

2. Eric D. Wish, "Drug Use in Arrestees in Manhattan" (Narcotic and Drug Research, Inc., New York, February 12, 1987).

3. Marcia R. Chaiken, "Crime Rates and Substance Abuse Among Types of Offenders," in Bruce D. Johnson and Eric Wish, eds., *Crime Rates Among Drug-Abusing Offenders* (Report to the National Institute of Justice, Washington, D.C., 1986), pp. 12–54; Jan Chaiken and Marcia R. Chaiken, "Who Gets Caught Doing Crime?" (Discussion paper, Bureau of Justice Statistics, Washington, D.C., 1985).

4. David P. Farrington, "Early Precursors of Frequent Offending," in James Q. Wilson and Glenn C. Loury, eds., *From Children to Citizens: Families, Schools, and Delinquency Prevention* (New York: Springer-Verlag, 1987), pp. 29–33.

5. John Kaplan, *The Hardest Drug: Heroin and Public Policy* (Chicago: University of Chicago Press, 1983), pp. 51–58.

6. David P. Farrington, "Offending From 10 to 25 Years of Age," in K. T. Van Dusen and S. A. Mednick, eds., *Prospective Studies of Crime and Delinquency* (Boston: Kluwer-Nijhoff, 1983); P. Wolf, "Delinquent Boys and Family Relations," in P. Wolf, ed., *Sequential Research* (Copenhagen: Micro Publications Social Science Series, 1984); Marvin E. Wolfgang, R. M. Figlio, and T. Sellin, *Delinquency in a Birth Cohort* (Chicago: University of Chicago Press, 1972).

7. Isabel Wilkerson, "Growth of the Very Poor Is Focus of New Studies," *New York Times*, December 20, 1987, p. 15.

8. Lee N. Robins, *Deviant Children Grown Up* (Baltimore, Md.: Williams & Wilkins, 1966); Lee N. Robins and K. S. Ratcliff, "Childhood Conduct Disorders and Later Arrest," in Lee N. Robins, P. J. Clayton, and J. K. King, eds., *The Social Consequences of Psychiatric Illness* (New York: Brunner/Mazel, 1980), pp. 248–63.

9. James Q. Wilson and Richard J. Herrnstein, *Crime and Human Nature* (New York: Simon & Schuster, 1985), pp. 463–64.

10. James Q. Wilson, *Thinking About Crime*, 1st ed. (New York: Basic Books, 1975), chap. 8, esp. pp. 177–78, 202.

11. Wilson and Herrnstein, *Crime and Human Nature*, chap. 12 and pp. 389–401; James Q. Wilson, *Thinking About Crime*, rev. ed. (New York: Basic Books, 1983), chap. 7.

12. Wilson, *Thinking About Crime*, 1st ed., p. 199.

13. Joan Petersilia, *Expanding Options for Criminal Sentencing* (Santa Monica, Calif.: Rand Corp., 1987).

14. Marvin E. Wolfgang and Paul E. Tracy, "The 1945 and 1958 Birth Cohorts: A Comparison of the Prevalence, Incidence, and Severity of Delinquent Behavior" (Paper delivered at the Conference on Public Danger, Dangerous Offenders, and the Criminal Justice System, Harvard University, Cambridge, Mass., 1982).

15. *Statistical Abstract of the United States, 1987* (Washington, D.C.: Government Printing Office, 1987), tables 13 and 16.

16. One advantage of coping with social problems by trying to change character rather than incentives is that wherever the former works it solves the problem of moral hazard. A moral hazard exists when an otherwise desirable compensation scheme induces undesirable behavior. Most welfare programs contain important moral hazards: if the benefits to single-parent families are too high, families will break up or fail to form to claim the benefits. Some drug abuse programs involve such hazards; for example, if addicts are offered low-priced drugs to keep them out of the black market, some will consume only part of their dosage and sell the rest. Some casual users will seek addict status to obtain low-priced drugs.

17. Wilson, *Thinking About Crime*, rev. ed., p. 209.

18. Ibid., pp. 201–4. That heroin use increases dramatically when the drug becomes cheaper is vividly shown by the 14 percent of U.S. ground troops in Vietnam who became heroin addicts and considerably more who became nonaddicted users. Moreover, doctors (who have easy access to drugs) are addicted to opiates at a rate twenty times greater than the population as a whole. See Kaplan, *The Hardest Drug*, p. 113

19. Mark H. Moore, "Policies to Achieve Discrimination in the Effective Price of Heroin," *American Economic Review* 63 (May 1973): 270–77.

20. Aristotle, *Nichomachean Ethics*, bk. 1, chap. 1, in Richard McKeon, ed., *The Basic Works of Aristotle* (New York: Random House, 1941).

21. Wilson and Herrnstein, *Crime and Human Nature*, chap. 8.

22. James Q. Wilson, "Raising Kids," *Atlantic Monthly*, September 1983, pp. 45–56.

23. See the review essays in Wilson and Loury, *From Children to Citizens*, by Rolf Loeber ("What Policy Makers and Practitioners Can Learn from Family Studies of Juvenile Conduct Problems and Delinquency"), Robert G. Wahler ("Contingency Management with Oppositional Children: Some Critical Teaching Issues for Parents"), Edward Zigler and Nancy W. Hall ("The Implications of Early Intervention Efforts for the Primary Prevention of Juvenile Delinquency"), and J. David Hawkins et al. ("Delinquency Prevention Through Parent Training").

24. Loeber, "Policy Makers," p. 95.

25. Lawrence J. Schweinhart, "Can Preschool Programs Help Prevent Delinquency?" in Wilson and Loury, *From Children to Citizens*, pp. 135–53.

26. James S. Coleman, Thomas Hoffer, and Sally Kilgore, *High School Achievement* (New York: Basic Books, 1982), pp. 159–78. See also Sabdra L. Hanson and

Alan Ginsburg, "Gaining Ground: Values and High School Success," *American Education Research Journal* (forthcoming).

27. Michael Rutter et al., *Fifteen Thousand Hours* (Cambridge, Mass.: Harvard University Press, 1979), chaps. 7 and 10.

28. Ibid., p. 186.

29. William J. Bennett, "Address Before the 1987 Texas Education Conference," January 16, 1987, as quoted in *New Consensus*, p. 104. A useful summary of the effective-schools literature is *What Works? Research About Teaching and Learning*, 2nd ed. (Washington, D.C.: U.S. Department of Education, 1987).

30. John E. Chubb and Terry M. Moe, "No School Is an Island: Politics, Markets, and Education," *Brookings Review*, Fall 1986, p. 28. The efforts of some states to provide greater parental choices in education are summarized in Chester E. Finn, Jr., "Education Choice: Theory, Practice, and Research" (Testimony before the U.S. Senate, Subcommittee on Intergovernmental Relations of the Committee on Governmental Affairs, October 22, 1985).

31. Coleman, Hoffer, and Kilgore, *High School Achievement*, chap. 3.

32. For a detailed discussion of research proposals, see David P. Farrington, Lloyd Ohlin, and James Q. Wilson, *Understanding and Controlling Crime* (New York: Springer-Verlag, 1986).

F. A. HAYEK

◆ ———————— ◆

Central Planning
The Fatal Conceit

◆ Even after seventy years of experience with socialism, it is safe to say that most intellectuals outside the areas where socialism has been tried—Eastern Europe and the Third World—remain content to brush aside what lessons might lie in economics, unwilling to wonder whether there might not be a reason why socialism, as often as it is attempted, never seems to work out as its intellectual leaders intended.

The doubts Jean-Jacques Rousseau cast on the institution of several—that is, private—property became the foundation of socialism and have continued to influence some of the greatest thinkers of our century, even as great a figure as Bertrand Russell. At least before the obvious economic failure of East European socialism, it was widely thought by such rationalists that a centrally planned economy would deliver not only social justice but also a more efficient use of economic resources. This notion appears eminently sensible at first glance. But it overlooks the fact that the totality of resources one could employ in such a plan *is simply not knowable to anybody* and therefore can hardly be centrally controlled.

Nonetheless, socialists continue to fail to face the obstacles in the way of fitting separate individual decisions into a common pattern conceived as a plan. The conflict between our instincts—which, since Rousseau, have become identified with morality—and the moral traditions that have sur-

This essay is adapted from F. A. Hayek, *The Fatal Conceit*, ed. W. W. Bartley III (London and New York: Routledge, 1988).

vived cultural evolution and serve to restrain these instincts is embodied in the separation now often drawn between certain sorts of ethical and political philosophy on the one hand and economics on the other. The point is not that whatever economists determine to be efficient is therefore right but that economic analysis can elucidate the usefulness of practices heretofore thought to be right—usefulness from the perspective of any philosophy that looks unfavorably on the human suffering and death that would follow the collapse of our civilization. It is a betrayal of concern for others, then, to theorize about the just society without carefully considering the economic consequences of implementing such views.

The intellectuals' vain search for a truly socialist community, which results in the idealization of, and then disillusionment with, a seemingly endless string of utopias—the Soviet Union, then Cuba, China, Yugoslavia, Vietnam, Tanzania, Nicaragua—should suggest that there might be something about socialism that does not conform to certain facts. But such facts, first explained by economists more than a century ago, remain unexamined by those who pride themselves on their rationalistic rejection of the notion that there could be any facts that transcend historical context or present an insurmountable barrier to human desires.

Meanwhile, among those who, in the tradition of Bernard Mandeville, David Hume, and Adam Smith, did study economics, there gradually emerged not only an understanding of market processes but a powerful critique of the possibility of substituting socialism for them. The advantages of these market procedures were so contrary to expectation that they could be explained only retrospectively, through analyzing this spontaneous formation itself. When this was done, it was found that decentralized control over resources, especially control through several property, leads to the generation and use of more information than is possible under central direction. Order and control extending beyond the immediate purview of any central authority could be attained by central direction only if, contrary to fact, those local managers able to gauge existing and potential resources were *also* currently informed of the constantly changing relative importance of such resources and could then communicate full and accurate details about this to some central planning authority in time for it to tell them what to do in the light of all the other, different, concrete information it had received from other regional or local managers—who of course, in turn, found themselves in similar difficulties in obtaining and delivering any such information.

Once we realize what the task of such a central planning authority would be, it becomes clear that the commands it would have to issue could not be derived from the information the local managers had recognized as important but could only be determined through direct dealings among individuals or groups controlling clearly delimited aggregates of means. The hypothetical assumption, customarily employed in theoretical descriptions of the market process (descriptions made by people who usually have no intention of supporting socialism), to the effect that all such facts (or parameters) can be assumed to be known to the explaining theorist, obscures all this, and consequently produces the curious deceptions that help to sustain various forms of socialist thinking.

The order of the extended economy is, and can be, formed only by a wholly different process—from an evolved method of communication that makes it possible to transmit not an infinite multiplicity of reports about particular facts but merely certain abstract properties of several particular conditions, such as competitive prices, which must be brought into mutual correspondence to achieve overall order. These communicate the different rates of substitution or equivalence that the several parties involved find prevailing between the various goods and services whose use they command. Certain quantities of any such objects may prove to be equivalents or possible substitutes for one another, either for satisfying particular human needs or for producing, directly or indirectly, means to satisfy them. Surprising as it may be that such a process exists at all, let alone that it came into being through evolutionary selection without being deliberately designed, I know of no efforts to refute this contention or discredit the process itself—unless one so regards simple declarations that all such facts can, somehow, be known to some central planning authority.

Indeed the whole idea of central control is confused. There is not and never could be a single directing mind at work; there will always be some council or committee charged with designing a plan of action for some enterprise. Though individual members may occasionally, to convince the others, quote particular pieces of information that have influenced their views, the conclusions of the body will generally not be based on common knowledge but on agreement among several views based on different information. Each bit of knowledge contributed by one person will tend to lead some other to recall yet other facts of whose relevance he has become aware only by his being told of yet other circumstances of which he did not know. Such a process thus remains one of making use of dispersed knowledge (and thus simulates trading, although in a highly inefficient way—a way usually lacking competition and diminished in accountability) rather than unifying the knowledge of a number of persons. The members of the group will be able to communicate to one another few of their distinct reasons; they will communicate chiefly conclusions drawn from their respective individual knowledge of the problem in hand. Moreover, only rarely will circumstances really be the same for different persons contemplating the same situation—at least insofar as this concerns some sector of the extended order and not merely a more or less self-contained group.

Perhaps the best illustration of the impossibility of deliberate rational allocation of resources in an extended economic order without the guidance by prices formed in competitive markets is the problem of allocating the current supply of liquid capital among all the different uses whereby it could increase the final product. The problem is essentially how much of the currently accruing productive resources can be spared to provide for the more distant future as against present needs. Adam Smith was aware of the representative character of this issue when, referring to the problem faced by an individual owner of such capital, he wrote: "What is the species of domestick industry which his capital can employ, and of which the produce is likely to be of the greatest value, every individual, it is evident, can, in his local situation, judge much better than any statesman or lawgiver can do for him."[1]

Comprehending the role played by the transmission of information (or of factual knowledge) opens the door to understanding the extended order. Yet these issues are highly abstract and are particularly hard to grasp for those schooled in the mechanistic, scientistic, constructivist canons of rationality that dominate our educational systems—and who consequently tend to be ignorant of biology, economics, and evolution. Our civilization depends, not only for its origin but also for its preservation, on this extended order of human cooperation, an order more commonly, if somewhat misleadingly, known as capitalism. To understand our civilization one must appreciate that the extended order resulted not from human design or intention but spontaneously: it arose from the unintended adoption of certain traditional and largely *moral* practices, many of which men tend to dislike, whose significance they usually fail to understand, whose validity they cannot prove, and which have nonetheless fairly rapidly spread by means of an evolutionary selection—the comparative increase of population and wealth—of those groups that happened to adopt them. The unwitting, reluctant, even painful adoption of these practices kept these groups together, increased their access to valuable information of all sorts, and enabled them to be "fruitful, and multiply, and replenish the earth, and subdue it" (Genesis 1.28). This process is perhaps the least-appreciated facet of human evolution.

The main point of my argument is, then, that the conflict between advocates of the spontaneous extended human order created by a competitive market, on the one hand, and those who demand a deliberate arrangement of human interaction by central authority based on collective command over available resources, on the other hand, is due to a factual error by the latter about how knowledge of these resources is and can be generated and utilized. As a question of fact, this conflict must be settled by scientific study. Such study shows that, by following the spontaneously generated moral traditions underlying the competitive market order (traditions that do not satisfy the canons or norms of rationality embraced by most socialists), we generate and garner greater knowledge and wealth than could ever be obtained or utilized in a centrally directed economy.[2]

Notes

1. Adam Smith, *An Inquiry into the Nature and Causes of the Wealth of Nations* (1776; Oxford: Oxford University Press, 1976).

2. For extended discussions of the concepts in this essay, see, in addition to *Fatal Conceit*, the following by F. A. Hayek: "The Use of Knowledge in Society," *American Economic Review* 35, no. 4 (September 1945): 519–30; "Competition as a Discovery Procedure," in Chiaki Nishiyama and Kurt R. Leube, eds., *The Essence of Hayek* (Stanford: Hoover Institution Press, 1984), pp. 254–65; "The Pretence of Knowledge," Nobel Memorial Lecture, Stockholm, December 11, 1974, reprinted in Nishiyama and Leube, *Essence of Hayek*, pp. 266–77; and *The Road to Serfdom* (Chicago: University of Chicago Press, 1944). On the relation between increases in wealth and in population, see chap. 8 of *Fatal Conceit*.—ED.

MARTIN ANDERSON

The New Capitalism

◆ Every now and then in history a new intellectual tide rises, sweeping aside old dogmas and traditional ideas. When it enters the political realm it can have the power and force of a revolution, radically changing national policies, toppling governments, and touching and affecting the daily lives of millions of people.

During the last twenty years we have witnessed such a revolution, perhaps not as important as the epoch-making one that ushered in the New Enlightenment, but one of such power and sweep that its impact is being felt in almost every country in the world. It was born in the United States in the late 1940s and early 1950s. By the 1960s it had caused the political rise of Barry Goldwater and Richard Nixon, and by the 1980s it carried Ronald Reagan to the crest of political power and became known as the Reagan Revolution.

The essence of the revolutionary idea was simple: statism, of whatever sort, be it communism, socialism, or dictatorship, was intellectually bankrupt, and capitalism, marked by individual freedom and private property, was the only sure, tested way to prosperity. Slowly, painfully the evidence has piled up in this century demonstrating beyond any reasonable doubt

Adapted from *Revolution*, copyright © 1988 by Martin Anderson, by permission of Harcourt Brace Jovanovich, Inc.

that controlled economies do not work and free ones do. The implications of this growing belief in the efficacy of capitalism are profound and perhaps incalculable.

Already we have seen the most populous nation on earth, China, shuck off basic elements of communist economic theory with ease and dispatch—and startlingly good results.

China was once the holy temple of communism. But now she is becoming an apostate. Instead of being guided by communist ideology and ethical commandments from Mao's red book, *Quotations from Chairman Mao Tse-tung*, China, in the early 1980s, adopted three new proverbs as the guiding principles for reforming its society.

The first principle was *shi shi qiu shi*, which means "seek truth from facts." It was a rejection of ideological dogma in favor of deductive reasoning.

The second principle was *yi shijian wei zhenli di weiyi biaozhun*, which means simply that "practice is the sole criterion of truth." A far cry from the thoughts of Mao Tse-tung, it meant that the ideological correctness of public policy is to be judged solely by whether or not the policy works, by whether or not it produces good results.

The third principle was *jiefang sixiang*, or "emancipate the mind from dogma." This was meant as a call for experimentation, urging the Chinese people to try new things even when the moral and political guidelines of the past would have condemned such experiments (and the person who tried them).

From the viewpoint of any communist, or any good statist ideologue for that matter, these three proverbs were intellectual heresy. To seek the truth from the facts of reality, to judge the rightness of a national policy by how well the policy works, and not to be bound by the past—this was an Aristotelian invitation to embrace capitalism.

Practically everywhere one looks, one sees a rising tide of capitalist philosophy and practice — in England and Canada, in New Zealand and France, in Angola and Vietnam, and even in the old granddaddy of communism itself, the Soviet Union.

In 1987 General Secretary Mikhail Gorbachev published an extraordinary book in the United States, *Perestroika*. Translated literally and narrowly, *perestroika* is the Russian word for "restructuring." But in Gorbachev's view the word has a more profound meaning. "Perestroika is a word with many meanings," he writes, "but if we are to choose from its many possible synonyms the key one which expresses its essence most accurately, then we can say thus: *perestroika is a revolution*." [1]

To deal with the failure of the communist economy, Gorbachev urges "radical reforms for revolutionary change." In an earlier (June 11, 1985) speech to the central committee of the Communist Party, Gorbachev admitted that

> Our system of material incentives is extremely confused, cumbersome, and inefficient . . . bonuses are frequently regarded as some kind of mechanical addition to wages paid to everybody without exception, regardless of the contribution made by a specific employee to the results achieved . . .
>
> Everything that is out-of-date must be boldly eliminated so that a, so to speak, cost-conscious economic mechanism can begin operating at full capacity, an economic mechanism that will stimulate economic development and literally rap the knuckles of sloppy economic planners . . .
>
> Times have changed.[2]

To what degree Gorbachev's plans for reforming the Soviet economy will be successful is unknown, but just the fact that they were proposed at all is extraordinary. And if he actually does what he has indicated he wants to do, then the results could also be extraordinary.

What is going on? Is it just coincidence that the conservatives were returned to power in England and Canada? That Ronald Reagan is president of the United States? That socialism failed miserably in France? That China blithely announced it was no longer doing business with communist economic theory? That the economy of the Soviet Union is staggering?

No, it is not coincidence. If you step back and take a long look at the changes in the ideological thinking of the nations of the world, patterns emerge.

For all of the twentieth century and stretching back into the nineteenth century, a tremendous intellectual and political battle has been fought over the question, What political system will bring a nation the greatest amount of happiness to the greatest number of its citizens? What political system will ensure their safety, give them the opportunity for material prosperity, and give them the freedom to develop and express their full potential in their personal interests, such as art, literature, sports, leisure, and work? During this period, two major ideologies have dominated, and driven, the major political changes in the world. One is communism and the other is capitalism. They are in direct competition with each other for the loyalties of people all over the world, and capitalism is winning.

At first the contest was unfair, because the early practice of a fledgling capitalism was compared to the dreamy ideals of a communism that had never been tried. The early practice of capitalism was often seen to be imperfect. In fact, many of the social and economic ills, especially poverty, that were in the process of being cured by capitalism were often erroneously attributed to it. The actual practice of capitalism was not fault-free, but it did work and it accomplished a great deal.

It was no contest at the beginning. The results of practical capitalism—no matter how spectacular—could not compete with the promised prowess of communism. Communism seemed to appeal particularly to intellectuals, who, unlike their less-talented brothers and sisters, could conceptually conjure what an ideal society might be like and what it would accomplish.

As capitalism began to grab hold in the societies of the old world, especially in England, and in the United States, enormous progress was made. But the incipient practice of capitalism did not create an ideal society overnight. What was left undone was the subject of growing, bitter criticism, especially by those who held out the idealistic goal of a communist society.

As time went on there were two major historical developments. First, more nations actually embraced communism—or to put it more accurately, had it fastened upon them by revolutionaries with guns. And so the world began to accumulate the experience of countries that had practiced communism. As some intellectuals, though not many, predicted, communism in real life was a disaster. It oppressed people brutally, was a poor producer of wealth, and fostered great disparities in the distribution of the wealth it did produce; it suppressed liberty and smothered human initiative and achievement.

At the same time a more mature, modern capitalism, exemplified by American capitalism, showed what a powerful vehicle capitalism was for enhancing individual liberty, generating economic prosperity, and providing for a strong national defense.

Now communism and socialism have been tried and tested for many years. The last 70 years have given us a massive social experiment unequaled in the history of the world. It has been incredibly costly in terms of human suffering and wasted resources, but terribly important in teaching us a most valuable lesson.

The theories of communism and socialism may sound good, but in practice they don't work. In practice they have had awful results, and a careful reexamination of their theories shows that the theories themselves aren't so good either. Consequently, during the last ten years a striking transformation has taken place in political philosophy worldwide. There has been a powerful resurgence in the belief that capitalism works.

During the first two-thirds of the twentieth century the theory of communism won the international political battle against the practice of early capitalism. Today it is becoming increasingly clear that a mature capitalism is superior in every way to mature communism. Capitalism's resurgence has been slow, but it has been powerful. Its strength is that it has worked.

The new intellectual force of capitalism has not proceeded swiftly or smoothly. Bits and pieces of capitalism have been introduced into socialist societies in anxious attempts to reap its benefits without having to admit the failures of their earlier statism. The socialist and communist leaders want the economic power of capitalism, but they also want to preserve their cultural heritage and, most especially, they want to hang on to their political power. As a result the course of the new capitalism has resembled that of a giant glacier—apparently quiet for years, now imperceptibly on the move again, flowing with unstoppable power.

As Professor Peter L. Berger said in his 1986 book, *The Capitalist Revolution,*

> Capitalism has become a global phenomenon . . . Capitalism has been one of the most dynamic forces in human history, transforming one society after another, and today it has become established as an international system determining the economic fate of most of mankind and, at least indirectly, its social, political, and cultural fate, as well.[3]

The evidence is overwhelming. The greater the degree to which a nation has practiced capitalism, the greater the degree to which it has achieved economic prosperity, ensured its national security, and increased the freedom of its citizens. On the other hand, the greater the degree to which a nation has practiced statism, whether it was fascism or a military dictatorship or communism, the worse it has fared. The fact that some communist dictatorships, such as the Soviet Union, are in the aggregate larger or more powerful than a smaller, freer country is not an advertisement for communism. The question to ask is, What might have been?

Look at any country in the world, take into account its natural assets—the size of its territory, its mineral wealth, the climate, and the size of its population—the accumulated historical evidence, especially during the forty-odd years since World War II, and you see that capitalism is better in all respects.

There is not a *single* example of a successful collectivist state, if you use the twin criteria of prosperity and freedom to measure them. Every statist society is fundamentally a slave society, a society in which most do the bidding of a few because of fear. The average citizen of a collectivist state lives in fear of the government, and the government thrives on the fear of its citizens.

Today, in the year 1988, we know that if socialist countries have prospered it has been in spite of their socialism. To prosper, extraordinary efforts are made on the part of the people to subvert and circumvent the system. The results have been devastating. The greater the degree to which a society is governed by the iron hand of the state, the greater the degree of failure.

One of America's most eloquent Democrats, Daniel Patrick Moynihan, put it this way in a commencement address at New York University in 1984:

> The truth is that the Soviet idea is spent. It commands some influence in the world; and fear. But it summons no loyalty. History is moving away from it with astounding speed. I would not press the image, but it is as if the whole Marxist-Leninist ethos is hurtling off into a black hole in the universe. They will be remembered for what? The death of Andrei Sakharov? Yelena Bonner? Are there Marxist-Leninists here and about in the world? Yes: especially when the West allows Communism to identify with nationalism. But in truth, when they do succeed, how well do they do? And for how long?

Tomorrow will demonstrate beyond any doubt that a capitalist society will increase in power relative to the alternatives of communism, dictatorship, and other forms of statism. Capitalism is the promise of tomorrow for the world, for those who will be able to take it.

In the United States capitalism has demonstrated in actual practice, not theory, that it is a more moral society, giving men and women a degree of freedom and liberty almost unthinkable in a noncapitalist society; that it is a more productive society; that it allows people to earn a level of material prosperity that only kings enjoyed not too long ago; and finally, that it produces a more powerful society, with the productive capacity and technological skills to fashion a defense force second to none in the world.

The idea of capitalism is now sweeping across the surface of the earth—across Western Europe, especially in France; across Eastern Europe; the Far East, in Hong Kong, Singapore, and Taiwan; across China; across Australia and New Zealand; South America; parts of Africa; and to a very limited degree even in the Soviet Union. There is a rising intellectual tide of what could be called the new capitalism.

The resurgence of capitalism is stronger and more vibrant and vital than it has ever been. The rush to capitalism is a phenomenon of the 1980s, born of frustration with failed statist economies, born of the burning envy of the power and success of capitalist economies, born of the fear of being left in the dust of the new capitalism.

There is one curious phenomenon of note in the ongoing struggle between capitalism and communism. Citizens of communist countries are not only referred to as communists; they call themselves communists. This is not true in the capitalist world. Often called capitalists in a pejorative way by others, those who live in capitalist countries rarely, if ever, call themselves capitalists. It is even true in America where nobody refers to himself as an American capitalist. But that may begin to change as the power of capitalism grows and becomes more widely appreciated. Then perhaps more people will proudly say, "I am a capitalist." We have French communists and Soviet communists and even American communists. It may not be long before we shall hear some say, "I am a French capitalist." "I am an English capitalist." "I am a Chinese capitalist." "I am an Indian capitalist." "I am an Italian capitalist." And perhaps some day there will be those who will say without fear, "I am a Russian capitalist."

The international capitalist community is growing steadily and rapidly. Today its strength is somewhat masked because of all the euphemisms used to describe it. But if these trends continue, the day will come when someone will say, "We are all capitalists now."

As long as the public policy and political change flow from the well of reigning, dominant intellectual beliefs, then the tide of the new capitalism will continue to rise. Only when and if there is a seismic shift to the left in the intellectual world will we see a reversal of the political changes we are now witnessing.

The ultimate irony of the twentieth century may be that a lasting worldwide political revolution was accomplished not by Trotsky and the communists, but instead by Reagan and the capitalists.

Notes

1. Mikhail Gorbachev, *Perestroika: New Thinking for Our Country and the World* (New York: Harper & Row, 1987); italics mine.

2. "Gorbachev Speaks on Economic Progress, Planning," *Foreign Broadcast Information Service: USSR National Affairs*, June 12, 1985, pp. R13–17.

3. Peter L. Berger, *The Capitalist Revolution: Fifty Propositions About Prosperity, Equality, and Liberty* (New York: Basic Books, 1986).

GEORGE SHULTZ

◆ ———————————————— ◆

National Success and International Stability in a Time of Change

◆ Americans, and people just about everywhere, now know that big changes are underway in the world—changes in virtually every subject from science to superpower relations. So understanding and managing change is crucial. The United States has been trying to do that in recent years. And we've had some success in doing so, because our society thrives on change. We are open to it, and we are ready for it.

The summit is one mark of our success. Arms control got the most attention, but the summit reflects hard work on human rights, on coping with conflicts around the world, and on trying for a more stable relation between the two superpowers.

We have been doing pretty well. But we cannot be satisfied to rest on our accomplishments. This is a time to try to deepen our understanding of the changes taking place, to look ahead, and to assess what needs to be done if we are to keep control of our own future.

The World Ahead

At this point in an essay about the world ahead, the reader can expect to be inundated with a tide of vague generalities—words like *interdependence*,

Portions of this essay were originally presented as a speech to the World Affairs Council of Washington, December 4, 1987.

exhortations like "the challenge of the global change," and recitations of the gee-whiz variety about artificial intelligence, genetic engineering, and robotics.

Maybe it's impossible, but we have to try to talk about the world ahead without getting bogged down in this stultifying vocabulary. In ancient China, when familiar words and ways of thinking no longer accurately described the realities of the day, philosophers spoke of the need to rectify names so that concepts would correspond to the new order of things.

This is one of those times. Developments in science and social organization are altering the world profoundly—too profoundly for conventional habits of thinking to grasp. History suggests that mankind rarely understands revolutionary change at the time it is coming about. When concepts eventually catch up with the pace of change, new definitions and descriptions are applied: the Agricultural Age, the Bronze Age, the Industrial Revolution were named long after the fact.

So if we are in such a time of transformation, what kind of age is it that were are entering? What do we need to know and do about it?

My purpose is not to offer a definitive analysis of the global trends now underway but to try to survey the present scene—in Emerson's words—from "an original relation to the universe." In this time of profound change, one of the hardest adjustments to make is intellectual adjustment. We must discard outdated habits of thinking and make room for new possibilities.

First of all, just how different is this era we have entered? From one point of view, it was the nineteenth century's radical intellectual, ideological, spiritual, moral, and social revolutions that shattered the eternal verities. In a way, we have not fully adjusted yet to those epic events.

Today's—and tomorrow's—revolutionary changes are of a different nature. They are characterized by greater size and speed; they are both centrifugal and centripetal in their impact, dispersing yet concentrating activities, influences, and decisions.

First, the very *material substances* that surround us in everyday life are being transformed. Physically, synthetic materials make objects lighter, stronger, and more durable. But they are changing societies and economies, too, because their emergence affects supply and demand for natural raw materials. One new material substance—ceramics—has led researchers around the world to superconductivity at new temperatures, which in turn may profoundly alter one foundation stone of all human activity: energy. Another such foundation—food—no longer limits by its production the possibility of world population growth. Biotechnology in agriculture has stood Malthus on his head.

The same scientific progress that has altered the nature of these basic substances has also accelerated the speed of human transactions. Time and space are calculated in ever-smaller units. Success in every field depends increasingly upon how quickly ideas can be transformed into reality. The speed at which information flows has already created a global financial market. Markets are no longer places but electronic networks.

Along with these alterations in substance and speed have come changes in *magnitude*. Scientific, economic, and political matters are global in dimension and enormous in extent. They are outstripping the traditional means by which governments dealt with them. The amount of money that changes hands in the global financial market in one day exceeds one trillion dollars—more than the entire budget of the U.S. government for a year. Such flows transcend national boundaries and can overwhelm rigid economic policies. Manufacturing processes similarly are becoming global in scale. I recently saw a snapshot of a shipping label for some integrated circuits produced by an American firm. It said, "Made in one or more of the following countries: Korea, Hong Kong, Malaysia, Singapore, Taiwan, Mauritius, Thailand, Indonesia, Mexico, Philippines. The exact country of origin is unknown." That label says a lot about where current trends are taking us.

The thread that runs through all these things is *knowledge*: its discovery, its rapid transmission as information, and the education needed to use it. Access to ideas, no matter where they are developed, becomes the key to scientific and economic progress. For example, the growth sector for employment is the so-called service sector, particularly in finance, data processing, software, engineering, and management consultation. *Services* is a misleading designation. These activities are centered on ideas but have all the characteristics of the production of what we traditionally call goods. So it is time, as the ancient Chinese would have recognized, for a rectification of names.

Changes in materials, magnitudes, knowledge, and the speed of its dissemination—the opportunities offered by these changes are immense. And the United States and other open societies are beautifully situated to make the most of this era ahead. But there are troubling implications of change to consider as well. Emerson would put it down to his principle of compensation—no aspect of progress comes free of some drawback.

For many nations, the emerging era means new problems. Countries that cannot or will not compete in the global marketplace and interact with ideas from other societies will find themselves falling behind the advanced innovators and producers. Some of those countries may be able to absorb what the innovators develop and may register moderate growth. But the quality and technological content of that growth will remain limited by the inability of such countries to adjust to rapid change.

Other nations—single commodity countries and agricultural and industrial subsistence economies—are in danger of becoming marginal participants in what we might call the information-age economy, living as in eras past. Some lack the human and physical infrastructure to create and exploit economic opportunities. Others are held back by the inflexible nature of their political and social systems.

Yet even those who fall further behind economically can partake of some of the fruits of the new age—fruits that unfortunately are not sufficiently forbidden. Wars in the Third World are being fought with increasing sophistication and firepower. The spread of modern technical skill coincides with the modern resurgence of age-old ethnic, religious, and communal conflict. Beyond the Iran-Iraq war, we see fighting in Sri Lanka, ethnic conflict in Fiji, the devastation of Lebanon, Sino-Indian border tensions, the New Caledonia and Cyprus disputes, and the continuing Arab-Israeli conflict.

Such tensions have always been part of human history. What is new is the heightened possibility that they will become wider and more deadly conflagrations through the misuse of relatively sophisticated weaponry. In the Iran-Iraq war, we see how readily available on the world arms market are missiles such as the Exocet, the SCUD, and the Silkworm. And many developing countries are becoming not just purchasers and users but adept manufacturers of military hardware considered highly advanced only a few years ago.

We have long feared the dangers of nuclear proliferation. Now we face a worldwide diffusion and use of chemical weapons—thus breaching the international moral consensus of more than half a century. But this growing capacity to acquire or produce and employ such weapons unfortunately is not the whole story. Violence itself is undergoing a qualitative change, as terrorists and narcotics traffickers spread new forms of destruction around the world. We now recognize the long, tough battle we are fighting with these modern day barbarians, equipped with effective weaponry and uninhibited by traditional norms of civilized conduct.

In centuries past, advances in science and technology and warfare often far outstripped the abilities of statesmen and politicians. Today political, economic, and social arrangements must be more closely harmonized with change. Drawing from the example of science, we must create a more just and decent social order from the elements of our understanding. Human society has no unique or preordained social pattern. Our God-given goal is to fulfill ourselves through the social and cultural institutions that we ourselves create and to leave this world a better place than when we entered.

Guidelines for Dealing with Today's Events

As we face this phalanx of changing conditions, what principles stand out for us? I see three clear guidelines for dealing with the size, speed, and complexity of events today.

First, a society must be open to this new age of knowledge and information; to resist it deadens hope of progress. Today's transformations are products of our own system of openness and creativity. What we face are not vast impersonal forces or trends that sway us against our will; they are challenges created by our own past achievements. They offer opportunities for a better future, but only if they can be exploited.

A subsidiary point: the eighteenth-century idea of democracy, with its qualities of openness, freedom, individual initiative, and innovation, remains the best way to deal with the stress and the opportunities of change.

Second, for decision makers, the margins for error are diminishing as the consequences of error increase in scope and gravity. Overcentralized plans and decisions increasingly will be inept. Thus the free operation of the marketplace—for goods and ideas—is the far more efficient arbiter of decisions.

And so entrepreneurial initiative in a market environment is the engine of development and change. Global economic problems will keep coming at us in waves; we must remain open as we face them or be swept away.

Third, the global nature of changes in science, in economics, in communication must be matched by political developments, particularly the strengthening and closer association of like-minded nations. To a greater degree than in revolutionary eras of the past, there is a synergistic interaction between scientific and technological advances and political, economic, and social developments, with each enhancing and accelerating the effect of change on the others.

So today, regional associations of nations are fast becoming an important and effective new milieu for political and economic interaction in the world.

The Drive Toward Democracy

How do things stand in applying these principles? Not bad. The most stirring political response to the new temper of our time has been the resurgence of democracy and the demand for political openness and participation.

Not so many years ago, democratic nations were thought to be a dwindling and embattled minority; today the idea of democracy is among the most important political forces of our time. Elites in the East and West recognize that advanced economic power comes from a high level of education, an openness to the world, a rational distribution of decision-making power, emphasis on individual initiative, decentralization of authority, greater freedom of information and association, and the right of the people to have a say in their own affairs and destiny.

Around the globe we see a powerful impulse toward democratic institutions and values. This recent phenomenon was first evident in Spain and Portugal a decade ago. Now, in Latin America, this drive has changed the complexion of the entire continent, from Argentina to El Salvador. In the Philippines, despite serious challenges, we see how tenaciously people are seeking to effect a transition to a new democratic way. In South Korea, there is a dramatic struggle to create new political institutions and achieve the peaceful transition of national leadership through open elections. And the Haitian people will not abide a return to the tyranny they so recently rejected.

Elsewhere the struggle continues, as in South Africa, where the structure of apartheid is under increasing siege, and in Afghanistan, Angola, Nicaragua, and Cambodia, where communist oppression has spawned resistance movements fighting for the rights denied them.

For the United States, these trends must be seen not only as an affirmation of the values we hold so firmly but also as a test. The transition to democracy is a difficult and fragile process. And it can be reversed.

Confronted by daunting internal and external challenges, new democracies will look to us for ideas, assistance, and understanding. In response, we cannot shut our eyes or close our doors. If we do, the lamp of democracy will go out in many lands.

Freedom: Turning to the Market

With the new surge of democratic feeling, others have come to recognize what we have known all along—that democracy and free markets go together. As our free political system looks out for basic justice and opportunity and provides a safety net in case of adversity, our free markets ensure that our economy will function effectively.

Free markets cannot function in an environment of stifling political regulation or interference. Measures that would isolate an economy from the world or disengage it from the global community do enormous harm. The disintegration of the trade and financial structures during the 1930s provides ample evidence on this score.

All nations share a common responsibility, and must work together, to promote market forces and to ensure the maintenance of an open international economic system. The objective of cooperation is not to achieve a fixed, predetermined result but to ensure that the free market is allowed to function.

There is real progress on all fronts here. The nations of Southeast and

Northeast Asia were in the vanguard, but now with every passing year we see formerly socialist or command economies, in Africa, Latin America, and Asia, shucking off those rigid and limiting policies and relying more and more on open market practices and individual incentives.

There is progress as well in overcoming the lingering sentiment that governments can get together and somehow dictate economic results. In today's world that simply cannot be done. Markets, not governments, determine economic results, and there is no way to overrule the market more than momentarily—especially given the vast quantities of goods, services, capital, information, and technology flowing across national boundaries today and every day.

However, governments can work together to promote procedures that allow markets to work more freely and efficiently—that's what we are doing, for example, in the General Agreement on Tariffs and Trade (GATT) talks in Geneva, in the annual economic summits, in the structural adjustment program of the Organization for Economic Cooperation and Development (OECD), and through the International Monetary Fund (IMF), the World Bank, and other international financial institutions.

The record of economic growth over the past four decades is one of amazing success. But at the same time, there are plenty of problems and challenges facing the world's free-enterprise market economies—just to name a few:

◆ The size of government—whether measured by spending or taxation or regulatory influence or income redistribution or price distortions—has become a real burden to the efficient functioning of the market. There are many stories to be told, from the unconscionably expensive and distorting farm programs to the detailed regulation of opening and closing hours of retail stores. But our own recent experience in trying to trim the budget deficit may bring it home most clearly. Once established, government programs are virtually impossible to eliminate—they spawn their own interest groups and become entrenched. Unless government is to grow without limits, we must find a way to make it shrink.

◆ The trade imbalances in the global economy represent another problem and are most likely a symptom of more fundamental imbalances that need to be corrected. I suspect that we, in the United States, are further along in facing up to our trade deficit than are many other countries whose economic growth has become all too dependent on an export surplus generally related to our deficit. Somehow people need to realize that it's not possible for every country in the world to have an export surplus at the same time. Our deficit has sort of the residual claimant of everybody else's surplus, and everybody says it must change. And I agree, and it will, and it is, and it could happen relatively fast. And my question is, when it does, are the countries that have been dining out to lunch on it ready?

Our challenge is to adopt policies at home that engender confidence in the strength of the U.S. economy and promote policies overseas that will strengthen the economies of our major trading partners. If we fail, the process of correction is likely to be acute and painful.

◆ Another problem: the extraordinary cycle of inflation and disinflation over the past two decades has left a legacy of inflated debt, depressed commodity prices, and stagnation in much of the developing world, especially in several countries close to home. The unpalatable mix of seeming political necessities and economic realities has made a debt workout hard slogging. Progress toward efficient market-oriented solutions to the debt problem has been demonstrated in some key developing countries. But the problem remains a serious one, calling for unusual political resolve in debtor countries and genuine ingenuity in the international community.

Each country must pursue market-oriented policies and get its own house in order if the international economic system is to thrive. This is especially true for the United States, since we are the largest player by far. The fact is that our size relative to that of other economies makes getting our house in order far more important for them than their housekeeping is for us. But we are not the only important player, and so others—Japan, Germany, the other OECD countries, the newly industrialized countries, indeed, all trading nations—must contribute to a stronger international system by strengthening their own economies.

New Political Groupings

A third emerging reality on the world scene is that political, technological, and economic power and influence have been dispersing horizontally. Ours is no longer a bipolar world—the U.S. and Soviet share of world economic output is decreasing as the growth rates of other countries have been more rapid.

In the future, more nations will have the economic and human resources to contend for political, technological, and commercial influence. Already Brazil, Korea, China, India, Israel, and the countries of the Association of Southeast Asian Nations (ASEAN), for example, have become movers and shakers in one or more commercial or technological areas. The increasing number of students from developing countries in advanced training programs—India alone has about 10 percent of the world's total enrollment in higher educational institutions—will put these countries in a position to create and take advantage of technological change.

In the new environment, the importance of regional country and functional groupings has been heightened. Regional, political, and religious blocs of nations—such as the Organization of American States, the Organization of African Unity, the South Asian Association of Regional Cooperation, the Non-aligned Movement, and the Islamic Conference—now provide platforms for a number of countries to exercise influence in global affairs. Not always the way we want, but, anyway, it's a vehicle.

Other regional organizations are taking on growing economic and political importance—from the eastern Caribbean to southern Africa, from the Americas to South Asia, from the Persian Gulf to the South Pacific. For example, the Pacific Basin, a region of phenomenal economic growth, is developing a web of cooperative realities. ASEAN is showing the way to regional cooperation and is taking on more and more of a political dimension beyond its initial focus on economic affairs.

Just as with the new trends toward democratization and open economies, these developments in political cooperation are outgrowths of our efforts and aspirations for a better world. The United States led the way after World War II in advocating the importance of the regional approach to the recovery of a devastated Europe.

Today the institutions that resulted are thriving: regional organizations such as the NATO alliance, the OECD, the European Economic Community, and the Western European Union; and functional organizations such as GATT, the IMF, the World Bank and regional development banks, and the effective functional organizations of the United Nations, such as those dealing with nuclear energy, health, and civil aviation.

This cooperation, which began in large measure by focusing on post–World War II reconstruction needs in Western Europe, is an inspiration and a model for regional and functional approaches to challenges around the world. It is vital to recall that these groupings originated in efforts to reduce barriers. New associations must stay true to that purpose rather than evolve with protectionist enclaves, which would spark devastating economic warfare.

Based on the clear success of the regional approach in advancing Western security and economic well-being, we are intensifying our efforts to strengthen regional cooperative efforts everywhere in meeting the common challenges we will face in the Information Age.

The East-West Dimension

What I have sketched out here is a picture of immense dynamism: of the creative energies of free peoples generating challenges that they—and increasing numbers of those who would emulate them—are meeting with considerable success. The West has no monopoly on clever people, and the world's centers of scientific creativity and economic power are proliferating.

Where in this picture do we find the nations of the communist world? The Soviet Union will remain our central security concern for the foreseeable future. U.S. military strength, our framework of alliances, and our other security ties remain central to peace in the world. But there is also emerging a new dynamism in the East-West relationship.

In this respect, the current ferment in the communist world is a remarkable political development. Perhaps nowhere is this more evident than in China, which can be seen to be undergoing a new era of rectifying names. The opening of a long-closed society to market forces, trade, technology, and ideas is bringing significant benefits for the Chinese people.

Certainly China and Western democracies are still divided over critical ideological issues. However, China has realized that the future belongs to those who open themselves up to global trends in the dissemination of knowledge, in the international economy, and in popular political participation.

Similar rethinking of old concepts and ways of doing things seems now to be underway in the Soviet Union and Eastern Europe. While the ultimate dimensions of this process remain to be seen, its potential importance is great. Despite the constraints of a rigidly centralized society and economy, the Soviet Union is a leading scientific force, for example, in space science, in various fields of medical research, and in theoretical disciplines. Its massive economy, for all its inefficiency, generates a per capita GNP of about eight thousand dollars.

But now Soviet leaders are telling their people that that is not enough—that the system they inherited essentially unchanged from Stalin must be restructured. As General Secretary Gorbachev stated in his June party plenum speech, "command forms of managing society put a brake on our movement." Whatever *perestroika* may finally come to mean, the terms in which it has been defined thus far suggest that Mr. Gorbachev and his colleagues understand that a closed society is a dead end for advanced development. And implicit in the parallel concept of *glasnost'* may be a recognition that the free flow of ideas and information that will fuel growth in the future requires greater intellectual and political freedom.

The most telling indicator will be the Soviet human rights situation. The world is looking for results that bear out the rhetoric—not only for the sake of the individuals and families involved but because human rights as practiced at home ultimately are related to international security. For a government that does not respect the rights it has guaranteed to its own people will not respect its international obligations and the general norms of the world community.

There is nothing in the new political thinking to date that suggests that the end of the adversarial struggle is at hand. What will new thinking mean for the people of Eastern Europe, who continue to strive for greater autonomy in dealing with their daunting socioeconomic agenda? And what about Afghanistan? Will Soviet leaders withdraw their troops and allow the Afghan people to decide by political means what kind of government, economy, and political system they desire? Will the Soviet Union play a constructive role in Cambodia, Korea, southern Africa, and the Persian Gulf?

The winds of change blowing from Moscow may prove as revolutionary as Mr. Gorbachev has declared. But in determining their ultimate impact, historians will look to the answers to questions such as those I've just raised.

But as for us today, the continuing reality before us means that U.S. political resolve must remain constant, our defense posture robust. With those parameters, the challenge to us is to be sensitive to any opportunities that the changes now under way in the Soviet Union and other communist countries may hold.

Conclusion

In this time of global challenge and change, nations of the world look intensively and searchingly at the relationship between the United States and the Soviet Union. That relationship today is meaty and substantial. A major reason for this is that we Americans stand up for our principles and our interests while remaining ready to test and to deal with changing realities in international life. This approach gets results, and we're going to stick with it.

In a world of blurring national boundaries, dispersed power, and new players vying for influence in international affairs, there will be a continuing need for U.S. engagement and leadership.

Our alliances and our friends, and the growing number of regional associations around the world, provide a foundation for problem solving on the scale demanded by the world ahead.

We must not falter on the economic front. We can take great satisfaction knowing that the message of economic freedom is at last being heard and acted upon in country after country around the world. If we ourselves yield to the temptation to return to isolation, protection, and structural rigidities, we betray this movement—and general prosperity in the era ahead will be a lost cause.

Economic progress and freedom go hand in hand. New democracies will require continuous support and encouragement. The United States has an immense stake in seeing that the democratic idea works. And those who resist totalitarian governments must be able to know without doubt that they will be able to look to the United States to back their legitimate pursuit of liberty and justice.

And finally, in this period of profound historical change, both the United States and the Soviet Union must make the most of opportunities to transform the adversarial character of the U.S.-Soviet relationship to one that is better for both our peoples and for the world at large.

We will leave it to future historians to give our age a name. Our task is to try to throw off outmoded concepts of the past as well as cloudy generalities about the future. What we need to see is the dynamism in the size, speed, and scope of global change. And most of all we need to see that this change is of our doing. We can manage it better than anyone. We have to have the courage to stand fast to our own principles: democracy, free enterprise, the cooperative association of responsible nations.

With this as our vision and guide, we face a bright future indeed.

B. R. INMAN

◆ ──────────── ◆

Intelligence in a Democratic Society

◆ History is full of examples of strong, often repressive, intelligence activities in monarchical and totalitarian regimes. Leaders of those regimes
understood the need for detailed knowledge of the activities, strengths, and
weaknesses of adversaries within their own countries and abroad if they
were to retain and expand their empires. Where it was useful to ensure
effectiveness, laws or regulations were put in place to facilitate intelligence
activities. Clandestine operations were often undertaken to permit the head
of state to deny knowledge of the operations if they were unsuccessful.

Intelligence is no less important in democratic societies, for they too
face both external threats to their interests and occasionally internal threats
from espionage and subversion. But maintaining and operating effective intelligence activities is much more complex in a democratic society, particularly in the absence of war to serve as a unifying purpose. In the earliest
days of the fight for independence, the leaders of the various colonies recognized the need for rigorous intelligence activities. George Washington organized intelligence collection, procured the services of those willing to spy
on behalf of the new republic, and dealt with the need to detect and uncover
the activities of traitors. He also understood the critical role of secrecy in
the effectiveness of intelligence organizations. Indeed as early as 1777 General Washington wrote: "The necessity for procuring good intelligence is
apparent and need not be further urged. All that remains for me to add is
that you keep the whole matter as secret as possible. For upon secrecy, suc-

cess depends in most enterprises of this kind, and for want of it they are generally defeated." [1]

The rigors of the fight for independence galvanized the colonial leaders to accept the need to derive information from their adversaries as well as the need to uncover the activity of those in their midst who were not committed to the cause of independence. The Congress established under the Articles of Confederation and the subsequent Constitutional Convention in 1787 recognized the need to provide secrecy for those activities whose exposure would jeopardize the ability to obtain such information. In the United States this was the first formal recognition of the need to protect intelligence sources and methods.

We have recognized and supported the basic rights of secrecy not only in the intelligence arena but also in such areas as attorney-client, doctor-patient, and reporter-source relations. The United States moved to protect these relations in the language of the Constitution and subsequently by law and by practice. Over the years the United States created a regime to ensure that intelligence activities would be conducted within the law. It is fundamental to the success of intelligence operations within a democracy that they be conducted effectively within the laws of the country.

U.S. history shows repeated trends of declining interest in obtaining intelligence and slacking concern for the environment necessary for successful intelligence operations when crises receded. Only during times of war did the United States establish vibrant intelligence operations, and rarely even during war were substantial efforts put in place to provide current analysis by trained professionals of the information being obtained. Similarly counterintelligence activities were given great attention when external efforts at espionage and subversion were obvious to the average citizen. As long periods of peace settled on the land, concern about foreign intelligence activities almost always receded, and the practices involved in trying to obtain information about U.S. citizens who might be collaborating with foreign governments came under renewed scrutiny out of usually valid concern for civil liberties.

World War II found the United States sorely unprepared to engage in a global conflict. Not only were our military forces inadequate and poorly trained, following long periods of inadequate budgets, but we were barely able to gather any information on the outside world or to provide timely, objective intelligence to the leadership. A vast effort was made during the war to obtain information on the economies, cultures, transportation systems, beaches, and harbors of many countries where military operations might need to be conducted or where facilities were necessary to support our war effort. Massive combat intelligence support activities played a critical role in the eventual successful prosecution of the war.

In the wake of World War II the leadership of the country set about, in a bipartisan manner, to create permanent peacetime intelligence organizations that would provide detailed knowledge of the outside world to permit those who governed to operate in the most knowledgeable manner. The National Security Act of 1946 provided the legal framework, and additional organizations were created by executive order. There was general agreement that collection activities should be managed for maximum efficiency, but competitive analytical efforts were encouraged to deal with assumptions that could easily produce inaccurate conclusions when fit together with the other bits and pieces of information about foreign activities collected by various methods. Concerns about the Cold War and about espionage and subversion activities also prompted a renewed focus on counterintelligence. But as subsequent events brought into question some of these activities, the pendulum began swinging away from a priority for counterintelligence activities toward a priority for ensuring the protection of civil liberties.

The years 1947–1959 saw massive investment by the U.S. government in its intelligence and counterintelligence activities. Major human and technical collection systems were put in place, as were competing analytical efforts to distill knowledge from the information gathered. An additional facet of intelligence activities, rising in prominence in World War II and reinforced in the late 1940s, was the conduct by the United States of covert operations abroad. This activity moved beyond the normal collection of information by overt and clandestine means and the analysis of that information. Eventually it put the Central Intelligence Agency (CIA) in an operational role in executing U.S. government policy by means other than diplomacy, but short of the overt use of force.

Congress facilitated the great intelligence buildup during the 1950s. Despite the early involvement with committees of the Congress created by the Articles of Confederation, Congress had taken a benign view of its role both as a consumer of intelligence and as overseer of intelligence activities. Programs were authorized and appropriations made on the advice of a few senior members of Congress. Few written records remain of the dialogue between leaders of the intelligence organizations and the members of Congress who authorized programs and appropriated funds.

The decade of the 1960s saw significant changes in the focus, the funding, and the governing process of the intelligence community. The overall size of covert activities reached a pinnacle in the early 1960s. Concern for the cost effectiveness of intelligence activities led to a greater reliance on official rather than unofficial cover for clandestine collection activities. In 1967 concern about the balance of payments caused the U.S. government to reduce its official presence abroad. By the turn of the decade the long slide in intelligence capabilities was well under way. In 1971 critical decisions were made to invest in remote collection assets to provide frequent observation of activities in denied areas of other countries. But unfortunately the decision was made to pay for these new sensors by giving up manpower from the agencies that collected and processed technically derived information. Further reductions were ordered during the years 1973–1975 as a punitive response for failing to predict the time of the Yom Kippur War in October 1973. Consequently by 1979 more than 40 percent of the manpower allocated to the U.S. intelligence community at the peak of its growth in the late 1950s had been removed. Even with the advent of modern communications and computing, productivity enhancements did not begin to compensate for the broad loss of manpower. The result was a sharply curtailed U.S. intelligence capability.

Beginning in 1967 with an exposé in *Ramparts* magazine alleging that the CIA was operating on its own out of control, followed by a series of disclosures in 1974 and 1975, public support for U.S. intelligence activities sharply deteriorated. What became clear to even the most casual observer was that no process was in place to arrest the loss of confidence or to ensure at least some focus on the adequacy of U.S. intelligence capabilities. The long-established view of the executive branch that intelligence information and intelligence activities were their proprietary instruments did not facilitate finding new approaches. Fearful of a backlash against its failure to act, Congress undertook an extended period of investigations of the activities of U.S. intelligence agencies over the previous 25 years. Two select committees, popularly known as the Church committee (in the Senate) and the Pike committee (in the House of Representatives), held extensive public and private hearings over a period of more than a year. Television coverage and lurid headlines with titillating stories helped create an image of rogue intelligence activities completely out of control.

Hidden from public view, a separate effort to come to grips with real problems was occurring in the Defense Appropriations Subcommittee of the House Appropriations Committee, under the leadership of the late Congressman George Mahon. Beginning in 1975 intensive budget hearings were held before that subcommittee, probing broadly and deeply the most sensitive intelligence operations of the U.S. government. Effective congressional oversight through the budget process over the details of U.S. intelligence operations began for the first time with those hearings. Over the succeeding thirteen years, I know of no incident where classified information provided to that subcommittee or its investigators was ever leaked or otherwise improperly used for partisan political advantage.

In an effort to rebuild public confidence in U.S. intelligence activities and to ensure their effectiveness, the Senate in 1976 and the House of Representatives in 1977 created permanent select committees on intelligence. Because these committees would operate as surrogates for the long-established committees, the membership was drawn from representatives of both political parties serving on the Foreign Relations, Armed Services, Appropriations, and Judiciary committees. Senate and House leaders from both parties served as ex officio members. Membership rotation was established as a central element, as was rotation of the chairmanship of the committee. Over time this has created a high level of experience within the Congress about the activities and capabilities of U.S. intelligence agencies. As that experience has grown, the committees have often moved to increase intelligence capabilities beyond the level proposed by the executive branch, particularly in periods of pressure on the overall size of the federal budget.

As Congress has worked to improve the process by which intelligence activities are authorized and funded, it has also focused on the need to create legislation to ensure that the necessary intelligence activities of the government can be performed under a properly constructed framework. The need to use technical means to investigate potential espionage activities by U.S. citizens and to monitor foreign intelligence operations within this country led to the enactment of the Foreign Intelligence Surveillance Act of 1978, creating a special court equipped to receive and examine classified information and to approve warrants for electronic surveillance. The genuine difficulty of prosecuting individuals for espionage in the light of defense efforts to expose intelligence activities as a means to blackmail the government into avoiding prosecution was bounded by the Classified Information Procedures Act, popularly known as graymail legislation. That act provided the legal framework to review information in camera to preclude its unauthorized exposure when the judge determined that it was irrelevant to the legitimate defense interest of an individual being prosecuted. The deliberate exposure of the names of U.S. clandestine agents in an effort to destroy their effectiveness was addressed directly by Congress with the enactment of the Intelligence Agent Identity Bill of 1982. Congress has modified the Freedom of Information Act to protect essential elements related to intelligence sources and methods from exposure under the auspices of the act by those with legitimate as well as illegitimate interests.

A long-term outgrowth of this oversight activity may be even more important for the effective performance of the U.S. government. As members of Congress have become exposed to U.S. intelligence activities under a framework permitting a detailed examination of both the collection activity and the intelligence itself, they have increasingly focused on the information provided on activities abroad that affect the interests of the United States. As committee membership has rotated, an increasing number of congressmen have become sustained users of intelligence products. They abide by congressional mandates that protect the information, but they are able to discuss intelligence issues with the executive branch and debate policy, drawing on the same basic data about foreign activities that the executive branch uses in shaping its policies and proposed operations. Over the long term, an informed government must ultimately operate more effectively and rationally in its dealings with the outside world.

The government has been less successful in establishing mechanisms for building a consensus on the desirability and effectiveness of U.S. covert operations. Covert operations do not normally derive from a careful determination that they are the most effective means to deal with a specific problem. They are most often undertaken when the executive branch becomes dissatisfied with the effectiveness of its diplomatic activities but is unwilling to use force overtly to protect or pursue its interests. Although it has usually been possible to maintain a bipartisan approach to the oversight of intelligence activities and the process of authorizing and appropriating funds for those activities, bipartisan agreement on many covert actions has been elusive to create and maintain. The select committees have proved over time to be effective forums for oversight and authorization when they pay careful attention to sustaining a bipartisan approach and maintaining effective security for the classified information they receive. But they have not been staffed, nor have new members been selected, to provide a forum for shaping policy on the covert operations of the U.S. government. If we are to avoid long-term damage to the effectiveness of U.S. intelligence activities in a troubled world, we must find more effective mechanisms for reaching a bipartisan consensus between the executive branch and Congress on the proper scope, oversight, and execution of covert operations.

The years 1981–1986 witnessed a major rebuilding of U.S. intelligence capabilities. Additional manpower was provided to all intelligence collection, analysis, and counterintelligence activities. We now appear to be heading into another long period of no growth or real reductions in expenditures. We will again hear many calls to focus on the cost effectiveness of all elements of government, including intelligence activities. But intelligence activities in a democratic society are inherently not cost effective. It is impossible to predict when religious fundamentalists or crosscurrents of cultural decay in other countries will spur activities inimical to the long-term interests of the United States and threatening to its citizens. Efforts to control expenses inevitably lead to pressure for shortcuts to get the job done by spending less money. It is possible to protect the security interests of the United States within the scope of enacted laws. But it is frequently more expensive in manpower needs and time than budget pressures would normally allow. An informed government offers the best prospect of dealing sensibly with threats abroad and at home.

In our efforts to reduce the federal deficit we must not destroy the capabilities that have been produced at great cost in both time and money, but we also must not short-circuit legal processes to secure classified information or cost effectiveness. A great nation will remain great only if it accurately assesses conditions in the outside world and deals with them intelligently. A democracy will remain vibrant only if it ensures that those activities undertaken on behalf of the nation are always conducted within the law. When legitimate needs cannot be accommodated under existing laws, then new legislation must be enacted. A determination by all branches of government and both political parties to provide legislation to permit effective intelligence activities is mandatory for the long-term health of this democracy.

Note

1. *Writings of George Washington* (Washington, D.C.: Government Printing Office, 1933), 16:330–32.

GERALD FORD

◆ ———————————————— ◆

Challenges to American Policy

◆ Thinking about America, when we are young, is an extension of thinking about our own future hopes and fears. Later on, the future of our children dominates our considerations and actions. As we become grandparents
we tend to think about America in terms of the promise our country holds
out to our grandchildren and countless others we shall never personally hug
and comfort, but whose peace and happiness is also our deep concern.

This shifting of perspective requires detachment from our customary
live coverage of current affairs and a comprehensive overview of America's
role in relatively recent history. The past is indeed prologue, though it never
really repeats itself, and from it we can take both comfort and forewarning.

The challenges to American policy for the remainder of this century are
as numberless as the sands of the seashore. I would not presume to rank in
urgency even the most obvious of them. But has it ever been otherwise?

Our forebears braved the raging oceans and the unknown shores. They
cast off the social shackles of the Old World and forged a new order of self-
government in which power proceeded from ordinary people to be sparingly
and temporarily vested in ordinary custodians of the common good.

They tamed the rivers, plowed the prairies, mined the mountains, and
manned the moon. They shed their blood on the altars of freedom from
absent overlords, freedom from human bondage, freedom from ideological
tyranny. They flung open the gates and shared their plenty with the poor
and the persecuted of all the world. As freedom flourished, so did the United
States of America.

But what about the slave markets, the broken Indian treaties, the sweat-shops, the lynch mobs, the gang wars, the robber barons, the corrupt city bosses, the labor racketeers, the rotten politicians, the drug and pornography peddlers? Who slaughtered the buffalo and the sperm whale, turned prairies into dust bowls, poured poisons into air and stream?

Yes, there have been ugly glitches in our pattern of growth, but as we contemplate the challenges ahead, it is important to remember that American society is extraordinarily resilient and self-correcting. As I said on the Fourth of July in 1976, "For America, the future is a friend."

In that future, hopefully before this century closes, I would like to see three important changes take place in this country. If they all cannot be fully accomplished, then, as President John Kennedy said that icy January day in 1961, "Let us begin."

◆ First, a return to fiscal responsibility by both the executive and legislative branches of our federal government to ensure the nation's economic health and competitive strength in the world.

◆ Second, a restoration of balance of power and cleaner lines of accountability among our political institutions to inhibit excessive partisanship and narrow the credibility gulf between Washington and the American people.

◆ Third, a resurgence of the innate confidence and sense of community that despite other differences make us all Americans and proud of it! This can both create and flow from coping with all the other challenges.

Let us start with our economy. Like the weather, everybody worries about it but nobody does much about it. Last year ended in a mood of premonition, political paralysis, and probably more public pessimism than usually accompanies the holiday season. But the major indices were promising: production, employment, inflation, even oil prices. Certainly there was no panic comparable to that which followed the Wall Street crash of 1929 and the bank closings and breadlines of the 1930s. The professional whistlers-in-the-dark saw nothing spookier than a mild recession, which depending on its timing would please some candidates and worry others.

However, no sooner did the dollar stop tobogganing in the world market and the stock market appear to hit bottom and start back up and our unfavorable trade balances get better than we found ourselves looking at another trillion-plus dollar federal budget this year and a third in fiscal 1989.

Both the majority controlling Congress and the president, squaring away at each other for the oncoming election contest, had spent the whole of 1987 reaching a "compromise" designed to trim our annual deficits (and thus slow the growth of our cumulative public debt—now exceeding $2 trillion) by a paltry $33.2 billion this fiscal year and $45.7 in 1989.

This not very bold or statesmanlike action passed by *one vote* in the House of Representatives amid a dense cloud of humbug as the chosen tribunes of the taxpayers hurried home for Christmas. It was a step in the right direction, but about as effective as Noah laying in a couple of spare buckets to prepare for the Flood.

When first elected to Congress I battled in vain against what we called a "whopping" peacetime budget of $42 billion submitted by President Truman for 1950. A quarter-century later, as president in an election year, I had to defend proposed spending of $394 billion, which I believed I had cut to the bone. Real inflation no longer explains most of the annual escalation of expenditures, but rather the huge federal entitlement programs whose growth is preordained by law and perpetuated by powerful political blocs of voters, whose wrath both parties fear.

Even if the cosmetic cures prescribed by the 100th Congress are not as phony as some suspect, they still point to a $150 billion budget deficit this year, assuming nothing gets any worse. Mark my words, unless we as a nation face up to the facts of fiscal reality and responsibility, and the sacrifices required to restore it, the economic time bomb we are sitting on will do us in as surely as any sudden enemy assault. We cannot go on living beyond our means by borrowing from future generations or being bailed out by foreign investors.

Without economic strength, military strength is essentially meaningless, and neither peace nor prosperity can be indefinitely sustained. Freedoms we cherish for ourselves and defend for others depend on a sound and growing economy at home.

To put the problem more personally, I have five precious granddaughters, aged three to ten. A recent survey showed that the average cost of a four-year college education is now about $75,000 and rising by 5 to 8 percent annually. Is it right to expect our great-grandchildren also to shoulder the costs of their grandparents' failure to balance the books of their generation?

We must leave them a better legacy. As we recover our national dedication to fiscal responsibility our worries about the personal security of our families, our dollars, our savings, and our ability to cope with future challenges will diminish proportionately.

If our elected policy makers have neglected their responsibilities and ducked the difficult decisions required in the economic sphere, they have strained even more the unwritten assumption of our Founding Fathers that the greatest happiness of the greatest number would be the end result of the political clashes and compromises among them.

Abraham Lincoln, no slouch at bare-knuckle politicking himself, warned that you cannot fool all the people all of the time. But in this day there is certainly no lack of trying. The tragic result is a disenchantment with "politics" that drives the best and the brightest of young leaders away from elective office and deprives the winning candidates of a meaningful mandate.

The so-called Credibility Gap, a phrase we enthusiastically pirated and turned against President Johnson in the 1960s, is no longer the exclusive property of any party or branch of the government. It is a rebuke to all leadership not wholly undeserved and a needless handicap in international bargaining.

Ever since Stalin, Americans have been saying, "Can we trust the Russians?" Today we also hear a swelling chorus in Europe, Asia, the Middle East, and Africa: "Can we depend on the Americans?" We must not only speak the truth to one another, but speak with a credible and a single voice to our allies and adversaries abroad.

It is highly ironic that even as we have been celebrating 200 years of constitutional governance, many Americans have had the uneasy feeling that our present-day political institutions are not working as well as they should. Most do not blame the Constitution, but rather the people managing our public affairs.

The story is told (which if not true, should be) that when the Founding Fathers finally agreed to the Constitution in 1787, Benjamin Franklin emerged from Independence Hall where he was surrounded by a crowd of curious citizens. One voice from the throng shouted: "What kind of government have you given us?" To which the sage of Philadelphia replied: "A republic, sir, *if you can keep it.*"

So, to point the finger of fault further, *we the people* are to blame, ultimately, for flawed policies and failed programs. We have both the right and the means to choose our temporary leaders and to fire them when they fail us. Unlike most of mankind, we get the kind of government we deserve.

This is an election year. My party affiliation is no secret. I am never happier than when I am campaigning. I believe fervently in the two-party system, but in this forum I would not want anything I write to be interpreted as subtle criticism or praise for those currently campaigning. I have walked too many miles in their shoes.

Difficult as it is to talk sense amid the clamor of a national campaign, it is harder still to get anyone to listen. So let us suppose we have hopped in a time machine to the day after the 1988 national elections are decided. What then should we expect, what will we demand, of the winners? Yes, and also of the losers?

We must expect and demand balance. One of the inspired compromises of 1787 was the idea of a separation of power among three coequal executive, legislative, and judicial branches. Each would check the excesses and balance the exercise of authority by the others. While certain responsibilities were specifically given to each branch, others were shared and many were deliberately left vague. This vagueness, together with a difficult but possible amendment process, accounts for the amazing durability of our Constitution.

The same vagueness has caused the pendulum of power to swing back and forth throughout our history. Two periods illustrate my point. After President Lincoln's assassination in 1865 and until President Theodore Roosevelt's election in 1901, Congress was the dominant force in government. It recovered this role after World War I and kept it until the Great Depression and World War II. Then tremendous power was vested in President Franklin D. Roosevelt and the executive branch—for good reason, I submit, because global war cannot be waged with more than 500 members of Congress calling the shots. Nor, may I add, can 535 senators and representatives publicly second-guess all the delicate negotiations of the president to reduce the danger of a nuclear shoot-out. But neither can Congress be cut out of the circuit altogether, nor is Congress likely to allow it.

What we really need is balance, not one extreme or another. The unstated but essential element of our constitutional system is comity, the assumption that the coequal sharers of power will act cooperatively and concertedly whenever the whole nation's vital interests are at stake.

We do not want an imperial presidency, but neither do we want an impotent presidency. We do not want an overbearing Congress any more than we want an obsequious Congress. During my quarter-century as a member of Congress, it was my bad luck to be in the minority for all but two years. Although I never achieved my ambition to be Speaker of the House, it was my good fortune to serve with three Speakers of the majority party who were first of all Americans—Sam Rayburn of Texas, John McCormack of Massachusetts, and Carl Albert of Oklahoma. Although in our government the Speaker wields power only slightly less than the president's, and no one has ever become Speaker without an impeccable record for party loyalty, all these formidable leaders of the loyal opposition stood solidly with Presidents Eisenhower and Nixon and with me in the pinches of international gamesmanship. So did their counterparts when Presidents Truman, Kennedy, and Johnson leveled with them and sought their support.

As truth is the glue that holds government together, cooperation and compromise are the gas and oil that make government go.

The same spirit of bipartisanship, or, more precisely, nonpartisanship, was shown by my Michigan political mentor Senator Arthur Vandenberg when he and other leaders of his party abandoned isolationism and supported President Truman's postwar initiatives of aid to Greece and Turkey, NATO, and the Marshall Plan. This consensus around the policies of containment and deterrence unquestionably saved Western Europe and brought us four decades without a major East-West war.

It is probably harmless, but we kid ourselves when we assert that American politics stops at the water's edge. What did generally stop in times past, and should stop in the future, is destructive partisan wrangling in the course of a crisis. The useful tradition of rallying 'round the Flag, of standing behind our president in troubled times, reached its peak after Pearl Harbor, began to unravel during the Korean War, and almost disappeared with Vietnam.

The war in Vietnam is receding into history, but some important lessons remain to be learned from it—more political than military. The first is that a government in which public opinion really matters cannot conduct sustained overseas combat without substantial citizen support and clearly stated objectives. This is particularly true when open telecommunications direct a round-the-clock barrage of gory battle images into citizens' homes and spread them simultaneously around the world.

Even with a firmer control of information and open dissent than Americans would ever tolerate, the Soviets feel the same erosion of home-front support for military intervention in Afghanistan that Presidents Johnson and Nixon faced over Southeast Asia. There are no checks and balances built into the Soviet constitution, but both instances prove that our Founding Fathers knew what they were doing when they gave the congressional body closest to the people the power to declare war and the commander in chief the power to wage and win it.

The second Vietnam lesson we should have learned (but evidently have not) is that when military force is used or contemplated, a president's hands should not be tied arbitrarily and automatically by the Congress. I refer specifically to the War Powers Resolution enacted in 1973 as a delayed reaction to frustrations over Vietnam.

I can speak with some experience on this, and more recent experiences surely bear me out. As a congressman I voted against the War Powers Resolution, despite my own reservations about the continuation of the war and probably contrary to the wishes of many of my constituents. As minority leader of the House, I led a losing effort to sustain President Nixon's veto. When I became president, I was more convinced than ever that the War

Powers Resolution is (1) unconstitutional, (2) impractical, and (3) needlessly constraining in the hard decisions a president has to make either to keep the peace or to restore it.

The provisions of the 1973 resolution are ingenious and, at first glance, not too unreasonable as an exercise in Vietnam hindsight. A president is required to notify Congress in a specific procedure when he commits U.S. armed forces to combat *or equips them* for participating in combat; after he informs he must consult with Congress; and then the resolution spells out what Congress can do, might do, or might not do about it. For 60 days it can, by majority vote in both houses, approve the commitment. Or, by concurrent resolution Congress can order the forces withdrawn. If after 60 days Congress does neither, the president *must call the whole thing off anyway*, without one member of the House or Senate having been compelled to stand up and be counted.

We can live with this kind of congressional "courage" when the pendulum of legislative-executive balance swings too far in domestic legislation. But we cannot afford it in national security crises. While I was in the Oval Office, six situations arose in which the War Powers Resolution arguably might have applied.

There were the emergency evacuations of American civilians and military personnel from Danang, Saigon, and Phnom Penh. Next came the S.S. Mayaguez incident in which an American merchant ship was fired upon, boarded, and its crew seized by Cambodian forces in international waters. Finally there were two evacuations of Americans from Lebanon under U.S. military cover. I refused to concede that the resolution applied to any of these actions. But I was careful to keep my relationship with my old friends in Congress cordial and considerate. So I went through the notification and consultation steps voluntarily.

This demonstrated how impractical the War Powers Resolution is. The Danang evacuation was forced upon us during the congressional Easter recess; not a single member of the bipartisan leadership was in Washington. Two were in Mexico, three in Greece, one in the Mideast, one in Europe, and two in China; the rest were scattered around the United States.

Just as we cannot have 535 commanders in chief, we cannot have 535 secretaries of state, arms control negotiators, peacemakers, and hostage rescuers. The Politburo or the Supreme Soviet may be able to bounce Mr. Gorbachev, but they don't all accompany him to summit meetings.

I well know that the Congress has its responsibilities and the president has his, having experienced both. The pressures on the president are unending and inexorable. Although he does have a lot of help, as President Truman noted by a sign on his desk: "The buck stops here."

The Congress sets its own timetables and deadlines and rarely meets them. The 100th Congress demonstrated this by its inability to pass a single one of the thirteen annual appropriation bills in 1987, though it was an off-election year in which things are more likely to get done than in even-numbered ones. The legislative branch of our balance-of-powers federal government has become increasingly inebriated with inertia. Its collective theme seems to be perpetuating itself and passing the buck for raw partisan advantage.

This should be a self-correcting excess, but it is complicated by a factor that the Founding Fathers apparently did not anticipate. For half the 40 years since 1948 (by no means an easy era) American voters have been experimenting with a new check and balance. Certainly our constitutional framework does not contemplate as normal a president of one party and a Congress of the other, but since 1948 only Presidents Kennedy, Johnson, and Carter have been completely spared that problem. President Eisenhower had his own party controlling Congress only two years, and President Reagan enjoyed the backstopping of the Senate majority for his first six years, but for both it made a dramatic difference. *Overall party responsibility* may be difficult, if not impossible, to restore today. But I believe our federal government works better all fish or all fowl, and that Presidents Truman, Eisenhower, Nixon, and Reagan would agree.

In politics, I reiterate, what we need is more balance, comity, give and take, reasonable compromise, and readiness to cooperate on the vital issues that affect the general welfare—indeed the survival—of our nation and the future of freedom in the world. We the people are entitled to less showmanship and more evident dedication by those we elect to speak for us in Washington.

There have been two high moments in the public half of my lifetime. They were neither receiving my first commission in the navy, nor my first election to the Congress, nor taking the oath of office as vice president or president of the United States.

They were September 2, 1945, the day *we*—all of us—won the war that gave our kind of civilization at least one more chance; and July 4, 1976, when amid the jubilant multitudes of Americans at Valley Forge, Philadelphia, New York, and Washington I fully realized for the first time the majestic meaning of "*We the People.*" Not quite two years had passed since I told an anxious nation: "My fellow Americans, our long national nightmare is over. Our Constitution works; our great Republic is a government of laws and not of men. Here the People rule." (I cribbed that final phrase from Thomas Jefferson, as presidents are fond of doing.)

My last part in the bicentennial celebration was a pilgrimage to Monticello, Jefferson's beautiful Virginia home. There I witnessed a naturalization ceremony and welcomed the new citizens with a story my favorite Sunday school teacher taught me, how the beauty of Joseph's coat was its many colors.

"To be an American," I told them,

> is to subscribe to those principles which the Declaration of Independence proclaims and the Constitution protects: the political values of self-government, liberty and justice, equal rights and equal opportunity. These beliefs are the secret of America's unity from diversity—in my judgment the most magnificent achievement of our first 200 years.
>
> "Black is beautiful" was a motto of genius which uplifted us far above its intention. Once Americans thought about it and perceived its truth, we began to realize that so are brown, white, red and yellow beautiful. Like Joseph's coat, all Americans are beautiful ... freely joined together by dedication to the United States of America.

Whatever future challenges we face, we can surmount them with this distinctively American spirit of unity in diversity, individuality in community, and hanging together rather than hanging separately.

There are numerous other challenges to American policy I have not mentioned, arguably more urgent and certainly more exciting than mine. Some are dangerous, some reassuring. The INF agreement, the free-trade pact with Canada, the future of NATO, the standoff in the Persian Gulf, the countdown in southern Africa, the unending battles against drugs and terrorism and famine and fanaticism and cruelty and disease.

As the election campaigns of 1988 get hotter and our differences of opinion get sharper, let's all remember to singe but never to burn. Remember, all of us, deep down and regardless of party or position or ancestry or faith, are striving together to create a more perfect Union, with liberty and justice for all.

We have an unwritten compact of respect for the convictions of others and faith in the decency of others that allows Americans the luxury of rugged political and economic competition without the savage scenes we see so often in less fortunate lands. Our challenges today, as they have been from our humble but heaven-blessed beginnings as one nation, must be to banish war from our shrinking world and hate from our expanding hearts.

The last word on challenges belongs, appropriately, to Abigail Adams, the first First Lady to live in the White House. Like one or two others, she is as well remembered and better beloved than her husband, President John Adams. In 1790, while John Adams was sweating out his eight years as vice president, Abigail wrote their son, John Quincy:

These are times in which a genius would wish to live. It is not in the still calm of life, or in the repose of a pacific station, that great challenges are formed . . . Great necessities call out great virtues.

That's telling it like it still is, Abigail!

JIMMY CARTER

◆ ——————————————— ◆

Challenges Old and New

◆ Many of our modern-day challenges are similar to those faced by our Founding Fathers: "to form a more perfect union, establish justice, provide for the common defense, promote the general welfare, and secure the blessings of liberty to ourselves and our posterity." In addition to seeking these goals as set forth in our Constitution, there have been dramatic unanticipated changes in our responsibilities during the last two centuries as the United States evolved from a nation that prided itself on remaining detached from the struggles of other countries to a society that finds itself at the center of world politics. Meeting this challenge of world leadership has been difficult for the United States for the last four decades and will remain so in the future.

After thwarting the imperialistic designs of Germany, Italy, and Japan, our country emerged from World War II as both the wealthiest and the most powerful nation on earth. The world can be thankful that despite its unmatched strength the United States has never sought world dominion in the manner of former leading powers, such as the Romans, the Arabs, or the French under Napoleon. One of our wartime allies, the Soviet Union, established a postwar empire. We did not. Instead we used our influence to encourage self-government and free enterprise. The end of colonialism and the economic miracles of Europe and Asia would not have taken place if the United States had not played such a role. Our example inspired the growth of democracy in other parts of the world.

Ironically some of today's most difficult challenges have arisen from our successes, not our failures. In effect, our policies have encouraged the rise of competitors, the most successful of whom also promote human rights, free enterprise, and democratic government. Sometimes Americans are disappointed because we expect too much. It tends to shake our confidence and national pride for us to realize that conflicting interests of strong allies—and even potential adversaries—can sometimes limit the exertion of our superior influence. Even when our desires are frustrated by others, the United States remains the most powerful nation on earth militarily, politically, economically, and, at times, morally. The rest of the world still looks to us for leadership as we face a future that is likely to be changing ever more rapidly.

As our forefathers warned, social ills relating to crime, unemployment, homelessness, malfeasance of public officials, and conflict among different ethnic groups can, when bad enough, bring on extreme reactions from the general public. Threats to civil liberties—including freedom of speech, the press, and religion—can result, as well-meaning people look for simple solutions to their problems. This is a challenge that the founders had to face, and it will still be with us in the 1990s.

Ours is a resilient nation, blessed with self-corrective features built into our system of government. Just within the last two decades we have successfully weathered the political and economic storms of Vietnam, the energy crisis, Watergate, the consequences of the Iranian revolution, a tripling of our national debt, massive trade imbalances, and the Iran-Contra scandals. Most of these crises were shocking and potentially damaging, but the United States has survived with its strength and influence intact.

The detection and analysis of historical trends can guide our leaders in preparation for the years ahead. In the Jimmy Carter Library we describe the evolution of the office of the U.S. president. One of the most interesting presentations is moving back in time from some of the significant events that took place during my own administration to see how they relate to prior actions of my predecessors in the twentieth century: from the decisions made by Theodore Roosevelt and the violent confrontations in the Panama Canal Zone under Lyndon Johnson through subsequent administrations to the final ratification of the new Panama Canal treaties in 1978; the Camp David accords and the Israeli-Egyptian peace treaty following four wars in 25 years and building on diplomatic efforts under Presidents Gerald Ford and Richard Nixon; the step-by-step evolution of SALT II, culminating more than 6 years of persistent negotiation with Soviet leaders; deregulation of oil, gas, transportation, banking and finance, and our nation's electronic communications, completing a cycle begun during the earliest days of the century; the ever-expanding impact of the New Deal and Great Society programs; and the reestablishment of normal diplomatic relations with China after an interval of 35 years. At least in retrospect, it is possible to detect a certain inevitability about these kinds of historic happenings.

Some of the evolutionary trends that we can now perceive are quite disturbing. In 1980 our government completed a three-year effort to look toward the beginning of the twenty-first century, attempting to predict some of the circumstances that might confront us unless corrective action is taken by the United States and other nations. Known as the *Global 2000* report, this document assessed the likely consequences of population growth, urbanization, soil erosion, deforestation, changes in composition of the upper atmosphere, acid precipitation, movement of refugees, air and water pollution, and the depletion of other natural resources. The beneficial impact of technological advances in such areas as food production, family planning, reforestation, education, communications, preventive health care, and new sources of energy were also considered. The most important unpredictable but alterable factor was U.S. government policy. It was obvious then and now that decisions made in Washington will have the most profound impact on the quality of life throughout the world.

The *Global 2000* report was subsequently abandoned and even disparaged in Washington, but it was adopted as a basis for ambitious studies in Japan and some of the more advanced countries in Europe. Their efforts have resulted, for instance, in continuing exploration of trade opportunities, using data related to natural resources, raw-material availability, consumer preferences, labor supplies, transportation systems, and government policies in consuming nations.

This information is giving those nations a growing advantage over ours in the highly competitive commercial world. We can meet the challenge by resuming our own analyses if our government, business and financial community, major universities, and basic and applied research capabilities are marshaled in concert. The highly respected and nonpartisan National Academy of Sciences would be a logical focus for this effort, with the responsibility of issuing an updated report to the public every four years or so. Such continuing assessments would help our leaders anticipate future challenges and deal with them more wisely. With all segments of our society acting independently but guided by the same data, our combined national efforts would likely be more effective.

Some of the greatest dangers to the global environment come from Third World nations, where economic development is considered more important than clean air. Even the nuclear threat plays second fiddle to the search for food and shelter. These starkly diverse concerns illustrate perhaps one of the most important problems that we face: the increasing disharmony and lack of understanding between the rich and the poor nations.

Some manifestations of these differences are already apparent, such as the explosion of Third World debt, massive immigration pressures from Mexico and other countries in this hemisphere, the increase in refugees, and revolutionary fervor in Central America and elsewhere. There are, of course, many other causes of these phenomena, but population growth and environmental deterioration are certainly significant in contributing to poverty, hopelessness, and disharmony.

We lack an adequate commitment to comprehend what is happening within the less-developed countries, to communicate with them, and to help alleviate their most critical problems. Such an effort, if successful, would bring to us great economic and political benefits. With careful planning and the cooperation of international agencies and recipient countries, this can be done overseas with relatively low funding levels.

The Carter Center, associated with Emory University in Atlanta, Georgia, is involved in some projects of this kind. Using seed developed in existing research centers, a modicum of fertilizer, coordination by a few experienced agricultural scientists, and field supervision by native extension workers, we are attempting to prevent a recurrence of starvation in some of the sub-Saharan countries of Africa. In order to minimize costs and the consumption of energy, no effort has been made to mechanize these farming operations. The farmers plant and cultivate their crops with pointed sticks and other simple hand tools. Now, on more than ten thousand small farms, production of basic food grains has tripled or quadrupled, encouraging both these farmers and their neighbors to help themselves.

Working closely with top officials in affected countries, we are also helping to immunize children against infectious diseases, teaching parents the benefits of oral rehydration therapy, and leading the effort to eradicate dracunculiasis, or guinea worm, a horrible tropical disease that afflicts about ten million people every year. The World Health Organization has recently targeted guinea worm as the second disease for global eradication. In addition, the Carter Center has a contract with the People's Republic of China to assist in a nationwide effort to rehabilitate disabled people. We are training specialists who will work with handicapped children and adults and helping the Chinese rapidly expand their production of high-quality artificial limbs.

These projects are being financed at relatively low cost by foreign philanthropists and supervised by senior advisers like Dr. Norman Borlaug, who won the Nobel peace prize in 1970 for bringing about the green revolution in India and Pakistan, and Dr. William Foege, former director of the Centers for Disease Control, who helped orchestrate the worldwide eradication of smallpox.

In every case there is a close working relationship with local government officials, specialists in the fields of health and agriculture, and citizens in the developing nations who benefit from the services provided. The procedures involved in these projects have proven to be cost-effective and have opened up a new dimension of understanding and cooperation with people who have been too often ignored in the past. Each partnership arrangement is designed to strengthen the ability of recipients to be more self-sufficient, not to change their life-style or to make them more dependent on outside assistance. There is no reason why our foreign-aid programs cannot be guided by similar principles.

It is obvious that one of the most challenging opportunities for us is to reduce the level of expenditures for armaments among all nations and devote at least a portion of these financial resources to alleviate the problems of poverty, starvation, and homelessness and to preventive health care both at home and abroad. Only the United States could successfully lead this effort.

Our nation should be the undisputed champion of peace, utilizing every possible means through negotiation and diplomacy to promote the settlement of regional disputes and the alleviation of suffering caused by armed conflict. There are times when we are able to participate directly, as with the shuttle diplomacy that ended the October 1973 war in the Middle East, the mediation of a peace treaty between Egypt and Israel, and the transition from Rhodesia to Zimbabwe. On other occasions we can support the efforts of others, such as the Vatican's successful resolution of the Beagle Channel dispute between Argentina and Chile. Instead of attempting to finance the Contra war, we could have hastened the move toward peace and democracy in Central America by positive involvement in the Contadora effort or the consummation of the plan orchestrated by President Oscar Arias of Costa Rica. Such a role as peacemaker would also help guarantee the incorporation of our own proposals at the negotiating table and the protection of our interests throughout the process.

We have too often ignored another major opportunity for the resolution of disputes: the international organizations created for this purpose, such as the United Nations, the Organization of American States, and the International Court of Justice. Instead, they have often been deliberately incapacitated by us and others. Lately, however, almost by default, the superpowers have turned to the United Nations as the best avenue through which peace might be pursued both between Israel and its neighbors and in the Gulf war. The best hope for progress in and around Palestine lies in an international peace conference predicated upon United Nations Resolutions 242 and 338 and sponsored by the five permanent members of the Security Council. Furthermore, in an unprecedented show of cooperation, these same nations have acted to end the war between Iran and Iraq by approving United

Nations Resolution 598 and calling upon the secretary-general to serve as a mediator. Beneficial results have not yet been realized, at least in part because of timidity or lack of zeal among the major nations in pursuing these goals. Nevertheless, with concerted support from among the powerful members of the Security Council, it might be possible for the United Nations to fulfill some of the world's expectations at its creation more than four decades ago.

One of the most interesting challenges is how to deal with the new and charismatic leader of the Soviet Union. Through his innovative approaches to old problems and his superb handling of public relations, or propaganda, General Secretary Mikhail Gorbachev has captured the imagination of many people in the world and become quite popular among our own closest allies and even within the United States. There is no reason for a U.S. president to yield center stage to any communist leader in seeking world peace, arms control, the enhancement of human rights, other humanitarian goals, or the strengthening of the United Nations or other international institutions.

Some of Gorbachev's actions and proposals have been symbolic, some substantive, and others perhaps superficial or false. His moratorium on the testing of nuclear explosives, pledge to honor all previously negotiated nuclear-arms agreements, objection to the deployment of destructive weapons in space, call for dramatic reductions in strategic nuclear arsenals, willingness to permit on-site inspections to verify compliance with agreements, release of some famous refuseniks, and promises to withdraw Soviet troops from Afghanistan have generated a great deal of excitement and appreciation in different nations. Predictably, all these moves have been carefully designed to benefit the Soviet Union. Some of them could also benefit us and other nations in the world.

It will require wise statecraft to sort through these kinds of proposals, to ascertain when the interests of both our nations can be well served by common efforts, when our best courses of action are inherently divergent, how to live with these differences and assure that the world understands our position, and how to use the tremendous advantages of our free and technologically advanced society to prevail in the peaceful competition that is inevitable between the superpowers.

In this process we will have to accommodate the burgeoning influence of such countries as China, Japan, and Brazil and deal with a more tightly aligned Europe that is already looking eastward and becoming equivocal about its singular commitments to the West.

I have supported the new treaty designed to eliminate intermediate-range nuclear forces (INF) from Europe and reduce the number of short-range tactical weapons and, when it was signed, immediately offered to help with its ratification by the U.S. Senate. However, it must be recognized that this INF agreement helps bring about a long-standing goal of Soviet leaders: to reduce the nuclear-deterrent capability of NATO and leave the Warsaw Pact nations with a clear preponderance of conventional forces. How to follow on with further reductions in weaponry that will bring a stable balance in nuclear *and* conventional forces is one of the most serious challenges that our nation must face. This will involve complex negotiations with a powerful and confident Gorbachev and the finest balancing of interests among our allies in Western Europe.

For the foreseeable future, the deterrent effect of nuclear weapons will continue to be beneficial. In pursuing the worthy goal of reducing strategic arsenals, we must be sure that additional stability results. The attraction of a potential first-strike advantage can be reduced by the use of mobile missile deployment, reduction in the warhead-to-launcher ratio, and deployment of the reduced number of missile launchers in relatively invulnerable sites. A penultimate goal for us to seek would be a few single-warhead missiles, the number balanced through negotiation among all the nuclear nations, deployed in deep silos on the sheltered side of mountains or submarines in safe havens, perhaps in inland seas. This would retain the advantages of nuclear deterrence while eliminating the temptation of a preemptive strike.

On the domestic scene, there is no challenge so great as the reduction of the unconscionable budget deficits, which have tripled our national debt during the last eight years and brought about unprecedented trade imbalances. So far foreign investors have been willing to finance our debt, but this convenient escape valve could easily be closed. The long-term consequences of these afflictions have yet to be comprehended, but they are likely to be more serious than is generally supposed.

No magic formula exists for bringing the federal budget back into balance, but it is not an impossible task. There is no doubt that we must have an increase in revenues and a substantial reduction in expenditures, reasonably balanced between defense and other items. Entitlement programs cannot be exempt. Here is the most vivid example of the need for a bipartisan sharing of responsibility for the evolution of a comprehensive plan, with the president bearing the onus of politically unpopular corrective steps. The U.S. public will accept such an approach if it is explained by a trusted executive and backed, even tacitly, by congressional leaders of both parties.

There is little doubt that the U.S. university system is the best on earth, but we face increasing challenges in educating our citizens of all ages. The average life expectancy of our fellow countrymen (those who do not smoke) is increasing rapidly: at a rate of seven hours a day, or two days a week. At the same time, people are retiring earlier, with many years of productive life ahead of them. Further education of adults is one means of ensuring that they can broaden their interests or be prepared for a gratifying second career. At the same time, education costs are rising, so that it is increasingly difficult for families of moderate means to afford a college education for their children.

Our elementary and high schools have been shocked by the responsibility of creating an equal society following the successful civil rights movement. Academic standards suffered from student demonstrations and the resulting permissiveness of the Vietnam War era. More and more children have less support at home as both parents work and the number of single-parent families increases. Discipline problems are demoralizing to both students and teachers. Our challenge is to reemphasize excellence in education while continuing to assure equality of opportunity for all our people.

Obviously, we need to emphasize the basics, but young Americans can give us some additional clues as to what might be done. Recently, on Christmas morning, our grandchildren received as gifts some small hand-held electronic games. I picked up one that simulated a football game and did my best to score 700. My nine-year-old grandson easily doubled my best effort. Then our daughter Amy's first try was 3200. It was obvious that the manipulation of controls and the reading of video screens was a generational ability that I could not equal.

With the advent of computers and other electronic devices, we have a new opportunity to reduce the costs of education, utilize more fully the talents of our superior teachers, provide for constant assessment of progress in the classroom, individualize instruction for students of varying interests and abilities, and more nearly match the abilities of our graduates with the needs for their talents in a changing world. Little work has been done to explore these new possibilities of our technological age. With proper leadership, our excessively lethargic educational establishment might be invigorated and inspired to explore new ways to teach students at all levels.

As unpleasant as the prospect is, we are almost certainly facing additional problems with energy supplies. The conservation legislation of the late 1970s is embedded in the laws of our nation and will continue to guarantee more efficient use of fuel and electric power for transportation, housing, manufacturing, and home appliances. Some faltering efforts still persist in seeking alternative sources of energy.

However, with the reduced oil prices that have resulted from global conservation efforts, a lackadaisical attitude is now causing a disturbing reversal in our nation's domestic production and importation of foreign oil. It is anticipated that by 1990 we will be importing about nine million barrels of oil per day, half our total consumption—and an all-time high. If present trends are not reversed by market forces or strong government action before 1995, two-thirds of the United States' oil will be imported, amounting to more than twelve million barrels per day. There is some doubt that this much will be readily available to us from overseas, a situation that could result in competition for scarce supplies, substantial increases in energy prices, and another wave of worldwide inflation.

It is possible, of course, to reverse the downward trend in U.S. oil production, which is now dropping about 30,000 barrels per day each month. However, only with substantial price increases can many of our domestic sources be profitably tapped. Most of our oil fields have been long exploited, and there are many marginal wells; in fact more oil wells are drilled in Texas than in all the rest of the world combined. (It costs about six times as much to produce a barrel of oil in the United States as in the Persian Gulf.) U.S. consumers will not join in the oil industry celebration of higher prices. I spent four years wrestling with these kinds of energy issues, one of my most unpleasant experiences in government. The same burden will almost certainly be borne by a future president.

There is no way to assess the dimensions of what might develop into the most serious health problem of all time: acquired immunodeficiency syndrome (AIDS). For a number of years this threat was acknowledged only in the United States and a few other industrialized countries. In Africa national leaders either did not recognize the seriousness of the problem or else they chose to conceal it. Now the World Health Organization (WHO), the Centers for Disease Control, and other similar sources of information have begun to divulge startling statistics based on their still-superficial epidemiological surveys. WHO projects that by 1990 more than 50 million people may be infected with the AIDS virus, 15 million of whom could be dying or already dead by 1995.

This is obviously a threat of almost indescribable magnitude, which will require the fullest support and cooperation of all nations in basic medical research, controlling the spread of the disease, and treating its victims. Although there is no known cure or vaccine for AIDS, in the United States we have recently launched an experimental program of education, detection of carriers of the virus, and prevention of the disease. We are now spending about one dollar per person on this project. In poor countries, however, such costs are almost prohibitive, and there are no mass media to bring needed messages to largely illiterate citizens. WHO is now trying to coordinate a global attempt to control AIDS by utilizing existing health and family-planning programs.

Our country has been a negative factor in this international effort by imposing special restrictions on family-planning efforts and by defaulting on treaty obligations to finance our share of WHO programs. At the beginning of 1988 the United States was more than $82 million in arrears in our pledges to WHO. As a rich and mighty nation with advanced medical and educational technology available to us, we should be in the forefront of this global effort to minimize the scourge of AIDS. This is certainly another example of helping others in order to help ourselves.

As president I made the protection of human rights an important factor in shaping U.S. foreign policy. Every ambassador was expected to be my personal representative in carrying out this goal, and our embassies in foreign capitals were known as havens for victims of oppression. We evolved a massive global organization to keep us informed about abuses by foreign leaders of their citizens. I often interceded personally with oppressors of the left and the right in an effort to correct some of the more serious cases of unwarranted arrest, the holding of prisoners incommunicado, extended incarceration without trial, torture of prisoners, and the killing or beating of innocent citizens. Heads of state who visited with me knew that their human rights record was being carefully scrutinized and realized that this was at least one of the factors that affected their relationship with the government of the United States.

The defense of human, or civil, rights was not restricted in application just to other nations but was considered to be a prime responsibility of all officials who served with me in administering the domestic affairs of our nation. This effort, which reflects the highest principles of our country, was compatible with the policies of presidents who preceded me.

The enhancement of human freedoms and the guarantee of individual rights is not an easy policy to evolve or to consummate. It is a real challenge to be as strong and consistent as possible and at the same time to accommodate the other factors that must be considered in dealing with conflicting interests at home and abroad. This is, however, a goal worth pursuing. Ours is often the only voice that can be truly significant. A lack of interest in Washington sends out a penetrating silence. This is what the oppressors most desire; it is what the victims most fear.

Human rights are not the same as motherhood, apple pie, or the Fourth of July. The issue cuts like a razor; it is often the cutting edge of societal change. It behooves our great and free country to hold high the banner of human rights. Again, we Americans reap rich benefits when we help others to be safe and free.

These are just a few of the opportunities for our country to provide world leadership during the remaining years of this century. There will certainly be many others that no one could anticipate. Despite their number or magnitude, there are no challenges that our nation cannot meet successfully if we wisely tap our tremendous natural and human resources and the unequaled soundness and resilience of our system of government.

RONALD REAGAN

◆ ———————————————— ◆

The United States and the World in the 1990s

◆ What will the world look like in the 1990s? It is always perilous to try to peer into the future, but for the statesman, this peril is an occupational hazard. To be successful, the statesman must design policies not only to meet the needs of today, but to anticipate—if not shape—the pattern of tomorrow. And our aim, as Americans, is to help shape the future in accordance with our fundamental ideals of liberty, progress, and peace.

I took office in 1981 facing three urgent foreign policy tasks:

◆ To restore our nation's economic strength and help reinvigorate the world economic system after the blows of the energy shocks, spiraling inflation, and global recession

◆ To restore our military strength after a decade when defense investment was neglected and the Soviet Union was allowed to overtake us in many crucial categories of military power

◆ To restore this nation's dynamism and self-confidence as a world leader after the wounds of Vietnam and a period when our adversaries were emboldened and our friends disheartened by American retreat

With the support of the American people, and in a bipartisan joint effort between the president and Congress, we made headway in all of these areas. *We put this nation back on the path of sustained economic growth with low inflation*, resulting in the longest continuous peacetime period of economic expansion in our history. We achieved this by measures to ease the burden of government on the natural productive forces of our economy—by bringing inflation and interest rates down, by income tax rate reductions and a historic tax reform, and by reducing the regulatory burden. Around the world we see today a revolution in economic thinking, as developed and developing nations alike—even to some degree in the communist world—are rediscovering that the wellspring of prosperity is the initiative and productivity of the individual, not the state. The United States remains the champion of a free, open, and fair international trading system. We have put forward major initiatives to lower trade barriers, promote economic development, improve monetary relations, and ease the problem of debt in the developing world.

We undertook a major rebuilding of America's military strength, from a larger, modernized navy to a vital program of strategic modernization, from more mobile and ready conventional forces to a potential revolution in strategic doctrine that holds the promise of blunting the threat of ballistic missile attack. We and our allies successfully carried out the 1979 North Atlantic Treaty Organization (NATO) decision to deploy U.S. intermediate-range nuclear forces (INF) in Europe, countering the menace of Soviet SS-20 missiles. On this foundation of resolve and strength, we have strengthened the peace and opened the way for unprecedented achievements in arms reduction.

Finally, and most important, we again see a vibrant America full of pride, patriotism, and faith in itself—an America putting behind it the period of retreat and taking up once again the role of vigorous leader of the free world. As Americans celebrated the centennial of the Statue of Liberty and the bicentennial of our Constitution, we drew fresh inspiration from our heritage. America is a very different country from what it was eight years ago.

Our own renewed pride in our democracy is today reinforced by the stirring sight of democracy thriving elsewhere. We see the ideology of totalitarianism discredited as never before and the spark of freedom brighter than ever before. The solidarity of our democratic alliances is strong. The democratic revolution spreading around the world inspires us by demonstrating anew the universal meaning of our most deeply held values. Courageous freedom fighters are resisting communist repression around the globe. Our rescue of Grenada, the blow we struck against Libyan terrorism, our defense of freedom of navigation in the Persian Gulf, and the pressure on the Soviet Union to leave Afghanistan show once again the results of America's willingness to act decisively and firmly in furtherance of its principles and interests.

In sum, we have restored the position of the United States in the world. The American people have made clear in unmistakable terms that they are not ready to go back to the policies of weakness and self-paralysis of the previous decade. Our country's retreat from responsibility during those years was one of the most destabilizing developments of the postwar era—and it must not be repeated.

I have always believed that the future belongs to America, that our best days lie ahead. Thus I believe we have set the stage for further achievements in foreign policy in the 1990s.

Successful policies are not abstract creations spun out of thin air. On the contrary, they are rooted in the historical forces at work in the world, correctly anticipating them and shaping them. We have taken advantage of historic opportunities to advance America's fundamental goals of liberty, security, and progress.

Economic Freedom and Prosperity

One lesson of the past ten years is that the societies that recovered most readily from the economic crisis of the 1970s were those that had the resilience and flexibility to respond to market forces. Our own policies played an important role, revitalizing our economy so that it would serve as a locomotive for world growth. But we were not alone. Worldwide we have witnessed a trend toward structural reform, the decentralization of decision making, and an easing of institutional rigidities—to give greater scope to market forces and to liberate the natural, indigenous productive forces in every society.

In some cases the results of this trend have been spectacular. Witness the extraordinary economic growth among the Four Tigers of Asia—the Republic of Korea, Singapore, Taiwan, and Hong Kong. But this trend goes well beyond these rapidly developing countries. At the Bonn Economic Summit in 1985, the leaders of the major industrial powers agreed unanimously that structural rigidities and excessive state control were the main obstacles to a revival of growth among the advanced countries. And at a special session of the United Nations General Assembly in 1986, African governments acknowledged that structural reforms were, for them too, the key to sustained growth and development. Perhaps most striking, we have seen, as I noted, a tentative recognition of these same realities in the communist world.

Today the world is on the threshold of yet another explosion of modernization. It's a new era, a new industrial revolution. In the past, economic development hinged on agricultural productivity or on increased industrialization. Today we are heading into the Information Age, in which technological advance depends more on advances in computers and telecommunications and the spread of their use. Knowledge, not machinery, is the key; information, not physical resources, is becoming the standard of exchange.

It is no coincidence that this new burst of innovation has originated in the free nations, where knowledge and information flow freely, where creativity is given free rein, where ideas flourish in a system of true openness. Nor is it an accident that this new industrial revolution poses a stark dilemma to a system that is terrified of the free flow of people, information, and ideas across national boundaries, a system that keeps photocopiers under lock and key as a threat to its monopoly of information. The communist system faces a clear choice: if it permits the conditions to develop that allow it to exploit information technology for economic growth, it risks a challenge to the party's monopoly of power; yet if it resists this new phase of modernization out of fear for its political control, it will fall further and further behind.

Probably it has no choice. As history moves on and the human mind continues to test the outer limits, these regimes will find they *cannot* resist the forces of change and the power of the human spirit.

Yet this wave of economic freedom that has swelled in the 1980s will carry us to greater prosperity in the 1990s only if we and other countries maintain and build upon the policies that keep faith with it.

Free trade is an absolute requirement for the rapid growth of the world economy as we enter the Information Age. The quick and easy exchange of goods, technologies, and ideas across national borders drives economic progress around the globe. For this reason I have remained firmly committed to free trade. We need no reminder that the protectionist Smoot-Hawley Act was a major factor in deepening and prolonging the Great Depression. Restricting trade is not the solution to American trade problems.

Instead we proposed, in February 1987, comprehensive legislation to ensure American competitiveness. This legislation would renew authority for negotiating agreements to remove trade barriers, reduce self-imposed export barriers, and amend a number of U.S. regulations and laws to promote international competition. Some of the proposals were included in separate versions of the Trade and International Economic Policy Reform Act of 1987 that have passed the Senate and the House of Representatives. Unfortunately other provisions in these bills would close U.S. markets or establish more restrictive legal procedures in the mistaken belief that these steps would reduce the U.S. trade deficit. At this writing we are working with the conference committees to produce a nonprotectionist bill, in full knowledge of how fragile the conditions for economic prosperity can be.

We have championed free trade at home, in our bilateral economic relations, and in multilateral negotiations in the General Agreement on Tariffs and Trade (GATT). It was the United States that took the lead in pushing for a historic new round of multilateral trade negotiations that began in the fall of 1986 in Uruguay. Our objective in these negotiations is to strengthen existing trade rules and extend them to areas such as agriculture, services, intellectual property, and investment, which have until now escaped meaningful international discipline.

In addition, we have succeeded in two truly historic efforts to establish free-trade areas. One is with Israel, and the second is with our largest trading partner, Canada. These agreements will expand the trade and investment of both parties by reducing or eliminating barriers.

Our efforts to broaden the boundaries of free trade have enjoyed substantial, though not total, success. At a minimum, worldwide economic growth in the 1990s requires the maintenance of the gains we have recently made. It would be a worthy goal for the next administration to reduce further the barriers to global economic interaction and global prosperity.

The Democratic Surge

In the mid-1960s, Nobel-Laureate-to-be Milton Friedman wrote *Capitalism and Freedom*, which traced the critical link between capitalism and economic prosperity on the one side and democracy and political freedom on the other. Given this link, it is not surprising that the trend to economic freedom in the 1980s has proceeded in parallel with an equally strong resurgence of democracy.

The United States can hardly claim credit for this resurgence—the credit is due those courageous people on almost every continent who have struggled to take control of their destiny. But America *can* take credit for having recognized, from the beginning, the power of the idea of freedom as a truly revolutionary force:

- ◆ In Poland in the early 1980s, we saw that 40 years of Soviet power had not snuffed out the dream of freedom, though that heroic effort was suppressed by martial law.

- ◆ In South and Central America in 1976, only a third of the people enjoyed democratic rule. Today over 90 percent of the population of Latin America lives in nations committed to democratic principles.

- ◆ In societies as far apart geographically and culturally as Argentina, Brazil, the Philippines, and the Republic of Korea, we have seen authoritarian rule give way to democracy.

◆ In South Africa the black majority has asserted its rights and its voice as never before, and the hated apartheid system is under greater pressure than ever before.

It is critical to understand that this is a continuing struggle both within the countries that have turned to democracy and in those that may one day in the future. And the policies of the next administration and the next Congress must give support, both moral and material, to this trend. Such support would vindicate our most deeply held values, serve our national interest, and help ensure that democracy will maintain its forward march through the next decade.

If the march of democracy is worldwide, the policy prescriptions may vary from case to case. In the National Endowment for Democracy we have a valuable new bipartisan institution that helps nurture the skills of democracy in many lands. In countries such as the Philippines and the Republic of Korea, we used our influence to encourage the transition to democratic rule. And in the Philippines we have provided moral, economic, and military assistance to aid the new democratic leadership in the face of economic problems and a brutal communist threat. In El Salvador and other Central American democracies we have likewise provided across-the-board assistance in the face of the threat from a communist neighbor sponsoring insurgent and subversive challenges even while talking peace.

If there is a common thread here, however, it is the need for an active, vigorous, and *sustained* American policy with the flexibility and resources to assist democratic friends around the world. Our foreign economic and security assistance programs are vital and deserve greater support.

The Revolt Against Totalitarianism

Closely related to the advance of democracy is another historic trend, perhaps even more remarkable: the unprecedented phenomenon of anticommunist insurgencies resisting totalitarian oppression throughout the developing world.

In the 1970s the Soviet Union and its clients overreached, at a time when America weakened itself by its internal divisions. Arrogantly they concluded in that period that the global "correlation of forces," as they like to put it, was shifting in their favor. Well, they were wrong. In the 1980s the Soviets and their clients have found it impossible to consolidate their gains—mainly because of the courageous forces of indigenous resistance, but also because of the revival of American and Western self-confidence. In Afghanistan, in Nicaragua, in Cambodia, in Angola, and elsewhere, resistance movements grew up to challenge communist regimes installed or maintained by the military power of the Soviet Union and its colonial agents.

Although the struggle against communist tyranny in the developing world is the achievement of the peoples involved, our support for their effort has been essential. Morally and strategically they deserve our assistance. The form and extent of our support should vary with the circumstances. As a popularly supported insurgency enjoys some natural military advantages, our help need not always be massive to make a difference. But it must be more than symbolic.

Nor are military solutions the goal of American policy here. We consider these wars tragic for their suffering victims and dangerous to world peace. For these reasons, in my October 1985 address to the United Nations General Assembly I put forward a plan for resolving by negotiations those regional conflicts in which Leninist regimes are making war against their own people. This initiative was meant to complement diplomatic initiatives already under way, to which the United States has given the strongest possible support. And I sought to engage the Soviet Union in a constructive dialogue.

We have made some progress, and there is a lesson here for American policy in the 1990s. Where we have received bipartisan support in the Congress, our policies have been effective. Where we Americans have been at odds among ourselves, we have courted failure.

The enormous pressure on the Soviet Union to withdraw from Afghanistan was the product of the heroism of the Afghan people and the courage of Pakistan, backed by overwhelming international political support. But our own substantial assistance to the freedom fighters played no small role. And this was a solidly bipartisan policy, with staunch congressional support.

Similarly, in Angola, Jonas Savimbi's UNITA freedom fighters have blunted repeated military offensives by the MPLA regime with its 40,000-man Cuban expeditionary force and Soviet combat advisers. There is hope there for a negotiated solution that would remove Cuban troops completely from Angola and promote national reconciliation within Angola.

Central America presents a different picture. It came to be almost universally accepted that democracy in Nicaragua is the core issue in the effort to bring peace to Central America. The United States has sought a negotiated solution to the turmoil in this region. Yet we have always recognized that this could not be achieved without leverage. Our support for the Nicaraguan Democratic Resistance has been an essential weapon for the Nicaraguan people in their fight to force the Sandinista Communists to live up to the promises of democracy and freedom made to the Organization of American States in 1979, promises they have repeated anew under the Guatemala peace accords of 1987. It is the pressure of the armed resistance that brought the Sandinistas to the peace table, and maintaining that pressure is the best hope for a real negotiation—and real democratization in Nicaragua.

America's support for those resisting totalitarianism may not involve very much in the way of resources, but the impact could be profound. The new Soviet leaders say they are open to "new thinking" and that they seek a breathing space internationally so they can concentrate on economic reform at home. If so, our task is to make clear their choice—to ensure that adventurism has a high cost and to maximize their incentives to help resolve those regional conflicts rather than persist in the pursuit of military solutions. If we meet our responsibility, we may indeed by our firmness help *make* this a turning point in Soviet policy—and in East-West relations.

Seeking Long-Term Strategic Stability

Let me turn now to another historic development—the arms reduction process and our efforts to ensure a stable strategic equilibrium for the long-term future.

Throughout the 1960s and the 1970s the arms control process was the repository of high hopes but a source of disappointment. It succeeded, at best, only in putting a cap on the growth of strategic arsenals—and wasn't all that successful in doing so. There were significant problems with Soviet violations. At times, the hopes for arms control were dashed by Soviet aggression in regional conflicts.

I sought to put the arms control process on a new and firmer basis. First, I approached arms control negotiations with a hard-nosed philosophy. We have not sought agreements for agreements' sake; rather, we have patiently worked for agreements that would truly enhance our national security and that of our allies. We will never sacrifice the security or interests of our allies just to reach an agreement with the Soviet Union. We have never forgotten that Soviet policy on human rights and on regional conflicts lay at the heart of the East-West conflict and that the weapons were really a symptom, not the cause, of the problem. We have had the courage to resist pressures on us to make unilateral concessions—a courage our allies displayed in following through with the deployment of INF missiles in 1983 and we displayed in resisting similar pressures for a nuclear freeze or an unverifiable moratorium on nuclear testing. We have also put a new and long-overdue emphasis on compliance with and verification of agreements. We have reported to Congress on repeated Soviet violations of existing treaties and have insisted on strict verification for any new agreements. In fact, the INF treaty contains—at our insistence—the most stringent verification regime in arms control history.

Second, the United States began to seek deep reductions in nuclear arsenals, not mere ceilings that codified a continuing buildup. The Soviets resisted this approach for years, but when they saw us standing firm, they began to come around. In December 1987 we and the Soviets reached a historic agreement that will eliminate an entire class of U.S. and Soviet intermediate-range nuclear missiles from the face of the earth, and we are making progress toward an even more significant agreement that will reduce the U.S. and Soviet strategic arsenals *by half.*

Third, and perhaps most important, I have put forward the prospect of a historic reorientation of nuclear strategy. The vigorous and promising program of research, development, and testing that constitutes my Strategic Defense Initiative (SDI) offers hope of making free-world security less reliant on the threat of offensive destruction and more reliant on deterrence based on defensive systems that threaten no one. Strategic defenses could offer the world a safer, more stable basis for deterrence—and we would welcome Soviet agreement for an orderly *joint* transition to a more defense-reliant world.

Perhaps among the most important legacies I will leave to my successors are these advances we have made in enhancing strategic security. They offer a fine starting point for further gains. But an element of caution is in order. Just as significant progress has been made, so future decisions can undo it. The next administration, with support from Congress, must remember that American national security requires an adequate defense budget, including strong support for SDI, firmness and patience in dealing with the Soviets, sensitivity to the vital concerns of our allies, and a clear vision of a better, safer future. All of these will be needed in full measure if we are to move from the dangers of mutual assured destruction to a world of mutually assured security.

Legacy for the Future

Lord Acton was right when he described history as the march of liberty. I believe future historians will look back with favor at the advances made during this period in the cause of political and economic freedom around the world. So too will they judge our efforts to establish a less-dangerous strategic equilibrium to ensure the peace that must accompany our freedom.

In closing, however, I must be frank. I am proud of what we have accomplished in our foreign policy but well aware that, in other circumstances, we could have done much more. My own achievements and disappointments have convinced me that a successful foreign policy requires a strong executive branch with the freedom to act decisively, as well as a cooperative relationship between the Congress and the executive.

In the 1970s the gridlock in executive-congressional relations led to the paralysis of American power. This paralysis in turn provided opportunities for the Soviets and their surrogates to make gains throughout the world. We cannot allow a recurrence of the self-inflicted disasters of the 1970s. We are a great power with vital international responsibilities, and the world becomes a more dangerous place when we cripple ourselves. A bipartisan consensus on this fundamental point is essential. No legacy would make me more proud than a bipartisan consensus that this nation will never again permit such a situation to come to pass.

Congress, of course, has a legitimate role in the foreign policy process, but only the president can *act*. Only he can respond quickly in a crisis or formulate a coherent and consistent policy in any region of the world or dimension of policy. Efforts to weaken the presidency only weaken the country.

And when the president acts, he must have at his command sufficient resources. The current assault on our foreign affairs budget is so devastating that we have neither adequate means nor enough flexibility to advance our purposes and meet our vital commitments. In fiscal year 1985 our foreign affairs budget was $26.3 billion. This figure dropped to $19.8 billion in fiscal 1986, $18.4 billion in fiscal 1987, and $17.8 billion in fiscal 1988. When accompanied by inflation and changes in the exchange rate of the dollar, these reductions represent a cut of 30 percent *since* 1985. They have cut into critical security and economic assistance programs and have forced us to close diplomatic missions abroad and otherwise reduce our foreign presence. Needless to say, these reductions are hamstringing our efforts to promote freedom at a time when the Soviets are outspending us two to one on foreign operations.

So I believe America and the free nations will be in a stronger position in the 1990s. But history won't do our work for us. We, after all, believe in the free will of human beings, not in deterministic theories of the forces of history. So our future is in our hands. But I have never doubted the capacities of free men and women to surmount their challenges and seize their opportunities. The future is bright for the cause of freedom.

Index